TO

LADY NEEDLEWORKERS

THROUGHOUT THE WORLD

This Book

IS DEDICATED BY THE AUTHORS,

IN THE HOPE THAT IT MAY AID IN THE PRODUCTION OF THOSE

ORNAMENTAL AND USEFUL ARTICLES

THAT ADD

ELEGANCE TO THE BOUDOIR,

AND

YIELD A PROFIT

TO THE

FANCY FAIR.

Treasures in Needlework

By MRS. WARREN and MRS. PULLMAN

A BERKLEY WINDHOVER BOOK
published by
BERKLEY PUBLISHING CORPORATION

Preface.

⟡

*Take up the pencil, let the needle move
Responsive to the ceaseless cares of love;
And we will ope instruction at the page
That best your glad attention may engage."*

⟡

THE art of Needlework in every form is well known to be as old as the hills; but in past ages the higher or picturesque gradations of it were confined to the delicate fingers of Queens and Court ladies. Matilda, the accomplished consort of William the Conqueror, has left a memorable achievement in the Bayeux Tapestry—a wondrous work truly, full of beauty, and most graphically presenting us with a history of the conquest. In our own times much has been done to raise the art of picturesque and useful Needlework in popular estimation; and it is gratifying to think that a spirit of emulation has been aroused, which must, sooner or later, render the knowledge of this art necessary to the perfection of womanly education.

"TREASURES IN NEEDLEWORK" is brought out to help this good tendency, and to meet the wishes of numerous Lady-Needleworkers, who have felt the want of a Book of Reference in which could be found plain and practical instructions, combined with workable patterns, in every species of Fancy and Ornamental Needlework. We believe this requirement is fully met in the following pages, abounding as they do with examples of the utmost variety, and in all styles.

Perhaps no contemporaneous issue of the press, even in these days of illustrated literature, can boast of so many really useful engravings, or

exhibit such manifest evidence of elaborate industry. Each design in
the book can be worked out: the directions are the result of actual
performance. They will, therefore, with the aid of the Errata (page x.),
be all-sufficient for the reproduction of the patterns.

It only remains to say, that no expense has been spared to render
the book worthy of universal acceptance. Upon the woodcuts and
designs above two thousand pounds have been expended. This outlay
does not include the cost of printing, paper, &c., nor any of the charges
incidental to publishing in this shape. A very large sale, not only in
"merrie England," but wherever fair fingers ply the needle, either for
ornamental or useful purposes, can alone recompense the enterprise that
now ventures to cast its bread upon the waters, earnestly entreating
those who may derive pleasure or profit from the book to extend to it
the kindness of a generous recommendation. "TREASURES IN NEEDLE-
WORK" is suitable to all ranks; its instructions can be carried out by all
capacities. Therefore let us hope, that while the work may grace the
Boudoir of the Peeress, it shall also penetrate into the Cottage of the
Peasant; that while it can become a source of useful recreation to the
rich, it may also prove a reliable aid to the industrious effort of the
poor.

CONTENTS.

CONTENTS.

ERRATA.

25.—A BABY'S KNITTED SOCK.—In 5th round, last line but one, read, 'left to right,' instead of 'right to left.'

,, 6th round, after the word 'the,' omit '1st loop;' read, 'same stitch as just knitted.'

63.—BREAD-CLOTH, PATTERN A LA REINE.—After 3rd row there should be no turning back.

80, 81.—NEAPOLITAN TIDY.—16th row, 3rd line, after '1 Sq,' read '3 L, 1 Sq.'

,, 49th row, 2nd line, after '21 L,' read '1 Sq,' instead of '2 Sq.'

    50th row, 3rd line, after '15 L,' read '5 Sq.'

91.—LADY'S POLKA.—8th line, after the word 'rib,' add 'in all 74 ribs.' The next five lines constitute one row.

,, 21st line of 2nd column, after the words 'arm-hole,' add 'knit 3 ribs.'

96, 102, 103.—A GENTLEMAN'S NIGHT-CAP.—In the pattern for side-pieces:

,, 2nd row, 1st line, K 4 instead of 5.

,, 6th row, 1st line, K 5 instead of 6.

,, 7th row, 1st line, K 6 instead of 7.

,, 8th row, 1st line, K 4 instead of 5.

,, 9th row, 1st line, K 7 instead of 8.

,, 10th row, 1st line, K 5 instead of 6.

,, 11th row, 2nd line, K 8 instead of 9, and add 'make 1.'

,, 27th row, 1st line, K 10; and after the word 'together,' in last line, add 'cotton round.'

,, 30th row, 1st line, K 5.

,, 38th row, 1st line, K 5.

,, 39th row, 2nd line, after the 1st 'together,' add 'bring forward.'

,, 40th row, 1st line, P 6.

,, 43rd row, 2nd line, instead of 'K 22,' K 2. In 4th line, after 'K 5,' omit 'Tf, K 2.' In 5th line, K 2 instead of K 3.

,, 46th row, 1st line, K 5.

,, 47th row, 1st line, add 'E 1' before the 'K 8.'

,, 58th row, last line, after 'P 3,' add 'together.'

100.—POLKA FOR A CHILD.—3rd line, 2nd column, knit 18 rows instead of 9; then afterwards, instead of 9 rows, knit 10. Again, instead of 9 rows, knit 18; instead of 4 rows, knit 16. In the next line, after the word 'encrease,' knit 9 ribs, instead of 17; then, instead of knitting 13 rows wherever desired, knit 14. Take off 12 ribs, instead of stitches, each side; then knit 14 rows on the back. Afterwards, take up a front, and knit 36 rows instead of 34. Cast on 57 stitches for the sleeves, and knit 24 rows instead of 19 in each place.

110, 111.—BALMORAL NECK-TIE.—2nd line, pearl alternately 8 rows.

,, 4th line, alternately 6 rows; omit the words 'work the same,' but add, 'work 2 rows;' then pearl and knit alternately 4 more rows. After the word 'white,' in 5th line, add, 'which does not require the 2 knitted rows, but knit and pearl alternately 6 rows.' 'Draw up the ends,' instead of 'dress up the beads.'

116.—PALM-LEAF EDGING.—3rd line, after the word 'loop,' add, 'in 1st 9 ch.'

,, 8th line, after the word 'worked,' add 'in 2nd 9 ch.'

,, 12th line, read, '2nd Dc stitch on the edge,' instead of '1st.'

,, 25th line, '6 ch,' instead of '5.'

,, 31st line, '2nd Dc,' instead of '1st.'

,, 36th line, after the '1st 11 ch,' add, 'of 2nd scallop.'

,, FISH SERVIETTE, 8th row, 3rd line, after the '3 Sq.' omit the '6 L.'

120.—CHEESE SERVIETTE.—4th row, after the word 'short,' make 7 ch, Dc into same loop.

,, 14th row, 1st line, substitute 'L' for 'E.'

123.—STILTON CHEESE SERVIETTE.—13th row after the second 6 L, read, '1 Sq.,' instead of '3.'

126.—DOYLEY FOR A SPIRIT STAND.—14th round, instead of '7 chain,' add '7 Dc.'

132.—LADY'S NETTED CAP.—1st line, after the word 'cotton,' add '16.'

,, 2nd column, 17th line, between the words 'and' * 'net,' place an asterisk; also, after the word 'repeat,' add 'from *, 18th line.

INTRODUCTORY CHAPTER.

In a retrospect of the Art of Needlework, whether of sewing, knitting or crochet, from the earliest period to the present time, it is impossible to estimate too highly the advantages of its domestic or ornamental character. In the one position, it brings daily blessings to every home, unnoticed, perhaps, because of its hourly silent application; for in a household each stitch is one for comfort to some person or other; and without its ever-watchful care home would be a scene of discomfort indeed. In its ornamental adaptation, it delights the eye, amuses the mind, nay, sometimes cheats grief of its sorrow; but, more than all, gives bread to thousands. The women of every nation, from time immemorial to the present, have beguiled their hours with the needle, from " the embroidered hangings of the temple, and the garments of fine needlework for kings' daughters," worked with gold, and silk, and precious stones, to the mocassins and festive ornaments of the savage embroidered with beads. Upon all classes and in all climes this simple instrument has bestowed a varied charm.

KNITTING is a chief source of employment to numbers of the peasantry of Europe; and in many parts of England the stockings and socks are knitted in the family, these being found much more durable than woven ones; and many articles also of great beauty and gossamer lightness are produced by nimble fingers and slender wires. A few specimens that have been recently imported from India, knitted by some modern Arachne, will almost challenge the spider's web for fineness. Much could be said in the praise of this branch of needlework, as adapted to every climate, whether we compare the delicate textures of the East, or the warm vests, socks, gloves, and neck-ties suitable to our colder climate; but for one peculiar quality, knitting should be held in reverence,—it is almost the sole employment and comfort of the indigent and aged blind; therefore all praise be to that art which can assuage a sorrow, or lighten an affliction.

NETTING, or KNOTTING as it was once termed, has its manifold uses. The art is of high antiquity, and the implements that have come down to us from bygone ages are much the same as those in present use. By it the fisher captures the shoals of fish which make so dainty an appearance on the table, and by it he entirely provides food and clothing for his family. By it the gardener preserves his fruits, the boy delights to catch the finny tribe, the fowler to trap his birds, and the pedlar to produce his cabbage-nets. Balloons have their silken coverings encased with it ; ladies make purses, caps, fringes, and "*golden nets for the hair which tangle lovers' hearts.*"

In the Museum at Berlin there still exist nets made by those fathers of all the arts, the Egyptians, three thousand years ago. Pliny mentions some nets which he had seen of so delicate a texture as to be easily passed through a man's ring, while a sufficient number could be carried by one person to surround a whole wood; each thread of these nets was composed of one hundred and fifty strands.

The women of Theurapia on the Bosphorus are, at this day, celebrated for their exquisitely fine netting, the ornamentation of which consists in raised flowers beautifully netted in the work. Most persons have seen the almost inimitable netting of those articles called Maltese mittens, so light as to be blown away by a breath, and so faultless that no join of the silk can be discovered in them.

CROCHÊT is the shepherd's knitting of primitive times, when the outer garments were made of the wool torn off the backs of the sheep by the brambles, which was collected, spun, and converted into warm clothing, with the aid of a hook neatly cut at the end of a stick. With the same shaped instrument of polished steel our elaborate designs are produced, and by it, probably more than three thousand years ago, Penelope wove the famous shroud of Laertes, as no other texture could have borne the constant "fretting" occasioned by the weaving and unweaving for so long a space of time:

> " All day she sped the long laborious toil,
>   But when the burning lamp supplied the sun,
>   Each night unravelled what the day begun,—
>   Three live-long summers did the fraud prevail."

In modern times, Queen Elizabeth and her bevy of maidens might possibly have amused themselves with this art; for John Taylor, in 1640, writes of needlework, thus—

> " All in dimension, ovals, squares, and rounds,
>   *   *   *   *   *   *
>   So that art seemeth nearly natural,
>   In forming shapes so geometrical."

By no other art than that of the needle can " shapes" so entirely geometrical be formed. Among the " treasures of needlework" in ancient times may be mentioned the corslet sent by Amasis, king of Egypt, to the Lacedæmonians, and described by Herodotus as made of linen with many figures of animals inwrought and adorned with gold and cotton-wool; each thread of this corslet was composed of three hundred and sixty threads.

Another " treasure" was the veil of Minerva embroidered by virgins, selected from the best families in Athens, which, after being carried in procession with great pomp and ceremony round the city, was hung up in the Parthenon, and consecrated to Minerva.

Coming to another age, a " treasure" still remains to us in the tapestry worked by Matilda, wife of William the Conqueror, highly valuable as an historical picture, and a truthful representation of the events which preceded and accompanied the Conquest. It is still preserved at Bayeux, in Normandy, and consists of a web of cloth upwards of two hundred feet in length, and about twenty inches in breadth, with borders top and bottom. The horses are worked in colours of blue, yellow, green, and red; but the whole is interesting and spirited.

In the Fishmongers' Hall, in London is a tolerably well-preserved specimen of needlework, on a linen ground. The work itself is splendid, and must have been magnificent when used as a pall at the funeral of Sir William Walworth, in 1381. It is now much faded in colour, and the gold dimmed by age; but altogether it is an exquisite specimen of needlework of that or any other period. We question if the very best of our embroiderers could produce anything resembling it.

Miss Linwood's "treasures" have long since been scattered among private individuals: such a collection can rarely, if ever, be brought together again. Each separate picture, faultless in its detail, and perfect in its completion, seems literally painted on the canvas with fine wool and the needle: the tints are unfaded and natural, or mellowed into rich and deepened beauty. The skin of the dogs in the "Woodman in a Storm" so exactly resembles life, that even after a minute inspection one cannot be persuaded but that it must have been carefully transferred from the animal's back to the picture. Such a collection was worthy of a nation.

To enumerate all the treasures of the needle, either known of or still in existence would be no easy task; and it is probable that the art will last as long as time itself,— o says the poet of two hundred years since:

> " —— till the world be quite dissolved and past,
> So long, at least, the needle's use shall last."

He also advises ladies to employ themselves with it in these words :

> " It will increase their peace, enlarge their store,
> To use their tongues less, and their needles more;
> The needle's sharpnesse profit yields and pleasure,
> But sharpnesse of the tongue bites out of measure."

There are many occasions in life when ladies desire to mark their esteem for a friend by some gift or token; and they are often puzzled in the choice of what to give or to work. Hence it is that no question is more frequently asked than, "What will be a suitable present for so-and so?" or, "What will be the most valuable things I can make for a Fancy Fair?"

In making gifts to individuals, the leading idea is, to assure them of our regard. That the gift is our own production, greatly adds to its value in the estimation of the recipient; and, indeed, there are many circumstances in which, when desiring to show gratitude for kindness, a lady may very properly offer a specimen of her own work, when a purchased gift would be either unsuitable or out of her power. For the same reason,—that it proves the receiver to have been an object of our thought and care,—any article evidently intended for that person only, is more welcome than such as might have been worked for anybody. The following list of articles, suitable for the respective purposes, will be found suggestive:—

PRESENTS FOR GENTLEMEN.

BRACES.—Embroidered on velvet, or worked on canvas, from a Berlin pattern.

CIGAR CASES.—Crochet. Velvet, and cloth appliqué, velvet, or cloth braided. Embroidered or worked in beads.

SLIPPERS.—Braided on cloth, morocco, or velvet; appliqué cloth and velvet; Berlin work.

SHAVING BOOKS, *especially useful.*—Braided. Worked in beads on canvas. Crochet, coloured beads, and white cotton, (washable.)

SMOKING CAPS.—Velvet braided richly; cloth, velvet and cloth appliqué. Netted and darned on crochet.

FRONTS FOR BRIDLES.—Crest embroidered with seed beads.

WAISTCOATS.—Braided on cloth or velvet. Embroidered.

PENWIPERS.—Worked in beads, and fringed. Appliqué velvet and cloth. Gold thread.

BOOKMARKERS.

PURSES.

SERMON CASES.

COMFORTERS. DRIVING MITTENS. SCARFS.

BRIDAL PRESENTS.

CHAIRS,—Embroidered in appliqué. Berlin work ditto. Braided ditto.

SOFA CUSHIONS.—Braided or embroidered.

SCREENS.—Raised cut Berlin work. Berlin work with beads.

HAND SCREENS.—Netted and darned. Appliqué. Crochet.

ANTIMACASSARS.

TABLE COVERS.—Cloth, with bead or Berlin borders. Cloth braided.

SET OF DISH MATS.—Worked in beads, with initials in the centre; border round; and grounded in clear white beads.

FANCY MATS.—For urns, lamps, &c.

OTTOMANS.—Braided. Appliqué, or embroidered.

FOOTSTOOLS.—Berlin or bead work. Braided.

WHATNOTS.—Braided. Berlin work.

DOYLEYS.—The set—bread, cheese, and table doyleys—worked in broderie and chain stitch.

WATCHPOCKETS.

NETTED CURTAINS.

FOR A BRIDE.

POINT-LACE COLLARS, CHEMISETTES, HANDKERCHIEFS, &c.

EMBROIDERED DITTO.

HANDKERCHIEF CASE or BOX.—On satin, embroidered or braided in delicate colours.

GLOVE BOX.—Worked in beads. Initials in centre; grounded with white beads.

SLIPPERS.—Braided or embroidered.

WORKBASKETS.—Netted and darned, or darned on filet, or crochet.

CARRIAGE BAGS.—Braided. Worked in Berlin work or beads.

PURSES.—Netted and darned, or crochet; delicate colours, as pink and silver.

PORTE-MONNAIE, or NOTE CASE.—Crest or monogram in centre, grounded in beads.

EMBROIDERED APRONS.—Worked in broderie-en-lacet. Braided, or embroidered.

TOILET CUSHIONS.—Crochet or netting.

RETICULES.—Darned netting; or embroidery.

CHRISTENINGS.

INFANTS' CAPS.—Point lace, crochet, or embroidery.

FROCKS.—Ditto.

QUILTS.—Crochet. Bead borders with motto, and drop fringe. Crest in the centre.

PINCUSHIONS.—Crochet, or embroidered satin.

BLANKETS.—Knitted with white wool, in double knitting,—a real " blessing to mothers."

These are a few of the leading and most useful presents. They are equally appropriate as offerings to a Fancy Fair.

In the choice of materials, much difficulty is often found, especially by those ladies who reside in the country. It is therefore necessary to allude to the cottons of Messrs. Walter Evans & Co., of Derby, manufacturers of the celebrated Boar's-Head Crochet Cotton, as those used exclusively in the following designs.

The fabrics of this firm have enjoyed a well-merited reputation for many years: we have used them ourselves for every design, because we have invariably found that they combined in an eminent degree the requisites of colour, evenness, and strength, so necessary for Fancy Work. Many have been manufactured expressly for the various styles of work which have become fashionable from time to time; and amongst these we may notice the Royal Embroidery Cotton, the Tatting Cotton, and the Patent Glacé (or Glazed) Thread, a new and exquisite material for every sort of plain work; the use of other cottons is liable to cause some confusion in working out their designs, owing to different makers employing various methods of numbering; for example, No. 10, Evans's Boar's-Head Cotton, is suitable for Beads No. 2 ; whilst No. 10 of other makers may prove either too fine or coarse for the purpose; and for the same reason other cottons might not work out the designs of the original dimensions.

So much for materials. A few words to those who desire to make their labours a source of profit.

Not a week passes without some dozens of inquiries as to where work can be disposed of; and we are obliged to say, that no Institution for this purpose exists in London. Some is disposed of at the Bazaars,—more is confided to the stand-keepers, for sale on commission,—and occasionally shops purchase a little, or give out work to those whom they may find competent. But the fact is, amateur needlework is like amateur painting, or drawing, or singing,—it is not of that quality which commands a price, however much flattering friends may extol it as charming and exquisite ! It requires care, patience, and perseverance, as well as instruction, to be a good workwoman. Being such, however, there is little doubt that employment could be found, —not so remunerative, perhaps, as to constitute a livelihood, but such as will afford an agreeable addition to a limited income.

Finally, whatever elucidations may be needed of any work or design in these pages, can always be obtained in those of the current numbers of the " *Family Friend*," addressed to the Editor of the Needlework Department, care of Messrs. Ward & Lock, 158, Fleet Street, London; and every material can be procured of Mrs. Pullan, 126, Albany Street, Regent's Park.

TREASURES IN NEEDLEWORK.

INSTRUCTIONS IN TATTING.

THIS art (which is among the best adapted for showing to advantage a pretty hand) had for a long period fallen into disuse in this country, till the beautiful specimens exhibited in the Exposition of Industry, in France, caused a revival of this ancient and (in olden time) frivolous amusement. Indeed, it was thought so trifling and useless an occupation, that our French friends designated it by the (then) appropriate term, *Frivolité*. It can, however, no longer be deemed frivolous or useless, for we have improved the hint given us by our ancestors, and are gratified to find it will admit of varied and elegant patterns.

The only necessary implements for tatting are a shuttle or short netting-needle, and a gilt pin and ring, united by a chain. The cotton used should be strong and soft. The only cotton we have found suitable for it is Evans's Tatting Cotton, manufactured expressly for the work by Messrs. W. Evans & Co., of Derby. It is so soft it never twists, and at the same time so strong that it will bear the peculiar *jerk* necessary to form the knot. There are three sizes, Nos. 1, 2, and 3. Attention should be paid to the manner of holding the hands, as on this depends the grace or awkwardness of the movement. Fill the shuttle with the cotton (or silk) required, in the same manner as a netting-needle. Hold the shuttle between the thumb and first and second fingers of the right hand, leaving about half a yard of cotton unwound. Take up the cotton, about three inches from the end, between the thumb and first finger of the left hand, and let the end fall in the palm of the hand; pass the cotton round the other fingers of the left hand (keeping them parted a little), and bring it again between the thumb and forefinger, thus making a circle round the extended fingers. There are only two stitches in tatting, and they are usually done alternately; this is therefore termed a *double stitch.*

The first stitch is called the *English stitch*, and made thus:—Let the thread between the right and left hands fall towards you; slip the shuttle under the thread between the first and second fingers; draw it out rather quickly, keeping it in a horizontal line with the left hand. You will find a slipping loop is formed on this cotton with that which went round the fingers. Hold the shuttle steadily, with the cotton stretched tightly out, and with the second finger of the left hand slip the loop thus made under the thumb.

The other stitch is termed *French stitch;* the only difference being, that instead of allowing the cotton to fall *towards* you, and passing the shuttle *downwards*, the cotton is thrown in a loop over the left hand, and the shuttle passed under the thread between the first and second fingers *upwards*. The knot must be invariably formed by the thread which passes round the fingers of the left hand. If the operation is reversed, and the knot formed by the cotton connected with the shuttle, the loop will not draw up. This is occasioned by letting the cotton from the shuttle hang loosely, instead of drawing it out and holding it tightly stretched. When any given number of these double stitches are done, and drawn closely together, the stitches are held between the first finger and thumb, and the other fingers are withdrawn from the circle of cotton, which is gradually diminished by drawing out the shuttle until the loop of tatting is nearly or entirely closed. The tatted loops should be quite close to each other, unless directions to the contrary are given.

The pin is used in making an ornamental edge, something like pearl edging, thus:—Slip the ring on the left-hand thumb, that the pin attached may be ready for use. After making the required number of

Infant's Cap Crown, in Tatting. By Mrs. Pullan.

double stitches, twist the pin in the circle of cotton, and hold it between the forefinger and thumb whilst making more double stitches; repeat. The little loops thus formed are termed *picots*.

Trefoil Tatting is done by drawing three loops up tightly, made close together, and then leaving a short space before making more. The trefoil is sewed into shape afterwards with a needle.

To join Loops.—When two loops are to be connected, a *picot* is made in the *first*, wherever the join is required. When you come to the corresponding part of the *second* loop, draw the thread which goes round the fingers of the left-hand through the picot with a needle, pulling through a loop large enough to admit the shuttle. Slip this through, then draw the thread tight again over the fingers, and continue the work. In many patterns—as in the Baby's Cap-crown which follows this article—a needle is used to work over, in button-hole stitch, the thread which passes from one loop to another. A long needle-ful of the same cotton or silk used for the tatting, is left at the beginning of the work, and a common needle used to buttonhole over bars wherever they occur.

Picots are also sometimes made with the needle and cotton in working over these bars.

INFANT'S CAP CROWN IN TATTING.

Materials.—Evans's Tatting Cotton, No. 3; Boulton's Steel Shuttle, No. 14; a very fine Pearling Pin; and a Reel of Evans's Mecklenburgh, No. 12, for the Mechlin wheel in the centre.

The Pattern consists of five loops, ten patterns being required to form the circle.

1st Pattern. — *1st Loop.* — 3 double stitches, 1 picot, 4 double stitches, 1 picot, 2 double stitches, 1 picot, 6 double stitches, 1 picot, 3 double stitches. Draw it up, leaving a bar of thread, on which 8 buttonhole stitches can be worked.

2nd Loop.—3 double stitches; join to the last picot of former loop, + 5 double

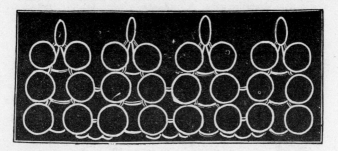

Edging in Frivolité.   By Mrs. Pullan.

stitches, 1 picot + twice, 3 double stitches. Draw it up a little tighter than the last.

3rd Loop.—3 double stitches, join to the last picot of 2nd loop, + 6 double stitches, 1 picot, + twice, 3 double. Draw it quite tight.

4th Loop.—Same as 2nd loop.

5th Loop.—3 double stitches, join to the last picot of 4th loop; 6 double stitches, 1 picot, 2 double stitches, 1 picot, 4 double stitches, 1 picot, 3 double stitches. Draw it up, but not tighter than 1st loop.

To work the buttonhole stitches, take a common sewing needle, with a very long piece of the same cotton; slip the needle through the picot, after the two double stitches of the first loop, draw it out, leaving a short end, on which do four common buttonhole stitches; catch up the next picot; make 6 buttonhole stitches, 8 buttonhole stitches on the bar of the 1st loop, 2 between that and the bar of 2nd loop, 6 on 2nd bar, 2 between that and bar of 4th loop, 6 on bar of 4th loop, 1 before the next; now slip the needle through the two stitches after the 1st loop, thus forming a bar, on which work back 6 buttonhole stitches, then 1 more between 4th and 5th loops, and 8 on the bar of 5th loop. Take the needle across to the base of the 1st loop, and work back 10 stitches; now work 6 buttonhole stitches on the thread connected with the shuttle, catch up the picot, work 8 buttonhole stitches, catch up the next picot, 4 buttonhole stitches, catch up 3rd picot, 4 buttonhole stitches; make a picot, 8 buttonhole stitches; make another picot, 6 buttonhole stitches.

Now resume the shuttle, leaving the needleful of cotton attached to the work.

2nd Pattern.—*1st Loop.*—Three double stitches, join to the last picot made with the needle and cotton; 4 double stitches join to the other picot made with the needle, 2 double stitches join to picot in the centre of the 5th loop of 1st pattern (which has been already caught up in working with the needle); 6 double stitches, 1 picot, 3 double stitches.

2nd, 3rd, 4th, and *5th Loops* to be done as in 1st pattern.

Then work the buttonhole stitches with the needle and cotton as before.

For the centre do ten loops thus :—

1st Loop.—Four double stitches, 1 picot, 6 double stitches; join to the last picot at the point of the 3rd loop of a pattern, 6 double stitches, 1 picot, 3 double stitches.

2nd Loop.—Four double stitches; join to the last picot of 1st loop 6 double stitches; join to the picot at the point of 3rd loop of a pattern; 6 double, 1 picot, 3 double stitches.

3rd, 4th, 5th, 6th, 7th, 8th, 9th, and *10th,* same as 2nd. These loops must not be drawn very tightly. The bars which connect them must be button-holed as those of the patterns.

These ten loops will form a small circle, within which a Mechlin wheel should be worked with the Mecklenburgh, No. 12. This wheel is one of our point-lace stitches, in which beautiful art full instructions will be found in another part. The crown when completed should be trimmed with the following narrow edge: —

1st Loop.—Four double stitches, + 1 picot, 2 double stitches + 4 times. Draw it up to form a semicircle.

2nd and all following Loops.—Two double stitches; join to the last picot of former loop 2 double stitches, + 1 picot, 2 double stitches + 4 times.

Draw up as 1st loop, and sew neatly round the crown.

EDGING IN FRIVOLITÉ.

Materials.—Evans's tatting cotton, Boulton's steel shuttle, and a pearling pin. The size of the cotton must depend upon the nature of the article which the edging is designed to trim. As a general rule, No. 1 is suitable for ladies' jupes, children's drawers, and other articles made in calico. No. 2 is a medium size, and will do for finer drawers, and generally for things made in jaconet or cambric muslin. No. 3 is very fine, and fit for infants' robes, caps, ladies' collars, &c.

1st Pattern.—Begin by threading the end of the cotton with a sewing needle. Double the cotton, allowing a long needleful on the needle; and holding the doubled end between the finger and thumb, do 14 buttonhole stitches with the needle. The thread can then be drawn up tight, so as not to leave a loop. Now begin with the shuttle.

1st Loop.—12 double stitches, 1 picot, 4 double, draw up the loop, but not tightly, and work with the needle on the bar of thread 10 buttonhole stitches.

2nd Loop. —With the needle, do 2 buttonhole stitches on the thread before beginning this loop. 4 double, join to the picot of the last; 8 double, 1 picot, 4 double. Draw this up like the first, and work on the bar 10 buttonhole stitches. 2 more on the thread before the

3rd Loop.—4 double; join to the picot; 9 double, 1 picot, 3 double. Draw up this loop rather tighter; work on it 7 buttonhole stitches, and 2 on the thread afterwards.

4th Loop.—(At the point.) 2 double, join to the picot, 12 double, 1 picot, 2 double. Draw this loop up *quite tightly.* Work 2 buttonhole stitches on the thread afterwards.

5th Loop.—3 double, join, 9 double, 1 picot, 4 double, draw up this like the third. Work on it 7 buttonhole stitches, and 1 on the thread afterwards. Slip the needle through between the two buttonhole stitches

after the second loop, and draw the thread through, allowing for a bar on which 6 buttonhole stitches can be worked. By doing these, the thread is brought back to the fifth loop; do one more buttonhole stitch on the thread, and proceed to the

6th Loop.—4 double, join ; + 4 double, 1 picot, + twice, 4 double. Draw it up, and work it with 10 stitches. Then join across to between the first and second loops, as after the fifth.

7th Loop.—4 double, join, 4 + double, 1 picot, + twice, 4 double. Take the needle across to the commencement of the first loop, and on the bar do 10 buttonhole stitches, 9 more buttonhole on the thread, join to the last picot, 9 buttonhole on the thread, make a picot, 9 more buttonhole. This completes one pattern.

1st loop of the 2nd pattern.—4 double, join to the picot on the thread, 4 double, join to the picot of the 7th loop, 4 double, 1 picot, 4 double. Draw it up and work on the bar 10 buttonhole stitches, and 2 after.

2nd Loop.—4 double, join to the picot, 4 double, join to the picot of the 6th loop, 4 double, 1 picot, 4 double. Draw it up, and work it like the last.

The remaining 5 loops are to be worked exactly like those of the first pattern. All subsequent ones are done like the second.

It may, perhaps, be permitted to us to observe that tatting, (or frivolité,) besides being very pretty, has the merit of wearing extremely well. It requires far less eyesight than crochet, and is much stronger than knitting, and is also, (as we trust we prove,) susceptible of great and elegant variations of design.

———◆———

MAXIMS FOR PARENTS AND TEACHERS. —Never give reproof, if it can be avoided, while the feelings of either party are excited. If the parent or teacher be not calm his influence is diminished, and a bad example is set. If the child is excited or provoked, he will not feel the force of argument or rebuke. On the other hand, do not defer too long. Seize the first favourable opportunity while the circumstances are fresh in the memory. Reprove each fault as it occurs, and do not suffer them to accumulate, lest the offender be discouraged by the amount.

INSTRUCTIONS IN CROCHET.

PERHAPS no kind of work has ever attained such popularity as *Crochet*. Whether as a simple trimming for drawers, as an elaborate quilt, or as a fabric, almost rivalling Point Lace, it is popular with every woman who has any time at all for fancy work, since it is only needful to understand the stitches, and the terms and contractions used in writing the descriptions of the different designs, to be enabled to work with ease the most beautiful pattern that ever appeared in crochet.

The names we give to the various stitches are the same which have been applied to them for years past in the "Family Friend," "Lady's Library," "Lady's Companion," and, in short, all the leading periodicals in which *work* forms a part. It will be found, therefore, that our *Treasure* is not only complete in itself, but that it forms a *Guide-Book* for all the periodicals which are at present popular.

In the first instance, the crochet hook should be very smooth, made of fine steel, and fixed in handles. The "*Tapered Indented*" Hook, which has been made at our suggestion, and has the *size* engraved on the handle, will be found convenient, from its quality, and saving trouble of referring to a guage.

The marks used in our crochet receipts are simple, consisting chiefly of Printer's marks, such as crosses, daggers, asterisks. They are used to mark repetitions. It will be seen that wherever a *mark* is used, another *similar* one is sure to be found; the repetition occuring between the two.

Sometimes one repetition occurs within the other. For instance : + 2 Dc, 4 Ch, miss 4, * 1 Dc, 1 Ch, miss 1, * three times, 5 Dc, + twice, it would at full length be—2 Dc, 4 Ch, miss 4, 5 Dc, 1 Ch, miss 1, 5 Dc, 1 Ch, miss 1, 5 Dc, 1 Ch, miss 1, 5 Dc, 2 Dc, 4 Ch, miss 4, 5 Dc, 1 Ch, miss 1, 5 Dc, 1 Ch, miss 1, 5 Dc, 1 Ch, miss 1, 5 Dc. There is another mode of abbreviating; but this can only be used where a row has a centre, both sides of which are alike, the latter being the same as the former, worked *backwards*. In this case the letters *b, a,* are employed, to show that in the latter part of the row the instructions must be reversed :—*b,* 7

Dc, 3 Ch, miss 2, 1 Dc, 2 Ch, miss 1, *a,* 1 Dc (the centre stitch), would be 7 Dc, 3 Ch, miss 2, 1 Dc, 2 Ch, miss 1, 1 Dc, miss 1, 2 Ch, 1 Dc, miss 2, 3 Ch, 7 Dc. A knowledge of these abbreviations is easily acquired, and much space is saved by them.

The stitches used are *Chain, Slip, Single, Double, Treble,* and *Long Treble Crochet.*

Chain Stitch is made by forming a loop on the thread, then inserting the hook, and drawing the thread through the loop already made. Continue this, forming a succession of stitches.

Slip Stitch is made by drawing a thread *at once* through any given stitch, and the loop on the needle.

Single Crochet (Sc).—Having a loop on the needle, insert the hook in a stitch, and draw the thread through in a loop. You then have two on the hook; draw the thread through both at once.

Double Crochet (Dc.)—Twist the thread round the hook before inserting it in the stitch, through which you draw the thread in a loop. There will then be three loops on the hook; draw the thread through two, and then through the one just formed, and the remaining one.

Treble Crochet (Tc), and *Long Treble* (long Tc), are worked in the same way; in treble the thread is put *twice;* in long treble *three times,* before inserting it into the stitch.

Square Crochet is also sometimes used. The squares are either open or close. An open square consists of one Dc, two Ch, missing two on the line beneath, before making the next stitch. A close square has three successive Dc. Thus, any given number of close squares, followed by an open, will have so many times three Dc, and *one over;* consequently any foundation for square crochet must have a number that can be divided by three, having one over.

To contract an Edge.—This may be done in Dc, Tc, or long Tc. Twist the thread round the hook as often as required, insert it in the work, and half do a stitch. Instead of finishing it, twist the thread round again, until the same number of loops are on, and work a stitch entirely; so that, for two stitches, there is only one head.

To join on a Thread.—Joins should be avoided as much as possible in open work. In joining, finish the stitch by drawing the new thread through, leaving two inches for both ends, which must be held in.

German Purse. By Mrs. Pullan.

To use several Colours.—This is done in single crochet. Hold the threads not in use on the edge of the work, and work them in. Change the colour by beginning the stitch in the old colour, and finishing it with the new, continuing the work with the latter holding in the old. If only one stitch is wanted in the new colour, finish one stitch, and begin the next with it; then change.

To join Leaves, &c.—When one part of a leaf or flower is required to be joined to another, drop the loop from the hook, which insert in the place to be joined; draw the loop through and continue.

To work over Cord.—Hold the cord in the left hand with the work, and work round it, as you would over an end of thread, working closely. When beads are used they must be first threaded on silk or thread, and then dropped, according to the pattern, on the *wrong* side of the work. This side looks more even than the other; therefore, when bead purses are worked from an engraving, they are worked the reverse of the usual way, viz., from right to left.

GERMAN PURSE.

MATERIALS.—2 skeins of very fine white netting silk; 6 skeins of the same sized silk, in any rich colour; an ounce of transparent white glass beads; 4 rows of blue steel, and a hank of gold beads. All the three to be the size called *seed* beads. For the garniture, two fringe ends of gold and blue steel, and gold rings.

THE style of purse of which this is a specimen, was introduced from Germany

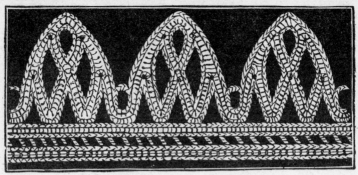

Gothic Edging, in Crochet. By Mrs. Pullan.

at the time of the Great Exhibition. The pattern is formed entirely in various sorts of beads, on a plain crochet ground. Frequently, there are six or seven different kinds of beads in one purse; but, as this is the first specimen we have given to our readers, we have selected a less complicated design. The way in which crochet, with beads, is done, is by dropping beads, wherever required, on the wrong side of the purse; and then turning the work, so that this side becomes the *right*. However many kinds of beads may be introduced, the mode of working is the same; only care must be taken to string them on in proper order. This, therefore, is the only difficult part of the process.

When transparent white, or silver beads are introduced, they are separately strung on white silk, which is worked in invisibly, and never appears at all—the white beads only being dropped on when required. Both silks must be *very* fine, or the small beads will not thread on them; and the crochet must be done as finely and tightly as possible.

Very rich blue, or scarlet, forms the prettiest ground for this purse. Preferring the former, my directions will apply to it. The contractions used are—B, (blue silk), S, (steel), G, (gold beads), W, (white beads).

Begin by threading the white beads on the white silk, half on each skein. On the blue silk thread the gold and blue steel in the following manner:—

1st Round.—141 gold, + 3 S, 4 G + twice, 3 S, 2 G, 3 S, 4 G, 3 S, 4 G, 3 S, 1 G. This brings you to the end of the first round, where steel beads are introduced.

2nd Round. + 1 G, 4 S, 5 G, 4 S, 5 G, 4 S, 1 G + twice.

3rd Round. + 1 G, 3 S, 4 G, 3 S, 4 G, 3 S, 1 G + twice.

4th Round. + 1 G, 2 S, 3 G, 2 S, 3 G, 2 S, 1 G + twice.

5th Round. + 1 G, 1 S, 4 G, 1 S, 4 G, 1 S, 1 G + twice.

6th Round.—Like the 5th.

Now thread on 256 more gold, and then begin on another skein of silk. They vary so much in size, and people crochet so differently, that it is impossible to say, exactly, what beads are to go on each skein; but, probably, two skeins will be required for each end, and two for the middle; therefore, use one skein before threading the beads on the next, as you can then more easily add on, or take off a few. The beads are now threaded for the first round of pines, and the scroll of gold between it and the next—58 gold.

1st Round with steel. + 1 G, 3 S, 4 G, 3 S, 4 G, 3 S, 1 G + twice.

2nd, 3rd, 4th, 5th, and 6th Rounds.—As before.

170 gold completes the end. The other must be done in the same manner.

With a very fine crochet-hook, make a chain of 110 stitches; close into a round; and work one round in Sc.

2nd Round. + 3 B, 3 G, 11 B, 1 G, 19 B, 1 G, 11 B, 3 G, 3 B + twice.

3rd Round. + (*b*) 2 B, 1 G, 3 B, 1 G, 3 B, 2 G, 4 B, 1 G, 1 B, 1 G, 4 B, 3 G (*a*), 3 B +. Work backward, from *a* to *b*, the 3 Blue silk after the *a* being the centre stitches of the row, or side of the round; and then again between the crosses.

4th Round. + (*b*) 2 B, 1 G, 2 B, 1 G, 3 B, 1 G, 2 B, 1 G, 2 B, 1 G 3 B, 1 G, 2 B, 1 G, 3 B, 1 G (*a*), 1 B +; *repeat* as before.

5th Round. + (*b*) 2 B, 1 G, 2 B, 1 G, 3 B, 1 G, * 2 B, 1 G, * 4 times, 3 B, 1 G (*a*), 3 B +; *repeat* as before.

6th Round. + (*b*) 3 B, 1 G, 2 B, 3 G, 4 B, 2 G, 3 B, 1 G, 2 B, 1 G, 3 B, 1 G (*a*), 3 B +; *repeat* as before.

7th Round. + 19 B, 2 G, 5 B, 1 G, 1 B, 1 G, 5 B, 2 G, 19 B + twice.

8th Round. + 26 B, 3 G, 26 B + twice.

9th Round.—Every stitch in silk, except that 1 bead is dropped on the centre of the 3 in the previous round.

10th Round.—All silk. Work in the end of the white silk.

11th Round. + 6 B, * 5 W (*beads*), 3 B, 1 G, 2 B, 1 G, 3 B, 1 G, 3 B, * twice, 5 W, 6 B + twice.

12th Round. + 5 B, * 7 W, 3 B, 2 G, 1 B, 3 G, 3 B * twice; 7 W, 5 B + twice.

13th Round. + 4 B, * 3 W, 3 G, 3 W, 4 B, 1 G, 5 B, * twice; 3 W, 3 G, 3 W, 4 B + twice.

14th Round. + 4 B, * 2 W, 1 G, 3 S, 1 G, 2 W, 2 B, 1 G, 1 B, 1 G, 5 B, * twice; 2 W, 1 G, 3 S, 1 G, 2 W, 4 B, * twice.

15th Round. + 3 B, * 2 W, 1 G, 4 S, 1 G, 2 W, 3 B, 1 G, 1 B, 1 G, 1 B, 1 G, 1 B, * twice; 2 W, 1 G, 4 S, 1 G, 2 W, 4 B + twice.

16th Round. + 3 B, * 2 W, 1 G, 3 S, 1 G, 3 W, 6 B, 2 G, 1 B, * twice; 2 W, 1 G, 3 S, 1 G, 3 W, 4 B + twice.

17th Round. + 3 B, * 2 W, 1 G, 2 S, 1 G, 3 W, 6 B, 1 G, 3 B, * twice; 2 W, 1 G, 2 S, 1 G, 3 W, 5 B + twice.

18th Round. + 3 B, * 2 W, 1 G, 1 S, 1 G, 3 W, 4 B, 1 G, 2 B, 1 G, 3 B, * twice; 2 W, 1 G, 1 S, 1 G, 3 W, 6 B + twice.

19th Round. + 3 B, * 2 W, 1 G, 1 S, 1 G, 2 W, 6 B, 2 G, 4 B, * twice; 2 W, 1 G, 1 S, 1 G, 2 W, 7 B + twice.

20th Round. + 3 B, * 2 W, 2 G, 2 W, 8 B, 1 G, 2 B, 1 G, 1 B, * twice, 2 W, 2 G, 2 W, 8 B + twice.

21st Round. + 4 B, * 2 W, 1 G, 2 W, 9 B, 2 G, 3 B, * twice, 2 W, 1 G, 2 W, 8 B, + twice.

22nd Round. + 4 B, * 2 W, 1 G, 2 W, 2 B, 2 W, 4 B, 1 G, 5 B, * twice; 2 W, 1 G, 2 W, 2 B, 2 W, 4 B, + twice.

23rd Round. + 5 B, * 4 W, 4 B, 1 W, 3 B, 1 G, 6 B, * twice; 4 W, 4 B, 1 W, 3 B, + twice.

24th Round. + 6 B, * 4 W, 3 B, 1 W, 1 B, 1 G, 1 B, 1 G, 4 B, 1 G, 2 B, * twice; 4 W, 3 B, 1 W, 3 B, + twice.

25th Round. + 7 B, * 4 W, 1 B, 1 W, 3 B, 1 G, 1 B, 4 G, 4 B, * twice; 4 W, 1 B, 1 W, 4 B, + twice.

26th Round. + 4 B, 2 G, 3 B, 3 W, * 8 B, 1 G, 2 B, 2 G, 3 B, 3 W, * twice; 5 B, + twice.

27th Round. + 2 B, 1 G, 1 B, 1 G, 16 B, 1 G, 1 B, 1 G, 16 B, 1 G, 1 B, 1 G, 9 B, 1 G, 2 B, + twice.

28th Round. + 3 B, 1 G, 1 B, 2 G, 3 B, * 1 G, 5 B, 1 G, 3 B, 1 G, 1 B, 4 G, 3 B, * twice; 1 G, 3 B, 1 G, 2 B, + twice.

29th Round. + 7 B, * 2 G, 2 B, 1 G, 4 B, 1 G, 2 B, 1 G, 6 B, * twice; 2 G, 2 B, 1 G, 1 B, 1 G, 3 B, + twice.

30th Round. + 6 B, * 2 G, 1 B, 4 G, 1 B, 2 G, 3 B, 2 G, 4 B, * twice; 2 G, 1 B, 4 G, 3 B, + twice.

31st Round. + 5 B, 1 G, 7 B, 2 G, 9 B, 1 G, 7 B, 2 G, 9 B, 1 G, 7 B, 1 G, 3 B, + twice.

32nd Round. + 14 B, 1 G, 1 B, 1 G, 16 B, 1 G, 1 B, 1 G, 15 B, 1 G, 3 B, + twice.

33rd Round.—Like 11th; but instead of the 6 B at end, 3 B, 1 G, 2 B.

34th Round.—Like 12th; but instead of 5 B at end, 2 B, 1 G, 2 B.

35th to 47th Round (inclusive).—Like 13th to 25th.

48th Round. + 9 B, 3 W, 7 B, 1 G, 8 B, 3 W, 7 B, 1 G, 8 B, 3 W, 5 B, + twice.

49th Round.—In blue silk, working in the white, which may be cut off, leaving an end for fastening. Repeat *backwards* from 9th to 2nd rounds, then a plain round. This finishes the end. Work to the centre of one side, and then 4 rounds; thus, 1 Dc, 1 Ch, miss 1, *repeat*, taking care that the Dc of one round comes over the chain of the previous one, and working *under*, not *in* the chain. Work backwards and forwards the same way for the opening, and then 4 rounds. Put on the slides before joining on the other end, which must be made separately. Close the end with a row of Sc, taking a stitch from each half of the round. Fasten on the garniture, and the Purse is complete.

GOTHIC EDGING, IN CROCHET.

MATERIALS.—Walter Evans & Co.'s Boar's Head Cotton, Derby, of any size suitable for the work to be trimmed. For Petticoat, No. 16—with Crochet-hook, No. 20. For coarser articles, No 4, or No. 8, with a Hook proportionably large.

MAKE a chain of the length required, the number of stitches being divisible by 17 : if a straight piece, add 5 more chains ; but if intended for trimming drawers, or similar articles, close into a round, without adding any extra stitches.

1st Row.—Sc.

2nd Row. + 1 Dc, 1 Ch, miss 1, + *repeat.*

3rd Row.—Sc.

4th Row.—5 Sc, putting the hook through both sides of the Ch, of the previous row, at every stitch + * 11 Ch, miss 2, 3 Sc, (under both sides of the Ch,) * 3 times, 2 Sc, + *repeat* for every pattern.

5th Row.—5 Sc, on 5, then on the first loop, 6 Sc on the first 6 of 11 Ch, + 1 Sc, 2 Dc, 1 Sc, on next, 4 Sc, on next 4, 1 Sc, on centre of 3 Sc. On the next loop, 5 Sc, on 5 chain ; 1 Sc, 2 Dc, 1 Sc, on the 6th Ch ; 5 Sc, on the next 5 ; 1 Sc, on centre of 3 Sc. On the next loop, 4 Sc, on 4 Ch ; 1 Sc, 1 Dc, on next Ch. Turn the work on the wrong side :— 8 Ch, 2 Sc, on the point of the 2nd loop ; 8 Ch, 2 Sc, on the 2 Dc, at the point of the 1st loop. Turn the work on the right side :—4 Sc, on 4 Ch ; 3 Sc, on the next ; 1 on each of the last 3. Miss the 2 Sc, at the point of the second loop ; and on the other chain of 8, 3 Sc, on the 1st 3, 2 Sc, on the next. Turn the work on the wrong side :—6 Ch, 2 Sc, at the point of the loop. Turn on the right side :—2 Sc, in the 1st ; 2 Ch, 2 Sc, in each of the next 2 ; 2 in the next 2. Sc down the chains of the half loops, taking care not to contract the edge at all. 5 Sc, on 5 Sc ; 3 Sc, on chain of the next loop ; 3 Ch, draw the loop through the corresponding part of the Sc of last loop. Slip back on the 3 Ch ; 3 Sc on 3 more chains of the loop. + *repeat* as often as may be required for the number of patterns.

THE WORK-TABLE FRIEND.

SOFA CUSHION IN TAPISSERIE D'AUXERRE.

MATERIALS.—A square of common black or white net ; 2 oz. of apricot-coloured Berlin wool ; 1 oz. of rich blue ditto ; and two hanks of large steel beads.

TAPISSERIE D'AUXERRE is the term applied to a new, and a very pretty sort of work with Berlin wool and net. The pattern is formed by darning the net, in various forms, and with different colours ; and, occasionally, beads are intermingled with the wool, as in the design now before us.

It will be remembered that all the ordinary kinds of net have meshes or holes of a hexagonal form, which affords peculiar facilities for radiating and star patterns.

Begin by running threads in the net, to mark the centres of the stars, using white cotton for black net, and some brilliant colour for white net. The first thread must be taken about fifteen holes from the selvage, and in the same direction. Run the needle in and out every second or third thread, and leave an inch or two of thread at each end. Miss thirty meshes, and run another thread along in the same way. The whole width of the net must thus be marked, by running a needleful of thread in every 31st mesh. Then do the same in the diagonal lines, at similar intervals, doing all those in one direction first. In beginning those in the opposite hue, see that the three threads cross each other always in one hole of the net, which they cannot fail to do if the first of them is begun properly, and the intervals of thirty holes have been maintained throughout. The net will then be seen to be divided into triangles in every part.

Begin the wool-work with the stars, which are done in apricot wool. Each star has six points. The centre is taken where the threads cross, the *spaces between* the threads being filled, whilst the lines occupied by those threads are left vacant. Reckon from the first clear mesh after the one the threads cross, and slip the needle up through the 10th hole beyond, making a knot in the wool to fasten on ; let the wool cross nine bars of net, parallel with one thread, and slip it under one bar near

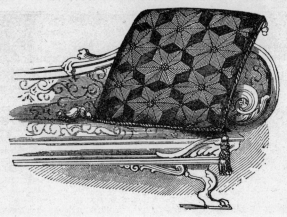

Sofa Cushion in Tapisserie D'Auxerre.—By Mrs. Pullan.

the centre, so as to take a similar stitch across nine bars, and on a line with the next dividing thread. Observe, there is no crossing any other dividing threads, these two stitches forming the base of one point of the star. Slip the needle into the next line of net, taking it a stitch higher, and

do two wool stitches across *eight* bars, on a line with and within the last. Within these two more must be worked, across seven bars; then six, five, four, three, two, one, till the space between two dividing threads is filled up in the form of a point. Slip the needle at the back to another division, and repeat; and so on until a com-

plete star is worked. All the others are to be done in the same way, taking as the centre the place where the threads cross.

The diamond-shaped spaces between the stars are to be filled with blue wool; or, the colours may be reversed if preferred; and, of course, any other two that will suit the furniture better, may be selected in preference. In working the diamonds, take the wool completely across each space, not in and out. The centre of every star is filled in with steel beads; or, it may be made of blue wool, in which case the work will wash extremely well.

The cushion may have both sides done in tapisserie, or the back may be covered with damask or moreen, to match with the furniture of the apartment. It must be trimmed with cord and tassels.

As the best mode of making up the pillow of a sofa cushion is not generally known, we will add the directions for this article :—

Cut out a square of stout calico, the *bias* way, the size intended for the pillow, and line it with fine, soft wadding, running them together at certain intervals, to prevent the wool getting rubbed away. Then make the calico thus lined into a case, which must be filled with down or feathers, and sewed up.

Sofa pillows made in this way are not

Rug, or Mat.

only much softer than ordinary ones, but they are not liable to become thin and out of shape; all needlework-covers should, therefore, invariably have the cushions made in this manner.

KNITTING, FOR RUGS OR MATS OF ANY SIZE.

THE wool which is to form the raised work is cut in even lengths; to cover a mesh with a groove, to admit the scissors, is the best way. The needles and material for the foundation must be proportioned to the article intended to be made. For a hearth or carriage-rug, the needles should be 8 or even a larger size. The material—fine, soft twine, or the coarsest woollen yarn—almost as coarse as moss yarn.

For an urn rug, the needles must be from 12 to 15, and the material the coarsest sewing cotton, very fine twine, or coarse strong, woollen yarn.

Set on the number of stitches you wish. Knit a row.

For the row at which you insert the wool.—Knit a stitch; take the wool to be worked in, in the left hand; put it *round* the foundation material, (which is held in the fingers of the right hand,) close to the right-hand needle; put the ends even together, and draw it under the right-hand needle, to the front. Knit a stitch, pass the wool back again, under the right-hand needle—then take another piece of the wool, and proceed as described above; repeat to the end of the row, then knit a plain row, and repeat the instructions given above for inserting the wool. For a hearth-rug, the wool to be inserted should be at least four times double.

HOLLY-BERRY DOYLEY.

Materials.—Messrs. W. Evans and Co.'s Boar's-head crochet cotton, No. 10, pale clear green, and imitation coral beads.

THREAD the coral beads on one reel of cotton, which you will put aside until you require it. The green you will thread on the other reel, and begin to work. 4 ch, close it into a round, and work 1 sc in each chain, and a chain stitch after each. 2nd. + 1 sc, 1 ch, miss none, + 8 times. Increase 8 stitches in each of the three following rounds, and then begin the pattern.

1st Pattern Round.—+ 2 stitches with beads, 1 cotton, 2 beads, 1 ch, 1 cotton, + 8 times.

2nd.—2 + beads, 1 ch, 1 cotton 2 beads, 2 cotton, + 8 times.

3rd.—+ 1 bead, 3 cotton, 1 ch, + 16 times.

4th.— + sc all round without any beads, and without increase.

5th.—+ 8 cotton, 1 ch, 1 bead, + 8 times.

6th.—+ 8 cotton and 1 ch, 2 beads, + 8 times.

7th.—+ 5 c, 2 b, 1 c, 1 ch, 5 b, + 8 times.

8th.—+ 4 c, 4 b, 1 ch, 5 b on 5, + 8 times.

9th.— + 4 c, 1 ch, 9 b, 1 c, + 8 times.

10th.—+ 2 c, 1 b, 1 ch, 1 c, 9 b, 2 ch, + 8 times.

11th.—+ 1 c, 3 b, 1 c, 5 b, 1 ch, 1 c, 5 b, 1 ch, + 8 times.

12th.—+ 1 c, 8 b, 3 c, 4 b, 2 c, 1 ch.

13th.—+ 1 c, 1 ch, 6 b, 4 c, 5 b, 3 c, + 8 times.

14th.—+ 2 c, 5 b, 4 c, 5 b, 1 ch, 5 c, + 8 times.

15th.—+ 3 c, 3 b, 1 ch, 2 c, 9 b, 3 c, + 8 times.

16th.—+ 5 c, 1 b, 1 c, 10 b, 1 c, 3 b, 1 c, + 8 times.

17th.—+ 1 b, 2 c, 1 ch, 1 c, 8 b, 4 c, 1 ch, 3 c, 3 b, + 8 times.

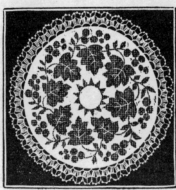

HOLLY-BERRY DOYLEY.

18th.—+ 5 b, 1 c, 7 b, 7 c, 1 b, 1 c, 1 b + 8 times.

19th.—+ 2 b, 7 c, 1 ch, 4 b, 6 c, 3 b 1 ch, 2 c, + 8 times.

20th.—+ 7 b, 12 c, 3 b, 4 c, + 8 times.

21st.—+ 1 b, 1 ch, 1 c, 2 b, 3 c, 1 b, join on the cotton with the coral beads, 4 c, 3 coral, 11 c, + 8 times.

22nd.—+ 4 c, 3 b, 5 c, 5 coral, 9 c, 1 ch, 1 b, + 8 times.

23rd.—+ 1 c, 2 b, 3 c, 2 b, 3 coral, 1 c, 5 coral on 5, 4 c, 2 b, 5 c, 1 ch, + 8 times.

24th.—+ 1 c, 2 b, 5 c, 5 coral (the centre 3 on 3), 1 c, 3 coral, 2 c, 1 coral, 1 c, 2 b, 6 cotton, + 8 times.

25th.—+ 3 c, 1 b, 4 c, 3 coral (on centre 3 of 5), 2 c, 3 coral, 1 c, 1 b, 1 c, 2 coral (on 2nd and 3rd of 3 coral), 2 c, 4 b, 1 ch, 2 c, + 8 times.

26th.—+ 15 c, 1 ch, 5 coral, on 3 and a cotton on each side, 1 c, 1 b, 2 c, 2 b, 1 ch, 6 c, + 8 times.

27th.—+ 16 c, 1 ch, 5 coral on 5, 1 c, 2 b, 2 c, 2 b, 6 c, + 8 times.

28th.—+ 18 c, 1 ch, 3 coral on centre 3 of 5, 3 c, 2 b, 9 c, 1 ch, + 8 times.

Do 2 rounds of cotton only, increasing 8 stitches in each round.

Border.—On the right side, work + 1 sc, 5 ch, miss 4, + all round.

2nd.—+ 3 dc under ch, 2 ch, 3 dc under same chain, + repeat all round.

3rd.—Work on the wrong side, sc under chain of 2, + 3 ch, with a bead on each sc between 3rd and 4th of 6 dc, 3 ch, with bead on each, sc under ch of 2, 3 ch with bead on each, sc under same ch, + all round. Fasten off.

This would be pretty with forget-me-not beads, instead of coral.

Pattern of Netted Lace.

PIECE OF NETTED LACE,

ADAPTED FOR COLLARS, CUFFS, AND TUCKERS FOR CHILDREN'S DRESSES.

Materials.—No. 20 Boar's-head for the above purposes, or No. 8 or 10 for Border for Curtains; bone mesh a quarter of an inch wide; steel mesh gauging, No. 13.

1st and 2nd Rows.—2 plain rows with the bone mesh.

3rd Row.—Plain row, steel mesh.

4th Row.—Steel mesh, cotton *twice* over the mesh, net a stitch into the 1st loop, cotton *once* over the mesh, net a stitch into the same loop, repeat.

5th and 6th Rows.—The same as the 4th.

7th Row.—Steel mesh, plain row.

8th Row.—Bone mesh, net 7 times into the 1st loop, miss 1 loop of last row, repeat.

9th Row.—Steel mesh, cotton *once* over the mesh, net into every loop of the 7 in last row, cotton *twice* over the mesh, miss the same loop as in last row repeat.

10th Row.—Same as last row.

11th Row.—Same mesh, cotton *once* over the mesh, net a stitch into the 1st loop, cotton *twice* over the mesh, net into the same loop; repeat this till the loop that was missed in last row, then with the cotton *twice* over the mesh, net into the next group of stitches, and repeat.

12th and 13th Rows.—Same as 11th row.

14th Row.—Same mesh, cotton twice over the mesh, net into the centre long loop of each group of stitches. It will be observed that the stitches decrease in every row till there will be only one stitch left at the termination of each group of stitches.

SULTANA, OR MOUCHOIR CASE.

IN 3 shades of rose-coloured Berlin wool With Penelope crochet, No. 2, and th darkest shade, make a chain of 66 loops.

1st Row.—Double crochet.

2nd Row.—Dc.

3rd Row.—With the second shade, work 3 long, 3 chain, miss 3, repeat.

4th Row.—With the lightest shade, work 3 long over the last 3 chain, miss 3, repeat.

5th Row.—With the same shade and in the same manner as the 3rd.

6th Row.—With the darkest shade, Dc.

7th Row.—Dc, work 5 loops with the darkest shade, and one with the lightest; repeat.

8th Row.—Dc, 4 dark, 2 light.

9th Row.—Dc, 3 dark, 3 light.

10th Row.—Dc, 2 dark, 4 light.

11th Row.—Dc, 1 dark, 5 light.

12th Row.—Dc, with the lightest shade.

Repeat the whole *reversed*, beginning at the 11th row and working up to the 1st, both inclusive. Work the other side in the same manner. To make it up, line the work with white satin; take a piece of rose-coloured satin for the back, and also a piece of white satin the same size,—between these quilt in a diamond pattern; any perfume that may be preferred, mixed with violet-powder; sew the worked part to the quilted satin, and trim all round with shaded cord. Affix a shaded tassel to each corner.

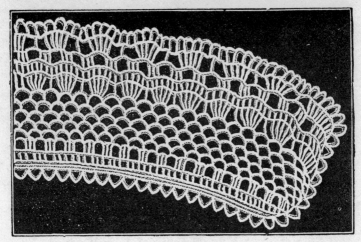

Crochet Cuff.

THE WORK-TABLE FRIEND.

CROCHET CUFF.

WITH Boar's head cotton, No. 30, and Penelope crochet, No. 4, make a chain of 130 stitches.

1st Row.—Dc.

2nd Row.—1 long, 1 chain, miss 1, *repeat.*

3rd Row.—3 *extra* long, 3 chain, miss 3, *repeat.*

4th Row.—5 chain, miss 3, 1 Dc, *repeat.*

5th Row.—1 Dc in centre of last 5 chain, 5 chain, *repeat.*

6th Row.—Same as 5th.

7th Row.—Same as 6th.

8th Row.—Same as 7th.

9th Row.—Work one extra long, and 2 chain, in every stitch of the first 5 chain in last row, 2 chain, 1 Dc in centre of next 5 chain, 2 chain, *repeat.*

10th Row. — 1 long, 1 chain, miss 1, *repeat.*

11th Row.—3 long, 5 chain, miss 5, *repeat.*

12th Row —5 long 2 chain, in every stitch of first 5 chain in last row, 4 chain, 1 long in centre of next 5 chain, 4 chain, *repeat.*

13th Row.—Work all round the cuff 5 chain, miss 3, *repeat.* It is to be worked from the right hand, cutting off the cotton at the end of each row—narrow satin ribbon to be drawn between the long and chain stitches in third row.

SOFA COVERING DENTELLE ANTIQUE.

Nos. 2 and 3 Penelope Crochet Hooks.* Amber border, in 4 thread wool; 8 reels of No. 6 Boar's Head; 4 shades of Amber, 10 skeins of the lightest, 8 of the remaining shades, the lightest to be bright lemon, the darkest, a direct scarlet orange.

Dc means Double Crochet; Sq. Squares. In describing this pattern, for the sake of brevity, and to greatly facilitate the work-

---

* The Penelope Crochet Hook is one in which the steel part runs through the handle, and is fastened at the end; it cannot, therefore, be pulled out. But the finish of the steel is far inferior, in our opinion, to that of Boulton's hooks, the only ones used by ourselves for either coarse or fine work. We have the number engraved on the ivory handle expressly for our friends.

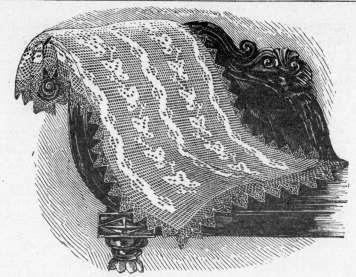

Sofa Covering Dentelle Antique. By Mrs. Warren.

ing, the open work between the thick parts of the pattern and on each side of it, is termed "*Squares*," each "*Square*" to be worked thus: 1 *long*, 2 *chain*, 1 *long into 3rd loop, and* 1 *long on long*, 2 *chain, repeat.* This will be readily understood, when it is observed that the 1st 5 rows are composed entirely of *Squares*.

1*st Row.*—Make a chain of 342 stitches, turn back, work 1 long, 2 chain, 1 long into 3rd loop, 114 (*Squares*) in this row.

2*nd Row.*—Commence with 5 chain on the 1st long of last row, leaving one end of the cotton a full ½ yard in length, this (5 *chain*) is equivalent to 1 long, 2 chain, and makes it less thick than working 1 long at the commencement of every row; 1 long on long, 2 chain, *repeat;* at the last stitch weave the end of cotton in last row into this stitch, this is to prevent any ends of cotton at the termination of the row.

3*rd Row.*—Tie the end of the cotton in a weaver's knot to the end of cotton that was left in last row, and work the same as last row, commencing in the 3rd loop of the 5 chain; be careful to work the knot into a long stitch, and not into a chain. The 4th and 5th rows are exactly the same, which

will be 5 rows of *Squares*. The cotton that is left at the beginning of the row should be of various lengths, or the knots will all come in one place.

6*th Row.*—7 Sq, * 12 long, this is in addition to the last long, formed by the last stitch of the 7 Sq, and this must be understood throughout the pattern, the instructions are to be *implicitly* followed, 5 Sq, 6 long, 5 Sq, *repeat* from * till within 7 Sq of the end, every row throughout this pattern must end with the same number of Sq as commenced.

7*th Row.*—5 Sq, * 24 long, 2 Sq, 3 long, 2 Sq, 3 long, 2 Sq, *repeat* from *.

8*th Row.*—5 Sq, 9 long, * 2 Sq, 15 long, 4 Sq, 15 long, *repeat* from *.

9*th Row.*—5 Sq, a row of long stitches, 1 long into every loop.

10*th Row.*—6 Sq, 3 long, * 4 Sq, 15 long, 2 Sq, 15 long, *repeat* from *.

11*th Row.*—7 Sq, * 3 long, 2 Sq, 3 long, 2 Sq, 24 long, 2 Sq, *repeat* from *.

12*th Row.*—8 Sq, * 6 long, 5 Sq, 12 long, 5 Sq, *repeat* from *.

13*th to* 17*th Rows.*—All rows of *squares*.

18*th Row.*—9 Sq, * 3 long, 21, Sq, *repeat* from *. (*This row must end with* 16 Sq.)

19th Row.—8 Sq, ✱ 3 long, 21 Sq, 3 long, *repeat* from ✱. (*This row ends with* 17 Sq.)

20th Row.—8 Sq, ✱ 6 long, 2 Sq, 1 chain miss 1 loop, 12 long, 1 chain, miss 1 loop, 8 Sq, 7 long, 1 chain, miss 1 loop, 2 Sq, *repeat* from ✱. (*This row ends with* 9 Sq.)

21st Row.—7 Sq, ✱ 3 long, 2 Sq, 3 long, 1 chain, miss 1 loop, 8 long, 1 chain, miss 1 loop, 6 long, 1 chain, miss one loop, 2 Sq, 6 long, 3 Sq, 9 long, 2 Sq, *repeat* from ✱. (*This row ends with* 9 Sq.)

22nd Row.—6 Sq, ✱ 3 long, 4 Sq, 1 chain, miss 1 loop, 5 long, 2 chain, miss 2 loops, 7 long, 2 Sq, 1 chain, miss 1 loop, 8 long, 2 chain, miss 2 loops, 11 long, 1 chain, miss 1 loop, 4 long, 2 chain, miss 2 loops, 1 long, *repeat* from ✱. (*This row. ends with* 10 Sq.)

23rd Row.—8 Sq,✱ 1 chain, miss 1 loop, 21 long, 1 chain, miss 1 loop, 2 Sq, 1 chain, miss 1 loop, 4 long, 1 chain, miss 1 loop, 13 long, 2 chain, miss 2 loops, 4 long, 1 chain, miss 1 loop, 4 long, 2 Sq, *repeat* from ✱. (*This row ends with* 10 Sq.)

24th Row.—8 Sq, ✱ 3 long, 2 chain, miss 2 loops, 8 long, 2 chain, miss 2 loops, 6 long, 4 Sq, 3 long, 2 chain, miss 2 loops, 8 long, 2 chain, miss 2 loops, 6 long, 4 Sq, *repeat* from ✱. (*This row ends with* 11 Sq.)

25th Row.—7 Sq, ✱ 1 chain, miss 1 loop, 4 long, 1 chain, miss 1 loop, 13 long, 2 chain, miss 2 loops, 4 long, 1 chain, miss 1 loop, 4 long, 2 Sq, 1 chain, miss 1 loop, 21 long, 1 chain, miss 1 loop, 2 Sq, *repeat* from ✱. (*This row ends with* 10 Sq.)

26th Row.—7 Sq, ✱ 1 chain, miss 1 loop, 8 long, 2 chain, miss 2 loops, 11 long, 1 chain, miss 1 loop, 4 long, 2 chain, miss 2 loops, 4 long, (*a*) 4 Sq, 1 chain, miss 1 loop, 5 long, 2 chain, miss 2 loops, 7 long, 2 Sq, *repeat* from ✱. (*This row should end at* (*a*), *and leave* 8 Sq.)

27th Row.—8 Sq, ✱ 6 long, 3 Sq, 9 long 2 Sq, 3 long, (*b*) 2 Sq, 3 long, 1 chain, miss 1 loop, 8 long, 1 chain, miss 1 loop, 6 long, 1 chain, miss 1 loop, 2 Sq, *repeat* from ✱ (*This row should end at* (*b*) *and will leave* 7 Sq.)

28th Row.—14 Sq, ✱ 7 long, 1 chain, miss 1 loop, 2 Sq, 6 long, (*c*) 2 Sq, 1 chain, miss 1 loop, 12 long; 1 chain, miss 1 loop, 8 Sq, *repeat* from ✱. (*This row should end at* (*c*) *and leave* 5 Sq).

29th Row.—19 Sq, ✱ 3 long, 21 Sq, *repeat* from ✱. (*This row ends with* 6 Sq.)

30th Row.—20 Sq, ✱ 3 long, 21 Sq, *repeat* from ✱. (*This row ends with* 5 Sq.)

Then work 5 rows of Squares, then commence at the first pattern again; there should be 2 patterns of leaves, and 3 of columns; then work 5 rows of Squares. Then at both ends, *under* every long stitch, work 3 Dc stitches, working 7 round the corner, and *under* every 2 chain at the sides, work 3 Dc stitches. With the lightest lemon work at the top and bottom only, 2 rows, thus,

1st Row.—Dc into the corner loop, 5 chain, Dc into 4th loop, *repeat*.

2nd Row.—Dc into centre loop of 5, 5 chain, *repeat*.

Then work 2 rows all round the same; at the corners, make 5 chain, and Dc twice into the same loop, therefore there will be 4 rows at both ends, and 2 rows only at the side.

Next shade.—Begin every row at the corner, but not at the same corner. 1 long into the centre loop of the 5 chain, ✱ 7 chain, 1 long into the same loop, *repeat* from ✱ twice more (*in all* 4 *long, and* 3 *chains of* 7), then 5 chain, Dc *under* the 2nd 5, 7 chain, Dc *under* the next 2nd 5, 5 chain, miss 1 chain of 5, *repeat*. (The long stitches with the 7 chains must always come at the extreme corner, therefore if there should be any chains of 5 too many for the complete pattern to come in at the corner in the one or two previous patterns, miss 2 chains of 5 instead of 1, immediately *under* the 5 *chain*, not *under* the 7).

Next shade.—✱ 1 long, *under* the 1st 7 chain, 5 chain, 1 long *under* the same, 5 chain, *repeat* from ✱ twice more, Dc *under both* chains of 7 and 5 in last and preceding rows (catching up both at once), 5 chain, *repeat*.

Darkest shade.—✱ 2 long *under* the 5 chain between the 2 long, making 5 chain between each, 3 chain, Dc *under* the 5 chain, 3 chain, *repeat* from ✱ again, 2 long *under* the next 5, making 5 chain between each, 5 chain, Dc exactly the same as in last row, 5 chain, *repeat*.

A pleasing addition may be made in this Tidy by working in the 3rd row of Squares, between the patterns, 7 long stitches in cotton, and 7 in amber shaded wool throughout the row alternately. The Tidy, when washed, must be made slightly blue, and when nearly dry (but of an equal dryness), must be pulled in form, folded double lengthways, and placed between linen folded double, with a heavy weight upon it; if got up in this manner, it will always look new; the wools also will bear washing the same as the cotton.

THE WORK-TABLE FRIEND.

WORK-TABLE COVER IN CROCHET.

12 shades of Amber, 12 shades of Scarlet, 8 skeins of each shade 4 thread Wool, Shaded Amber, Scarlet, and Green, of each, ½ an oz., two reels of Drab Boar's Head cotton, No. 6. Nos. 2 and 3 Penelope Hooks. Dc means Double Crochet. (*It is important that the shades of wool are bright, and that yellow greens are always avoided; otherwise, that which is really elegant becomes vulgar.*)

1st Row.—With lightest Scarlet make a chain of 11 stitches, unite the ends, (*twist the wool twice over the hook, for all the long stitches throughout, until directed to the contrary,*) work *under* the circle, (*that is, into the space and not through the chain,*) 24 long with 1 chain between each long stitch, (*to commence this it is better, after uniting the ends, to make 6 chain ; this is equal to 1 long and 1 chain, and must be reckoned with the 24 long ; these long stitches, it will be observed, are double the length of the ordinary long, and should be considerably longer than ½ an inch, and must never be used unless specially directed,*) draw the wool to the back, tie it neatly and securely, this must be done at every row.

2nd Row.—Next shade, Dc *under* the 1 chain, * 5 chain, Dc *under* next : 3 chain, 3 long with 1 chain between each, *under* next ; 3 chain, Dc *under* next, repeat from *.

3rd Row.—Next shade, 3 long with 1 chain between each *under* the 5 chain ; 1 chain, Dc between 1st long ; 5 chain, Dc between next long ; 1 chain, *repeat.*

4th Row.—Next shade, same as last, only making 5 long instead of 3.

5th Row.—Shaded Amber, 5 long *under* the chain, 1 chain, Dc between 2nd long, 5 chain, Dc between next long, 1 chain, *repeat.*

6th Row.—Next shade, 7 long with 1 chain between each, *under* the 5 chain ; 1 chain, Dc between 1st long, 7 chain, Dc between 3rd long ; 1 chain, *repeat.*

7th Row.—Shaded Amber, same as last row, only making 9 long instead of 7, and Dc between 2nd long instead of 1st.

8th Row.—Next shade Scarlet, 11 long with one chain between each ; *under* the 7 chain ; 1 chain, Dc between 3rd long ; 7 chain ; Dc between 3rd long ; 1 chain ; *repeat.*

9th Row.—Shaded Amber, same as last row only Dc between 4th long instead of 3rd, still making 7 chain and Dc between 3rd long.

10th Row.—Next shade Scarlet, 11 long, with 1 chain between each *under* the 7 chain ; 1 chain ; Dc between 2nd long, 5 chain, Dc between 2nd long, 7 chain, Dc between 3rd long, 5 chain, Dc between 2nd long, 1 chain, *repeat.*

11th Row.—Shaded Amber, 11 long *under* the 7 chain as before ; (*in every row there must be 1 chain between each long,*) 1 chain, Dc *under* the 5 chain ; 5 chain ; Dc between 4th long ; 7 chain, Dc between 3rd long ; 5 chain ; Dc *under* 5 chain ; 1 chain, *repeat.*

12th Row.—Next shade Scarlet, same as last row.

13th Row.—Shaded Amber, 11 long *under* the 7 chain as before, 1 chain, Dc *under* the 5 chain ; 5 chain, Dc between 2nd long for twice, (*that is, 5 chain, Dc between 2nd long and 5 chain, Dc between next 2nd long : this must be understood throughout wherever the term "for twice," or "for three times," or more, is used.*) 7 chain, Dc between 3rd long ; 5 chain, Dc between 2nd long, 5 chain, Dc *under* 5, 1 chain, *repeat.*

14th Row.—Next shade Scarlet, 11 long *under* the 7 chain as before, 1 chain, Dc *under* the 5 chain ; 5 chain, Dc *under* the 5 chain ; 5 chain, Dc between the 2nd long stitch for twice ; 7 chain, Dc between 3rd long, 5 chain, Dc between 2nd long, 5 chain, Dc *under* 5 chain for twice, 1 chain, *repeat.*

15th Row.—Shaded Amber, 11 long *under* the 7 chain as before, 1 chain, Dc *under* 5 chain ; 5 chain, Dc *under* 5 chain for twice, 5 chain, Dc between 2nd long for twice, 7 chain, Dc between 3rd long, 5 chain, Dc between 2nd long 5 chain, Dc *under* 5 chain for three times, 1 chain *repeat.*

16th Row.—Next Scarlet, 11 long *under* the 7 chain as before, 1 chain, Dc *under* 5 chain ; 5 chain, Dc *under* 5 for three times ; 5 chain, Dc between 3rd long ; 7 chain ; Dc between 5th long, 5 chain, Dc *under* 5 for four times, 1 chain, *repeat.*

17th Row.—Shaded Amber, same as last row.

18th Row.—Next shade Scarlet, same as last row, only making 9 chain instead of 7.

19th Row.—Shaded Amber same as last row.

20th Row.—Darkest Scarlet, same as last row.

(*Damp well and lay it between a linen cloth, and place a heavy weight upon it.*)

C

Table Cover. By Mrs. Warren.

(*Crochet or knitting must never be ironed, but when pressing is directed, it must always be managed as before-mentioned.*)

21*st Row.*—(*Now use the 12 shades of Amber alternately, with the 12 shades of Scarlet, using them in gradation, and beginning with the palest Lemon ;*) 11 long as before, *under* the 9 chain, 1 chain, Dc *under* 5 ; 5 chain, Dc *under* 5, for 3 times, 5 chain ; Dc between 2nd long, for twice, 7 chain, Dc between 3rd long ; 5 chain, Dc between 2nd long ; 5 chain ; Dc *under* 5 for 4 times, 1 chain, *repeat.*

22*nd Row.*—Next shade to the darkest Scarlet, 11 long as before, 1 chain, Dc *under* 5 ; 5 chain, Dc *under* 5, for 4 times, 5 chain, Dc between 2nd long twice : 7 chain, Dc between 3rd long, 5 chain, Dc between 2nd long ; 5 chain, Dc *under* 5 for 5 times, 1 chain, *repeat.*

23*rd Row.*—Next shade Amber same as last row, only making 5 chain, Dc *under* 5, for 5 times and 6 times.

24*th Row.*—Next shade, Scarlet, same as last row, making 5 chain, and Dc *under* every 5 chain.

Lamp Mat.   By Mrs. Warren.

25th Row.—Next Amber, 11 long as before, 1 chain; Dc *under* 5 chain ; 5 chain, Dc *under* 5, for 4 times, then Dc *under* next 5, without any chains between, 5 chain, Dc *under* 5 twice, 5 chain Dc between 2nd long twice, 7 chain Dc, between 3rd long, 5 chain, Dc between 2nd long, 5 chain Dc *under* 5, for 3 times, Dc *under* next 5 without chains between 5 chain Dc *under* 5, for 4 times, 1 chain, *repeat.*

26th Row.—Next, Scarlet same as last row, omitting the 5 chains, exactly over the same place, as last row.

27th Row.—Next Amber, the same.

28th Row.—Next Scarlet, the same.

29th Row.—Next Amber, the same.

30th Row.—Next Scarlet, the same.

31st Row.—Next Amber, 11 long as before, 1 chain, Dc *under* 5 ; 5 chain, Dc *under* every 5 chain ; work over the 11 long, as in last row, and Dc *under* every 5 chain.

32nd Row.—Next Scarlet, the same.

33rd Row.—Next Amber, the same.

34th Row.—Next Scarlet, 11 long as before, 1 chain, Dc *under* 5, 5 chain, Dc *under* 5, for 5 times, Dc *under* next 5 without any chain between, 5 chain, Dc *under* 5 chain, for 4 times ; 5 chain, Dc between 2nd long for twice, 7 chain, Dc between 3rd long, 5 chain, Dc between 2nd long, 5 chain, Dc *under* 5 for 5 times, Dc *under* next 5, 5 chain, Dc *under* 5, for 5 times, 1 chain, *repeat.*

35th Row.—Next Amber, the same.

36th Row.—Next Scarlet, the same as 31st *row.*

37th Row.—Next Amber, 11 long as before, 1 chain, Dc *under* 5 ; 5 chain, Dc *under* 5, for 6 times, Dc *under* next 5, 5 chain. Dc *under* 5, for 4 times, 5 chain, Dc between 2nd long, for twice, 7 chain, Dc between 3rd long, 5 chain, Dc between 2nd long, 5 chain, Dc *under* 5, for 5 times, Dc *under* next 5, 5 chain, Dc *under* 5, for 6 times, 1 chain, *repeat,*

38th Row.—Next, Scarlet, same as 31st row.

39th Row.—Next, Amber, 11 long as before, 1 chain, Dc *under* 5 ; 5 chain, Dc *under* 5, for 6 times, Dc *under* next 5, 5 chain, Dc, *under* 5, for 5 times ; 5 chain

Dc between 2nd long, for twice ; 7 chain, Dc between 3rd long, 5 chain, Dc between 2nd long, 5 chain, Dc *under* 5, for 6 times, Dc *under* next 5, 5 chain, Dc *under* 5, for 6 times, 1 chain, *repeat,*

39th Row.—Next Scarlet, same as 31st row.

40th Row.—Next Amber, 11 long as before, 1 chain, Dc *under* 5 ; 5 chain, Dc *under* 5, for 7 times, Dc *under* next 5, 5 chain, Dc *under* 5, for 5 times, 5 chain, Dc between 2nd long, for twice, 7 chain, Dc between 3rd long, 5 chain, Dc between 2nd long, 5 chain, Dc *under* 5, for 6 times, Dc under next 5, 5 chain, Dc *under* 5, for 7 times, 1 chain, *repeat.*

41st Row.—Lightest Scarlet, same as 31st row.

42nd Row.—Darkest Amber. 11 long ʌs before, 1 chain Dc *under* 5 chain ; 5 chain Dc *under* 5 for eight times, Dc *under,* next 5, 5 chain Dc *under* five for five times ; 5 chain Dc between 2nd long for twice ; 7 chain Dc between 3rd long, 5 chain Dc between 2nd long, 5 chain ; Dc *under* five for seven times ; Dc *under* next 5 5 chain Dc *under* five for seven times, 1 chain *repeat.*

For the Border.

(*The Cotton and Wool must now be once over the Hook, which will make the ordinary long stitch. No. 3 Hook. Care must be taken not to draw the Cotton too tightly, both Wool and Cotton should work easily together.*)

1st Row.—Drab Cotton—Dc on the Dc, immediately before the 7 chain on the Scarlet point, 8 chain Dc on next Dc ; 7 chain Dc *under* next 5, 7 chain, Dc *under* 5 for six times more * 1 chain, 1 long *under* next 5. *Repeat* from * twice more, 7 chain, Dc *under* five for five times. Dc between 2nd long for twice, 8 chain Dc between 3rd long, 7 chain, Dc between 2nd long, 7 chain, Dc *under* five for six times, 1 chain, 3 long with 1 chain between each *under* the 3 chain of 5 as before, 7 chain, Dc *under* 5 for six times, 7 chain, *repeat.*

2nd Row.—Begin at a Scarlet point, 6 long with 5 chain between each, *under* the 8 chain ; 5 chain ; Dc *into* fourth loop of the 7 chain, 7 chain, Dc *into* fourth loop of 7 chain, for six times. 1 long *under* each 1 chain, with 5 chain between each ; Dc *into* fourth loop of 7 chain, 7 chain, Dc *into* 4th loop of 7 chain 6 times, 5 chain *repeat.*

3rd Row.—2 long ; 5 chain, 2 more long *under* the first 5 chain between the first two long stitches, 2 chain, *repeat* this four times more, Dc into the centre loop of 7 (*omit the 5 chain*) 7 chain, Dc *into* centre of 7, 5 times ; 2 long, 5 chain, 2 more long *under* the 5 chain, 2 chain ; 2 long, 5 chain, 2 more long *under* the next 5. Dc *into* centre loop of 7. 7 chain, Dc *into* centre loop of 7 for five times (*omit the 5 chain*) 1 chain *repeat.*

4th Row.—2 long, 5 chain, 2 more long *under* the first ; 5 chain between the 4 long 5 chain *repeat* this four times more (*omit the 5 chain*) 2 chain Dc *into* centre loop of 7, 7 chain Dc *into* centre of 7 for four times—Dc *under* 5 chain, 7 chain Dc *under* next 5 ; Dc *into* centre loop of 7. 7 chain Dc *into* centre loop of 7 for four times ; 2 chain *repeat.*

5th Row.—Work over the point as in the last row, only making 6 long instead of 4 ; and 5 chain, Dc *into* centre loop of 7 instead of 2 chain, then 7 chain, Dc *into* centre loop of 7, for three times ; 5 chain Dc *into* centre of 7, 5 chain Dc *into* centre of 7. 7 chain Dc *into* centre of 7 for three times, 5 chain *repeat.*

6th Row.—Green shaded wool. * 3 long, 5 chain, 3 more long *under* the 5 chain, between the first 6 long, 5 chain, Dc *under* 5 ; 5 chain, *repeat* from * four times more, (*omitting the Dc and 5 chain the last time.*) Dc *into* centre loop of 7. 7 chain, Dc *into* centre loop of 7 for twice, 5 chain, Dc *into* 5 ; 5 chain, Dc *into* 7, 7 chain Dc *into* 7 for twice, 5 chain, *repeat.*

7th Row.—Shaded Scarlet. Dc *under* the first 5 chain between the first 6 long ; 5 chain, Dc *under* every 5 chain (*over the point omit working the Dc into the last 5 chain after the last long*) make 7 chain instead, Dc *under* 7, 7 chain, Dc *under* 7, * 3 chain, 1 long *under* next. *Repeat* from * twice more, 3 chain, Dc *under* 7, 7 chain, Dc *under* 7, 7 chain *repeat.*

8th Row.—Shaded Green. 7 chain Dc *under* every 5 chain and 7 chain, and *under* the first 3 chain, 7 chain, Dc on 2nd long, 7 chain, Dc *under* last 3 chain, then continue 7 chain, Dc under every 7 chain and 5 chain.

Damp thoroughly well, and place it open between double linen, taking care to pull the points and edges well ; and place a heavy weight upon it, and let it remain a day or two.

Convolvulus-Pattern Mat for Flower-Vase. By Mrs. Warren.

CONVOLVULUS-PATTERN MAT FOR FLOWER-VASE.

4 Thread Wool Shaded Amber, Violet, Scarlet, Blue, and Green; 1 skein of each. 2 skeins of White, 3 shades of bright Emerald Green, 2 skeins of each shade. No. 2 Penelope hook. 3 yards of ordinary-sized White Blind Cord.

WITH shaded Violet work 14 Dc stitches over the end of the cord; double it round, in as small a circle as possible.

1st Row.—Work 2 stitches into every loop.

2nd and 3rd Rows.—Increase 1 in every 3rd. (*All the rows afterwards increase* 1 *in every 6th.*) Work 6 rows of this shade.

Now 2 rows of Amber, then 2 rows of Green. Cut off the cord, and Dc over the end very neatly.

Border.

Commence in a different place with **darkest** Green: make 5 chain, and Dc into every 4th loop. (*There must be* 48 *chains of* 5.)

1st Row.—Twist the wool twice over the hook for all the long stitches in every row. 7 long, with 1 chain between each, *under* a 5 chain; (3 *chain, miss one chain of* 5;) Dc into next 5 chain, Dc *under* every next 5 chain for 3 times, 3 chain, *repeat*.

2nd Row.—Next shade. 1 long, with 1 chain between each, *under* every 3rd and 1st chain in last row, (*making in all* 9 *long* ;) 3 chain, Dc *under* 5 chain ; 5 chain ; Dc *under* 5 for twice ; 3 chain, *repeat*.

3rd Row.—Lightest shade. 1 long, with 2 chains between each, *under* every 3rd and 1st chain; 3 chain, Dc *under* 5 ; 5 chain, Dc *under* 5, 3 chain, *repeat*.

For the Flowers ; eight will be required.— With White make a chain of 7, unite the ends, work *under* the circle 15 long, with the wool twice over the hook, making 2 chains between each long. (*To commence these long stitches make* 7 *chain ; this is*

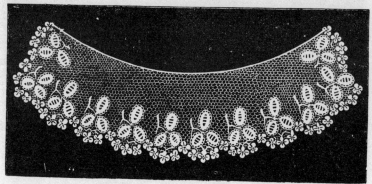

Point de Bruxelles Collar.   By Mrs. Warren.

equivalent to 1 *long,* 2 *chain.*) After the 15th long, make 2 chain, and crochet into the 1st long, (*not cut off the wool,*) but on this long stitch, make 1 long, with wool once over the hook; then 1 chain and 1 long *under* every 2 chain, commencing with the next 2 chain, (*therefore there will be at the beginning, an extra long stitch;*) unite neatly, draw the wool down to the back of the stitch, and tie securely.

1*st Flower.*—With shaded Scarlet. *Under* every 1 chain, work 1 long, with 3 chain between each; unite neatly, and tie securely at the back, making the knot as little seen as possible.

2*nd Flower.*—White centre, shaded Violet edge. (*The edge is the last row.*)

3*rd Flower.*—Blue centre, shaded Amber edge.

4*th Flower.*—All shaded Scarlet.

5*th Flower.*—Violet centre, Amber edge.

6*th Flower.*—All Amber.

7*th Flower.*—White centre, Blue edge.

8*th Flower.*—Blue centre, Scarlet edge.

Sew each of these flowers between each shell of Green, with Green wool.

PATCHWORK.

MANY improvements may be made in the old style of patchwork that most of us have been accustomed to see for years, when visiting the cottages and rooms of the poor; the same old, quaint, hexagonal shape, has haunted us wherever we have been, and in anticipation of some improvement in the designs at present used, we venture to intrude a few remarks, trusting that our numerous friends will not take them amiss.

The materials necessary for patchwork are such portions of wearing apparel, whether of cloth, calico, linen, Holland, silk, velvet, cotton prints, &c., as would otherwise be thrown away, or saved for the rag-man. No matter how small the portion, it has its use. The next necessary article is some stiff paper,—old envelopes, backs of letters, brown paper, &c.,—to form the shapes; and lastly, the design-shapes, cut out in tin, and the designs themselves.

The materials should be arranged into shades and qualities. After having been cut to the requisite sizes, and the irregularities of the edges neatly remedied; when this is done, they are ready for use.

The patterns may be varied *ad infinitum,* if the person possess the least talent for drawing and designing; but for the sake of those who may not be thus gifted, we submit the following simple and effective designs, to be executed in any of the materials.

To make the Patchwork.—The pattern should be placed before the person, and the shades being selected, the several pieces arranged so as to form the design, and the edges then neatly sewn together; after which, they are either pressed, or ironed, the papers removed, and the lining proceeded with.

When silks and velvets are employed, it improves the effect to combine the two, taking the silk for the lighter, and the velvet for the darker shades ; or as in figs. 5, 6, 8, and 11, to have silk for the lighter shades, and two velvets for the others, shaded to pattern.

A very pretty effect is produced by combining Holland and calico, silk and satin, silk or satin and velvet, and rough and fine cloth.

The various articles that may be manu-factured, are quilts in coloured and white calico; anti-macassars in silks; ottomans in silks and velvets, silks and cloth ; table-covers in silks and cloth ; cushions for chairs or sofas, in silks ; and mats rugs, and carpets, in cloth.

We have seen many useful white quilts for children's cots made from the cuttings remaining after shirt making. The centre might be of Holland and calico, pattern 10, fig. 5, and then fig. 7, with a fringe border, knitted. Numerous rugs might be made in coloured cloths, to look equal to carpets, for poor people, and wear much better.

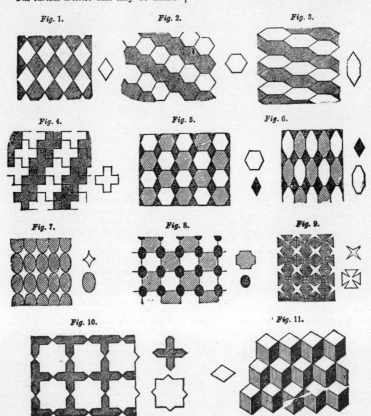

Fig. 1.   Fig. 2.   Fig. 3.
Fig. 4.   Fig. 5.   Fig. 6.
Fig. 7.   Fig. 8.   Fig. 9.
Fig. 10.   Fig. 11.

Carriage Bag.　By Mrs. Warren.

THE WORK-TABLE FRIEND.

DESIGN FOR A CARRIAGE BAG.

2 oz. of shaded Scarlet. 1 oz. each of 2 shades of bright Emerald Green; one to be 3 shades darker than the other. 1 oz. of light Drab or Stone. All 8 thread Wool. No. 1 Penelope Hook. A foundation bag with clasp, 12½ in. wide, 10 in. in depth, from the top of the clasp to the bottom. This bag is worked entirely in Dc or Double Crochet.

MAKE a chain a trifle longer than the bag, measuring from the clasp on one side, round to the opposite side.

Now work 9 rows of *Ridged Crochet,* in Scarlet, which is worked thus:—

1st Row.—After the chain, turn, and work a row of Dc, then after the last stitch, make 1 chain; this is to turn, and must never be worked into.

2nd Row.—Turn back, and work into the back loops instead of the front; do this 9 times.

Now work the following rows in plain Dc, without turning back, beginning at one end every time.

†One row of dark Green.
One row of light.

One of dark Green.
Three rows of Drab.
One row of 7 stitches Scarlet, 1 stitch light Green.
One row of 6 stitches Scarlet, (*the first time only,*) 3 stitches dark Green; afterwards, 5 Scarlet stitches instead of 6.
One row of 7 stitches Scarlet, 1 light Green.
Three rows of Drab.
One row dark Green.
One row light Green.
One row dark Green. †
Four rows of Scarlet ridged Crochet.
* One row Green ridged.
One row Scarlet ridged.

Work from * 4 times more, that is, 6 rows of Green, and 6 rows of Scarlet, using the two colours alternately.

Four rows of Scarlet ridged.

This forms the centre stripe. Now work from † to † again; then nine rows of Scarlet ridged. Damp, and lay between linen, under a heavy weight; then make up on the foundation, which may be procured at any Berlin house.

A Baby's Knitted Sock.　By Mrs. Warren.

A BABY'S KNITTED SOCK.

No. 40 Boar's Head cotton. 3 needles, No. 24.

CAST on 98 stitches, 42 on one needle, and 28 on each of the others.

Knit and rib alternate stitches for 44 rows.

1st Round.—Knit 2, bring forward, take 2 together, knit 1, bring forward, take 2 together, knit 5, take two together, bring forward, and *repeat*.

2nd Round.—Pearl 5, thread forward, knit 1, thread forward, take 2 together, knit 3, take 2 together, thread forward, knit 1, thread forward, *repeat*.

3rd Round.—Knit 2, thread forward, take 2 together, knit 1, thread forward, knit 3, thread forward, take 2 together, knit 1, take 2 together, thread forward, knit 3, thread forward, *repeat*.

4th Round.—Pearl 5, thread forward, knit 5, thread forward, take 3 together, thread forward, knit 5, thread forward, *repeat*.

5th Round.—Knit 2, thread forward, take 2 together, knit 1; pull 6 stitches from left to right, over 1; thread forward, knit 1, thread forward, knit 1; pull 6 stitches from right to left, over 1; thread forward, knit 1, thread forward, *repeat*.

6th Round.—Pearl 5, knit 1, pearl 1 in the 1st loop, knit 5, pearl 1. knit 1 in the next loop, *repeat*.

Repeat the pattern 11 times; this will be the length for the leg. Then divide the stitches for the heel. With 2 needles, knit and pearl every alternate row. When there are 26 rows on the needles, begin to decrease, by knitting two stitches together, each side of the middle stitches, till there are only 32 on the needles; knit these together for the top of the heel. Take up 30 stitches on one side of the heel, and continue the pattern in front as before; take up 30 on the other side of the heel; this will form the foot of the sock. Continue to knit plain for the back of the foot, and the pattern for the front of the sock, taking care to knit 2 together every other row, at the end of the plain stitches, each side of the heel, for 3 rows; then miss 3 rows, and take 2 together for two rows. When there are 10 patterns done, then knit plain all round 18 rows, take 2 together on both sides of the sock, at the back and front; every other row 14 times; then every row till there are only eighteen stitches on the needles, when cast off.

COMBINATION DESIGNS.

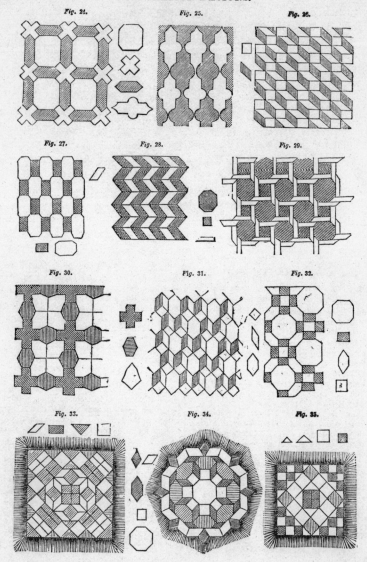

Fig. 24.   Fig. 25.   Fig. 26.

Fig. 27.   Fig. 28.   Fig. 29.

Fig. 30.   Fig. 31.   Fig. 32.

Fig. 33.   Fig. 34.   Fig. 35.

Musnud for a Sofa.

COMBINATION DESIGNS.

We again give a series of Combination Patchwork Designs, which will be found very useful in connexion with those which occur, in various other places, amongst our Treasures.

AN ELEGANT MUSNUD FOR A SOFA.

The materials required, consist of braid of various hues, purse-silk of different shades, bed-ticking, feathers, down, horsehair, or worsted ends; the design-shapes, some cord for pipings, the various coloured cloths, silks, &c., and a curtain-ring or a piece of cardboard for the centre.

The size varies from 15 to 18 inches in diameter, according to taste.

The colours cannot be fixed, because it depends much upon taste, but we have made the elegant musnud given above, by placing cobalt as the right hand centre-piece, then (proceeding from right to left) white, salmon, purple, crimson, amber, pea-green, and madder-brown. The han-

dles are amber, the side brown, and the back purple.

It is better, in combining or arranging all colours for patchwork, to keep as near as possible to the harmony observed by Nature; therefore, to attend to the same order displayed in the case of a refracted ray of light, viz., violet, indigo, blue, green, yellow, orange, and red, adding, in this case, white, to represent the ray in its natural state before refraction or dispersion of its colours took place.

To make the Musnud.—Cut two circles of fifteen or eighteen inches in diameter in bed-ticking, and a strip of the same material three inches deep, and thrice the length of the diameter; make into the usual shape, and stuff with feathers, down, horsehair, or the refuse ends of worsted. Cut out two handles as in the design, of the same material, and sew them on. Rub the *inside* of the bed-ticking with a lump of bees'-wax previous to making up the musnud, (as it prevents the feathers and dust working through,) and tack the centre down.

Cut out the back in a piece of purple

moreen, or any other material, then cut
four strips of brown cashmere, each three
inches deep and five long, join these neatly
together to form the side, and braid the
following design in bright yellow on it,
finishing the veining of the leaves in chain-
stitch with purse silk.

The wedge-shaped pieces should now be
cut out in the various coloured cloths, &c.,

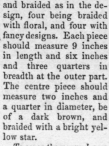

and braided as in the de-
sign, four being braided
with floral, and four with
fancy designs. Each piece
should measure 9 inches
in length and six inches
and three quarters in
breadth at the outer part.
The centre piece should
measure two inches and
a quarter in diameter, be
of a dark brown, and
braided with a bright yellow star.

To cover the musnud, sew
the pieces neatly together,
and cover the joining with
narrow strips of dark-
brown cloth, braided in
bright yellow to resemble
a chain; cover the curtain
ring, or a circu-
lar piece of card-
board, with the
central piece, and
sew it on.

Now affix the
pipings cut cross-
ways out of brown
cloth, and cover
the handles with amber-coloured
material, braid and pipe them; join
the back to the side with an intervening piping, slip the musnud
into the lower covering, and sew on the
top.

In *braiding* the patterns, we recommend
the same arrangement of colours as will be
found in page 33, adding the following:—

The purple ground should have a scarlet
braid.

The brown, yellow.

In finishing the braiding, it will require
the occasional aid of some chain-stitch
work in purse-silk, for the veinings of the
leaves. stamens, tendrils, &c.

THE WORK-TABLE FRIEND.

LADY'S NIGHT-CAP IN CROCHET.

1 Reel No. 16, 4 reels of 20 Boar's Head Cotton.
Penelope Hook No. 4.

WITH 16 cotton make a chain of 360
stitches, turn back, work 1 long, 2 chain,
1 long into 3rd loop. There must be 113
Squares, and must measure, without
stretching, full 20 inches: it must be
worked firmly, and worked forwards and
back, till otherwise directed.

2nd Row.—1 long on long, 2 chain,
repeat.

3rd, 4th, 5th, and *6th Rows* the same as
2nd.

7th Row.—No. 20 cotton. 1 long upon
long, 2 chain for 4 times, 2 chain, Dc on
next long, * 2 chain, miss 2 squares
(cotton twice over the hook for all the
long stitches forming the flutes) till the
end; 10 long with 2 chain between
each, under the next 2 chain (which will
be the 3rd square), 2 chain, Dc upon 3rd
long, repeat from * 20 times more, making
in all 21 Flutes, till within 4 squares of the
end, when work as at beginning.

8th Row.—1 long on long, 2 chain for 4
times, 2 chain, Dc on Dc, * 2 chain, (twist
the cotton twice over the hook), 1 long,
with 2 chain between each, under every 2
chain, making in all 11 long; 2 chain, Dc
on Dc, repeat from *.

9th Row.—Same as 8th, only having 12
long.

From 9th to 14th the same, only making
in every row the 1st long of the flute come
under the 2nd 2 chain; therefore every row
after the 9th will be decreased till in the
4th row there will only be 7 long.

15th Row.—3 Dc stitches under every 2
chain for 4 times, miss 1 chain of two, 2
Dc under every 2 chain, excepting the 2
chain on each side the Dc stitch, between
the flutes (this will draw them up). Make
both ends alike.

16th Row.—Cut off the cotton, and begin
on the right side of the chain for the

Insertion :

1 long, 2 chain, 1 long into 3rd loop for 4
times; then 5 chain, Dc into every 3rd
loop. (Make both ends alike.)

17th Row.—Turn back every row, till
otherwise directed, 1 long, 2 chain, 1 long

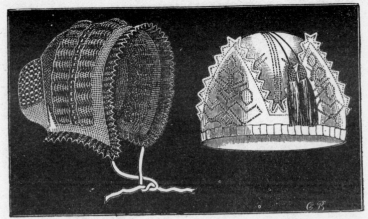

Lady's and Gentleman's Night-Caps, in Crochet. By Mrs. Warren.

on long for 4 times, 5 chain, Dc under centre of every 5 chain. (Make both ends alike ; this must be done in every row.)

18*th Row.*—1 long on long, 2 chain for 4 times, 1 chain, 5 long under 2nd 5, * 1 chain, 1 long under next 5, 1 chain, 5 long under next 5, repeat from *.

19*th Row.*—1 long on long, 2 chain for 4 times, 5 chain, Dc under the 2nd 1 chain ; * 6 chain, Dc under next 1 chain (this will be the other side of the 1 long), 5 chain, Dc under 1 chain, repeat from *.

20*th Row.*—1 long on long, 2 chain for 4 times, 5 chain, * 3 Dc under the centre of the 6 chain, 5 chain, repeat from *.

21*st Row.*—Cut off the cotton, and begin t the right side of the chain (still turning back at every row), 1 long on long, 2 chain for 4 times, * 5 chain, Dc under centre of 5, 5 chain, Dc under the 3 Dc stitches, repeat from *.

22*nd Row.*—1 long on long, 2 chain for 4 times, 3 chain, Dc under 5, * 5 chain, Dc under 5, repeat from *.

23*rd Row.*—1 long on long, 2 chain 4 times, * 2 chain, Dc under 5, repeat from *.

24*th Row.*—Under every 2 chain work 3 Dc stitches.

25*th Row.*—Cut off the cotton, com-

mence at the other end ; 1 long, 2 chain, 1 long into 3rd loop.

Now work from the 7th to the 15th rows, including both.

34*th Row.*—Cut off the cotton, begin at the right side of the chain ; Dc on all the Dc and over the first flute (this is the commencement of the slope) ; then 1 long, * 2 chain, 1 long into 3 loop, repeat from *. Make both ends alike at every row.

35*th Row.*—The cotton must be fastened off at every row, and each row commenced at the same end ; Dc on all the Dc and 1st 2 chain, * 5 chain, Dc under every 2 chain, repeat from *.

36*th Row.*—Dc over the Dc, 5 chain, miss 1 chain of 5, Dc under centre of 2nd 5, * 5 chain, Dc under centre of 5, repeat from *.

37*th Row.*—Dc over the Dc, and over 1st 5 chain, 7 chain, miss one chain of 5, * Dc under centre of 5, 5 chain, repeat from *.

38*th Row.*—Dc over the Dc, and over the 7 chain, 7 chain, miss 1 chain of 5, Dc under next, * 5 chain, Dc under 5, repeat from *.

39*th Row.*—Same as last row.

40*th Row.*—Dc under 1st 5 chain, 5 chain, Dc under 5 till the last 5 chain ; then Dc under 7 chain, and turn back.

Superb Table-Cover, in Patchwork.

41st Row.—5 chain, Dc under 5 till last 5 chain; after which Dc under 7 chain, turn back.

42nd Row.—5 chain, Dc into centre of every 5. After the Dc under the last 5 chain, make 5 chain, Dc into every 4th loop down the thick Dc part.

43rd Row.—Turn back, 5 chain, Dc under every 5, working down the thick part of the other end, as in last row.

44th Row.—Turn back 5 chain, Dc under 5 up to the end of the thick part of the Dc, to match the other side, and fasten off.

45th Row.—5 chn., Dc under 5 all the row.

46th Row.—Turn back 3 chain, Dc under every 5, repeat.

47th Row.—Turn back, 3 Do under every 3 chain, repeat.

For the "Horse-shoe" or Crown.

1st Row.—With 20 cotton make a chain of 151 stitches, turn back, 1 long, 2 chain, 1 long into 3rd loop, repeat. This should measure 7½ to 8 inches. Turn back every row; there should be 50 squares.

Work 3 more rows of squares, which is 1 long upon long, 2 chain, repeat.

5th Row.—5 chain, Dc under every 2 chain, repeat.

6th Row.—5 chain, Dc under every 5 chain.

7th Row.—* 1 long under 1st 5 chain, 1

chain, 5 long under next 5, 1 chain, repeat from *. This row must end with 5 long.

8th Row.—5 chain, Dc under every 1 chain, repeat. This row ends with the 5 chain over the 5 long, Dc into last long.

9th Row.—1 long, 5 chain, * 2 long with 3 chain between each, under the 2nd 5 chain (this will be the 5 chain that appears like a loop of 5), 5 chain, repeat from *. The last 1 long to be worked into the last stitch of the 5 long.

10th Row.—* 5 long under the 5 chain, 1 chain, 1 long under the 3 chain, 1 chain, repeat from *. These 3 rows form one pattern.

Continue working the last 3 rows till there are 7 patterns, or 7 rows of groups of long stitches.

11th Row.—As at 8th.

To decrease or round the top of the "horse-shoe."

1st Row.—5 chain, 2 long with 3 chain between each, under the 2nd 5 chain (this will be the 5 chain like a loop of 5), * 5 chain, 2 long with 3 chain between each, under the next 5, repeat from *. Make both ends alike in every row.

2nd Row.—5 Dc under the 5 chain, 1 chain, 1 long under the 3 chain, * 1 chain, 5 long under 5, 1 chain, 1 long under 3, repeat from *.

3rd Row.—5 chain, Dc under the 2nd 1 chain, 5 chain, Dc under every 1 chain.

Work these 3 rows till there are only 14 groups of long stitches along the top. The "horse-shoe" terminates with the row of long stitches.

Now begin at the other end of the "horse-shoe" at the foundation chain, and work very tightly 7 more rows of 1 long on long, 2 chain.

Now sew the "horse-shoe" into the front in the ordinary way, as if it were muslin, sewing each side up plain for the space of a little more than a nail, and allowing the fullness to be equal. Fasten in all ends securely, and work along the back of the cap, at the bottom (from ear to ear), or from corner to corner, thus :—1 long, 2 chain (all the chains must be tight), 1 long under every long stitch till the Dc stitches which form the slope, work along these the same at equal distances ; along the "horse-shoe" make 1 long, 2 chain, 1 long under every second 2 chn. Make both sides alike.

Turn back 5 chain, 1 long under 2nd 2 chain (this rounds the corner), * 2 chain,

1 long under every 2 chain, repeat from * Make both corners alike.

Turn back 5 chain, 1 long under 1st 2 chain, * 1 chain, 1 long under next, repeat from * till the "horse-shoe," when work as in last row. Make both sides alike.

Another row the same, only when opposite the thick Dc part of the slope, work 7 long without making a chain between; this draws it in still more. Cut off the cotton, commence at the other end, still working along the back.

2 Dc stitches under every 1 chain, 1 Dc between every long stitch where there are no chains, 3 Dc under every 2 chain.

Now work along the front of the Cap 3 Dc under every 2 chain, drawing them tightly : cut off the cotton. Commence for the

Border

at the right hand side of the cap (beginning just round the corner) where the 5 chains are made. (Twist the cotton twice over the hook for the long stitches in this row only) into these spaces, and under the chains, 20 long with 2 chain between each ; these should come at the extreme corner. Now under every 3 Dc stitches, which will be into each space between the long stitches, work * 3 long with 2 chain between each, 2 chain, repeat from *, making both corners alike, but along the back of the cap work only 2 long instead of 3.

2nd Row.—1 long, 5 chain, 1 long under every 2 chain.

3rd Row.—1 long, 5 chain, 1 long under 5 till after the 4th flute in the front ; then 5 chain, Dc under 5 (this will decrease the border along the forehead) till within 4 flutes of the end, when work as at beginning ; work round the corner the same till after the 1st flute at the ear, when work the Dc stitch instead of the long.

4th Row.—1 long, 5 chain, 1 long under 5, all round the cap.

5th Row.—5 long under the 5 chain, 3 chain, 1 long under next 5, 3 chain repeat.

6th Row.—Dc under 3 chain, * 7 chain, Dc under every 3 chain, repeat from *.

This makes one of the most comfortable caps that can be imagined, and is admirably adapted for ladies who have a great deal of hair ; while, if required smaller, it may be worked very tightly, or with 28 Boar's Head ; but for a useful and com-

mon-sized cap, work according to the instructions. The trouble of working, which
is but slight, is well recompensed in its
production.

PATCHWORK TABLE-COVER.

THE Table-cover now submitted to the
readers of the *Treasures* may be taken as
an admirable specimen of Patchwork, at
once harmonious in design and effective in
execution; and Patchwork being still popular with a large number of ladies, it may
serve to give them an idea, by the aid of
which they may convert to useful account
spare pieces of cloth, velvet, &c.

The materials necessary for its formation
are, braid of various widths and hues, purse-
silk of different shades, bright coloured
cloth, yellow or crimson fringe, and the
design shapes, in tin or mill-board.

The size of the cloth will necessarily vary
with the table to be covered, but an ordinary loo or square table will require one
six feet square.

The centre-piece should be six inches in
diameter, and of a bright mulberry colour;
immediately surrounding this is the fillet,
of white or bright blue, with the motto,
buckle, pendant, &c., worked in silk; then
succeeds the second circle of the centre,
composed of eight pieces of the same coloured cloth as the central piece; next comes
the second band, of bright scarlet, in four
compartments, and then the wedge-shaped
pieces.

The outer circle of wedge-shaped pieces
is composed of twenty-four pieces of various
colours; and for the guidance of those who
may not have any idea of the arrangement
of them, respecting their colours, we sub-
join the following, to be placed in the order
they are given — cobalt, green, scarlet,
yellow, drab, white, cobalt, &c., &c.

It should be observed, that the colours
should be placed diametrically opposite
one another; that is to say, cobalt should
face cobalt, green face green, &c. &c., by
these means a uniformity of design will be
preserved.

These wedge-shaped pieces should be
eight inches long, and every alternate one

braided, as in the following figure, but
each piece having a dif-
ferent pattern; thus there
will be twelve plain and
twelve braided.

The ground should be
eleven inches deep, from
the apex of the wedge-
pieces to the edge of the
border pieces, composed
of four separate portions,
and of a bright mulberry,
drab, or blue.

The corner pieces
may be omitted, if
thought proper, but
it is economical to
construct them in the
semblance of a group
of flowers, as in the an-
nexed : — because the
portions of the cloth re-
maining from the cut-
tings of the other shapes
can now be appropria-
ted; thus the remnants of blue will form
corollas, the green calices and leaves, requir-
ingly the additional aid of a chain stitch
in silk to form the veinings of the leaves,
stamens, &c.

Or the attached de-
sign will give a fin-
ish to the corners,
and, from the pecu-
liarity of its form, be
greatly in keeping
with the other parts
of the table-cover.
It may be con-
structed from such
parts as will necessarily remain after cutting out the wedge-shaped pieces. By some
persons this corner-piece may be preferred,
as in closer unison with the central design.

The Border Pieces are
fifty-six in number, and
partake of the same co-
lours as the outer circle.
They should be four and
a half inches wide, and
five inches long, and all
braided with a different
pattern on each side of
the border; thus there will be fourteen
different patterns required—thirteen for the

consecutive pieces, and one for each corner piece.

Our engraver has thrown in various designs, some of which may be impractical, but will aid the mind in designing various embellishments to these squares.

The Fringe may be crimson or bright yellow, according to taste.

The Crest.—It will improve the effect of the cloth, if the crest is cut out in white cloth, and sewed on; after which such parts as require it may be either worked in silk, or touched up with coloured marking-inks.

The Braiding.—Much of the beauty of the patterns will depend upon the arrangement of colours, as the greater the contrast the more beautiful the effect.

The cobalt grounds should have scarlet braid patterns.

The green, yellow braid.

The scarlet, yellow or purple.

The yellow, blue or crimson.

The drab, yellow.

The white, mulberry or green;

so that the *tout ensemble* may present a most beautiful grouping of colours, with a uniformity of design.

The lining may be of light blue, salmon, or mulberry, stitched to such points of the work as shall not interfere with the pattern. In this we would recommend the adoption of such stitching as the design lays down, so that it may serve the double purpose of strength and beauty.

In conclusion, we may mention that the addition of a tassel to each corner would give a more decided finish to the cloth, and assist in making it hang well, especially if loaded with a bullet.

THE ACORN.—If an acorn be suspended by a piece of thread within half an inch of the surface of some water contained in a hyacinth glass, and so permitted to remain without being disturbed, it will, in a few months, burst, and throw a root down into the water, and shoot upwards its straight and tapering stem, with beautiful little green leaves. A young oak tree growing in this way on the mantel-shelf of a room is a very elegant and interesting object.

THE WORK-TABLE FRIEND.

A PLAIN KNITTED STOCKING.

Evans's Boar's Head Cotton. No. 24, or Fine Lamb's Wool; 4 Needles. No. 16.

(A turning in two rows, because at every second round the seam-stich is pearled.)

Cast on 40 stitches on each of 2 needles, and 41 on the 3rd needle; the 41st (or odd stitch) is always the seam-stitch at the back of the stocking. Every alternate row of the seam stitch must be pearled, as if it were a straight piece instead of round knitting. *To form the welts*—which are the rounds of ribbed stitches, at the top of every sock or stocking, to prevent their curling up—K 4, P 4 (or turn 4), there will be 40 ribs and 1 odd stitch (which is the seam-stitch), K 60 rows or 30 turnings, then narrow at the seam-stitch; K 6 rows or 3 turnings more, and narrow 6 or 3 more, and narrow; K 3 turnings and widen, K 3 more and widen, K 2 more and widen, K 10 turnings or 20 rows and narrow, K 4 turnings and narrow, K 4 more and narrow, K 3 and narrow, K 3 and narrow, K 2 and narrow till the leg is small enough. *For the heels*, take half the stitches on the seam needle, being an equal number on each side the seam, and K 22 turnings or 46 rows, then cast half these stitches off; then double the heel the two right sides together, and bind the stitches one over the other, pick up the stitches that are under the heel on one needle, having the other two needles in front, decrease or narrow one stitch on each side the heel for 3 rows, then K 100 rows, then narrow by K 2 + 6 times at regular divisions; then K 12 rows and narrow at every 6th stitch, then sew the tops together.

A MAT FOR A TOILET CANDLESTICK.

Two Reels Evans's Boar's Head Cotton; No. 3 Penelope Hook.

1st Row.—11 chain, unite (this forms a circle), * 9 chain, Dc *under* the circle, *repeat* from * 7 times more (in all 8 chains of 9). Each row must be commenced afresh.

2nd Row.—Dc into the centre loop of the 9 chain, 9 chain, *repeat.*

D

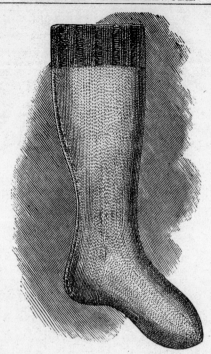

A Plain Knitted Stocking. By Mrs. Warren.

3rd Row.—1 L into every loop of the 9 chain, omitting the Dc stitches.

4th Row.—5 L in the 5th loop of the 9 L, 5 chain, 1 Dc between the two groups of 9 L (that is, just over the Dc stitches in 2nd row), 5 chain, *repeat.*

5th Row.—Dc on Dc, 5 chain, 7 L, the 1st into the 5th loop of the 5 chain, 5 chain, *repeat.*

6th Row.—Dc on Dc, 7 chain, 9 L, the 1st into 5th loop of the 5 chain, 5 chain, *repeat.*

7th Row.—Dc on Dc, 9 chain, 11 L, the 1st into the 7th loop of the 7 chain, 9 chain, *repeat.*

8th Row.—9 L, the 1st on 2nd L, 5 chain, Dc into 4th loop, 5 chain, Dc into 7th loop of the 2nd, 9 chain, 5 chain, *repeat.*

9th Row.—7 L, the 1st on 2nd L, * 5 chain, Dc into centre loop of 5 chain, repeat from * twice more, 5 chain, *repeat* from beginning.

10th Row.—5 L, the 1st on 2nd L, 7 chain, miss 1 chain of 5, 5 L into centre loop of next 5, 2 chain, 5 L into centre loop of next 5, 7 chain, *repeat.*

11th Row.—3 L, the 1st into the 2nd L, 7 chain, 5 L, the 1st into 8th loop, 3 chain, 5 L, the 1st on next, 7 chain, *repeat.*

12th Row.—1 L on 2nd of the 3 L, 7 chain, 7 L, the 1st into 7th loop, 5 chain, 7 L, the 1st on 2nd L, 7 chain, *repeat.*

13th Row.—1 Dc immediately before the 1 L, then 2 more Dc (1 into each loop, making in all 3 Dc), 5 chain, 7 L, the 1st into 6th loop, 5 chain, Dc into centre loop of 5 chain, 5 chain, 7 L, the 1st on 2nd L, 5 chain, *repeat.*

14th Row.—5 Dc *over* the 3 Dc (that is, 1 immediately before and after the 3 Dc),

A Mat for a Toilette Candlestick.   By Mrs. Warren.

5 chain, 7 L, the 1st into 4th loop, 5 chain, Dc into centre loop of 5, 5 chain, Dc into centre loop of next 5, 5 chain, 7 L, the 1st on 2nd L, 5 chain, *repeat.*

15th Row.—7 Dc *over* the 7 L, 14 chain, *repeat.*

16th Row.—Dc *over* the Dc stitches, 14 L in every 14 chain, *repeat.*

17th Row.—Fringe.—Dc in a loop *, 40 chain, Dc into next loop, *repeat* from *.

BOOKS, PRICES OF.—Jerome states that he had ruined himself by buying a copy of the works of Origen. A large estate was given for one on Cosmography, by Alfred, about A.D. 872. The *Roman de la Rose* was sold for above £30; and a Homily was exchanged for 200 sheep and five quarters of wheat; and they usually fetched double or treble their weight in gold. They sold at prices varying from £10 to £40 each, in 1400. In our own times, the value of some volumes is very great. A copy of Macklin's Bible ornamented by Mr. Tomkins, has been declared worth 500 guineas. A yet more superb copy is at present insured in a London office for £3000. *Il Decamerone* of Boccacio, edition of 1471, was bought at the Duke of Roxburgh's sale by the Duke of Marlborough for £2260, June 17, 1812. A copy of the " Mazarin Bible," being the first edition and first book ever printed (by Guttemberg at Mentz in 1455) was sold at auction in London, in April 1846, for £500. This copy, the only one known to exist, except 19 in public libraries, is now in a private library in New York.

INSTRUCTIONS IN MODERN POINT LACE.
AMONGST the various kinds of lace which
are now fashionable, that termed POINT
is at once the most beautiful and the most
valuable. This arises partly from the circumstance of the choicest specimens being
heirlooms in noble families, and having
descended through many generations; for
we may observe that comparatively little
is the production of modern times.

During the last few years point lace has
risen into greater favour than ever in the
fashionable world, and hence has arisen a
demand for it which promises to make the
manufacture one of the best channels for
developing female industry. For this
reason we are anxious to give our readers
the clearest instructions for the practice
of an art which offers many advantages;
not merely because it requires no greater

amount of accomplishment than that com-
prised in a thorough knowledge of plain
needlework, but also because the cheapness of the materials employed places it,
more than almost any other kind of fancy
work, in the power of the humblest.

Point lace is always worked on a foundation of some description· this foundation
is used to form the outline of the design,
and is generally either some sort of braid
or coarse thread. Sometimes linen is
used for this purpose. The pattern is
drawn on coloured paper, which is lined
with stout calico, or some other material.

When braid is employed, the design is
made, as much as possible, in a few continuous lines; but if thread is employed
for the outlines, this is not of so much
consequence. French-white cotton-braid
is run on rather closely, the stitches being

Point Lace Collar.—By Mrs. Pullan.

taken *across* the braid, to prevent it from stretching. When fastening on or off a small piece is turned in, underneath, as neatly as possible. The needle passes through the lined paper at every stitch. It is not requisite to sew the braid very closely, as all the threads have afterwards to be cut to detach the work from the paper. When coarse thread is used as an outline the paper is lined with merino or alpaca, as either of these substances will allow the needle to return through the same hole in the paper. A fine thread is used for laying on the coarser one, which it crosses at every stitch. The outline threads are afterwards covered with button-hole stitch.

When the outlines are formed, the whole is worked into a solid mass by means of some of the various stitches for which we shall give instructions.

The effect of the lace, when worked, as well as its durability, depends in a great measure on the cottons employed. From the great difference between the hand-spun threads used two centuries ago, and the machine-spun cottons of our own time, it was a work of considerable difficulty to procure such a selection of materials as would really answer the purpose. Some kinds were not to be procured at all, and had to be made expressly for the work, which was done by Messrs. Walter Evans & Co., of Derby, who have, by our direction, manufactured complete sets of cottons and threads, of those sizes required for point lace. They are arranged in boxes, elegantly labelled, and are termed Evans's Point Lace cottons.

It is requisite to be very particular in using, in each receipt, the cottons named for each stitch in that design, as the same stitch is worked in any one of the cottons, according to the style and size of the pattern.

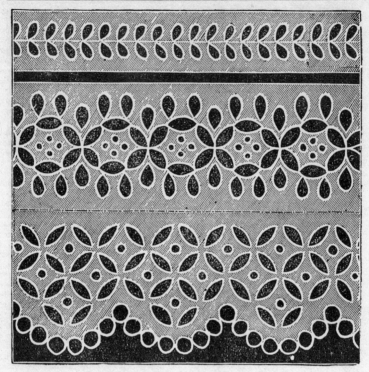

Chemisette in Broderie Anglaise.—By Mrs. Pullan.

Although there appeared to be a great variety of stitches in our present instructions and the accompanying diagrams, we can assure our friends that a great many yet remain to be given at a future time, as they become more *au fait* at the work, which we recommend to their attention as at once the most beautiful branch of needlework, and the one offering the best prospect for remuneration to those who desire to turn their labour to account.

There are four very simple stitches which are used as a finish to the outer edge of a pattern. The first of these is Brussels' Edge, which is formed by a succession of stiches worked on the edge of the braid, exactly in the same manner as an ordinary buttonhole, but not drawing the thread tightly, only instead of being taken close together, they are made at intervals, varying from the eighth to the twelfth of an inch, according to the size of the pattern. It is necessary to observe that all these stitches are worked either wider or closer, as the pattern varies ; and for the same stitch a coarser cotton may be used in a large article than is allowed for a small or delicate piece of work.

Little Venetian Edging.—To form this edge make one stitch as in the preceding, and in the loop thus formed work one tight buttonhole stitch.

Venetian Edge.—This is done exactly like the last, only four buttonhole stitches must be worked in the loop instead of one.

Sorrento Edge.—This edging is found in the most ancient foreign lace. It is worked more or less closely according to the dimensions of the design. It consists of two stitches, done exactly like little Venetian, but at irregular distances, the second being only half the length of the first.

Flowers or scrolls are filled in with various stitches, more properly called *laces*.

We shall begin by describing the easiest, which is

Brussels Lace.—Work a row of Brussels edging in the space which is to be filled, then another line, from right to left, passing the needle every time through a loop of the first row. Repeat this backwards and forwards till the part is finished. In working the last row attach each stitch to the braid.

English Lace is generally used to fill a large space. Make a certain number of diagonal bars, one-eighth of an inch apart, across the part to be filled in, and pass the needle under the thread a sufficient number of times to make it appear as a single thread returning to the commencement of the thread. These bars being made, cross them in the opposite direction by others at the same distance apart, and in twisting the thread back, work a small spot wherever the bars cross each other, by passing the needle alternately under and over the threads, five or six times. Twist the threads twice round each other in bringing the needle to the next cross, and repeat until a spot is made at each crossing.

Open English.—Commence as in the preceding, but when the two lines of diagonal bars are made, a line of perpendicular and one of horizontal threads must be added. The spot will thus be worked on eight threads instead of four. These lines in this lace should be about five to an inch.

English Rosette.—This forms a large spot, one only being used in a space, and the size must be in proportion to the part to be filled in. The space is crossed with four, six, or eight twisted threads. Twist the last only to the centre, and join all together by one or two tight buttonhole stitches. Then pass the needle round one thread and under the next, then round that and under the succeeding, continuing thus till the rosette is formed as large as

the space requires. Stop at the single thread, twist round it, and fasten off.

Venetian Lace is made by working consecutive rows of Venetian edging, not backwards and forward, but always from left to right; fastening off at the end of each row. If the space is small the needle can be run in the braid back to the place where the next line is to be begun.

Valenciennes Lace.—This lace has a heavy appearance, but forms an elegant contrast with the lighter stitches. Any space to be thus filled has a number of radiating threads meeting in one common centre, and very closely darned with extremely fine cotton.

Mechlin Lace.—This is one of the most complicated, but at the same time most beautiful stitches we have.

It is worked thus:—A number of diagonal bars, each of a single thread, cross each other in the space to be filled up, at the distance of one-quarter of an inch from each other. Work all the bars in one direction, in buttonhole stitch. Then begin in the opposite direction, the same way, and work about six stitches past the crossing of the two. Pass the thread loosely round the cross twice, slipping the needle under one and over the other thread to form a circle. Work in buttonhole stitch to the middle of a quarter, then make a dot thus: instead of drawing the thread tight, as usual, put a pin in the loop, and keep it about the eighth of an inch long, and, on the loop thus held, work three buttonhole stitches; then take out the pin, and continue the round. These dots are sometimes omitted in every alternate round.

Henriquez Lace.—This must be always done in fine thread. Make a diagonal bar across the space you wish to fill, and return your needle to the point from which you began, by twisting the thread back again. Make another line parallel with this one, about the tenth of an inch distant; twist it over four times, and on the single and double thread form a square spot, by darning the three backwards and forwards about six times. Twist your needle round the single thread about a quarter of an inch, and form another spot; repeat this to the end of the line. Make similar ones at about a quarter of an inch apart through the space. Cross these lines with others in the opposite direction, worked in the same way, taking care that in crossing the lines the thread is twisted between the first and second bars, so that a small square may be left clear.

Cordovan Lace.—This is similar to Henriquez lace, but not so troublesome. Make two twisted bars, the tenth of an inch apart, and a third single one, in going back on which work the spots on two twisted threads and the single one. Cross these by similar ones; the crossing of the threads will, in this, form a diamond of four holes.

Swiss Lace is always worked in a square or succession of squares, each of which is filled up in the following manner:—Having fastened on the thread, bring it to one corner, then carry it to the opposite corner completely across the square, and twist it closely back to the first; a second twisted bar must then be made parallel with the first, connecting the same two corners. Run on the foundation to one of the two vacant corners, and carry the thread to the opposite one, passing the needle *under* the two bars already made. Twist back four times over this thread, then passing the needle over one of the former bars, twist the thread three times between this and the next, in order to keep the two bars apart, and four times more to complete the bar. A second must then be taken to correspond with this. The four radiating spaces are then filled in with close darning, like Valenciennes lace, leaving a space in the centre in the form of a diamond.

Connecting Bars are used to unite different parts of the lace, where no filling is required. The simplest of these is—

Sorrento Bar.—Pass the thread from one part to another; fasten it tightly, and twist the thread back on the bar thus formed, until it appears as much twisted as a cable.

Point D'Alençon Bars are similar to the common herring-bone stitch, only the needle is passed under the last thread after every stitch, before taking another, which twists the two together. If the space is wide, two twists will be necessary.

Venetian Bars.—Take a thread across the space two or three times, and work them over in buttonhole stitch. If it is a cross-bar, work the buttonhole stitch half the length; make the opposite bar, and

work it; and if you require another, do the same before finishing the first bar.

Edged Venetian Bars.—These are done as the preceding, and edged on each side with Brussels or Sorrento edging.

Dotted Venetian Bars.—Pass the thread across the space two or three times; make four buttonhole stitches on the bar thus formed; put a needle in the fourth, and draw it out till it will admit of three or four buttonhole stitches being worked on it. Repeat this the whole length of the bar.

English Bars are used to connect two opposite edges. Pass the needle backwards and forwards between the two edges, four times each way, always putting the needle in the *under* side of the edge. These bars may be radiated by missing a stitch more on one side than on the other.

Raleigh Bars.—This is found in some of the most ancient pieces of Point lace. It is formed thus:—Pass the thread across twice, beginning from the left. Work on these threads a few buttonhole stitches. Pass the needle over bar, and bring it out to the right of the new loop; do not draw it up, but keep the loop under the left thumb, and pass the needle eight times through the loop—thus the right-hand side of the loop will be twisted. Now remove the thumb and draw it up. Slip the needle up between the two threads which form the bar, and continue the buttonhole stitches. The dot is repeated at intervals as often as required, according to the length of bar.

POINT LACE COLLAR.

Materials. — W. Evans's & Co's Point Lace Cottons, and No. 7 French-white Cotton braid.

THE section given of this Collar consists of one end and a single pattern beyond. Being of the full size, the perfect collar may readily be drawn from it, by proceeding in the following manner:—

Cut out a bit of tracing-paper in the shape of half a collar, of ample size; then, having made a copy of our engraving, transfer the pattern to the tracing-paper, by laying over the latter some of the prepared blackened paper sold in drawing shops for the purpose, and then, place the design over this, going over all the outlines with a hard pencil, which leaves the pattern on the tracing-paper. As but one flower besides the corner one is given, this must be moved as often as is required to repeat it. Begin at the centre of the collar, placing the flower so that it forms the middle, and drawing from the centre to the corner. The tracing-paper being so transparent, the design is as clear on the wrong side as on the right, so that when one-half has been drawn on coloured paper, the other may also be obtained by turning the pattern. It is necessary to ink the coloured paper pattern before lining it with calico.

With regard to the colour to be selected for working on, we recommend green or blue, in preference to a brighter tint, as being less trying to the eyes. The calico is made to adhere to the paper by thin flour paste.

The large flowers in this design are filled alternately with English lace, worked in Evans's Boar's Head Cotton, No. 70, and Venetian lace, done in the same thread.

The ground of the part round the neck is Brussels lace, done in Evans's Boar's Head, No. 90.

The edging is Sorrento, worked at intervals of the eighth and the sixteenth of an inch between the stitches. Evans's Mecklenburgh thread, No. 100, is the material to be employed. This thread is also to be used for the Raleigh and Venetian bars which form the ground.

The English rosette and Mechlin wheel which fill up the small flowers, alternately are done in Evans's Mecklenburgh thread, No. 120.

CHEMISETTE IN BRODERIE ANGLAISE.

THE term Broderie Anglaise (*English Embroidery*), is applied to the heavy open-work which is now so fashionable for morning dress. The pattern is formed entirely of a succession of holes, variously arranged, and worked round. The edge is finished in buttonhole stitch.

To prepare this work, select a good and fine jaconet or French muslin, and tear off strips for the length required, allowing each to be at least one inch wider than the extreme width of the pattern. The strips must, of course, be torn on the width of the muslin, and the object of separating them is to secure a regularity in marking the design, as it is much more difficult to draw the pattern perfectly straight on a large piece of muslin.

Draw the design on good writing-paper, from the section given in the engraving, and ink it clearly; when it is dry, lay it under the muslin, put weights to keep it down, and trace the pattern on the material with a mixture of stone-blue dissolved in *very* thin gum-water, or white sugar and water, using a fine sable brush, or soft quill pen. When one length of the paper is marked over, move it along to the next piece of plain muslin, taking care that there are no breaks or defects in the pattern.

To work the Broderie.—With fine scissors, cut out all the holes of a small piece of the pattern—not at the marks, but *within* them, to allow a little for turning in, in working them round. For working, turn in the edge, by rolling it slightly with the thumb, as is done in common whipping, and sew it closely round. To pass from one hole to another, slip the needle on the wrong side.

The border is finished with the button-hole stitch, the outline having previously been traced in cotton. The holes being so small are not cut out, but made by piercing the muslin with a stiletto. The habit-shirt contains three different patterns: an edging, which trims the collar, and piece of insertion down the front, and the two insertions, the narrowest of which is used for the collar.

The piece of work down the front is attached to the habit-shirt at the top only; this allows of its being worn with either a close or an open gilet.

The materials for this work are very fine jaconet muslin, and Evans's Embroidery Cotton, No. 50.

———◆———

IT might, methinks, somewhat abate the insolence of human pride, to consider, that it is but increasing or diminishing the velocity of certain fluids in the animal machine, to elate the soul with the gayest hopes, or sink her into the deepest despair; to depress the hero into a coward, or advance the coward into a hero.—*Fitz-osborne.*

Net for the Hair, with Gold Border.—By Mrs. Warren.

NET FOR THE HAIR, WITH GOLD BORDER.

THREE skeins of hair-brown purse silk: 1 hank of gold twist: ½ a yard of elastic. No. 9 mesh: No. 2 Penelope hook.

NET a foundation of 10 stitches (*or* 12, *if a larger net is required*) upon a No. 9 mesh, then net 20 rows, or 10 diamonds; there must be 10 diamonds every way. Then cut it off from the foundation, and pin it in the centre to a heavy weight; then net 1 stitch into every loop all round, and next 16 rows, or 8 diamonds.

For the Crochet Border.

1st Row.—1 L into every loop, with 5 chain between each.

2nd Row.—11 L under a 5 chain, 5 chain, 1 L on next L, 5 chain, miss 1 chain of 5, *repeat.*

3rd Row.—9 L, the 1st on 2nd of the 11 L in last row, 5 chain, 3 L, the 1st into 6th loop, 5 chain, *repeat.*

4th Row.—7 L, the 1st on 2nd of the 9 L, 5 chain, 5 L, the 1st into 6th loop, 5 chain, *repeat.*

5th Row.—5 L, the 1st on the 2nd L of the 7, 6 chain, 5 L, with 1 chain between each, the 1st to come on the 1st of the 5 L, 6 chain, *repeat.*

6th Row.—3 L, the 1st on 2nd of the 5 L, 7 chain, 5 L over the L, with 2 chain between each, 7 chain, *repeat.*

7th Row.—1 L, the 1st on 2nd of the 3 L, 8 chain, 3 L on the L, with 3 chain between each L, 2 chain, 1 L into same loop as the last L, 3 chain, 1 L on L, 3 chain, 1 L on L, 8 chain, *repeat.*

8th Row.—Gold Border. Use a very large hook, and under the 1st 8 chain work with the gold twist 8 L (*these L stitches must be worked very loosely, and be more than an inch in length*); 3 chain, 8 L *under*

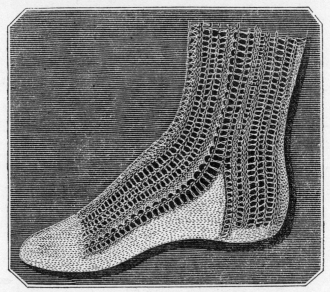

Child's Open-Knit Sock.—By Mrs. Warren.

next 8 chain, 7 chain, Dc *under* the 2 chain, 8 chain, *repeat. (This row may be omitted altogether if preferred.)* The elastic is to be run in at the last row of diamonds, and then joined.

CHILD'S OPEN-KNIT SOCK.

Evans's Boar's Head Cotton No. 28. Needles 19 or 20.

Cast on 84 stitches, 42 on one needle, and 21 on each of the other two ; then knit 2 stitches and pearl 2, for 50 rows. Then commence the Pattern.

1st Row.—K 2 +, K 1, K 2 +, K 1, Tf, K 1, Tf, K 1, Tf, K 1, Tf, K 1, K 2 +, K 1, K 2 +, Tf, K 2 +, Tf, K 2 +, Tf, K 2 +.

2nd Row.—Knitted plain.

Knit these 2 rounds for 90 rounds ; then divide the knitting in half, and take 2 patterns, or 42 stitches, for the heel. Knit 28 rows of the pattern, pearling the back rows instead of knitting them: knit and **pearl alternately 12 rows**; divide the heel in half, and knit it together. Pick up 22 stitches on *each* side of the heel.

Continue the pattern in front, and knitting the back rows plain : knit 2 together at the beginning and end of the plain stitches every fourth round for 28 rounds, thus decreasing 7 times ; knit 34 rounds more without decreasing ; knit plain all round, decreasing in this round 4 times, that is, at the beginning and end of back, and at the beginning and end of the front, in every 3rd round, till there are but 8 stitches left ; divide them in half, and knit them together.

Knowledge of books in recluse men is like that sort of lantern, which hides him who carries it, and serves only to pass through secret and gloomy paths of his own ; but in the possession of a man of business, it is a torch in the hand of one who is willing and able to show those who are bewildered, the way which leads to prosperity and welfare.

KNITTED TOILET CUSHION OR OTTOMAN —SEXAGON SHAPE.

No. 16 Evans's Boar's Head Cotton: No. 14 Needles, No. 18 Needles.

CAST on 2 stitches with No. 18 needles; knit backwards and forwards, encreasing 1 at the beginning of each row until there are 5 stitches on the needle.

1st Row.—K 2, Tf, K 1, Tf, K 2.

2nd Row.—Pearled: every alternate row is pearled.

3rd Row.—K 1, Tf, K 2 +, Tf, K 1, Tf, K 2 +, Tf, K 1.

5th Row.—K 1, Tf, K 1, Tf, K 2 +, Tf, K 1, Tf, K 2 +, Tf, K 1, Tf, K 1.

7th Row.—K 1, Tf, K 2 +, Tf, K 2 +, Tf, K 3, Tf, K 2 +, Tf, K 2 +, Tf, K 1.

9th Row.—K 1, Tf, K 2 +, Tf, K 2 +, Tf, K 5, Tf, K 2 +, Tf, K 2 +, Tf, K 1.

11th Row.—K 1, Tf, K 2 +, Tf, K 2 +, Tf, K 7, Tf, K 2 +, Tf, K 2 +, Tf, K 1.

13th Row.—K 1, Tf, K 2 +, Tf, K 2 +, Tf, K 3, K 2 +, Tf, K 4, Tf, K 2 +, Tf, K 2 +, Tf, K 1.

15th Row.—K 1, Tf, K 2 +, Tf, K 2 +, Tf, K 3, K 2 +, Tf, K 1, Tf, K 2 +, K 3, Tf, K 2 +, Tf, K 2 +, Tf, K 1.

17th Row.—Same as 15th.

19th Row.—K 1, Tf, K 2 +, Tf, K 2 +, Tf, K 1, Tf, K 3, K 2 +, Tf, K 1, Tf, K 2 +, K 3, Tf, K 1, Tf, K 2 +, Tf, K 2 +, Tf, K 1.

21st Row.—K 1, Tf, K 2 +, Tf, K 2 +, Tf, K 3, Tf, K 3, K 2 +, Tf, K 1, Tf, K 2 +, K 3, Tf, K 3, Tf, K 2 +, Tf, K 2 +, Tf, K 1.

23rd Row.—K 1, Tf, K 2 +, Tf, K 2 +, Tf, K 5, Tf, K 3, K 2 +, Tf, K 1, Tf, K 2 +, K 3, Tf, K 5, Tf, K 2 +, Tf, K 2 +, Tf, K 1.

25th Row.—K 1, Tf, K 2 +, Tf, K 2 +, Tf, K 7, Tf, K 3, K 2 +, Tf, K 1, Tf, K 2 +, K 3, Tf, K 7, Tf, K 2 +, Tf, K 2 +, Tf, K 1.

27th Row.—K 2 +, Tf, K 1, Tf, K 2 +, Tf, K 3, K 2 +, Tf, K 4, Tf, K 2 +, K 3, Tf, K 2 +, K 2, K 2 +, Tf, K 3, K 2 +, Tf, K 4, Tf, K 1, Tf, K 2 +, Tf, K 2 +.

29th Row.—K 2 +, Tf, K 1, Tf, K 2 +, Tf, K 3, K 2 +, Tf, K 1, Tf, K 2 +, K 3, Tf, K 2 +, K 5, K 2 +, Tf, K 3, K 2 +, Tf, K 1, Tf, K 2 +, K 3, Tf, K 1, Tf, K 2 +, Tf, K 2 +.

31st Row.—K 2 +, Tf, K 1, Tf, K 2 +,

Tf, K 2 +, K 2, K 2 +, Tf, K 1, Tf, K 2 +, K 2, K 2 +, Tf, K 2 +, K 3, K 2 +, Tf, K 2 +, K 2, K 2 +, Tf, K 1, Tf, K 2 +, K 2, K 2 +, Tf, K 1, Tf, K 2 +, Tf, K 2 +.

33rd Row.—K 2 +, Tf, K 1, Tf, K 2 +, Tf, K 2 +, K 2, K 2 +, Tf, K 1, Tf, K 2 +, K 2, K 2 +, Tf, K 5, Tf, K 2 +, K 2, K 2 +, Tf, K 1, Tf, K 2 +, K 2, K 2 +, Tf, K 1, Tf, K 2 +, Tf, K 2 +.

35th Row.—Same as 33rd.

37th Row.—K 2 +, Tf, K 1, Tf, K 2 +, Tf, K 2 +, K 2, K 2 +, Tf, K 1, Tf, K 2 +, K 13, K 2 +, Tf, K 1, Tf, K 2 +, K 2, K 2 +, Tf, K 1, Tf, K 2 +, Tf, K 2 +.

39th and 41st Rows.—Same as 37th.

43rd and 45th Rows.—Same as 33rd.

47th Row.—K 2 +, Tf, K 1, Tf, K 2 +, Tf, K 2 +, K 2, K 2 +, Tf, K 1, Tf, K 2 +, K 3, Tf, K 7, Tf, K 3, K 2 +, Tf, K 1, Tf, K 2 +, K 2, K 2 +, Tf, K 1, Tf, K 2 +, Tf, K 2 +.

49th Row.—K 2 +, Tf, K 1, Tf, K 2 +, Tf, K 3 +, K 1, K 2 +, Tf, K 1, Tf, K 2 +, K 1, K 2 +, Tf, K 2 +, K 5, K 2 +, Tf, K 2 +, K 1, K 2 +, Tf, K 1, Tf, K 2 +, K 1, K 3 +, Tf, K 2 +, Tf, K 1, Tf, K 2 +.

51st Row.—K 2 +, Tf, K 1, Tf, K 2 +, Tf, K 3 +, K 1, K 2 +, Tf, K 2, K 2 +, Tf, K 2 +, K 2, Tf, K 2 +, K 1, K 2 +, Tf, K 2 +, K 2, Tf, K 2 +, K 1, K 3 +, Tf, K 2 +, Tf, K 1, Tf, K 2 +.

53rd Row.—K 2 +, Tf and K 2 + 3 times, K 3, K 2 +, Tf, K 2 +, K 2, Tf, K 1, Tf, K 2, K 2 +, Tf, K 2 +, K 3, K 2 +, Tf and K 2 + 3 times.

55th Row.—K 2 +, Tf and K 2 + 3 times, K 1, K 2 +, Tf, K 2 +, K 3, Tf, K 1, Tf, K 3, K 2 +, Tf, K 2 +, K 1, K 2 +, Tf and K 2 + 3 times.

57th Row.—K 2 +, Tf, K 2 +, Tf, K 2 +, Tf, slip 1, K 2 +, pass the slip stitch over, Tf, K 3 +, K 3, Tf, K 1, Tf, K 3, K 3 +, Tf, S 1, K 2 +, pass the slip stitch over, Tf and K 2 + 3 times.

59th Row.—K 2 +, Tf, K 2 +, Tf, K 3 +, Tf, K 3 +, K 3, Tf, K 1, Tf, K 3, K 3 +, Tf, K 3 +, Tf, K 2 +, Tf, K 2 +.

61st Row.—K 2 +, Tf and K 2 + 3 times, K 3, Tf, K 1, Tf, K 3, K 2 +, Tf and K 2 + 3 times.

63rd Row.—Same as 61st.

65th Row.—K 2 +, Tf and K 2 + 3

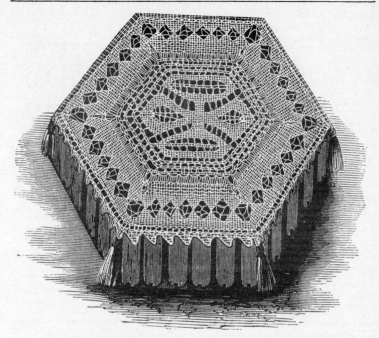

Knitted Toilet Cushion or Ottoman—Sexagon Shape.—By Mrs. Warren.

times, K 3, Tf, K 2 +, K 2, K 2 +, Tf
and K 2 + 3 times.

67th Row.—K 2 +, Tf and K 2 + 3
times, K 5, K 2 +, Tf and K 2 + 3
times.

69th Row.—K 2 +, Tf and K 2 + 3
times, K 3, K 2 +, Tf and K 2 + 3
times.

71st Row.—K 2 +, Tf and K 2 + 3
times, K 1, K 2 +, Tf and K 2 + 3
times.

73rd Row.—K 2 +, Tf, K 2 +, Tf, K
2 +, Tf, S 1, K 2 +, pass the slip stitch
over, Tf and K 2 + 3 times.

75th Row.—K 2 +, Tf, K 2 +, Tf, K
3 +, K 2 +, Tf, K 2 +, Tf, K 2 +.

77th Row.—K 2 +, Tf, K 2 +, Tf, K
2 +, K 3 +, Tf, K 2 +.

79th Row.—K 2 +, Tf, K 3 +, Tf, K
3 +.

81st Row.—K 2 +, K 1, K 2 +.

Knit 3 together.

Pick up 26 stitches on one of the six
sides, having the right side in front.

1st and *2nd Rows.*—Knit plain.

3rd Row.—Encrease 1; pearl the remainder.

4th Row.—Encrease 1; knit all.

5th Row.—Pearled.

6th Row.—Knitted.

7th Row.—K 2, Tf, K 2 +.

8th Row.—Pearled.

9th Row.—K 2 +, * Tf, K 1, Tf, S 1, K
2 +, pass the slip stitch over; *repeat* from
* to the end, where Tf, K 2.

10th Row.—Pearled.

11th Row.—As 7th Row.

12th and *13th Rows.*—Pearled.

14th Row.—Encrease 1; knit remainder.

15th Row.—Encrease 1; pearl all.

16th and *17th Rows.*—Knitted.

Cast off. In knitting each of the Bor-

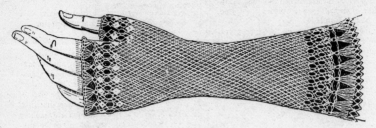

Netted Mitten.--By Mrs. Warren.

ders on the other five sides, pick up one stitch at the beginning of each row, from the side of the one last knitted; and in order to prevent it encreasing, knit it into the 1st stitch.

For the Edging.

Cast on 5 stitches with No. 14 needles.

1st Row.—K 1, Tf, K 2 +, Tf, K 2.

2nd Row.—K 2; pearl remainder.

3rd Row.—K 1, Tf, K 2 +, Tf, K 1, Tf, K 2.

4th Row.—Same as 2nd.

5th Row.—K 1, Tf, K 2 +, Tf, K 1, Tf, continue K 2 +, Tf, K 2.

6th Row.—Same as 2nd.

7th Row.—K 1, Tf, K 2 +; knit the remainder plain.

8th Row.—Cast off all but 5 stitches, which knit plain.

This Edging is to be sewed round.

For the Sides.—No. 18 Needles.

Cast on 30 stitches : knit 8 rows plain.

9th Row.—K 4, P 22, K 4.

10th Row.—Knitted.

11th Row.—Same as 9th.

12th Row.—Knitted.

13th Row.—S 4, K 22, turn the knitting round, and pearl 22, leaving 4 stitches at each end of the needle. *Repeat* these two rows until 24 ridges can be counted from the 12th row.

Next row the same as 9th.

Next row knitted.

Next row the same as 9th.

Next row knitted.

Repeat from the 9th row four times more, till there are 5 patterns; then knit 8 plain rows, and cast off.

Knit 5 pieces more exactly the same;

then join together, and sew round the cushion.

Make six tassels of cotton, and sew to each corner; but chenille tassels of the same colour as the draperies of the room, or the lining of the cushion, look best.

To make the cushion up, cut six pieces of cardboard for the sides, and a piece for the bottom the same size as the top of the cushion, to be covered with coloured silk or cambric. Then make a similar shape in calico, only a size smaller, and fill it with bran; place it in the cardboard frame, and cover it; then place the knitting over, and sew it round the bottom.

This cushion may be converted into an ottoman for a room, if No. 12 knitting pins be used for the cushion, and a bullion Fringe for the Edge; also using Berlin wool for the top, and at the sides shades of wool to harmonize with the top, making each of the five flutings at the side of one shade.

NETTED MITTEN.

Four skeins of the very finest Purse Silk that can be procured, the size of 50 Evans's Boar's Head Cotton, for black mittens; or for summer wear. 45 Evans's Boar's Head Cotton. For a large hand use No. 17 Pin, or for a small one use No. 19 Pin; also No. 10 Pin.

BEGIN on a foundation of 78 loops.

Net 14 rounds, or 7 diamonds.

Decrease, by netting 2 loops together once in every fourth round for 6 times, but not always in the same place.

There should now be 38 rounds, or 19 diamonds, from the foundation.

Then net 54 rounds without decreasing, making 46 diamonds from the foundation.

Now net 2 into the 1st loop, the remainder of the round without encreasing—thus encreasing once only in the round.

Net 3 rounds.

Net 1; net 2 into the 2nd loop; net the remainder without increasing, till within 3 loops of the end; net 2 into the 1st of these; net the other two plain.

Net 3 rounds.

Net 2; net 2 into the 3rd loop; net the remainder without encreasing, till 4 from the end; net two into the 1st of these; net the 3 without encreasing.

Net 3 rounds.

Continue thus to encrease twice in every 4th round, leaving 2 more loops each time between the double stitches (*thus, after leaving first* 3 *and them* 5 *between, as just directed, next leave* 7, *then* 9, *&c.*), till there are 100 loops all round; now divide the Mitten in half, taking as the middle the centre diamond between the double stitches.

Count 13 loops on each side of this diamond, making in the whole 27 loops; join these together for the thumb.

On these 27 loops net 10 rounds, or 5 diamonds; then one pattern of Leaf Netting, thus:—Net * 5 in the 1st loop, 5 in the 2nd; net 3 loops plain; *repeat* from * all round.

Next round; net the 11 loops together; net 4 plain; *repeat* all round. These two rounds complete one pattern of Leaf Netting.

Net 2 plain rounds.

Net 1 pattern round of Leaf Netting.

Net 2 plain rounds.

Take a No. 10 pin, and net 6 stitches in 1 loop, miss 3 loops, *repeat.*

Take the smaller pin, and net 1 plain round.

This finishes the edge at the top of the thumb.

Cut off the silk or cotton, and fasten it on at the hand.

Net 20 plain rounds, or 10 diamonds; net the edge as directed for the thumb.

Cut the Mitten from the foundation. Fasten the silk on to this point, which is the arm, and commence the Border and Edging:—

Net 1 pattern of Leaf Netting.

Net 2 rounds plain.

Net 1 pattern of Leaf Netting, using No. 10 pin in the 1st round, and the smaller pin in the 2nd round.

With No. 10 pin net 10 loops in one, miss 4 loops, *repeat.*

With No. 10 pin net 1 round plain.

With smaller pin net 1 round plain.

SOURCES OF DIFFERENCES OF OPINION.

A GREAT portion of the opinions of mankind are notoriously propagated by transmission from one generation to another, without any possible option on the part of those into whose minds they are instilled. A child regards as true whatever his teachers choose to inculcate, and whatever he discovers to be believed by those around him. His creed is thus insensibly formed, and he will continue in after-life to believe the same things, without any proof, provided his knowledge and experience do not happen to impinge on their falsehood. Mere instillation is sufficient to make him believe any proposition, although he should be utterly ignorant of the foundation on which it rests, or the evidence by which it is supported. It may create in his mind a belief of the most palpable absurdities; things, as it appears to others, not only contradicted by his reason, but at variance with the testimony of his senses; and in the boundless field which the senses do not reach, there is nothing too preposterous to be palmed on his credulity. The religious opinions of the majority of mankind are necessarily acquired in this way: from the nature of the case they cannot be otherwise than derivative, and they are as firmly believed, without the least particle of evidence, as the theorems of Euclid by those who understand the demonstrations. Men do not suspect their religious creed to be false, because the grounds of its truth or falsity lie altogether without the pale of their knowledge, and remote from the path of their experience; and because, when they have been accustomed to connect certain ideas together in their infancy, it grows beyond the power of their imagination to disjoin them. Nor is it merely definite opinions which are acquired in this manner, but a thousand associations are established in the mind, which influence their judgments in matters with which they subsequently become conversant.

Thus the external circumstances in which men are placed unavoidably occasion, without any choice on their part, the chief diversities of opinion existing in the world.

D EEP LACE IN CROCHET.

THE WORK-TABLE FRIEND.

DEEP LACE IN CROCHET.

For trimming mandarine sleeves, &c. Like all other crochet lace, this pattern may be used for many different purposes, and may be made of various sizes, according to the cotton employed for it.

It is very suitable for mandarine sleeves, for working which we would advise W. Evans and Co.'s Boar's Head crochet cotton, No 24, with Boulton's crochet hook, No 20. For petticoats, W. Evans and Co.'s Boar's Head crochet cotton, No 12, with a hook about No 16; and for children's drawers, No 30 cotton may be used.

The pattern, as will be seen in the engraving, consists of a series of deep scallops, each comprising five wheels. They are done in the order in which they are marked alphabetically.

A. 4 Ch; close into a round with A Sc, stitch in the first chain. Do another Sc. stitch in that chain, and two in each of the other three. Then slip stitch in every one of the eight Sc.

7 Ch. Tc behind the first stitch, + 3 Ch. Tc behind the next, + 6 times. 3 Ch. slip on the 4th of 7 Ch. Sc. all round, so there will be 32 stitches. Fasten off.

B. Do this exactly like the last, except that, when 24 of the last round are done, you will make a chain of 2, draw the loop through the opposite stitch of A, slip back on the 2 chain, and finish the round of Sc. Fasten off.

C. Like B, joining on to A at the

eighth stitch from that where A and B are joined.

D. Do all but the last round like the previous ones. Then,—one Sc, 2 Ch, join to the last stitch of wheel B; slip stitch back, 4 Sc, 7 Ch, join to the 4th of the 7 Sc in the quarter of B; slip back 3 of the 7; 3 Ch, join to the corresponding place of A, slip back: 3 Ch, join to the same part of C, slip back; slip back on the remaining ones of the 7 : 4 more Sc on the wheel, join to C, and finish the round with Sc.

E is a wheel made like the previous ones, and joined, *without* the two chains, to C and D, at the fifth stitch of each,—from where the two are united together.

These five form one scallop. All the following ones on the same line as B are done like it. All those on the line with D are repetitions of the same receipt. J, and the others at the point, are like E.

Do as great a length as may be required, before putting the scallop on the heading. For the former, Sc on the side of the wheel C, + 4 Ch, miss 3, Dc on the 4th; 5 Ch, Dc on the wheel E, at the 5th stitch, from where it joins to C, 5 Ch, miss 4, Dc on 5th, 5 Ch, miss 3, Dc on 4th, 5 Ch, miss 2, Dc on 3rd, 5 Ch, miss 3, Dc on 4th, 5 Ch, miss 4, Dc on 5th, 5 Ch, Dc on wheel D, the 4th stitch from where that joins to H, 4 Ch, Sc on the 2 Ch that join D and H, + repeat.

Round each scallop do thus :—1 Sc, 3 Dc under the 4 Ch; + 4 Dc, 2 Ch, 4 Dc, + under every chain of five; 3 Ch, 1 Sc, under the chain of 4.

For the Heading. Dc on the 11th stitch of the wheel, reckoning from where it joins the one preceding it, + 5 Ch, miss 4, Dc on the 5th; 8 Ch, Dc on the 6th stitch of the next wheel, from the join.

2nd Row. Sc on every stitch.

EMBROIDERED NOTE-CASE.

Materials.—A piece of fawn-coloured kid, 8 inches by 18; a small quantity of fine gold bullion and thread; 5 shades of blue green, and the same number of yellow green embroidery silk, 7 shades of crimson, and 3 of lilac ditto, with a very few steel beads No. 2.

The engraving gives the group of

flowers the full size; the design may therefore be traced from it, prepared, and marked on the kid. The note-case is about six inches long, and four wide, the outside of the pockets being made of the same piece as the backs. Both the backs are embroidered in simple patterns. They may be done alike, or otherwise, as may be preferred.

Line the kid with fine new linen, before placing it in a frame to be worked. This is to prevent the needle from tearing the leather, as it is apt to do when the stitches are very close to each other. The embroidery of this pattern is extremely simple. All the leaves are composed of two shades of green; some of the large ones have three, and the variety of tint is produced by selecting different shades for the leaves which are nearest to each other. A large light leaf may be worked with the three lightest yellow-greens, having the darkest of those greens for the veining. Close to this leaf, another might be made of the

E

three darkest shades of blue green, the veining being gold. A third leaf of the same group could be worked in the darkest yellow greens. Invariably the lower part of a leaf, and that nearest the stem are the darkest; but there should be no abrupt transitions. The stitches should be blended by taking those of one shade irregularly —short and long alternately, and then working in those of the next shade with them. The veinings are either in the darkest silks or in gold. The small leaves are not veined, and the stitches are taken parallel and close together. The stems are done in half-polka stitch. The tendrils are done in gold cord, laid on and sewed over, the ends only being drawn through the kid. The large flower is a dahlia, worked in shades of crimson;—as in Nature, the outer leaves are the darkest. The stitches are all taken radiating from the centre of the flower. Care must be taken, in working every part, to preserve the edges as clear and perfect as possible. The eye of the flower is made of loops of gold bullion,—each about a quarter of an inch long, threaded on a needleful of silk. After threading each piece, the needle must be drawn down in the same place it was brought up, the bullion thus forming a little loop. Six of these with a steel bead in the centre, form the eye of the flower. The buds are made by forming a circle of gold bullion, and placing a steel bead in the centre of each.

The other flower is worked in lilac silks, and has a single bead in the centre.

These note-cases may be made up at a bookbinder's; but the process is so simple, a little ingenuity will enable anybody to do it at home. Line the kid with scarlet silk, having previously cut it to exactly the size required, allowing a quarter of an inch every way for turning in. Cut two slits nearly at the edge of each pocket, to place loops of leather for the pencil. On one side a slit must be made about half an inch from the top, three quarters of an inch long. Leave rather more than an inch, and cut another. On the other side the slits must be made where the leather is uncut in this one. Pieces of leather, large enough to allow a pencil to slip in, are secured in these slips by means of gum. Gum in slips of leather for the sides of the pockets, and fold over the turnings. A few sheets of paper, cut the proper size, with an outside one covered with silk like the lining, are held in the book by a bit of white ribbon fastened to the back.

Any bookbinder with whom you may be in the habit of dealing, would stamp the outlines of the cover and pocket. This should be done before making up, but it may be dispensed with.

A COVER FOR A FOOTSTOOL OR SOFA PILLOW.

IN CROSS STITCH, BERLIN WORK.

For a Footstool, take half a yard of Penelope Canvas, containing 12 double threads to the inch. For a Sofa Pillow, three quarters of a yard of Penelope Canvas, containing 9 double threads to the inch. Seven shades of Scarlet, 4-thread Berlin wool, 2 shades of Drab, or nearly a Stone-colour, 1 white, 1 Imperial Blue, 2 shades of Green: 1 Lighter Green silk. Two bunches of Steel Beads, 2 of Gold, 2 of Black Glass Beads the same size as the Steel, which should be No. 12 or 14. The Beads are to be sewn on with cotton.

Explanation of terms:—For the Scarlet wools, DC is the darkest Claret, almost a Black; C is Claret, the next shade; Garnet is the next shade; Ruby is the next; DS, or dark Scarlet, is the next; MS, or military Scarlet, is the next; Rose is the lightest shade; making in all seven shades. LDb, or light Drab, which must be very close to white; Db, or the second shade of Drab, which must be of middle tint. Wt. or White. S, or Steel. B, or Black. LG for light Green; DG, dark Green; G, Gold.

The directions here given are for one corner, and the opposite one; afterwards, the remaining two corners can, of course, be very readily worked.

Commence at the right-hand corner of the canvas, working from the right-hand to the left. Every row must be commenced afresh, and not worked forwards and back.

1st Row.—67 stitches of DC.

2nd Row.—55 DC, 5 Wt, 7 DC.

3rd Row.—2 DC, 1 LDb, 1 Db, 1 S, 10 DC, 5 G, 23 DC, 1 Wt, 9 DC, 8 Wt, 1 DC, 1 Wt, 4 DC.

4th Row.—1 DC, 1 LDb, 1 Db, 1 S, 10

DC, 1 G, 1 Db, 4 B, 8 DC, 1 Wt, 11 DC, 2 Db, 2 Wt, 6 DC, 3 Wt, 6 Db, 4 Wt, 3 DC.

5th Row.—1 DC, 1 LDb, 1 Db, 1 S, 7 DC, 3 G, 1 Db, 1 S, 5 Db, 1 B, 6 DC, 2 Wt, 1 Db, 8 DC, 3 Db, 1 S, 1 Db, 1 Wt, 5 DC, 2 Wt, 2 Db, 4 S, 3 Db, 1 Wt, 1 Db, 1 Wt, 1 DC, 1 Wt, 1 DC.

6th Row.—1 DC, 1 LDb, 1 Db, 1 S, 6 DC, 1 G, 2 S, 1 Db, 1 S, 7 Db, 1 B, 2 DC, 2 S, 1 DC, 1 Wt, 2 Db, 1 Wt, 4 DC, 1 Db, 1 DC, 3 Db, 1 LDb, 1 S, 1 Db, 1 Wt, 7 C, 1 Wt, 2 Db, 3 LDb, 2 S, 2 Db, 1 S, 1 Db, 1 Wt, 1 Db, 1 Wt (A). (*In the 3rd and 4th corners, from this mark, it will be observed that the latter portion of this row, and some of the succeeding ones, have been already worked in the 1st and opposite corner.*) Miss 6 stitches of canvas, then work 6 Wt.

7th Row.—1 DC, 1 LDb, 2 Db, 1 S, 4 DC, 1 G, 1 S, 1 Db, 1 S, 1 Db, 1 S, 5 Db, 1 B, 2 Db, 1 B, 2 DC, 1 G, 1 S, 1 Db, 1 S, 1 Db, 2 Wt, 2 DC, 3 Db, 3 LDb, 1 S, 2 Db, 1 Wt, 5 C, 1 Wt, 2 C, 1 Wt, 4 Db, 2 LDb, 1 S, 1 Db, 1 S, 1 Db, 1 Wt, 1 S, 1 Db, miss 3 stitches of canvas, then 1 Db, miss 1 stitch of canvas, then 2 Wt, 4 Db, 1 Wt.

8th Row.—1 DC, 2 LDb, 2 Db, 2 S, 2 G, 1 S, 1 Db, 1 S, 2 Db, 1 S, 2 Db, 2 LDb, 1 Db, 1 B, 3 Db, 3 C, 1 G, 2 S, 2 Db, 1 Wt, 2 C, 1 Db, 1 Wt, 1 Db, 2 G, 1 S, 2 Db, 2 Wt, 4 C, 3 Wt, 2 C, 2 Wt, 4 Db, 1 LDb, 2 S, 2 Db, 1 S, 1 Db, miss 2 stitches of canvas, 3 Db, 1 Wt, 2 Db, 1 S, 2 Db, 1 Wt.

9th Row.—2 DC, 2 LDb, 3 Db, 2 S, 2 Db, 1 S, 1 Db, 1 LDb, 1 S, 2 Db, 2 LDb, 1 Db, 1 B, 3 Db, 3 C, 1 G, 1 S, 3 Db, 1 Wt, 1 C, 1 Db, 1 S, 1 Db, 2 S, 3 Db, 1 Wt, 1 Db, 3 C, 1 Wt, 1 C, 1 Wt, 1 Db, 2 Wt, 3 C, 6 Db, 1 G, 1 S, 1 Db, 1 S, 1 Db, miss 1 stitch of canvas, 2 Db, 1 S, 3 Db, 1 S, 1 Db, 2 Wt.

10th Row.—1 DC, 2 LDb, 2 Db, 1 LDb, 1 Db, 1 S, 2 Db, 1 LDb, 2 Db, 2 LDb, 1 S, 3 Db, 1 DC, 1 B, 2 Db, 1 LDb, 3 C, 1 G, 1 S, 1 Db, 1 S, 1 Db, 1 Wt, 2 Db, 2 S, 1 G, 1 Db, 1 S, 1 Db, 2 Wt, 4 C, 2 Wt, 1 Db, 1 S, 1 Db, 1 Wt, 2 C, 2 Db, 3 S, 3 Db, 1 G, 1 S, 1 Db, 1 Wt, miss 1 stitch of canvas, 2 Db, 1 S, 2 Db, 1 S, 2 Db, 3 Wt.

11th Row.—2 DC, 4 LDb, 3 Db, 2 LDb, 1 Db, 3 LDb, 4 DC, 1 C, 1 B, 2 Db, 1 LDb, 2 C, 1 G, 3 S, 1 Db, 1 Wt, 2 Db,

2 S, 1 G, 1 S, 3 Db, 2 C, 1 G, 3 C, 1 Wt, 2 Db, 1 S, 1 Db, 1 Wt, 3 C, 3 Db, 2 LDb, 2 S, 1 G, 1 S, 1 Db, 2 Wt, 1 Db, 1 S, 2 Db, 1 S, 2 Db, 1 Wt, 1 Db, 1 Wt.

12th Row.—5 DC, 2 LDb, 1 Db, 1 LDb, 1 DC, 4 LDb, 4 DC, 2 C, 1 B, 2 Db, 1 LDb, 2 C, 2 S, 5 Db, 1 S, 2 G, 1 S, 3 Db, 2 C, 1 Db, 2 S, 1 Db, 1 Wt, 2 Db, 1 S, 1 Db, 2 Wt, 6 C, 1 Db, 3 LDb, 1 S, 1 G, 1 S, 2 Db, 4 S, 2 Db, 2 Wt.

13th Row.—6 DC, 2 LDb, 3 DC, 2 LDb, 4 DC, 2 C, 1 B, 2 Db, 2 LDb, 1 C, 2 S, 2 G, 2 G, 10 G, 1 Db, 2 S, 4 Db, 2 S, 2 Db, 1 Wt, 7 C, 2 Db, 2 LDb, 1 G, 3 S, 2 G, 3 Db, 5 Wt.

14th Row.—16 DC, 3 C, 1 B, 1 Db, 2 LDb, 2 S, 2 G, 2 S, 4 Db, 2 S, 1 G, 4 Db, 1 S, 5 G, 3 S, 3 Db, 1 Wt, 4 C, 4 Wt, 2 Db, 1 LDb, 2 G, 1 S, 2 G, 1 Db, 1 S, 1 Db, 1 S, 3 Db, 2 Wt.

15th Row.—15 DC, 3 C, 1 B, 1 S, 2 Db, 2 LDb, 6 G, 2 Wt, 2 Db, 1 S, 1 G, 1 Db, 2 Wt, 1 Db, 1 S, 1 G, 2 S, 3 G, 3 Db, 2 Wt, 3 Garnet, 2 Wt, 5 Db, 2 S, 3 G, 2 S, 1 Db, 1 S, 2 Db, 3 Wt.

16th Row.—14 DC, 4 C, 2 B, 4 Db, 1 LDb, 1 G, 4 S, 1 G, 2 Blue, 1 Wt, 2 Db, 1 S, 1 G, 2 Blue, 1 Wt, 1 Db, 1 S, 1 G, 1 Db, 2 S, 2 G, 1 Db, 2 Wt, 5 Garnet, 4 Db, 3 S, 1 LDb, 1 S, 1 G, 1 S, 1 Wt, 3 Db, 2 Wt.

17th Row.—3 DC, 6 LDb, 4 DC, 4 C, 1 B, 1 S, 4 Db, 1 LDb, 1 G, 1 S, 1 Db, 1 G, 1 Db, 2 S, 1 G, 2 Blue, 1 Wt, 2 Db, 1 S, 1 G, 2 Blue, 1 Wt, 1 Db, 1 S, 1 G, 2 Db, 1 S, 2 G, 5 Garnet, 2 Wt, 1 Db, 3 S, 1 Db, 1 LDb, 1 S, 1 LDb, 1 Db, 1 S, 1 Db, 2 Wt, 3 Db, 2 Wt.

18th Row.—2 DC, 1 LDb, 5 Db, 2 LDb, 1 DC, 1 LDb, 4 C, 1 B, 1 S, 2 Db, 3 LDb, 1 G, 2 S, 3 Blue, 1 Db, 1 S, 1 G, 3 Blue, 2 Db, 1 S, 1 G, 3 Blue, 1 Db, 1 S, 1 G, 1 Blue, 2 Db, 1 S, 2 G, 3 Garnet, 2 Wt, 6 Db, 1 LDb, 1 S, 1 LDb, 1 Db, 1 Wt. miss 1 stitch of Canvas, 1 S, 5 Wt.

19th Row.—2 DC, 7 Db, 1 LDb, 1 Db, 2 LDb, 2 C, 1 B, 1 S, 2 Db, 2 LDb, 2 G, 1 S, 5 Blue, 1 Wt, 1 S, 1 G, 2 Blue, 2 Wt, 1 Db, 1 S, 1 G, 2 Blue, 2 Wt, 1 S, 1 G, 2 Blue, 1 Db, 1 S, 1 G, 1 S, 1 G, 2 Garnet, 6 Wt, 2 Db, 1 LDb, 1 S, 3 Db, 1 Wt, miss 1 stitch of canvas, 1 S.

20th Row.—2 DC, 10 Db, 1 LDb, 1 C, 1 B, 1 S, 2 Db, 1 LDb, 2 Blue, 2 G, 6 Blue, 1 Db, 1 S, 1 G, 2 Blue, 1Wt, 2 Db, 1 S, 1 G, 2 Blue, 1 Wt, 1 Db, 1 S, 1 G, 1

A Cover for a Footstool or Sofa Pillow.—By Mrs. Warren.

Blue, 2 Wt, 1 S, 1 G, 1 Db, 1 S, 1 G, 2 Garnet, 4 Wt, 2 Db, 1 LDb, 1 S, 2 Db, 5 Wt, miss 2 stitches of canvas, 1 S.

21st Row.—3 DC, 4 Db, 1 B, 5 Db, 1 C, 2 B, 3 Db, 2 LDb, 8 Blue, 1 S, 1 G, 4 Blue, 1 Db, 1 S, 1 G, 4 Blue, 1 S, 1 G, 2 Blue, 1 Wt, 1 Db, 1 S, 1 G, 2 Db, 1 S, 1 G, 5, Garnet, 2 Db, 1 LDb, 1 S, 2 Db, 3 Wt, 2 B, 1 S, 5 B.

22nd Row.—4 DC, 4 Db, 1 B, 4 Db, 1 B, 1 S, 5 Db, 1 LDb, 26 Blue, 1 S, 1 G, 1 Blue, 1 LDb, 2 Db, 1 S, 1 G, 2 Garnet, 3 B, 1 Db, 1 LDb, 1 S, 2 Db, 4 Wt, 2 S, 1 B, 5 S, 3 B.

23rd Row.—5 DC, 1 Db, 1 LDb, 2 Db, 1 B, 2 Db, 2 S, 2 Db, 5 LDb, 7 Blue, 4 LG, 18 Blue, 1 LDb, 2 Db, 1 S, 2 B, 3 S, 4 Db, 2 Wt, 1 S, 4 Db, 1 B, 3 DB, 1 S, 2 B, 2 S, 2 B.

24th Row.—5 DC, 1 Db, 2 LDb, 1 Db, 1 B, 1 Db, 2 B, 2 Db, 4 LDb, 3 Blue, 1 LG, 2 Silk, 2 Blue, 5 LG, 4 Blue, 1 LG, 13 Blue, 2 LDb, 1 Db, 5 S, I Wt, 2 Db, 3 Wt, 3 Ruby, miss 2 stitches of canvas, 1 B, miss 5 stitches of canvas, 1 B, 5 S, 2 B.

25th Row.—5 DC, 1 Db, 1 LDb, 2 Db, 1 B, 1 S, 1 B, 2 Db, 2 LDb, 5 Blue, 3 LG, 2 Silk, 1 DG, 2 LG, 1 DG, 2 LG, 1 Blue, 5 LG, 1 Silk, 3 Blue, 1 G, 3 S, 4 Blue, 2 LDb, 1 Db, 2 S, 3 Db, 9 Ruby, miss 2 stitches of canvas, 1 B, miss 6 canvas, 2 S, 1 Db, miss 1 canvas, 2 S.

26th Row.—4 DC, 1 S, 2 Db, 1 S, 1 Db, 1 B, 1 3, 1 B, 1 Db, 6 LDb, 2 Blue, 2 LG, 1 DG, 1 LG, 1 Silk, 1 DG, 1 LG, 1 DG, 6 LG, 3 Blue, 2 Silk, 1 Blue, 1 G, 4 Db, 1 S, 3 Blue, 2 LDb, 1 Db, 1 S, 5

A Blind Tassel Cover.—By Mrs. Warren.

Db, 4 S, 3 Ruby, miss 1 stitch canvas, 1 B, miss 8 canvas, 2 Db.

27th Row.—4 DC, 2 S, 1 Db, 3 S, 1 B, 2 Db, 1 LDb, 2 Db, 4 LDb, 1 Blue, 2 LG, 1 DG, 1 LG, 1 Silk, 2 DG, 3 LG, 1 DG, 7 Blue, 1 Silk, 1 G, 1 S, 5 Db, 3 Blue, 2 LDb, 1 Db, 1 S, 1 Db, 9 Ruby, 4 S.

28th Row.—4 DC, 1 S, 1 B, 4 S, 1 B, 1 Db, 1 LDb, 4 Db, 2 LDb, 2 Blue, 2 LDb, 1 LG, 1 Db, 1 LDb, 1 B, 1 S, 1 Db, 1 LG, 1 DG, 4 Silk, 5 Blue, 1 G, 1 S, 2 Db, 2 LDb, 1 Db, 1 Blue, 3 LDb, 1 Db, 2 S, 13 Ruby.

29th Row.—4 DC, 1 S, 2 B, 2 S, 1 B, 6 Db, 2 LDb, 2 Blue, 1 Db, 2 LDb, 1 Db, 1 LDb, 1 B, 1 S, 1 Db, 1 S, 1 Db, 1 LG, 2 DG, 3 Silk, 2 Blue, 3 G, 1 S, 2 Db, 2 LDb, 1 Db, 4 LDb, 1 Db, 1 S, 1 G, 13 Ruby.

30th Row.—5 DC, 1 S, 2 B, 1 S, 1 B, 2 Db, 1 S, 1 Db, 4 LDb, 2 Blue, 1 Db, 1 LDb, 2 Db, 1 LDb, 2 B, 1 S, 1 Db, 1 S, 1 Db, 2 LG, 1 DG, 2 Silk, 1 Blue, 5 G, 1 S, 4 Db, 3 LDb, 1 Db, 2 S, 1 G, 11 Ruby, 2 DS.

31st Row.—2 DC, 5 Db, 1 S, 2 B, 1 Db, 1 S, 1 Db, 4 LDb, 3 Blue, 1 S, 1 Db, 1 S, 1 Db, 1 LDb, 1 Wt, 1 S, 2 Db, 1 S, 2 Db, 1 LG, 1 Silk, 1 LG, 1 Silk, 2 G, 3 B, 1 G, 2 S, 6 Db, 2 S, 1 G, 9 Ruby, 5 DS.

32nd Row.—1 DC, 3 Db, 2 S, 1 B, 1 Db, 1 S, 1 B, 2 S, 2 Db, 1 LDb, 2 Blue, 3 LG, 2 S, 1 B, 1 Wt, 1 Db, 1 LDb, 1 Wt, 2 S, 1 LDb, 2 Db, 3 silk, 1 Blue, 2 B, 3 S, 2 B, 1 G, 7 S, 1 G, 7 Ruby, 8 DS.

33rd Row.—1 DC, 5 Db, 1 S, 1 B, 1 S, 1 B, 1 S, 2 Db, 1 LDb, 1 G, 1 Blue, 5 LG, 1 S, 1 B, 1 LDb, 1 Wt, 1 Db, 3 Wt, 1 LDb, 1 Db, 2 LG, 2 Blue, 1 G, 2 S, 4 Db, 9 G, 5 Ruby, 11 DS.

34th Row.—2 DC, 2 Db, 1 LDb, 2 Db, 1 S, 2 B, 1 S, 2 Db, 1 LDb, 1 B, 1 G, 1 Blue, 1 LG, 3 DG, 2 Db, 1 B, 1 LDb, 2

Wt, 1 Db, 1 Wt, 1 LDb, 1 Db, 4 LG, 1 Blue, 1 G, 1 S, 1 Db, 2 LDb, 2 Db, 3 S, 1 B, 4 S, 1 Wt, 2 Ruby, 13 DS.

35th Row.—3 DC, 1 S, 1 Db, 1 LDb, 1 Db, 1 S, 2 B, 1 S, 1 Db, 1 LDb, 1 B, 1 G, 1 Blue, 4 silk, 2 LDb, 1 Db, 1 B, 1 LDb, 1 Wt, 1 Db, 1 LDb, 1 S, 1 Db, 1 LDb, 1 DG, 2 LG, 1 Blue, 1 S, 1 Db, 2 LDb, 1 Ruby, 2 Db, 2 LDb, 2 S, 1 B, 1 S, 2 LDb, 1 Db, 1 LDb, 1 Wt, 14 DS.

36th Row.—3 DC, 1 S, 1 Db, 2 LDb, 1 S, 1 B, 1 S, 1 Db, 1 LDb, 1 B, 1 G, 2 Blue, 4 silk, 2 LDb, 1 Db, 3 B, 1 S, 1 Db, 2 LDb, 2 DG, 1 LG, 1 Blue, 1 S, 1 Db, 1 LDb, 2 Ruby, 1 Db, 2 LDb, 1 S, 1 Db, 1 LDb, 1 S, 1 B, 1 S, 2 LDb, 3 Wt, 13 DS.

37th Row.—3 DC, 1 S, 2 Db, 1 LDb, 1 Db, 1 S, 1 B, 1 S, 1 Db, 1 LDb, 1 B, 1 G, 6 B, 4 Db, 1 silk, 4 Db, 3 LG, 2 Blue, 1 S, 1 Db, 1 LDb, 2 Ruby, 2 LDb, 1 S, 1 Db, 3 L Db, 1 B, 1 S, 1 LDb, 1 Wt, 16 DS.

38th Row.—3 DC, 2 S, 2 Db, 1 S, 2 B, 1 S, 2 LDb, 1 B, 1 G, 6 Blue, 2 S, 1 LG, 3 silk, 1 LG, 6 Blue, 1 S, 2 Db, 2 Ruby, 1 Db, 1 LDb, 1 Db, 3 LDb, 1 Db, 1 S, 1 B, 1 Db, 2 LDb, 15 DS.

39th Row.—4 DC, 3 S, 4 B, 1 S, 1 Db, 1 LDb, 1 B, 1 G, 6 Blue, 1 S, 1 B, 2 LG, 1 silk, 3 LG, 5 Blue, 1 S, 2 Db, 3 Ruby, 2 Db, 1 LDb, 1 Db, 1 LDb, 2 Db, 1 B, 1 LDb, 1 Db, 1 LDb, 1 Wt, 14 DS.

40th Row.—6 DC, 2 S, 3 B, 1 S, 1 Db, 1 LDb, 1 B, 1 G, 5 Blue, 1 G, 1 S, 2 B, 2 LG, 2 silk, 1 LG, 5 Blue, 1 G, 1 S, 2 Db, 2 Ruby, 4 Db, 1 LDb, 1 Db, 1 LDb, 1 B, 1 LDb, 1 Wt, 1 LDb, 1 Wt, 11 DS, 3 MS.

41st Row.—5 DC, 3 Db, 2 S, 1 B, 1 S, 1 Db, 2 LDb, 1 B, 1 G, 3 Blue, 2 G, 1 S, 1 B, 2 Blue, 3 LG, 6 Blue, 2 G, 1 S, 2 Db, 2 Ruby, 1 DS, 3 Db, 1 LDb, 1 Db, 2 LDb, 2 Wt, 8 DS, 6 MS.

42nd Row.—4 DC, 1 Db, 3 S, 2 B, 1 S, 2 Db, 1 LDb, 2 B, 1 G, 1 Blue, 1 G, 3 Db, 1 S, 1 B, 9 Blue, 1 G, 3 B, 1 S, 2 Db, 1 Ruby, 2 DS, 3 Db, 1 LDb, 1 Db, 2 LDb, 1 Wt, 6 DS, 9 MS.

43rd Row.—5 DC, 2 MS, 1 S, 3 B, 2 S, 1 MS, 2 LDb, 2 B, 1 G, 1 MS, 2 LDb, 2 MS, 1 S, 1 B, 8 Blue, 3 G, 1 B, 1 G, 1 MS, 1 Ruby, 4 DS, 1 MS, 1 DS, 1 Wt, 2 LDb, 2 Wt, 3 DS, 12 MS.

44th Row.—4 DC, 2 Db, 1 S, 2 B, 2 S, 1 B, 1 S, 2 Db, 2 LDb, 2 B, 4 LDb, 1 Db, 1 S, 1 B, 8 Blue, 1 G, 1 S, 1 G, 1 S, 1 B,

3 S, 5 DS, 1 Wt, 1 LDb, 2 Wt, 2 DS, 14 MS.

45th Row.—4 DC, 1 Db, 7 S, 1 B, 1 S, 2 Db, 2 LDb, 1 Db, 4 LDb, 1 Db, 1 S, 1 B, 7 Blue, 1 G, 1 S, 1 Db, 1 S, 1 G, 1 B, 2 Db, 2 S, 4 DS, 3 Wt, 1 DS, 16 MS.

46th Row.—3 DC, 2 Db, 2 S, 3 Db, 3 S, 1 B, 2 S, 4 Db, 2 LDb, 2 Db, 1 S, 1 B, 7 Blue, 1 G, 1 S, 1 Db, 1 S, 2 G, 1 B, 2 Db, 2 S, 4 DS, 1 Wt, 1 DS, 17 MS.

47th Row.—4 DC, 1 Db, 1 S, 2 Db, 2 LDb, 1 Db, 3 S, 2 B, 3 S, 4 Db, 1 S, 2 B, 6 Blue, 1 G, 1 S, 3 Db, 1 S, 1 G, 1 S, 1 B, 2 S, 6 DS, 18 MS.

48th Row.—4 DC, 6 Db, 1 LDb, 2 Db, 3 S, 3 B, 4 S, 2 B, 6 Blue, 1 G, 2 S, 2 Db, 1 LDb, 1 Db, 1 G, 1 Db, 2 S, 6 DS, 19 MS.

49th Row.—5 DC, 1 Db, 3 C, 3 Db, 2 S, 3 Db, 2 S, 5 B, 2 LDb, 1 Db, 2 S, 2 G, 2 S, 2 Db, 2 LDb, 1 Db, 1 S, 1 G, 1 Db, 1 S, 4 DS, 20 MS.

50th Row.—5 DC, 5 C, 1 LDb, 1 S, 1 C, 2 LDb, 1 Db, 1 S, 2 Db, 2 S, 2 Db, 2 LDb, 5 Db, 1 S, 2 Db, 2 LDb, 2 Db, 1 S, 1 G, 1 Db, 1 S, 1 Db, 1 S, 2 DS, 21 MS.

51st Row.—5 DC, 7 C, 2 LDb, 3 Db, 1 LDb, 3 Db, 2 Garnet, 1 B, 2 LDb, 1 Db, 1 LDb, 1 Db, 1 LDb, 1 Db, 1 S, 1 Db, 3 LDb, 1 Db, 1 S, 1 Db, 1 G, 3 Db, 1 S, 1 DS, 19 MS, 3 Rose.

52nd Row.—5 DC, 8 C, 4 LDb, 6 Garnet, 1 B, 1 S, 2 LDb, 1 Ruby, 1 LDb, 1 Db, 1 S, 1 Db, 1 LDb, 1 DS, 1 LDb, 2 Db, 1 S, 1 Db, 2 S, 1 Db, 1 S, 1 DS, 17 MS, 6 Rose.

53rd Row.—5 DC, 9 C, 8 Garnet, 1 B, 2 S, 3 Ruby, 1 LDb, 2 Db, 2 LDb, 1 DS, 1 LDb, 1 Db, 1 LDb, 2 Db, 1 S, 1 Db, 1 S, 2 DS, 15 MS, 8 Rose.

54th Row.—5 DC, 9 C, 8 Garnet, 1 B, 1 S, 4 Ruby, 4 LDb, 2 DS, 3 LDb, 1 Db, 1 LDb, 1 S, 2 Db, 1 S, 4 MS, 10 Rose.

55th Row.—5 DC, 5 Wt, 4 C, 7 Ruby, 1 B, 2 S, 5 Garnet, 1 LDb, 2 Garnet, 2 DS, 1 LDb, 1 DS, 2 LDb, 2 Db, 1 S, 1 Db, 1 S, 13 MS, 11 Rose.

56th Row.—5 DC, 1 Wt, 2 Db, 3 Wt, 2 C, 1 Wt, 7 Garnet, 1 B, 2 S, 8 Ruby, 4 DS, 1 LDb, 3 Db, 1 S, 1 Db, 1 S, 12 MS, 12 Rose.

57th Row.—5 DC, 1 Wt, 2 Db, 1 Wt, 1 Db, 1 Wt, 1 C, 3 Wt, 6 Garnet, 2 B, 1 S, 7 Ruby, 6 DS, 1 LDb, 2 Db, 1 LDb, 1 S, 11 MS, 13 Rose.

58th Row.—5 DC, 1 Wt, 1 Db, 1 S, 2

Db, 3 Wt, 1 Db, 1 Wt, 5 Garnet, 1 B, 1 S, 2 B, 7 Ruby, 6 DS, 4 Db, 12 MS, 14 Rose.

59th Row.—5 DC, 1 Wt, 2 Db, 1 S, 2 Db, 2 Wt, 1 Db, 1 Wt, 1 Garnet, 1 Wt, 3 Garnet, 1 B, 2 S, 8 Ruby, 7 DS, 3 LDb, 12 MS, 14 Rose.

60th Row.—5 DC, 2 Wt, 2 Db, 1 S, 2 Db, 1 Wt, 2 Db, 3 Wt, 2 Garnet, 1 B, 1 S, 1 Db, 7 Ruby, 9 DS, 1 LDb, 12 MS, 15 Rose.

61st Row.—5 DC, 1 C, 2 Wt, 2 Db, 1 S, 2 Db, 1 S, 1 Db, 1 LDb, 1 Db, 1 Wt, 2 Garnet, 1 B, 1 S, 1 Db, 7 Ruby, 10 DS, 12 MS, 15 Rose.

62nd Row.—5 DC, 2 C, 3 Db, 1 S, 2 Db, 1 S, 3 Db, 1 Wt, 2 Garnet, 1 B, 1 S, 1 Db, 7 Ruby, 10 DS, 11 MS, 16 Rose.

63rd Row.—5 DC, 1 C, 2 Db, 2 S, 1 Db, 1 S, 1 Db, 1 S, 3 Db, 1 Wt, 2 Garnet, 1 S, 2 B, 7 Ruby, 9 DS, 12 MS, 16 Rose.

64th Row.—5 DC, 2 C, 3 Db, 2 S, 1 G, 1 Db, 1 S, 1 Db, 2 Wt, 1 Garnet, 1 S, 1 B, 1 S, 1 Db, 2 B, 5 Ruby, 9 DS, 12 MS, 15 Rose.

65th Row.—5 DC, 3 C, 3 Db, 2 S, 1 G, 1 S, 2 Wt, 2 S, 1 Garnet, 1 B, 1 S, 1 Db, 2 Ruby, 1 B, 3 Ruby, 9 DS, 12 MS, 17 Rose.

66th Row.—5 DC, 5 C, 1 Wt, 1 Db, 1 S, 2 G, 2 S, 2 Garnet, 2 Wt, 1 S, 1 Db, 3 Ruby, 1 S, 1 Ruby, 11 DS, 12 MS, 17 Rose.

67th Row.—5 DC, 1 Wt, 3 Db, 2 Wt, 1 Db, 2 S, 2 G, 1 S, 3 Db, 2 Wt, 1 Db, 3 Ruby, 1 S, 1 Ruby, 10 DS, 12 MS, 17 Rose.

Now count 67 stitches across to the opposite corner, and begin at the right hand, working from right to left, and work again from 1st row; after this opposite corner is worked, there can be no difficulty about the other corners, if care be always taken to begin at a corner, and work from right to left. Now work all round, in herring-bone stitch, 1 row Blue, 1 row Rose colour, then a row 4 stitches Rose colour, 4 Blue. To work this herring-bone stitch, take up one stitch of canvas only on the needle, and make the stitch 3 stitches of canvas in depth; then take up another stitch of canvas on the needle, consequently the three rows will take up 9 stitches in depth of canvas.

A BLIND TASSEL-COVER.

No. 10 or 12 Evans's Boar's Head Cotton. No. 3 Penelope Hook.

1st Row.—Make 15 chain, unite, work 15 Dc stitches round.

2nd Row.—1 L, 2 chain, 1 L into every Dc stitch; after the last 2 chain, unite into the 1st L. (*The cotton must now be cut off at the end of every row.*)

3rd Row.—5 chain, Dc on every L stitch; 15 chains of 5, in this row.

4th Row.—5 chain, Dc in centre loop of every 5 chain.   [every 5.

5th Row.—3 chain, Dc in centre loop of every 3.   [of every 7.

6th Row.—7 chain, Dc in centre loop of

7th Row.—3 chain, Dc into centre loop

8th Row.—3 L in the centre loop of the 3 chain, 1 chain, *repeat.*

9th Row.—3 L in the centre L stitch, 2 chain, *repeat.*

There will be 75 stitches in this row.

For the Border.

Begin on a L stitch; 37 chain, turn back, 1 L into 9th loop from hook, * 1 L, 2 chain, 1 L into 3rd loop, *repeat* from * 9 times more (*in all,* 10 *spaces*); this forms the vein of leaf: 1 chain, Dc into loop where commenced, 1 chain, turn the work round on the finger, 7 Dc up the side of the vein; this will bring to the 3rd L stitch of vein. Then 25 L stitches up to the point in the 26th loop, work 4 L, 3 chain, 4 more L into same loop, then 25 L stitches down, then 7 Dc stitches down to the loop where commenced; turn on wrong side, 5 chain, Dc into 4th loop up the side of the leaf, 5 chain, Dc into 4th loop; then 5 chain, 1 L into 4th loop till the last of the 25 L, then 5 chain, 1 L into centre loop of the 3 chain, 5 chain, 1 more L into same loop; then 5 chain, 1 L on 1st of the 25 L, then 5 chain, 1 L into every 4th loop for 6 times; then 5 chain, Dc into 4th loop, 5 chain, Dc into 4th loop, 5 chain, Dc into loop where commenced. Turn on the right side: 5 Dc *under* every 5 chain all round; lastly, Dc into loop where commenced, then 12 Dc into the 12 loops of 9th row.

Now 37 chain, and work another leaf, but uniting into the 1st leaf for 7 times; that is, after making the first 5 Dc stitches, unite into the 5th Dc stitch of first leaf; *repeat* this 6 times more.

THE WORK-TABLE FRIEND.

INSTRUCTIONS IN EMBROIDERY.

EMBROIDERY, properly speaking, includes every sort of ornamental work done with a sewing needle of any kind; but, in its popular acceptation, it applies only to the ornamentation of any article by the eye or from drawn or marked patterns—whatever may be the material, or combination of materials employed; Berlin work, or canvass work, on the contrary, is the usual designation of all kinds of embroidery on canvass, *done by counting threads,* and frequently by the aid of a painting on checked paper.

Although these two different sorts of work are really equally entitled to the designation of *embroidery,* yet for the sake of making our instructions as intelligible as possible, we will adopt the popular terms, and confine our present remarks to that sort of embroidery which is not executed by the stitch, supplying all that is so done at pp. 147-149, under the term of "canvas-work."

After the innumerable specimens of embroidery shown in every department of the Great Exhibition, from the collar worked by an Irish peasant for 3d., and exhibited for cheapness, to the magnificent bed of Messrs. Faudel and Phillips, the mere working of which cost many hundreds of pounds, we need not say that every sort of material may be used for embroidery. The most ordinary are muslin, cambric, velvet, satin cloth, and leather. The simplest style of embroidery is that termed *Application,*— that is, where the pattern is in one material, laid on another which forms the ground. In this way muslin is worked on net (as in the Swiss collar given at p. 422); velvet is laid on cloth, or on another velvet, and so on, the edges being either sewed over, or ornamented with fancy cord, braid, gold thread, or any other appropriate material.

Another very easy style of ornamentation is that known as braiding. Braids of many kinds are used. Children's dresses are worked with narrow silk or worsted braid, the latter being also used for ladies' aprons, flounces, &c. Gold and silver braid enter largely into various sorts of decorative needlework, and the Victoria braid, which has something of the appearance of satin stitch, is generally known. We ourselves imported from the Continent a new braid, for application, and other purposes, termed the Albert braid. We shall shortly give a design for a cap, in which this braid will be used.

Patterns for braiding are usually scrolls and arabesques; anything, in short, where the pattern is formed in continuous lines appropriate for this sort of work. There is considerable art required to achieve putting on braid evenly and firmly. The stitches should be taken across the braid, but not to either edge. This makes it lie flat. The usual way of braiding is to run the needle along the centre of the braid, taking several stitches at a time. The edges, when this is done, invariably rub up, and soon look shabby, besides that the braid looks sometimes wide, and sometimes narrow.

But the most elaborate kinds of embroidery are those which represent flowers, fruit, and other devices on any material; and these may be divided into white and coloured embroidery.

White embroidery, or embroidery on muslin, is used for a great variety of articles of ladies' dress. The collar, given in p. 404 of this volume, is a specimen. The simplest, and at present the most fashionable kind, is termed Broderie Anglaise, a design for which accompanies these instructions. In this style the pattern is formed of holes cut out of the muslin, and sewed over with embroidery cotton. The great art in working broderie, is to make the holes all of the same size, and to take the stitches closely and regularly.

Satin stitch is a smooth raised work, used for leaves, flowers, &c. It is done by first tracing the outlines accurately with soft cotton, then taking stitches from point to point of the part to be raised so as to have the greatest thickness of cotton in the centre, and sewing it over, in stitches taken close together, and completely across the part outlined. The veining of leaves is generally formed by taking the stitches from the vein to the edge, first on one side and then on the other. The borders of embroidered muslin collars, &c., are usually finished with button-hole stitch, worked either the

EMBROIDERED SLIPPER, BY MRS. PULLAN.

width of an ordinary button-hole, or in long stitches, and raised like satin stitch. Eyelet-holes are made by piercing round holes with a stiletto, and sewing them round.

There are many fancy stitches introduced into muslin work, but these require to be practically taught.

The kind of frame on which muslin is most easily worked, consists of two hoops of wood, about eight inches in diameter. One is rather smaller than the other. On it the muslin is stretched, and the larger one being slipped over it, and fitting tightly, keeps the muslin in its place. This is the mode used throughout the Irish and Scotch work counties.

Satin and velvet are embroidered in coloured silks, gold and silver bullion, pearls, &c. A very fashionable style is the work with *ombré* silks. This term is applied to silk or wool dyed in various shades of one colour. *Chiné* silk is silk dyed in shades of various colours. These shades are either long or short. For small patterns the short are almost universally used.

The most delicate kinds of embroidery are worked with fine netting silk, one

strand of which is drawn out. **This** makes the silk appear softer and richer.

It requires considerable care to work well with ombré silks, to avoid incorrect shading. Nature should be followed as closely as possible. Not only must the form be carefully preserved, but the lights and shades must be disposed in an artistic manner. For instance: the point of a leaf is never the darkest part, nor should the lower leaves and flowers of a group of the same kind be light.

We have elsewhere described pounced patterns, and the mode of preparing and using them. It may be useful to add, that where a design consists of a series of repetitions, a single pattern is prepared and moved for every fresh length. When a design has sections which resemble each other, as the quarters of a sofa cushion, or any similar thing, one section only is pounced, the paper being moved from quarter to quarter.

It is to be remembered that both sides of a pounced pattern may be equally used. Thus, for the Apron given in p. 425 the design for one-half only is marked on the paper.

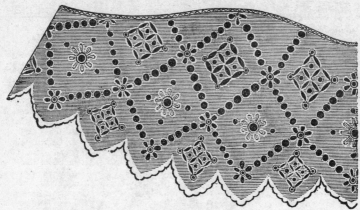

MANDARIN SLEEVE, IN BRODERIE ANGLAISE, BY MRS. PULLAN.

THE WORK-TABLE FRIEND.

EMBROIDERED SLIPPER.

Materials.—Black velvet; ombré olive silk, of the coarsest size; blue ditto, and gold thread, about the size of W. Evans & Co.'s Boar's Head sewing cotton. No. 4.

WE have selected this design as one of the simplest specimens of embroidery, from the few colours employed, and the easiness of the stitches. Our space does not permit us to give the full size of the pattern, and indeed this must necessarily vary with the dimensions of the slipper to be worked, but the design is to be increased so as completely to cover the front of the shoe, and the scroll must be reversed for the second. The heel is also worked with a scroll and flowers drawn to correspond with the front, but long and narrow. Pounced patterns suitable for either a lady's or a gentleman's slipper can be obtained; or the velvet may be worked at a warehouse.

The scroll is worked with the olive silk, in close chain stitch, care being taken to join on a new needleful at the same part of a shade as you left off the last one. This forms the greatest difficulty in working with ombré silks, as the sudden transition from light to dark, or vice versâ, has the worst possible effect.

The gold thread we have named in the list of materials, is useful for the diamonds seen within a part of the scroll. It is laid on the velvet, and sewn over with fine silk of the same colour; the ends being drawn through the velvet at the extremities of the lines.

The flowers are first worked in soft cotton, and then in ombré blue silk. The threads must be close together, and lying in the direction indicated in the engraving, for every part.

Silk in short shades should be chosen for this slipper, and we think that velvet with a silk face would be found sufficiently good for ordinary purposes, the other materials being of an inexpensive sort, and the work very rapidly done. It is, indeed, selected especially for our more juvenile friends, who may wish to make acceptable presents to papa or mamma without incurring too much expense, or losing too many play-hours.

TRUE ZEAL is a sweet, heavenly, and gentle flame, which maketh us active for God, but always within the sphere of love. —*Cudworth.*

MANDARIN SLEEVE, IN BRODERIE ANGLAISE.

Materials.—French Muslin, and W. Evans and Co.'s Embroidery Cottons, Nos. 40 and 50.

COMPELLED, by the size of our pages, either to present this pattern on a limited scale, or to show only a very small section of it, we have chosen the former method as being the one which gives the best idea of the design. Though our friends who are sufficiently good artists, may enlarge the pattern for themselves to the required dimensions, namely (for the *half* sleeve), 6 inches deep, by 9 wide. This is for the worked part only; the muslin sleeve must be cut sufficiently long to reach to the shoulder. Ladies who are not able, or inclined, to mark the patterns for themselves may have it done for them. The width we give is for the deepest part of the sleeve. The shape is that known as Mandarin, and is intended exclusively for in-door wear.

To work the sleeve, begin by tacking the end on a square of *toile ciré*, and working the edge in scalloped button-hole stitches; the surface must be raised by running tracing-threads close together, in the space to be afterwards covered with overcast. All those parts of the engraving which are perfectly black are to be cut out in the form indicated, and sewed over very closely and rather thickly. The small eyelet-holes are pierced with a stiletto, and sewed round; then a circle of thread is run outside this, and closely sewed.

The stars of eight points are worked in satin-stitch. Each point is a small leaf, with a vein up the centre nearly to the top. This is made by taking each stitch from the centre to the edge only, instead of completely across the leaf, as far as the vein is to extend.

The hem-stitch at the top of the work is very simple. First, with coarse embroidery cotton, run two parallel lines, about the eighth of an inch apart. Take the stiletto,—make two small holes close to the lower line, and one, between them, close to the upper. Sew over the threads between, in every direction; make another hole near the upper line, sew over between it and the last lower;—then one below, continued until the whole length is done.

THE WORK-TABLE FRIEND.

KNITTING INSTRUCTIONS.

BY MRS. PULLAN.

ALTHOUGH the art of knitting is known perhaps more generally than almost any other kind of fancy work, still, as the knowledge is not universal, and there have been of late years great improvements in many of the processes, we hope that a short account of all the stitches, and the elementary parts of the craft, will be welcomed by many of our friends; and most seriously would we recommend them to attain *perfection* in this branch of work, because, above all others, it is a resource to those who, from weak eyes, are precluded from many kinds of industrial amusement, or who, as invalids, cannot bear the fatigue of more elaborate work. The fact is, that knitting does not require eyesight at all; and a very little practice ought to enable any one to knit whilst reading, talking, or studying, quite as well as if the fingers were unemployed. It only requires that the fingers should be properly used, and that one should not be made to do the duty of another.

The implements used for knitting are rods or pins of ivory, bone, or steel. The latter are most commonly used, and should have tapered points, without the least *sharpness* at the extremity.

Fig. 1. *The first process in casting on.*—Hold the end of cotton between the first and second fingers of the left hand, bring it over the thumb and forefinger, and bend the latter to twist the cotton into a loop; bend the needle in the loop; hold the cotton attached to the reel between the third and little fingers of the right hand, and over the point of the fore finger; bring the thread round the needle, by the slightest possible motion; bend the needle towards you, and tighten the loop on the left-hand finger, in letting it slip off to form the *first* stitch.

Fig. 2. Now take that needle, with the loop on it, in the left hand, and another in the right. Observe the position of the hands. The left hand needle is held between the thumb and the second finger, leaving the forefinger free, to aid in mov-

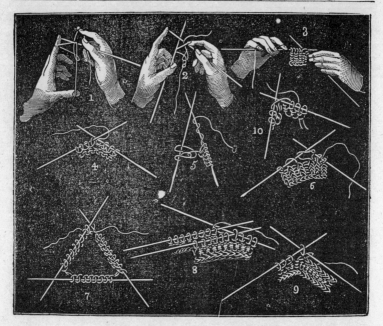

KNITTING INSTRUCTIONS, BY MRS. PULLAN.

ing the points of the needles. This mode of using the forefinger, instead of employing it merely to hold the needle, is the great secret of being able to knit without looking at the work, for so extremely delicate is the sense of touch in this finger, that it will, after a little practice, enable you to tell the sort of stitch coming next, in the finest material, so that knitting becomes merely mechanical. The engraving indicates the mode in which the right hand needle should be held. Insert the point in the loop, bringing it behind the other needle, slip the thread round it, bring the point in front, and transfer the loop to the left hand needle, without withdrawing it from the right hand. Repeat the process for any number of stitches required.

Fig. 3. *Plain knitting.*— Slip the point of the right hand needle in a loop, bring the thread round it, and, with the forefinger, push the point of the needle off the loop, so that the thread just twisted round forms a new one on the right hand.

Fig. 4. *Purling.*—The right hand needle is slipped in the loop *in front of* the left hand one, and the thread, after passing between the two, is brought round it; it is then worked as before. The thread is always brought forward before beginning a purled stitch, unless particular directions to the contrary are given.

Fig. 5. *The mode of making stitches.*—To make one, merely bring the thread in front before knitting, when, as it passes over the needle, it makes a loop; to make two, three, or more, pass the thread *round the needle in addition,* once for 2, twice for 3, and so on.

Fig. 6. *To decrease.*—Take one stitch off without knitting; knit one, then slip the point of the left hand needle in the unknitted stitch and draw it over the other. It is marked in receipts d. 1. To decrease 2 or more, slip 1, knit 2, 3, or more together, *as one*, and pass the slip-stitch over.

Fig. 7. *The way to join a round.*—Four or five needles are used in round work, such as socks, stockings, &c. Cast on any given number of stitches on one needle, then slip another needle in the last stitch, before casting any on it; repeat for any number. When all are cast on, knit the first 2 stitches off on to the end of the last needle. One needle is always left unused in casting on for a round.

Fig. 8. *The way of joining the toe of a sock, or any similar thing.*—Divide all the stitches on to two needles, hold both in the left hand, as if they were one, and in knitting take a loop off each one, which knit together.

Fig. 9. *To cast off.* — Knit 2 stitches; with the left hand needle draw the first over the second; knit another; repeat. Observe that the row before the casting-off should never be very tightly knitted.

Fig. 10. This shows the mode of knitting three stitches together, so that the centre one shall be in front. Slip 2 off the needle together, knit the third, and draw the others over together.

To raise a stitch, is to knit the bar of thread between the two stitches, as one.

The abbreviations used are: K, knit; P, purl; D, decrease (Fig. 6); K 2 t, knit two together; P 2 t, purl two together; M 1, make one.

Take care to have needles and cotton or wool that are suitable to each other in size. The work of the best knitter in the world would appear ill done if the needles were too fine or too coarse. In the former case, the work would be close and thick; in the latter it would be too much like a cobweb. The *numbers* we give for needles are according to the Eagle cardboard gauge.

BROAD KNITTED LACE.

Materials. W. Evans & Co.'s Boar's-head cotton, No. 50. Boulton's knitting-needles, No. 23. 2 needles.

Cast on 55 stitches, and do one plain row.

1st Pattern Row.—Slip 1, K 3, K 2 t, + M 1, K 1, M 1, D 1, K 5, K 2 t, + 4 times; M 1, K 1, M 1, D 1, K 4, M 2, K 2

2nd Row.—K 3, P 1, K 1, P to the end.

3rd Row.—Slip 1, K 2, K 2 t, + M 1, K 3, M 1, D 1, K 3, K 2 t, + 4 times, M 1, K 3, M 1, D 1, K 7.

4th Row.—Cast off 2, K 1, purl to the end.

5th Row.—Slip 1, K 1, K 2 t, + M 1, K 5, M 1, D 1, K 1, K 2 t, + twice; M 1, raise 1, M 1, D 1, K 1, K 2 t, M 1, raise 1, M 1, D 1, K 1, K 2 t, M 1, K 5, twice, M 1, K 2 t, K 1, M 2, K 2.

6th Row.—Like 2nd Row.

7th Row.—Slip 1, K 2 t, + M 1, K 7, M 1, D 2, + twice; M 1, K 3, M 1, D 2, M 1, K 3, M 1, D 2, M 1, K 7, M 1, D 2 M 1, K 7, M 1, K 6.

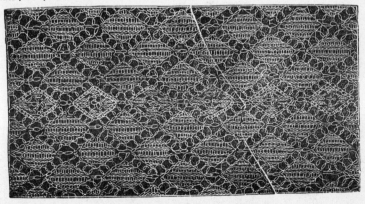

BROAD KNITTED LACE, BY MRS. PULLAN.

8th Row.—Like 4th Row.

9th Row.—Slip 1, K 1, + M 1, D 1, K 5, K 2 t, M 1, K 1, + twice; M 1, D 1, K 5, K 2 t, M 1, K 1, M 1, D 4, K 5, K 2 t, M 1, K 2, M 2, K 2.

10th Row.—Like 2nd Row.

11th Row.—Slip 1, K 2, + M 1, D 1, K 3, K 2 t, M 1, K 3, + twice; M 1, D 2, M 1, K 3 twice; M 1, D 1, K 3, K 2 t, M 1, K 3, M 1, D 1, K 3, K 2 t, M 1, K 7.

12th Row.—Like 4th Row.

13th Row.—Slip 1, K 3, + M 1, D 1, K 1, K 2 t, M 1, K 5, + twice; M 1, D 2, K 1, K 3 t, M 1, K 5, M 1, D 1, K 1, K 2 t, twice; M 1, K 4, M 2, K 2.

14th Row.—Like 2nd Row.

15th Row.—Slip 1, K 4, + M 1, D 2, M 1, K 7, + 4 times; M1, D 2, M 1, K to the end.

16th Row.—Like 4th Row.

When sufficient is done to go easily round the top of a dress, in the form of a bertha, take up all the stitches at the plain edge, and knit a few rows, quite plain, backwards and forwards, which will form a band to tack inside the dress.

ROUND MAT FOR A CANDLE LAMP.

This is all worked in Dc over White Linen Blind Cord of the usual size ; 1 oz. each of Shaded Green and Shaded Scarlet 4, thread wool; ½ an ounce of 8 thread Shaded Green; ditto five shades of Light Scarlet, five of Dark Scarlet, five of Yellow, five of Violet, five of Pink, one skein of each. Three skeins of White, one of very pale Lemon, all 4 Thread Berlin Wool. One Mesh ⅝ of an inch wide ; Nos. 1 and 2 Penelope Hooks.

Twelve yards of Blind Cord.

With the Shaded Scarlet work about nine or twelve stitches in Dc over the end of the Blind Cord ; form it round in as small a circle as possible; now work round this, increasing the first round by working two stitches into every loop ; work eight rounds with this colour, increasing as may be necessary, but always by working two stitches into a loop, and not by making a chain. These eight rounds will include the first circle. Now three rounds of Shaded Green, still increasing where required; then three rounds of Scarlet; then

three rounds of Green; then three rounds of Scarlet ; then three rounds of Green. This will complete the mat. Cut off the cord, and fasten the end in neatly, then with the same wool commence in a different place.

For the Border.

1st Row.—Dc into a loop, 5 chain, Dc into every fourth loop round the Mat. 87 chains of 5.

2nd Row.—With 8 thread wool. No. 1 Penelope Hook. Dc under the 5 chain, 3 chain, miss 1 chain of 5, 4 long with 3 chain between each, under next 5, 3 chain repeat.

3rd Row.—In the centre, 3 chain between the long stitches, work 5 long, then 3 chain, Dc under 3; 5 chain, Dc under 3; 3 chain, Dc under 3, 5 chain, Dc under 3; 3 chain, miss 1 chain of 5, repeat.

For the Dahlias.

Net on a piece of string, or Boar's Head Cotton No. 6, over the mesh, all the shades separately, only before taking off the mesh slip off four loops, and sew them at the point securely and neatly with fine silk precisely the same colour as the different shades. Cut some rounds of foundation muslin 1¾ inches in diameter. Sew the lightest shade (for instance, yellow) round the circle of muslin, drawing it rather tightly, to give roundness to the Dahlia ; then take the four remaining shades and sew round successively.

The white Dahlia must have pale Lemon only in the centre. By sewing the darkest shade outside, sometimes there will be more variety, and the wool can all be worked up. Twelve Dahlias will be sufficient for the mat, which must be sewed round the edge of the mat, leaving the border extending beyond the Dahlias.

(This is one of the prettiest Mats that can be made, and is really beautiful for a Fish Globe.)

A FRENCH wife wrote this affectionate and laconic letter to her husband : " Je vous écris parceque je n'ai rien à faire: Je finis, parceque je n'ai rien à dire." I write to you, because I have nothing to do : I end my letter, because I have nothing to say.

THE WORK-TABLE FRIEND.

BREAD CLOTH, PATTERN A LA REINE.

THREE reels of No. 16 Boar's Head cotton, or, if a larger size is required, use No. 12; No. 4 Penelope hook, or No. 3 for No. 12 cotton.

L, long stitch; Sq, squares; Dc, double crochet.

1st Row.—Make a chain of 261 stitches, turn back, work 1 long, 2 chain, 1 long into 3rd loop; there must be 87 Sq, or squares.

2nd and *3rd Rows.*—1 Long upon long, 2 chain, *repeat*; this row forms 3 rows of squares.

4th Row.—3 Sq, 6 L, 3 Sq, 24 L, 10 Sq, 6 L, 5 Sq, 12 L, 5 Sq, 9 L, 5 Sq, 12 L, 5 Sq, 6 L, 10 Sq, 24 L, 3 Sq, 6 L, 3 Sq.

5th Row.—3 Sq, 6 L, 1 Sq, 9 L, 2 Sq, 6 L, 3 Sq, 9 L, 7 Sq, 9 L, 3 Sq, 18 L, 2 Sq, 6 L, 3 Sq, 6 L, 2 Sq, 18 L, 3 Sq, 9 L, 7 Sq, 9 L, 3 Sq, 6 L, 2 Sq, 9 L, 1 Sq, 6 L, 3 Sq.

6th Row.—5 Sq, 6 L, 1 Sq, 6 L, 3 Sq, 3 L, 5 Sq, 6 L, 7 Sq, 3 L, 3 Sq, 6 L, 2 Sq, 12 L, 7 Sq, 12 L, 2 Sq, 6 L, 3 Sq, 3 L, 7 Sq, 6 L, 5 Sq, 3 L, 3 Sq, 6 L, 1 Sq, 6 L, 5 Sq.

7th Row.—5 Sq, 3 L, 3 Sq, 3 L, 4 Sq, 3 L, 6 Sq, 6 L, 4 Sq, 6 L, 3 Sq, 6 L, 3 Sq, 9 L, 2 Sq, 9 L, 2 Sq, 9 L, 3 Sq, 6 L, 3 Sq, 6 L, 4 Sq, 6 L, 6 Sq, 3 L, 4 Sq, 3 L, 3 Sq, 3 L, 5 Sq.

8th Row.—4 Sq, 3 L, 2 Sq, 6 L, 5 Sq, 6 L, 2 Sq, 3 L, 2 Sq, 3 L, 1 Sq, 15 L, 2 Sq, 3 L, 2 Sq, 6 L, 2 Sq, 6 L, 2 Sq, 15 L, 2 Sq, 6 L, 2 Sq, 6 L, 2 Sq, 3 L, 2 Sq, 15 L, 1 Sq, 3 L, 2 Sq, 3 L, 2 Sq, 6 L, 5 Sq, 6 L, 2 Sq, 3 L, 4 Sq.

9th Row.—4 Sq, 3 L, 10 Sq, 3 L, 3 Sq, 6 L, 3 Sq, 3 L, 4 Sq, 6 L, 6 Sq, 6 L, 2 Sq, 6 L, 1 Sq, 6 L, 2 Sq, 6 L, 6 Sq, 6 L, 4 Sq, 3 L, 3 Sq, 6 L, 3 Sq, 3 L, 10 Sq, 3 L, 4 Sq.

10th Row.—4 Sq, 3 L, 4 Sq, 9 L, 3 Sq, 6 L, 8 Sq, 3 L, 1 Sq, 9 L, 6 Sq, 6 L, 4 Sq, 9 L, 4 Sq, 6 L, 6 Sq, 9 L, 1 Sq, 3 L, 8 Sq, 6 L, 3 Sq, 9 L, 4 Sq, 3 L, 4 Sq.

11th Row.—4 Sq, 3 L, 3 Sq, 12 L, 3 Sq, 6 L, 4 Sq, 6 L, 1 Sq, 3 L, 1 Sq, 6 L, 5 Sq, 9 L, 3 Sq, 6 L, 5 Sq, 6 L, 3 Sq, 9 L, 5 Sq, 6 L, 1 Sq, 3 L, 1 Sq, 6 L, 4 Sq, 6 L, 3 Sq, 12 L, 3 Sq, 3 L, 4 Sq.

12th Row.—4 Sq, 6 L, 2 Sq, 9 L, 3 Sq, 12 L, 3 Sq, 6 L, 4 Sq, 18 L, 5 Sq, 9 L, 5 Sq, 9 L, 5 Sq, 18 L, 4 Sq, 6 L, 3 Sq, 12 L, 3 Sq, 9 L, 2 Sq, 6 L, 4 Sq.

13th Row.—5 Sq, 3 L, 2 Sq, 21 L, 2 Sq, 9 L, 2 Sq, 3 L, 3 Sq, 3 L, 2 Sq, 3 L, 7 Sq, 9 L, 2 Sq, 9 L, 2 Sq, 9 L, 7 Sq, 3 L, 2 Sq, 3 L, 3 Sq, 3 L, 2 Sq, 9 L, 2 Sq, 21 L, 2 Sq, 3 L, 5 Sq.

14th Row.—5 Sq, 3 L, 3 Sq, 15 L, 3 Sq, 3 L, 2 Sq, 6 L, 8 Sq, 9 L, 2 Sq, 12 L, 2 Sq, 6 L, 1 Sq, 6 L, 2 Sq, 12 L, 2 Sq, 9 L, 8 Sq, 6 L, 2 Sq, 3 L, 3 Sq, 15 L, 3 Sq, 3 L, 5 Sq.

15th Row.—6 Sq, 3 L, 10 Sq, 6 L, 4 Sq, 9 L, 2 Sq, 6 L, 4 Sq, 12 L, 3 Sq, 6 L, 1 Sq, 6 L, 3 Sq, 12 L, 4 Sq, 6 L, 2 Sq, 9 L, 4 Sq, 6 L, 10 Sq, 3 L, 6 Sq.

16th Row.—7 Sq, 3 L, 5 Sq, 6 L, 3 Sq, 3 L, 4 Sq, 12 L, 3 Sq, 6 L, 5 Sq, 39 L, 5 Sq, 6 L, 3 Sq, 12 L, 4 Sq, 3 L, 3 Sq, 6 L, 5 Sq, 3 L, 7 Sq.

17th Row.—8 Sq, 6 L, 2 Sq, 9 L, 3 Sq, 6 L, 4 Sq, 9 L, 3 Sq, 6 L, 1 Sq, 6 L, 17 Sq, 6 L, 1 Sq, 6 L, 3 Sq, 9 L, 4 Sq, 6 L, 3 Sq, 9 L, 2 Sq, 6 L, 8 Sq.

18th Row.—3 Sq, 6 L, 5 Sq, 12 L, 4 Sq, 9 L, 2 Sq, 12 L, 6 Sq, 6 L, 1 Sq, 6 L, 2 Sq, 6 L, 3 Sq, 6 L, 2 Sq, 6 L, 1 Sq, 6 L, 6 Sq, 12 L, 2 Sq, 9 L, 4 Sq, 12 L, 5 Sq, 6 L, 3 Sq.

19th Row.—3 Sq, 9 L, 5 Sq, 3 L, 4 Sq, 9 L, 1 Sq, 18 L, 10 Sq, 6 L, 1 Sq, 12 L, 1 Sq, 12 L, 1 Sq, 6 L, 10 Sq, 18 L, 1 Sq, 9 L, 4 Sq, 3 L, 5 Sq, 9 L, 3 Sq.

20th Row.—5 Sq, 9 L, 4 Sq, 3 L, 1 Sq, 3 L, 1 Sq, 6 L, 4 Sq, 9 L, 15 Sq, 6 L, 3 Sq, 6 L, 15 Sq, 9 L, 4 Sq, 6 L, 1 Sq, 3 L, 1 Sq, 3 L, 4 Sq, 9 L, 5 Sq.

21st Row.—5 Sq, 15 L, 2 Sq, 3 L, 61 Sq, 3 L, 2 Sq, 15 L, 5 Sq.

22nd Row.—5 Sq, 3 L, 2 Sq, 9 L, 2 Sq, 3 L, 1 Sq, 3 L, 55 Sq, 3 L, 1 Sq, 3 L, 2 Sq, 9 L, 2 Sq, 3 L, 5 Sq.

23rd Row.—4 Sq, 3 L, 4 Sq, 6 L, 2 Sq, 3 L, 1 Sq, 3 L, 55 Sq, 3 L, 1 Sq, 3 L, 2 Sq, 6 L, 4 Sq, 3 L, 4 Sq.

24th Row.—4 Sq, 3 L, 2 Sq, 12 L, 2 Sq, 3 L, 12 Sq, 6 L, 3 Sq, 6 L, 1 Sq, 6 L, 3 Sq, 9 L, 4 Sq, 6 L, 5 Sq, 9 L, 4 Sq, 3 L, 12 Sq, 3 L, 2 Sq, 12 L, 2 Sq, 3 L, 4 Sq.

25th Row.—4 Sq, 3 L, 2 Sq, 9 L, 3 Sq, 3 L, 1 Sq, 6 L, 8 Sq, 3 L, 1 Sq, 3 L, 2 Sq, 3 L, 1 Sq, 3 L, 2 Sq, 3 L, 2 Sq, 3 L, 2 Sq, 3 L, 5 Sq, 3 L, 4 Sq, 3 L, 1 Sq, 18 L, 10 Sq, 6 L, 1 Sq, 3 L, 3 Sq, 9 L, 2 Sq, 3 L, 4 Sq.

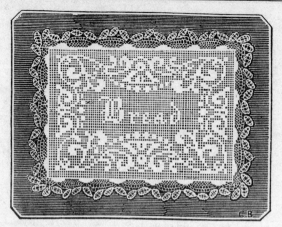

Bread Cloth, Pattern à la Reine. By Mrs. Warren.

26th Row.—4 Sq, 6 L, 6 Sq, 3 L, 2 Sq, 6 L, 7 Sq, 3 L, 2 Sq, 3 L, 4 Sq, 12 L, 4 Sq, 6 L, 5 Sq, 3 L, 3 Sq, 6 L, 4 Sq, 3 L, 1 Sq, 3 L, 10 Sq, 6 L, 2Sq, 3 L, 6 Sq, 6 L, 4 Sq.

27th Row.—5 Sq, 6 L, 3 Sq, 6 L, 12 Sq, 3 L, 2 Sq, 3 L, 4 Sq, 3 L, 1 Sq, 3 L, 4 Sq, 3 L, 1 Sq, 3 L, 2 Sq, 3 L, 1 Sq, 6 L, 3 Sq, 6 L, 3 Sq, 3 L, 1 Sq, 6 L, 15 Sq, 6 L, 3 Sq, 6 L, 5 Sq.

28th Row.—4 Sq, 18 L, 4 Sq, 6 L, 8 Sq, 3 L, 1 Sq, 3 L, 5 Sq, 6 L, 5 Sq, 6 L, 3 Sq, 6 L, 1 Sq, 6 L, 2 Sq, 6 L, 3 Sq, 3 L, 1 Sq, 6 L, 1 Sq, 3 L, 9 Sq, 6 L, 4 Sq, 18 L, 4 Sq.

29th Row.—3 Sq, 6 L, 2 Sq, 3 L, 5 Sq, 12 L, 7 Sq, 3 L, 26 Sq, 6 L, 1 Sq, 3 L, 1 Sq, 3 L, 1 Sq, 9 L, 9 Sq, 12 L, 5 Sq, 3 L, 2 Sq, 6 L, 3 Sq.

30th Row.—4 Sq, 18 L, 4 Sq, 6 L, 9 Sq, 3 L, 27 Sq, 3 L, 2 Sq, 3 L, 1 Sq, 6 L, 11 Sq, 6 L, 4 Sq, 18 L, 4 Sq.

31st Row.—5 Sq, 6 L, 3 Sq, 6 L, 14 Sq, 3 L, 25 Sq, 6 L, 2 Sq, 3 L, 1 Sq, 6 L, 15 Sq, 6 L, 3 Sq, 6 L, 5 Sq.

32nd Row.—4 Sq, 6 L, 6 Sq, 3 L, 2 Sq, 6 L, 10 Sq, 3 L, 24 Sq, 6 L, 2 Sq, 3 L, 1 Sq, 6 L, 10 Sq, 6 L, 2 Sq, 3 L, 6 Sq, 6 L, 4 Sq.

33rd Row.—4 Sq, 3 L, 2 Sq, 9 L, 3 Sq, 3 L, 1 Sq, 6 L, 10 Sq, 3 L, 24 Sq, 6 L, 2 Sq, 3 L, 1 Sq, 3 L, 11 Sq, 6 L, 1 Sq, 3 L, 3 Sq, 9 L, 2 Sq, 3 L, 4 Sq.

34th Row.—4 Sq, 3 L, 2 Sq, 12 L, 2 Sq, 3 L, 38 Sq, 12 L, 1 Sq, 3 L, 4 Sq, 3 L, 10 Sq, 3 L, 2 Sq, 12 L, 2 Sq, 3 L, 4 Sq.

35th Row.—4 Sq, 3 L, 4 Sq, 6 L, 2 Sq, 3 L, 1 Sq, 3 L, 37 Sq, 3 L, 4 Sq, 12 L, 9 Sq, 3 L, 1 Sq, 3 L, 2 Sq, 6 L, 4 Sq, 3 L, 4 Sq.

36th Row.—5 Sq, 3 L, 2 Sq, 9 L, 2 Sq, 3 L, 1 Sq, 3 L, 55 Sq, 3 L, 1 Sq, 3 L, 2 Sq, 9 L, 2 Sq, 3 L, 5 Sq.

37th Row.—5 Sq, 15 L, 2 Sq, 3 L, 61 Sq, 3 L, 2 Sq, 15 L, 5 Sq.

Now work as at 20th row; afterwards as 19th, 18th, 17th, &c. and so on to the 1st row.

Under the 2 chain, or into the spaces between each long stitch, work 3 Dc stitches all round, making 7 Dc at each corner.

For the Border.

1st Row.—Dc into 4th loop at corner, 5 chain, *repeat* in same loop twice more (*in all, 3 chains of* 5), 5 chain, Dc on 1st long, 5 chain, Dc on 2nd long, * 24 Dc (*these, with the last Dc, will form* 25, *and will extend over eight spaces*), 5 chain, Dc on a long stitch for 7 times (*this will extend over seven spaces*), *repeat* from *, making all corners alike.

Music Stool Couverette.   By Mrs. Warren.

2nd Row.—23 Dc, the 1st on 2nd Dc, 3 chain, Dc *under* 5 chain, 5 chain, Dc *under* 5 for 6 times, 3 chain *repeat.*

3rd Row—21 Dc, the 1st on 2nd Dc, 5 chain, Dc *under* every 5 chain, 5 chain *repeat.*

4th Row.—19 Dc, the first on 2nd Dc (*this must be on the* 21 *Dc previous to the corner*), 3 chain, Dc *under* 5, 5 chain, 1 long *under* 5 for 3 times, 5 chain, 1 long *under* the same last 5 again (*this is at extreme corner*), 5 chain, 1 long *under* 5 for twice, 5 chain. Dc *under* 5, 3 chain, * 19 Dc as before, 3 chain, Dc *under* 5, 5 chain, 1 long *under* 5 for 5 times, 5 chain, Dc *under* 5, 3 chain, *repeat* from *.

5th Row.—9 Dc, the 1st on 6th Dc, 7 chain, 1 long, with 5 chain between each, *under* every 3 and 5 chain, 7 chain. *repeat.*

Encrease at the corners in this **row** the same as the last.

The leaves are worked, and **attached** to the Border from left hand to right.

Begin on last long stitch of **corner** (*which will be immediately in front of the corner*). Make 18 chain, turn back, 1 long into 6th loop from hook, 3 chain, 1 long into 4th loop for twice, 3 chain, Dc *into* loop where commenced (*this forms the veins of the leaf*); 1 chain to cross, turn **it** round on the finger, always keeping it on the right side; Dc *under* the opposite 3 chain, * 5 chain, Dc on long stitch, *repeat* from * twice more, 7 chain, Dc on opposite long, 5 chain, Dc on long for twice, 5 chain, Dc into the 1 chain, 3 chain to cross, turn it round on the finger, Dc *under* opposite 5 chain, 5 long *under* same, 5

F

chain, Dc on Dc, crochet into next long stitch of Border. (*To do this, take out the hook from loop of leaf, insert it into loop of long stitch of Border, draw the loop from which the hook was withdrawn through the loop of long stitch, and continue.*) 4 Long *under* next chain of 5, crochet into next long of Border, 1 long *under* same 5, Dc on Dc, 5 long *under* next 5, Dc on Dc, 9 long *under* the 7 chain, Dc on Dc; work down the other side of leaf, without attaching it to Border (*the last Dc must be under the last 5 chain*). Draw the cotton to the back of the leaf, tie it securely and so that the ends of cotton are not seen on the right side; this must be done at the end of every leaf.

2nd Leaf.—Commence upon the next long of Border, and work the same, attaching it first upon next long of Border, secondly into centre loop of the 5 chain at extreme corner, and lastly after the last Dc stitch which is *under* the last 5 chain; crochet it into the centre loop of third compartment of former leaf.

3rd Leaf.—Commence on next long, attach it first upon next long, secondly upon next long, and lastly, as in former leaf.

4th Leaf.—Commence upon next long, attach it first upon next long, secondly upon 1st of the 9 Dc, thirdly at the 3rd long of the third compartment, into the centre loop of the 9 Dc, and lastly as in the former leaf: this is now round the corner.

5th Leaf.—* Commence on next long, attach first on next long, secondly on next long, and lastly after the last Dc stitch, under the last 5 chain; make another Dc into the centre of the 3 chain which crosses the bottom of the leaf; then Dc into the centre loop of the 9 long of former leaf.

6th Leaf.—Commence on next long, attach first on next long, secondly on next long, lastly into centre loop of 3rd compartment of former leaf.

7th Leaf.—Begin on next long, attach first on next long, secondly on 1st Dc stitch, thirdly after the 3rd long in the 3rd compartment of leaf, Dc into centre loop of the 9 Dc stitches, lastly into the 3rd compartment of former leaf: now *repeat* from *, working all corners as at beginning.

MUSIC STOOL COUVERETTE.

Seven Shades of Scarlet, 4 Thread Berlin Wool, 4 Skeins of each, 8 Skeins of bright Green, 3 Reels of No. 10 Drab Boars' Head Cotton, No. 2 and 3 Penelope Hooks.

1st Row.—With darkest Scarlet make 12 chain, unite and *into* every chain work 1 long with 2 chain between each; there must be 12 long. Cut off the ends, draw it to the back and tie neatly. (*This must be done at every row.*)

2nd Row.—Same shade. Dc *under* a 2 chain, 5 chain, 3 long *under* next 2 chain, 5 chain, *repeat*.

3rd Row.—Cotton, Dc *under* 5 chain, 7 chain, Dc *under* 5 chain, 5 chain, *repeat*, (*the 5 chain must come over the long stitches.*)

4th Row.—Next shade Scarlet. 5 double long with 1 chain between each *under* the 5 chain, 5 chain, Dc *under* 7 chain, 5 chain, *repeat*.

5th Row.—Next shade. Dc on Dc, *, 5 chain, 1 long *under* 5 chain, 2 long *under* every 1 chain, 1 long *under* 5 chain, 5 chain, Dc on Dc, *repeat* from * 5 times more.

6th Row.—Lightest shade but one. 1 long on every long with 1 chain between each, 5 chain, Dc on Dc, 5 chain, *repeat*.

7th Row.—With Green. Dc *under* the 1st 1 chain, *, 17 chain, turn back 1 long *into* 8th loop from the Hook, 5 chain, 1 long into 5th loop, 4 chain, Dc into the loop where commenced, 1 chain to cross, turn round on the finger, Dc *under* the opposite 4 chain of Green, 4 long *under* the same, Dc on long stitch, 5 long *under* the 5 chain, Dc on long stitch, 9 long *under* the chains at top, Dc on long stitch, 5 long *under* the 5 chain, Dc on long, 4 long *under* the 4 chain, Dc *under* the same, Dc through the one chain that crossed and through the loop where commenced, 4 Dc, that is, 1 Dc *under* every chain for 4 times, *repeat* from * again, then 4 Dc as before, then *repeat* again, then 7 chain, and *repeat* from beginning.

8th Row.—Cotton. Dc on 1st long of the 9 long at point of leaf, 5 chain, Dc into every alternate loop 4 times more, 3 chain, and *repeat* over the next leaf. (*There will be 4 chains of 5 over every leaf, with 3 chain between each leaf.*)

(Continued at Page 70.)

THE WORK-TABLE FRIEND.

D'OYLEY FOR A ROUND CRUET STAND, OR FOR A D'OYLEY.

If intended for a Cruet Stand, use No. 12, or if for a D'Oyley, No. 16 Evans's Boar's Head Cotton. No. 4 Penelope Hook.

1st Row.—Make 13 chain, unite, *, 9 chain, Dc *under* this circle, *repeat* from * 9 times more, in all 10 loops of 9 chains, regulate them, and fasten off; every round must be commenced afresh.

2nd Row.—5 long *under* the 9 chain, 1 chain, *repeat* 9 times more.

3rd Row.—3 Dc *under* the 1 chain, 7 chain, *repeat.*

4th Row.—5 Dc *under* the 7 chain, 7 chain, *repeat.*

5th Row.—6 Dc *under* the 7 chain, 7 chain, *repeat.*

6th Row.—The same, only making 7 Dc.

7th Row. 1st *Row of Leaves.*—Begin in centre loop of 7 chain. § 8 chain; make 7 Dc down this chain of 8, (*this is for centre of leaf.*) 1 chain to cross, Dc *into* opposite side of chain, 9 chain Dc *into* next loop, 9 chain Dc *into* next loop but one, 9 chain Dc *into* next loop but one, 9 chain Dc *into* next loop, 9 chain Dc *into* same loop ; there will now be 5 chains of 9; 11 chain Dc *into* loop at top of leaf, 9 chain Dc *into* next loop down the other side, 9 chain Dc *into* same, * 9 chain Dc *into* next loop but one, *repeat* from * again, 9 chain Dc *into* last loop, 5 chain, turn round on the finger, Dc *into* centre loop of 1st 9 chain, † 2 chain Dc *into* next, *repeat* from † twice more, 3 chain Dc *into* next, 4 chain Dc *into* 11 chain, 4 chain Dc *into* 9 chain, 3 chain Dc *into* 9, 2 chain Dc *into* 9 for 3 times, 5 chain Dc *into* the bottom of the leaf and through the 1st Dc stitch ; 5 chain Dc *into* centre loop of the 7 chain. (*In the* OUTSIDE *circle of leaves do this twice, then* 5 chain Dc *on* Dc), 5 chain Dc *into* centre loop of 7 chain, *repeat* from §.

8th Row.—Dc *under* 1st 2 chain in leaf, * 5 chain Dc *under* next, 5 chain Dc *under* 3 chain, 5 chain Dc *under* 4 chain, 7 chain Dc *under* 4 chain, 5 chain Dc *under* 3 chain, 5 chain Dc *under* 2 chain for 3 times, 3 chain Dc *under* 1st 2 chain of next leaf, 5 chain Dc *under* next 2 chain, *repeat* from *. (*When this row is finished pull out the leaves well at the points.*)

9th Row.—(*Great care must be taken to work this Row tight ; the edge must not be in the least full*).—7 Dc *under* the 7 chain at top of the leaf, Dc on Dc, 5 Dc *under* each of the 5 chain for 3 times, making a Dc on Dc between each 5 Dc, then Dc *into* the 2nd Dc stitch of next leaf, and work the same up the leaf; (*by doing this one 5 chain in each leaf is missed.*)

10th Row.—Dc *into* centre loop of the 7 Dc stitches at point of leaf, 5 chain, 1 long *into* centre loop of 5 Dc stitches, 5 chain, 1 double long *into* centre of next five, 5 chain, 1 double long *into* centre loop of the Dc stitch in the other leaf, 5 chain, 1 long *into* centre of next five, 5 chain, *repeat.*

11th Row.—*Under* the 5 chain, that is, between the two leaves, work 5 Dc, then 7 long *under* the other 5 chain, making a Dc stitch on every Dc and long stitch in previous row, *repeat.* This row must be worked tightly, and kept quite flat.

12th Row.—* Dc into the Dc stitch on the top of the leaf, and work as at 7th row, only at the end there will be an additional chain of 5, *repeat* from *.

The next leaf will come immediately above the point of the former one, on the Dc stitch ; there will be 20 leaves instead of 10.

13th Row.—Same as 8th.

14th Row.—Same as 9th, only omitting the Dc on Dc.

CHEESE CLOTH

3 reels of No. 10 Bones, Boar's Head cotton. No. 3, Penelope Hook.

MAKE 11 chain, unite the ends, and *under* the circle work 18 long with 1 chain between each.

2nd Row.—1 long into every loop, with 1 chain between each long.

3rd Row.—1 long on long, 2 chain, *repeat.*

4th Row.—1 long on long, 3 chain, *repeat ;* these 4 rows may be worked without cutting off the cotton, after which the cotton must be cut off and fastened at every row.

5th and 6th Rows.—Begin each row in a different place. 1 long on long, 4 chain, *repeat.* Continue working the same, but encreasing 1 chain between every long stitch

D'Oyley for a Cruet Stand, or for a D'Oyley.   By Mrs. Warren.

in every row, till there are 7 chain between every long: this will be at the 9th row.

10th Row.—There are now 36 spaces. Tie a piece of cotton into the loop of every 4th long stitch for the temporary purpose of marking each division. 12 leaves will be required to go round the circle, each leaf occupying 3 spaces. Commence in the 4th loop of the centre 7 chain between the two pieces of cotton, make 14 chain, turn back 1 long into 3rd loop from the bottom (*not from the Hook*), 11 chain, 1 long into same loop; now 13 chain, 1 long into same loop; 11 chain, 1 long into same loop, 11 chain, Dc into same loop: this makes the foundation of a leaf of 5 compartments; now make 1 chain to cross the stem; *under* the chains in the 1st compartment work 3 Dc 4 long, 4 double long (*the double long is made by twisting the cotton twice over the Hook instead of once*) 4 long; *under* the chain in next compartment work 4 long, 5 double long, 4 long; *under* the centre compartment work 5 long, 7 double long, 5 long; *under* the next compartment

4 long, 5 double long, 4 long; *under* the last work 4 long, 4 double long, 4 long, 3 Dc, Dc through the last chain of leaf, and into the centre loop of the 7 chain, where the leaf was commenced (*this can be done with one stitch*) draw the cotton to the back and tie it neatly and securely.

To form and join the Second Leaf.

Commence in the centre chain of 7 between the two ends of cotton. Make the 5 compartments exactly as in 1st leaf, make 1 chain to cross the stem; *under* the chains in 1st compartment work 3 Dc, 4 long, 2 double long. Crochet into the 2nd long stitch at right hand, draw out the end of cotton, then crochet into the 2nd double long of first leaf; do it in this manner (*after 2nd double long of 2nd leaf, withdraw the Hook from the loop, insert it in the loop of the long stitch of the round; then pull the cotton through, withdraw the Hook again, insert it into 2nd double long of 1st leaf, draw the cotton through this loop*), and continue working 2 more double long, 4 long, and

Cheese Cloth. By Mrs. Warren.

continue working the other compartments the same as in 1st leaf.

11th Row.—1 long on the 1st of the 7 double long at the point of the leaf, 7 chain, 1 long on last long, 7 chain, 1 long on the last long of the same compartment, 7 chain, 1 long on centre double long of·next compartment, 5 chain, 1 long on centre double long of compartment of next leaf, 7 chain, 1 long on 1st long of next compartment, 7 chain, *repeat.*

12th Row.—Begin on the 1st long stitch at point of leaf, 9 Dc the 1st on the 1st long, 6 chain, 1 long on long, 6 chain, 1 long on long, 5 chain, 1 long on long, 6 chain, 1 long on long, 6 chain, *repeat.*

13th Row.—7 Dc the 1st on 2nd Dc, 5 chain, 1 long upon long for 4 times, 5 chain, *repeat.*

14th Row.—The same as last row, only making 5 Dc instead of 7.

15th Row.—1 long, 2 chain, miss 2 loops, *repeat.* There should be 136 spaces, or squares.

16th and 17th Rows.—1 long on long, 3 chain, *repeat.*

18th, 19th, and 20th Rows.—1 long on long, 4 chain, *repeat.*

21st Row.—4 Dc *under* every 4 chain all round.

22nd Row.—*Commence on a long stitch, make 27 chain, turn back 1 long into 8th loop, 5 chain, 1 long into 6th loop, 5 chain, 1 long into 6th loop, 5 chain, Dc into 6th loop *(this makes the foundation of leaf).* make 1 chain to cross Dc into same loop as last Dc, now make 18 long into the 18 chain up the side of the leaf, now 2 long into 1 loop for 4 times; then Dc down the side of the leaf, Dc through the leaf, and into the 1 chain of stem, also Dc into the loop where the leaf was commenced, work 8 Dc along the 21st row; this will bring to a long stitch.

For the Flower.

Make 11 chain, turn back 5 Dc down the chain, make 1 to cross, 5 Dc up the chain *(this forms the calyx),* 7 chain, 1 long into centre of calyx, 7 chain, 1 long into same place, 7 chain, Dc into same place, Dc round the calyx, taking care to Dc through 1 chain of stem; Dc *under* 1st 7 chain, 7 long *under* same chain, Dc *under* same, re-*peat* the same *under* the other 2 chains of 7, Dc down the calyx and stem ; and into loop where commenced, then work 8 Dc along the 21st row, then *repeat* from *.

To join the Leaves and Flowers together.

At the 3rd long stitch of 1st flower Dc into the loop immediately above the 2nd long stitch in the foundation of the leaf; and at the 12th long stitch. In the 3rd and every alternate leaf Dc into 4th long stitch of flower.

23rd Row.—Dc into the point of a leaf, 11 chain, Dc into the point of the next flower, 11 chain, *repeat*.

24th Row.—A row of Dc all round, taking care not to work on the Dc stitches.

MUSIC STOOL COUVERETTE.
(Continued from Page 66.)

9th Row.— Cotton, No. 3 Hook. 5 chain, Dc into every 5 chain all round.

10th Row.—(*Work with cotton till further directed*). Under the 5 chain at point of leaf work 9 long with 1 chain between each, 5 chain, Dc *under* 2nd 5, 5 chain, miss 1 chain of 5, *repeat*.

11th Row.—15 long, beginning on the 1st 1 chain, 5 chain, Dc on Dc, 5 chain, *repeat*.

12th Row.—13 long, beginning on 2nd long, 6 chain, Dc on Dc, 6 chain, *repeat*.

13th Row.—11 long, beginning on 2nd long, 7 chain, Dc on Dc, 7 chain, *repeat*.

14th Row.—9 long, beginning on 2nd long, 7 chain, Dc into 5th loop, 7 chain, Dc into 4th loop from Dc stitch, 7 chain, *repeat*.

15th Row.—7 long, beginning on 2nd long, 7 chain, Dc into 4th loop, 7 chain, Dc into centre loop of 7, 7 chain, Dc into 5th loop from Dc stitch, 7 chain, *repeat*.

16th Row.—5 long, beginning on 2nd long, 7 chain, Dc into centre loop of every 7 chain, 7 chain, *repeat*.

17th Row.—3 long, beginning on 2nd long, and work as before.

18th Row.—Dc into centre loop of 7 chain, 7 chain, *repeat*.

Work 9 more rows the same as last, or if required larger, work more rows the same. Damp and press well.

For the Border.

1st Row.—5 chain, Dc into centre loop of every 7 chain.

2nd Row.—1 long on Dc stitch, 5 chain, *repeat*.

3rd and 4th Rows.—1 long on long, 5 chain, *repeat*.

5th Row.—7 long, the 1st on a long stitch, *, 5 Sq, (*these are formed by working 5 chain, 1 long on long, repeat,*) 6 long, re-*peat* from *.

6th Row.—19 long, arranged so that the 1st 7 of the 19 long shall come in the Sq, previous to the 7 long in last row, * 3 Sq, 18 long, *repeat* from *.

7th Row.—7 Long, the 1st on the 7th long, * 5 Sq, 6 long, *repeat* from *. (*This is the same as 5th row*).

8th Row.—Now work the 3 following rows the same as the last 3, beginning at the 6th Sq from the 7 long stitches in last row.

Now 3 rows more, the same as last 3.

1 Row of squares.

Green Wool *, 3 double long, 3 chain, 3 more, double long *under* a 5 chain, 5 chain, Dc on 2nd long, 5 chain, miss 1 chain of 5. *Repeat* from *.

Green. 3 double long, 3 chain, 3 more double long *under* the 3 chain, 5 chain, Dc *under* 5, and Dc *under* next 5, 5 chain, *repeat*.

Green. Dc *under* the 3 chain, 5 chain, Dc *under* 5 chain, 3 chain, Dc *under* next 5, 5 chain, *repeat*.

Darkest Scarlet. *Under* the 3 chain work 3 double long, 3 chain, 3 more double long *under* the same; 5 chain, Dc *under* the Dc stitch at the top of the long stitches, 5 chain, *repeat*.

Next shade. 3 double long, 3 chain, 3 more double long *under* the 3 chain, 5 chain, Dc *under* 5, Dc *under* next 5, 5 chain, *repeat*.

Work the 4 next shades the same as last row.

Lightest shade. 5 double long, with 5 chain between each long, *under* the 3 chain, 5 chain, Dc *under* 5, Dc *under* next 5, 7 chain, Dc *under* 3 chain, 7 chain, Dc *under* 5, Dc *under* next 5, 5 chain, *repeat*.

Cotton. *, 2 long with 5 chain between each *under* the 1st 5 chain between the double long, 5 chain, *repeat* from * 3 times more, but make 7 chain the last time, Dc *under* the Dc on the top of the 3 chain, 7 chain, *repeat* from beginning.

Cotton. 1 long *under* the 1st 5 chain, 5 chain, *repeat* the same *under* every 5 chain, 7 chain, Dc on Dc, 7 chain, *repeat*, Double and press the sides after damping.

THE WORK-TABLE FRIEND.

MAT FOR HYACINTH GLASS.

(*Designed by Mrs. Warren.*)

FOUR yards of ordinary White Blind Cord, or Skirt Cord same size. ⅛ an oz. of 4 Thread Shaded Scarlet Berlin Wool. 4 Shades of Scarlet, the lightest to be a military Scarlet, 2 Skeins of each. 2 Skeins of Maize, 1 of bright Lemon or Sulphur colour, 1 of white; 3 Shades of bright Green, 2 Skeins of each. No. 2 Penelope Hook.

WITH Shaded Scarlet work 14 Dc stitches over the end of the cord, double it in as small a circle as possible, then in the next row work 2 Dc stitches into every loop, taking care to cover the cord; work a sufficient number of rounds to fit the bottom of the glass; then one row additional; after that work a row, and gently draw the cord, so as to make the row stand up round the edge. Work 4 more rows, taking care not to encrease. With the same wool work on the top of the last row 5 chain, Dc *into* every 4th loop, taking care to leave 36 chains of 5, fasten off the wool neatly, and take the darkest shade of scarlet.

1st Row.—*Under* a 5 chain work 3 double long, 3 chain, 3 more double long (*all under the 5 chain*) 5 chain, Dc *under* 5, and Dc *under* next 5, 5 chain, *repeat*.

2nd Row.—Next shade. *Under* the 3 chain, work 3 double long, 3 chain, 3 more double long *under* the same, 3 chain, Dc *under* 5 chain, Dc *under* next 5, 3 chain, *repeat*.

3rd and 4th Rows.—With the 2 next shades work the same as last row.

For the Flowers.

White Wool. Make 7 chain, unite, and *under* this circle work 12 double long with 1 chain between each.

Maize. 1 double long *under* every 1 chain, with 1 chain between each.

Next row same colour. Work the same, only make single long instead of double.

Lemon. *Under* each 1 chain work thus: put the hook *under* the chain as for Dc, but instead of pulling it through two loops, pull it through the loop that is on the hook, still keep this last loop on the hook, and pull the wool through this again, *repeat* again *under* the 1 chain, thus making 2 stitches *under* every 1 chain; fasten off

very neatly, and pull the flower well. (*The edge of the Flower must be worked very loosely.*)

For Leaves.

With darkest green make 11 chain, turn back, work 10 Dc down, leave this shade on, and take the next shade, work Dc all round, taking care to work at the extreme point, 2 Dc into same loop, with 1 chain between each. Lightest Green, work the same. Then take the darkest, and make 15 chain, turn back, and work 10 Dc down, then work this leaf the same as the 1st leaf. The leaves and flowers are to be sewed on as in the Engraving, taking care to pull the border well up round the glass, or if it should have been worked loosely, some pieces of wire pulled from black ribbon wire, and sewed inside between the patterns of the Border, will obviate the defect.

TOILETTE CUSHION.

(*Designed by Mrs. Warren.*)

2 Reels of No. 20 Evans's Boar's Head Cotton; No. 4 Penelope Hook.

1st Row.—Make a chain of 159 stitches, turn back, work 1 long, 2 chain, 1 long into 3rd loop; this should form 53 Sq, or squares.

2nd Row.—1 Long on long, 2 chain, repeat. Cut off the Cotton at every row, and weave in the end.

3rd Row.—46 Sq, 3 L, 6 Sq.

4th Row.—36 Sq, 3 L, 9 Sq, 3 L, 6 Sq.

5th Row.—3 Sq, 12 L, 4 Sq, 3 L, 2 Sq, 9 L, 5 Sq, 9 L, 2 Sq, 3 L, 3 Sq, 9 L, 3 Sq, 3 L, 8 Sq. 6 L, 5 Sq.

6th Row.—2 Sq, 6 L, 1 Sq, 21 L, 1 Sq, 3 L, 2 Sq, 9 L, 2 Sq, 3 L, 2 Sq, 9 L, 3 Sq, 3 L, 2 Sq, 6 L, 2 Sq, 3 L, 5 Sq, 3 L, 2 Sq, 6 L, 5 Sq.

7th Row.—1 Sq. 6 L, 3 Sq, 15 L, 6 Sq, 3 L, 2 Sq, 3 L, 2 Sq, 3 L, 5 Sq, 6 L, 1 Sq, 3 L, 1 Sq, 9 L, 6 Sq, 6 L, 1 Sq, 6 L, 2 Sq, 3 L, 2 Sq.

8th Row.—1 Sq, 6 L, 4 Sq, 3 L, 8 Sq, 3 L, 3 Sq, 3 L, 1 Sq, 6 L, 5 Sq, 6 L, 1 Sq, 3 L, 9 Sq, 3 L, 1 Sq, 18 L, 3 Sq.

9th Row.—1 Sq, 3 L, 1 Sq, 21 L, 5 Sq, 6 L, 3 Sq, 3 L, 1 Sq, 6 L, 5 Sq, 6 L, 1 Sq, 3 L, 7 Sq, 6 L, 2 Sq, 3 L, 1 Sq, 6 L, 5 Sq.

Mat for Hyacinth Glass.   By Mrs. Warren.

10th Row.—2 Sq, 3 L, 1 Sq, 21 L, 4 Sq, 6 L, 3 Sq, 3 L, 1 Sq, 6 L, 1 Sq, 3 L, 3 Sq, 6 L. 1 Sq, 3 L, 1 Sq, 3 L, 5 Sq, 6 L, 2 Sq, 3 L, 1 Sq, 6 L, 5 Sq.

11th Row.—2 Sq, 6 L, 1 Sq, 3 L, 4 Sq, 6 L, 3 Sq, 6 L, 2 Sq, 6 L, 1 Sq, 9 L, 4 Sq, 6 L, 1 Sq, 6 L, 6 Sq, 6 L, 2 Sq, 3 L, 1 Sq, 6 L, 5 Sq.

12th Row.—3 Sq, 21 L, 1 Sq, 3 L, 3 Sq, 6 L, 3 Sq, 3 L, 1 Sq, 6 L, 5 Sq, 6 L, 1 Sq, 3 L, 7 Sq, 6 L, 1 Sq, 6 L, 1 Sq, 6 L, 1 Sq, 3 L, 3 Sq.

13th Row.—4 Sq, 24 L, 3 Sq, 6 L, 3 Sq, 3 L, 1 Sq, 6 L, 5 Sq, 6 L, 1 Sq, 3 L, 2 Sq, 3 L, 4 Sq, 6 L, 2 Sq, 3 L, 1 Sq, 9 L, 4 Sq.

14th Row.—2 Sq, 3 L, 7 Sq, 3 L, 4 Sq, 6 L, 2 Sq, 3 L, 2 Sq, 6 L, 5 Sq, 9 L, 4 Sq, 3 L, 3 Sq, 6 L, 1 Sq, 6 L, 1 Sq, 6 L, 5 Sq.

15th Row.—2 Sq, 6 L, 2 Sq, 6 L, 2 Sq, 3 L, 2 Sq, 3 L, 2 Sq, 6 L, 3 Sq, 6 L, 6 Sq, 3 L, 1 Sq, 9 L, 2 Sq, 3 L, 3 Sq, 6 L, 2 Sq, 3 L, 1 Sq, 6 L, 5 Sq.

16th Row.—2 Sq, 12 L, 1 Sq, 9 L, 4 Sq, 6 L, 1 Sq, 15 L, 6 Sq, 3 L, 3 Sq, 12 L, 5 Sq, 3 L, 2 Sq, 3 L, 1 Sq, 6 L, 1 Sq, 6 L, 2 Sq.

17th Row.—40 Sq, 12 L, 3 Sq, 15 L, 1 Sq.

18th Row.—39 Sq, 3 L, 2 Sq, 3 L, 8 Sq, 3 L, 1 Sq.

19th & 20th Rows.—2 Rows of Sq.

If the Cushion is required larger than this, work 4 rows of Sq more on each side.

3 Dc stitches *under* every 2 chain all round, with 7 Dc at each corner.

Dc into centre Dc stitch of the 7 at the corner (to work down the long side), ∗ 9 chain, Dc into same loop, 11 chain, Dc into same loop, 9 chain, Dc into same; make 1 chain to cross, turn round on the finger, 11 Dc *under* the 1st 9 chain, 13 Dc *under* the **11, 11 Dc *under* the 9; ∗ now 3**

Toilette Cushion. By Mrs. Warren.

Dc along last row; this will bring to 1st long stitch. Now *repeat* from * to * again; now 9 Dc along last row, this brings to 4th long (*after this reckon 4 long, exclusive of the one last worked upon*); † make another leaf, joining it after the 6th Dc, into the 6th Dc of former leaf, now 12 Dc worked tightly, now *repeat* from † (*there will now be 12 Dc between each leaf*). (*On one side of each corner, a leaf will come on the 5th long; on the other side it will be on the 4th.*)

On the short side there will be one space too little; to obviate this, about the centre of this side work 9 Dc instead of 12, working the leaf on the 3rd long instead of 4th; then continue working on the 4th long.

2nd Row.—In the centre loop at the point of each leaf work another leaf, then 5 chain, Dc on the loop where the two leaves are joined, 5 chain, *repeat*. Join the leaves together in the same manner and place as last row.

3rd Row.—Make one leaf in the centre loop of leaf at extreme corner; then 5 chain, Dc into 6th loop from this; now make another leaf, then 5 chain, Dc between the 2 leaves of last row, 5 chain, *repeat* as in last row, making both sides of each corner alike. At each corner there will be 3 leaves round the corner leaf of last row.

4th Row.—Same as 2nd row.

The back may be worked in as many rows of squares as there are rows in the front, then joined nicely round.

For the Cushion, cut two pieces of thin calico rather longer than the work, fill it not too hard with bran.

When washing is required, let it be made of good colour, then roll in linen very tightly for an hour; afterwards pull it out well, and lay between linen, under a weight.

"THIRTEEN TO DINNER."

THERE is a prejudice existing, generally, on the pretended danger of being the thirteenth at table. If the probability be required, that out of thirteen persons, of different persons, of different ages, one of them, at least, shall die within a year, it will be found that the chances are about one to one that one death, at least, will occur. This calculation, by means of a false interpretation, has given rise to the prejudice, no less ridiculous, that the danger will be avoided by inviting a greater number of guests, which can only have the effect of augmenting the probability of the event so much apprehended.

CROCHET ANTIMACASSAR.

Boar's head cotton, No. 8; steel crochet, No. 16.

Each row must be commenced at the same end.

Make a chain of 277 stitches.

1st Row. 1 treble, 5 chain, miss 5, 12 treble, 5 chain, miss 5, 1 treble, 5 chain, miss 5, 12 treble, 5 chain, miss 5, repeat—end with 1 treble.

To avoid repetition after every chain of 5, you must miss 5 of the preceding row.

2nd Row. 2 treble, *, 5 chain, 3 treble, 5 chain, 17 treble, 5 chain, 3 treble, 5 chain, 3 treble, repeat from * end with 2 treble.

3rd Row. 3 treble*, 5 chain, 3 treble, 5 chain, 15 treble, 5 chain, 3 treble, 5 chain, 5 treble, repeat from * end with 3 treble.

4th Row. 4 treble*, 5 chain, 3 treble, 5 chain, 13 treble, 5 chain, 3 treble, 5 chain, 7 treble, repeat from * end with 4 treble.

5th Row. 5 treble*, 5 chain, 3 treble, 5 chain, 11 treble, 5 chain, 3 treble, 5 chain, 9 treble, repeat from * end with 5 treble.

6th Row. 6 treble*, 5 chain, 3 treble, 5 chain, 9 treble, 5 chain, 3 treble, 5 chain, 11 treble, repeat from * end with 6 treble.

7th Row. 7 treble*, 5 chain, 3 treble, 5 chain, 7 treble, 5 chain, 3 treble, 5 chain, 13 treble, repeat from * end with 7 treble.

8th Row. 8 treble*, 5 chain, 3 treble, 5 chain, 5 treble, 5 chain, 3 treble, 5 chain, 15 treble, repeat from * end with 8 treble.

9th Row. 9 treble*, 5 chain, 3 treble, 5 chain, 3 treble, 5 chain, 3 treble, 5 chain, 17 treble, repeat from * end with 9 treble.

Commence again at 1st row, and continue until you have worked the required length. Then work a row of Double Crochet all round, and add a fringe.

THE WORK-TABLE FRIEND.

POINT DE BRUXELLES COLLAR, IN CROCHET.

No. 30, Boar's Head cotton. No. 4, Penelope Hook.

To make the Sprigs.—Make a chain of 29 stitches, *, turn back, work 1 long into 5th loop; 2 chain; 1 long into 3rd loop twice; 2 chain; Dc into 3rd loop; turn the work on the finger; 2 chain; (*this forms the foundation of the leaf*); work long stitches round this foundation, working 2 long into every chain round the point; (*the last stitch must be a Dc stitch*); 5 chain, Dc into every alternate loop round the leaf; 4 Dc down the stem of the leaf.

2nd Leaf.—15 chain, repeat from *; turn the work on the finger; 1 chain, Dc into the other edge of the stem.

3rd Leaf.—Make 15 chain, and repeat from * to * again.

Stem.—15 chain, turn back, work 8 Dc stitches, make 8 chain, Dc into the fifth chain of 5, in last leaf; 5 chain, Dc into the next 2nd chain of 5.

For Calyx.—7 chain, turn back, work 5 Dc †, turn the work on the finger, make 1 chain to cross, and work 5 Dc up.

1st Flower.—7 chain, Dc on top of calyx, 9 chain, Dc into same loop, 7 chain, Dc into same loop; Dc round the calyx; *under* the 7 chain work 11 long, Dc *under* same chain; Dc *under* 9 chain; 13 long *under* same; Dc *under* same; Dc *under* 7 chain; 11 long *under* same; Dc down the calyx †, to the point of the leaf. (*In the 2nd and 3rd flower, Dc down the stem to the point of the leaf.*

2nd Flower.—11 chain, turn back, work 5 Dc down, and repeat from † to †; 6 chain, Dc into 4th long stitch of the last leaf of the flower just made.

3rd Flower.—11 chain, turn back, work 5 Dc, then repeat from † to † again. (*In this flower, work down to the Dc stitch in the last leaf of the 2nd flower; then Dc into next 2nd 5 chain of leaf.*)

4th Flower.—9 chain; Dc into 4th long stitch of the last leaf of last flower; then Dc into the 3rd 5 chain of top leaf; 11 chain, turn back 5 Dc; then repeat from † to † again, (*omitting to work down the stem;*) Dc into 3rd 5 chain of leaf from last Dc stitch. This sprig is worked continuously, without cutting off the cotton.

Cut out in Brussels net of good quality, the shape of a collar that may be approved of; (12 sprigs will be required for a good shape;) sew these sprigs round the collar with very fine cotton, arranging them as in engraving. Be careful to sew round the serrated edges of the leaves, as well as the thick parts; then cut out the net at the back.—This collar, if worked nicely, will be difficult to distinguish from Brussels Point of great value: it may be washed and starched as any other collar.

THE WORK-TABLE FRIEND.

KNITTED BED QUILT, IN STRIPES.

To be knitted in stripes, and sewn together. Needles No. 12; Evans's Boar's Head Cotton No. 0.

The Broad Stripe.

Cast on 67 stitches.

1st Row.—K 3, Tf and K 2 + 5 times, K 1, P 2, K 4, P 2, K 2, Tf, K 2 +, K 1, K 2 +, K 9, K 2 +, K 1, K 2 +, Tf, K 2, P 2, K 4, P 2, K 1, K 2 +, Tf and K 2 + 4 times, Tf, K 3.

2nd Row.—K 3, Tf and K 2 + 5 times, P 1, K 2, P 4, K 2, P 2, Tr,* P 2 +, P 1, P 2 +, P 3, K 1, P 3, P 2 +, P 1, P 2 +, Tr, P 2, K 2, P 4, K 2, P 1, P 2 +, Tf and K 2 + 4 times, Tf, K 3.

3rd Row.—K 3, Tf and K 2 + 5 times, K 1, P 2, K 2, Tf, K 2, P 2, K 2, Tf, K 2 +, K 1, K 2 +, K 5, K 2 +, K 1, K 2 +, Tf, K 2, P 2, K 2, Tf, K 2, P 2, K 1, K 2 +, Tf and K 2 + 4 times, Tf, K 3.

4th Row.—K 3, K 2 +, Tf and K 2 + 4 times, P 1, K 2, P 2. Tr, P 1, Tr, P 2, K 2, P 2, Tr, P 2 +, P 1, P 2 +, P 1, K 1, P 1, P 2 +, P 1, P 2 +, Tr, P 2, K 2, P 2, Tr, P 1, Tr, P 2, K 2, P 1, P 2 +, Tf and K 2 + 4 times, K 3.

5th Row.—K 2, K 2 +, Tf and K 2 + 4 times, K 1, P 2, K 2, Tf, K 3, Tf, K 2, P 2, K 2, Tf, K 2 +, K 1, K 2 +, K 1, K 2 +, K 1, K 2 +, Tf, K 2, P 2, K 2, Tf, K 3, Tf, K 2, P 2, K 1, K 2 +, Tf, K 2 + 4 times, K 2.

6th Row.—K 3, Tf and K 2 + 4 times, P 1, K 2, P 2, Tr, P 5, Tr, P 2, K 2, P 2, Tr, P 2 +, K 1, P 2 +, P 2 +, Tr, P 2, K 2, P 2, Tr, P 5, Tr, P 2, K 2, P 1, P 2 +, Tf and K 2 + 3 times, Tf, K 3.

7th Row.—K 3, K 2 +, Tf and K 2 + 3 times, K 1, P 2, K 2, Tf, K 7, Tf, K 2, P 2, K 2, Tf, K 3 +, K 1, K 3 +, Tf, K 2, P 2, K 2, Tf, K 7, Tf, K 2, P 2, K 1, K 2 +, Tf and K 2 + 3 times, K 3.

8th Row.—K 4, Tf and K 2 + 3 times, P 1, K 2, P 2, Tf, K 9, Tf, P 2, K 2, P 1, P 2 +, Tr, P 3 +, Tr, P 2 +, P 1, K 2, P 2, Tr, P 9, Tr, P 2, K 2, P 1, P 2 +, Tf and K 2 + twice, Tf, K 4.

9th Row.—K 2, K 2 +, Tf and K 2 +

---

* *Tr* means *thread round*, so as to make a stitch, as the thread is already forward in purling.

---

3 times, K 1, P 2, K 2, Tf, K 1, Tf, K 9, Tf, K 1, Tf, K 2, P 2, K 2, K 2 +, K 2 +, K 1, P 2, K 2, Tf, K 1, Tf, K 9, Tf, K 1, Tf, K 2, P 2, K 1, K 2 +, Tf and K 2 + 3 times, K 2.

10th Row.—K 3, Tf and K 2 + 3 times, P 1, K 2, P 2, Tr, P 3, Tr, P 9, Tr, P 3, Tr, P 2, K 2, P 1, P 2 +, P 2, K 2, P 2, Tr, P 3, Tr, P 9, Tr, P 3, Tr, P 2, K 2, P 1, P 2 +, Tf and K 2 + twice, Tf, K 2.

11th Row.—K 3, K 2 +, Tf and K 2 + twice, K 1, P 2, K 2, Tf, K 2 +, K 3, Tf, K 2, K 2 +, K 1, K 2 +, K 2, Tf, K 3, K 2 +, Tf, K 2, P 2, K 4, K 2, P 2, Tf, K 2 +, K 3, Tf, K 2, K 2 +, K 1, K 2 +, K 2, Tf, K 3, K 2 +, Tf, K 2, P 2, K 1, K 2 +, Tf and K 2 + twice, K 3.

12th Row.—K 4, Tf and K 2 + twice, P 1, K 2, P 2, Tr, P 2 +, P 4, Tr, P 1, P 2 +, K 1, P 2 +, P 1, Tr, P 4, P 2 +, Tr, P 2, K 2, P 4, K 2, P 2, Tr, P 2 +, P 4, Tr, P 1, P 2 +, P 1, P 2 +, P 1, Tr, P 4, P 2 +, Tr, P 2, K 2, P 1, P 2 +, Tf, K 2 +, K 4.

13th Row.—K 2, K 2 +, Tf and K 2 + twice, K 1, P 2, K 2, Tf, K 1, Tf, K 2, K 2 +, K 9, K 2 +, K 2, Tf, K 1, Tf, K 2, P 2, K 4, P 2, K 2, Tf, K 1, Tf, K 2, K 2 +, K 9, K 2 +, K 2, Tf, K 1, Tf, K 2, P 2, K 1, K 2 +, Tf, K 2 +, Tf, K 2 +, Tf, K 2.

14th Row.—K 3, Tf and K 2 + twice, P 1, K 2, P 2, Tr, P 3, Tr, P 2, P 2 +, P 3, K 1, P 3, P 2 +, P 2, Tr, P 3, Tr, P 2, K 2, P 4, K 2, P 2, Tr, P 3, Tr, P 2, P 2 +, P 3, K 1, P 3, P 2 +, P 2, Tr, P 3, Tr, P 2, K 2, P 1, P 2 +, Tf, K 2 +, Tf, K 3.

15th Row.—K 3, Tf and K 2 + twice, K 1, P 2,* K 2, Tf, K 5, Tf, K 2, K 2 +, K 5, K 2 +, K 2, Tf, K 5, Tf, K 2, P 2,* K 2, P 4, *repeat* from * to * ; then K 1, K 2 +, Tf, K 2 +, Tf, K 3.

16th Row.—K 3, Tf and K 2 + twice, P 1, K 2,* P 2, Tr, P 2 +, P 5, Tr, P 2, P 2 +, P 1, K 1, P 1, P 2 +, P 2, Tr, P 5, P 2 +, Tr, P 2, K 2,* P 4, K 2, *repeat* from * to * ; then P 1, P 2 +, Tf, K 2 +, Tf, K 3.

17th Row.—K 3, Tf and K 2 + twice, K 1, P 2,* K 2, Tf, K 2 +, K 6, Tf, K 2, K 2 +, K 1, K 2 +, K 2, Tf, K 6, K 2 +, Tf, K 2, P 2,* K 4, P 2, *repeat* from * to * ; then K 1, K 2 +, Tf, K 2 +, Tf, K 3.

18th Row.—K 3, Tf and K 2 + twice,

P 1, K 2,* P 2, Tr, P 1, Tr, P 2, P 2 +,
P 5, P 2 +, K 1, P 2 +, P 5, P 2 +, P
2, Tr, P 1, Tr, P 2, K 2,* P 4, K 2, *repeat*
from * to *; then P 1, P 2 +, Tf, K 2 +,
Tf, K 3.

19th Row.—K 3, Tf and K 2 + twice,
K 1, P 2,* K 2, Tf, K 3, Tf, K 2, K 2 +,
K 3, K 2 +, K 1, K 2 +, K 3, K 2 +,
K 2, Tf, K 3, Tf, K 2, P 2,* K 4, P 2,
repeat from * to *; then K 1, K 2 +, Tf,
K 2 +, Tf, K 3.

20th Row.—K 3, Tf and K 2 + twice,
P 1, K 2,* P 2, Tr, P 5, Tr, P 2, P 2 +,
P 3, K 1, P 3, P 2 +, P 2, Tr, P 5, Tr,
P 2, K 2,* P 4, K 2, *repeat* from * to *;
then P 1, P 2 +, Tf, K 2 +, Tf, K 3.

21st Row.—K 3, Tf and K 2 + twice,
K 1, P 2,* K 2, Tf, K 2 +, K 5, Tf, K 2,
K 2 +, K 5, K 2 +, K 2, Tf, K 5, K 2
+, Tf, K 2, P 2,* K 4, P 2, *repeat* from *
to *; then K 1, K 2 +, Tf, K 2 +, Tf,
K 3.

22nd Row.—K 3, Tf and K 2 + twice,
P 1 K 2,* P 2, Tr, P 2 +, P 6, Tr, P 2,
P 2 +, P 3, P 2 +, P 2, Tr, P 6, P 2 +,
Tr, P 2, K 2,* P 4, K 2, *repeat* from * to *;
then P 1, P 2 +, Tf, K 2 +, Tf, K 3.

23rd Row.—K 3, Tf, K 1, Tf, K 2 +,
Tf, K 2, P 2,* K 2, Tf, K 2 +, K 9, K 2
+, K 1, K 2 +, K 9, K 2 +, Tf, K 2, P
2,* K 4, P 2, *repeat* from * to *; K 2, Tf,
K 2 +, Tf, K 1, Tf, K 3.

24th Row.—K 4, Tf and K 2 + twice,
Tr, P 2, K 2,* P 2, Tr, P 2 +, P 1, P 2
+, P 7, K 1, P 7, P 2 +, P 1, P 2 +,
Tr, P 2, K 2,* P 4, K 2, *repeat* from * to *;
P 2, Tf, K 2 + twice, Tf, K 4.

25th Row.—K 3, Tf and K 2 + 3 times,
Tf, K 2,* P 2, K 2, Tf, K 2 +, K 1, K 2
+, K 4, K 2 +, K 1, K 2 +, K 4, K 2
+, K 1, K 2 +, Tf, K 2,* P 2, K 4, *re-*
peat from * to *; then P 2, K 2, Tf and K
2 + 3 times, Tf, K 3.

26th Row.—K 4, Tf and K 2 + 3 times,
Tr, P 2, K 2,* P 2, Tr, P 2 +, P 1, P 2
+, P 2, P 2 +, K 1, P 2 +, P 2, P 2 +,
P 1, P 2 +, Tr, P 2, K 2,* P 4, K 2, *re-*
peat from * to *; P 2, Tf, K 2 + 3 times,
Tf, K 4.

27th Row.—K 3, Tf and K 2 + 4 times,
Tf, K 2, P 2,* K 2, Tf, K 2 +, K 11, K
2 +, Tf, K 2, P 2,* K 2, Tf, K 2, P 2,*
repeat from * to *; then K 2, Tf and K 2
+ 4 times, Tf, K 3.

28th Row.—K 4, Tf and K 2 + 4 times,
*Tf, P 2, K 2, P 2, Tr, P 2 +, P 1, P 2

+, P 2, K 1, P 2, P 2 +, P 1, P 2 +,
Tr, P 2, K 2, P 2,* Tr, P 1, *repeat* from *
to *; then Tf and K 2 + 5 times, K 2.

29th Row.—K 2, K 2 +, Tf and K 2 +
4 times,* Tf, K 2, P 2, K 2, Tf, K 2 +,
K 1, K 2 +, K 3, K 2 +, K 1, K 2 +,
Tf, K 2, P 2, K 2,* Tf, K 3, *repeat* from *
to *, Tf and K 2 + 5 times, K 3.

30th Row.—K 3, K 2 +, Tf and K 2 +
4 times,* Tr, P 2, K 2, P 2, Tr, P 2 +,
P 1, P 2 +, K 1, P 2 +, P 1, P 2 +, Tr,
P 2, K 2, P 2,* Tr, P 5, *repeat* from * to *;
Tf and K 2 + 5 times, K 2.

31st Row.—K 2, K 2 +, Tf and K 2 +
4 times,* Tf, K 2, P 2, K 2, Tf, K 2 +,
K 2 +, K 1, K 2 +, K 2 +, Tf, K 2, P
2, K 2,* Tf, P 7, *repeat* from * to *; Tf
and K 2 + 5 times, K 3.

32nd Row.—K 2, K 3 +, Tf and K 2 +
4 times,* Tr, P 2, K 2, P 2, Tr, P 3 +,
K 1, P 3 +, Tr, P 2, K 2, P 2,* Tr, P 9,
repeat from * to *; Tf and K 2 + 5 times,
K 2.

33rd Row.—K 2, K 2 +, Tf and K 2 +
4 times,* Tf, K 2, P 2, K 2, Tf, K 3 +,
K 2 +, Tf, K 2, P 2, K 2,* Tf, K 1, Tf,
K 9, Tf, K 1, *repeat* from * to *; then Tf
and K 2 + 5 times, K 2.

34th Row.—K 2, K 2 +, Tf and K 2 +
4 times, Tr, P 2, K 2, P 2, P 2 +, P 2 +,
P 2, K 2, P 2, Tr, P 3, Tr, P 9, Tr, P 3,
Tr, P 2, K 2, P 2,* Tr, P 2, K 2, P 2, K
2, P 2, Tf and P 2 + 5 times, K 2.

35th Row.—K 2, K 2 +, Tf and K 2 +
4 times,* Tf, K 2, P 2, K 1, K 2 +, K 2
+, K 1, P 2, K 2,* Tf, K 2 +, K 3, Tf,
K 2, K 2 +, K 1, K 2 +, K 2, Tf, K 3,
K 2 +, *repeat* from * to *; then Tf and K
2 + 5 times, K 2.

36th Row.—K 2, K 2 +, Tf and K 2 +
4 times, Tf, P 2, K 2, P 4, K 2, P 2, Tr,
P 2 +, P 4, Tr, P 1, P 2 +, K 1, P 2 +,
P 1, Tr, P 4, P 2 +, Tr, P 2, K 2, P 4,
K 2, P 2, Tf and K 2 + 5 times, K 2.

37th Row.—K 2, K 2 +, Tf and K 2 +
4 times, Tf, K 2, P 2, K 4, P 2, K 2, Tf,
K 1, Tf, K 2, K 2 +, K 9, K 2 +, K 2,
Tf, K 1, Tf, K 2, P 2, K 4, P 2, K 2, Tf
and K 2 + 5 times, K 2.

38th Row.—K 2, K 2 +, Tf and K 2 +
4 times, Tr, P 2, K 2, P 4, K 2, P 2, Tr,
P 3, Tr, P 2, P 2 +, P 3, K 1, P 3, P 2
+, P 2, Tr, P 3, Tr, P 2, K 2, P 4, K 2,
P 2, Tf and K 2 + 5 times, K 2.

39th Row.—K 2, K 2 +, Tf and K 2 +
4 times, Tf, K 2, P 2, K 4, P 2, K 2, Tf,

Knitted Bed Quilt, in Stripes.　By Mrs. Warren.

K 5, Tf, K 2, K 2 +, K 5, K 2 +, K 2, Tf, K 5, Tf, K 2, P 2, K 4, P 2, K 2, Tf and K 2 + 5 times, K 2.

40th Row.—K 2, K 2 +, Tf and K 2 + 4 times, Tf, P 2, K 2, P 4, K 2, P 2, Tr, P 2 +, P 5, Tr, P 2, P 2 +, P 1, K 1, P 1, P 2 +, P 2, Tr, P 5, P 2 +, Tr, P 2, K 2, P 4, K 2, P 2, Tf and K 2 + 5 times, K 2.

41st Row.—K 2, K 2 +, Tf and K 2 + 4 times, Tf, K 2, P 2, K 4, P 2, K 2, Tf, K 2 +, K 6, K 2, K 2 +, K 1, K 2 +, K 2, Tf, K 6, K 2 +, Tf, K 2, P 2, K 4, P 2, K 2, Tf and K 2 + 5 times, K 2.

42nd Row.—K 2, K 2 +, Tf and K 2 + 4 times, Tr, P 2, K 2, P 4, K 2, P 2, Tr, P 1, Tr, P 2, P 2 +, P 5, P 2 +, K 1, P 2 +, P 5, P 2 +, P 2, Tr, P 1, Tr, P 2, K 2, P 4, K 2, P 2, Tf and K 2 + 5 times, K 2.

43rd Row.—K 2, K 2 +, Tf and K 2 + 4 times, Tf, K 2, P 2, K 4, P 2, K 2, Tf, K 3, Tf, K 2, K 2 +, K 3, K 2 +, K 1, K 2 +, K 3, K 2 +, K 2, Tf, K 3, Tf, K 2, P 2, K 4, P 2, K 2, Tf and K 2 + 5 times, K 2.

44th Row.—K 2, K 2 +, Tf and K 2 + 4 times, Tr, P 2, K 2, P 4, K 2, P 2, Tr, P 5, Tr, P 2, P 2 +, P 3, K 1, P 3, P 2 +, P 2, Tr, P 5, Tr, P 2, K 2, P 4, K 2, P 2, Tf and K 2 + 5 times, K 2.

45th Row.—K 2, K 2 +, Tf and K 2 + 4 times, Tf, K 2, P 2, K 4, P 2, K 2, Tf, K 2 +, K 5, Tf, K 2, K 2 +, K 5, K 2 +, K 2, Tf, K 5, K 2 +, Tf, K 2, P 2, K 4, P 2, K 2, Tf and K 2 + 5 times, K 2.

46th Row.—K 2, K 2 +, Tf and K 2 + 4 times, Tr, P 2, K 2, P 4, K 2, P 2, Tr, P 2 +, P 6, Tr, P 2, P 2 +, P 3, P 2 +, P 2, Tr, P 6, P 2 +, Tr, P 2, K 2, P 4, K 2, P 2, Tf and K 2 + 5 times, K 2.

47th Row.—K 2, K 2 +, Tf and K 2 + 4 times, Tf, K 2, P 2, K 4, P 2, K 2, Tf, K 2 +, K 9, K 2 +, K 1, K 2 +, K 9, K 2 +, Tf, K 2, P 2, K 4, P 2, K 2, Tf and K 2 + 5 times, K 2.

48th Row.—K 2, K 2 +, Tf and K 2 + 4 times, Tr, P 2, K 2, P 4, K 2, P 2, Tr, P 2 +, P 1, P 2 +, P 7, K 1, P 7, P 2 +, P 1, P 2 +, Tr, P 2, K 2, P 4, K 2, P 2, Tf and K 2 + 5 times, K 2.

49th Row.—K 2, K 2 +, Tf and K 2 +
4 times, Tf, K 2, P 2, K 4, P 2, K 2, Tf,
K 2 +, K 1, K 2 +, K 4, K 2 +, K 1,
K 2 +, K 4, K 2 +, K 1, K 2 +, Tf, K
2, P 2, K 4, P 2, K 2, Tf and K 2 + 5
times, K 2.

50th Row.—K 2, K 2 +, Tf and K 2 +
4 times, Tr, P 2, K 2, P 4, K 2, P 2, Tr,
P 2 +, P 7, K 1, P 7, P 2 +, Tr, P 2,
K 2, P 4, K 2, P 2, Tf and K 2 + 5
times, K 2.

Begin again at the 1st row.

The Narrow Stripe.

Cast on 49 stitches.

1st Row.—K 3, Tf and K 2 + 3 times;*
take the 4th stitch on your left-hand needle,
as if you were going to knit it, draw the
cotton through it without slipping it, then
through the 3rd, then through the 2nd,
then the 1st, then slip them all off; K 4
plain, repeat from * 3 times, Tf and K 2
+ 3 times, K 2.

2nd Row.—Pearled.

3rd Row.—Same as 1st, only K 4 plain
before drawing the cotton through the 4th,
and omit the 4 plain at the end.

4th Row.—Pearled.

Begin again at the 1st row.

DOYLEY.

Evans's Boar's Head Cotton No. 16.   No. 4
Penelope Hook.

1st Round.—13 chain, unite, * 9 chain,
Dc under the circle, repeat from * 7 times
more, in all, 8 loops of chains; regulate
them, and fasten off. (Each round must be
commenced afresh.)

2nd Round.—5 L under the 9 chain,
1 chain, repeat 7 times more.

3rd Round.—Dc under a 1 chain, 9
chain, Dc under same, 5 chain, repeat.

4th and last Round.—Dc under the centre
of the 9 chain, make 52 chain, turn back,
1 L into 8th loop from hook, * 2 chain, 1
L into 3rd loop, repeat from * 14 times
more; then 2 chain, Dc under the 9 chain

where commenced (*this forms vein of leaf*), 1 chain, turn round on the finger, Dc *under* the opposite 2 chain of the 52; 5 chain, Dc on every L stitch of vein till the last L at the top, there make 5 chain, Dc into centre loop of the 7 chain at top, 7 chain, Dc into same loop, 5 chain, Dc on every L stitch till the end; then make 5 chain, Dc into the 1 chain, 1 chain, turn round on the finger; Dc *under* the 1st 5 chain, 3 L *under* every 5 chain, but under the 7 chain at the top work 11 L; after the last 3 L at the termination of leaf, Dc *under* the 5 chain, and Dc *under* the 9 chain where commenced, make 1 chain, turn round on the finger, Dc on the 1st Dc stitch previous to the L stitches (*a*); then work 15 more Dc on 15 of the L stitches, then 15 L on the L. Then work 18 DbL (or Double Long) on the L stitches till the 11 at the point, † then work 2 DbL into every loop of the 11 L, then 18 more DbL, 15 L and 16 Dc down the side of the leaf, Dc through the 1 chain, and *under* the 9 chain where commenced with the same stitch; 7 chain, Dc *under* next 9 chain; now *repeat* at beginning of 4th round until the letter (*a*). Then make 9 Dc instead of 15, unite into 9th loop of outside round of 1st leaf, make 13 chain, Dc into 12th loop of 1st leaf from where the two leaves were united, turn back, Dc into each of the 1st 2 loops of the 13 chain, 2 L, 1 DbL, 2 L, 1 Dc successively in the loops; then make 14 chain, Dc into 6th loop of 1st broad leaf; then in the 14 chain work 2 Dc, 2 L, 2 DbL, 2 L, 1 Dc successively; now 16 chain, Dc into next 6th loop of 1st broad leaf; work the same as last, only making 3 DbL instead of 2. Now 18 chain, unite into 6th loop of broad leaf; work the same, only making 4DbL instead of 3; now make 22 chain, unite into 6th loop of broad leaf; work the same, only making 5 DbL instead of 4; 13 chain, unite into 5th loop from point of small leaf last made, 2 Dc, 2 L, 2 DbL, 1 L, 1 Dc successively in the loops, 10 chain, unite into 9th loop from hook, 1 chain, turn round on the finger, Dc *under* this circle, and *under* the same, work 19 L stitches, after which Dc *under* the circle, and Dc into last Dc stitch of last leaf; make 10 chain, turn back, 2 Dc, 2 L, 2 DbL, 2 Dc, Dc into loop at termination of last leaf, Dc down the stem to termination of next leaf on the opposite

side; make 8 chain, unite into point of last leaf, make 5 more chain, turn back, work 2 Dc, 2 L, 5 DbL, 2 L, 1 Dc, Dc into loop where the 8 chain commenced; Dc down the stem to the termination of next leaf, 12 chain, turn back, 2 Dc, 2 L, 4 DbL, 2 L, 1 Dc, Dc into loop where commenced, Dc down the stem to the loop where next leaf was commenced; 10 chain, turn back, 2 Dc, 2 L, 2 DbL, 2 L, 1 Dc, Dc into loop where 10 chain commenced, Dc down the stem to the loop where next leaf was commenced, 9 chain, turn back, 2 Dc, 2 L, 1 DbL, 2 L, 1 Dc, Dc into loop where 9 chain commenced, Dc down the stem to next leaf, 7 chain, turn back, 2 Dc, 3 L, 1 Dc, Dc into loop where 7 chain commenced; Dc down the stem to the part where the two broad leaves were joined; now work 6 Dc more on 6 of the L stitches of the 2nd broad leaf, then 6 L stitches, and unite into point of 1st small leaf; now 6 more L stitches, and unite into point of 2nd small leaf; now 3 L and 3 DbL, and unite into point of next small leaf; now 6 more DbL, and unite into point of next leaf; 6 more DbL, and unite into point of next leaf (which is the last); now work DbL till the 11 L of last round, then repeat from †.

TO WORK FROM A SMALL ENGRAVED SQUARE CROCHET PATTERN.

As crochet patterns (of antimacassars, &c.) are frequently given, on a scale which renders them difficult to work, we should advise a piece of *point* paper, as it is technically called, in which the squares are of a large size, to be procured, and the design to be copied on it, *dotting* the pattern down, which will be found much clearer than filling the squares with the pen.

Point paper may be procured having 6 to 12 squares to the inch. 8 squares to the inch give a very large and clear scale.·

NEAPOLITAN-PATTERN TIDY.

THIS Tidy may be worked in Drab cotton centre, and wool border, or in plain White; if the latter, 8 reels of Boar's Head cotton, No. 10; if the former, 4 reels of Drab cotton, No. 6, 7 shades of Emerald Green, 4 thread Berlin wool, 6 skeins of each, 1 shade of bright military scarlet, 12 skeins. Nos. 2 and 3 Penelope Hooks.

WITH No. 3 hook make a chain of 273 stitches, turn back, work 1 long, 2 chain

1 long into 3rd loop, repeat. There must be 91 Sq or squares.

In the next row work 1 long upon long, 2 chain, repeat.

There must be three rows of squares.

4th Row.—37 Sq, 4 L, 53 Sq.

5th Row.—36 Sq, 12 L, 51 Sq.

6th Row.—35 Sq, 6 L, 1 Sq, 9 L, 9 Sq, 15 L, 6 Sq, 18 L, 24 Sq.

7th Row.—35 Sq, 6 L, 1 Sq, 9 L, 9 Sq, 18 L, 3 Sq, 15 L, 1 Sq, 12 L, 22 Sq.

8th Row.—34 Sq, 9 L, 1 Sq, 3 L, 1 Sq, 6 L, 8 Sq, 3 L, 2 Sq, 3 L, 1 Sq, 3 L, 3 Sq, 6 L, 1 Sq, 3 L, 1 Sq, 6 L, 1 Sq, 9 L, 21 Sq.

9th Row.—22 Sq, 9 L, 2 Sq, 9 L, 4 Sq, 3 L, 3 Sq, 3 L, 1 Sq, 6 L, 8 Sq, 9 L, 2 Sq, 6 L, 1 Sq, 6 L, 1 Sq, 6 L, 5 Sq, 9 L, 20 Sq.

10th Row.—21 Sq, 15 L, 1 Sq, 12 L, 3 Sq, 9 L, 2 Sq, 9 L, 2 Sq, 12 L, 2 Sq, 12 L, 1 Sq, 6 L, 1 Sq, 3 L, 4 Sq, 6 L, 1 Sq, 9 L, 22 Sq.

11th Row.—21 Sq, 15 L, 1 Sq, 12 L, 3 Sq, 12 L, 1 Sq, 3 L, 1 Sq, 3 L, 1 Sq, 15 L, 2 Sq, 6 L, 4 Sq, 3 L, 1 Sq, 3 L, 2 Sq, 3 L, 1 Sq, 15 L, 23 Sq.

12th Row.—21 Sq, 6 L, 4 Sq, 15 L, 2 Sq, 6 L, 5 Sq, 3 L, 1 Sq, 6 L, 1 Sq, 6 L, 3 Sq, 12 L, 1 Sq, 3 L, 1 Sq, 3 L, 1 Sq, 9 L, 1 Sq, 9 L, 24 Sq.

13th Row.—22 Sq, 3 L, 1 Sq, 9 L, 2 Sq, 9 L, 3 Sq, 12 L, 1 Sq, 6 L, 1 Sq, 3 L, 1 Sq, 6 L, 4 Sq, 6 L, 3 Sq, 27 L, 26 Sq.

14th Row.—19 Sq, 9 L, 1 Sq, 18 L, 1 Sq, 9 L, 2 Sq, 6 L, 3 Sq, 3 L, 2 Sq, 3 L, 1 Sq, 6 L, 2 Sq, 6 L, 1 Sq, 18 L, 33 Sq.

15th Row.—18 Sq, 12 L, 1 Sq, 21 L, 1 Sq, 6 L, 3 Sq, 12 L, 1 Sq, 6 L, 5 Sq, 12 L, 3 Sq, 21 L, 29 Sq.

16th Row.—18 Sq, 12 L, 1 Sq, 21 L, 1 Sq, 6 L, 8 Sq, 12 L, 2 Sq, 15 L, 3 Sq, 3 L, 1 Sq, 3 L, 15 L, 27 Sq.

17th Row.—19 Sq, 9 L, 1 Sq, 24 L, 1 Sq, 3 L, 4 Sq, 9 L, 1 Sq, 15 L, 1 Sq, 15 L, 3 Sq, 3 L, 1 Sq, 6 L, 4 Sq, 6 L, 26 Sq.

18th Row.—24 Sq, 21 L, 1 Sq, 3 L, 3 Sq, 30 L, 1 Sq, 15 L, 1 Sq, 12 L, 1 Sq, 3 L, 2 Sq, 12 L, 4 Sq, 6 L, 20 Sq.

19th Row.—20 Sq, 12 L, 1 Sq, 24 L, 3 Sq, 3 L, 4 Sq, 18 L, 1 Sq, 9 L, 1 Sq, 18 L, 1 Sq, 3 L, 3 Sq, 9 L, 2 Sq, 6 L, 21 Sq.

20th Row.—19 Sq, 18 L, 2 Sq, 15 L, 2 Sq, 3 L, 7 Sq, 15 L, 1 Sq, 9 L, 1 Sq, 18 L, 1 Sq, 3 L, 1 Sq, 3 L, 3 Sq, 3 L, 2 Sq, 6 L, 21 Sq.

21st Row.—20 Sq, 21 L, 3 Sq, 15 L, 8 Sq, 12 L, 1 Sq, 6 L, 1 Sq, 21 L, 1 Sq, 9 L, 1 Sq, 9 L, 2 Sq, 6 L, 21 Sq.

22nd Row.—22 Sq, 27 L, 3 Sq, 9 L, 1 Sq, 12 L, 2 Sq, 9 L, 1 Sq, 6 L, 1 Sq, 18 L, 3 Sq, 15 L, 4 Sq, 6 L, 20 Sq.

23rd Row.—33 Sq, 3 L, 3 Sq, 21 L, 2 Sq, 6 L, 1 Sq, 3 L, 1 Sq, 18 L, 14 Sq, 15 L, 15 Sq.

24th Row.—37 Sq, 27 L, 5 Sq, 15 L, 1 Sq, 3 L, 1 Sq, 3 L, 9 Sq, 9 L, 19 Sq.

25th Row.—38 Sq, 21 L, 2 Sq, 9 L, 1 Sq, 9 L, 2 Sq, 3 L, 1 Sq, 6 L, 7 Sq, 6 L, 1 Sq, 3 L, 20 Sq.

26th Row.—31 Sq, 6 L, 4 Sq, 27 L, 1 Sq, 3 L, 1 Sq, 3 L, 4 Sq, 12 L, 2 Sq, 9 L, 3 Sq, 6 L, 2 Sq, 3 L, 3 Sq, 3 L, 16 Sq.

27th Row.—30 Sq, 12 L, 4 Sq, 27 L, 1 Sq, 6 L, 1 Sq, 21 L, 5 Sq, 12 L, 6 Sq, 9 L, 15 Sq.

28th Row.—20 Sq, 21 L, 2 Sq, 18 L, 4 Sq, 15 L, 6 Sq, 3 L, 2 Sq, 36 L, 1 Sq, 3 L, 5 Sq, 9 L, 16 Sq.

29th Row.—18 Sq, 30 L, 1 Sq, 21 L, 8 Sq, 15 L, 1 Sq, 9 L, 1 Sq, 12 L, 2 Sq, 3 L, 2 Sq, 3 L, 7 Sq, 9 L, 17 Sq.

30th Row.—17 Sq, 60 L, 5 Sq, 21 L, 1 Sq, 12 L, 1 Sq, 6 L, 2 Sq, 3 L, 2 Sq, 3 L, 5 Sq, 15 L, 18 Sq.

31st Row.—16 Sq, 30 L, 1 Sq, 3 L, 1 Sq, 9 L, 1 Sq, 15 L, 4 Sq, 18 L, 1 Sq, 18 L, 3 Sq, 3 L, 3 Sq, 3 L, 2 Sq, 18 L, 20 Sq.

32nd Row.—16 Sq, 24 L, 2 Sq, 6 L, 1 Sq, 9 L, 1 Sq, 15 L, 3 Sq, 21 L, 1 Sq, 18 L, 3 Sq, 3 L, 2 Sq, 3 L, 1 Sq, 15 L, 23 Sq.

33rd Row.—15 Sq, 21 L, 2 Sq, 9 L, 1 Sq, 12 L, 1 Sq, 18 L, 2 Sq, 21 L, 1 Sq, 18 L, 1 Sq, 15 L, 1 Sq, 15 L, 24 Sq.

34th Row.—15 Sq, 3 L, 6 Sq, 12 L, 2 Sq, 15 L, 1 Sq, 39 L, 2 Sq, 18 L, 1 Sq, 18 L, 1 Sq, 3 L, 1 Sq, 6 L, 24 Sq.

35th Row.—16 Sq, 24 L, 4 Sq, 15 L, 1 Sq, 15 L, 2 Sq, 12 L, 5 Sq, 15 L, 1 Sq, 18 L, 2 Sq, 6 L, 25 Sq.

36th Row.—29 Sq, 15 L, 1 Sq, 12 L, 7 Sq, 9 L, 2 Sq, 15 L, 1 Sq, 15 L, 1 Sq, 9 L, 25 Sq.

37th Row.—30 Sq, 15 L, 1 Sq, 9 L, 6 Sq, 18 L, 6 Sq, 15 L, 1 Sq, 9 L, 2 Sq, 12 L, 19 Sq.

38th Row.—26 Sq, 9 L, 3 Sq, 12 L, 1 Sq, 9 L, 5 Sq, 24 L, 1 Sq, 24 L, 1 Sq, 6 L, 2 Sq, 6 L, 1 Sq, 9 L, 18 Sq.

39th Row.—24 Sq, 6 L, 3 Sq, 9 L, 3 Sq,

6 L, 2 Sq, 6 L, 4 Sq, 27 L, 1 Sq, 21 L, 1 Sq, 6 L, 1 Sq, 9 L, 3 Sq, 3 L, 18 Sq.

40th Row.—23 Sq, 3 L, 5 Sq, 18 L, 5 Sq, 6 L, 4 Sq, 24 L, 1 Sq, 18 L, 1 Sq, 6 L, 2 Sq, 3 L, 1 Sq, 3 L, 1 Sq, 9 L, 18 Sq.

41st Row.—23 Sq, 3 L, 6 Sq, 30 L, 1 Sq, 3 L, 3 Sq, 45 L, 6 Sq, 3 L, 4 Sq, 6 L, 18 Sq.

42nd Row.—24 Sq, 3 L, 2 Sq, 9 L, 2 Sq, 30 L, 2 Sq, 6 L, 1 Sq, 21 L, 3 Sq, 3 L, 3 Sq, 12 L, 1 Sq, 6 L, 1 Sq, 12 L, 18 Sq.

43rd Row.—22 Sq, 6 L, 1 Sq, 21 L, 9 Sq, 12 L, 4 Sq, 12 L, 2 Sq, 6 L, 1 Sq, 24 L, 4 Sq, 6 L, 19 Sq.

44th Row.—21 Sq, 6 L, 1 Sq, 21 L, 4 Sq, 27 L, 8 Sq, 3 L, 1 Sq, 3 L, 2 Sq, 3 L, 1 Sq, 24 L, 1 Sq, 12 L, 19 Sq.

45th Row.—20 Sq, 6 L, 1 Sq, 18 L, 2 Sq, 18 L, 5 Sq, 3 L, 4 Sq, 18 L, 1 Sq, 3 L, 2 Sq, 3 L, 1 Sq, 24 L, 1 Sq, 6 L, 21 Sq.

46th Row.—20 Sq, 6 L, 1 Sq, 12 L, 2 Sq, 18 L, 2 Sq, 21 L, 2 Sq, 21 L, 2 Sq, 6 L, 2 Sq, 27 L, 23 Sq.

47th Row.—19 Sq, 9 L, 1 Sq, 9 L, 1 Sq, 18 L, 4 Sq, 15 L, 1 Sq, 3 L, 2 Sq, 24 L, 4 Sq, 3 L, 1 Sq, 24 L, 1 Sq, 9 L, 19 Sq.

48th Row.—19 Sq, 6 L, 1 Sq, 9 L, 1 Sq, 18 L, 3 Sq, 3 L, 3 Sq, 9 L, 1 Sq, 3 L, 2 Sq, 21 L, 1 Sq, 15 L, 2 Sq, 21 L, 1 Sq, 12 L, 18 Sq.

49th Row.—18 Sq, 6 L, 1 Sq, 9 L, 1 Sq, 18 L, 1 Sq, 3 L, 2 Sq, 21 L, 2 Sq, 3 L, 2 Sq, 18 L, 1 Sq, 9 L, 1 Sq, 9 L, 3 Sq, 12 L, 5 Sq, 6 L, 17 Sq.

50th Row.—18 Sq, 3 L, 1 Sq, 30 L, 2 Sq, 6 L, 3 Sq, 12 L, 1 Sq, 6 L, 3 Sq, 9 L, 3 Sq, 9 L, 1 Sq, 15 L, 15 Sq, 3 L, 1 Sq, 15 L, 17 Sq.

51st Row.—18 Sq, 3 L, 1 Sq, 30 L, 3 Sq, 24 L, 1 Sq, 6 L, 2 Sq, 3 L, 5 Sq, 12 L, 1 Sq, 18 L, 3 Sq, 6 L, 2 Sq, 6 L, 1 Sq, 6 L, 16 Sq.

52nd Row.—19 Sq, 30 L, 6 Sq, 15 L, 1 Sq, 6 L, 3 Sq, 9 L, 2 Sq, 15 L, 1 Sq, 18 L, 3 Sq, 6 L, 1 Sq, 3 L, 2 Sq, 9 L, 16 Sq.

53rd Row.—20 Sq, 27 L, 1 Sq, 3 L, 7 Sq, 6 L, 1 Sq, 6 L, 3 Sq, 9 L, 2 Sq, 15 L, 1 Sq, 21 L, 3 Sq, 3 L, 1 Sq, 3 L, 1 Sq, 3 L, 2 Sq, 3 L, 16 Sq.

54th Row.—20 Sq, 24 L, 2 Sq, 27 L, 1 Sq, 6 L, 4 Sq, 6 L, 1 Sq, 3 L, 1 Sq, 15 L, 2 Sq, 18 L, 3 Sq, 9 L, 1 Sq, 12 L, 16 Sq.

55th Row.—20 Sq, 3 L, 3 Sq, 9 L, 1 Sq, 3 L, 2 Sq, 21 L, 1 Sq, 12 L, 3 Sq, 6 L, 1 Sq, 3 L, 1 Sq, 15 L, 2 Sq, 18 L, 5 Sq, 15 L, 17 Sq.

56th Row.—23 Sq, 3 L, 4 Sq, 27 L, 1 Sq, 9 L, 1 Sq, 3 L, 3 Sq, 3 L, 1 Sq, 6 L, 1 Sq, 12 L, 5 Sq, 9 L, 28 Sq.

57th Row.—22 Sq, 3 L, 5 Sq, 24 L, 1 Sq, 12 L, 1 Sq, 3 L, 3 Sq, 3 L, 1 Sq, 9 L, 1 Sq, 6 L, 9 Sq, 9 L, 25 Sq.

58th Row.—22 Sq, 3 L, 4 Sq, 21 L, 2 Sq, 12 L, 1 Sq, 6 L, 3 Sq, 3 L, 1 Sq, 9 L, 2 Sq, 3 L, 8 Sq, 9 L, 26 Sq,

59th Row.—22 Sq, 6 L, 3 Sq, 15 L, 2 Sq, 15 L, 2 Sq, 3 L, 5 Sq, 9 L, 11 Sq, 6 L, 1 Sq, 15 L, 22 Sq.

60th Row.—23 Sq, 9 L, 1 Sq, 9 L, 2 Sq, 18 L, 2 Sq, 6 L, 5 Sq, 6 L, 1 Sq, 3 L, 10 Sq, 6 L, 2 Sq, 15 L, 21 Sq.

61st Row.—26 Sq, 30 L, 3 Sq, 6 L, 6 Sq, 6 L, 1 Sq, 12 L, 7 Sq, 3 L, 3 Sq, 18 L, 20 Sq.

62nd Row.—27 Sq, 21 L, 4 Sq, 6 L, 7 Sq, 3 L, 3 Sq, 15 L, 10 Sq, 15 L, 20 Sq.

63rd Row.—26 Sq, 3 L, 9 Sq, 9 L, 8 Sq, 3 L, 1 Sq, 6 L, 2 Sq, 15 L, 33 Sq.

64th Row.—26 Sq, 3 L, 4 Sq, 18 L, 11 Sq, 15 L, 4 Sq, 18 L, 28 Sq.

65th Row.—27 Sq, 27 L, 13 Sq, 39 L, 29 Sq.

66th Row.—29 Sq, 15 L, 16 Sq, 33 L, 30 Sq.

67th Row.—52 Sq, 15 L, 34 Sq.

68th, 69th, and *70th,* all rows of Squares. Work 3 Dc stitches under every 2 chain at the two sides, and under every long stitch on the other two sides, working 7 Dc stitches at each corner.

If wool is used for border, it should commence now. With No. 2 hook work thus, lightest Green :—

1st Row.—Into the 4th Dc stitch at corner make 5 long, 3 chain, 5 long into same loop, 5 chain, 2 long successively ; the 1st on 1st long, * 1 chain, miss 1 loop, 2 long successively, 5 chain, miss 3 loops, 2 long successively, repeat from *.

(This row must not be repeated, but work instead, as at A.)

2nd Row.—Scarlet. 5 long under the 3 chain at corner, 3 chain, 5 long under same, 7 chain, * 1 long on 1st long ; then 1 long on last long, 6 chain, repeat from *

3rd Row.—Scarlet. 5 long under the 3 chain at the corner, (5 chain,) 5 long under same 3 chain, Dc under both 5 and 7

G

Neapolitan-pattern Tidy. By Mrs. Warren.

chain, (catching up both at once), 3 chain, * 1 long on long, 3 chain, 1 long on next long, **3** chain, Dc under both chains, 3 chain, repeat from *.

A. Now instead of 1st row, work thus, with next Green:—5 long under the **5** chain at corner, 3 chain, 5 more long under same, 5 chain, 1 long on last of the 5 long, 3 chain, 1 long on Dc stitch. 5 chain, * 1 long on long, 3 chain, 1 long on next long, 5 chain, repeat from *. (Make both sides of the corner alike.) Now continue working 2nd, 3rd, and A rows till there are 7 patterns, or 21 rows, using the Green in shades for the A row only.

Edge—which must be of cotton, whether the border be of wool or otherwise.

1*st Row.*—5 long, with 5 chain between each long stitch, under the 5 chain at the corner, **3** chain, Dc under 3 chain, * 5 chain, Do under 3 chain, between the 2

long, 3 chain, 5 long, with 5 chain between each long, under the next 3 chain, between the long stitches, 3 chain, Dc under the **3** chain, between the 2 long, repeat from *.

2*nd Row.*—* **7** long under the 1st 5 chain at corner, Dc on 1st long, repeat from * 3 times more, omit the Dc the last time, 3 chain, Dc under 5, 3 chain, miss a chain of 3, repeat.

3*rd Row.*—Dc on Dc, between the shells, 3 chain, Dc on 4th long, * 7 chain, Dc on next 4th long after the Dc stitch in last row, repeat from * twice more, **3** chain, repeat.

BE KIND.—Hard words are like hail-stones in summer, beating down and de-stroying what they would nourish were they melted into drops.

ROSE-PATTERN ANTIMACASSAR.

Materials.—8 reels of the deep pink Boar's-head crochet cotton of Messrs. W. Evans and Co. of Derby; 6 oz. of rich purple beads, No. 2.

THE design is worked alternately in close and open stripes. In the former, the pattern is produced by beads.

Make a chain of the required length with the cotton on which the beads are threaded, and work on it one row of sc.

1st Pattern Row.—+ 14 b, 6 c, 1 b, + repeat throughout the length, in this and all following rows.

2nd.—+ 14 b, 5 c, 2 b, +.

3rd.—+ 12 c, 2 b, 5 c, 2 b, +.

4th.—+ 10 b, 2 c, 2 b, 2 c, 5 b, +.

5th.—+ 10 b, 2 c, 2 b, 1 c, 6 b, +.

6th.—+ 8 b, 2 b, 2 c, 2 b, 1 c, 2 b, 2 c, 2 b, +.

7th.—The same.

8th.—+ 5 c, 16 b, +.

9th.—+ 4 c, 17 b, +.

10th.—+ 4 c, 2 b, 2 c, 2 b, 2 c, 2 b, 1 c, 2 b, 4 c, +.

11th.—The same.

12th.—+ 2 c, 8 b, 2 c, 2 b, 1 c, 2 b, 4 c, +.

13th.—+ 1 c, 8 b, 3 c, 2 b, 1 c 2 b, 4 c, +.

14th.—+ 1 c, 2 b, 1 c, 2 b, 6 c, 2 b, 1 c, 2 b, 4 c, +.

15th.—+ 1 c, 2 b, 1 c, 10 b, 1 c, 2 b, 4 c, +.

16th.—The same.

17th.—+ 1 c, 2 b, 12 c, 2 b, 4 c.

18th.—+ 1 c, 16 b, 4 c, +.

19th.—The same.

20th.—Sc.

Now with a reel on which there are no beads, and working on the right side, do the open stripe from the engraving, in open square crochet. Repeat the two stripes alternately, terminating with the one in beads. Do a row of open square crochet at each edge, and knot in a handsome fringe.

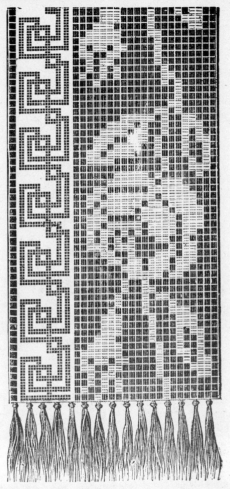

ROSE-PATTERN ANTIMACASSAR.

Other colours may be used, instead of those we have designated; but the purple beads, which are exceedingly rich and new will be found particularly beautiful.

PENDENT PINCUSHION.

PENDENT PINCUSHION, IN APPLICATION.

Materials.—A piece of dark-blue cloth, on which a bright scarlet is appliqué, according to the form seen in the engraving. Also black Albert braid, gold braid, gold thread, cord and tassels.

THIS toilet-cushion is in a style which is new, even on the Continent, and has never yet been introduced into this country. It is intended to be suspended against the wall, by the side of the toilet-glass; and being so extremely convenient, we doubt not it will be very generally patronised by our readers.

It is very easily made:—A piece of cloth about 4 inches by 7, and on which cloth or velvet of another colour is applied, is procured. The edges of the pattern are finished with gold braid, which is seen in the engraving, represented by a white line. The black lines indicate Albert braid, edged on one side with gold thread.

To make up the cushion, take a thin piece of wood, rather smaller than the cloth, and lay on one side a bag, filled with bran, of the same size. Tack this down, with a piece of calico at the other side of the back. Stretch the embroidered cloth over the stuffed side, and a piece of silk of the same colour over the other. Turn in the edges, sew them together, and finish with a cord all round. Add the tassels and cord by which it is to be suspended.

We recommend that great care should be employed in putting on the gold braid, which must cover the edges of the red cloth completely. The ends, of course, must be drawn on the wrong side; and before being mounted, we advise the back being lightly brushed with gelatine.

Antique Point Lace Collar.—By Mrs. Pullan.

ANTIQUE POINT COLLAR.

Materials.—3½ yards of Italian Braid, and the Point lace cottons of Messrs. W. Evans and Co., of Derby.

The braid which forms the outline of this Collar is made of linen, and is precisely similar to that used for the same purpose many centuries ago. The pattern is to be drawn on coloured paper and lined with Glazed Calico.

Each flower is outlined with a separate piece of braid, the ends being neatly turned in; and the braid being wide, it is necessary to run it on at each edge. A single line of braid goes completely round the collar, forming the scallops of one edge, and the inner row for the neck.

The edging consists of two rows of Sorrento, of which one is worked on the other. It is done with Evans's Mecklenburgh, No. 100.

The Raleigh and edged Venetian bars which form the ground, are done in Evans's Mecklenburgh, No. 120; and the small flowers and veinings of the leaves are in the same material.

The leaves are filled in completely with Brussels lace, done in Evans's Boar's Head, No. 90, and the Venetian bars which form the veinings are worked over it.

The centre of the flower is done in English lace, worked in Evans's Boar's Head, No. 70, surrounded by a line of buttonhole stitch; and the space between that and the braid is filled up with Venetian lace, done in the same cotton.

About twelve flowers, including those at the ends, will make a good-sized collar. The two flowers in the centre must lean in opposite directions, as must all the others, to make the ends correspond. If the plan of drawing the pattern, which we have recommended, be followed, this effect will be produced without any trouble

FLOWERS IN CROCHET—FLEUR-DE-LIS.—BY MRS. PULLAN.

FLOWERS IN CROCHET.

FLEUR-DE-LIS.

Materials.—Berlin wool, White, light Yellow; 2 shades of Yellow Green, and 2 of Vert d'Islay, ditto. Of the latter colour, the lightest shade manufactured must be one, and the other must be considerably darker. Green and White florists' wire, and fine common ditto.

AGAIN it is necessary to introduce a new crochet stitch, which we will call short treble crochet. It occupies the same medium between the Dc and the Tc, that the Short double crochet (described in the receipt for the Narcissus), does between a Sc and a Dc stitch.

Begin the short treble crochet (Stc), exactly like a double crochet stitch, but when three loops are on the hook, instead of drawing the wool through *two* at once, draw it only through *one*, so that you have still *three* loops on the needle. Now, pass the wool round the hook, and draw it through two loops; repeat this, and the stitch is completed.

The texture of this flower being so delicate, one of the strands of the white wool may be drawn out, before it is worked; or very good Shetland wool may be substituted for the Berlin. It is not necessary to make the wool for the leaves finer than it is bought.

THE LEAVES.—The darkest, for which the dark yellow-green wool is used, must be made thus: 45 chain. Take a piece of the fine common wire, half a yard long, and work it in, in the same way as you do the florist's wire in the Narcissus. (See page 405 of this volume.) Slip the end in the last chain stitch, and work 3 Sc, 3 Sdc stitches, 6 Dc, 18 Stc, 6 Dc, 4 Sdc, 4 Sc. Bend the wire, and work on the other side of the chain, 4 Sc, 4 Sdc, 6 Dc, 18 Stc, 6 Dc, 3 Sdc, 3 Sc, 1 slip stitch in the last stitch of the chain. Bend the wire, and work on the other side 5 Sc, 5 Sdc, 5 Dc, 11 Tc, 5 Dc, 8 Sdc, 4 Sc, 2 Sc, in the next, 1 Ch. Again bend the wire and do 2 Sc in the same stitch on the other side, 4 more Sc, 8 Sdc, 5 Dc, 11 Tc, 5 Dc 5 Sdc, 5 Sc, 1 slip stitch. Fasten off.

EMBROIDERED ANTI-MACASSAR.—BY MRS. PULLAN.

Take another piece of the wire, half the length, and work round the leaf, 8 slip stitches, 29 Sc, 8 slip, 1 slip in the 1 Ch at the points, 1 Ch, 8 Slip on the other side, 29 Sc, 8 Slip. This is the largest and darkest leaf.

Take the lighter shade of green, of the same tint as the last, and a piece of the common wire not quite half a yard long. Make 40 chain stitches. Slip the end of the wire in the last, and work as before. 3 Sc, 3 Sdc, 25 Dc, 4 Sdc, 4 Sc. Bend the wire, 4 Sc, 4 Sdc, 25 Dc, 3 Sdc, 3 Sc, 1 slip stitch in the last. Bend the wire; 5 Sc, 5 Sdc, 16 Dc, 8 Sdc, 4 Sc, 2 Sc in one, 1 Ch; bend the wire. 2 Sc in one, on the other side; 4 Sc, 8 Sdc, 16 Dc, 5 Sdc, 5 Sc, 1 slip stitch. Fasten off.

Take another piece of wire, not quite half as long. Join on the same wool at the eighth stitch from the base of the leaf, and work 24 Sc, holding in the wire, 8 slip stitches, 1 slip stitch in the chain stitch; bend the wire, and do another slip

stitch in the same chain stitch, 8 slip, 23 Sc, 1 slip. Cut off the wool, and fasten the ends.

SMALLEST LEAF.—Use the same shade of green. 30 Ch. Take a piece of wire rather shorter than that in the last leaf, and place it as before. 3 Sc, 5 Sdc, 13 Dc, 5 Sdc, 3 Sc. Bend the wire, and work over it on the other side of the chain, 3 Sc, 5 Sdc, 13 Dc, 5 Sdc, 3 Sc; 1 slip stitch in the last chain. Bend the wire, and work on the other side, 8 Sc, 3 Sdc, 8 Dc, 3 Sdc, 6 Sc, 2 Sc in the last stitch 1 Ch; bend the wire down the other side, and work as before, 2 Sc in one, 6 Sc, 3 Sdc, 8 Dc, 3 Sdc, 8 Sc, 1 slip stitch. Fasten off. Take a piece of wire half the length; join on your wool at the 7th stitch from the base of the leaf; 15 Sc, 8 slip, 1 slip in the 1 ch, 1 ch; bend your wire, and work on the other side of the leaf in the same way, ending with a slip stitch.

THE FLOWER.—35 chain. Take about

one-third of a yard of white Florist's wire; slip it into the last stitch, and work on the chain, 1 Sc, 2 Sdc, 26 Dc, 2 Sdc, 2 Sc, 1 Ch, bend the wire down the other side of the chain, on which, 2 Sc, 2 Sdc, 26 Dc, 2 Sdc, 2 Sc, 1 slip stitch. Bend the wire up the other side, and do 3 Sc, 2 Sdc, 3 Dc, 16 Stc, 6 Dc, 2 Sdc, 2 Sc, 3 Sc, on the 1 chain; work down the other side with the wire, 2 Sc, 2 Sdc, 6 Dc, 16 Stc, 3 Dc, 2 Sdc, 3 Sc, 1 slip. Fasten off. Every flower requires 6 petals.

THE BUD.—The same wool, and a rather shorter piece of the same wire. 25 chain. Place the wire as before. 3 Sc, 2 Sdc, 15 Dc, 2 Sdc, 2 Sc, in one chain. On the other side, 2 Sc, in one, 2 Sdc, 15 Dc, 3 Sdc, 3 Sc, 1 slip stitch.

Work up the other side, 4 slip stitches, 1 Sc, in every other stitch all round the petal, except the last four, which slip like the first.

Now slightly draw the wire, to give the proper concave form to the petal. It will be very desirable to have a flower before you when working, in order to imitate it with the greater exactness.

Three petals are required for each bud.

THE STAMENS.—Cut eight pieces of the white wire. Take some of the light yellow wool, which you will split in half and use only two strands. Make 7 chains very tightly, and on them do 6 Sc, working in the wire. Then slip both ends of the wire to the centre of this little morsel, which exactly resembles an anther, while the wire will do for the stem.

Each flower requires 6 stamens, and each bud two.

THE PISTIL. — The faintest tinge of blueish green is the proper shade for the little balls at the top of the pistil. Take a very little bit of wire, and wind, in the centre of it, a very small ball of the pale green wool. The ball must be the size of a very small pea. When this is made, twist the end of the wool with the two bits of wire to form one stem. Make three of these.

Take the three and fasten them together, with 8 inches of stronger wire to support them, by covering the whole with the same light green wool. When you have done about 1½ inches, roll a bit of jewellers' cotton round the wire, to form a small oblong ball, which also cover with the wool. Fasten off.

To MAKE UP THE SPRAY.— For the flowers, take the pistil, and arrange round it the six stamens, and three of the petals. Twist the green wool round them, and then add the other three petals. Continue to twist the wool round, half a *long* finger length.

Make up every flower in the same way.

For the buds, arrange the three petals round the stamens, so that they may nearly close over them; take a piece of the strong wire, a quarter of a yard long, wind some wool round it, and round the ends of wire belonging to the smallest bud; then round a second, and third, if you have them, then add a flower, continue winding round the thick wire, add another flower, and when all the flowers are put on, add the leaves, one after another, beginning with the *lightest*.

Observe that the flowers, buds, and leaves, with the exception of the one bud at the summit, must be placed regularly and alternately on different sides of the thick wire, that forms the stem, as is seen in Nature.

EMBROIDERED ANTI-MACASSAR.

Materials.—1¼ yards of book muslin; 3 skeins of Shetland wool; and 12 skeins of Berlin ditto. The Shetland wool is to be of three different shades, and the Berlin may match any one of them; or mohair braid may be used instead of Shetland wool.

THIS anti-macassar is of the same shape as the one in crochet given in a subsequent part of this volume; that is, a kind of bag, made for slipping over the top of a chair. The front is ornamented either with braid run on, or with chain stitch, the latter being rather the most work; but having a far better effect than the former. The initials we have selected are given to show the way in which *any* initials may be arranged for the centre. The pattern for the border is given in the engraving with the utmost accuracy, but requires, of course, to be greatly enlarged, and marked on the muslin in the way we have already described in our "Instructions in Embroidery," (page 56.)

The width of the anti-macassar, at the widest part, is 26 inches; a margin is left beyond the border, of about one inch, and the depth is 18 inches. The back of the anti-macassar may be of either worked or plain muslin. The two tucks are run together, near the edges, on the wrong side, then turned on the right, and a row of chain stitch worked at the extreme edge. All the border is done with one shade of the Shetland wool; but the monogram should be in two or three shades, according to the number of letters, each letter being done in one shade. When the muslin is braided, one shade only need be employed. The Russian mohair braid is the best adapted for this purpose; it washes well, and is easily put on; but the chain stitch is certainly prettier. Marked muslin may be readily finished for either oblong or oval anti-macassars: and those who wish it, can have any initials marked for them.

The BORDER.—Take a bone mesh half-an-inch wide, and do a strip of common diamond netting, wide enough for the border of the anti-macassar. Do four plain rows, and in the fifth work three stitches in one. In the sixth row, take three stitches together. Repeat these two rows, and knot a handsome fringe in the loops of the last.

The border is composed entirely of Berlin wool; the depth of the fringe is four inches.

As many may not know how the knotting of fringe is performed, we give the following information:—

Wind the wool on cotton as often as you may wish, round a card of any given width, and slip it carefully off, without cutting either end. Draw all the loops of one edge through the loops of netting, sufficiently far to allow the loops of the other edge to be drawn through them, and tightly pulled. The ends must then be cut.

A GENTLEMAN'S NIGHT-CAP.

WITH 4 Needles, No. 18. Evans's Knitting Cotton, No. 16.

CAST on 240 stitches, that is, 80 on each of 3 needles.

Knit 4 inches plain.

To condense this description as much as possible, it will be better to use abbreviations; thus, thread forward will be "Tf,' knit will be "K."

1st Row.—K 1, Tf, K 2 together 3 times, K 33.

2nd Row.—K plain; repeat these two rounds for one inch; then commence the Pattern as follows:—

Pattern.

1st Row.—K 1, Tf, K 2 together 3 times, K 14, K 2 together, Tf, K 1, Tf, K 2 together, K 14, repeat to the end of the round.

2nd Row.—K 20 K 2 together, Tf, K 3, Tf, K 2 together, K 13.

3rd Row.—K 1, Tf, K 2 together 3 times, K 12, K 2 together, Tf, K 5, Tf, K 2 together, K 12.

4th Row.—K 18, K 2 together, Tf, K 7, Tf, K 2 together, K 11.

5th Row.—K 1, Tf, K 2 together 3 times, K 10, K 2 together, Tf, K 9, Tf, K 2 together, K 10.

6th Row.—K 16, K 2 together, Tf, K 3, K 2 together, Tf, K 1, Tf, K 2 together, K 3, Tf, K 2 together, K 9.

7th Row.—K 1, Tf, K 2 together 3 times, K 8, K 2 together, Tf, K 3, K 2 together, Tf, K 3, Tf, K 2 together, K 3, Tf, K 2 together, K 8.

8th Row.—K 14, K 2 together, Tf, K 3, K 2 together, Tf, K 5, Tf, K 2 together, K 3, Tf, K 2 together, K 7.

9th Row.—K 1, Tf, K 2 together 3 times, K 6, K 2 together, Tf, K 3, K 2 together, Tf, K 7, Tf, K 2 together, K 3, Tf, K 2 together, K 6.

10th Row.—K 12, K 2 together, Tf, K 3, K 2 together, Tf, K 9, Tf, K 2 together, K 3, Tf, K 2 together, K 5.

11th Row.—K 1, Tf, K 2 together 3 times, K 4, K 2 together, Tf, K 3, K 2 together, Tf, K 11, Tf, K 2 together, K 3, Tf, K 2 together, K 4.

12th Row.—K 10, K 2 together, Tf, K 3, K 2 together, Tf, K 4, K 2 together, Tf, K 1, Tf, K 2 together, K 4, Tf, K 2 together, K 3, Tf, K 2 together, K 3.

13th Row.—K 1, Tf, K 2 together 3 times, K 2, K 2 together, Tf, K 3, K 2 together, Tf, K 4, K 2 together, Tf, K 3, Tf, K 2 together, K 4, Tf, K 2 together, K 3, Tf, K 2 together, K 2.

14th Row.—K 13, K 2 together, Tf, K 4, K 2 together, Tf, K 5, Tf, K 2 together, K 4, Tf, K 2 together, K 6.

15th Row.—K 1, Tf, K 2 together 3

Lady's Claret Polka. By Mrs. Warren.

times, K 6, K 2 together, Tf, K 10, K 2 together, Tf, K 4, K 2 together, Tf, K 7.

16*th Row.*—K 14, Tf, K 2 together, K 10, Tf, K 2 together, K 4, Tf, K 2 together, K 6.

17*th Row.*—K 1, Tf, K 2 together 3 times, K 7, Tf, K 2 together, K 10, Tf, K 2 together, K 4, Tf, K 2 together, K 6.

18*th Row.*—Same as 16th.

19*th Row.*—K 1, Tf, K 2 together 3 times, K 7, Tf, K 2 together, K 8, Tf, K 2 together, K 6, Tf, K 2 together, K 6.

20*th Row.*—K 14, Tf, K 2 together, K 7, K 2 together, Tf, K 7, Tf, K 2 together, K 6.

21*st Row.*—K 1, Tf, K 2 together 3 times, K 7, Tf, K 2 together, K 6, K 2 together, Tf, K 8, Tf, K 2 together, K 6.

22*nd Row.*—K 14, T f, K 2 together, K 5, K 2 together, Tf, K 9, Tf, K 2 together, K 6.

23*rd Row.*—K 1, Tf, K 2 together 3 times, K 7, Tf, K 2 together, K 4, K 2 together, Tf, K 10, Tf, K 2 together, K 6.

24*th Row.*—K 14, Tf, K 2 together, K 5, Tf, K 2 together, K 9, Tf, K 2 together, K 6.

25*th Row.*—K 1, Tf, K 2 together 3 times, K 7, Tf, K 2 together, K 5, Tf, K 2 together, K 9, Tf, K 2 together, K 6

26*th Row.*—Same as 24th.

27*th Row.*—Same as 25th.

28*th Row.*—K 7, K 2 together, K 6, Tf, K 2 together, K 5, Tf, K 2 together, K 6, K 2 together, Tf, K 6, K 2 together.

29*th Row.*—K 1, Tf, K 2 together 3

times, K 8, Tf, K 2 together, K 5, Tf, K 2 together, K 4, K 2 together, Tf, K 8.

30th Row.—K 7, K 2 together, K 7, Tf, K 2 together, K 5, Tf, K 2 together, K 2, K 2 together, Tf, K 7, K 2 together.

Continued at Page 95.

LADY'S CLARET POLKA, IN BRIOCHE

STITCH, (which is :—Wool forward, slip a stitch, knit 2 together: the same backwards and forwards).

9 Skeins of Claret Fleecy. No. 8 Pins. 4 thread. 4 skeins of Grey Fleecy.

CAST on 238 stitches, that is, 234 for 78 ribs, and 4 over, 2 on each side, to be knitted plain.

Knit a plain row, take off 14 stitches on to a string each side.

Knit 18 rows, taking up 1 stitch off the string every row; when every 3rd stitch is taken up, knit the 3 as 1 rib.

Knit 21 ribs, decrease a rib (*by taking 3 stitches together, pass the last stitch of the last rib, over*), knit 1 rib, decrease a rib.

Knit 26 ribs, decrease a rib, knit 1 rib, decrease a rib, knit 21 ribs.

Knit 14 rows.

Knit 22 ribs, decrease a rib, knit 1 rib, decrease a rib, knit 24 ribs, decrease, knit 1 rib, decrease, knit 22 ribs.

Knit 12 rows.

Knit 21 ribs, decrease, knit 1 rib, decrease, knit 22 ribs, decrease, knit 1 rib, decrease, knit 21 ribs.

Knit 8 rows.

Knit 20 ribs, decrease, knit 1 rib, decrease, knit 20 ribs, decrease, knit 1 rib, decrease, knit 20 ribs.

Knit 8 rows.

Knit 19 ribs, decrease, knit 1 rib, decrease, knit 18 ribs, decrease, knit 1 rib, decrease, knit 19 ribs.

Knit 8 rows.

Knit 18 ribs, decrease, knit 1 rib, decrease, knit 16 ribs, decrease, knit a rib, decrease, knit 18 ribs.

Knit 8 rows.

Knit 17 ribs, decrease, knit 1 rib, decrease, decrease every alternate rib 7 times, decrease, knit 1 rib, decrease, knit 17 ribs.

Knit 14 rows.

Knit 18 ribs, encrease (*by picking up the 2 back stitches on the left-hand needle, thread forward, slip 1, knit 1*), knit 7 ribs, encrease, knit 18 ribs.

Knit 14 rows.

Knit 18 ribs, encrease, knit 9 ribs, encrease, knit 18 ribs.

Knit 14 rows.

Knit 18 ribs, encrease, knit 11 ribs, encrease, knit 18 ribs.

Knit 12 rows.

Knit 4 ribs, encrease, Knit 41 ribs, encrease, knit 4 ribs.

Knit 2 rows.

Knit 19 ribs, encrease, knit 13 ribs, encrease, knit 19 ribs.

Knit 6 rows.

Knit 5 ribs, encrease, knit 43 ribs, encrease, knit 5 ribs.

Knit 8 rows.

Knit 6 ribs, encrease, knit 14 ribs, encrease, knit 15 ribs, encrease, knit 14 ribs, encrease, knit 6 ribs.

Knit 8 rows.

Knit 7 ribs, encrease, knit 45 ribs, encrease, knit 7 ribs.

Knit 5 rows.

Knit 16 ribs, cast off 3 ribs for arm-hole, encrease, knit 17 ribs, encrease, knit 3 ribs, cast off 3 ribs, knit 16 ribs.

Take off the fronts on to a string.

Knit 12 rows.

Knit 3 ribs, encrease, knit 19 ribs, encrease, knit 3 ribs.

Knit 16 rows.

Encrease 1 rib each side, and Knit 16 rows.

K 2 stitches, pull the first over the 2nd, knit a stitch, pass the 2nd over the 3rd, finish the row, and knit the odd stitch into the last rib: do this 10 times, that is, at the beginning of each row; this will make 20 rows, leaving 9 ribs in the middle for the neck.

Take up the fronts.

Knit 28 rows. Encrease a rib.

Knit 16 rows.

Decrease at the side nearest the shoulder 3 ribs; then decrease equally both sides till to a point.

For the Sleeves.

Cast on 81 stitches, knit 22 rows, encrease a rib at the beginning of the row. Knit 60 rows, decrease the last rib of the 60th row, knit 22 rows.

Finish with 5 rows of Grey Fleecing in shades, working long stitches in Crochet.

WINTER CAP.

7 Shades of Scarlet, 4 thread, Berlin Wool, 6 skeins of all but the 2 darkest shades; 2 of these. No. 2 Penelope Hook.

1st Row.—With lightest make 9 chain,

unite the ends *under* the chain, work * 5
chain, Dc *under* the circle, *repeat* from
* 7 times more. Cut off the Wool, and
tie neatly at the back ; this must be done
at every row.

2nd Row.—Same shade, Dc *under* 5, 5
chain *repeat.*

3rd Row.—*Under* the 5 chain work 2
long, 3 chain, 2 long *under* same, 3 chain
Dc on Dc, 3 chain *repeat.*

4th Row.— *Under* the 3 chain between
the 4 long work 2 long, 3 chain, 2 more
long *under* same, 3 chain, Dc *under* 3 chain,
Dc *under* next 3, 3 chain, *repeat.*

5th Row.—The same.

6th Row.—The same, only making 4
chain instead of 3.

7th Row.—The same, only making 5
chain.

8th Row.—Next shade. *Under* the 5
chain between the 4 long, work 2 long, 5
chain, 2 long *under* same, 5 chain, Dc
under 5, 5 chain, Dc *under* 5, 5 chain repeat.

9th Row.—*Under* the 5 chain between
the 4 long, work 2 long 5 chain, 2 more
long *under* same, 5 chain, Dc *under* 5, 5
chain, 2 long, 5 chain, 2 more long *under*
next 5, 5 chain, Dc *under* 5, 5 chain, re-
peat.

10th Row.—2 long, 5 chain, 2 more long
under the 5 chain, at the point, 5 chain,
Dc *under* 5, Dc *under* next 5, 5 chain, 2
long, 5 chain, 2 more long *under* next 5, 5
chain, Dc *under* 5, Dc *under* next 5, 5
chain, *repeat.*

11th Row.—Work at a point as before,
then 5 chain, Dc *under* 5 for twice, 5 chain,
2 long, 5 chain, 2 more long *under* next 5,
5 chain, Dc *under* 5 for twice, 5 chain, re-
veat.

12th Row.—Work on the longest point
as before, then 5 chain, Dc *under* 5 for
twice, Dc *under* next 5, 5 chain, 2 long,
5 chain, 2 more long *under* next 5, 5 chain,
Dc *under* 5, Dc *under* next 5, 5 chain, Dc
under 5, 5 chain, *repeat.*

13th Row.—Next shade, 2 long, 5 chain,
2 more long *under* the 5 chain at point,
then 5 chain, Dc *under* 5 3 times, 5 chain,
repeat.

14th Row. — Work at point as before,
then 5 chain, Dc *under* 5 for twice, Dc
under next 5, 5 chain, Dc *under* 5, 5 chain,
repeat.

15th Row.—The same.

16th Row — The same, only making 6
long instead of 4 at each point.

17th Row.—Work at point the same as
last row, then 5 chain, Dc *under* every 5
chain, 5 chain, *repeat.*

18th Row.—Next shade, the same.

19th Row.—The same at point as before,
then 5 chain, Dc *under* 5 for 3 times, Dc
under next 5, 5 chain, Dc *under* 5 for twice,
5 chain, *repeat.*

Damp and press under a heavy weight.

20th Row.—Work at point as before, then
5 chain, Dc *under* 5 for twice, 3 chain, 1
long *under* 5 for twice, 3 chain, Dc *under*
5, 5 chain, Dc *under* 5, 5 chain, *repeat.*

21st Row.—*Under* the 5 chain at point
work 5 Dc * 11 chain, 5 Dc *under* next 5
chain at point, *repeat* from *.

22nd Row—5 chain, Dc into every 3rd
loop.

23rd Row.—Commence on a point * 1
double long (*that is, with the Wool twice
over the Hook*) *under* the 5 chain, 5 chain,
repeat from * over 5 points, there will be
about 22 or 23 double long, then 5 chain,
Dc *under* 5 for 5 points. there will be about
26 Dc stitches, this forms the front of the
Cap. Then 5 chain, *repeat* from * to *
again, then 5 chain, Dc *under* 5 for 3 points,
there will be about 14 Dc stitches.

24th Row.—Next shade ; along the front
Dc *under* 5 chain, 3 chain ; over the ears
work as in last row, and at the back Dc
under 5, 5 chain, *repeat.*

25th Row.—1 long, 5 chain, 1 long *under*
every 5 chain round the cap, making 3
chain along the front.

26th Row. —Same as last row.

27th Row —Next shade ; *under* the 3
chain across the front work *, 2 long, 4
chain, 2 more long *under* same, 4 chain,
Dc *under* next 5, 4 chain, *repeat* from *,
under next 3 chain. Round the remainder
of cap make 5 chain instead of 4.

28th Row.—Darkest shade ; *under* the 5
chain between the 4 long in front, work 2
long, 3 chain, 2 long *under* same, 3 chain,
Dc *under* 4 chain, Dc *under* next 4, 3
chain, *repeat.*

On the ears, and at the back, work *under*
the 5 chain between the 4 long, 2 long, 5
chain, 2 more long *under* same, 3 chain,
Dc *under* 5, 3 chain, *repeat.*

Round the head of the Cap run 2 rows
of narrow satin ribbon as in engraving,
and place a satin bow behind.

FOOTSTOOL, WITH BEAD EMBROIDERY.

THE WORK-TABLE FRIEND.

FOOTSTOOL, WITH BEAD EMBROIDERY.

Materials.—Canvas, with beads, No. 2, of the following colours :—Chalk, opal, and clear white; aqua-marine, fawn, black, bronze (3 shades), blue (2 shades), also two hanks of steel beads, No. 7, and 2 ditto, uncut gold, of the same size. Put the beads on with Evans's Boar's Head cotton, No. 16.

In the engraving we give rather more than a quarter of the entire design, the space in the centre being intended either for the monagram of the proprietor, or for a small spray (such as a rose with buds and leaves), to be worked to correspond with the rest of the design.

Our readers will observe that we have not enumerated *greens* among the colours required for this pattern. The reason is, that the ground being blue, the green would not look well close to it. Should, however, any other tint be chosen for the ground, the leaves may be worked in their natural colours.

The scroll forming the corner of the design is worked in bronze, with gold and black. The engraving indicates the colours with sufficient accuracy to allow the worker to follow it. Those parts which are quite white are to be done in gold beads ; the depth of shading shows where the three tints of bronze come in, and the darkest part is in black. This, it will be observed, in order to give the effect of folds, always comes close to the lightest.

To produce variety in the shades of the leaves, a different set of colours are taken alternately. The flowers are very light, chalk being taken for the outer tint (represented in the engraving as perfectly white), clear white for the rest, steel for the third, and black for the fourth. When black occurs in the leaves and flowers, the squares are left of that colour.

In the centre of the flower will be seen some cross-bars. These indicate the medium bronze and gold.

The colours composing the leaf are chalk, clear white, aqua-marine, steel, and black. The first and last named are engraved to correspond. Steel is taken as the next shade to black, then aqua-marine, and clear white as *next* to chalk.

Fawn-colour and opal are introduced, instead of aqua-marine, and blue-white for the intermediate leaf. This gives a very pleasing variety in the arrangement, and contributes greatly to the effect.

Should a rose, with foliage, be chosen for the centre, the shades of the flower may be of either aqua-marine or fawn. The foliage should be of bronze, shaded with the same colours as the scroll.

As the four quarters of the design correspond precisely, the work has only to be reversed for the remaining portions. A rich dark blue forms the ground as far as the outer circle of the leaves, the inner part being filled in with a lighter (or turquoise) shade.

A novelty, called the railway footstool, has lately been introduced, which is so convenient for travellers, and so well adapted to this piece of work, that we think ourselves justified in naming it to the reader. It consists of a stuffed cushion, with a wooden frame, and folding legs; the work is sewed over the stuffed part, and it is then sufficiently portable to be slipped into a travelling bag, and taken out when in the carriage. It is certainly one of the nicest inventions of modern times.

To do bead-work nice be sure to stretch the canvas *evenly* in a frame, and to select it of such a size that the beads will cover two threads each way. Of course, they must all be sewed on *in the same direction*, and the thread be firm and well fastened in and off. If these directions are attended to, bead-work will be found infinitely more durable than Berlin-work.

About an ounce of each kind of bead will be required, except blue, of which you should have four ounces of each shade.

BISHOP SLEEVE IN APPLICATION AND EMBROIDERY.

Materials.— Fine Cambric muslin; Eugénie braid; Messrs. W. Evans and Co.'s Royal Embroidery cotton, Nos. 12 and 26; and Boar's Head sewing cotton, No. 70.

THE newest and most fashionable form of sleeve is an embroidered full sleeve, set in a narrow band, to be worked to correspond. The muslin is about three-eighths of a yard, to half a yard

deep, but only so much is embroidered as appears below the sleeve of the robe. The

BISHOP SLEEVE.

edge is overcast in button-hole stitch, as if the scallops were to be cut out, which, however, is not done. We would advise those ladies who set a value on their own work, and desire to preserve their sleeves from being torn by the laundress, to have the bishop sleeves made open, the sides and top simply hemmed, and the band sewed on at the bottom; then, after washing, the sides can be lightly tacked together, and again undone when they are soiled.

The Eugénie is a pretty, and extremely soft and pliable fancy tape, which we have recently brought from Paris. The design being marked on the muslin, the tape is tacked down, as seen in the engraving, and the edges neatly and closely run. All the other parts of the design should also be traced, and the small wheels run round two or three times. Then all the bars are to be worked with the coarsest embroidery cotton, after which the edges of the braid may be closely button-holed, the centres of the wheels pierced and overcast, and the scalloped border completed.

The flowers seen in various parts are worked on the muslin, the centre being cut out and filled with English lace, done with Boar's Head cotton No. 70. Each bar of overcast is done on a single thread, carried across from one part to the other, and button-holed back. The object in doing this *before* the rest of the work, is to be able to run the thread from one part to another without trouble, as the subsequent working conceals all these threads.

This sort of work is well adapted for petticoats. Ordinary linen tape may then be used, instead of the fancy kinds, but it must be of a very soft description.

The design we have given might readily be converted into an insertion by reversing the upper part for the lower, instead of putting the scallop at the bottom. Many petticoats now are trimmed in this way, with an *entre deux* above the hem instead of a scalloped border, as it is much more durable, and not so liable to tear.

We have many patterns in this style, any of which will be found extremely appropriate.

CROCHET INSERTION.

Materials.—Messrs. W. Evans's & Co.'s Boar's Head crochet cotton, No. 20, 24, or 30.

MAKE a chain of any length required, and form it into a round if for drawers, or any similar purposes.

1st Row.—Dc.
2nd Row.—+ 1 Dc, 5 Ch, miss 4. + repeat all round.
3rd Row.—+ Sc on 3rd of 5 Ch, 4 Ch, slip on Sc stitch, 9 Ch, + repeat all round.
4th Row.—Sc on 5 of 9 Ch, + 5 Ch, Sc on 5th of next 9 Ch, + all round.
5th Row.—+ Sc on 3rd of 5 Ch, 7 Ch, + repeat all round.
6th Row.—+ 3 Dc, beginning on 3rd of 7 Ch, 7 Ch, + repeat all round.
7th Row.—+ Sc on centre of 7 Ch, 5 Ch, + repeat all round.
8th Row.—+ Sc on centre of 5 Ch, 9

BEAD AND CROCHET WORK.

Ch, slip-stitch on 5th, 4 more chain. + repeat all round.
9th Row.—+ Sc on the slip-stitch of last row, 5 Ch, + repeat all round.
10th Row.—+ 1 Dc on centre of 5 Ch, 4 Ch, + repeat all round.
11th Row.—Dc.

CROCHET INSERTION.

To be worked from the engraving in square crochet. This pattern is very suitable for bead work.

Initial letters.—Evans's Royal Embroidery cotton, No. 60, is suitable for cambric.

A GENTLEMAN'S NIGHT-CAP.

Continued from Page 91.

31st Row.—K 1, Tf, K 2 together 3 times, K 2 together, K 7, Tf, K 2 together, K 7, K 2 together, Tf, K 7, K 2 together.
32nd Row.—K 7, K 2 together, K 7, Tf, K 2 together, K 5, K 2 together, Tf, K 7, K 2 together.
33rd Row.—K 1, Tf, K 2 together 3 times, K 2 together, K 7, Tf, K 2 together K 3, K 2 together, Tf, K 7, K 2 together
34th Row.—K 7, K 2 together, K 7. Tf K 2 together, K 1, K 2 together, Tf, K 7 K 2 together.
35th Row.—K 1, Tf, K 2 together

times, K 2 together, K 7, Tf, K 3 together, Tf, K 7, K 2 together.

36th Row.—K 7, K 2 together, Tf, K 2
together, K 11, K 2 together, Tf, K 2
together.

37th Row.—K 1, Tf, K 2 together 3
times, K 2, Tf, K 2 together, K 9, K 2
together, Tf, K 2.

38th Row.—K 7, K two together, K 1,
Tf, K 2 together, K 7, K 2 together, Tf,
K 1, K 2 together.

39th Row.—K 1, Tf, K 2 together 3
times, K 2 together, K 1, Tf, K 2 together, K 5, K 2 together, Tf, K 1, K 2 together.

40th Row.—K 7, K 2 together, K 1, Tf,
K 2 together, K 3, K 2 together, Tf, K 1,
K 2 together.

41st Row.—K 1, Tf, K 2 together 3
times, K 2 together. K 1, Tf, K 2 together, K 1, K 2 together, Tf, K 1, K 2 together.

42nd Row.—K 7, K 2 together, K 1, Tf,
K 3 together, Tf, K 1, K 2 together.

43rd Row.—K 1, Tf, K 2 together
three times, K 2 together, K 3, K 2 together.

44th Row.—K 7, K 2 together, K 1, K
2 together.

45th Row.—K 1, Tf, K 2 together 3
times, K 3 together.

46th Row.—K 6, K 2 together.

47th Row.—K 1, Tf, K 2 together, Tf,
K 2 together, K 2 together.

48th Row.—K 1, K 2 together, Tf, K 2
together, K 1.

49th Row.—K 1, K 3 together, K 1.

50th Row.—K 3 together.

Knit all together. This will form the
Cap: the side pieces must be knitted
thus :—Cast on 1 stitch, knit it, increase 1,
knit; then continue to increase 1 at the
beginning of each row till there are 12
stitches on the needle, then commence the
Pattern.

Pattern for Side Pieces.

(E for Encrease, P for Pearl.)

1st Row.—E 1, K 5, Tf, K 2 together,
K 5.

2nd Row.—E 1, K 5, P 2 together, cotton round the needle, P 1, Tf, K 6.

3rd Row.—E 1, K 4, K 2 together, Tf,
K 3, Tf, K 6.

4th Row.—E 1, K 4, P 2 together, cot
ton round the needle, P 5, Tf, K 6.

5th Row.—E 1, K 4, K 2 together, Tf,
K 7, Tf, K 6.

6th Row.—E 1, K 6, P 1, cotton round
the needle, P 2 together, P 5, P 2 together, Tf, K 6.

7th Row.—E 1, K 7, Tf, K 2 together,
K 5, K 2 together, Tf, K 2 together, K 5.

8th Row.—E 1, K 5, P 2, cotton round,
P 2 together, P 5, P 2 together, cotton
round, P 1, K 6.

9th Row.—E 1, K 8, Tf, K 2 together,
K 5, K 2 together, Tf, K 7.

10th Row.—E 1, K 6, P 2, cotton round,
P 2 together, P 5, P 2 together, cotton
round, P 2, K 6.

11th Row.—E 1, K 8, Tf, K 2 together,
K 5, K 2 together, Tf, K 9.

12th Row.—E 1, K 6, P 3, cotton round,
P 2 together, P 5, P 2 together, cotton
round, P 3, K 6.

13th Row.—E 1, K 10, Tf, K 2 together,
K 3, K 2 together, Tf, K 11.

14th Row.—E 1, K 6, P 6, cotton round,
P 2 together, P 1, P 2 together, cotton
round, P 6, K 6.

15th Row.—E 1, K 6, K 2 together, Tf,
K 1, Tf, K 2 together, K 2, Tf, K 3 toge-
ther, Tf, K 2, K 2 together, Tf, K 1, Tf,
K 2 together, K 7.

16th Row.—E 1, K 6, P 2 together, cotton round, P 3, cotton round, P 2 together, P 2, cotton round, P 1, cotton round,
P 2, P 2 together, cotton round, P 3, cotton round, P 2 together, K 6.

17th Row.—E 1, K 5, K 2 together, Tf,
K 5, Tf, K 2 together, K 5, K 2 together,
Tf, K 5, Tf, K 2 together, K 6.

Continued at Page 101

LADY'S UNDER SLEEVE.

THIS Sleeve may be made in No. 20 Boar's
Head Cotton, and with No. 4 Penelope Hook, of
any size, by increasing the number of rows, and
makes a pretty Sleeve for Summer; or, if made
in 4 thread White Berlin Wool, with cotton Border, and Ribbon the colour of the Robe, drawn
through the centre, it makes an excellent warm
Sleeve for Winter, and has the advantage of
washing; or, if made in fine Black Purse Silk,
and No. 3 Penelope Hook, with Grey Silk Border, is a good Mourning Sleeve. The engraved
Sleeve is made with 7 shades of Scarlet, 4 thread
Berlin Wool, and No. 2 Penelope Hook.

WITH darkest shade make a chain of 61
stitches, unite, and work a round of Dc.

2nd Row.—Same colour, 1 long, 1 chain, miss 1 loop, repeat.

3rd Row.—Dc under the 1 chain, 5 chain, repeat.

4th Row.—Dc under 5, 5 chain, repeat.

5th Row.—Next shade, Dc under 5 chain, 5 chain, Dc under 5, 5 chain, Dc under same 5, 5 chain, repeat.

6th Row.—Dc under 5, 5 chain, repeat.

Continue working 2 rows of every shade (excepting the lightest), the same as the 6th row.

Take the lightest shade, work 5 long under the 5 chain, 5 chain, miss 1 chain of 5, repeat.

Same shade, 5 long on the long, 5 chain, repeat.

Next darker shade, Dc on 1st long, 5 chain, Dc on last long, 5 chain, repeat.

Same shade, Dc under the 5 chain, 5 chain, repeat.

Continue working all the shades the same as last row, working 2 rows of each shade; after the 2 last rows of the darkest shade, with the same colour work 1 long under the 5 chain, 2 chain, repeat.

Same colour, 1 long under the 2 chain, chain, repeat.

Same colour, work rather loosely 1 Dc under every 1 chain. (This is the part which is attached to the long sleeve.)

For the Border at the Wrist.

1st Row.—With military Scarlet, Dc into a loop of the foundation chain, * 5 chain, Dc into 2nd loop, repeat from *.

2nd Row.—Same shade, Dc under 5, 5 chain, repeat.

3rd Row.—Same shade, 3 long under a 5 chain, 3 chain, 3 more long under same, 3 chain, Dc under 5, 3 chain, repeat.

4th Row.—Second shade darker, 3 long under the 3 chain, between the 6 long, 3 chain, 3 more long under same, 3 chain, Dc under 3 chain, and Dc under next 3 chain, 3 chain, repeat.

5th Row.—Darkest shade; the same, only making 2 chain after the 6 long instead of 3.

Draw two rows of narrow Scarlet satin Ribbon through the 2 rows of the lightest shade, in the centre of the Sleeve, and a piece of Elastic through the Wrist.

LADY'S NECK TIE.

3 Shades of fine Chenelle, Scarlet or Blue; 5 skeins of the lightest, 1 of the next shade, 3 of the darkest, or military Scarlet. Or 3 shades of 4 thread Berlin Wool, 5 skeins of the lightest, 1 of the next shade, and 4 of military Scarlet, 5 skeins of common Black Purse Silk, rather fine. No. 2 Penelope Hook.

WITH military Scarlet make a chain 14 nails in length, turn back, Dc into 10th stitch; then 5 chain, Dc into every 6th stitch. There must be 65 loops. (The loops are the spaces formed between each Dc stitch.) This forms the foundation. Cut off the wool, tie it neatly.

2nd Row.—Same colour, Dc under the loop or space at the extreme end, 5 chain, 3 long under same loop or space, 5 chain, 3 more long under same, 5 chain, Dc under same, 5 chain, * 3 long under next loop or space, 5 chain, 3 more long under same, 5 chain, Dc under next loop or space, 5 chain, repeat from *. Work round both sides of the foundation the same. (This makes an admirable substitute for braid on children's dresses or pinafores.)

3rd Row.—Black silk; under the 5 chain at the extreme end work 3 long, 5 chain, 3 more long under the same, 5 chain, Dc under same, 5 chain, 3 long, 5 chain, 3 more long under same (all this to be worked under the 5 chain at the extreme end), * 5 chain, Dc under next 5, Dc under next 5, 5 chain, 3 long under next 5, 3 chain, 3 more long under same, repeat from *, working both ends alike.

4th Row.—Next shade Scarlet, Dc under a 5 chain, 5 chain, and Dc under every 5 chain all round.

5th Row.—Black silk; under the 5 chain, that is, between the groups of Black stitches, work 3 long, 4 chain, 3 more long under same, 4 chain, Dc on Dc on the top of the group of Black stitches, 4 chain, repeat. Round the ends work thus:—Dc on Dc on the top of the 1st group of long stitches on the right hand side, 5 chain, miss 1 chain of 5, 3 long under next chain of 5, 5 chain, 3 more long under same, 5 chain, Dc on next Dc, 5 chain, 3 long under next 5, 5 chain, 3 more long under same, 5 chain, Dc on 2nd Dc, 4 chain; now continue as at the beginning of this row.

6th Row.—Lightest shade Scarlet; twist

H

Winter Cap, Neck Tie, and Under Sleeve. By Mrs. Warren.

the wool twice over the hook for all the long stitches in this row only. Begin *under* the 1st chain of 4, between the 6 long, round the corner at right hand, 7 long with 1 chain between each, 1 chain, Dc *under* 5, 5 chain, Dc *under* next 5, 1 chain, 7 long with 1 chain between each, *under* next 5, 1 chain, Dc on Dc, * 1 chain, 7 long, with 1 chain between each, *under* the 4 chain, 1 chain, Dc on Dc, *repeat* from *, making both ends alike.

7th Row.—Black silk, Dc into the centre loop of the 5 chain at the end, 5 chain, 1 long between 1st long, * 5 chain, 1 long between next long, *repeat* from * four times more, making in all 6 long: this will extend over one scallop; now 1 long between the 1st long of next scallop, † 5 chain, 1 long between next long, *repeat* from † 4 times more; then continue over the next scallop, taking care that there are no chains between the 2 scallops; make both ends alike.

Pull the edge well out, and, if made of wool, damp well, and press between linen, under a very heavy weight.

T. C.—Centre Piece.

T. C.—Corner Piece.

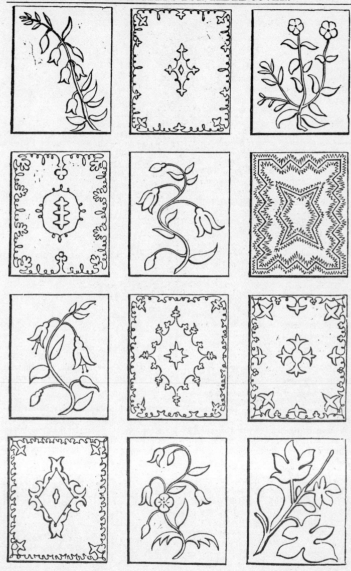

EXPLANATION OF STITCHES.

CHAIN STITCH, is made by forming a loop, and drawing one loop through the other.

DC or DOUBLE CROCHET, is made by inserting the hook through the loop, and drawing the cotton through, then draw the cotton through the two loops, and again through two, there will then be one loop on the hook.

LONG STITCH, is made by *first* twisting the cotton over the hook, then insert the hook into the loop, draw the cotton through, then through two loops, and again through two, there will then be 1 loop on the hook.

DOUBLE LONG is made by first twisting the wool or cotton twice over the hook, and drawing it through 2 loops successively for 3 times.

BRIOCHE STITCH is—Wool forward, slip a stitch, knit 2 together, the same backwards and forwards.

NEW CROCHET CHAIN.—Take any two colours, fasten them together, make a loop with *both*, then holding them a little apart, work with each colour alternately: the loop thus left on what has hitherto been the *wrong* side of the chain, constitutes a new and pretty face to it. In working, care must be taken not to twist the wools or cottons.

POLKA FOR A CHILD

OF SIX YEARS OLD, IN BRIOCHE STITCH.

No. 9 Pins—or if required for one younger, No. 10 or 12 Pins. 7 Skeins of fleecy 4 thread, ¼ lb. of shaded 4 thread Berlin wool, Sable Colour, or Grey. 1 pair Steel Pins No. 14.

CAST on with No. 9 Pins 181 stitches, that is, 177 for 59 ribs, and 4 over, 2 of each side, to be knitted plain.

Knit 2 plain rows.

Take off 11 stitches on each side, on to a string, knit 18 rows, taking up 1 stitch off the string on to the pin every row; when every 3rd stitch is taken up, knit the 3 as 1 rib, knit 17 ribs; then decrease a rib (*by taking 3 stitches together, and pass the last stitch of the last rib over*), knit 1 rib, decrease 1 rib, knit 19 ribs, decrease, knit 1 rib, decrease, knit 17 ribs.

Knit 9 rows.

Knit 16 ribs, decrease, knit 1 rib, de-

crease, knit 17 ribs, decrease, knit 1 rib, decrease, knit 16 ribs.

Knit 9 rows.

Knit 15 ribs, decrease, knit 1 rib, decrease, knit 15 ribs, decrease, knit 1 rib decrease, knit 15 ribs.

Knit 9 rows.

Knit 14 ribs, decrease, knit 1 rib, decrease, knit 15 ribs, decrease, knit 1 rib, decrease, knit 14 ribs.

Knit 9 rows.

Knit 13 ribs, decrease, knit 1 rib, decrease, decrease every alternate rib 6 times, decrease, knit 1 rib, decrease, knit 13 ribs.

Knit 4 rows.

Knit 13 ribs, encrease, knit 17 ribs, encrease, knit 13 ribs.

Knit 13 rows.

Knit 13 ribs, encrease, knit 11 ribs, encrease, knit 13 ribs.

Knit 13 rows.

Knit 13 ribs, encrease, knit 13 ribs, encrease, knit 13 ribs.

Knit 13 rows.

Take off 12 stitches each side, on to a string, for the fronts, knit 1 rib, encrease, knit 15 ribs, encrease, knit 1 rib.

Knit 13 rows.

Knit 1 rib, encrease, knit 17 ribs, encrease, knit 1 rib.

Knit 20 rows.

Decrease on each side the back, and knit 8 rows.

Knit 2 stitches, pull the first over the 2nd, knit a stitch, pass the 2nd over the 3rd, finish the row, and knit the odd stitch into the last rib; do this at the beginning of each row, until there are but 5 ribs left on the pin, now cast off.

Take up a front, and knit 34 rows, encrease on the side nearest the shoulder.

Knit 8 rows.

Decrease 1 rib, knit 2 rows, then decrease equally both sides the front till to a point.

For the Sleeves.

Cast on 51 stitches, knit 19 rows, encrease a rib at the beginning of next row, knit 34 rows, decrease the last rib of the 34th row, knit 19 rows, and cast off.

For the Border.

Wind the shaded Wool in two balls; cast on 9 stitches with No. 14 Pins, knit a plain row, then place the point of the needle in the 1st stitch, bring the wool round the 2nd finger of left hand, forming a loop, place

Polka for a Child of Six Years old. By Mrs. Warren.

it between the points of the needle, and knit it off with the other ball of Wool; knit all the row in the same manner, this will form a row of loops; in returning, knit a plain row with both ends of Wool double; now continue the row of loops, Or it may be finished with 4 rows of long stitches in Crochet, worked in four shades of Grey Fleecy.

This Border is to be sewed round the Polka.

A GENTLEMAN'S NIGHT-CAP.

Continued from Page 96.

18*th Row.*—E 1, K 5, P 2 together, cotton round, P 7, cotton round, P 2 together, P 3, P 2 together, cotton round, P 7, cotton round, P 2 together, K 5.

19*th Row.*—E 1, K 6, Tf, K 2 together, K 5, K 2 together, Tf, K 2 together, K 1, K 2 together, Tf, K 2 together, K 5, K 2 together, Tf, K 7.

20*th Row.*—E 1, K 6, P 1, cotton round P 2 together, P 5, P 2 together, cotton round, P 3 together, cotton round, P 2 together, P 5, P 2 together, cotton round, P 1, K 6.

21*st Row.*—E 1, K 7, Tf, K 2 together, K 5, K 2 together, Tf, K 1, Tf, K 2 together, K 5, K 2 together, Tf, K 8.

22*nd Row.*—E 1, K 6, P 2, cotton round, P 2 together, P 5, P 2 together, cotton round, P 1, cotton round, P 2 together, P 5, P 2 together, cotton round, P 2, K 6.

23*rd Row.*—E 1, K 9, Tf, K 2 together, K 4, K 2 together, Tf, K 1, Tf, K 2 together, K 4, K 2 together, Tf, K 10.

24*th Row.*—E 1, K 6, P 5, cotton round, P 2 together, P 3, P 2 together, cotton round, P 1, cotton round, P 2 together, P 3, P 2 together, cotton round, P 5, K 6.

25*th Row.*—E 1, K 7, Tf, K 2 together, K 3, Tf, K 2 together, K 9, K 2 together, Tf, K 3, K 2 together, Tf, K 8.

26*th Row.*—E 1, K 6, P 3, cotton round, P 2 together, P 3, cotton round, P 2 together, P 7, P 2 together, cotton round, P 3, P 2 together, cotton round, P 3, K 6.

27th Row.—E 1, K 11, Tf, K 2 together, K 3, Tf, K 2 together, K 5, K 2 together, Tf, K 3, K 2 together, Tf, K 11.

28th Row.—E 1, K 6, P 7, cotton round, P 2 together, P 3, cotton round, P 2 together, P 3, P 2 together, cotton round, P 3, P 2 together, P 7, K 5.

29th Row.—E 1, K 8, Tf, K 2 together, K 3, Tf, K 2 together, K 3, Tf, K 2 together, K 1, K 2 together, Tf, K 3, K 2 together, Tf, K 3, K 2 together, Tf, K 9.

30th Row.—E 1, K 6, P 2, P 2 together, cotton round, P 1, cotton round, P 2 together, P 3, cotton round, P 2 together, P 3, cotton round, P 3 together, cotton round, P 3, P 2 together, cotton round, P 3, P 2 together, cotton round, P 1, cotton round, P 2 together, P 2, K 5.

31st Row.—E 1, K 6, K 2 together, Tf, K 3, Tf, K 2 together, K 3, Tf, K 2 together, K 7, K 2 together, Tf, K 3, K 2 together, Tf, K 3, Tf, K 2 together, K 7.

32nd Row.—E 1, K 5, P 1, P 2 together, cotton round, P 5, cotton round, P 2 together, P 3, cotton round, P 2 together, P 5, P 2 together, cotton round, P 3, P 2 together, cotton round, P 5, cotton round, P 2 together, P 1, K 5.

33rd Row.—E 1, K 5, K 2 together, Tf, K 7, Tf, K 2 together, K 3, Tf, K 2 together, K 3, K 2 together, Tf, K 3, K 2 together, Tf, K 7, Tf, K 2 together, K 6.

34th Row.—E 1, K 5, P 2, cotton round, P 2 together, P 5, P 2 together, cotton round, P 2 together, P 3, cotton round, P 2 together, P 1, P 2 together, cotton round, P 3, P 2 together, cotton round, P 2 together, P 5, P 2 together, cotton round, P 2, K 5.

35th Row.—E 1, K 7, Tf, K 2 together, K 5, K 2 together, Tf, K 5, Tf, K 3 together, Tf, K 5, Tf, K 2 together, K 5, K 2 together, Tf, K 8.

36th Row.—E 1, K 5, P 3, cotton round, P 2 together, P 5, P 2 together, cotton round, P 3, P 2 together, cotton round, P 3, cotton round, P 2 together, P 3, cotton round, P 2 together, P 5, P 2 together, cotton round, P 3, K 5.

37th Row.—E 1, K 8, Tf, K 2 together, K 5, K 2 together, Tf, K 2. K 2 together, Tf, K 5, Tf, K 2 together, K 2, Tf, K 2 together, K 5, K 2 together, Tf, K 9.

38th Row.—E 1, K 6, P 4, Tf, P 2 toge-

ther, P 5, P 2 together, Tf, P 3, Tf, P 2 together, P 3, P 2 together, Tf, P 3, Tf, P 2 together, P 5, P 2 together, Tf, P 4, K 5.

39th Row.—E 1, K 9, Tf, K 2 together, K 5, K 2 together, K 4, Tf, K 2 together, K 1, K 2 together, Tf, K 4, Tf, K 4, Tf, K 2 together, K 5, K 2 together, Tf, K 10.

40th Row.—E 1, K 5, P 4, cotton round, P 2 together, P 5, P 2 together, cotton round, P 5, cotton round, P 3 together, cotton round, P 5, cotton round, P 2 together, P 5, P 2 together, cotton round, P 4, K 6.

41st Row.—E 1, K 11, Tf, K 2 together, K 3, K 2 together, Tf, K 15, Tf, K 2 together, K 3, K 2 together, Tf, K 12.

42nd Row.—E 1, K 5, P 8, Tf, P 2 together, P 1, P 2 together, Tf, P 17, cotton round, P 2 together, P 1, P 2 together, Tf, P 8, K 5.

43rd Row.—E 1, K 7, K 2 together, Tf, K 1, Tf, K 2 together, K 22, Tf, K 3 together, Tf, K 2, K 2 together, Tf, K 1, Tf, K 2 together, K 5, Tf, K 2, K 2 together, Tf, K 1, Tf, K 2 together, K 3, Tf, K 3 together, Tf, K 2, K 2 together, Tf, K 1, Tf, K 2 together, K 8.

44th Row.—E 1, K, 5, P 2, K 2 together, Tf, P 3, Tf, K 2 together, P 2, cotton round, P 1, cotton round, P 2, P 2 together, cotton round, P 3, cotton round, P 2 together, P 3, P 2 together, cotton round, P 3, cotton round, P 2 together, P 2, cotton round, P 1, cotton round, P 2 together, cotton round, P 3, cotton round, P 2 together, P 2, K 5.

45th Row.—E 1, K 6, K 2 together, Tf, K 5, Tf, K 2 together, K 5, K 2 together, Tf, K 5, Tf, K 2 together, K 5, K 2 together, Tf, K 5, Tf, K 2 together, K 7.

46th Row.—E 1, K 6, P 1, P 2 together, cotton round, P 7, cotton round, P 2 together, P 3, P 2 together, cotton round, P 7, cotton round, P 3 together, cotton round, P 7, cotton round, P 2 together, P 3, P 2 together, cotton round, P 7, cotton round, P 2 together, P 1, K 5.

47th Row.—K 8, Tf, K 2 together, K 5, K 2 together, Tf, K 2 together, K 1, K 2 together, Tf, K 2 together, K 5, K 2 together, Tf, K 1, Tf, K 2 together, K 5, K 2 together, Tf, K 2 together, K 1, Tf, K 2 together, K 5, K 2 together, Tf, K 18.

48th Row.—K 6, P 2, cotton round, P 2 together, P 5, P 2 together, cotton round, P 3 together, cotton round, P 2 together,

P 6, cotton round, P 3, cotton round, P 6, P 2 together, cotton round, P 3 together, cotton round, P 2 together, P 5, P 2 together, cotton round, P 2, K 6.

49th Row.—K 8, Tf, K 2 together, K 5, K 2 together, Tf, K 1, Tf, K 2 together, K 6, Tf, K 5, Tf, K 6, K 2 together, Tf, K 1, Tf, K 2 together, K 5, K 2 together, Tf, K 8.

50th Row.—K 6, P 2, cotton round, P 2 together, P 5, P 2 together, cotton round, P 1, cotton round, P 2 together, P 6, cotton round, P 2 together, P 3, P 2 together, cotton round, P 6, P 2 together, cotton round, P 1, cotton round, P 2 together, P 5, P 2 together, cotton round, P 2, K 6.

51st Row.—K 9, Tf, K 2 together, K 4, K 2 together, Tf, K 1, Tf, K 2 together, K 4, K 2 together, Tf, K 1, Tf, K 2 together, K 1, K 2 together, Tf, K 1, Tf, K 2 together, K 4, K 2 together, Tf, K 1, Tf, K 2 together, K 4, K 2 together, Tf, K 9.

52nd Row.—K 6, P 4, cotton round, P 2 together, P 11, P 2 together, cotton round, P 3, cotton round, P 3 together, cotton round, P 3, cotton round, P 2 together, P 11, P 2 together, cotton round, P 4, K 6.

53rd Row.—K 11, Tf, K 2 together, K 9, K 2 together, Tf, K 5, Tf, K 1, Tf, K 5, Tf, K 2 together, K 9, K 2 together Tf, K 11.

54th Row.—K 6, P 6, cotton round, P 2 together, P 7, P 2 together, cotton round, P 2 together, P 11, P 2 together, cotton round, P 2 together, P 7, P 2 together, cotton round, P 6, K 6.

55th Row.—K 13, Tf, K 2 together, K 5, K 2 together, Tf, K 2 together, K 11, K 2 together, Tf, K 2 together, K 5, K 2 together, Tf, K 13.

56th Row.—K 6, P 8, cotton round, P 2 together, P 3, P 2 together, cotton round, P 1, cotton round, P 2 together, P 2, P 2 together, cotton round, P 1, cotton round, P 2 together, P 2, P 2 together, cotton round, P 1, cotton round, P 2 together, P 8, K 6.

57th Row.—K 15, Tf, K 2 together, K 1, K 2 together, Tf, K 3, Tf, K 2 together, K 2 together, Tf, K 3, Tf, K 2 together, K 2 together, Tf, K 3, Tf, K 2 together, K 1, K 2 together, Tf, K 15.

58th Row.—K 6, P 10, cotton round, P 3 together, cotton round, P 5, cotton round, P 2 together, cotton round. P 5, cotton round, P 2 together, cotton round, P 5, cotton round, P 3, cotton round, P 10, K 6.

59th Row.—K 14, K 2 together, Tf, K 3, Tf, K 2 together, K 3, K 2 together, Tf, K 2 together, K 3, K 2 together, Tf, K 2 together, K 3, K 2 together, Tf, K 3, Tf, K 2 together.

60th Row.—K 6, P 7, P 2 together, cotton round, P 5, cotton round, P 2 together, P 4 cotton round, P 2 together, P 1, P 2 together, cotton round, P 4, P 2 together, cotton round, P 5, cotton round, P 2 together, P 7, K 6.

61st Row.—K 12, K 2 together, Tf, K 7, Tf, K 2 together, K 4, Tf, K 3 together, Tf, K 4, K 2 together, Tf, K 7, Tf, K 2 together, K 12.

62nd Row.—K 6, P 8, cotton round, P 2 together, P 3, P 2 together, cotton round, P 15, cotton round, P 2 together, P 3, P 2 together, cotton round, P 8, K 6.

63rd Row.—K 15, Tf, K 2 together, K 1, K 2 together, Tf, K 17, Tf, K 2 together, K 1, K 2 together, Tf, K 15.

64th Row.—K 6, P 10, Tf, P 3 together, Tf, P 19, Tf, P 3 together, P 10, K 6.

Knit 10 rows, cast off.

For the Band.

Cast on 20 stitches, Knit 9 rows, Pearl 9 rows, till sufficient is knitted to go round the cap.

Pattern for Edging

To be sewed on all of the 4 pieces, after the pieces are joined together; they are then to be sewed on the Cap, and afterwards the band sewed on, then finished with a tassel at the top.

1st Row.—Cast on 5 stitches, K 3, Tf, K 2.

2nd Row.—K 2, cotton round, P 1, cotton round, P 1, keep cotton in front, and K 2 together.

3rd Row.—K 3, Tf, K 3, Tf, K 2.

4th Row.—K 2, cotton round, P 5, cotton round, P 1, keep the cotton in front, K 2 together.

5th Row.—K 3, Tf, K 2 together, K 3, K 2 together, Tf, K 2.

6th Row.—K 3, cotton round, P 2 together, P 1, P 2 together, cotton round, P 2, keep cotton in front, K 2 together.

7th Row.—K 5, Tf, slip 1, K 2 together, pass the slipped stitch over, Tf, K 4.

8th Row.—Cast off all but 5 stitches, K 2, Tf, K 2 together.

CROCHET EDGING.

Materials.—Messrs. W. Evans and Co.'s Boar's Head crochet cotton, No. 12, or 14 for petticoats, or of any higher or lower number, according to the purpose to which the work is intended.

1st Row.—Dc.

2nd Row.—Sc on a stitch, + 4 Ch, Sc under next, 9 Ch, miss 5 Dc, Sc on 6th, + repeat to the end.

3rd Row.—+ 7 Dc under loop of 4, miss 2 of the 9 Ch, slip-stitch very loosely on the next 3, 4 Ch, slip on same as last, slip-stitch on the next 2, +.

4th Row.—+ 7 Dc in loop of 4, 2 Ch, Sc on 3rd of 7 Dc in previous row, 4 Ch, Sc in next, 2 Ch, +.

5th Row.—Slip on 5th of 7 Dc, + 9 Ch, slip on 5th of 9, 4 more Ch, slip on 3rd, 4th, and 5th of next 7 Dc, + repeat to the end. These two rows must be repeated for any depth required.

Last rows, which must always be done after a repetition of the 4th. + Sc on 4th of 7 Dc, 12 Ch, + repeat to the end.

Work the small loops by slip-stitch on Sc of last row, + 4 Ch, miss 2, Sc on 3rd, + throughout the entire length.

THE WORK-TABLE FRIEND.

KNITTED TABLE-COVER, OR COVER FOR SOFA PILLOW.

Twelve reels of No. 6 Evans's Boar's Head Cotton; five pins, No. 12 pins. Or, 19 shades of any colour Wool; No. 8 pins.

Explanation of Terms :—Tf, thread forward ; +, together ; K, knit ; P, pearl.

KNIT 6 rounds of each shade.

Cast on 2 stitches on *each* of the 4 pins, bring the wool forward at the *beginning* and in the *middle* of each pin ; then K one plain round. Repeat these two rounds till there are 34 stitches on *each* pin.

1st Fancy Round.—Tf, K 6, K 2 +, Tf, K 9 ; *repeat* all round.

Every alternate row being plain knitting, it will be unnecessary to repeat this direction.

3rd Round.—Tf, K 4, K 2 +, K 2 +, Tf, K 1, Tf, K 9.

5th Round.—Tf, K 1, K 2 +, K 2 +, K 2 +, Tf, K 1, Tf, K 1, Tf, K 1, Tf, K 9.

7th Round.—Tf, K 2, K 3 +, Tf, K 1, Tf and K 2 + 3 times, Tf, K 9.

9th Round.—Tf, K 1, K 3 +, Tf, K 1,

Tf and K 2 + 4 times, Tf, K 2, K 2 +, Tf, K 5.

11th Round.—Tf, K 3 +, Tf, K 3 +, Tf and K 2 + 4 times, Tf, K 1, K 2 +, Tf, K 1, Tf, K 5.

13th Round.—Tf, K 1, Tf and K 2 + 7 times, Tf, K 1, Tf, K 2 +, Tf, K 5.

15th Round.—Tf, K 1, Tf and K 2 + 11 times, K 3.

17th Round.—Tf, K 1, Tf and K 2 + 12 times, K 2.

19th Round.—Tf, K 1, Tf and K 2 + 13 times, K 1.

21st Round.—K 1, Tf and K 2 + 6 times, Tf, K 2, Tf and K 2 + 7 times.

23rd Round.—Tf and K 2 + 7 times, Tf, K 3, Tf and K 2 + 5 times, Tf, K 3 +.

25th Round.—Tf, K 3 +, Tf and K 2 + 6 times, Tf, K 4, Tf and K 2 + 5 times, Tf, K 1.

27th Round.—The same, only knitting 5 instead of 4.

29th Round.—The same, only knitting 6 instead of 4.

31st Round.—The same, only knit 7.

33rd Round.—The same, only knit 8.

35th Round.—The same, only knit 9.

37th Round.—Tf, K 3 +, Tf and K 2 + 6 times, Tf, K 4, Tf, K 6, Tf and K 2 + 4 times, Tf, K 3 +.

39th Round.—Tf, K 3 +, Tf and K 2 + 6 times, Tf, K 4, Tf, K 1, Tf, K 7, Tf and K 2 + 3 times, Tf, K 3 +.

41st Round.—Tf, K 3 +, Tf and K 2 + 6 times, Tf, K 6, Tf, K 9, Tf, K 2 +, Tf, K 2 +, Tf, K 3 +.

43rd Round.—Tf, K 3 +, Tf and K 2 + 6 times, Tf, K 9, Tf, K 8, Tf, K 2 +, Tf, K 3 +.

45th Round.—Tf, K 3 +, Tf and K 2 + 6 times, Tf, K 9, Tf, K 1, Tf, K 9, Tf, K 3 +.

47th Round.—Tf, K 3 +, Tf and K 2 + 6 times, Tf, K 9, Tf, K 1, Tf, K 2 +, Tf, K 9, K 2 +.

49th Round.—K 2 +, Tf, K 3 +, Tf and K 2 + 5 times, Tf, K 11, Tf, K 1, Tf, K 12.

51st Round.—K 3, Tf, K 3 +, Tf and K 2 + 4 times, Tf, K 13, Tf, K 13.

53rd Round.—K 5, Tf, K 3 +, Tf and K 2 + 3 times, Tf, K 17, Tf, K 10.

55th Round.—K 7, Tf, K 3 +, Tf, K 2 +, Tf, K 2 +, Tf, K 17, Tf, K 1, Tf, K 10.

Knitted Table-Cover, or Cover for Sofa Pillow.   By Mrs. Warren.

57th Round.—K 9, Tf, K 3 +, Tf, K 2 +, Tf, K 17, Tf, K 1, Tf, K 2 +, Tf, K 10.

59th Round.—K 11, Tf, K 3 +, Tf, K 17, Tf, K 1, Tf, 2 +, Tf, K 2 +, Tf, K 10.

61st Row.—K 14, Tf, K 18, Tf and K 2 + 3 times, K 10.

63rd Round.—K 15, Tf, K 19, Tf, K 2 +, Tf, K 2 +, K 11.

65th Round.—K 16, Tf, K 20, Tf, K 2 +, K 12.

67th Round.—K 17, Tf, K 27, Tf, K 2 +, K 5.

69th Round.—K 18, Tf, K 25, K 2 +, Tf, K 1, Tf, K 2 +, K 4.

71st Round.—K 19, Tf, K 24, K 2 +, Tf, K 1, Tf, K 2 +, Tf, K 2 +, K 3.

73rd Round.—K 20, Tf, K 23, K 2 +, Tf, K 1, Tf and K 2 +, 3 times, K 2.

75th Round.—K 21, Tf, K 22, K 2 +, Tf, K 1, Tf and K 2 + 4 times, K 1.

77th Round.—K 22, Tf, K 24, Tf and K 2 +, 4 times, K 2.

79th Round.—K 23, Tf, K 25, Tf and K 2 +, 3 times, K 3.

81st Round.—K 24, Tf, K 28, Tf, K 2 +, K 4.

Cast off rather loosely.

For the Border.

Cast on 8 stitches on one needle.

1st Round.—K 2, Tf and K 2 **+ 3** times.

2nd Round.—K 2, P 1, *repeat to the end,* and K the two last stitches.

3rd Round.—K 2, * Tf and K 2 +, *repeat from *.

4th and *5th Rounds.*—Plain.

6th Round.—Cast off all but eight stitches.

Knit one point in each of six shades, and sew the Border on easily.

Mohair Cap, for morning wear. By Mrs. Warren.

MOHAIR CAP, FOR MORNING WEAR.

Two skeins of Hair-brown Mohair. No. 1 Penelope Hook.

MAKE 21 loose chain stitches; turn back, and work 4 chain, Dc into every 3rd loop: each row must be worked very loosely. Now continue working this backwards and forwards till there are 34 rows, but decreasing 1 chain of four at the *beginning of every row*. This forms half the cap. Fasten off, and begin on the other side of the 21 chain, and work the other half.

Now make 7 or eight yards of loose chain, which forms a chain gimp; sew this with the same mohair all round the cap. Now, round this edge make 5 chain, Dc *under* every alternate loop; making round the ears, 7 chain.

Form the remainder of this chain gimp into two rosettes, and then work thus:—

Dc into a loop, 5 chain, Dc into next loop, till the rosette is finished. Or rosettes of very narrow brown satin ribbon are preferable.

A SPARE DIET.

DR. TROHCHIN, physician to a former Duke of Orleans, was celebrated for having studied the influence of the moral upon the physical man, the necessity of managing the strength, of proportioning the resources to the means, and the advantage of combating the principle of the disease, by removing out of the way whatever might contribute to cherish and irritate it. Spare diet was almost always one of the first of his prescriptions. "'Tis the best way," he said, " to cut off the enemy's provisions: that is already a great point gained."

Watch Pocket.—By Mrs. Warren.

DOUBLE-PRIMROSE MAT.

Three shades of Violet—three skeins of the darkest, and six skeins of the other two shades; and two skeins of dark Green—4-thread wool. Half an ounce of two shades of Green-spangled wool. Nos. 1 and 2 Penelope hooks; one quarter of a yard of black velvet; a piece of stout cardboard measuring seven inches every way.

For the Primroses.

Darkest violet. With No. 2 hook make 7 chain, unite (*this forms a small circle*); make 3 chain, and then *under* this circle work 18 L without any chains between; fasten off into the 3rd loop of the 3 chain.

There will now be the appearance of 19 L. Each shade must be worked separately.

2ndly.—Next shade: 7 chain, unite, 7 chain, Dc *under* the circle for 5 times (*in all*, 5 *chains of* 7); then Dc *under* 1st 7 chain, * 7 L *under* same, Dc *under* same, Dc *under* next 7; *repeat* from *.

3rdly.—Lightest shade: 9 chain, unite; work same as last, only making 6 chains of 8 instead of 5 chains of 7.

Now, with darkest shade, sew these separate pieces together in the centre, having the lightest shade outside. Make 7 pieces of each shade, which will form 21 Flowers.

Double-Primrose Mat.—By Mrs. Warren.

For the Leaves.

For Veins : use darkest green wool, and No. 1 hook ; make 11 chain, turn back, work 10 Dc down, 13 chain, turn back, work 12 Dc down, Dc into last Dc stitch of 1st vein, 15 chain, turn back, work 14 Dc down, Dc into last Dc stitch of last vein ; 13 chain, turn back, work 12 Dc down, Dc into last Dc stitch of last vein ; 11 chain, turn back, work 10 Dc down ; Dc into last Dc stitch of *first vein.* Join on the darkest spangled wool, and turn round on the finger.

With No. 2 *hook* make 3 chain, Dc into 2nd loop ; *repeat* this up the side of the vein, and at the *point* Dc into top loop, 3 chain, Dc into same loop ; then 3 chain, Dc into every 2nd loop till within 2 chain of the bottom, *miss these* 2 *chains,* and Dc into 3rd loop of next vein, without making any chains between. Work over all the other veins in the same manner ; and when at the termination where the stem of the leaf should be, Dc into the centre of all the veins ; then 3 chain, Dc *under* every 3 chain up the side of the veins, as before,

but without working the extra 3 chain at the top of the point ; then work down the side of the vein till within one chain of 3 at the bottom ; *omit this,* and, without making any chains between, Dc *under* 2nd chain of 3 on next vein. *Repeat* the same over all the veins ; then, when this row is completed, *after the last Dc stitch,* Dc on Dc in centre of all the veins, and Dc *under* next 3 chain : thus there will be 3 Dc stitches successively, without chains between.

Join on next shade, and work another row precisely the same, only making 5 chain over each point.

Seven of these leaves will be required. Each leaf, if not worked smoothly, may be damped, and pressed under a heavy weight.

Sew the flowers on to the leaves with the darkest violet. Then, having first prepared a round foundation of cardboard, seven inches in diameter, with the velvet gummed on the cardboard, sew these leaves round the Mat ; afterwards gum on the back a round piece of paper or black cambric— the latter is best.

WATCH POCKET.

Five needles, No. 15; Evans's Boar's Head Cotton, No. 14.

CAST on 3 stitches on the 1st needle, 2 on the 2nd, 3 on the 3rd, and 4 on the 4th. Bring the thread forward at the *beginning* of the first and 3rd needles, and at the *beginning* and in the middle of the 2nd and 4th needles. Then knit one plain round.

Repeat these two rounds till there are 22 stitches on the 1st and 3rd, and 40 stitches on the 2nd and 4th; then—

1st Round.—Tf, K 3, Tf, K 3, * Tf, K 2 +, K 2, *repeat* from * to the end of the 2nd needle; then begin as at the commencement of the round, and *repeat* again from * till the end of the 4th needle.

2nd Round.—Plain.

3rd Round.—Tf, K 1, Tf, K 3 +, *repeat* all round.

4th Round.—Plain.

5th Round.—K 1, Tf, K 2 +, K 1.

Knit 3 plain rounds, and cast off.

Knit 2 rounds thus; fold one in half, and sew it to the other round where the row of four holes comes.

For the Edging.

Cast on 5 stitches.

1st Round.—K 1, Tf, K 2 +, K 1, Tf, K 1.

2nd Round.—K 1, Tf, K 5.

3rd Round.—K 1, Tf, K 2 +, K 3, Tf, K 1.

4th Round.—K 1, Tf, K 7.

5th Round.—K 1, Tf, K 2 +, K 5, Tf, K 1.

6th Round.—K 1, Tf, K 9.

7th Round.—K 1, Tf, K 2 +, K 4, K 2 +, Tf, K 2 +.

8th Round.—K 2 +, Tf, K 2 +, K 6.

9th Round.—K 1, Tf, K 2 +, K 2, K 2 +, Tf, K 2 +.

10th Round.—K 2 +, Tf, K 2 +, K 4.

11th Round.—K 1, Tf, K 2 +, K 2 +, Tf, K 2 +.

12th Round.—K 2 +, Tf, K 2 +, K 2.

Sew the Edging round the outside circle, and round the upper half of the circle in front, which forms the Pocket.

Make two tassels, and sew on each side; and trim with ribbon. Cover a piece of whalebone the size of the diameter of the round, and sew it across the centre of the back; boring a hole at each end with a large needle, and fastening the ends of the bone securely.

D'OYLEY.

No. 16 Evans's Boar's Head Cotton. No. 4 Penelope Hook.

1st Round.—13 chain, unite, * 9 chain, Dc *under* this circle, *repeat* from * 7 times more, (in all 8 chains of 9), tie in a knot at the back, and cut off the cotton, which must be done at every row.

2nd Round.—7 L *under* the 9 chain, 5 chain, *repeat*.

3rd Round.—Dc *under* the 5 chain, 5 chain, Dc *under* same, 7 chain, *repeat*.

4th Round.—Dc into centre loop of the 5 chain, 13 chain, * turn back, Dc into 9th loop from hook (this forms a circle), 1 chain, turn round on the finger, Dc *under* the circle, work 5 L, 3 Dble L, 1 chain, 3 Dble L, 5 L, Dc *under* same, 13 chain, *repeat* from * again ; then make 11 chain, and *repeat* from 1st * again ; then 2 Dc down the stem, Dc into the circle of 2nd Berry, make 10 chain, *repeat* from 1st * again, Dc into the circle again, and Dc down the stem and into the circle of 1st Berry, then make 10 chain and repeat as last Berry, Dc down the stem and under the 5 chain, where the Spray was commenced ; 9 Dc *under* the 7 chain, 1 chain, and to make the 2nd Spray of Berries *repeat* from beginning again ; only after the 3 Dble L in the 1st Berry make 3 chain instead of 1 chain, and Dc into the 1 chain of last Berry of the last Spray ; then 3 Dc *under* the 3 chain, then finish the Berry the same as in 1st Spray. For 2nd Berry *repeat* as before, only after the 3 Dble L make 7 chain instead of 1 chain, and Dc into the 1 chain of next Berry in last Spray ; now finish the other Berries also as in last Spray.

5th Round.—Dc into the 1 chain on the top of the Berry at a point, 9 chain, 1 L on 1st of the 3 Dble L on next Berry, 9 chain, 1 L into 5th Dc of the 9 Dc, 9 chain, 1 L on last of the 3 Dble L in next Berry, 9 chain, *repeat* from *.

6th Round.—Dc on the Dc at the point of the Berry *, 9 chain, 1 L on L, *repeat* from * twice more, 9 chain, *repeat* from beginning.

7th Round.—The same as last round, only making 10 chain instead of 9.

8th Round.—10 Dc *under* every 10 chain.

9th Round.—Begin on a Dc stitch over a L stitch, make 27 chain, (turn back) 1 L

D'oyley. By Mrs. Warren.

into the 7th loop, 2 chain, 1 L into 3rd loop, 2 chain, 1 Dble L into 3rd loop of 2 chain, 1 Dble L into 3rd loop, 2 chain, 1 Dble L into 3rd loop, 2 chain, 1 L into 3rd loop, 2 chain, 1 L into 3rd loop, 2 chain, Dc into last loop, 1 chain, turn round on the finger, Dc under the 1st 2 chain, 3 L *under* same, 3 L *under* next 2, and 3 L *under* next 2; now 3 Dble L *under* each of the 3 next compartments, 3 L *under* next compartment, 5 L *under* the chain at the point, 3 chain, 5 more L *under* same; now work down the side of the leaf the same as just completed after the last 3 L, make a Dc *under* the same, 2 chain, then 10 Dc

over the Dc till the next L stitch or Dc stitch over the point of the Berry, make 27 chain and *repeat* another leaf, (but after the 1st 3 Dble L, unite with 6th Dble L of the leaf last made.)

THE BALMORAL NECK TIE, IN CHIN-CHILLA COLOURS.

No. 6 Knitting Pins; Chinchilla Colour and White or Black 4-thread Berlin Wool, 6 skeins of the darkest shade, 5 of the second shade, 3 of the third, and 7 white.

Cast on 100 stitches in the darkest shade, and knit and pearl alternately 9 rows, then join on the white and knit and pearl alter-

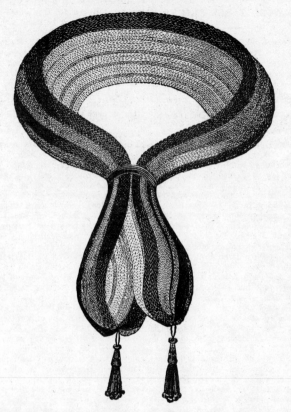

The Balmoral Neck Tie, in Chinchilla Colours. By Mrs. Warren.

nately **7** rows, join on the next shade and work the same; then the white, then the lightest shade; then white, then the next darkest shade; then white, and lastly, the darkest shade, and cast off; dress up the beads and finish with tassels, and secure it at the neck with a scarf ring. The wrong or plain side of the coloured stripes is the right side of the tie.

———

HOPE is the most beneficial of all the affections; and doth much to the prolong-ation of life, if it be not too often frustrated; but entertaineth the fancy with an expectation of good; therefore they which fix, and propound to themselves some end as the mark and scope of their life, and continually, and by degrees go forward in the same, are for the most part long-lived: insomuch, that when they are come to the top of their hope, and can go no higher therein, they commonly droop, and live not long after. So that *hope is a leaf-joy, which may be beaten out to a great extent, like gold.—Lord Bacon.*

THE WORK-TABLE FRIEND.

FLOWER VASE MAT—SWEET-PEA PATTERN.

(Designed by Mrs. Warren.)

3 Shades of Amber, the lightest to be a bright Yellow, 4 skeins of each shade; 3 shades of bright Green, 2 skeins of each; 2 skeins of White, 3 of bright Pink, 1 skein of shaded Green, 1 of shaded Pink—all 4 thread Berlin Wool. 1 Reel of No. 10 Evans's Drab Boar's Head Cotton. 4 Yards of White Skirt Cord, the size of White Blind Cord. Nos. 1 and 2 Penelope Hooks.

1st Row.—With Drab Cotton, and No. 2 Hook, work over the Cord in Dc, 3 rounds, working 2 stitches into every loop; then one row of shaded Green, and one row of Cotton for twice more; then one row of shaded Pink, then 7 rows of shaded Green; making in all 15 rows of Cord, encreasing as may be required. Cut off the Cord, and fasten neatly; then with same Wool make 5 chain, Dc into every 4th loop. (*This forms first row of Border.*)

2nd Row.—With Drab Cotton. *Under* the 5 chain work 4 long, with 5 chain between each, 5 chain, *repeat* all round.

Now 3 rows thus:—1 Long *under* a 5 chain, 5 chain, *repeat.* There will be 4 rows of Cotton.

6th Row.—Darkest Amber. With No. 1 Hook work loosely 2 stitches *under* every 5 chain, the same precisely as directed for the Edge of the Sweet-Pea; keep the right side of the Mat in front, double this edge down towards the wrong side of Mat, and work between every long stitch, 1 stitch the same as last row. (*There will be a row of long stitches in front, and a row at the back; therefore the number of stitches will be exactly the same as 1st row.*) Lastly, double this row down again, take the next shade and work the same. There will be three rows of this raised border or stitch upon the surface of the Cotton rows. Now divide this as equally as may be into 11 divisions. Pin the point of each division on to the Pink row of Cord, pulling the edge out round and well, and sewing the two dark amber edges together.

For the Sweet-Peas.

These flowers, with the exception of Edge, must be worked very tight.

Centre of Pea.—With White make 11 chain, unite; *under* this circle work 20 long, with 1 chain between each; unite, draw the wool to the back, and tie neatly.

Next Petal.—Pink. 11 Chain, unite; *under* this circle work 20 double long, with 1 chain between each; unite, and fasten the Wool. With shaded Pink, and No. 1 Hook, work the Edge thus:—

Put the Hook *under* the chain between the long stitches, draw the Wool through, and then through the loop on the Hook; then twist the Wool over the Hook, and draw it through the loop on the Hook. (*This forms 1 stitch.*) Work 1 stitch *under* every 1 chain. This must be worked loosely, but not so loosely as the Edge of the Mat.

Outside Petal.—With White, the same as last; then make an additional row thus:—After the double long stitches, with Pink work 2 long *under* every 1 chain, with 1 chain between each; when nearly half-way round, work 4 Dc stitches, that is, 1 *under* every 1 chain, with 1 chain between each, then continue round as before. Then with shaded Pink, and No. 1 Hook, work as last Petal. Double all the Petals together in the shape of a half-moon, and sew them together at the place where all the joins come, sewing the point of the White centre *doubled,* down to the two Pink Petals.

For the Green Leaves, work exactly as directed for the leaves of the Hyacinth.

Sew each Flower by the part where the stem would be, on to the Pink row of Mat, and between each flute of the Border; place the Green leaves *under* the other point of the Flower, as in the Engraving; with 1 stitch sew the point of the Flower, and the two leaves, down to the Edge of Cord; then sew the points of the Leaves to the Border, and pull it well out all round.

(*All the sewing must be done with Wool the same colour as the portion to be sewed.*)

POINT-LACE COLLAR IN CROCHET.

(Designed by Mrs. Warren.)

Nos. 20, 28, or 34, Evans's Boar's Head Cotton, No. 4 Penelope Hook.

Each spray is worked tightly, without cutting off the cotton till it is finished.

1st Flower.—Make 16 chain, turn back, work 5 Dc down this chain, 1 chain, (*this*

Flower Vase Mat—Sweet-Pea Pattern.   By Mrs. Warren.

chain is to cross the stem), turn on the finger, *keeping the chain always on the right side*), 5 Dc up (*this forms the foundation of calyx*), 8 chain, 1 L into same loop as last Dc, * 5 chain, 1 L into same loop, repeat from * twice more; then 8 chain, Dc into same loop, 3 chain to cross (*turn on the finger*), Dc *under* the 8 chain, 7 chain, Dc *under* same, † 3 chain, Dc *under* next 5, 7 chain, Dc *under* same, repeat from † twice more; then 3 chain, Dc *under* 8 chain, 7 chain, Dc *under* same, Dc down the calyx, Dc through the loop that crossed, and through the stem, with the same stitch; 1 chain to cross, Dc up the calyx, 3 chain, ‡ 7 L *under* the 7 chain, 1 chain, Dc *under* 3 chain, 1 chain, repeat from ‡ over the flower, making 3 chain instead of 1 the last time; Dc down the Calyx, Dc through the chain that crossed, and through the stem, with the same stitch (*this last stitch must be done always at the termination of every flower and leaf, whether directed or not, whenever the calyx of flower is to be worked down*); Dc down the stem.

1st Leaf.—22 Chain, turn back, 1 L into 5th loop from hook; then 3 chain, I L into 4th loop for 3 times, then 3 chain, Dc into 4th loop (*this forms the vein of leaf*), 1 chain to cross, turn on the finger, * 5 chain, Dc on L stitch, repeat from * 3 times more, 5 chain, Dc *under* 5 chain at point of leaf, 7 chain, Dc *under* same, and work down the side of the leaf the same; at the end make 1 chain to cross (*turn on the finger*) Dc *under* the 5 chain, 5 L *under* same, Dc *under* same; work this round the leaf, making 7 L *under* the 7 chain at point of leaf, but joining at 3rd L of 3rd compartment of leaf, into the 3rd L from calyx of last compartment of flower, make 18 chain instead of 16.

2nd Flower.—Repeat as at 1st flower, but joining at the outside row the 1st L into 3rd L of last compartment but one of 1st leaf; and at the 6th L of same compartment of flower, into the 3rd compartment from point of last leaf; then finish the flower, working 6 Dc down the stem.

2nd Leaf.—Make 27 chain, and work as at 1st leaf, only there will be 27 chain; but join at 3rd L of 2nd compartment of leaf, into 3rd L from calyx of last compartment of flower.

3rd Leaf.—Make 26 chain, and work another leaf, but in the outside row make

I

Point-Lace Collar in Crochet.   By Mrs. Warren.

1 chain to cross, Dc *under* 5, 3 L *under* same, join into 3rd L of 1st compartment of last leaf; 2 more L *under* same 5, Dc *under* same, Dc *under* next 5, 3 L *under* same, crochet into 3rd L of next compartment of last leaf.

3rd Flower.—12 Chain; and make another flower, joining at 3rd L of outside of flower, into the third L of compartment of leaf nearest the point of last finished leaf; finish the flower, Dc down the calyx and stem to the leaf that was left unfinished, and continue working the same as the other leaves; only, in the 3rd L of the compartment of leaf which is nearest to the point of leaf, join into 3rd L of last compartment of last flower; then finish the leaf, 6 chain, Dc into the termination of the stem of 2nd flower, 9 chain, Dc into the termination of calyx of 1st flower, and proceed to 4th flower.

4th Flower.—16 Chain, and make as the others, only joining at 4th L of outside row of flower, into the 3rd L of last compartment of last leaf, and at 3rd L of next compartment of flower; join into 3rd L of 3rd compartment of last leaf. (*In the last spray of all, at this place finish the flower; and, at the last of the 7 L, join into the 4th L of 1st flower.*) At the 4th L of 4th compartment of this flower, make 12 chain, and make a

5th Flower, joining at 1st L, into 4th L of 3rd compartment of last flower; and at 6th L of same compartment of flower, into 3rd L of 2nd compartment of leaf from the point; and at 3rd L of 2nd compartment of flower, into 3rd L of compartment of leaf nearest, the point; finish the flower, crochet down the calyx, and 4 Dc down the stem; then finish the 4th flower, crochet down the

calyx, and 4 Dc down the stem; join into 4th L of 1st compartment of 1st flower.

In the last spray of all, omit the 5th and 6th flowers.

6th Flower.—12 Chain; and make another flower, joining at 1st L of outside row, into 3rd L of last compartment of 4th flower; and in the last compartment of this flower, at the last of the 7 L, crochet into 4th L of 2nd compartment of 1st flower; fasten off without working down the stem; this completes one spray. Fasten the ends securely and neatly, and proceed to join the sprays together.

2nd Spray.—Make 16 chain; and work another flower as at 1st flower, then make another leaf as at 1st leaf, as far as the 3rd L stitch of 3rd compartment of outside row; then join into 3rd L of last compartment of the flower just made; continue the leaf till the 3rd L in 1st compartment after the point, then join into 4th L of 3rd compartment of 6th flower in last spray; now finish the leaf.

2nd Flower.—18 Chain; make another flower as in last spray, but in the outside row, at the 1st L of 1st compartment of flower, join into 3rd L of 2nd compartment of last leaf from the stem; and in 6th L of same compartment, join into 3rd L of next compartment of leaf; and at 4th L of next compartment of flower, join into 4th L of 2nd compartment of 6th flower in last spray; and at 4th L of next compartment, join into the termination of the stem of 5th flower; and at 4th L of next compartment, join into last L of last compartment of 5th flower; finish the flower, working 6 Dc down the stem. Make 27 chain; and make another leaf:—

I

2nd Leaf.—Work the same as 2nd leaf in last spray, joining at 3rd L of 2nd compartment, into 3rd L of last compartment of last flower; and at 3rd L of 4th compartment of leaf, join into 4th L of 4th compartment of 5th flower of last spray; now finish the leaf, and turn to the directions for 3rd leaf; and finish the spray according to the instructions given for the **1st spray.**

To join the leaves or flowers by uniting the stitches together, do thus:—Withdraw the hook from the loop, insert it in the loop of the flower or leaf already worked, and draw the loop from whence the hook was withdrawn through this loop, pulling the cotton tightly, and then continue working.

If No. 20 cotton is used, 7 sprays will be required; if No. 28, 8 sprays; if No. 34, 9 sprays.

Now take the straight side of the Collar, the right side in front; 1 L into the point of 2nd compartment of 1st flower, * 5 chain, Dc into next point, 5 chain, Dc into next point, 5 chain, 1 L where the flower and leaf are joined, 5 chain, Dc into next point of L, 5 chain, Dc into next point, 5 chain, Dc into next point, 5 chain, 1 L into next point of flower (*but not where the leaf and flower are joined*), 5 chain, 1 L into next half point of flower immediately before the place where the two flowers are joined together, 5 chain, 1 L into next half point immediately after where the two are joined, 5 chain, repeat from * ; continue this till the point of leaf at the extreme end of the Collar.

The following rows, all but the last, must be worked very tightly. Turn back, 7 chain, Dc *under* 5, * 5 chain, Dc *under* 5, repeat from * along the Collar; at the end, after the last Dc, make another 5 chain, and Dc into the long stitch at the end; this is to prevent losing a 5 chain.

Turn back, work another row the same, but not work into the additional 5 chain.

Turn back, work the same.

Now 4 Dc *under* every 5 chain, worked moderately tight. Fasten the ends in securely. In washing this Collar it should not be stiffened, but washed and made slightly blue, then rolled in linen for an hour; afterwards pulled out, and laid between dry linen, and then put under a heavy weight.

PEN-WIPER.

This Pen-wiper is a round of cloth, the braiding pattern of which is worked in beads, edged with gold thread; claret, green, or violet cloth, with black beads, looks well. The fringe is knitted thus:—Thread black beads on silk of the same colour, and use two fine knitting needles. Cast on 7 stitches, and do 1 plain row.

1st.—Slip 1, make 1, slip 5 beads up the silk, knit 2 together, make 1, slip 6 up, knit 2 together, make 1, slip 7 up, knit 2 together.

2nd.—Slip 1, + make 1, knit 2 together, + 3 times.

Repeat these two rows alternately until enough is done to go round the cloth. The button is a most elegant little decoration, called the Alliance.

PIN-CUSHION.

This pin-cushion is in patchwork, made of velvet, silk, and satin, in as many bright and varied colours as possible. The principal pieces, of which there are twelve, are pentagons, or **five-sided figures.**

THE WORK-TABLE FRIEND.

PALM-LEAF EDGING, WORKED THE SHORT WAY.

(Designed by Mrs. Warren.)

IF this Edge is required instead of Fringe, for Bed Furniture, use No. 2 or 4 Evans's Boar's Head Cotton; if for Border of Toilette Covers or Bread Cloths, use No. 10, and No. 3 Penelope Hook; if required for trimming Children's Drawers, &c., use No. 20 Evans's Boar's Head Cotton, with No. 4 Penelope Hook.

9 Chain, Dc into 1st loop, * 9 chain, withdraw the hook from the loop, insert it into the 4th loop from the Dc stitch just made, and draw the loop from whence the hook was withdrawn tightly through (this forms a single crochet or plain stitch); 9 chain, Dc into 4th loop from last Dc stitch just worked, repeat from *; when this has been done 6 times, it will then have the appearance of 3 chains of 5 along the edge; now 11 chain (make these 11 only, rather loose), Dc on 1st Dc stitch on the edge, 5 chain, Dc on next Dc stitch, † 11 chain, 1 plain into 1st loop of the 1st 11 chain, 11 Dc under the 2nd 11 chain, repeat into next loop from †, and into every loop of the 1st 11 chain, repeating twice into the 6th loop, which forms the point of the Edge; therefore there will be 12 of these Dc leaves in every 1st 11 chain; 6 chain, 1 plain into last Dc stitch of the Edge, close by the 11 Dc, 9 chain, 1 plain into 4th loop from last Dc stitch, 9 chain, Dc into 4th loop from last Dc, Dc into the loop of the 5 chain nearest the last of the 11 Dc stitches, 9 chain, 1 plain into 4th loop from last Dc stitch, 9 chain, Dc into 4th loop from last plain stitch, repeat this 4 times more; it must look like 3 chains of 5 from the last scallop; 11 chain, Dc on 1st Dc on the top of the Edge, 5 chain, Dc on next, 11 chain, 1 plain into 1st loop of 1st 11 chain, 11 Dc under the last 11 chain, 1 plain into last of the 11 Dc of last scallop, 11 chain, 1 plain into next loop of the 1st 11 chain, 11 Dc under the last 11 chain, 1 plain into last of the next 11 Dc of last scallop, and continue this scallop as the last.

When the Edge is required wider, as in the engraving, work along the Edge thus:—Dc on Dc, 7 chain, Dc on Dc, repeat.

Next Row.—5 Chain, Dc into centre loop of 7, repeat

FISH SERVIETTE.

THE size of this Serviette is twenty-one inches long, and seventeen inches wide: if required smaller, use No. 12 or 16 Evans's Boar's Head Cotton. For the size now given, use four reels of No. 8 Evans's Boar's Head Cotton, and No. 3 Penelope Hook.

1st Row.—Make 25 chain, turn back, 1 L into 1st loop, * 2 chain, miss 2 loops, 1 L into 3rd loop, repeat from * till the end, where join, and cut off the cotton: this must be done at every row. (There should be 10 L stitches.)

2nd Row.—3 L, with 3 chain between each L, under the long stitch at the end; then * 2 chain, 1 L on L, repeat from * all round, making both ends alike.

3rd Row.—1 L into every loop, with 1 chain between each, over the end, beginning on the 1st of the 4 L at the end (there will be 13 L over the end); then 1 chain, 25 L without chains between, 1 chain, repeat.

4th Row.—1 L into every loop all round, beginning on the first of the 25 L.

5th Row.—Begin on the same place that the last row was finished (for this row only), that is, on the first of the 25 L in 3rd row; 1 L, 2 chain, 1 L into 3rd loop, 2 chain; repeat this 7 times more, in all, 8 Squares; then 1 chain, 1 L into every loop, with 1 chain between each, for 28 times: then 2 chain, and repeat all round alike, making 8 Sq; it will then appear as if there were 29 L round each end.

6th Row.—1 L on L, 2 chain, repeat all round; there will be 72 L round.

7th Row.—(There are now 8 Sq on each side, reckoning from the 5th row.) Now 7 L, the 1st on the 1st L of the 3rd Sq of the 8 Sq at the side; then 2 chain, 1 L on L, 2 chain for 33 times, then 2 chain, 7 L as before, and repeat.

8th Row.—13 L, the 1st on the 1st L previous to the 7 L in last row; now 5 Sq, * 6 L, 3 Sq, 6 L, repeat from * four times more; then 5 Sq, 12 L, 5 Sq, and repeat from the first * again.

9th Row.—7 L, the 1st on the 4th of the 13 L, † 5 Sq, 1 L into same loop as the long stitch formed by the last Sq, 12 L, 1 L into same loop as last L, * 2 chain, miss 2 loops, 15 L (the 2 first and 2 last L into the same loop), repeat from * 3 times more, 5 Sq, 6 L, repeat from †.

10th Row.—9 L, the 1st on the 5th of the 15 L, and working the 2 first and 2 last

Palm-Leaf Edging, Worked the Short way.   By Mrs. Warren.

into one loop; * 2 chain, 1 L into 2nd loop, 2 chain, 1 L into 2nd loop, 2 chain, 1 L on 1st of the 15 L, 2 chain, 1 L into 2nd loop, 2 chain, 9 L worked as before, *repeat* from * 3 times more; then 2 chain, 1 L into 2nd loop, 2 chain, 1 L on last of the 15 L, 12 Sq, 2 chain, 1 L into 2nd loop, 2 chain, *repeat* from the begining.

11th Row.—1 L, 2 chain, 1 L into every alternate loop, over every 9 L in last row; then 2 chain, 1 L on L on all the open parts all round.

12th Row.—1 L on L, 2 chain all round. *(This is a row of Squares.)*

13th Row.—7 L immediately over the 7 L at the side in the 9th row, 6 Sq, 1 L into same loop as the last L of the last Sq, * 5 chain, miss 5 loops, 2 L into 6th loop, 2 chain, 1 L on L, 2 chain, 2 L on next L, *repeat* from * 10 times more (*the last time will terminate with 5 chain, 2 L into 6th loop*); then 6 Sq, 6 L, 6 Sq, 1 L into same loop as last Sq; now *repeat* from the first *.

14th Row.—13 L, the 1st on the 1st L before the 7 L in last row, 5 Sq; now work over the end exactly the same as last row; then 5 Sq, 12 L, 5 Sq, *repeat*.

15th Row.—7 L, the 1st on the 4th of the 15 L, 6 Sq, 2 L into next loop, * 5 chain, 2 L on next L, 1 L into next loop, 2 chain, 1 L on L, 2 chain, 1 L on next L, 2 L into next loop, *repeat* from * 10 times more (*the last time will end with 5 chain, 2 L on next L, 1 L into next loop*); 6 Sq, 6 L, 6 Sq, *repeat* from the first *.

16th Row.—14 Sq, beginning on the last of the last 3 L, 2 L on L, * 5 chain, 3 L on the 3 L, 1 L on L, 2 chain, 3 L on L, *repeat* from * 10 times more (*the last time*

will end with 3 L); then *repeat* from the beginning.

17th Row.—14 Sq over the Squares, 1 L into next loop, 2 L into next loop, * 5 chain, 2 L on next L, 2 L into successive loops, 2 chain, 1 L on L, 2 chain, 2 L on next 2 L, 2 L into next loop, *repeat* from * as before, then repeat from beginning.

18th Row.—14 Sq as before, 3 L over the L, * 5 chain, 4 L on the L, 2 chain, 1 L on L, 2 chain, 4 L over the L, *repeat* from * ; make both sides alike.

19th Row.—7 L on the 7 L in 15th row, * 6 Sq, then *repeat* over the end the same as last row; then 6 Sq, 6 L, and *repeat* from *.

20th Row.—13 L, beginning on the 1st L before the 7 L, † 5 Sq, 4 L over the L, 5 chain, * 2 L into next loop, 3 L into successive loops, 2 chain, 1 L on L, 2 chain, 3 L on L, 2 L into next loop, 5 chain, *repeat* from †, ending with 5 chain, 4 L over the four L, 5 Sq, 12 L, *repeat* from *.

21st Row.—4 L on the last 4 L, 6 Sq, 6 L, 6 Sq, 4 L on L, 5 chain; now work the same as in last row, only making 6 L instead of 5, always working the encreased stitch into the loop nearest the 5 chain, *repeat* round the end, then *repeat* from the beginning.

22nd Row.—14 Sq, beginning on the last of the 4 L, 4 L on L, 5 chain; now the same as last row, only making 7 L instead of 6.

23rd Row.—14 Sq, over the Sq, 4 L over the L, 1 L into same loop as last (*therefore there are 5 L on the 4 L*); then 5 chain, and work the same as last row, only making 8 L instead of 7.

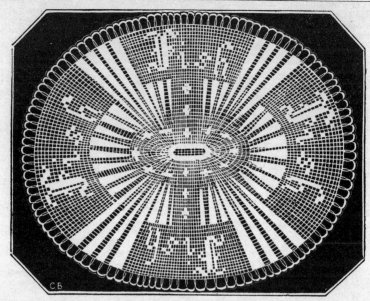

Fish Serviette. By Mrs. Warren.

24th Row.—(*Great care must be taken with this row, as the omission of one loop, or the addition of a stitch, would destroy the pattern.*) 14 Sq over the Sq, 2 chain, 1 L into every alternate loop, with 2 chain between each, for 15 times, * 5 chain, 9 L on the 8 L, 5 chain, 9 L, *repeat* from * again; then 5 chain, 1 L into every alternate loop, with 2 chain between each, for 50 times; then *repeat* from the first * twice; then 5 chain, 1 L into every alternate loop, with 2 chain between each, 16 times; then 14 Sq over the Sq. (*There must be 44 spaces on each side, formed by the 1 L, 2 chain; and 49 over each end.*)

25th Row.—Commence at the side, on the 1st L of the 44 spaces, 4 Sq, 3 L, 3 Sq, 3 L, 35 Sq, * 5 chain, 9 L on the 9 L, 5 chain, 9 L, *repeat* from * again; then 5 chain, 7 Sq, 3 L, 3 Sq, 3 L, 37 Sq; *repeat* from the first * twice; then 5 chain, and *repeat* from the beginning.

26th Row.—(*Begin every row on the side, but not on the same side every time.*) 5 Sq, 3 L, 2 Sq, 6 L, 34 Sq, * 5 ch, 9 L over

the 9 L, 5 chain, 9 L, *repeat* from * again, 5 chain, 8 Sq, 3 L, 2 Sq, 6 L, 36 Sq, 5 chain, *repeat* from the first * twice, then 5 chain, and *repeat* from beginning.

27th Row.—5 Sq, 3 L, 3 Sq, 3 L, 5 Sq, 6 L, 5 Sq, 6 L, 7 Sq, 12 L, 3 Sq, 3 L, 5 Sq, * 5 chain, *repeat* over the stripes as in last row, then 5 chain, 8 Sq, and *repeat* from * to *, only at both ends of the Serviette make 7 Sq instead of 5 the last time, then 5 chain, *repeat* over the stripes, then 5 chain, and *repeat* from beginning.

28th Row.—5 Sq, * 3 L, 3 Sq, 3 L, 4 Sq, 3 L, 2 Sq, 6 L, 2 Sq, 3 L, 1 Sq, 3 L, 6 Sq, 6 L, 2 Sq, 6 L, 2 Sq, 3 L, * 5 Sq, 5 chain, *repeat* over the stripes in last row, then 5 chain, 8 Sq, *repea* from * to *, 7 Sq, 5 chain, work over the stripes, then 5 chain, *repeat* from beginning.

29th Row.—5 Sq, * 3 L, 2 Sq, 6, 1. 5 Sq, 3 L, 7 Sq, 3 L, 6 Sq, 6 L, 1 Sq, 3 L, 1 Sq, 9 L, * 6 Sq, 5 chain, work over the stripes as before, 5 chain, 8 Sq, *repeat* from * to *, 8 Sq, 5 chain, work over the stripes 5 chain, *repeat* from beginning.

30th Row.—6 Sq, * 6 L, 1 Sq, 3 L, 2 Sq, 6 L, 2 Sq, 3 L, 6 Sq, 3 L, 1 Sq, 3 L, 4 Sq, 6 L, 1 Sq, 3 L, * 10 Sq, 5 chain, work over the stripes as before, 5 chain, 9 Sq, *repeat* from * to *, 12 Sq, 5 chain, work over the stripes, 5 chain, and *repeat* from the beginning.

31st Row.—9 Sq, * 3 L, 4 Sq, 6 L, 7 Sq, 6 L, 3 Sq, 3 L, 1 Sq, 6 L, 1 Sq, 3 L, * 10 Sq, 5 chain, work over the stripes, 5 chain, 12 Sq, *repeat* from * to *, 12 Sq, 5 chain, work over the stripes as before, 5 chain, *repeat* from beginning.

32nd Row.—9 Sq, * 3 L, 17 Sq, 3 L, 2 Sq, 6 L, 1 Sq, 3 L, 1 Sq, 3 L, * 8 Sq, 5 chain, work over the stripes as before, 5 chain, 12 Sq, *repeat* from * to *, 10 Sq, 5 chain, work over the stripes, 5 chain, *repeat* from the beginning.

33rd Row.—9 Sq, * 3 L, 18 Sq, 12 L, 1 Sq, 6 L, * 9 Sq, 5 chain, work over the stripes as before, 5 chain, 12 Sq, *repeat* from * to * again, 11 Sq, 5 chain, work over the stripes, 5 chain, and *repeat* from the beginning.

34th Row.—5 Sq, * 6 L, 1 Sq, 3 L, 14 Sq, 3 L, 6 Sq, 6 L, 1 Sq, 3 L, * 10 Sq, 5 chain, work over the stripes as before, 5 chain, 8 Sq, *repeat* from * to * again, 12 Sq, 5 chain, work over the stripes, 5 chain, *repeat* from the beginning.

35th Row.—6 Sq, * 6 L, 22 Sq, 6 L, 1 Sq, 3 L, * 10 Sq, 5 chain, work over the stripes as before, 5 chain, 9 Sq, *repeat* from * to * again, 12 Sq, 5 chain, work over the stripes as before, 5 chain, *repeat* from the beginning.

36th Row.—26 Sq, * 6 L, 2 Sq, 6 L, 1 Sq, 3 L, * 10 Sq, 5 chain, work 11 L over each 9 L in the stripes, thus: 4 L into successive loops, 3 L into next loop, 4 L into successive loops, still working the 5 chain between each stripe; after the last stripe, 5 chain, 29 Sq, *repeat* from * to *, then 12 Sq, work over the stripes as before, then 5 chain, *repeat* from the beginning.

37th Row.—25 Sq, * 3 L, 1 Sq, 6 L, 1 Sq, 3 L, 1 Sq, 3 L, 3 Sq, 3 L, * 7 Sq, 5 chain, 5 L on one L, 3 L into next loop, 5 L on the L, 5 chain, *repeat* this over the stripes, then 5 chain, 28 Sq, *repeat* from * to * again, then 9 Sq instead of 7, work over the stripes as before, then *repeat* from the beginning.

38th Row.—28 Sq, * 6 L, 3 Sq, 9 L, * 8 Sq, 5 chain, 6 L over the L. 3 L into next loop, then 6 L again, *repeat* this over the stripes, then 31 Sq, *repeat* from * to *, then 10 Sq instead of 8, work over the stripes as before, then *repeat* from the beginning.

39th Row.—44 Sq on the side, 5 chain, 16 L over the 15 L, that is, encreasing 1 in the centre of the 15 L; 49 Sq over the end, work over the stripes as before, and *repeat* from the beginning.

40th Row.—The same as last row, only not encreasing.

For the Border.

Begin on the side, as before, on the 1st L of the Sqs, 22 chain, Dc on 3rd L, * 5 chain, withdraw the hook from the loop, insert it into the 6th loop of the 22 chain, and draw the loop of the 5 chain through; 17 chain, miss 1 L, Dc on next, *repeat* from * till the last of the Sqs at the side, then *repeat* the same on the 1st L of the 16, then on every 5th L, then on last L, then again on the 1st L of the next 16, and continue till the 49 Sq at the end, where *repeat* the same as at the side, but in the centre of the 49 Sq, that is, after the 24 Sq, Dc into next long instead of alternate L, then continue the same as before.

2nd Row.—7 Dc on the top of each 17 chain, beginning in the 3rd loop from where the 2 chains of 17 are joined together, (if the border should be too full over the stripes), make 5 Dc instead of 7, beginning on the 4th loop from the join.

HISTORY.

It is the resurrection of ages past; it gives us the scenes of human life, that, by their actings, we may learn to correct and improve. What can be more profitable to man, than by an easy charge and a delightful entertainment, to make himself wise by the imitation of heroic virtues, or by the evitation of detested vices? where the glorious actions of the worthiest treaders on the world's stage shall become our guide and conduct, and the errors that the weak have fallen into shall be marked out to us as rocks that we ought to avoid. It is learning wisdom at the cost of others; and, which is rare, it makes a man the better for being pleased.

THE WORK-TABLE FRIEND.

CHEESE SERVIETTE, WITH LETTERS.

(Designed by Mrs. Warren.)

Six reels of No. 8 Evans's Boar's Head cotton. No. 3 Penelope hook.

1st Row.—12 chain, unite, and then 7 chain, Dc into every alternate loop; there will be 6 chains of 7. Tie securely at the back, and cut off; this must be done at every row, unless where directed to the contrary.

2nd Row.—Dc into the centre loop of the 7 chain, 7 chain, Dc into same loop, 7 chain, *repeat.*

3rd Row.—Dc into centre loop of 7 chain, 7 chain, Dc into same loop, 5 chain, *repeat.*

4th Row.—Dc into the centre loop of the 7 chain that appears short, 8 chain, Dc into centre loop of next 7 chain, 8 chain, *repeat.*

5th Row.—Dc into the centre loop of the 7 chain, 3 chain, 8 L in the 8 chain, 1 L on Dc stitch, 8 L in the 8 chain, 3 chain, *repeat.*

6th Row.—17 L over the 17 L, 4 chain, Dc on Dc stitch, 7 chain, Dc into same loop, 4 chain, repeat.

7th Row.—Same as last, only making 5 chain instead of 4.

8th Row.—Same as last, only making 6 chain instead of 5.

9th Row.—Dc into centre loop of 7, 6 chain, 19 L, the 1st in the loop before the L in last row, 6 chain, *repeat.*

10th Row.—3 Dc, the 1st in the 1st loop before the Dc stitch, 6 chain, 21 L worked as before, 6 chain, *repeat.*

11th Row.—5 Dc on the Dc, beginning in the loop before the Dc in last row, 6 chain, 23 L, 6 chain, *repeat.*

12th Row.—3 Dc, the 1st on 2nd Dc, 7 chain, 25 L worked as before, 7 chain, *repeat.*

13th Row.—1 L on 1st Dc, 4 chain, 1 L on last Dc, 6 chain, 27 L worked as before, 6 chain, *repeat.*

14th Row.—1 E, 2 chain, 1 L with 2 chain between each, into every alternate loop on the 27 L, making in all 13 Sq; 5 chain, 1 L upon L, 1 chain, 1 L into every loop, with 1 chain between each, into the next 5 loops, 5 chain, *repeat.*

Now write on 6 separate pieces of paper, about an inch square, each letter forming the word " CHEESE," and sew each letter separately, in rotation, on each thich division of the work.

Instead of cutting off the cotton at every row, the letters may now be worked thus, and if carefully done, the joining cannot be perceived:—In the 1st Sq that is directed in any row, instead of working 1 L, make 5 *chain*, 1 *L into 3rd loop*; this 5 chain is equivalent to 1 L, 2 chain. In concluding the row, after the last 2 chain, unite into the 3rd loop of the first 5 chain; this will be found to form as perfect a Sq as in any other part, the 3 chain being a substitute for the 1 L.

15th Row.—Begin on the commencement of the H division 3 Sq, 3 L, 9 Sq, * 5 chain, 1 L on L, 1 L into every loop for the remaining 10 loops, 5 chain, 13 Sq on the Sq, *repeat* from * all round.

16th Row.—Exactly the same as last row.

17th Row.—Begin on the same division —2 Sq, 3 L, 10 Sq, * 5 chain, 5 L on the L, 3 chain, miss one loop, 5 L on L, 5 chain, 13 Sq over the Sq, *repeat* from * all round. Cut off the cotton at this row, and fasten neatly.

18th Row.—Begin on the last E division of the word "CHEESE," and continue commencing at this division till all the letters are finished. 3 Sq, 18 L, 4 Sq, * 5 chain, 6 L, the 1st into the 5th loop of the 5 chain, 4 chain, 6 L, the 1st on next L, 5 chain, *. S division—3 Sq, 12 L, 4 Sq, 3 L, 1 Sq, *repeat* from * to * again; then over the 2 E divisions work 3 Sq, 18 L, 4 Sq, working between all the letters as from * to *. H division—1 Sq, 6 L, 2 Sq, 9 L, 3 Sq, 3 L, 1 Sq. C division—3 Sq, 18 L, 4 Sq, *repeat* from * to * again.

19th Row.—Division E—2 Sq, 3 L, 4 Sq, 12 L, 2 Sq, * 5 chain, 7 L, the 1st into 5th loop, 5 chain, 7 L, the 1st on next long, 5 chain, *. S division—2 Sq, 6 L, 1 Sq, 21 L, 1 Sq, *repeat* from * to * between all the letters. Work over the 2 E divisions as at 1st E. H division—1 Sq, 6 L, 1 Sq, 3 L, 1 Sq, 9 L, 2 Sq, 3 L, 1 Sq. C division—2 Sq, 3 L, 4 Sq, 12 L, 2 Sq.

20th Row.—E division—1 Sq, 3 L, 7 Sq, 6 L, 2 Sq, * 5 chain, 8 L, the 1st into 5th loop, 6 chain, 8 L, the first upon next L, 5 chain, * *repeat* from * *to* * between all the letters. S division—1 Sq, 6 L, 3

Cheese Cloth. By Mrs. Warren.

Sq, 15 L, 2 Sq. The 2 E divisions as at 1st. H division—1 Sq, 6 L, 5 Sq, 9 L, 2 Sq. C division—1 Sq, 3 L, 7 Sq, 6 L, 2 Sq.

21st Row.—E division—7 Sq, 3 L, 1 Sq, 9 L, 1 Sq, * 5 chain, 9 L, 7 chain, 9 L, 5 chain, *repeat* from * between all the letters. S division—1 Sq, 6 L, 4 Sq, 3 L, 5 Sq. Over the E division as at 1st. H division—1 Sq, 6 L, 4 Sq, 3 L, 1 Sq, 3 L, 3 Sq. C division—7 Sq, 3 L, 1 Sq, 9 L, 1 Sq.

22nd Row.—6 Sq, 6 L, 2 Sq, 6 L, 1 Sq, * 5 chain, 2 L into 5th loop, 7 L into successive loops, 2 L into next loop, 7 chain, 2 L on 2nd L, 7 L into successive loops, 2 L into next loop, 5 chain, *repeat* from * between each letter. S division—1 Sq, 3 L, 1 Sq, 21 L, 3 Sq. E divisions—6 Sq, 6 L, 2 Sq, 6 L, 1 Sq. H division—1 Sq, 6 L, 3 Sq, 6 L, 1 Sq, 3 L, 3 Sq. C division—6 Sq, 6 L, 2 Sq, 6 L, 1 Sq.

23rd Row.—2 Sq, 6 L, 2 Sq, 6 L, 2 Sq, 6 L, 1 Sq; work between each letter the

same as last row, only making 9 L instead of 7 between the increased stitches. S division—2 Sq, 3 L, 1 Sq, 21 L, 2 Sq. E divisions—2 Sq, 6 L, 2 Sq, 6 L, 2 Sq, 6 L, l Sq. H division—1 Sq, 12, L, 1 Sq, 6 L, 1 Sq, 3 L, 1 Sq, 3 L, 1 Sq. C division—6 Sq, 6 L, 2 Sq, 6 L, 1 Sq. In the last division after the 13 L, make 2 chain, 5 L, the 1st into the third loop from last long; 2 chain, and work the 13 stitches as before; this forms the stop between the first and last letters. Work it also in the two following rows:—

24th Row.—1 Sq, 3 L, 1 Sq, 6 L, 1 Sq, 6 L, 2 Sq, 6 L, 1 Sq. Work the same as last row between all the letters, only making 11 L instead of 9. S division—2 Sq, 6 L, 1 Sq, 3 L, 4 Sq, 6 L, 1 Sq. Work over the two E divisions as at 1st. H division—2 Sq, 6 L, 2 Sq, 6 L, 1 Sq, 6 L, 2 Sq. C—6 Sq, 6 L, 2 Sq, 6 L, 1 Sq.

25th Row.—4 Sq, 3 L, 1 Sq, 6 L, 2 Sq,

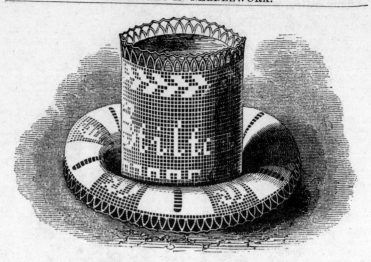

Stilton Cheese Serviette. By Mrs. Warren.

6 L, 1 Sq. Work between all the letters as before, only making 13 L instead of 11. S—3 Sq, 21 L, 1 Sq, 3 L, 1 Sq. The E divisions—4 Sq, 3 L, 1 Sq, 6 L, 2 Sq, 6 L, 1 Sq. H division—6 Sq, 6 L, 1 Sq, 3 L, 3 Sq. C—6 Sq, 6 L, 2 Sq, 6 L, 1 Sq.

26th Row.—3 Sq, 3 L, 2 Sq, 6 L, 2 Sq, 6 L, 1 Sq. Continue working as before, but increasing between all the letters. S division—4 Sq, 24 L, 1 Sq. E divisions —3 Sq, 3 L, 2 Sq, 6 L, 2 Sq, 6 L, 1 Sq. H—6 Sq, 6 L, 1 Sq, 3 L, 3 Sq. C—6 Sq, 6 L. 2 Sq, 6 L, 1 Sq.

27th Row.—2 Sq, 6 L, 2 Sq, 3 L, 3 Sq, 3 L, 2 Sq. Continue working and increasing as before between all the letters. S—2 Sq, 3 L, 7 Sq, 3 L, 2 Sq. Work over the 2 E divisions as at first. H—2 Sq, 6 L, 2 Sq, 6 L, 1 Sq, 3 L, 3 Sq. C—2 Sq, 6 L, 2 Sq, 3 L, 3 Sq, 3 L, 2 Sq.

28th Row.—1 Sq, 3 L, 1 Sq, 9 L, 3 Sq, 3 L, 3 Sq. Work and increase between all the letters as before. S—2 Sq, 6 L, 2 Sq, 6 L, 2 Sq, 3 L, 2 Sq. E divisions— 1 Sq, 3 L, 1 Sq, 9 L, 3 Sq, 3 L, 3 Sq. H—1 Sq, 3 L, 1 Sq, 6 L, 1 Sq, 3 L, 1 Sq, 3 L, 2 Sq, 3 L, 1 Sq. C—1 Sq, 3 L, 1 Sq, 9 L, 3 Sq, 3 L, 3 Sq.

29th Row.—4 Sq, 3 L, 2 Sq, 6 L, 4 Sq.

Work and increase between all the letters as before. S—2 Sq, 12 L, 1 Sq, 9 L, 3 Sq. E divisions—4 Sq, 3 L, 2 Sq, 6 L, 4 Sq. H—4 Sq, 6 L, 3 Sq, 6 L, 2 Sq. C— 4 Sq, 3 L, 2 Sq, 6 L, 4 Sq.

30th Row.—Over the letters work Sqs; then 5 chain, Dc in all the L stitches, then 4 Dc into the 4 loops of the 7 chain, another Dc into the same loop, then 3 Dc in the remaining 3 loops, then Dc over the L stitches, 5 chain, and *repeat.*

31st Row.—1 L on L, 3 chain over the letters, 1 L, 3 chain, 1 L into 3rd loop, over 5 chains and Dc stitches: there must be 216 L stitches.

For the Border.

1st Row.—Begin on the 1st L of a letter division—* 23 chain, miss 2 Sq, Dc on 3rd L, 3 more Dc, each into successive loops; *repeat* from * all round.

2nd Row.—12 Dc upon the 23 chain, 1 chain, 1 more Dc into same loop, 11 Dc down, 2 chain, *repeat.*

3rd Row.—12 Dc in the 12 Dc, 1 Dc, chain, 1 more Dc into the increased loop, 12 Dc down, * 4 Dc up the next 12 Dc, but here join into the 5 loop of the previous scallop, by withdrawing the hook from the loop, inserting it into the 5th loop, drawing the loop of the 2nd scallop through; then 9 Dc up, I Dc, 1 chain, 1 more Dc into the increased loop, 12 Dc down.

4th Row.—Dc into the increased loop at the top of the scallop, 11 chain, *repeat.*

5th Row.—6 Dc into the 1st 6 loops of the 11 chain, 1 chain, Dc into same loop, 5 Dc in the remaining loops; be careful not to work into the Dc stitches.

Pull the border well out, and when washed, lay it for some hours in linen; then pull it well out, lay it between a linen cloth, and place a heavy weight upon it. This Serviette should be placed on a soup plate, the Border will then fall over the sides.

STILTON CHEESE SERVIETTE.

Same cotton and hook.

1st Row.—Make a chain 324 stitches, unite the ends; now work a row of L stitches, 1 into every loop. The whole of this must be worked without cutting off the cotton, care being taken, as in the former Serviette, that when a L stitch or more is directed at the beginning of any row, then make 3 chain, which is equal in length to 1 L; and when Sqs are directed, make the 1st Sq as 5 chain, which is equal to 1 L, 2 chain.

2nd Row.—1 L, 2 chain, 1 L into 3rd loop.

3rd Row.—10 L, * 2 Sq, 12 L, *repeat* from *.

4th Row.—2 Sq, * 3 L, 2 Sq, *repeat* from *.

5th Row.—The same.

6th Row.—2 Sq, 12 L, *repeat.*

7th, 8th, 9th, 10th.—4 rows of Sqs.

11th Row.—9 Sq, 9 L, 3 Sq, 6 L, 3 Sq, 9 L, 2 Sq, 9 L, 1 Sq, 3 L, 3 Sq, 3 L, 3 Sq, 18 L, 13 Sq, 6 L, 1 Sq, 6 L, 4 Sq, 9 L, 2 Sq, 6 L, 3 Sq, 6 L, 3 Sq, 6 L, 4 Sq, 6 L, 4 Sq, 12, L, 4 Sq, 3 L, 7 Sq.

12th Row.—8 Sq, 3 L, 2 Sq, 3 L, 2 Sq, 3 L, 2 Sq, 3 L, 1 Sq, 3 L, 2 Sq, 3 L, 1 Sq, 3 L, 2 Sq, 3 L, 1 Sq, 3 L, 3 Sq, 3 L, 2 Sq, 3 L, 4 Sq, 12 L, 10 Sq, 3 L, 1 Sq, 3 L, 2 Sq, 3 L, 3 Sq, 3 L, 2 Sq, 3 L, 1 Sq, 3 L, 1 Sq, 3 L, 2 Sq, 3 L, 1 Sq, 3 L, 2 Sq, 3 L, 1 Sq, 3 L, 3 Sq, 3 L, 1 Sq, 3 L, 3 Sq, 6 L, 1 Sq, 21 L, 7 Sq.

13th Row.—10 Sq, 6 L, 3 Sq, 3 L, 5 Sq, 6 L, 3 Sq, 6 L, 3 Sq, 3 L, 3 Sq, 3 L, 1 Sq, 3 L, 7 Sq, 6 L, 12 Sq, 3 L, 2 Sq, 3 L, 3 Sq, 3 L, 2 Sq, 3 L, 3 Sq, 3 L, 4 Sq,

3 L, 4 Sq, 3 L, 5 Sq, 3 L, 2 Sq, 6 L, 3 Sq, 15 L, 8 Sq.

14th Row.—10 L, 6 Sq, 3 L, 1 Sq, 3 L, 1 Sq, 3 L, 2 Sq, 3 L, 3 Sq, 3 L, 1 Sq, 3 L, 2 Sq, 3 L, 1 Sq, 3 L, 1 Sq, 3 L, 2 Sq, 6 L, 7 Sq, 3 L, 1 Sq, 9 L, 11 Sq, 3 L, 1 Sq, 6 L, 1 Sq, 3 L, 1 Sq, 3 L, 2 Sq, 3 L, 3 Sq, 3 L, 4 Sq, 3 L, 4 Sq, 3 L, 1 Sq, 3 L, 3 Sq, 3 L, 2 Sq, 6 L, 4 Sq, 3 L, 8 Sq, 8 L.

15th Row.—10 L, 6 Sq, 6 L, 3 Sq, 6 L, 4 Sq, 6 L, 3 Sq, 6 L, 3 Sq, 6 L, 1 Sq, 3 L, 6 Sq, 6 L, 2 Sq, 6 L, 11 Sq, 6 L, 1 Sq, 6 L, 2 Sq, 9 L, 3 Sq, 9 L, 3 Sq, 3 L, 4 Sq, 6 L, 3 Sq, 9 L, 1 Sq, 3 L, 1 Sq, 21 L, 6 Sq, 8 L.

16th Row.—* 10 L, 30 Sq, 3 L, 6 Sq, 6 L, 2 Sq, 6 L, 25 Sq, 3 L, 4 Sq, 3 L, 10 Sq, 3 L, 3 Sq, 3 L, 1 Sq, * 21 L, 5 Sq, 8 L.

17th Row.—*Repeat* from * to * in last row; then 3 L, 4 Sq, 6 L, 5 Sq, 8 L.

18th Row.—33 Sq, 3 L, 6 Sq, 6 L, 2 Sq, 6 L, 24 Sq, 3 L, 5 Sq, 3 L, 4 Sq, 3 L, 4 Sq, 3 L, 5 Sq, 21 L, 1 Sq, 3 L, 7 Sq.

19th Row.—29 Sq, 3 L, 2 Sq, 3 L, 7 Sq, 6 L, 2 Sq, 6 L, 29 Sq, 3 L, 1 Sq, 3 L, 15 Sq, 24 L, 7 Sq.

20th Row.—30 Sq, 6 L, 4 Sq, 6 L, 2 Sq, 3 L, 3 Sq, 3 L, 30 Sq, 3 L, 16 Sq, 3 L, 7 Sq, 3 L, 7 Sq.

21st Row.—35 Sq, 3 L, 1 Sq, 9 L, 3 Sq, 3 L, 47 Sq, 6 L, 2 Sq, 6 L, 2 Sq, 3 L, 8 Sq.

22nd Row.—38 Sq, 3 L, 2 Sq, 6 L, 48 Sq, 12 L, 1 Sq, 9 L, 9 Sq.

23rd, 24th, 25th, 26th Rows.—4 rows of Sqs.

27th Row.—10 L, * 3 Sq, 9 L, *repeat* from *.

28th Row.—1 Sq, * 9 L, 3 Sq, *repeat* from *.

29th Row.—2 Sq, * 9 L, 3 Sq, *repeat* from *.

30th Row.—7 L, * 3 Sq, 9 L, *repeat* from *.

31st Row.—4 L, * 3 Sq, 9 L, *repeat* from *.

32nd Row.—3 Sq, 9 L, *repeat.*

33rd Row.—A row of Sqs.

Work the Border the same as Cheese Serviette.

A row of Dc may be worked tightly upon the row of long stitches; and if considered more convenient, 4 rows of Squares may be worked on this end, to admit of a string being drawn through, and tied at the bottom of the cheese.

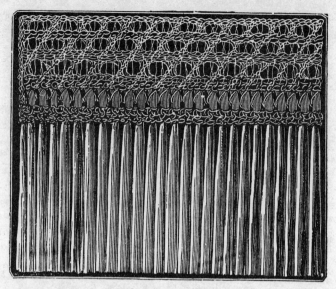

Handsome Fringe for a Toilet Cover or Anti-Macassar. By Mrs. Warren.

THE WORK-TABLE FRIEND.

HANDSOME FRINGE FOR A TOILET COVER OR ANTI-MACASSAR.

No. 0 Evans's Boar's Head Cotton ; No. 14 Needles.

Cast on 12 stitches, and K 1 plain row.

1st Row.—P 1, * cotton in front, turn it twice over the needle, and bring it in front again, P 2 +, *repeat* from * twice more, turn the cotton to the back ; now cut some cotton into lengths, two fingers long (*this should be previously done*), take 4 of these lengths, double them exactly in half, hang them in the centre over the right hand needle, hold the ends back, K 2 stitches ; bring the ends in front, K 2 more stitches, turn the ends to the back, K 1.

2nd Row.—K 4, K 3 loops + twice (4 of these loops are formed by the fringe), K the remainder of the stitches, taking off the cotton that is twice over the needle as one stitch.

3rd Row.—P 7, turn the cotton to the back, hang on the fringe, and finish the row as 2nd row.

4th Row.—K 4, K 3 loops together twice, K the remainder. Now repeat the pattern from 1st row.

THE BALMORAL SLEEVE.

Two ounces of 4-thread Berlin Wool if the sleeve is required to be very warm, or one ounce of Shetland for an in-door sleeve ; both should be in 3 shades, that will either match or harmonise well with the colour of the dress. If the sleeve is made of Shetland Wool, the first 4 rows of the pattern should be worked in Berlin Wool ; also the 16th, 17th, and 18th rows. The remainder work loosely and in Dble L stitches. If in 4-thread Wool, it must be worked tightly. No. 2 Penelope Hook.

1st Row.—Make 81 chain, unite, work a row of Dc (it should now measure 2 nails).

2nd Row.—1 L, 1 chain, miss 1 loop, *repeat* (the wool need not be cut off at any of the rows, but the termination of the rows should be marked by tying in a piece of wool of a different colour).

3rd Row.—1 row Dc.

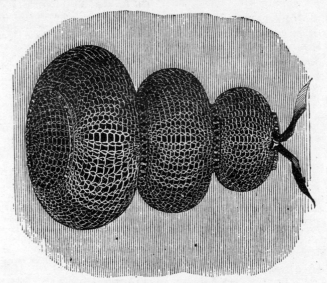

The Balmoral Sleeve. By Mrs. Warren.

4th Row.—2 L into 1 loop, with 1 chain between each, 1 chain, miss 1 loop, *repeat*.

5th Row.—2 L, with 2 chain between each *under* the 1 chain, between the 2 L, 2 chain, *repeat*.

6th Row.—The same, only making 3 chain instead of 2.

7th Row.—The same, only making 4 chain instead of 3.

8th, 9th, 10th, 11th, and 12th Rows.—The same, only making 5 chain instead of 4.

13th Row.—The same, only making 4 ch.

14th Row.—The same, only making 3 chain.

15th Row.—The same, only making 2 chain.

16th Row.—The same, only making 1 chain.

17th Row.—1 L *under* every chain, without any chain between.

18th Row.—1 L, 1 chain, miss 1 loop, *repeat*.

19th Row.—A row of Dc.

For 2nd Puff.—Now *repeat* from 4th row, only miss 2 loops instead of 1, but make 1 chain between each, and at 8th row make only 3 rows with the 5 chain between each, instead of 5 rows.

For 3rd Puff.—*Repeat* as at 4th row exactly, but at 8th row work only 1 row, with 5 chain between, and at the row of L stitches, with 1 L, 1 chain, miss 1 loop, make the L stitches Dble L; this is to run the ribbon in, or a piece of elastic is preferable, with a bow in the centre; in each insertion between the puffs, elastic may be used.

Every human creature is sensible of the propensities to some infirmity of temper, which it should be his care to correct and subdue, particularly in the early period of life; else, when arrived at a state of maturity, he may relapse into those faults which were originally in his nature, and which will require to be diligently watched and kept under, through the whole course of life; since nothing leads more directly to the breach of charity, and to the injury and molestation of our fellow-creatures, than the indulgence of an ill temper.—*Dr. Blair.*

THE WORK-TABLE FRIEND.

D'OYLEY FOR A SPIRIT STAND.

No. 30, Evans's Boar's Head Cotton; No. 4 Penelope Hook. (If coarser cotton is used the D'Oyley will be too large.)

1st Round.—7 chain, unite; under this circle work 7 chain, Dc under same for 6 times, (*making in all 6 chains of 7.*) Cut off the cotton every round until further directed.

2nd Round.—* Dc under 7 chain, 3 chain, Dc under 7, 7 chain, repeat from * twice more.

3rd Round.—Under the 7th chain work 5 L, 5 chain, 5 more L under same, 3 chain, Dc under 3 chain, 3 chain, *repeat.*

4th Round.—Under the 5 chain work 5 L, 5 chain, 5 more·L under same, 3 chain, Dc under 3 chain, 3 chain, Dc under 3, 3 chain, *repeat.*

5th Round.—Work at corner as in last row, then 5 chain, Dc under 3, 5 chain, Dc under 3, 5 chain, Dc under 3, 5 chain, *repeat.*

6th Round.—Work at corner as before, then 6 chain, Dc under every 5, 6 chain, *repeat.*

7th Round.—Work at corner as before, then 7 chain, Dc under 6 chain, 7 chain, Dc under 6, 9 L under next 6 chain, Dc under next, 7 chain, Dc under next, 7 chain, *repeat.*

8th Round.—Work at corner as before, 7 chain, Dc under 7 4 times, 7 chain, 4 L, the 1st on 1st L, 1 chain, miss 1 loop, 4 L, 7 chain, Dc under 7 for twice, 7 chain, *repeat.*

9th Round.—Work at corner as before, then 7 chain, Dc under 7 for 3 times, 7 chain, Dc under 1 chain, 7 chain, Dc under 7 for 3 times, 7 chain, *repeat.*

10th Round.—Corner as before, then 7 chain, Dc under every 7 chain, 7 chain, *repeat.*

11th Round.—Corner as before, 7 chain, Dc under 7 for twice, 11 L under next 7, Dc under next 7, 7 chain, Dc under 7 for twice, 11 L under next 7, Dc under next 7, 7 chain, Dc under 7, 7 chain, *repeat.*

12th Round.—Corner as before, 7 chain, Dc under 7 twice, 7 chain, 5 L, the 1st on 1st L, 1 chain, miss 1 loop, 5 L, 7 chain, Dc under 7 twice, 7 chain, 5 L, the 1st on 1st L, 1 chain, 5 more L, 7 chain, Dc under 7 for twice, 7 chain, *repeat.*

13th Round.—7 Dc under the 5 chain at corner, 7 chain, 7 Dc under the 7 chain, 1 chain, 7 Dc under the 7 chain, 1 chain, 7 Dc under the 1 chain, 5 chain, Dc under 1 chain, 5 chain, 7 Dc under the 7 chain, 1 chain, 7 Dc under next 7, 1 chain, 7 Dc under next 7, 5 chain, Dc under 1 chain, 5 chain, 7 Dc under 7 chain, 1 chain, 7 Dc under 7 chain, 1 chain, 7 Dc under 7 chain, 7 chain, *repeat.*

14th Round.—Work 14 L into the 7 chain at corner, then 1 L into every loop, including all the Dc stitches. (*Be careful to work into every loop, and reckon that there are no more stitches on one side than the other.*)

15th Round.—Tie an end of cotton (*for a mark*) into the 8th loop of the 14 L at corner, then reckon 28 loops on each side of this; commence in the 28th loop from this cotton, now work 56 long and 2 L into the centre loop at corner, in all 58 long stitches round this corner, now 2 chain 1 L into every 3rd loop, thus making 21 squares. (*Should there be an extra stitch, which with the utmost care will sometimes happen, it must come into this part and not round the corners.*)

16th Round.—1 L into every loop, with 1 chain between each round the L stitch at the corner (*count that there are 57 spaces, that is, the space between each L stitch*) then 1 L on 2 chain for 21 squares, then *repeat;* (*this will set full, but will work out.*)

17th Round.—1 L on 2 chain all round. (*Write the three letters* B, R, G, *each on a separate piece of paper, sew* B *on to one corner, then* R, *then* G, *but not on the row of long stitches.*)

Letter Rows.

1st Row.—Begin on the 1st of the 58 long, at B corner, 6 Sq, 12 L, 4 Sq, 3 L, (*this brings to* R *corner,*) 73 Sq, 3 L, 2 Sq, 6 L, 4 Sq, 9 L, 74 Sq, this brings to G corner, 6 L, 2 Sq, 9 L, 2 Sq, 3 L, 50 Sq, (*not cut off the Cotton now throughout the rows, but make 5 chain; this is equivalent to* 1 L, 2 *chain, and at the end of the Row, after the last 2 chain, simply draw the cotton through the 3rd loop of this 5 chain, it will then be a perfect square.*)

2nd Row.—5 Sq, 3 L, 4 Sq, 3 L, 1 Sq, 12 L, 72 Sq, (R *corner,*) 18 L, 2 Sq, 3 L, 1 Sq, 6 L, 73 Sq, (G *corner*) 3 L, 3 Sq, 3 L, 1 Sq, 12 L, 51 Sq.

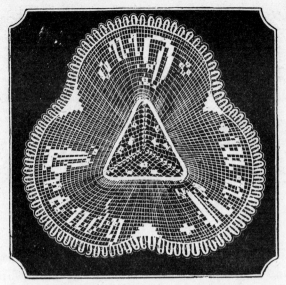

D'Oyley for a Spirit Stand. By Mrs. Warren.

3rd Row.—9 Sq, 3 L, 1 Sq, 3 L, 2 Sq, 6 L, 25 Sq, 3 L, 47 Sq, (R *corner,*) 6 L, 1 Sq, 6 L, 1 Sq, 3 L, 2 Sq, 6 L, 72 Sq, (G *corner,*) 3 L, 3 Sq, 6 L, 3 Sq, 3 L, 52 Sq.

4th Row.—*8 Sq, 6 L, 1 Sq, 3 L, 2 Sq, 6 L, *25 Sq, 3 L, 55 Sq, (R *corner,*) 6 L, 1 Sq, 3 L, 2 Sq, 6 L, (G *corner,*) 71 Sq, 6 L, 3 Sq, 6 L, 2 Sq, 3 L, 53 Sq.

5th Row.—Repeat from * to * in last row; then 26 Sq, 3 L, 49 Sq, (R *corner,*) 6 L, 1 Sq, 3 L, 2 Sq, 3 L, 72 Sq, (G *corner,*) 6 L, 3 Sq, 6 L, 1 Sq, 12 L, 4 Sq, 3 L, 46 Sq.

6th Row.—8 Sq, 6 L, 1 Sq, 3 L, 2 Sq, 3 L, 28 Sq, 3 L, (R *corner,*) 48 Sq, 6 L, 1 Sq, 3 L, 1 Sq, 3 L, 73 Sq, (G) 6 L, 3 Sq, 9 L, 3 Sq, 6 L, all Sq.

7th Row.—7 Sq, 9 L, 1 Sq, 3 L. 1 Sq, 3 L, 1 Sq, 6 L, 27 Sq, 3 L, 46 Sq, (R) 9 L, 1 Sq, 6 L, 1 Sq, 3 L, 64 Sq, (G) 6 L, 6 Sq, 6 L, 3 Sq, 6 L, 4 Sq, 6 L, 20 Sq, 6 L, all Sq.

8th Row.—6 Sq, 3 L, 1 Sq, 6 L, 1 Sq, 3 L, 3 Sq, 6 L, 1 Sq, 6 L, 1 Sq, 6 L, 4 Sq, 6 L, 4 Sq, 6 L, 1 Sq, 6 L, 4 Sq, 3 L, 1 Sq, 3 L, 2 Sq, 6 L, 1 Sq, 6 L, 1 Sq, 6 L, 14 Sq, 3 L, (R) 22 Sq, 3 L, 1 Sq, 6 L, 1 Sq, 3 L, 2 Sq, 6 L, 5 Sq, 6 L, 1 Sq, 6 L, 4 Sq, 6 L, 1 Sq, 6 L, 1 Sq, 6 L, 23 Sq, 3 L, (G) 15 Sq, 6 L, 2 Sq, 6 L, 4 Sq, 6 L, 3 Sq, 6 L, 4 Sq, 6 L, 2 Sq, 6 L, 4 Sq, 6 L, 1 Sq, 6 L, 5 Sq, 6 L, 2 Sq, 6 L, 15 Sq, 3 L, 10 Sq.

9th Row.—8 Sq, 6 L, 1 Sq, 3 L, 3 Sq, 6 L, 2 Sq, 6 L, 1 Sq, 3 L, 3 Sq, 3 L, 1 Sq, 3 L, 3 Sq, 3 L, 1 Sq, 6 L, 1 Sq, 3 L, 3 Sq, 3 L, 2 Sq, 3 L, 1 Sq, 3 L, 1 Sq, 6 L, 1 Sq, 3 L, 13 Sq, 9 L, (R) 14 Sq, 6 L, 8 Sq, 6 L, 1 Sq, 3 L, 2 Sq, 6 L, 4 Sq, 3 L, 1 Sq, 3 L, 2 Sq, 3 L, 3 Sq, 3 L, 1 Sq, 6 L, 1 Sq, 6 L, 1 Sq, 3 L, 5 Sq, 6 L, 15 Sq, 9 L, (G) 14 Sq, 6 L, 2 Sq, 6 L, 4 Sq, 9 L, 2 Sq, 6 L, 4 Sq, 6 L, 1 Sq, 3 L, 1 Sq, 3 L, 3 Sq, 3 L, 1 Sq, 6 L, 1 Sq, 3 L, 5 Sq, 6 L, 2 Sq, 6 L, 14 Sq, 9 L, 9 Sq.

10th Row.—8 Sq, 3 L, 1 Sq, 3 L, 4 Sq, 6 L, 2 Sq, 3 L, 5 Sq, 12 L, 5 Sq, 3 L, 2 Sq, 3 L, 3 Sq, 3 L, 2 Sq. 3 L, 3 Sq, 3 L, 2 Sq 3 L, 12 Sq, 15 L, (R) 11 Sq, 18 L,

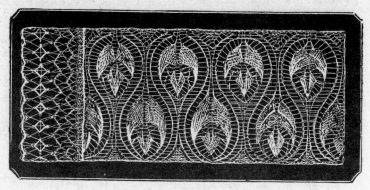

Knitted Pattern for Curtains. By Mrs. Warren.

5 Sq, 9 L, 1 Sq, 3 L, 2 Sq, 6 L, 6 Sq, 3 L, 2 Sq, 3 L, 5 Sq, 3 L, 2 Sq, 3 L, 2 Sq, 3 L, 3 Sq, 18 L, 12 Sq, 15 L, (G) 15 Sq, 6 L, 7 Sq, 6 L, 2 Sq, 3 L, 5 Sq, 6 L, 3 Sq, 3 L, 5 Sq, 3 L, 2 Sq, 3 L, 7 Sq, 6 L, 15 Sq, 15 L, 8 Sq.

11th Row.—8 Sq, 18 L, 1 Sq, 3 L, 3 Sq, 3 L, 5 Sq, 3 L, 2 Sq, 3 L, 1 Sq, 3 L, 3 Sq, 3 L, 2 Sq, 3 L, 1 Sq, 3 L, 1 Sq, 3 L, 1 Sq, 3 L, 4 Sq, 3 L, 2 Sq, 3 L, 10 Sq, 2 chain, miss 1 Sq, 3 Dc under next, 16 Dc over the Dc, 3 Dc under next Sq, 2 chain, miss 1 L, 1 L on next, 11 Sq, 6 L, (R) 8 Sq, 6 L, 1 Sq, 3 L, 2 Sq, 6 L, 2 Sq, 3 L, 3 Sq, 3 L, 1 Sq, 6 L, 1 Sq, 3 L, 3 Sq, 3 L, 2 Sq, 3 L, 2 Sq, 3 L, 1 Sq, 3 L, 3 Sq, 6 L, 12 Sq. Now work as at former side. (G) 22 Sq, 12 L, 5 Sq, 6 L, 4 Sq, 3 L, 1 Sq, 3 L, 3 Sq, 3 L, 2 Sq, 3 L, 1 Sq, 3 L, 20 Sq. Work the same as the other side; then 6 Sq.

12th Row.—7 Sq, 3 L, 4 Sq, 9 L, 4 Sq, 6 L, 4 Sq, 6 L, 1 Sq, 6 L, 4 Sq, 6 L, 1 Sq, 6 L, 2 Sq, 6 L, 5 Sq, 6 L, 1 Sq, 3 L, 9 Sq, 2 chain. Now work as at last row, only Dc over all the Dc stitches; then 2 chain 21 Sq, (R) 9 L, 3 Sq, 9 L, 4 Sq, 6 L, 1 Sq, 6 L, 4 Sq, 6 L, 1 Sq, 6 L, 1 Sq, 6 L, 17 Sq, 2 chain. Work over the Dc stitches as before; then 2 chain, 23 Sq, (G) 21 L, 6 Sq, 6 L, 4 Sq, 6 L, 1 Sq, 6 L, 20 Sq. Work at side as before; then 5 Sq, and fasten off.

13th Row.—Dc on the L stich imme-diately after the Dc stitches *before* the letter (B); 2 chain, Dc on next L, 2 chain; Dc on next L, 3 chain, 1 L on L, 9 Sq, now 39 Sq, making 3 chain instead of 2 ; then 5 Sq, with 2 chain instead of 3 ; 3 L on the last 3 L of last rows, 5 Sq, with 2 chain between each, 3 chain, Dc on next L, † 2 chain, Dc on next L, *repeat* from † twice more (4 *Dc in all*). Turn back, 7 chain, 3 Dc *under* 3 chain, 2 chain, 1 L on L for 6 times, 3 L, 2 chain, 1 L on L for 3 times, 48 Sq, making 3 chain instead of 2 ; 3 chain, 3 Dc *under* 2 chain, 5 chain, Dc on last L ; fasten off without working over the Dc stitches. Now work at both other corners the same, only making all squares, with 3 chain between each L in-stead of 2, till within and before 9 squares of the Dc stitches, where make 2 chain in-stead of 3. Turn back, and where there are 2 chain, there make 2 chain ; and where there are 3, there make 3.

For the Border.

Three Dc *under* every 2 and 3 chain, and 5 Dc *under* every 5 and 7 chain ; but not work over the 27 Dc stitches.

For the Leaves.

Dc on the 1st of the 27 Dc stitches at the side, 12 chain, turn back, 1 L into 9th loop from hook ; 3 chain, Dc into the loop where commenced, 1 chain to cross, turn round on the finger, Dc *under* the opposite

3 chain, 5 L *under* same, 5 L *under* the chains at point of leaf; 3 chain, 5 more L *under* same, 5 L *under* the 3 chain, Dc *under* same, Dc into same loop where commenced; * 3 chain, Dc into 3rd loop, 3 chain, Dc into 3rd loop, 3 chain, Dc into 3rd loop.

2nd Leaf.—12 chain, and work exactly the same as the last, but uniting after the 1st 5 L, into the 3rd L of last leaf; then *repeat* from * until the long stitches are reached, then work the same until 12 Leaves are made; then make 8 Leaves with only 2 chains of 3 between each Leaf (*this is round the corner*). Now work down the side as before.

The number of Leaves, that is, one more or less, is immaterial.

After washing, the D'Oyley should be pulled quite flat, and laid to press between linen, without stiffening, with a heavy weight upon it.

KNITTED PATTERN FOR CURTAINS.

No. 4 Evans's Boar's Head Cotton; No. 12 Pins.

Thirty eight stitches form one Pattern.

Cast on 400 stitches; this will make ten patterns, and ten stitches each side must be knitted plain at the commencement and end of each row.

1st Row.—K 1, Tf, K 1, K 2 +, Tf, K 6, K 2 +, K 14, K 2 +, K 6, Tf, K 2 +, K 1, Tf, K 1, *repeat* to the end.

2nd Row.—P 1, Tf, P 1, P 2 +, Tf, P 6, P 2 +, P 14, P 2 +, P 6, Tf, P 2 +, P 1, Tf, P 1.

3rd Row.—Same as 1st.

4th Row.—Same as 2nd.

5th Row.—Tf, K 2, Tf, K 2 +, K 1, Tf, K 6, K 2 +, K 12, K 2 +, K 6, Tf, K 1, K 2 +, Tf, K 2.

6th Row.—Tf, P 2 +, P 1, Tf, P 2 +, P 1, Tf, P 6, P 2 +, P 10, P 2 +, P 6, Tf, P 1, P 2 +, Tf, P 1, P 2 +, Tf, P 1.

7th Row.—K 2, Tf, K 2 +, K 1, Tf, K 2 +, K 1, Tf, K 6, K 2 +, K 8, K 2 +, K 6, Tf, K 1, K 2 +, Tf, K 1, K 2 +, Tf, K 1.

8th Row.—P 2, Tf, P 2 +, P 1, Tf, P 2 +, P 1, Tf, P 6, P 2 +, P 6, P 2 +, P 6, Tf, P 1, P 2 +, Tf, P 1, P 2 +, Tf, P 3.

9th Row.—K 4, Tf, K 2 +, K 1, Tf, K 2 +, K 1, Tf, K 5, K 2 +, K 6, K 2 +, K 5, Tf, K 1, K 2 +, Tf, K 1, K 2 +, Tf, K 3.

10th Row.—P 4, Tf, P 2 +, P 1, Tf, P 2 +, P 1, Tf, P 5, P 2 +, P 4, P 2 +, P 5, Tf, P 1, P 2 +, Tf, P 1, P 2 +, Tf, P 5.

11th Row.—K 1, K 2 +, K 3, Tf, K 2 +, K 1, Tf, K 2 +, K 1, Tf, K 4, K 2 +, K 4, K 2 +, K 4, Tf, K 1, K 2 +, Tf, K 1, K 2 +, Tf, K 3, K 2 +.

12th Row.—P 5, Tf, P 2 +, P 1, Tf, P 2 +, P 1, Tf, P 4, P 2 +, P 2, P 2 +, P 4, Tf, P 1, P 2 +, Tf, P 1, P 2 +, Tf, P 6.

13th Row.—K 7, Tf, K 2 +, K 1, Tf, K 2 +, K 1, Tf, K 3, K 2 +, K 2, K 2 +, K 3, Tf, K 1, K 2 +, Tf, K 1, K 2 +, Tf, K 6.

14th Row.—P 7, Tf, P 2 +, P 1, Tf, P 2 +, P 1, Tf, P 3, P 2 +, P 2 +, P 3, Tf, P 1, P 2 +, Tf, P 1, P 2 +, Tf, P 8.

15th Row.—K 1, K 2 +, K 6, Tf, K 2 +, K 1, Tf, K 2 +, K 1, Tf, K 2, K 2 +, K 2 +, K 2, Tf, K 1, K 2 +, Tf, K 1, K 2 +, Tf, K 1, K 6, K 2 +.

16th Row.—P 8, Tf, P 2 +, P 1, Tf, P 2 +, P 1, Tf, P 1, P 2 +, P 2 +, Tf, P 1, Tf, P 1, P 2 +, Tf, P 1, P 2 +, Tf, P 9.

17th Row.—K 1, K 2 +, K 7, Tf, K 2, Tf, K 1, Tf, K 2 +, K 1, Tf, K 2 +, K 2 +, Tf, K 1, K 2 +, Tf, K 1, Tf, K 2, Tf, K 7, K 2 +.

18th Row.—P 2 +, P 7, Tf, P 2, Tf, P 3, Tf, P 2 +, P 1, Tf, P 2, Tf, P 1, P 2 +, Tf, P 3, Tf, P 2, Tf, P 7, P 2 +, P 1.

19th Row.—K 1, K 2 +, K 6, Tf, K 1, K 2 +, Tf, K 2 +, K 1, Tf, K 2 +, K 1, Tf, K 2, Tf, K 1, K 2 +, Tf, K 1, K 2 +, K 2, Tf, K 2 +, K 1, Tf, K 6, K 2 +.

20th Row.—P 2 +, P 5, Tf, P 1, P 2 +, Tf, P 2, P 2 +, P 2, Tf, P 2 +, P 1, Tf, P 2, Tf, P 1, P 2 +, Tf, P 2, P 2 +, P 2, Tf, P 2 +, P 1, Tf, P 5, P 2 +, P 1.

21st Row.—K 1, K 2 +, K 5, Tf, K 2, Tf, K 3, K 2 +, K 2, Tf, K 2 +, K 1, Tf, K 2, Tf, K 1, K 2 +, Tf, K 2, K 2 +, K 3, Tf, K 2, Tf, K 5, K 2 +.

22nd Row.—P 2 +, P 4, Tf, P 1, P 2 +, Tf, P 8, Tf, P 2 +, P 1, Tf, P 2, Tf, P 1, P 2 +, Tf, P 8, Tf, P 2 +, P 1, Tf, P 4, P 2 +, P 1.

23rd Row.—K 1, K 2 +, K 4, Tf, K 3 +, K 3, K 2 +, K 4, Tf, K 2 +, K 1, Tf, K 2, Tf, K 1, K 2 +, Tf, K 4, K 2 +, K 3, K 3 +, Tf, K 4, K 2 +.

J

KNITTED PATTERN FOR CURTAINS.

—

24th Row.—P 2 +, P 3, Tf, P 5, P 2 +, P 4. Tf, P 2 +, P 1, Tf, P 2, Tf, P 1, P 2 +, Tf, P 4, P 2 +, P 5, Tf, P 3, P 2 +, P 1.

25th Row.—K 1, K 2 +, K 2, Tf, K 5, K 2 +, K 5, Tf, K 2 +, K 1, Tf, K 2, Tf, K 1, K 2 +, Tf, K 5, K 2 +, K 5, Tf, K 2, K 2 +.

26th Row.—P 2 +, P 6, P 2 +, P 6, Tf, P 2 +, P 1, Tf, P 2 +, Tf, P 1, P 2 +, Tf, P 6, P 2 +, P 6, P 2 +, P 1.

27th Row.—K 2 +, K 6, K 2 +, K 6, Tf, K 2 +, K 1, Tf, K 2, Tf, K 1, K 2 +, Tf, K 6, K 2 +, Tf, K 7.

28th Row.—P 7, P 2 +, P 6, Tf, P 2 +, P 1, Tf, P 2, Tf, P 1, P 2 +, Tf, P 6, P 2 +, P 7.

29th Row.—K 7, K 2 +, K 6, Tf, K 2 +, K 1, Tf, K 2, Tf, K 1, K 2 +, Tf, K 6, K 2 +, Tf, K 7.

30th Row.—As 28th.

31st Row.—K 6, K 2 +, K 6, Tf, K 1, K 2 +, Tf, K 2, Tf, K 2, Tf, K 2 +, K 1, Tf, K 6, K 2 +, Tf, K 6.

32nd Row.—P 5, P 2 +, P 6, Tf, P 1, P 2 +, Tf, P 1, P 2 +, Tf, P 1, Tf, P 2 +, P 1, Tf, P 2 +, P 1, Tf, P 6, P 2 +, P 5.

33rd Row.—K 4, K 2 +, K 6, Tf, K 1, K 2 +, Tf, K 1, K 2 +, Tf, K 3, Tf, K 2 +, K 1, Tf, K 2 +, K 1, Tf, K 6, K 2 +, K 4.

34th Row.—P 3, P 2 +, P 6, Tf, P 1, P 2 +, Tf, P 1, P 2 +, Tf, P 5, Tf, P 2 +, P 1, Tf, P 2 +, P 1, Tf, P 6, P 2 +, P 3.

35th Row.—K 3, K 2 +, K 5, Tf, K 1, K 2 +, Tf, K 1, K 2 +, Tf, K 7, Tf, K 2 +, K 1, Tf, K 2 +, K 1, Tf, K 2 +, K 5, K 3.

36th Row.—P 2, P 2 +, P 5, Tf, P 1, P 2 +, Tf, P 1, P 2 +, Tf, P 9, Tf, P 2 +, P 1, Tf, P 2 +, P 1, Tf, P 5, P 2 +, P 2.

37th Row.—K 2, K 2 +, K 4, Tf, K 1, K 2 +, Tf, K 1, K 2 +, Tf, K 3, K 2 +, K 1, K 2 +, K 3, Tf, K 2 +, K 1, Tf, K 2 +, K 4, K 2 +, K 2.

38th Row.—P 1, P 2 +, P 4, Tf, P 1, P 2 +, Tf, P 1, P 2 +, Tf, P 11, Tf, P 2 +, P 1, Tf, P 2 +, P 1, Tf, P 4, P 2 +, P 1.

39th Row.—K 1, K 2 +, K 3, Tf, K 1, K 2 +, Tf, K 1, K 2 +, Tf, K 13, Tf, K 2 +, K 1, Tf, K 2 +, K 1, Tf, K 3, K 2 +, K 1.

40th Row.—P 2 +, P 3, Tf, P 1, P 2 +, Tf, P 1, P 2 +, Tf, P 15, Tf, P 2 +, P 1, Tf, P 2 +, P 1, Tf, P 3, P 2 +.

41st Row.—K 2 +, K 2, Tf, K 1, K 2 +, Tf, K 1, K 2 +, Tf, K 6, K 2 +, K 1, K 2 +, K 6, Tf, K 2 +, K 1, Tf, K 2 +, K 1, Tf, K 2, K 2 +.

42nd Row.—P 2 +, P 1, Tf, P 1, P 2 +, Tf, P 1, P 2 +, Tf, P 17, Tf, P 2 +, P 1, Tf, P 2 +, P 1, Tf, P 1, P 2 +.

43rd Row.—K 2 +, Tf, K 1, K 2 +, Tf, K 1, Tf, K 2, Tf, K 7, K 2 +, K 1, K 2 +, K 7, Tf, K 2, Tf, K 1, Tf, K 2 +, K 1, Tf, K 2 +.

44th Row.—P 1, Tf, P 1, P 2 +, Tf, P 3, Tf, P 2, Tf, P 7, P 2 +, P 1, P 2 +, P 7, Tf, P 2, Tf, P 3, Tf, P 2 +, P 1, Tf, P 1.

45th Row.—K 1, Tf, K 1, K 2 +, Tf, K 1, K 2 +, K 2, Tf, K 2 +, K 1, Tf, K 6, K 2 +, K 1, K 2 +, K 6, Tf, K 1, K 2 +, Tf, K 2, K 2 +, K 1, Tf, K 2 +, K 1, Tf, K 1.

46th Row.—P 1, Tf, P 1, P 2 +, Tf, P 2, P 2 +, P 2, Tf, P 2 +, P 1, Tf, P 5, P 2 +, P 1, P 2 +, P 5, Tf, P 1, P 2 +, Tf, P 2, P 2 +, P 2, Tf, P 2 +, P 1, Tf, P 1.

47th Row.—K 1, Tf, K 1, K 2 +, Tf, K 2, K 2 +, K 3, Tf, K 2, Tf, K 5, K 2 +, K 1, K 2 +, K 5, Tf, K 2, Tf, K 3, K 2 +, K 2, Tf, K 2 +, K 1, Tf, K 1.

48th Row.—P 1, Tf, P 1, P 2 +, Tf, P 8, Tf, P 2 +, P 1, Tf, P 4, P 2 +, P 1, P 2 +, P 4, Tf, P 1, Tf, P 8, Tf, P 2 +, P 1, Tf, P 1.

49th Row.—K 1, Tf, K 1, K 2 +, Tf, K 4, K 2 +, K 3, K 3 +, Tf, K 4, K 2 +, K 1, K 2 +, K 4, Tf, K 3 +, K 3, K 2 +, K 4, Tf, K 2 +, K 1, Tf, K 1.

50th Row.—P 1, Tf, P 1, P 2 +, Tf, P 4, P 2 +, P 5, Tf, P 3, P 2 +, P 1, P 2 +, P 3, Tf, P 5, P 2 +, P 4, Tf, P 2 +, P 1, Tf, P 1.

51st Row.—K 1, Tf, K 1, K 2 +, Tf, K 5, K 2 +, K 5, Tf, K 2, K 2 +, K 1, K 2 +, K 2, Tf, K 5, K 2 +, K 5, Tf, K 2, K 1, Tf, K 1.

52nd Row.—P 1, Tf, P 1, P 2 +, Tf, P 6, P 2 +, P 6, P 2 +, P 1, P 2 +, P 6, P 2 +, P 6, Tf, P 2 +, P 1, Tf, P 1.

A Lady's Netted Cap. By Mrs. Warren.

53rd Row.—K 1, Tf, K 1, K 2 +, Tf, K 6, K 2 +, K 7, K 2 +, K 6, K 2 +, K 6, Tf, K 2 +, K 1, Tf, K 1.

54th Row.—P 1, Tf, P 1, P 2 +, Tf, P 6, P 2 +, P 14, P 2 +, P 6, Tf, P 2 +, P 1, Tf, P 1.

Begin again at 1st Row.

For the Edging.

Cast on 17 stitches.

1st Row.—K 4, Tf, K 1, K 2 +, Tf, K 1, K 2 +, Tf, K 3, Tf, K 4.

2nd Row.—K 4, Tf, K 5, Tf, K 2 +, K 1, Tf, K 2 +, K 1, Tf, K 4.

3rd Row.—K 4, Tf, K 1, K 2 +, Tf, K 1, K 2 +, Tf, K 1, Tf, K 2 +, K 1, K 2 +, Tf, K 1, Tf, K 4.

4th Row.—K 4, Tf, K 3, Tf, K 3 +, Tf, K 3, Tf, K 2 +, K 1, Tf, K 2 +, K 1, Tf, K 4.

5th Row.—K 5, K 2 +, Tf, K 1, K 2 +, Tf, K 11, Tf, K 4.

6th Row.—K 2 +, K 3, Tf, K 2 +, K 1, K 2 +, Tf, K 1, Tf, K 2 +, K 1, K 2 +, Tf, K 1, K 2 +, Tf, K 1, K 2 +, Tf, K 1, K 2 +, K 4.

7th Row.—K 4, Tf, K 2 +, K 1, Tf, K 2 +, K 1, Tf, K 3 +, Tf, K 3, Tf, K 3 +, Tf, K 3, K 2 +.

8th Row.—K 2 +, K 3, Tf, K 2 +, K 3, K 2 +, Tf, K 1, K 2 +, Tf, K 1, K 2 +, Tf, K 2 +, K 3.

9th Row.—K 3, K 2 +, Tf, K 2 +, K 1, Tf, K 2 +, K 1, Tf, K 2 +, K 1, K 2 +, Tf, K 3, K 2 +.

10th Row.—K 2 +, K 3, Tf, K 3 +, Tf, K 1, K 2 +, Tf, K 1, K 2 +, Tf, K 2 +, K 3.

11th Row.—K 3, K 2 +, Tf, K 2 +, K 1, Tf, K 2 +, K 2, Tf, K 3, K 2 +.

12th Row.—K 2 +, K 3, Tf, K 1, Tf, K 2 +, K 1, Tf, K 2 +, K 1, Tf, K 4.

Screen for a Flower-Pot and Saucer. By Mrs. Warren.

A LADY'S NETTED CAP.

THREE reels Evans's Boar's Head cotton: three steel meshes, Nos. 10, 14, and 12; two flat bone or wood meshes (the latter preferable), one three-eighths of an inch wide, the other three-quarters of an inch. Netting needle No. 14.

WITH the narrowest flat mesh net on a string 35 stitches, and draw up quite tight, for the crown.

No. 14 Mesh.—Net 4 rounds, or 3 diamonds.

Broadest flat Mesh.—1 round.

No. 12 Mesh.—2 rounds, or 1 diamond.

Broadest Mesh.—4 stitches into each loop of last row (*that is*, 4 knots).

No. 14 Mesh.—4 rounds, or three diamonds deep.

Narrow flat Mesh.—1 round.

Same Mesh.—1 round, taking 3 loop of last round into 1 knot.

Same Mesh.—Net 3 stitches into every loop.

No. 12 Mesh.—Net 1 plain row all round. This finishes the crown.

Count 91 diamonds, or stitches, for the front, which must now be worked forwards and back.

No. 12 Mesh.—1 plain stitch, 3 more stitches into same loop (*there must be 4 knots*), 1 plain into next, 3 more into same, *repeat*; finish the row with 1 plain stitch. (*Observe that every row must be begun and ended with 1 plain stitch.*)

There must be but little cotton on the needle for this row (*or wind over the mesh an end of cotton 100 times; this is a guide for the length of cotton required for the row; then thread a large darning needle with this*), and net 1 plain stitch; then take up 7 loops, and net into 1 stitch; *repeat*, and end the row with a plain stitch. Continue these rows alternately till there are 14 rows, or seven patterns.

Same Mesh.—1 row plain.

Narrowest flat Mesh.—Net a row.

Same Mesh.—1 row, netting 3 loops of last row into 1 knot.

Same Mesh.—Net 3 stitches into every loop of last row.

No. 12 Mesh.—Net 6 rows more of the pattern rows, or three patterns.

Same Mesh.—Plain row all round the Cap.

For the Border.

Widest flat Mesh.—Net into every loop all round 6 stitches, or 5 knots.

No. 14 Mesh.—5 rounds, or 4 diamonds deep all round.

No. 10 Mesh.—1 round, 1 stitch into every alternate loop, that is, missing 1 stitch, or diamond, all round.

When washed, the Cap should be drawn up with ribbon.

SCREEN FOR A FLOWER-POT AND SAUCER.

THIRTY-TWO small common Curtain Rings measuring six-eighths of an inch across the ring; sixty-four of the next size larger; and sixteen of the next size, which must measure exactly one inch across. (*The number of rings here given is for a Flower-pot measuring six inches across the top.*) Half an ounce each of shaded Violet and Amber 4-thread Berlin Wool. No. 2 Penelope Hook.

Take the Amber wool, and 16 of the smallest rings; Dc under each of the rings, covering them well, and joining the first and last stitch neatly, then fastening off at the back in a firm but almost imperceptible knot. Now, with cotton as nearly the colour as may be, sew these rings together in couples. Now take the Violet Wool, and work the same with the other 16 rings, joining them in the same manner; but be careful with all, to sew them where the wool has been joined. Now take the next size, and work and join exactly the same. Then take the largest sized ring, work 8 only with each colour; then join them together in stripes, that is, a stripe of Violet and Amber alternately. (*Be careful that the joining does not show on the right side.*) Now take 16 of the middle-sized rings, and work them all with Amber only, then sew them on to the bottom row of the small-sized rings. This row of one colour will cover the space between the Flower-pot and saucer. Now take 16 of the same-sized rings, and work them alternately—Amber and Violet in this manner. In-

stead of plain Dc round the ring, work thus, 2 Dc under the ring; now 3 L, 3 ch, 3 more L, then 2 Dc stitches; *repeat this all* round the ring, till there are 7 points. Now join them in alternate colours by two of the points, leaving 1 point only, to sew to the last row of rings. This row will fall over the outside of the saucer, and completely conceal it.

This is exceedingly pretty for hiding the unsightliness of the common Flower-pot, and may be made of any size, if the measure be taken about an inch and a quarter from the bottom of the Flower-pot; but the rings should never be of larger size than the dimensions here given. There is a most important advantage, also, in this ornament: the rings can at any time be re-covered, or may be made available for any household purpose.

HANDSOME TRIMMING FOR DRAWERS.

Materials.— Evans's Mecklenburgh thread No. 8, with Boulton's crochet hook, No. 18.

MAKE a chain of the length required and close it into a round, on which work one round of Sc.

2nd.—Open square crochet.

3rd.—Sc.

4th.—Sc, + 7 Ch, miss 4, 1 Sc, + repeat all round, taking care the number of loops can be divided by 4.

5th.—Cover 3 loops, and half the 4th closely with Sc, working under each; turn 7 Sc, Sc on loop, 7 Ch, Sc on next, 7 Ch, Sc on next (which is the first of the round). Turn, 3 Ch, slip stitch on 2nd and 3rd of them, now cover two of the loops and half the 3rd with Sc; turn make 2 loops over the 3; turn, 3 Ch, slip on 2 of 3, cover one loop and half the next with Sc; turn, one loop of 7 Ch, across, between the 2; turn, 3 Ch, slip on 2, half cover the loop, 3 Ch, slip on 2, finish covering the loop. Make another picot (of 3 Ch, on which 2 are slipped at the end of every loop). Finish covering the half loops, and proceed in the same way with the next 4. Repeat to the end, from the 5th.

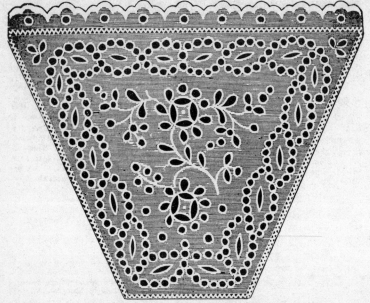

STOMACHER OF A CHILD'S DRESS, BY MRS. PULLAN.

THE WORK-TABLE FRIEND.

STOMACHER OF A CHILD'S DRESS.

Materials. French muslin, with Messrs. Walter Evans & Co.'s royal embroidery cotton, No. 50, and Boar's-head sewing cotton, No. 60.

THIS pattern may be enlarged to suit a child of any age. For a child of a year old, or more, it may be increased to double its present size, every part being proportionably enlarged. Should it be desirable to make it yet larger, the number of the scrolls, flowers, &c., should also be increased, as the holes should not be of more than certain dimensions.

Nothing can be simpler than the pattern, or more easy to enlarge. Take a piece of tracing paper, sufficiently large for a full-sized body ; rule lines for the top, waist, and sides. Mark the centre, and with a pencil lightly trace the scroll of one-half in simple lines. Correct any little irregularity, and from the one-half

trace the other. The stems of the spray may then be put in the centre. After this is done, draw the pattern perfectly, eyelet holes, leaves, and flowers. Take a sheet of blue tracing paper ; lay it with the blue side on muslin, and the clear paper over it, and draw the pattern. Tack it on *toile ciré*, and it is ready to work. Trace every part twice round, and sew it over. For the open-hem, sew a straight line at each edge, and within these two, pierce a succession of holes, first at one edge, and then at the other, with a very coarse needle, and sew over the threads between every two holes. They are so arranged that a hole at one edge falls just between two at the other edge.

For the trimming of the sleeves, &c., the design given at the top of the frock, or any other simple and pretty broderie edging may be used

THE WORK-TABLE FRIEND.

LADIES' CARRIAGE-BAG.

IN BERLIN WORK.

Materials.—No. 16 French Cotton Canvas, 15 inches wide, by 26 long; 4 ozs. of Claret Berlin wool; 1 hank of large steel beads, 4 ozs. of chalk-white, 4 ozs. of turquoise blue, and 2ozs. of black;—all these beads are of a size considerably larger than seed-beads.

THE pattern is formed entirely in beads. It consists of wide and narrow stripes alternately; the former contains an elegant pair, bending first to the left and then to the right, the ground being filled in entirely with Berlin wool. The narrow stripes consist of beads only.

Those who select the materials for themselves, must be particularly careful so to assort the canvas with the beads that each one of the latter may just cover two threads of canvas in each direction, equivalent to a cross stitch. If the canvas be too fine, the beads will look crowded, and the effect will be spoilt; if it be coarser than it ought to be, they will not cover the threads.

It would seem almost superfluous to *say* that every material we give in our receipts may be obtained, were it not for the letters we daily receive asking whether such and such things really do exist. Perhaps therefore it may gratify our Friends to know that every design we give, is drawn from some article worked by ourselves, with the same materials we prescribe: those materials are, therefore, in all cases *to be had;* but as, in accordance with our promise, we do not limit our designs to the works already known in England, but are constantly receiving novelties from Paris, Berlin, and Vienna, besides having new sorts of material made expressly for our Friends, it is quite possible that there may be a little difficulty in obtaining novel articles; but a reference to ourselves will at once enable subscribers to procure specimens of them.

Divide the canvas in half, for the two sides of the bag, and herringbone all the edges of each.

For the narrow stripe, being the border, up the sides, beginning at the lowest left hand corner.

1st Row.—1 blue, 1 black, 2 white, 2 blue.

2nd Row.—1 blue, 2 black, 1 white, 2 blue.

3rd Row.—2 blue, 2 black, 2 blue.

4th Row.—2 blue, 1 white, 2 black, 1 blue.

5th Row.—2 blue, 2 white, 1 black, 1 blue. Repeat these five rows up the sides and between every two broad stripes.

Broad Stripe.—*1st Row.*—Wool only, 23 cross stitches.

2nd Row.—11 wool, 1 blue, 11 wool.

3rd Row.—8 wool, 1 blue, 1 wool, 3 blue, 1 wool, 1 blue, 8 wool.

4th Row.—7 wool, 4 blue, 1 black, 4 blue, 7 wool.

5th Row.—4 wool, 4 blue, 1 white, 1 blue, 3 black, 1 blue, 1 white, 4 blue, 4 wool.

6th Row.—4 wool, 1 blue, 2 black, 1 blue, 2 white, 1 blue, 1 black, 1 blue, 2 white, 1 blue, 2 black, 1 blue, 4 wool.

7th Row.—4 wool, 1 blue, 2 black, 1 blue, 3 white, 1 blue, 3 white, 1 blue, 2 black, 1 blue, 4 wool.

8th Row.—4 wool, 4 blue, 3 white, 1 blue, 3 white, 4 blue, 4 wool.

9th Row.—2 wool, 2 blue, 4 white, 1 blue, 5 white, 1 blue, 4 white, 2 blue, 2 wool.

10th Row.—3 wool, 2 blue, 4 white, 1 blue, 1 white, 1 steel, 1 white, 1 blue, 4 white, 2 blue, 3 wool.

11th Row.—2 wool, 2 blue, 1 black, 1 blue, 4 white, 3 steel, 4 white, 1 blue, 1 black, 2 blue, 2 wool.

12th Row.—1 wool, 2 blue, 3 black, 2 blue, 1 white, 5 steel, 1 white, 2 blue, 3 black, 2 blue, 1 wool.

13th Row.—Like 11th.

14th Row.—Like 10th.

15th Row.—Like 9th.

16th Row.—Like 8th.

17th Row.—4 wool, 1 blue, 2 black, 1 blue, 3 white, 1 blue, 3 white, 1 blue, 2 black, 3 blue, 2 wool.

18th Row.—4 wool, 1 blue, 2 black, 1 blue, 2 white, 1 blue, 1 black, 1 blue, 2 white, 1 blue, 2 black, 1 blue, 1 white, 2 blue, 1 wool.

19th Row.—4 wool, 4 blue, 1 white, 2 blue, 1 black, 2 blue, 1 white, 4 blue, 2 white, 1 blue, 1 wool.

20th Row.—6 wool, 5 blue, 1 black, 1 white, 5 blue, 3 white, 1 blue, 1 wool.

21st Row.—6 wool, 4 blue, 1 white, 2 blue, 2 white, 1 black, 8 white, 1 blue, 1 wool.

LADIES' CARRIAGE-BAG, BY MRS. PULLAN.

22nd Row.—6 wool, 1 blue, 5 white, 1 black, 7 white, 2 blue, 1 wool.

23rd Row.—6 wool, 1 blue, 5 white, 2 black, 5 white, 3 blue, 1 wool.

24th Row.—6 wool, 1 blue, 4 white, 2 blue, 2 black, 6 white, 1 blue, 1 wool.

25th Row.—6 wool, 2 blue, 2 white, 2 blue, 2 white, 1 black, 1 blue, 4 white, 2 blue, 1 wool.

26th Row.—7 wool, 4 blue, 3 white, 1 black, 7 blue, 1 wool.

27th Row.—9 wool, 1 blue, 4 white, 1 black, 1 white, 4 blue, 3 wool.

28th Row.—3 wool, 3 blue, 3 wool, 1 blue, 3 white, 1 blue, 1 black, 4 white, 2 blue, 2 wool.

29th Row.—2 wool, 2 blue, 1 white, 1 blue, 2 wool, 2 blue, 2 white, 2 blue, 1 black, 5 white, 1 blue, 2 wool.

30th Row.—2 wool, 1 blue, 1 white, 2 blue, 3 wool, 4 blue, 1 white, 1 black, 1 blue, 4 white, 1 blue, 2 wool.

31st Row.—2 wool, 1 blue, 1 white, 1 blue, 4 wool, 3 blue, 2 white, 1 black, 2 blue, 2 white, 2 blue, 2 wool.

32nd Row.—2 wool, 1 blue, 1 white, 2 blue, 3 white, 1 blue, 3 white, 1 black, 2 white, 4 blue, 3 wool.

33rd Row.—2 wool, 1 blue, 2 white, 5 blue, 2 white, 1 blue, 1 black, 3 white, 1 blue, 5 wool.

34th Row.—2 wool, 2 blue, 5 white, 3 blue, 1 black, 1 blue, 3 white, 1 blue, 5 wool.

35th Row.—3 wool, 1 blue, 6 white, 2 black, 1 white, 1 blue, 2 white, 2 blue, 5 wool.

36th Row.—3 wool, 2 blue, 4 white, 1 blue, 3 white, 4 blue, 6 wool.

37th Row.—4 wool, 6 blue, 3 white, 1 blue, 9 wool.

38th Row.—9 wool, 5 blue, 9 wool.

For the next pine, work from the first to the sixteenth row (inclusive of both), exactly like those already given ; the remaining rows must be worked backwards, beginning at the end of each, and working to the commencement.

The third pine is worked like the first.

When both sides are done, the bag should either be mounted at a carpet-bag manufacturer's or by the worker. The sides are usually of leather. We have given a size which we think generally useful; but it may be made larger or smaller according to fancy. Done on fine canvas, with seed-beads, it is very pretty for a hand reticule.

SHORT PURSE IN CROCHET.

Materials.—2 skeins of fine Crimson Netting Silk; 2 skeins of Black ditto; 4 skeins of Gold Thread, of the same size; a yard of fine Crimson Cord; 2 small Bullion Slides, and a very handsome Tassel of Gold, Crimson and Black intermingled. Use Boulton's Crochet-hook. No. 23,—or, if you work loosely, No. 24.

MAKE a chain of 6 stitches, with the crimson, silk and close it into a round, on which work another round of crimson increasing to 12 stitches.

2nd Round.—Gold Sc, increasing to 24 stitches.

3rd Round.—Gold, increasing to 36 stitches.

4th Round.—Black, + 2 Sc on 2, 2 Ch, Miss 1, + 12 times.

5th Round.—Black, + 1 Sc on the second of the two in last round, 2 Sc on the first of the two chain, 2 Ch, + 12 times.

6th Round.—Black, + Sc on the 2nd and 3rd of the three Sc of last round, and on the first chain, 3 Ch, + 12 times.

7th Round.—Black, + 1 Sc on 2nd Sc, 1 on the 3rd, 2 Sc on the first chain stitch, 3 Ch, + 12 times.

8th Round.—Black, + Sc on the three last of 4 Sc, and on the first chain, 4 Ch, + 12 times.

Join on the gold thread, and cut off the black. As only very short ends can be left, the knot must be very carefully made, and the following will be found the best. Make a small slip knot close to the end of the new colour, and pass the end of the old one through the loop, then tighten the slip knot, as much as possible, by drawing both threads *of the new colour* at once. This forms the most secure knot possible, for every kind of work, as the ends may be cut off quite close.

9th Round.— + Miss 1 Sc, Sc on each

SHORT PURSE IN CROCHET,
BY MRS. PULLAN.

of the three others, and on the first chain, 4 Ch, + 12 times.

10th Round.— + Miss 1 Sc, Sc on the next 3, and on 1 Ch, 5 Ch, + 12 times.

11th Round.—Crimson, + Miss 1 Sc, Sc on each of the next two, 2 Sc on next, 1 Sc on Ch, 5 Ch, + 12 times.

12th Round.—Crimson, + Miss 1 Sc, Sc on each of the other four, and on the first Ch, 5 Ch, + 12 times.

13th Round.—Gold. Like 12th.

14th Round.—Like 13th.

15th to 19th Round.—Like the 12th, but with the black silk, and worked rather looser. There will now be 120 stitches in the round, which is the full size of the purse.

20th Round.—Gold. Like 12th.

Join on the crimson, without cutting off the gold, and do. for the

21st Round.— + 1 crimson, 1 gold, + 60 times. Cut off the gold.

22nd, 23rd, and 24th Rounds.—Sc with crimson only.

25th Round.—Join on the gold, which must be worked with the crimson, + 9 crimson, 1 gold, 10 crimson, + 6 times.

26th Round.—Join on the black also, + 3 crimson, 1 gold, 2 crimson, 1 black, 1 crimson, 3 gold, 1 crimson, 1 black, 2 crimson, 1 gold, 4 crimson, + 6 times.

27th Round.— + 2 crimson, 3 gold, 1 crimson, 2 black, 1 crimson, 1 gold, 1 crimson, 2 black, 1 crimson, 3 gold, 3 crimson, + 6 times.

28th Round.— + 3 crimson, 1 gold, 2 crimson, 3 black, 1 crimson, 3 black, 2 crimson, 1 gold, 4 crimson, + 6 times. Cut off the gold.

29th Round.— + 6 crimson, 3 black, 1 crimson, 3 black, 7 crimson, + 6 times.

30th Round.— + 2 crimson, 4 black, 1 crimson, 2 black, 1 crimson, 2 black, 1 crimson, 4 black, 3 crimson, + 6 times.

31st Round.— + 3 crimson, 4 black, 1 crimson, 1 black, 1 crimson, 1 black, 1 crimson, 4 black, 4 crimson, + 6 times.

32nd Round.—Join on the gold, + 2 crimson, 1 gold, 1 crimson, 4 black, 1 crimson, 1 gold, 1 crimson, 4 black, 1 crimson, 1 gold, 3 crimson, + 6 times.

33rd Round.— + 1 crimson, 3 gold, 4 crimson, 3 gold, 4 crimson, 3 gold, 2 crimson, + 6 times.

34th like *32nd Round.*—After which cut off the gold.

35th like *31st;* *36th* like *30th;* *37th* like *29th.* Join on the gold. *38th* like *28th;* *39th* like *27th;* *40th* like *26th;* *41st,* like *25th.*

42nd, 43rd, and 44th, all crimson.

45th Round.—Join on the gold, and do one gold stitch and one crimson alternately all round.

46th Round. — Gold. Fasten off the crimson.

47th Round.—Black. + 5 Sc, 5 Ch, Miss 5, + all round.

48th and three following *Rounds,* with black; + 5 Sc, beginning always on the second Sc of the previous round, 5 Ch, + repeat.

52nd and *53rd Round.*—Same with gold.

54th and *55th Round.*—Same with crimson.

56th and *57th Round.*—Same with gold.

58th to *62nd Round* (inclusive).—The same with black.

63rd to *68th Round.*—All black, + 1 Dc, 1 Ch, Miss 1, + all round. Fasten off.

This is the top of the purse. The lace edging which falls back, below the strings, is then worked on the 66th *Round,* thus,—

With the crimson silk, + 5 Dc in one chain, 1 Ch, Miss 4, + repeat.

2nd Round.—Gold. Sc on every Dc, and under every chain.

3rd Round.—Crimson, + 5 Dc, over the third of the 5 Dc, 1 Ch, + repeat.

4th Round.—Gold. Sc on every Dc, and under every chain. Fasten off neatly.

Two rounds of open crochet being thus left, above the lace, the crimson cord is to be run in there, for the strings; the ends of the cord to be finally sewed together, and the joins concealed by the small bullion slides.

The purse is to be finished by sewing on a very handsome French tassel at the bottom of the purse.

HADROT LAMP-COVER.

Materials —Rich Crimson and Stone-coloured Berlin Wool, 16 skeins of each; 4 of Boulton and Son's knitting-needles, No. 15.

Cast 24 stitches on one needle, with the crimson wool, and 36 on each of two others; join into a round, and do one inch thus. + knit 2, purl 2 + repeat all round.

Fasten on the Stone.

1st Round. + Knit 2, + miss 1, knit 1, + 6 times, knit 1, purl 3 + 8 times.

2nd Round. + Knit 15, purl 3 + 8 times.

3rd Round. + Knit 2 twice, knit 11, knit 2 twice, purl 3, + 8 times.

4th Round. + Knit 2 twice, knit 9, knit 2 twice, purl 3 + 8 times.

5th Round. Knit 2 twice, knit 7, knit 2 twice, purl 3, + 8 times.

There being now the same number of stitches that there were at the beginning, repeat this pattern with the stone wool, three times more; then fasten on the crimson, and repeat it. Do four stripes of each colour which will be sufficient for

the large part of the lamp, when you will decrease by knitting two stitches together at the beginning and end of every shell, (that is, between the purled stitches,) until only three plain are left between the purled three.

Then with the crimson, do about 2 inches thus,—+ Knit 3, purl 3, + repeat. Cast off very loosely.

For the netted frill, work on a foundation, with the stone wool, a round large enough to set *full* round the bottom of the cover, do about five rounds, with a small bone mesh, and stone wool; then two rounds with crimson. Take a mesh twice as large, and work two stitches in every one; then with the fine mesh two rounds of stone.

Sew it round the base of the cover.

These covers may be made of any two colours that will suit the draperies of the room. For a large lamp add 24, 36, or 48 stitches, and repeat between the crosses so many times more as you have a greater number of twelves.

These covers are extremely useful in protecting the French bronze of the Hadrot lamps from the dust, which greatly injures them.

———

HADROT LAMP COVER, BY MRS. PULLAN.

CHEMISETTE, IN ANTIQUE POINT.

Materials.—W. Evans & Co.'s Point Lace cottons, and 3 yards of Italian braid.

THIS design must be enlarged to any dimensions that may be required. Perhaps fourteen inches may be considered a good average length for the front, not of course reckoning up to the shoulder; but it depends entirely on whether the dress be worn very open or not.

If one-half be drawn on tracing paper, the pattern of the other side of the chemisette will be obtained from the wrong side of the drawn design

The outlines of all the flowers, leaves, and buds, are made in Italian braid, the stem being in the same material. It is necessary to fasten off the braid at every separate leaf; and these and the buds should be outlined before the stems and large flowers are done, as, by referring to the engraving, it will be seen that the flowers form continuations and terminations to the stems. The branches are all

CHEMISETTE
IN ANTIQUE POINT,
BY MRS. PULLAN.

done separately, beginning with the upper one.

The top of the flower and bud are outlined in No. 1 Mecklenburgh thread. This, also, is done before the braiding. The entire ground is in Raleigh bars.

The filling up is as follows: — The leaves are worked in Brussels lace, with Evans's Boar's Head, No. 70. Over the lace the veinings are done with Mecklenburgh thread, No. 100. The best way of doing the veinings is to take a thread three times along the length of the leaf, *ending at the point;* then cover these threads with close button-hole stitch, as far as the first branch; run the needle through the braid at the proper place, and work back on that single bar of thread to the main stem, on which continue until you come to the next side veining, which work like the first.

The whole of the veinings are thus done without breaking off the thread.

The buds are worked in close, fine English lace with W. Evans and Co.'s Boar's Head Cotton, No. 100. The single spot at the upper part, and the Brussels lace are done with the same cotton.

The petals are done in Venetian lace, with W. Evans and Co.'s Boar's Head, No. 70. The Mecklin wheels in Mecklenburgh 160.

Down each front a few rows of close foundation stitch may be worked with small spaces left at intervals, for the button-holes, which should be very small and to correspond with each other.

A collar, to match with this habit-shirt, might very readily be formed of the flowers and buds. Being rather solid work, the paper is better lined with Alpaca than with calico.

ORIGIN OF THE HUMAN RACE.—I believe that the origin of the human race is not connected with any given place, but is to be sought everywhere over the face of the earth; and that it is an idea more worthy of the power and wisdom of the Creator, to assume that he gave to each zone and each climate its proper inhabitants, to whom that zone and climate would be the most suitable, than to assume that the human species has degenerated in such innumerable instances.—*Niebuhr.*

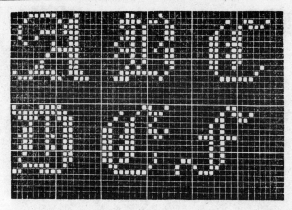

LETTERS IN SQUARE CROCHET, BY MRS. PULLAR.

LETTERS IN SQUARE CROCHET.

IN fulfilling our promise to give specimens of letters in crochet, it is scarcely necessary to add any instructions, the mode of working square crochet being so generally known. Those who are not acquainted with it may, however, refer to our "Instructions in Crochet," in another part of this work.

We would suggest, however, that mottoes worked in beads, in the same manner as the border of the Anti-macassar given elsewhere, are pretty for various purposes; and for these, the Alphabet we are now giving, and one of small letters which will follow, may be easily made available. Our friends will remember, however, that beads can only be used for this purpose, in working *Sc*, and also that such work is invariably done on the wrong side.

SLIPPERS IN ORIENTAL EMBROIDERY.

Materials.—Rich Green, Blue, or Black Velvet; 2 ozs. of Bright and Dead Bullion Gold; Gold Spangles; Seed Pearls; Gold-coloured Floss, and China Silk.

THE quantity of velvet required for these slippers must depend, of course, on the size required. Seven-sixteenths of a yard will be ample for ladies' slippers, unless the foot to wear them is of a most unusual size; and the width of velvet is sufficient to allow of both coming out of it. The velvet should be of the richest description, with a short, thick, close pile,—not merely because it is much more durable, but also because it is much more easy to work.

We trust that none of our friends will be deterred from attempting this beautiful style of work, either by the grandeur of the name, or by any imaginary difficulty in gold embroidery. True, the most striking specimens of oriental embroidery in the Great Exhibition were such as would require the wealth of Crœsus, and the years of Methuselah, for any one person to accomplish; but the beauty of the embroidery was not better displayed in them than in the tasteful trifles which almost any one may accomplish, — the slippers, cigar-cases, and lounging-caps, which are so well calculated for birthday presents, parting gifts, and souvenirs of friends.

Of such is the slipper of which we now give the design. The scrolls which form the outlines of the pattern are in raised gold embroidery; the diagonal stones are worked in gold bullion, the stars are in spangles, and in the centre of each diamond is a single seed pearl.

SLIPPERS IN ORIENTAL EMBROIDERY, BY MRS. PULLAN.

Begin by transferring the design to strong writing-paper, and pricking the outlines to form a pounced pattern. Then mark the velvet as you would any other kind of embroidery. Care must be taken to do this without injuring the pile of the velvet. Place the slippers in a frame, and cover all the scrolls with layers of thick soft cotton, tacked down with yellow silk. The cotton is not threaded and taken through the velvet, but merely *laid over*,—being thicker along the middle of the width of the scroll, than at the edges. It should be kept quite within the edges of the pattern, and is covered with yellow floss. A smooth raised surface is thus obtained, forming a bed over which the gold bullion is to be laid.

Doubtless the majority of our readers know the sort of gold which is termed bullion; but as there may be some who are not acquainted with it, we may as well describe it. It is a continuous *tube* of very fine gold wire, either plain or fancy. The tube is either smaller or larger, as may be required; the finest only is used in gold embroidery. When worked, it is cut into lengths, and the needle, threaded with waxed silk, run through the tube. The gold should be of the purest quality manufactured; common gold, though looking well at first, tarnishes almost immediately.

To lay on the gold, thread a long sewing-needle, with waxed silk, attach it to the velvet on the wrong side, and bring it up on the right at the end of a scroll. Cut off sufficient bullion to cover that end; thread it on, and draw the needle through the velvet on the wrong side. Continue to work the whole scroll in this manner,—the bits of bullion being laid on parallel with each other and as close together as possible. Three bits of brilliant, and four of dead gold come alternately throughout. The engraving shows the direction in which they are laid.

The bars which mark the diamonds are done entirely in dead gold, the pieces being all of the same length, namely sufficiently long to go from cross to cross. At a short distance from the point where four meet, as many spangles are sewed on, the silk being covered with short bits of the bright bullion, all four stitches meeting in the centre. To conceal this, another spangle is added thus,—slip the needle through it, cut off about the sixth of an inch of bright bullion, thread it on the needle, which pass again through the eye of the spangle, the bullion thus forming a little loop above the spangle.

A single seed pearl is sewed in every diamond.

Slippers so richly ornamented in front are seldom embroidered at the sides; those ladies who may wish it done can, however, add a strip of diamonds down to correspond with the centre of the front.

For gentlemen there should be no trimming round the top of the slipper, but for ladies it may be finished in the following manner. Lay a gold fringe all round the top, *to fall over the foot*, and at the heading of it a satin ribbon, box-plaited along the centre, with a seed-pearl in every plait. The ribbon should not be more than three-quarters of an inch wide.

The family crest forms a very suitable front for a gentleman's slipper, in this sort of embroidery.

THE DREAM OF LIFE.—How few of us at the close of life can say, " I have filled and occupied the position to which I looked forward when a boy!" In the onward progress of life, how often in some stray moment of thought and reflection, do we not find ourselves inquiring, "Is this as I hoped,—have I enacted my dream?" And the answer is invariably—No! We look forward in childhood—and only look forward—without reflection. We build up gorgeous palaces, we sketch a career of life all gold and sunshine,—what are they, and where are they, when years sober us?

THE WORK-TABLE FRIEND.

POINT LACE INSERTION.

Material. — W. Evans & Co's Point Lace Cottons, and No. 7 French-white Cotton braid.

A PERFECT section of this design is given, and is to be repeated as often as required. If a short piece is wanted—such as a length for the front of a chemisette—it is well to draw the whole of it on a slip of paper; but when any continuous piece is to be made, draw only such a length as may be conveniently held in the hand, and when that is worked, remove the lace, and work again on the same pattern, folding up the finished piece, and tacking it in muslin or silver paper, to keep it clean, whilst working the remainder. Of course, when long pieces of lace are to be produced, the braid must not be cut off until the whole is done. As many pieces are to be used as there are continuous lines in the design. In the one before us, four pieces will be wanted, namely, one for each edge, and two for the scroll. They are wound on cards. The ground is Brussels lace, worked in Evans's Boar's Head, No. 120; the English lace in Evans's Boar's Head, 100; the Venetian lace in the same; the Mechlin wheels in Evans's Mecklenburgh, 120, and the Venetian and English bars in Evans's Mecklenburgh, 100. The Venetian edging in the same thread as the Venetian lace, and the Valenciennes in Evans's Boar's Head, No. 150.

To join Point lace edgings or insertions to muslin or net, make a very narrow hem of these latter; and laying the narrow braid which forms the edge of the Point lace over the hem, run them both together. A row of Venetian or Brussels edge may then be worked, connecting the muslin and braid at every stitch.

TRIMMING FOR A MANDARIN SLEEVE IN TATTING.

Materials. — Evans's Tatting Cotton, No. 1; Boulton's Steel Shuttle; a Pearling-pin; and Evans's Tatting Cotton, No. 3.

The Scallop.—Having filled the shuttle with the tatting cotton, leaving a very long needleful, on which a coarse needle is threaded, begin

Point Lace Insertion.—By Mrs. Pullan.

The 1st Set of Five Loops.—14 double stitches, + 1 picot, 2 double + twice. Draw up the loop tightly. With the needle, work on the thread attached to the shuttle 6 buttonhole stitches; make a picot on the needleful of thread, 6 more buttonhole stitches.

2nd Loop.—2 double. join to the last picot of the first loop; 2 double, join to the next; 10 double, + 1 picot, 2 double + twice; draw it up tightly. Work 4 buttonhole stitches on the thread.

3rd Loop.—2 double, join ; 2 double, join ; 14 double; 1 picot, 2 double, 1 picot, 2 double. Work 4 buttonhole stitches on the thread.

4th Loop.—Like 2nd. After this, work 6 buttonhole stitches on the thread, and connect with the picot made *after* the 1st loop, by slipping the needle through it ; then 6 more buttonhole stitches on the thread.

5th Loop.—2 double, join ; 2 double, join ; 5 double ; 1 picot, 5 double, 1 picot, 2 double, 1 picot, 2 double; draw it up tightly. Slip the needle across to the close of the 1st loop, and work back on the bar 12 buttonhole stitches. This completes the 1st set of five.

The buttonhole bar between this and the next is done thus : + 4 buttonhole stitches, .join to picot of 5th loop + twice ; 16 buttonholes,* 1 picot on the thread connected

with the shuttle, 4 buttonhole stitches,* twice.

The 2nd Set of Five Loops.—1st Loop. 2 double, join to picot last made ; 2 double, join to the next ; 5 double, join to picot on the 5th loop : 5 double ; + 1 picot, 2 double + twice. Draw it up tightly.

The intermediate spaces, and the other 4 loops, are done like those of the 1st set ; but on the bar made to connect this set with the next, only 9 buttonhole stitches are worked where 16 were made on the former one ; and, on the 5th loop, instead of 10 double, do 7 double, 1 picot 3 double.

The 3rd Set of Five Loops.—1st Loop. 2 double, join ; 2 double, join ; 3 double, join ; 7 double ; + 1 picot, 2 double + twice ; draw it up tightly. The 4 remaining loops are worked like those of the 2nd set ; but, after drawing up the 5th, instead of making a bar across to the 1st, work on the thread 4 buttonhole stitches, and connect with the last picot ; then slip the needle across to the corresponding part of the connecting bar between the 2nd and 3rd, and work back on the thread 6 buttonhole stitches. Do the remaining part of this bar like the last.

The 4th Set of Five Loops.—Like the 3rd, except the 5th loop, which is made thus : —2 double, join ; 2 double, join ; + 5 double, 1 picot + twice, 2 double, 1 picot,

Trimming for a Mandarin Sleeve in Tatting.—By Mrs. Pullan.

2 double. Draw it up like the rest, and work a connecting bar exactly like that between the 1st and 2nd sets.

The 5th Set of Five Loops.—Like the 2nd except the 5th loop. 2 double, join; 2 double, join; 14 double. Draw it up.

These 5 sets form one scallop. All the scallops are worked separately; and, when finished, they are tacked in their proper places on a piece of coloured paper, cut out in the shape of a Mandarin sleeve, with a sprig in each Vandyke; and the whole formed into a lace by working Venetian lace in all the vacant spaces, connecting it to the picots, and other parts of the tatting. A line is also made as an inner edge, by laying 4 parallel lines of cotton on the paper, and working them into a braid, by darning them backwards and forwards with Mecklenburgh, No. 80.

The Sprig.—Leave a few inches of the thread on the shuttle, and take a separate and very long needleful of thread for the buttonhole work.

First Leaf. 1st Loop.—6 double, + 1 picot, 3 double + twice; draw it up tightly. With the needle, work 8 buttonhole stitches, *leaving a few inches of the thread.*

2nd Loop.—3 double, join; + 3 double, 1 picot + twice, 3 double. Draw it up, and work afterwards like the 1st.

K

3rd Loop.—3 double, join; 3 double, 1 picot, 4 double, 1 picot, 2 double. Draw it up tightly, and work 5 buttonhole stitches afterwards.

4th Loop.—2 double, join; 3 double, 1 picot, 2 double, 1 picot, 2 double, 1 picot, 3 double, 1 picot, 2 double. Draw it up, and work 5 stitches.

5th Loop.—2 double, join; 4 double, 1 picot, 3 double, 1 picot, 3 double. Draw it up, slip the needle to the closing of the 3rd loop, and work back on it 5 buttonhole stitches; then 8 more between this and the 6th loop, which is made like the 2nd. Work after this in the same manner.

7th Loop.—3 double, join; 3 double, 1 picot, 6 double. Draw it up tightly, and work 1 buttonhole stitch to close the leaf.

Work with the needle on the two ends of thread, backwards and forwards, about three-fourths of an inch for a stem. Begin the second leaf with a space of cotton between, and do it like the first, omitting the 2nd and 6th loops. Leave another space of cotton, and work the flower, commencing at the centre.

The Flower. + 3 double, 1 picot, + 5 times, 3 double. Draw it up tightly. Make 6 small loops thus:—5 double, 1 picot, 5 double. Draw it up into a semicircular form, the bar of thread at the base being equal to the space of 3 double stitches. Work all along these in buttonhole, with the needle, doing 5 stitches on the loop, and 2 between it and the next, slipping the needle through a picot of the centre loop, after the first of the 2 buttonhole. Now work in braid stitch up the stem till opposite the small leaf, which repeat. Continue until you are opposite the large leaf; leave a length of thread for its stem; repeat the large leaf; then braid down the stem, and the flower is made.

It will be remembered, that flowers, **stars**, or any other patterns in Tatting, may be made at any intervals from each other without breaking off the thread. This affords a facility for the formation of stems and connecting bars.

———◆———

The surest way of governing, both a private family and a kingdom, is for a husband and a prince to yield at certain times something of their prerogative.

THE WORK-TABLE FRIEND.

HAND-SCREEN IN CROCHET.

Materials—2 skeins of coarse purse silk, blue, green, or crimson; 2 skeins of gold thread, the same size; half-a-yard of white satin; half-a-yard of silk to match the netting silk; 3 yards of ornamental cord; some stout cardboard, and wadding; a pair of handles.

WITH the silk make a chain of eight stitches, close it into a round, and work on it 16 stitches in Sc.

2nd Round.—+ 1 Ch, miss none, 1 Dc, + 16 times.

3rd Round.— + 2 Ch, Dc on Dc, + 16 times.

4th Round.— + 3 Ch, Dc on Dc, + 16 times.

5th Round.— + 4 Ch, Dc on Dc, + 16 times.

6th Round.— + 9 Ch, miss 6, Tc under the 7th, + 11 times missing 7 three times, instead of six.

7th Round.— 8 Ch, + 5 Dc, the centre one coming over the Tc of last round, 6 Ch, + repeat all round. End with 7 Ch.

8th Round.— + 7 Dc, 5 centre coming over the five of last round, 6 Ch, + all round. End with eight chain.

9th Round.— + 9 Dc, one coming over each Dc, and one at each side, 6 Ch, + all round. Join on the gold, and work it in to the last 9 Dc, ending with 9 chain, made with the gold thread.

10th Round.— In this round all the Dc are made with silk, and the chain with gold. At the conclusion of it, fasten off the silk, and work with gold only. + 11 Dc, coming as the nine, 9 Ch + 10 times; 11 Dc as before.

11th Round.— + 4 Ch, Dc on the centre of 9 Ch, 4 Ch, Dc on the first of 11 Dc, 4 Ch, Tc on the centre of 11 Dc, 4 Ch, Dc on the last of 11 Dc, + all round.

12th Round.— + 7 Ch, 3 Dc, the centre over the 1 Dc on the 9 Ch, 7 Ch, 3 Dc, the centre over the Tc + all round.

13th Round.—Dc over the centre of every three Dc, and on the 4th of every 7 Ch, with 5 Ch between, in every instance. End with 5 Ch.

14th Round.— + 3 Dc, the 2nd coming on the 1 Dc over 7 Ch, 9 Ch, + repeat all round. End with 7 Ch, and join on the silk, which use for the remainder.

**HAND-SCREEN IN CROCHET,
BY MRS. PULLAN.**

15th Round.— + 7 Dc, over 3 Dc and 2 Ch on each side, 5 Ch + all round.

16th Round.—+ 11 Dc, over 7 Dc and 2 Ch on each side, 3 Ch, + all round.

17th Round.— + 13 Ch, over 11, and 1 chain on each side, 3 Ch; + all round.

18th Round.— + 3 Ch, miss 3, 1 Dc, + all round.

19th Round.—All Dc, increasing enough to make the work quite flat.

To make up the screen, cut out a round of cardboard, the size of the crochet; lay wadding on both sides of it, and cover it with the satin on one side, and with the silk on the other, bringing this latter a little over the edge. Sew them together;

put on the crochet, over the white satin, and trim it with two rounds of cord.

In the pattern, two different kinds of cord are used. Both are crimson and white, and they are laid so that the twist is *reversed.*

The handles are put on with gilt nails.

Many screens are trimmed with a deep silk fringe, which has a very rich and beautiful effect.

EMBROIDERED HANDKERCHIEF.

Materials.—1 square of fine French cambric, with W. Evans & Co.'s scarlet and white embroidery cotton, No. 50.

WE give the corner of this handkerchief the full size, as the pattern can be traced from it, and only requires to be repeated for the whole border. The edge, it will be seen, is formed of two scallops, worked in graduated button-hole stitch, and intersecting each other. One of these should be worked in scarlet cotton, and the other in white; but as scarlet is rather expensive, the tracing of the whole should be done with white, as well as the running in of the threads which raise the surface for the satin stitch. The eyelet-holes, after being traced, are cut out, and worked round in button-hole stitch. The flowers are done as in Broderie Anglaise. Either the flowers or the eyelet-holes should be done in scarlet.

We have selected the initial E as being one of the most generally useful. It has a very beautiful effect, when worked. The outlines of the letter are intended to represent the branches of a tree, and may be done in scarlet embroidery; the grapes are formed of very small eyelet-holes, which, with the stem, are sewed over. The leaves are in very fine and delicate satin stitch, and the veinings are worked in scarlet cotton. The fruit, leaves, and tendrils, are white.

Handkerchiefs embroidered in colours should be done on fine, but *thick* cambric: not the transparent kind; for which, not being used in evening toilette, they are not suitable.

For instructions in marking and working embroidery, see another part of this volume.

INSTRUCTIONS IN CANVASS WORK.

THE necessity for giving the additional stitches in Point Lace, prevented us from

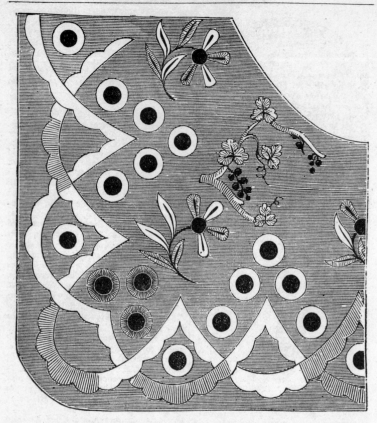

EMBROIDERED HANDKERCHIEF, BY MRS. PULLAN

fulfilling our promise to complete the subject of Embroidery, by giving directions for that branch of it which is usually called *Canvass*, or *Berlin Tapestry* work. Our present article will be confined wholly to this subject; and we will begin by describing the materials usually employed.

CANVASS of some kind forms the foundation on which every kind of Berlin or tapestry is worked. It is a fabric woven generally of cotton or silk, and known as German, French, Penelope, and silk **canvass.**

Fine canvass has the threads close and fine; in coarse canvass they are thick and far apart. The sizes are distinguished by numbers, which are given according to the number of threads in the inch. It follows that the size of a piece of work depends wholly on the canvass employed,—a fact not unfrequently forgotten by those who order designs to be drawn to fill a certain space. Imagine, for instance, that a coat of arms is to be drawn, to be worked for the back of a chair. Unless the size of the canvass on which it is to be done, it is impossible to draw it satisfactorily; for supposing that the width of the drawing were 100 cross stitches, it would be about 14 inches wide; if worked on No. 12 canvass, and worked on No. 40, it would be just 5¾ inches. If done in tent-stitch, it would be just half the size each way; nor are the numbers of canvass I have given the extremes of either coarse or fine.

The coarsest canvass in general use is No. 6, which has 9 threads in an inch. From that number up to 24 (progressing by 2, 6, 8, 10, &c.) there are always three threads more than the number of the canvass, in the inch. 30 has 31 threads only; 40 has but 35, and 50 only 37. This is the finest canvass in general use.

To enable our friends to select patterns and canvass that will really suit them, we give the following Table:

In No. 6 canvass, 100 stitches make 21 inches				
No. 8	,,	,,	,, 18	,,
No. 10	,,	,,	,, 15¼	,,
No. 12	,,	,,	,, 13½	,,
No. 14	,,	,,	,, 11½	,,
No. 16	,,	,,	,, 10½	,,
No. 18	,,	,,	,, 9¾	,,
No. 20	,,	,,	,, 8¾	,,
No. 22	,,	,,	,, 8	,,
No. 24	,,	,,	,, 7½	,,
No. 30	,,	,,	,, 6¾	,,
No. 40	,,	,,	,, 5¾	,,
No. 50	,,	,,	,, 5½	,,

in cross stitch.

Any pattern worked in tent - stitch occupies *one-half* the width and length that it would take if cross stitch were used.

GERMAN COTTON CANVASS is distinguished by every tenth thread being yellow. This is convenient for counting, but the canvass itself is of very inferior quality, the squares are not true, and it is not nearly so strong as the French canvass. In consequence of these defects, it is not much used.

French Cotton Canvass is that generally used; and to it the scale we have given more particularly refers.

Silk canvass (sometimes called Berlin canvass), is not made in nearly so many sizes as the common sort; those most in use have 21, 29, 34, and 40 threads to the inch.

Silk canvass is chiefly used for pieces that are not to be grounded. It requires great care in working, as the threads and wools must not be carried from one part to another, at the back of the work, lest they should be seen through the canvass.

Penelope canvass takes its name from presenting the appearance of canvass that has been worked, and the work picked out again. Every two threads are nearly close together, and have a space between them and the next two. It can only be worked in cross stitch.

INFANT'S BLANKET.

Materials.—1½ lb. of 6 thread fleecy, and 2 coarse knitting needles.

CAST on 200 stitches.

1st row + knit 4, purl 4 + alternately to the end. 2nd row the same, always beginning with the same stitches you ended with. 3rd like 1st. 4th like 2nd. Now reverse these. Begin by purling 4 to come over the knitted 4, and *vice versa*; and let the 5th, 6th, 7th, & 8th rows have purled stitches where the four first were knitted, and knit over purled, to form a check. Repeat these eight rows three times. Now knit the first and last 24 in the same way, but the intermediate ones thus + knit 1, bring the thread in front, slip 1 from the back, put the thread back, + repeat to within 24, finish like the end. The next row the same. Knit the stitches you slipped before, and slip those you knitted.

Do this until sufficient is knitted for a bassinet quilt, and then do 24 rows like the first, and fasten off.

PROMISES.—There is a sort of people in the world of whom the young and inexperienced stand much in need to be warned. These are the sanguine promisers. They may be divided into two sorts. The first are those who, from a foolish custom of fawning upon all those they come in company with, have acquired a habit of promising to do great kindness, which they have no thought of performing. The other are a sort of warm people, who, while they are lavishing away their promises, have really some thought of doing what they engage for; but afterwards, when the time of performance comes, the sanguine fit being gone off, the trouble or expense appears in another light; the promiser cools, and the expectant is bubbled, or perhaps greatly injured by the disappointment.

CURIOUS ANTIQUE LACE, MADE IN THE FIFTEENTH CENTURY.

THE WORK-TABLE FRIEND.

INSTRUCTIONS IN ANTIQUE POINT.

WE now present our readers with instructions for working some of the more complicated stitches used in the old point lace; and, in doing so, we beg distinctly to disavow any wish to take to ourselves credit for the invention of any one of them; we do not profess to be the *inventor* of stitches that were worked hundreds of years ago; we are contented to claim the merit of reviving an art which was almost lost; of following closely in the footsteps of three admirable needlewomen, whose works we endeavour to imitate, but do not hope to excel; and we do claim the credit of adapting, to the modern forms of dress, those exquisite stitches and elegant designs, the production of which formed the glory and pride of our ancestresses. The study of antique point lace is one so full of interest, that once taken up it becomes a sort of passion. Those who understand its peculiarities and value its power to gratify the dealers in curiosities, are confident of the due appreciation of any peculiarly scarce and beautiful specimen, therefore are certain to offer it to the connoisseur; and hence it has happened that we have become the fortunate possessors of rare pieces of old lace, which form a constant and most interesting study. The results are given to our readers, certainly, not as *inventions* of our own, or as point lacework,—a title which is simply an absurdity; but as veritable antique point, resembling as nearly as possible the valuable old points which is considered in many great families as so inestimable an heirloom; the sort of lace celebrated not only from forming a part of the costume of the

"Fair dames and ancient knights"

of other days, but also from having been deemed not unworthy to exercise the skill and taste of some of the greatest painters, who designed many of the most valuable specimens of this exquisite style of work.

The great difficulty we have had to

VICTORIA LACE COLLAR. BY MRS. PULLAN.

surmount has arisen from the difference between the threads used in those days and those produced in our own. Even this, however, we have now surmounted, through the kindness of Messrs. W. Evans and Co., of Derby, who have manufactured various kinds of thread and cotton expressly for point lace, with a degree of care that leaves nothing to be desired on this head. To ourselves belongs the rest; what the fingers of our ancestresses achieved, it is surely not unreasonable to hope that ours may accomplish: it only requires that we should be as good plain needlewomen as they were, for the finest and most delicate point lace is but a modification of *sewing*, requiring no extraordinary talents but industry and perseverance.

The most valuable lace is that in which the pattern, being drawn on paper or any other substance, is outlined entirely in thread. Some lace is outlined in cotton braid. Some in a *lace braid*, made of linen, and known to our readers under the term *Italian* braid; some is worked on the linen itself, the threads of which are partially drawn out; but all these have less work, and are consequently less valuable than that in which a simple thread forms the outlines of the pattern. A thread has been manufactured expressly for this work, termed Evans's Mecklinburgh thread, No. 1.

To Prepare and Outline the Pattern.—Draw it on coloured paper. which line with two or three thicknesses of alpaca, or merino, tacked under it. Thread a fine needle with No. 100 Mecklenburgh thread, in which make a knot; lay the end of the No. 1 Mecklenburgh over the beginning of one of the inked lines, run the needle through the alpaca and paper into the line on one side of the thread, and, (letting the fine thread cross the coarse,) bring the needle *through the same hole*, on to the wrong side. Take similar stitches throughout the pattern, at the distance of about the eighth of an inch from each other, always making one at the extremity of every point and corner, so that the outlines are made with the utmost exactness. When you wish to join the ends of an outlining thread, lay one over the other.

Outlines made in thread possess the advantage of being made in separate sections, if necessary, instead of running them in continuous lines as is always done with French braid.

We shall now give our readers some new stitches; adding that many others will be discovered in the process of the work.

THE STITCHES. — No. 1 foundation stitch. This stitch is the one in which all those parts of the lace are worked, which are perfectly solid, and have no fancy stitches in them. Take a bar of thread parallel with that of the foundation, and over them work Brussel lace stitches, doing them as closely together as possible. For the second row, take a thread parallel with the first, and work a similar row: taking a stitch between every two stitches of the former. The bars of thread should be about the sixteenth of an inch apart, if very fine work be required and more distant, if the pattern be on a large scale. Each time that you come to the outline thread, twist the needle twice round it, before taking the next bar across.

No. 2. OPEN DIAMONDS. 1st Row. + 8 close Brussels stitches; miss the space of one stitch, + repeat throughout the length.

2nd Row. + Miss the first two of the eight stitches; do five close button-hole, miss the last two; do two close Brussels on the loop formed in the last row by missing a stitch; + repeat.

3rd Row. Do two close Brussels in every loop formed in last row, and also over the centre of the five close—that is, after the second and the third.

4th Row. 5 close Brussels (crossing over the five of 2nd row), and two in the loop over the two of that row.

5th Row. This is like the first: there are eight close Brussels stitches done, 4 of which come over the five of last row, and two on the loop on each side, then miss the space of the two stitches of last row. For this stitch repeat the last four rows as often as may be required.

No. 3. CLOSE DIAMONDS.

1st Row. Brussels lace, worked quite closely.

2nd Row. + 8 close Brussels, miss 2, + repeat.

3rd Row. + Miss the two first of eight, do five close Brussels, which will be finished just before the two last of eight; miss them, do 2 close Brussels on the loop of last row, + repeat.

4th Row. + 8 close Brussels, 4 of which come over the five, and two on the loop at each end of it, miss the two worked over the loop, + repeat.

These four rows join one line of diamonds. In filling up any space, always let the diamonds of one pattern fall just between those of the last. This might be done (if the width of the space were not increased).

No. 4. BARCELONA LACE.

1st Row. Work a row of Sorrento edging, the long loop of which shall be long enough to hold four close Brussels stitches, and the other half that length.

2nd Row. 4 close Brussels on each long stitch, missing the short one altogether.

3rd Row. Take a stitch on to the bar of third between the first four and the second, work a tight button-hole stitch on it; do another in the same; repeat on every bar of thread.

For this lace, repeat the second and third rows alternately.

No. 5. FAN LACE.

1st Row. 6 close Brussels, miss the space of six—Repeat.

2nd Row. 6 close stitches on every side of last row.

3rd Row. 6 close Brussels on every loop of thread, missing all the stitches of last row.

4th Row. 6 over the six, and six more on the loop.

5th Row. + 6 close stitches on those worked on the loop, miss the next six + repeat.

For all future patterns, repeat the third, fourth, and fifth rows only: They may be worked backwards and forwards.

No. 6. SPOTTED LACE.

1st Row. + 2 close Brussels, leave the space of two, + repeat.

2nd and following Rows. 2 close Brussels in every loop, missing the stitches of the last row.

No. 7. ANTWERP LACE. The first and second rows are the same as for open diamonds (No. 2).

3rd Row. + 1 close on the centre of five close, 5 close over the two close and the loops on each side of them. + repeat.

4th Row. + 5 close over two close, 2 close over five. + repeat.

Repeat these four rows as often as necessary.

No. 8. SEVILLE LACE.

1st Row. + 9 close Brussels, miss the space of two, + repeat.

2nd and all following Rows. + Miss the two first stitches of nine, work one after the second and all the others, and one more on the loop on which the eighth will be worked. + repeat.

No. 9. CADIZ LACE.

1st Row. + 6 close stitches, miss the space of two, 2 close, miss the space of two, + repeat.

2nd Row. Miss all the stitches of the last row, whether two or six, and on every space between work two stitches.

Repeat these two rows alternately for Cadiz Lace.

It will be observed that the common button-hole stitch (Brussels lace), is the only one required for all these laces, the patterns being formed by the various spaces left.

CURIOUS POINT LACE OF THE FIFTEENTH CENTURY.

Materials. — W. Evans and Co.'s Point Lace Cottons, and No. 1 Mecklenburgh Thread.

THIS lace is copied from some very valuable specimens, lent to us by a distinguished lady, in whose family they had been heirlooms for some hundreds of years. It is distinguished by a grotesqueness of forms, and a solidity of workmanship, characteristic of the period.

The outlines are done entirely in W. Evans and Co.'s Mecklenburgh thread, No. 1; the solid parts are done in foundation stitch, worked with No. 160 of the same thread, over bars done in No. 100. The cups of the acorns are done in close diamonds; the acorns in foundation stitch with the holes left, as in the engraving. Some of the leaves are done in the same manner, others have open spaces, in which Sorrento bars are crossed. When the stems are open, the outlines are overcast, after the bars within them have been done. All those parts which are pearled, must also be overcast, and the pearling is made of small Raleigh No. 3. The large flower is filled in, principally with open English lace; a stitch given in another part of this volume. The ground is made in plain Raleigh bars, or Venetian bars.

One of the flowers has a Mecklin wheel in the centre; the other has an English

point: the petals are done in close diamond-stitch.

One entire pattern of this lace is given in the engraving; and, in working it, the copy should be kept before the eye, and followed as closely as possible.

VICTORIA LACE COLLAR.

Materials.—Some fine Bobbinet; a piece of Victoria Braid, No. 7; and W. Evans and Co.'s Tatting Cotton, No. 1; and Boar's Head Sewing Cotton, No. 50.

Victoria lace is the name applied to net braided with the material once termed *Coronation* braid. It is composed of alternate thick and thin sections; and, when laid on, has something of the appearance of satin stitch. It is usually done by the eye, the thick part of the engraving designating the same in the braid: but those who cannot do it in this manner, may draw the pattern on coloured paper, cut out in the shape of the collar, or other article to be worked, and tack the net on it, having previously whipped the edges.

In putting on the braid, the needle is slipped through the thick and soft parts, and the stitch taken *over* the thin ones, which are of so hard a substance that a needle will not readily pass through them.

The ends are drawn through the braid.

The edging is done in tatting, thus :— 1 drab, + 1 pink, 1 double, + 9 times, draw it up. Every loop is done in the same way.

UNRESERVED communication is the lawful commerce of conjugal affection, and all concealment is contraband. It is a false compliment to the object of our affection, if, for the sake of sparing them a transient uneasiness, we rob them of the comfort to which they are entitled of mitigating our suffering, by partaking it. All dissimulation is disloyalty to love: besides, it argues a lamentable ignorance of human life, to set out with an expectation of health without interruption, and happiness without alloy. When young persons marry with the fairest prospects, they should never forget that infirmity is bound up with their very nature, and that in bearing one another's burdens, they fulfil one of the highest duties of the union.—*Mrs. H. More.*

COLLAR IN SPANISH ROSE POINT, BY MRS. PULLAN.

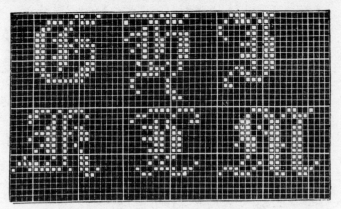

LETTERS IN SQUARE CROCHET, BY MRS. PULLAN.

THE WORK-TABLE FRIEND.

COLLAR IN SPANISH ROSE POINT.

Materials.—Walter Evans & Co.'s Point-lace cottons, Moravian thread; and No. 1, Mecklenburgh thread.

THE section given of this collar is one-fourth of the entire length, two patterns forming one half, and being reversed for the remainder.

The whole of the pattern is done in the close thick stitches of which we have already given diagrams and descriptions. Some parts are done wholly in foundation stitch, with the exception of the veinings, which are formed by doing one or two lines like the SPOTTED LACE. Open diamond and Antwerp lace are done with W. Evans's and Co.'s Mecklenburgh thread; No. 160. So is the foundation stitch; but the *bars* on which it is worked are done with Mecklenburgh, No. 120. The Spanish rose point stitch is a close button-hole stitch, worked over many threads of Moravian. The little loops are made thus: having worked the space for one loop, take the thread back to the beginning and cover the bar thus made with button-hole stitch; then do a small piece more of the thick part, and repeat. As the thickness is gradually shaped to a point at each end, it is necessary to cut some of the Moravian threads shorter. They are

tacked together, and form a sort of cushion, and the button-hole stitches are taken over them, but not through the lace. The little wheels in the bars of the ground-work (so characteristic of old Point), are covered with buttonhole-stitch, dotted with Raleigh bars. The edge is outlined, and worked in the same manner.

ANTI-MACASSAR IN CROCHET.

Materials.—Six reels of W. Evans and Co.'s Boar's-head cotton, No. 8, and 50 rows of turquoise beads, No. 2. Boulton and Son's crochet-hook, No. 16.

THIS Anti-Macassar being similar in style to others already given, although, of course, totally different in design, we have not thought it necessary to give an engraving of it. Thread all the beads on *one* reel of cotton; with another reel make a chain of 244 stitches, and do one row of Dc.

2nd Row.—A close square at each end, and all the rest open.

3rd Row.—1 close square, 1 open, Dc all but the last six stitches; 2 Ch, Miss 2, 4 Dc.

4th to 9th Row.—1 close, 1 open, 1 close, at each end; all the intermediate open.

10th Row.—1 close, 1 open, 1 close, 14 open, 1 close, 3 open, 1 close, 6 open, 1 close, 12 open, 1 close, 4 open, 1 close, 8 open, 2 close, 21 open, 1 close, 1 open, 1 close.

11th Row.—1 close, 1 open, 1 close, 15 open, 2 close, 2 open, 1 close, 5 open, 2 close, 2 open, 1 close, 2 open, 2 close, 3 open, 1 close, 4 open, 2 close, 4 open, 1 close, 2 open, 2 close, 12 open, 1 close, 9 open, 1 close, 1 open, 1 close.

12th Row.—1 close, 1 open, 1 close, 17 open, 4 close, 1 open, 1 close, 2 open, 2 close, 1 open, 2 close, 3 open, 2 close, 2 open, 1 close, 4 open, 1 close, 6 open, 1 close, 1 open, 2 close, 7 open, 1 close, 1 open, 1 close, 1 open, 1 close, 10 open, 1 close, 1 open, 1 close.

13th Row.—1 close, 1 open, 1 close, 16 open, 1 close, 4 open, 2 close, 2 open, 2 close, 1 open, + 2 close, 3 open, + twice; 3 close, 1 open, 1 close, 1 open, 3 close, 2 open, 3 close, 7 open, 1 close, 2 open, 2 close, 11 open, 1 close, 1 open, 1 close.

14th Row.—1 close, 1 open, 1 close, 20 open, 1 close, 2 open, 2 close, 1 open, 4 close, 4 open, 2 close, 2 open, 4 close, 1 open, 4 close, 2 open, 1 close, 7 open, 1 close, 1 open, 3 close, 2 open, 1 close, 10 open, 1 close, 1 open, 1 close.

15th Row. — This being the first decreased row, must be begun thus,—1 slip stitch, 1 Sc, 2 Dc, 2 Ch, miss 2; the last three stitches forming the open square, the process is to be reversed at the end. In future rows, we shall say, decrease one (or more), at each end ; to decrease two, make your slip stitch on the 4th of the previous row, to decrease these, it must be on the 7th and so on, the other end corresponding. Decrease 1 as above, 1 close, 9 open, + 1 close, 7 open, + twice, 4 close, 7 open, + 6 close, 1 open, + twice, 1 close, 2 open, 2 close, 1 open, 3 close, 2 open, 2 close, 12 open, 1 close. Decrease.

16th Row.—1 close (over open), 1 open, 1 close, 9 open, 1 close, 6 open, 2 close, 5 open, 3 close, 1 open, 1 close, 7 open, 6 close, 1 open, 6 close, 3 open, 2 close, 1 open, 1 close, + 2 open, 2 close, + twice ; 10 open, 1 close, 1 open, 1 close.

17th Row.—1 close, 1 open, 1 close, 9 open, 1 close, 1 open, 1 close, 5 open, 1 close, 2 open, 2 close, 6 open, 2 close, 1 open, 2 close, 3 open, 11 close, 4 open, 4 close, 18 open, 1 close, 1 open, 1 close.

18th Row.—1 close, 1 open, 1 close, 10 open, 2 close, 1 open, 1 close, 4 open, 4 close, 6 open, 5 close, 5 open, 2 close, 3

open, 2 close, 5 open, 1 close, 1 open, 2 close, 19 open, 1 close, 1 open, 1 close.

19th Row.—Decrease one, 1 close, 12 open, 2 close, 1 open, 1 close, 2 open, 2 close, 1 open, 2 close, 2 open, 2 close, 1 open, 5 close, 1 open, 2 close, 1 open, 2 close, 2 open, 1 close, 2 open, 5 close, 1 open, 2 close, 21 open, 1 close, decrease one.

20th Row.—1 close (over open), 1 open, 1 close, 10 open, 1 close, 2 open, 4 close, 1 open, 4 close, 2 open, + 3 close, 1 open, + twice, 3 close, 2 open, 2 close, 3 open, 7 close, 2 open, 3 close, 4 open, 1 close, 12 open, 1 close, 1 open, 1 close.

21st Row.—1 close, 1 open, 1 close, 12 open, + 1 close, 2 open, + twice ; 2 close, 2 open, 9 close, 1 open, 5 close, 1 open, 11 close, 3 open, 1 close, 1 open, 4 close, 13 open, 1 close, 1 open, 1 close.

22nd Row.—Decrease one, 1 close, 14 open, 1 close, 7 open, 6 close, 2 open, 7 close, 1 open, 5 close, 1 open, 3 close, 5 open, + 1 close, 2 open, + twice ; 2 close, 11 open, 1 close. Decrease.

23rd Row.—1 close (over open), 1 open, 1 close, 22 open, 4 close, 1 open, 2 close, 2 open, 4 close, 3 open, 4 close, 1 open, 3 close, 6 open, 1 close, 2 open, 1 close, 3 open, 1 close, 9 open, 1 close, 1 open, 1 close.

24th Row.—1 close, 1 open, 1 close, 17 open, 2 close, 2 open, + 1 close, 3 open, + twice ; 2 close, 1 open, 1 close, 2 open, 3 close, 1 open, 4 close, 3 open, 2 close, 1 open, 2 close, 18 open, 1 close, 1 open, 1 close.

25th Row.—1 close, 1 open, 1 close, 15 open, 1 close, 1 open, 4 close, 2 open, 4 close, 3 open, 1 close, 1 open, 6 close, 1 open, 4 close, 3 open, 5 close, 18 open, 1 close, 1 open, 1 close.

26th Row.—Decrease one, 1 close, 16 open, + 2 close, 1 open, + twice ; 5 close, 4 open, 1 close, 1 open, + 4 close, 1 open, + twice ; 3 close, 1 open, 1 close, 1 open, 1 close, + 1 open, 2 close, + twice, 13 open, 1 close. Decrease 1.

27th Row.—1 close (over open), 1 open, 1 close, 12 open, 1 close, 2 open, 4 close, 2 open, 6 close, 3 open, 1 close, 1 open, 5 close, 6 open, 1 close, 1 open, 5 close, 2 open, 2 close, 13 open, 1 close, 1 open, 1 close.

28th Row. — Decrease 1, 1 close, 13 open, 2 close, 2 open, 2 close, 3 open, 3 close, 1 open, 3 close, 2 open, 2 close, 1 open, 3 close, + 1 open, 2 close, + twice; 2 open, 2 close, 1 open, 2 close, 2 open, 1 close, 1 open, 2 close, 11 open, 1 close. Decrease 1.

29th Row.—1 close (over open), 1 open, 1 close, 11 open, 1 close, 1 open, 1 close, 6 open, 1 close, 3 open, 9 close, 3 open, 3 close, 1 open, 3 close, 8 open, 1 close, 2 open, 2 close, 9 open, 1 close, 1 open, 1 close.

30th Row.—Decrease 1, 1 close, 10 open, 1 close, 7 open, 4 close, 2 open, 4 close, 1 open, 5 close, 2 open, 7 close, 22 open, 1 close. Decrease 1.

31st Row.—1 close (over open), 1 open, 1 close, 18 open, 2 close, 1 open, 1 close, 1 open, 4 close, 1 open, 5 close, 4 open, 1 close, 1 open, 1 close, 2 open, 1 close, 20 open, 1 close, 1 open, 1 close.

32nd Row.—Decrease one at each end of this and every following row, till further directions. Decrease 1, 1 close, 16 open, 2 close, 1 open, 1 close, + 1 open, 2 close, + twice; 2 open, 3 close, 2 open, 1 close, 1 open, 7 close, 1 open, 2 close, 18 open, 1 close. Decrease 1.

33rd Row.—Decrease 1, 1 close, 16 open, 1 close, 3 open, 2 close, 6 open, 2 close, 2 open, 1 close, + 1 open, 3 close, + twice; 1 open, 1 close, 1 open, 3 close, 14 open, 1 close. Decrease 1.

34th Row.—Decrease 1, 1 close, 13 open, 2 close, 4 open, 2 close, 2 open, 1 close, 1 open, 1 close, 3 open, 1 close, 2 open, 1 close, + 1 open, 2 close, + twice; 2 open, 1 close, 4 open, 1 close, 12 open, 1 close. Decrease 1.

35th Row.—Decrease 1, 1 close, 11 open, 1 close, 5 open, 2 close, 2 open, 5 close, 2 open, 2 close, + 5 open, 1 close, + twice; 15 open, 1 close. Decrease 1.

36th Row.—Decrease 1, 1 close, 21 open, 1 close, 1 open, 1 close, 3 open, 2 close, 5 open, 1 close, 20 open, 1 close. Decrease 1.

37th Row.—Decrease 1, 1 close, 19 open, 5 close, 2 open, 2 close, 4 open, 1 close, 1 open, 1 close, 18 open, 1 close. Decrease 1.

38th Row.—Decrease 1, 1 close, 19 open, 1 close, 1 open, + 1 close, 4 open, + twice; 1 close, 19 open, 1 close. Decrease 1.

39th Row.—Decrease 1, 1 close, 19 open, 1 close, 5 open, 1 close, 3 open, 1 close, 19 open, 1 close. Decrease 1.

40th Row.—Decrease 1, 2 close, 16 open, 1 close, 28 open, 2 close. Decrease 1.

41st Row.—Decrease 1, 1 open, 2 close, 41 open, 2 close, 1 open. Decrease 1.

42nd Row.—Slip 1, 1 Sc, Dc over open squares, 2 open, 2 close, 37 open, 2 close, 2 open, 5 Dc, 1 Sc, 1 Slip.

43rd Row.—Slip 1, 1 Sc, Dc over open, 2 open, 3 close, 31 open, 3 close, 2 open, finish as 42nd.

44th Row.—Slip 1, 1 Sc, Dc over open, 3 open, 4 close, 23 open, 4 close, 3 open, finish as 42nd.

45th Row.—Begin and end as last ; 4 open over close, 4 close, 15 open, 4 close, 4 open.

46th Row.—Begin and end as last. Open squares over 4 close, and close over all the open.

47th Row.—Begin and end as last. Open squares over all the close

48th Row.—Work over the open squares only in Dc, beginning and ending with a Sc stitch.

———

BEAD BORDER.—Work on the wrong side. 4 Sc at the beginning and end of every row, and the following pattern repeated 6 times, and as far as the + once more.

1st Row.—5 beads, 2 cotton, 1 bead, 6 cotton, 3 beads, 5 cotton, + 6 cotton, 3 beads, 4 cotton.

2nd Row.—1 cotton, 5 beads, 1 cotton, 2 beads, 4 cotton, 4 beads, 5 cotton, + 5 cotton, 1 bead, 3 cotton, 1 bead, 3 cotton.

3rd Row.—1 cotton, 2 beads, 2 cotton, 5 beads, 3 cotton, 2 beads, 1 cotton, 1 bead, 5 cotton, + 8 cotton, 1 bead, 1 cotton, 1 bead, 2 cotton.

4th Row.— + 2 cotton, 3 beads, + twice ; 2 cotton, 2 beads, 1 cotton, 2 beads, 5 cotton, + 6 cotton, 3 beads, 2 cotton, 1 bead, 1 cotton, 1 bead, 1 cotton.

5th Row.—4 cotton, 3 beads, 1 cotton, 3 beads, 1 cotton, 2 beads, 1 cotton, 1 bead, 6 cotton, + 3 cotton, 5 beads, 3 cotton, 1 bead, 1 cotton.

6th Row.—2 cotton, 6 beads, 1 cotton, 2 beads, 1 cotton, 1 bead, 1 cotton, 3 beads, 5 cotton, + 3 cotton, 5 beads, 2 cotton, 1 bead, 2 cotton.

7th Row.—2 cotton, 2 beads, 2 cotton, 3 beads, 1 cotton, 1 bead, 1 cotton, 1 bead, 1 cotton, 4 beads, 4 cotton, + 3 cotton, 5 beads, 1 cotton, 3 beads, 1 cotton.

8th Row.—3 cotton, 3 beads, 4 cotton, 3

beads, 1 cotton, 1 bead, 1 cotton, 2 beads, 4 cotton, + 1 cotton, 12 beads.

9th Row.—4 cotton, 6 beads, 1 cotton, 3 beads, 1 cotton, 2 beads, 5 cotton, + 5 beads, 3 cotton 5 beads.

10th Row.—6 cotton, 5 beads, + 1 cotton, 2 beads, + twice; 5 cotton, + 4 beads, 2 cotton, 1 bead, 2 cotton, 4 beads.

11th Row.—10 cotton, 2 beads, 2 cotton, 1 bead, 1 cotton, 2 beads, 4 cotton, + 4 beads, + 1 cotton, 1 bead, + twice; 1 cotton, 3 beads, 1 cotton.

12th Row.—2 beads, 5 cotton, 7 beads, 8 cotton, + 1 cotton, 3 beads, + 2 cotton, 1 bead, + 3 times.

13th Row.—2 cotton, 7 beads, 5 cotton, 3 beads, 5 cotton, + 3 cotton, 2 beads, 3 cotton, 3 beads, 2 cotton.

14th Row.—1 cotton, 1 bead, 2 cotton, 3 beads, 2 cotton, 2 beads, 1 cotton, 3 beads, 1 cotton, 6 beads, + 1 cotton, 11 beads, 1 cotton.

15th Row.—1 bead, 3 cotton, 2 beads, 1 cotton, 7 beads, 1 cotton, 4 beads, 2 cotton, 1 bead; + 6 beads, 1 cotton, 5 beads, 1 cotton.

16th Row.—4 cotton, 4 beads, 1 cotton, 3 beads, 10 cotton, + 1 cotton, + 5 beads, 1 cotton, + twice.

17th Row.—9 cotton, 2 beads, 11 cotton, 2 cotton, 3 beads, 3 cotton, 3 beads, 2 cotton.

Turn the work on the right side ; do one row of Dc ; then one row thus,—+ 1 Dc, 3 Ch, 3 beads, + repeat to the end, finishing with a Dc.

Knot a fringe of twelve strands (24 ends,) under every chain of the last row.

CORAL-BORDERED HANDKERCHIEF.

Materials.—A square of French cambric, two skeins of Evans's Royal Embroidery cotton, No. 30, and six skeins of scarlet ditto. One piece of toile ciré.

THIS handkerchief is extremely easy to work, and is at the same time remarkably pretty. In the section we give (see p. 226) every part is the full size, and the design may therefore be traced from it, and repeated as often as may be required for the handkerchief. The scallop, and the centre part of the letters, is done in raised work, the former being overcast, and the latter in satin-stitch. This raised work is produced by running with soft cotton, backwards and forwards in the parts to be raised until there is a sufficient thickness, which is then to be covered with close open stitches, either overcast, or simply sewed across the space. The work is always raised most in the widest parts. As this tracing is not at all seen, and it uses a considerable quantity of cotton, it is advisable to do it with the white, which is very much cheaper than the scarlet. All the work that is seen is to be done in scarlet. The coral branches are done in simple chain-stitch, as are the outlines of the initials. It is very rapidly done, and extremely effective.

POINT-LACE UNDER-SLEEVE.

Materials.—The point-lace cottons of Messrs W. Evans and Co. of Derby, and a piece of white cotton French braid, No. 7

THE sleeve itself is made of the worked part forming the cuff. The point goes up the arm towards the elbow, and it fastens round the wrist. A small bell-sleeve, with a deep lace-trimming to match, is worn over the tight sleeve; and being warmer this style is much more suitable for winter than that previously worn.

The principal stitch is Brussels-lace, which is done with W. Evans and Co.'s Boar's-head cotton, No. 70. The English lace is done with No. 100. The Mecklenwheels with Mecklenburg, No. 120. The Raleigh and other bars which form the ground, in No. 100 Mecklenburgh. The English bars in the same thread.

SIMPLE COLLAR, IN SATIN STITCH.

Materials.—Fine book muslin, and W. Evans and Co.'s Moravian cotton.

WE have designed (see engraving, p. 184) one of the simplest patterns for practice in embroidery on muslin. The whole of it is done in raised satin-stitch, the only open part being the eyelet-holes in the small wreath. After being traced with common embroidery cotton, it is to be worked in Moravian, by which means it is very quickly done. The muslin should be tacked on a piece of toile ciré

KNITTING-BAG.

Materials—8 yards of cotton cord; 3 straw-coloured silk tassels, and 2 yards of cord to correspond; 1 skein of filoselle to match; 1 skein of light green filoselle; 4 skeins of black Berlin wool; 7 shades of green Berlin wool, and 7 of lilac ditto (2 skeins of each); No. 13 Boulton's crochet hook, and a mesh one-third of an inch wide.

WORK on the end of the cord, with black wool, 10 stitches, which form into a round, on which work 20 stitches.

2nd Round. — Darkest green wool. Crochet all round, increasing sufficiently to make the work perfectly flat.

3rd Round.—With the next shade of wool, do the same.

4th Round.—Next shade of wool. Do the same, having 60 stitches in the round.

5th Round.—Next shade of green, and darkest lilac, + 1 lilac, 6 green, on 5 + 10 times.

6th Round.—Next shade of both colours + 1 lilac, 7 green, on 6 + 10 times.

7th Round.—Next shades, + 2 lilac, over 1, 1 lilac over green, 5 green, 1 lilac, + 10 times. This is not quite flat.

8th Round.—Next shades. This round begins the side, and the cord is held in the proper position for that purpose. There is no increase in the *number* of stitches; but they are not quite so close together as in the former round, + 4 lilac, 3 green (coming over the centre of 5 green), 2 lilac, + 10 times.

9th Round.—Next shade of lilac, green filoselle, + 1 green over the centre of 3 green, and all the rest lilac, working 9 stitches over 8, + 10 times.

10th Round. — With the lightest lilac work a round, having the same number of stitches; but holding in the cord as tightly as possible to contract the bag.

11th Round. — Same lilac; darkest green. Contract the round still more, + 4 green, 8 lilac, 2 green, + 7 times.

12th Round.—Change to the lightest lilac but one, and the next darkest green, altering the lilac to óne darker, and the green to one lighter in every future round. Join on the straw silk, + 4 straw, 2 green, 4 lilac, 4 green, + 7 times. Hold the cord looser.

13th Round.— (Holding the cord still looser) + 2 green, 2 straw, 2 green, 2 lilac, 2 green, 2 lilac, 2 green + 7 times.

KNITTING-BAG, BY MRS. PULLAN.

14th Round.— + 4 green, 4 lilac, 2 green, 2 lilac, 2 green, + 7 times.

15th Round.—(Lightest green), + 1 green, 5 lilac, 2 green, 5 lilac, 2 green, + 7 times. There is an increase of seven stitches in this round; the cord is also held sufficiently slack to increase the bag a little. The remaining rounds are not increased.

16th Round. — (Green filoselle, and darkest lilac but one), + 6 silk, 9 lilac, + 7 times.

17th Round.—Darkest lilac only, without increase. Then do four rounds with the black wool. At the end, cut the cord in a slanting way, so that the top may terminate gradually.

Thread a needle with the darkest green wool, and net all round the top of the bag a single round of common netting; do another round with each shade of green wool, to the lightest : about 24 stitches should be sufficient for the top of the bag. In the last round of netting, the cords are run to draw it up: and the part where the crochet and netting join is trimmed with fringe. A tassel is added at the bottom.

THE WORK-TABLE FRIEND.

HANDSOME LAMP-MAT

Materials. 6 yards of crochet cord; 1 ball of white crystal twine; 4 shades of crimson Berlin, 2 skeins each ; 1 lighter shade, 4 skeins : dark green Berlin, 4 skeins; white Fleury, all 6-thread, 1 skein ; black ditto, 1 skein ; 4 shades crimson ditto, 1 skein each ; 4 shades green ditto, 1 skein each : also 4 bone knitting-needles, and one of W. Boulton & Son's crochet-hooks, No. 15.

This mat may be considered as a proof of the marvellous improvements which have been made of late years in materials for the work-table. It introduces to our readers the beautiful crystal twine which has so rich and brilliant an effect in many styles of crochet. It is a recent invention of Messrs. Faudel and Phillips (the exhibitors of the magnificent tapestry bed in the Great Crystal Palace), a firm to whose exertions in bringing out constantly new materials for every sort of work, our friends are so frequently indebted. This crystal twine is made in various colours : we have selected *white* as the groundwork of the present mat. Another great improvement is seen in the variety of shades in which fleecy work is now dyed. A very few years ago, black, white, and some single harsh colours, were all that could be obtained ; now it rivals even Berlin in

the variety and softness of its tints ; and when we consider that for fringes and many other things, it is far better suited than Berlin wool, the advantage this gives to the worker may readily be appreciated.

With the crystal work 12 stitches on the end of the cord, and close it into a round. Be careful to keep the round perfectly flat.

1st Round.—26 stitches.

2nd Round.—42 stitches. Join on the green wool.

3rd Round. —+ 3 crystal, 1 green, 1 green over the cord of *last* round, as well as this. 2 green, 2 crystal, + 6 times, working 9 stitches over every 7 of last round. Join darkest crimson.

4th Round. — + 4 crystal over 3, 1 green, 4 darkest crimson (over 2 green), 1 green over green, 2 crystal + 6 times. Join next crimson.

5th Round. — + 4 crystal, 1 green over green, 5 crimson over 4, 1 green, 3 crystal over 2, + 6 times. Join on next crimson.

6th Round. — + 4 crystal over 4, 1 green over green, 3 crimson, 1 crimson over 2 cords, 3 more crimson (all 7 coming over 5 of last round), 1 green on green, 3 crystal + 6 times. Join on the next crimson.

7th Round.— + 6 crystal, over 4 crystal, and 1 green, 1 green over crimson, 2 crimson on 1, 1 crimson over 2 cords (as before), 1 crimson, 1 crimson over 2 cords 2 crimson on 1, 1 green on crimson, 4 crystal, + 6 times. Join on the lightest crimson.

8th Round.— + 5 crystal, 1 green over crystal, 2 crimson, 1 green, 1 crimson, crimson over 2 cords, and just between the two long stitches of last round, 1 crimson, 1 green, 2 crimson, 1 green (on crystal), 3 crystal, + 6 times.

9th Round.— + 4 crystal, 4 green (which are worked with the wool to cover the cord, and the chain part to be of the crystal), 1 crystal, 1 green (in the common way), 1 crimson over long stitch of last round, 1 green, 1 crystal, 4 green and crystal, as before, the last coming over a crystal, 3 crystal over 2, + 6 times.

10th Round.—All crystal, increasing enough to keep the mat quite flat, with a single green stitch over the crimson one of last round.

11th Round.—All crystal.

HANDSOME LAMP-MAT, BY MRS. PULLAN.

12th Round.— 2 crystal, and 2 of the lightest crimson alternately, all round. Fasten off.

Observe that the wool is to be passed at the back, from one pattern to another, not worked in, as is generally done with colours, as they would show through, and the effect of the pure white would be spoilt.

For the five fans: all done with the crystal. Make a chain of 10 stitches, and close it into a round, work under it in Sc; then 13 Ch, miss 3, Dc on the 4th, + 1 Ch, miss 1 Dc on 2nd + 4 times; 2 Ch, Sc under the round, + slip back on the last five stitches; 7 Ch, miss 3, Dc on 4th, + 1 Ch, miss 1, Tc on next, + 3 times, 1 Ch, miss 1, Dc on next, 2 Ch, Sc under the round, + 6 times. Sc all round this fan, doing 2 Sc under every *one* chain, and six under the three at each point. Five fans will just go round the centre of the mat.

For the Fringe. — First cut the coloured fleecy into pieces, 2½ inches long, keeping all the shades separate. With the black fleecy, cast on 72 stitches, + 24 on each of three needles. Close it into a round. Take a bit of the darkest green wool, twist a loop in the centre of it, *without a knot*, and put it over the left-hand needle, with one end towards you; knit the loop with the stitch, bring the other end forward, and knit another stitch without any green wool. Put in, thus,

L

+ six pieces of the darkest green, then
the same number of the darkest crimson
+ 3 times. Purl one round, increasing
two stitches in every twelve. In the next
round, take the succeeding shade of the
colours, and do 7 pieces in each section.
Purl the next round, increasing two in
every fourteen. Then take the third
shade, and put in eight pieces in each
section. Purl a round, without increase,
and put in eight more pieces, in every
division of the next round, using the same
shade. Purl a round, increasing every
sixteen to eighteen; knit in 9 pieces of
the lightest shade in each section; purl
another round; then put in more wool;
knit one round, and cast off. Sew the
knitted fringe round the mat, comb it out
very nicely, and then put on the fans.

VERY DURABLE SHORT PURSE,

Materials. 1 hank of steel beads, No. 5: some
transparent white glass ditto; 2 skeins of white
silk, and 2 of green. For a garniture, that termed
a *Diable* mount; and a fringe which may be made
by the working of the beads and bugles. W.
Boulton & Son's crochet-hook, No. 24.

THREAD the steel beads on one skein of
white silk, and about four rows of white
on the green. The remainder of the
white on the other skein of white silk.
The lower part of this purse is done in Sc ;
a spray of leaves, in white, outlined and
veined with steel beads, form the pattern,
on a green ground. The little spots are
in the glass beads, threaded on green.

With the green silk, make a chain of
112 stitches; close it into a round; join
on the white silk, working it in, and dropping from it a steel bead, when desired.

1st Round.— + 38 green, 1 steel, 17
green +. This forms one side, or half
the round. In this, therefore, and in all
following rounds, the pattern within the
marks, is to be worked *twice*.

2nd Round.— Like 1st.

3rd Round.— + 37 green, 1 steel, 18
green +.

4th Round.— + 22 green, 1 steel, 14
green, 1 steel, 5 green, 2 glass, 8 green, 2,
glass, 1 green +.

5th Round.— + 21 green, 1 steel, 3
green, 2 steel, 10 green, 1 steel, 4 green, 4
glass, 6 green, 4 glass +.

6th Round.— + 3 green, 5 steel, 13
green, 1 steel, 2 green, 1 steel, 1 green, 1

VERY DURABLE SHORT PURSE,
BY MRS. PULLAN.

steel, 2 green, 4 steel, 3 green, 1 steel,
5 green, 4 glass, 6 green, 4 glass +.

7th Round.— + 4 green, 1 steel, 3 white,
4 steel, 10 green, 4 steel, 2 green, 1 steel,
4 green, 1 steel, 1 green, 1 steel, 7 green,
2 glass, 8 green, 2 glass, 1 green +.

8th Round.— + 4 green, 1 steel, 7
white, 3 steel, 10 green, 3 steel, 5 green,
1 steel, 1 green, 1 steel, 20 green +.

9th Round.— + 4 green, 1 steel, 1 white, 2 steel, 7 white, 2 steel, 16 green, 2 steel, 3 green, 2 glass, 8 green, 2 glass, 6 green +.

10th Round.— + 4 green, 1 steel, 1 white, 3 steel, 8 white, 1 steel, 14 green, 1 steel, 4 green, 4 glass, 6 green, 4 glass, 5 green +.

11th Round.— + 4 green, 1 steel, 2 white, 3 steel, 8 white, 1 steel, 6 green, 7 steel, 5 green, 4 glass, 6 green, 4 glass, 5 green +.

12th Round.— + 4 green, 1 steel, 2 white, 4 steel, 4 white, 1 steel, 3 white, 1 steel, 4 green, 1 steel, 7 white, 2 steel, green, 2 glass, 8 green, 2 glass, 6 green +.

13th Round.— + 3 green, 1 steel, 4 white, 3 steel, 3 white, 2 steel, 4 white, 1 steel, 2 green, 1 steel, 4 white, 1 steel, 5 white, 1 steel, 21 green +.

14th Round.— + 3 green, 1 steel, 5 white, 3 steel, 2 white, 2 steel, 4 white, 1 steel, 2 green, 1 steel, 3 white, 3 steel, 5 white, 1 steel, 7 green, 2 glass, 8 green, 2 glass, 1 green +.

15th Round.— + 3 green, 1 steel, 6 white, 3 steel, 1 white, 2 steel, 4 white, 1 steel, 2 green, 1 steel, 2 white, 4 steel, 6 white, 1 steel, 5 green, 4 glass, 6 green, 4 glass +.

16th Round.— + 3 green, 1 steel, 7 white, 2 steel, 1 white, 2 steel, 4 white, 1 steel, 2 green, 1 steel, 2 white, 4 steel, 7 white, 1 steel, 4 green, 4 glass, 6 green, 4 glass +.

17th Round.— + 3 green, 1 steel, 8 white, 1 steel, 1 white, 1 steel, 5 white, 1 steel, 3 green, 1 steel, 1 white, 3 steel, 9 white, 1 steel, 4 green, 2 glass, 8 green, 2 glass, 1 green +.

18th Round.— + 4 green, 1 steel, 8 white, 1 steel, 6 white, 1 steel, 3 green, 5 steel, 10 white, 1 steel, 16 green.

19th Round.— + 4 green, 1 steel, 8 white, 1 steel, 5 white, 1 steel, 3 green, 3 steel, 1 white, 2 steel, 11 white, 1 steel, 7 green, 2 glass, 6 green +.

20th Round.— + 4 green, 1 steel, 8 white, 1 steel, 2 white, 3 steel, 3 green, 2 steel, 3 white, 7 steel, 7 white, 1 steel, 5 green, 4 glass, 5 green +.

21st Round.— + 5 green, 1 steel, 7 white, 3 steel, 5 green, 1 steel, 1 green, 1 steel, 3 white, 3 steel, 1 white, 4 steel, 7 white 1 steel, 4 green, 4 glass, 5 green.

22nd Round.— + 6 green, 2 steel, 3 white, 1 steel, 2 green, 1 steel, 3 green, 1 steel, 2 green, 1 steel, 4 white, 2 steel, 2 white, 5 steel, 6 white, 1 steel, 4 green, 2 glass, 6 green +.

23rd Round.— + 8 green, 6 steel, 3 green, 3 steel, 3 green, 1 steel, 4 white, 2 steel, 2 white, 6 steel, 5 white, 1 steel, 12 green +.

24th Round.— + 15 green, 2 steel, 1 green, 1 steel, 5 green, 1 steel, 8 white, 5 steel, 4 white, 3 steel, 8 green, 2 glass, 1 green +.

25th Round.— + 2 green, 2 steel, 10 green, 1 steel, 2 white, 1 steel, 7 green, 2 steel, 17 white, 2 steel, 6 green, 4 glass +.

26th Round.— + 1 green, 1 steel, 2 green, 1 steel, 5 green, 4 steel, 2 white, 1 steel, 1 white, 3 steel, 6 green, 4 steel, 10 white, 3 steel, 8 green, 4 glass +.

27th Round.— + 4 green, 1 steel, 4 green, 1 steel, 5 white, 1 steel, 5 white, 2 steel, 8 green, 10 steel, 12 green, 2 glass, 1 green +.

28th Round.— + 3 green, 2 steel, 3 green, 1 steel, 4 white, 2 steel, 1 white, 2 steel, 5 white, 1 steel, 6 green, 1 steel, 25 green +.

29th Round.— + 2 green, 1 steel, 1 green, 2 steel, 2 green, 1 steel, 3 white, 8 steel, 4 white, 1 steel, 5 green, 1 steel, 17 green, 2 glass, 6 green +.

30thRound.—+ 2 green, 2 steel, 1 green, 1 steel, 2 green, 1 steel, 1 white, 6 steel, 1 white, 5 steel, 2 white, 1 steel, 5 green, 1 steel, 16 green, 4 glass, 5 green +.

31st Round.— + 5 green, 1 steel, 2 green, 1 steel, 2 white, 3 steel, 2 white, 1 steel, 1 white, 3 steel, 3 white, 1 steel, 6 green, 1 steel, 2 green, 8 steel, 5 green, 4 glass, 5 green +.

32nd Round.— + 4 green, 1 steel, 3 green, 1 steel, 7 white, 1 steel, 7 white, 1 steel, 6 green, 1 steel, 1 green, 1 steel, 8 white, 1 steel, 5 green, 2 glass, 6 green +.

33rd Round.— + 3 green 1 steel, 4 green, 1 steel, 7 white, 2 steel, 6 white, 1 steel, 6 green, 1 steel, 1 green, 1 steel, 8 white, 2 steel, 12 green +.

34th Round.— + 3 green, 1 steel, 4 green, 2 steel, 6 white, 3 steel, 5 white, 1 steel, 3 green, 5 steel, 10 white, 1 steel, 9 green, 2 glass, 1 green +.

35th Round.— + 3 green, 1 steel, 3 green, 1 steel, 1 green, 1 steel, 6 white, 4 steel, 4 white, 1 steel, 3 green, 1 steel, ., white, 2 steel, 5 white, 3 steel, 1 white, 1 steel, 8 green, 4 glass +.

36th Round.— + 4 green, 3 steel, 2 green, 1 steel, 7 white, 4 steel, 3 white, 1 steel, 3 green, 1 steel, 3 white, 2 steel, 3 white, 4 steel, 2 white, 1 steel, 8 green, 4 glass +.

37th Round.— + 6 green, 1 steel, 3 green, 1 steel, 7 white, 4 steel 2 white, 1 steel, 3 green, 1 steel, 2 white, 4 steel, 1 white, 1 steel, 7 white, 1 steel, 8 green, 2 glass, 1 green +.

38th Round.— + 4 green, 2 steel, 5 green, 1 steel, 7 white, 3 steel, 2 white, 1 steel, 3 green, 1 steel, 2 white, 3 steel, 1 white, 4 steel, 5 white, 1 steel, 11 green +.

39th Round.— + 2 green, 2 steel, 8 green, 1 steel, 7 white, 3 steel, 1 white, 1 steel, 3 green, 1 steel, 2 white, 4 steel, 2 white, 5 steel, 2 white, 1 steel, 3 green, 2 glass, 6 green +.

40th Round.— + 5 green, 4 steel, 4 green, 2 steel, 10 white, 1 steel, 3 green, 1 steel, 2 white, 4 steel, 2 white, 5 steel, 2 white, 1 steel, 1 green, 4 glass, 5 green +.

41st Round.— + 3 green, 2 steel, 4 white, 1 steel, 4 green, 4 steel, 7 white, 1 steel, 4 green, 1 steel, 2 white, 4 steel, 2 white, 4 steel, 2 white, 1 steel, 1 green, 4 glass, 5 green +.

42nd Round. — + 2 green, 1 steel, 7 white, 1 steel, 2 green, 1 steel, 4 green, 2 steel, 5 white, 1 steel, 5 green, 1 steel, 2 white, 3 steel, 5 white, 2 steel, 2 white, 1 steel, 1 green, 2 glass, 6 green +.

43rd Round. — + 2 green, 1 steel, 8 white, 2 steel, 7 green, 3 steel, 2 white, 1 steel, 6 green, 1 steel, 13 white, 1 steel, 9 green +.

44th Round. — + 1 green, 1 steel, 9 white, 6 steel, 6 green, 3 steel, 7

POINT-LACE STITCHES, BY MRS. PULLAN.

green, 1 steel, 13 white, 1 steel, 5 green, 2 glass, 1 green +

45th Round.— + 1 green, 1 steel, 3 white, 4 steel, 2 white, 2 steel, 4 white, 1 steel, 6 green, 1 steel, 9 green, 14 steel, 4 green, 4 glass +.

46th Round.— + 1 green, 1 steel, 2 white, 6 steel, 1 white, 1 steel, 5 white, 1 steel, 3 green, 2 steel, 2 green, 1 steel, 26 green, 4 glass +.

47th Round.— + 1 green, 1 steel, 5 white, 2 steel, 1 white, 3 steel, 4 white, 1 steel, 3 green, 1 steel, 1 green, 1 steel, 1 green, 1 steel, 27 green, 2 glass, 1 green +.

48th Round.— + 1 green, 1 steel, 7 white, 1 steel, 1 white, 4 steel, 2 white, 1 steel, 4 green, 3 steel, 31 green +.

49th Round.— + 1 green, 1 steel, 6 white, 2 steel, 2 white, 2 steel, 3 white, 1 steel, 5 green, 1 steel, 4 green, * 2 glass, 8 green, * twice ; 2 glass, 6 green +.

50th Round.— + 2 green, 1 steel, 4 white, 3 steel, 6 white, 1 steel, 5 green, 1 steel, 4 green, * 4 glass, 6 green, * twice ; 4 glass, 5 green +.

51st Round.— + 2 green, 1 steel, 3 white, 3 steel, 6 white, 1 steel, 1 green, 1 steel, 2 green, 2 steel, 5 green, * 4 glass, 6 green, * twice ; 4 glass, 5 green +.

52nd Round. — + 2 green, 1 steel, 2 white, 3 steel, 6 white, 1 steel, 5 green, 4 steel, 7 green, 2 glass, * 8 green, 2 glass, * twice ; 6 green +.

53rd Round. — + 2 green, 1 steel, 2 white, 2 steel, 5 white, 2 steel, 5 green, 2 steel, 35 green +.

54th Round. — + 2 green, 1 steel, 1 white, 1 steel, 2 white, 2 steel, 5 green, * 2 glass, 8 green, * 4 times, 2 glass, 1 green +.

55th Round. — + 2 green, 1 steel, 6 white, 1 steel, 2

green, * 4 glass, 6 green, • 4 times;
4 glass +.

56th Round.— + 2 green, 1 steel, 3
white, 3 steel, 3 green, • 4 glass, 6 green,
• 4 times , 4 glass.

57th Round.— + 2 green, 4 steel, 7
green, • 2 glass, 8 green, • 4 times; 2
glass, 1 green +.

Do one round of Sc with the green, and
22 stitches more ; this will be the proper
centre of one side of the purse, and will
throw the white spots equally on both sides
of the beads. Join on the white silk with
beads threaded on, and work from this
centre backwards and forwards thus.

1st Round.—5 Ch, (with a bead dropped
on every one,) Miss 3, Sc in the fourth.

2nd and all succeeding Rounds.—5 Ch, Sc
under chain of last row. At the end,
after Sc under the last loop, 5 Ch, Tc to
make the line even. Do about 16 rows of
this work, and sew on the top, the slip
being in the middle of one side. Join up
the end with a row of Sc, taking two
stitches together. Add the fringe, which
may be either bought or made.

THE WORK-TABLE FRIEND.

SWISS LACE COLLAR.

Materials.—A piece of very fine book-muslin,
large enough for a large collar; some fine bobbinet, the same size, with W. Evans & Co.'s
embroidery cotton, No. 80, and Boar's Head
Sewing Cotton, No. 70.

A SECTION of this design being given, the
collar must be enlarged to double the
width from it. This may appear very
large, but it must be remembered that
this sort of work invariably shrinks very
much, so that if it be drawn smaller, great
disappointment is likely to ensue when the
article is washed.

The pattern must first be drawn completely on coloured paper, and inked. Then
lay it under the muslin, and keep it in its
place by means of weights. Trace the
design on the muslin with a very fine sable
brush, dipped in a solution of indigo and
thin gum-water. Remove the paper pattern, and tack the net under the muslin.
It is then ready to be worked.

Some ladies do the work without any
more substantial lining, but we prefer using
a piece of oil-skin tacked under it, to
keep it firm. The net should have all
stiffness taken out of it before it is worked.

With the fine embroidery cotton trace
the whole of the pattern, taking very
short stitches, and attaching the net to
the muslin at every stitch. Then do
the outer edge in the neatest possible
buttonhole stitch. All the outlines are
formed by small holes made between two
rows of sewing. They are to be done in
working the second row, by piercing small
holes in the muslin with a needle, at
intervals of about the sixth of an inch, and
sewing over the little spaces between them.
After doing one, sew the bit of the edge
till you come to the next ; work that, then
another hole, and so on.

The large petals of the flowers have an
open piece of lace in each ; in the smaller
petals a raised spot is worked with soft
cotton.

When all the collar is completed, the
superfluous muslin, which was left as a
margin to the collar, must be cut away,
and also all those parts which are between
the sprays, the net only being left for a
ground. Lace-scissors must be used for
this purpose, as, from the closeness of the
pattern, great care is requisite to prevent
the net from being cut with the muslin.

LADY'S TRAVELLING BAG, IN STRAW-WORK.

Materials.—A strip of French canvass, No. 14,
5½ inches wide ; half an ounce each of five shades
of green Berlin wool; 36 yards of straw beading;
quarter of a yard of wide Green Glacé silk, to
match with one of the darker shades of wool;
sarsnet to line the same ; a piece of stout cardboard ; 1½ yards of fancy straw trimming an inch
wide; and 1½ yards of satin ribbon to match the
silk.

THESE baskets are at once among the
prettiest and the most useful of the day.
They are generally made of plain straw,
instead of Berlin-work ; but the latter has
so elegant an appearance that we are sure
our friends will think it well repays them
for the little extra trouble.

It is to be understood that the lower
part alone is done on canvass ; the upper
part is a bag of silk ; the joining of the
two is concealed by a piece of wide fancy
straw laid on.

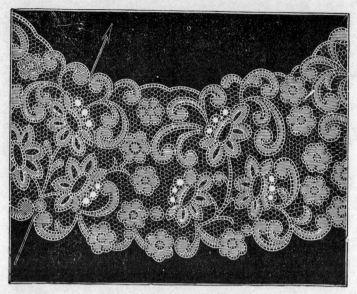

Swiss Lace Collar. By Mrs. Pullan.

Narrow canvass is to be used for the bags in preference to a strip of the same width cut from a broader piece, because the selvages add so much to the strength of the basket.

Work across the width, first from right to left and then from left to right, so that the straw beading need not be cut at the end of the rows.

The pattern contains 20 rows. Begin with the darkest shade, and change at the 5th, 9th, 13th and 17th; at the commencement of the next pattern (the 21st row) resume the darkest shade.

1st Row.—Hold one end of the straw beading over two threads of the canvass, and work thus :—

1st Row.—6 stitches taken across the straw in a straight line; consequently, across two upright threads of canvass, but not crossing any in the width; miss 3 threads, 12 stitches, miss 5 threads, 4 stitches, miss 3 threads, 2 stitches, miss 9 threads, 2 stitches, miss 11 threads, 10 stitches, miss 3 threads, 6 stitches.

[In future rows it will be understood that *threads* are missed, and that *s* signifies stitches.]

2nd Row.—Worked the reverse way. 4 s, miss 7, 6 s, miss 7, 8 s, miss 9, 4 s, miss 5, 4 s, miss 3, 8 s, miss 7, 4 s.

3rd Row.—6 s, miss 3, 10 s, miss 3, 6 s, miss 3, 6 s, miss 7, 2 s, miss 3, 2 s, miss 5, 12 s, miss 3, 6 s.

4th Row.—16 s, miss 7, 4 s, miss 7, 2 s, miss 3, 12 s, miss 3, 20 s.

5th Row.—20 s, miss 3, 8 s, miss 3, 6 s, miss 9, 2 s, miss 9, 14 s.

6th Row.—6 s, miss 3, 10 s, miss 3, 2 s, miss 11, 2 s, miss 13, 4 s, miss 3, 10 s, miss 3, 6 s.

7th Row.—4 s, miss 7, 16 s, miss 9, 2 s, miss 3, 2 s, miss 3, 2 s, miss 5, 2 s, miss 5, 6 s, miss 7, 4 s.

8th Row.—6 s, miss 3, 8 s, miss 11, 6 s, miss 3, 8 s, miss 7, 14 s, miss 3, 6 s.

9th Row.—20 s, miss 11, 2 s, miss 3, 2 s, miss 5, 6 s, miss 3, 2 s, miss 5, 16 s.

10th Row.—14 s, miss 5, 10 s, miss 3, 2 s, miss 3, 2 s, miss 3, 6 s, miss 3, 22 s.

Lady's Travelling Bag, in Straw-work.   By Mrs. Pullan.

11*th Row.*—6 s, miss 3, 10 s, miss 11, 2 s, miss 9, 2 s, miss 3, 4 s, miss 5, 12 s, miss 3, 6 s.

12*th Row.*—4 s, miss 7, 8 s, miss 3, 4 s, miss 5, 4 s, miss 9, 8 s, miss 7, 6 s, miss 7, 4 s.

13*th Row.*—6 s, miss 3, 12 s, miss 5, 2 s, miss 3, 2 s, miss 7, 6 s, miss 3, 6 s, 10 s, miss 3, 6 s.

14*th Row.*—20 s, miss 3, 12 s, miss 3, 2 s, miss 6, 4 s, miss 6, 16 s.

15*th Row.*—14 s, miss 9, 2 s, miss 9, 6 s, miss 3, 8 s, miss 3, 20 s.

16*th Row.*—6 s, miss 3, 10 s, miss 3, 4 s, miss 13, 2 s, miss 11, 2 s, miss 3, 10 s, miss 3, 6 s.

17*th Row.*—4 s, miss 7, 6 s, miss 5, 2 s, miss 5, 2 s, miss 3, 2 s, miss 3, 2 s, miss 9, 16 s, miss 7, 4 s.

18*th Row.*—6 s, miss 3, 14 s, miss 7, 8 s, miss 3, 6 s, miss 11, 8 s, miss 3, 6 s.

19*th Row.*—16 s, miss 5, 2 s, miss 3, 6 s, miss 5, 2 s, miss 3, 2 s, miss 11, 20 s.

20*th Row.*—22 s, miss 5, 6 s, miss 3, 2 s, miss 3, 2 s, miss 3, 10 s, miss 5, 14 s.

This completes one pattern, and must be repeated as often as desired for the size of the basket.

Cut out in cardboard an oval, pointed at both ends, about 12 to 14 inches long, and 3½ to 5 wide. Cover this with silk on both sides, and sew the straw-work all round it, having previously added a silk bag to the canvass. The cardboard should be sewed in very strongly, and the seam may be covered with straw beading.

The handle, which is made of the fancy straw, should be stiffened with a bit of wire ribbon, and firmly sewed on the centre of each side of the basket. The fancy straw is also to be put round the top of the canvass to conceal the joining of it with the silk.

WATCHPOCKET, BY MRS. PULLAN.

THE WORK-TABLE FRIEND.

WATCH-POCKET.

Materials—1 ball of silver crystal twine; 1 ditto of pink; 1 skein of light green crystal wool; 1½ yards of green satin ribbon; and 2 mother-of-pearl watch-hooks.

OBSERVE that the two balls of twine will make two pairs or more of watch-pockets.

With the white twine make a chain of 7 stitches, close it into a round, and work under it as many stitches as you can in Dc. Continue to work round and round, until a piece 2 inches in diameter is made. Fasten off with 1 Sc, 1 slip, to make the round perfectly even.

Join on the pink twine, and Sc all round, having 80 stitches altogether.

2nd Round.— + 4 Sc, 10 Ch, 9 Sc, on the chain, Sc on the round. + 16 times.

3rd Round.— + Sc on 2nd of 4 Sc, 3 Ch, Dc under 3rd of 10 Ch; 3 Ch, Dc under the same. Miss 1, Dc under the next,

GENTLEMAN'S PURSE, BY MRS. PULLAN.

2 Ch, Dc under the same, Dc under the point 3 Ch, Dc under the same stitch. Miss 1, Dc under the 2nd, 2 Ch, Dc under the same, miss 1 Dc under the 2nd, 3 Ch, Dc under the same, 3 Ch, + 16 times.

4th Round.—With the green wool + Sc under the 2nd chain of 3, 2 Ch, Dc under the next Ch, 3 Ch, Dc under the same; Dc under the next (which is the chain at the point), 3 Ch, Dc under the same, Dc under the next, 3 Ch, Dc under the same, Dc under the next. + 16 times. Fasten off the green wool. Join on the pink twine.

5th Round.—Sc between every 2 Dc, with 3 chain between.

This completes the round. The bows in the centre are made with the silver twine, thus:—16 Ch, form into a round, + 1 Sc, 12 Ch, 11 Sc on the Ch, Sc on the round, + 8 times.

6th Round.—Sc all round every one of these points, catching up a thread at the edge of the white circle, at the extremity of each one, joining them at equal distances. With the green wool work on the edge of the white round, + Sc, 3 Ch, miss 1, + all round.

To make up the watchpocket, cut a round piece of cardboard, 2 inches in diameter, and cover it with silk on both sides. Sew it under the white round, then, with a strong needle and thread, fasten on the hook, sewing down beneath it the chain which formed the foundation of the bows.

Add the ribbon, to suspend the pocket.

We have given a pretty combination of colours, but any others may be used that would harmonize with the furniture of the bed.

GENTLEMAN'S PURSE.

Materials—3 skeins of rich claret-brown purse silk, 1 skein of brilliant cerise ditto, 1 skein of white, 6 strings of transparent white glass beads, and a hank of steel ditto of the same size, with a few steel bugles, and two slides.

THREAD about four strings of steel beads on the white silk, and four more on the brown; also, the white beads on the cerise. With the white silk, make a chain of 120 stitches, join into a round and work one round of Sc.

1st Pattern round.— + 10 silk, 1 bead, 3 silk, 1 bead, 3 silk, 1 bead, 11 silk, + 4 times.

2nd Round.— + 6 silk, 1 bead, 2 silk, 2 beads, 2 silk, 3 beads, 2 silk, 2 beads, 2 silk, 1 bead, 7 silk, + 4 times.

3rd Round.— + 6 silk, 1 bead, 2 silk, 3 beads, 1 silk, 3 beads, 1 silk, 3 beads, 2 silk, 1 bead, 7 silk, + 4 times.

4th Round.— + 6 silk, 2 beads, 1 silk, 11 beads, 1 silk, 2 beads, 7 silk, + 4 times.

5th Round.— + 3 silk, 1 bead, 1 silk, 19 beads, 1 silk, 1 bead, 4 silk, + 4 times. Join on the brown silk.

6th Round.— + 3 white (silk), 1 bead, 1 white, 5 beads, 1 brown, 3 beads, 1 brown, 3 beads, 1 brown, 5 beads, 1 white, 1 bead, 4 white, + 4 times.

7th Round.— + 3 white, 3 beads, 1 brown, 2 beads, 2 brown, 1 bead, 5 brown, 1 bead, 2 brown, 2 beads, 1 brown, 3 beads, 4 white, + 4 times.

8th Round.— + 3 white, 3 beads, 1 brown, 1 bead, 13 brown, 1 bead, 1 brown, 3 beads, 4 white, + 4 times.

9th Round.— + 2 white, 4 beads, 1 brown, 1 bead, 6 brown, 2 beads off the brown, 5 brown, 1 bead, 1 brown, 4 beads, 2 white, 1 bead, + 4 times. The word *steel*, will indicate a steel bead off the brown silk, in future rounds.

10th Round.— + 2 white, 1 bead, 1 brown, 1 bead, 8 brown, 1 steel, 1 brown, 1 steel, 8 brown, 1 bead, 1 brown, 1 bead, 2 white, 1 bead, + 4 times.

11th Round.— + 1 white, 2 beads, 1 brown, 1 bead, 8 brown, 1 steel, 1 brown, 3 steel, 6 brown, 1 bead, 1 brown, 2 beads, 1 white, 1 bead, + 4 times.

12th Round.— + 1 white, 2 beads, 10 brown, 1 steel, 1 brown, 1 steel, 1 brown, 1 steel, 8 brown, 2 beads, 2 white, + 4 times.

13th Round.— + 2 steel, 12 brown, 4 steel, 9 brown, 2 steel, 1 white, + 4 times. Fasten off the white.

14th Round.— + 2 steel, 7 brown, 2 steel, 2 brown, 1 steel, 13 brown, 3 steel, + 4 times.

15th Round.— + 1 steel, 7 brown, 8 steel, 12 brown, 2 steel, + 4 times.

16th Round.— + 1 steel, 6 brown, 4 steel, 2 brown, 1 steel, 1 brown, 3 steel, 1 brown, 2 steel, 1 brown, 2 steel, 4 brown, 1 steel, 1 brown, + 4 times.

17th Round.— + 1 steel, 6 brown, 1 steel, 1 brown, 3 steel, 1 brown, 2 steel, 4 brown, 5 steel, 4 brown, 1 steel, 1 brown, + 4 times.

18th Round.— + 1 steel, 9 brown, 1 steel, 2 brown, 3 steel, 3 brown, 4 steel, 5 brown, 1 steel, 1 brown, + 4 times.

19th Round.— + 14 brown, 6 steel, 10 brown, + 4 times.

20th Round.— + 14 brown, 1 steel, 15 brown, + 4 times.

21st Round.— + 7 brown, 3 steel, 3 · brown, 2 steel, 15 brown, + 4 times.

22nd Round.— + 8 brown, 3 steel, 1 brown, 5 steel, 13 brown, + 4 times.

Join on the cerise silk, and drop a white bead from it, whenever directed.

23rd Round.— + 11 brown, 1 white, 1 brown, 7 white, 3 brown, 2 white, 5 brown, + 4 times.

24th Round.— + 9 brown, 12 white, 1 brown, 1 white, 7 brown, + 4 times.

25th Round.— + 9 brown, 1 white, 1 brown, 13 white, 6 brown, + 4 times.

26th Round.— + 11 brown, 11 white, 8 brown, + 4 times.

27th Round.— + 10 brown, 4 white, 4 cerise, 6 white, 6 brown, + 4 times.

28th Round.— + 9 brown, 4 white, 5 cerise, 4 white, 2 brown, 2 white, 4 brown, + 4 times.

29th Round.— + 9 brown, 4 white, 5 cerise, 6 white, 6 brown, + 4 times.

30th Round.— + 7 brown, 5 white, 6 cerise, 5 white, 7 brown, + 4 times.

31st Round.— + 8 brown, 4 white, 6 cerise, 6 white, 6 brown, + 4 times.

32nd Round.— + 6 brown, 6 white, 5 cerise, 4 white, 9 brown, + 4 times.

33rd Round.— + 6 brown, 1 steel, 5 white, 5 cerise, 3 white, 1 brown, 2 white, 7 brown, + 4 times.

34th Round.— + 5 brown, 7 white, 4 cerise, 3 white, 2 brown, 3 white, 6 brown, + 4 times.

35th Round.— + 6 brown, 2 white, 2 brown, 2 white, 4 cerise, 3 white, 3 brown, 1 white, 7 brown, + 4 times.

36th Round.— + 6 brown, 1 steel, 3 brown, 2 white, 4 cerise, 3 white, 3 brown, 1 white, 1 brown, 1 steel, 5 brown, + 4 times.

37th Round.— + 5 brown, 2 steel, 3 brown, 3 white, 3 cerise, 2 white, 1 brown, 2 white, 3 brown, 1 steel, 5 brown, + 4 times.

38th Round.— + 5 brown, 2 steel, 3 brown, 3 white, 2 cerise, 2 white, 1 brown, 4 white, 1 brown, 2 steel, 5 brown, + 4 times.

39th Round.— + 4 brown, 3 steel, 1 brown, 5 cerise, 2 cerise, 2 white, 2 brown, 2 white, 2 brown, 2 steel, 5 brown, + 4 times.

40th Round.— + 4 brown, 3 steel, 3 white, 2 brown, 2 white, 1 cerise, 3 white, 5 brown, 3 steel, 4 brown, + 4 times.

41st Round.— + 4 brown, 1 steel, 1 brown, 1 steel, 2 brown, 1 white, 2 brown, 2 white, 1 cerise, 2 white, 2 brown, 1 white, 3 brown, 3 steel, 4 brown, + 4 times

42nd Round.— + 4 brown, 1 steel, 1 brown, 3 steel, 1 white, 2 brown, 3 white, 1 cerise, 1 white, 1 brown, 1 steel, 1 brown, 1 white, 2 brown, 3 steel, 4 brown, + 4 times.

43rd Round.— + 5 brown, 6 steel, 5 white, 1 cerise, 3 white, 1 brown, 1 white, 2 brown, 2 steel, 4 brown, + 4 times.

44th Round.— + 6 brown, 4 steel, 1 brown, 11 white, 1 steel, 1 brown, 2 steel, 4 brown, + 4 times.

45th Round.— + 8 brown, 1 steel, 1 brown, 4 white, 2 brown, 6 white, 1 steel, 1 brown, 1 steel, 5 brown, + 4 times.

46th Round.— + 7 brown, 1 steel, 2 brown, 1 white, 2 brown, 1 white, 2 brown, 5 white, 4 steel, 5 brown, + 4 times.

47th Round,— + 6 brown, 2 steel, 2 brown, 3 steel, 8 brown, 3 steel, 1 brown, 1 steel, 4 brown, + 4 times. Fasten off the cerise.

48th Round.— + 5 brown, 2 steel, 1 brown, 2 steel, 10 brown, 2 steel, 1 brown, 2 steel, 4 brown, + 4 times.

49th Round.— + 4 brown, 1 steel, 2 brown, 1 steel, 1 brown, 5 steel, 2 brown, 4 steel, 2 brown, 2 steel, 4 brown, + 4 times.

50th Round.— + 9 brown, 2 steel, 2 brown, 7 steel, 1 brown, 4 steel, 5 brown, + 4 times.

51st Round.— + 10 brown, 2 steel, 4 brown, 1 steel, 13 brown, + 4 times.

52nd Round.— + 17 brown, 3 steel, 10 brown, + 4 times,

53rd Round.— + 18 brown, 3 steel, 9 brown, + 4 times.

Do the other end like this: then for the centre, backward and forwards, + 2 Dc, 2 Ch, miss 2, + end with 2 Dc. Every following row, + 2 Dc, under chain 2 Ch, +.

Crochet up the ends with white silk, and make the fringes of steel beads and bugles.

The rings are to be slipped over the middle before the second end is sewed on.

ALWAYS BUSY. — The more a man accomplishes the more he may. An active tool never grows rusty. You always find those men who are the most forward to do good, or to improve the times and manners, always busy. Who starts our railroads, our steamboats, our machine shops, and our manufactories? Men of industry and enterprise. As long as they live they work, doing something to benefit themselves and others. It is just so with a man who is benevolent—the more he gives, the more he feels to like giving. We go for activity—in body, in mind, in everything. Let the gold grow not dim, nor the thoughts become stale. Keep all things in motion. We should rather that death should find us scaling a mountain than sinking in a mire—breasting a whirlpool than sneaking from a cloud.

BERLIN TRAVELLING BAG.

(à mille raies.)

Materials.—Penelope canvass, No. 6, 1½ yard, and the following wools and silks:—Wool—black, 2 ozs.; light blueish green, 3 ozs.; scarlet, 1½ oz.; 4 shades lilac, ½ oz. each; 5 shades scarlet, ½ oz. each; 5 shades crimson, ½ oz. each; 5 shades yellow, ½ oz. each. Floss—1 lilac, 1 crimson, 1 scarlet; all lighter than the lightest wool.

In writing the receipt for this bag, I shall distinguish the shades of each colour by numbers, from 1 to 5, No 1 being the darkest.

By referring to the engraving it will be seen that the bag has 4 broad stripes, and three narrow ones, intervening, with a half stripe at each edge. These narrow stripes are in black and scarlet, the scarlet part being marked in the centre stripe.

2. The ground, (marked 3) is in light green wool. Work entirely with double wool.

Each side of the bag is 140 squares (or stitches) wide, and proportionally long, a narrow stripe goes up the centre occupying 12 stitches, and is worked thus:

1st Row.—2 black, 8 scarlet, 2 black.

2nd Row.—2 black, 2 scarlet, 1 black, 2 scarlet, 1 black, 2 scarlet, 2 black.

3rd Row.—2 black, 1 scarlet, 2 black, 2 scarlet, 2 black, 1 scarlet, 2 black.

4th Row.—5 black, 2 scarlet, 5 black.

5th Row.—Like 4th.

6th Row.—2 black, miss 1, 2 black, 2 scarlet, 2 black, miss 1, 2 black.

7th Row.—1 black, miss 2, 2 black, 2 scarlet, 2 black, miss 2, 1 black.

8th, 9th, and *10th Rows.*—Miss 3, 2 black on black, 2 scarlet on scarlet, 2 black on black, miss 3.

11th Row.— Like 7th.

12th Row.—Like 6th.

13th and *14th Rows.*—Like 4th.

15th Row.—Like 3rd.

16th Row.—Like 2nd.

17th and *18th Row.*—Like 1st.

Repeat these eighteen rows up to the top: miss 22 squares on each side, and

* To enable ladies in the country to obtain, without difficulty, the proper materials for the Work-Table designs in this volume, Mrs. PULLAN will supply any of them by post. (See her announcements on the wrapper of each Number of the "FAMILY FRIEND."

repeat the stripes: miss 22 more, and repeat as much of the stripe as you can, which will be 7 stitches of the twelve, and allow a single row of black all round.

In the directions for the broad stripe, I shall use the *initials* of the colours. C. crimson, S. scarlet, L. lilac, Y. yellow: Work from left to right.

1st Row.—Miss 3, 1 s 1, 1 floss, miss 3, 1 s 2, 1 floss, miss 3, 1 s 3, 1 floss, miss 3, 1 y 3, 1 y 5, miss 2.

2nd Row.—Miss 3, 2 s 1, 1 floss, miss 2, 2 s 2, 1 floss, miss 2, 2 s 3, 1 floss, miss 3, 1 y 5, miss 2.

3rd Row.—Miss 3, 2 s 1, 1 s 3, 1 floss, miss 1, 2 s 2, 1 s 4, 1 floss, miss 1, 2 s 3, 1 s 5, 1 floss, miss 5.

4th Row.—Miss 3, 2 s 1, 2 s 3, 1 floss, 2 s 2, 2 s 4, 1 floss, 2 s 3, 2 s 5, 1 floss, miss 4.

5th Row.—Miss 3, 1 s 1, 3 s 3, 2 s 2, 3 s 4, 2 s 3, 3 s 5, 1 floss, miss 3.

6th Row.—Miss 3, 2 s 1, 3 s 3, 1 s 2, 4 s 4, 1 s 3, 5 s 5, 1 floss, miss 2.

7th Row.—Miss 3, 2 s 1, 3 s 3, 5 s 4, 6 s 5, 1 floss, miss 2.

8th Row.—Miss 3, 2 s 1, 3 s 3, 1 s 2, 4 s 4, 1 s 3, 5 s 5, miss 3.

9th Row.—Miss 3, 2 s 1, 3 s 3, 2 s 2, 3 s 4, 2 s 3, 3 s 5, miss 4.

10th Row.—Miss 3, 2 s 1, 2 s 3, miss 1, 2 s 2, 2 s 4, miss 1, 2 s 3, 2 s 5, miss 2, 1 lilac floss, miss 2.

11th Row.—Miss 3, 2 s 1, 1 s 3, miss 1, 1 lilac floss, 2 s 2, 1 s 4, miss 2, 2 s 3, 1 s 5, miss 2, 2 lilac floss.

12th Row.—Miss 3, 2 s 1, miss 1, 1 lilac floss, 2 l 2, 2 s 2, miss 3, 2 s 3, miss 2, 1 l floss, 1 l 4, 1 l floss, miss 2.

(Observe *lilac* 4 is the lightest shade of that colour, black being taken for the darkest.)

13th Row.—Miss 3, 1 s 1, miss 1, 1 l floss, 2 l 2, 1 s 2, miss 3, 1 l floss, 1 s 3, miss 2, 1 l floss, 2 l 4, 1 l floss, miss 2.

14th Row.—Miss 4, 1 l floss, 3 l 2, 1 l floss, miss 2, 1 l floss, 1 l 3, 1 l floss, miss 1, 1 l floss, 3 l 4, 1 l floss, miss 2.

15th Row.—Miss 3, 1 l floss, 1 black, 2 l 2, 1 l floss, miss 1, 1 l floss, 2 l 3, 2 l floss, 4 l 4, 1 l floss, miss 2.

16th Row.—Miss 3, 2 black, 3 l 2, 1 l floss, 1 l 1, 3 l 3, 1 l floss, 5 l 5, 1 l floss, miss 2.

17th Row.—Miss 3, 2 black, 3 l 2, 2 l 1, 3 l 3, 1 l 2, 5 l 5, 1 l floss, miss 2.

BERLIN TRAVELLING BAG, BY MRS. PULLAN.

18th Row.—Miss 3, 2 black, 3 1 2, 2 1 1, 3 1 3, 2 1 2, 4 1 5, 1 1 floss, miss 2.

19th Row.—Miss 3, 2 black, 3 1 2, 2 1 1, 3 1 3, miss 1, 2 1 2, 3 1 5, 1 floss, miss 2. Begin crimson floss.

20th Row.—Miss 4, 2 black, 2 1 2, 2 1 1, 3 1 3, miss 1, 2 1 2, 3 1 5, 1 crimson floss, miss 2.

21st Row.—Miss 5, 2 black, 1 1 2, 2 1 1, 3 1 3, miss 1, 2 1 2, 2 1 5, 2 c floss, miss 2.

22nd Row.—Miss 6, 2 black, 2 1 1, 3 1 3, 1 c 4, 2 1 2, 1 1 5, 1 c floss, 1 c 3, 1 c floss, miss 2.

23rd Row.—Miss 7, 1 black, 2 1 1, 2 1 3, 2 c 4, 2 1 2, 1 c floss, 2 c 3, 1 c floss, miss 2.

24th Row.—Miss 8, 2 1 1, 1 1 3, 3 c 4, 1 1 2, 1 c floss, 3 c 3, 1 c floss, miss 2.

25th Row.—Miss 9, 1 1 1, (the last lilac,) 3 c 4, 1 c floss, 4 c 3, 1 c floss, miss 2.

26th Row.—Miss 6, 1 c 3, miss 2, 5 c 4, 5 c 3, 1 c floss, miss 2.

27th Row.—Miss 5, 2 c 3, 1 c 2, 5 c 4, 1 c 2, 5 c 3, 1 c floss, miss 2.

28th Row.—Miss 4, 1 c 1, 2 c 3, 2 c 2, 3 c 4, 1 c 2, 1 c 1, 5 c 3, 1 c floss. miss 2.

29th Row.—Miss 3, 2 c 1, 2 c 3, 1 c 4, 2 c 2, 1 c 4, 1 c 2, 2 c 1, 5 c 3, 1 c floss, miss 2.

30th Row.—Miss 3, 2 c 1, 2 c 3, 2 c 4, 3 c 2, 2 c 1, 5 c 2, 1 c floss, miss 2.

31st Row.—Miss 3, 2 c 1, 2 c 3, 1 c 2, 2 c 4, 1 c 2, 1 c 4, 2 c 1, 5 c 3, 1 c floss, miss 2.

32nd Row.—Miss 3, 2 c 1, 2 c 3, 2 c 2, 3 c 4, 2 c 1, 5 c 3, miss 3.

33rd Row.—Miss 3, 2 c 1, 3 c 3, 2 c 2, 3 c 4, 2 c 1, 3 c 3, miss 1, 1 c floss, miss 2.

34th Row.—Miss 4, 2 c 1, 2 c 3, miss 1, 2 c 2, 2 c 4, 1 c 5, 2 c 1, 1 c 3, miss 1, 2 c floss, miss 2.

35th Row.—Miss 5, 2 c 1, 1 c 3, miss 2,

FLOWERS IN CROCHET—THE JESSAMINE—BY MRS. PULLAN.

2 c 2, 1 c 4, 2 c 5, 1 c 1, miss 1, 1 c floss, 1 c 5, 1 c floss, miss 2.

36th Row.—Miss 6, 2 c 1, miss 2, 1 y 2, 2 1 2, 3 1 5, 1 1 floss, 2 1 5, 1 1 floss, miss 2.

37th Row.—Miss 7, 1 c 1, miss 2, 2 y 2, 1 1 2, 1 1 3, 5 1 5, 1 1 floss, miss 2.

38th Row.—Miss 10, 2 y 2, 1 y 4, 2 1 2, 4 1 5, 1 1 floss, miss 2.

39th Row.—Miss 3, 1 y floss, miss 4, 1 y 2, miss 1, 2 y 2, 2 y 4, 2 1 3, 3 1 5, 1 1 floss, miss 2.

• *40th Row.*—Miss 3, 1 y 1, 1 y floss, miss 3, 4 y 2, 3 y 4, 2 1 3, 2 1 5, 1 1 floss, miss 2.

41st Row.—Miss 3, 2 y 1, 1 y floss, miss 2, 4 y 2, 3 y 4, 1 y floss, 2 1 3, 1 1 5, 1 1 floss, miss 2.

42nd Row.—Miss 3, 2 y 1, 1 y 3, 1 y floss, miss 1, 4 y 3, 3 y 4, 1 y floss, miss 1. 2 1 3, 1 1 floss, miss 2.

43rd Row.—Miss 3, 2 y 1, 2 y 3, 1 y floss, 2 y 2, 1 y 4, 1 y 2, 3 y 4, 1 y floss, miss 2, 1 1 3, 1 1 floss, miss 2.

44th Row.—Miss 3, 2 y 1, 3 y 3, 2 y 2,

3 y 4, 1 y 3, 1 y 4, 1 y floss, miss 3, 1 1 floss, miss 2.

45th Row.—Miss 3, 2 y 1, 3 y 3, 2 y 2, 3 y 1, 2 y 3, 1 y 5, 1 y floss, miss 5.

46th Row.—Miss 3, 2 y 1, 3 y 3, 2 y 2, 3 y 4, 2 y 3, 2 y 5, 1 y floss, miss 4.

47th Row.—Miss 3, 2 y 1, 3 y 3, 2 y 2, 3 y 4, 2 y 3, 3 y 5, 1 y floss, miss 3.

48th Row.—Miss 3, 2 y 1, 3 y 3, 2 y 2, 3 y 4, 2 y 3, 4 y 5, 1 y floss, miss 2.

49th Row.—Like 48th.

50th Row.—Miss 4, 2 y 1, 2 y 3, miss 1, 2 y 2, 2 y 4, miss 1, 2 y 3, 3 y 5, 1 y floss, miss 2.

51st Row.—Miss 5, 2 y 1, 1 y 3, miss 2, 2 y 2, 1 y 4, miss 2, 2 y 3, 2 y 5, 1 y floss, miss 2.

52nd Row.—Miss 6, 2 y 1, miss 3, 2 y 2, miss 3, 2 y 3, 1 y 5, 1 y floss, miss 2.

53rd Row.—Miss 3, 1 scarlet floss, miss 3, 1 y 1, 1 s floss, miss 3, 1 y 2, 1 s floss, miss 3, 1 y 3, 1 s floss, miss 3, 2 y 3, 1 y floss, miss 2. Repeat from the 1st.

The third, (or middle one,) of the five shades of scarlet, must be the same as that in the narrow stripes. The yellow is shaded into a sort of olive-brown, both scarlet and crimson into brown.

The second stripe should be begun at the 15th row of the first, and after the 53rd you should go on from the 1st. The third stripe may begin at the 29th row, and the fourth at the 44th row. By this arrangement the brilliancy of the pattern is much increased, the colours falling in different parts of the stripe, instead of in the same line across the bag.

The grounding should be done last. One row of black is to be worked completely round each side of the bag. The sides may have leather, as in an ordinary carpet bag, or be simply sewed together.

THE JESSAMINE.

Materials. A reel of white cannetille; a little coarser wire: a skein of pure white floss silk; a small skein of yellow ditto; green Berlin wool of three shades:—rather a yellow green is required, and the shades must not be very light.

FOR THE FLOWER. — With the white floss silk, make a chain of eight stitches; take a piece of cannetille a nail long, and place it under the last chain. Crochet down the chain, working over the wire doubled, 7 Sc. Draw the silk through the last loop, and fasten off. This makes one petal, and five will be required for each flower. To make up the flower, take a finger-length of the coarser wire, bend the end of it down closely in the form of a hook, and wind round the top a piece of yellow floss silk, two or three times. Then pinch the wire close together, and wind the silk round both sides of the wire, a little way. Round this head arrange the petals one by one, winding a little white silk round each. Continue to wind the white silk round, for about ¾ of an inch, and then cover the remainder of the stem with a light green wool. Do every flower in the same manner. About five will be required for a small spray.

THE FOLIAGE.—The leaves of the jessamine grow in sets; each small branch has a leaf at the point, and six others, placed in twos, at the sides. Several of these sets, made of the various shades of green, are arranged on a spray, care being taken that the *lightest* shall always be the

highest, and the darkest at the end of the stem.

1st Leaf. (For the points of the set.) Make 16 Ch, fold a bit of wire in the form of a hook. Slip the end in the last chain, and work down it 6 Sc, 2 Sdc, 5 Dc, 1 Sdc, 2 Sc; draw the wool through, and fasten off.

2nd Leaf. (Two required). 13 Ch, bend a bit of wire, and work over it, down the chain, 4 Sc, 3 Sdc, 5 Dc, 1 Sc. Fasten off.

3rd Leaf. (Four required). 10 Ch; bend the wire as before; work on it, 3 Sc, 3 Sdc, 2 Cc, 1 Sdc, 1Sc; fasten off.

When the seven leaves are made, take a piece of the coarser wire, three inches long; slip the point in the end of the first leaf, fasten it to the fine wire stem of the leaf, by winding some wool of the same shade round it very evenly; place the next two leaves a little way down the stem, opposite each other, and continue winding, covering in the ends of their stems; place the other four leaves in pairs in the same way, and wind round the wool, to the end of the wire.

Several of these sets of leaves should be made, and then flowers and leaves are to be arranged in a tasteful manner, on a coarse wire.

OUR MOTHER.—Children ought to love, obey, and honour their parents. Let your mother, in particular, who in your tender years has the more immediate charge of you, be on earth the most sacred object of your affections. Let her be your friend and chief confidant. Conceal nothing from her, but make her acquainted with the company which you keep, the books which you read, and even the faults which you commit. Happy is the son and particularly the daughter, who are not afraid to communicate to their mother their more secret thoughts. While they remain thus artless and undisguised, they are free from danger. Children, obey your parents in youth; but whenever you are no longer under their care, let not your reverence abate. If by the providence of God you should rise above them in the world, grow not ashamed of them. While they are bending under the infirmities of old age, still continue to treat them with respect as well as affection.

POINT-LACE FOR AN ALTAR-CLOTH, BY MRS. PULLAN.

POINT-LACE FOR AN ALTAR-CLOTH.

Materials. No. 7 white cotton French braid; and the Point-lace cottons of Messrs. W. Evans and Co., of Derby.

THE pattern here given is a copy of a very old piece of lace, and is designed for the border of an altar-cloth. It is, however, well adapted for any lace trimming, and might readily be arranged in the form of a collar.

The following stitches and threads are to be used.

A single spot of English lace is worked in every alternate point. This must be done with W. Evans & Co.'s Mecklenburgh thread, No 80. The intermediate points are nearly filled (as will be seen in the engraving), with foundation-stitch, done in Mecklenburgh, No 160. Between the two parallel lines of braid forming the scallop, is worked a double row of English lace, in W. Evans & Co.'s Boar's-head cotton, No 90. The Venetian bars which make the groundwork, are done in the Mecklenburgh 100.

The close diamonds, and other stitches in the centre of the scallops, are to be worked from the engraving, entirely in Mecklenburgh thread, No. 140

NETTED TIDY.

Two reels of No. 10 Evans's Boar's Head Cotton, and two reels of No. 16. No. 6 round wooden mesh; a broad mesh 2 inches wide. No. 16 Netting Needle.

WITH No. 6 mesh, and No. 10 cotton net a piece of netting eighty-seven diamonds every way; then, with No. 16 cotton, darn a row of diamonds.

Then commence darning the pattern, beginning at each corner. Great care must be taken to run in the ends securely, or when washed, they will all come out.

For the Fringe.

Take No. 20 knitting cotton, 4-thread, and, with the broad mesh, net 4 stitches into every diamond; then, after it is washed, cut the Fringe.

This should be very slightly stiffened, and afterwards undergo the same process as directed for Crochet work.

CROCHET FLOWERS—THE POPPY.—BY MRS. PULLAN.

CROCHET FLOWERS.

THE POPPY.

Materials.—Deep scarlet wool, as nearly as possible the colour of the poppy; and some fine white cannetille, and black floss silk, with a mesh three-quarters of an inch wide.

SPLIT the wool in half to make the petals lighter. Make 7 chain. Take a finger-length of wire, and work over it on the chain 1 Sdc, 2 Dc, in each of the next 3 stitches, 3 Dc in the next, 3 in the next. On the other side of the chain, still holding in the wire, do 4 Dc in the same stitch as you have just made 3, 3 Dc•in the next, 2 Dc in each of the next three, 1 Sdc in the next, 3 Sc to take the wool above the first Sdc.

Work now all round this petal, inserting the hook always under both sides of the chain, holding in the wire.

1 Sdc on Sdc, 1 Dc on the same, 1 Dc on each of the next 7, 2 Dc on each of the next 11, 1 Dc on each of the next 7, 1 Dc and 1 Sdc on the next. Make a slip-stitch, and fasten off.

Four of these petals are required for each flower.

FOR THE STAMENS.—With the floss silk make a chain 1½ inch long; then thread a needle with half a yard of the silk left at the end of the chain, and work on it, over the mesh, *taking the stitches as closely together as possible.* Withdraw the mesh, cut the fringe, and roll it as tightly round as possible, so that the chain part shall be a very small ball; give this a stitch to secure it. Take a bit of fine wire, two fingers long, slip it through the chain, and bend it in the form of a hair-pin. Cover a very small bit of it, at the top, with green wool; then arrange the petals round, and fasten them to the stem by winding the wool very closely all round to the end of the wire.

M

THE WORK-TABLE FRIEND.

INSTRUCTIONS IN NETTING.

THE art of netting is one of the simplest and prettiest with which a lady's fingers and leisure time can be employed. The implements are extremely simple, the stitches few and readily to be understood, and the patterns formed, with or without the aid of a common sewing needle, are very elegant and durable. One thing is especially to be noted in netting. Each stitch is, in itself, so firmly made, and so independent of all the others, that the accidental breakage does not in the least affect them. This, we know, is not the case with crochet; and the disastrous consequences of " dropping a stitch " in knitting are known to every worker.

By the aid of our diagrams, we trust to make our descriptions perfectly intelligible to the reader.

The implements used in netting are, a netting needle and a mesh. The former is a long steel or bone bar, split at each end, and with a hole through which the end of the cotton is drawn and fastened, before being wound round the needle. In filling a netting needle with the material with which you intend to work, be careful not to make it so full that there will be a difficulty in passing it through the stitches. The size of the needle must depend on the material to be employed, and the fineness of the work. Steel needles are employed for every kind of netting except the very coarsest. They are marked from 12 to 24, the latter being extremely fine. The fine meshes are usually also of steel; but, as this material is heavy, it is found better to employ bone or wooden meshes when large ones are required. Many meshes are flat; and in using them the *width* is given, but round ones are measured by the same ivory gauge as is used for knitting needles.

The first stitch in this work is termed *diamond* netting (Fig. 1), the holes being in the form of diamonds. To do the first row, a stout thread, knotted to form a round, is fastened to the knee with a pin, or passed over the foot, or on the hook sometimes attached to a work cushion for the purpose. The end of the thread on the needle is knotted to this, the mesh being held in the left hand on a line with

it. Take the needle in the right hand; let the thread come over the mesh and the third finger, bring it back under the mesh, and hold it between the thumb and first finger. Slip the needle through the loop over the third finger, under the mesh and the foundation thread. In doing this a loop will be formed, which must be passed over the fourth finger. Withdraw the third finger from the loop, and draw up the loop over the fourth, gradually, until it is quite tight on the mesh. The thumb should be kept firmly over the mesh while the stitch is being completed. When the necessary number of stitches is made on this foundation, the future rows are to be worked backwards and forwards. To form a *round*, the first stitch is to be worked immediately after the last, which closes the netting into a circle.

ROUND NETTING (Fig. 2) is very nearly the same stitch. The difference is merely in the way of putting the needle through the loop and foundation, or other stitch. The engraving shows that, after passing the needle through the loop, it must be brought out, and put *downwards* through the stitch. This stitch is particularly suitable for gentlemen's purses.

SQUARE NETTING is exactly the same stitch as diamond netting, only it is begun at a corner, on one stitch, and increased (by doing two in one) in the last stitch of every row, until the greatest width required is attained. Then, by netting two stitches together at the end of every row, the piece is decreased to a point again. When stretched out, all the holes in this netting are perfect squares.

GRECIAN NETTING (Fig. 3). Do one plain row. First pattern row. Insert the needle in the first stitch, as usual, and, without working it, draw through it the second stitch, through the loop of which draw the first, and work it in the ordinary way. This forms a twisted stitch, and the next is a very small loop formed of a part of the second stitch. Repeat this throughout the row.

The second row is done plain.

The third like the first; but the first and last stitches are to be done in the usual manner, and you begin the twisting with the second and third loops.

The fourth is plain. Repeat these four rows as often as required.

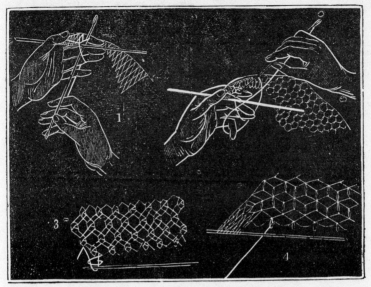

INSTRUCTIONS IN NETTING, BY MRS. PULLAN.

Use No. 20 mesh for the fancy rows, and No. 14 for the plain.

HONEYCOMB NETTING (Fig. 4). After a plain row, first row, net in the usual way the second loop, then the first. Repeat, working the loops alternately throughout the row.

Second row, plain.

Third, do one plain stitch, and then repeat the first row.

Fourth, plain.

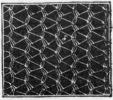

HERRINGBONE NETTING (Fig. 5). To make this stitch, do every row like the first of the last pattern, taking the second stitch *first*, and the first second.

Square and diamond netting are frequently ornamented by having patterns darned on them, in simple darning or in various point stitches, in which we hope shortly to instruct our readers. In the latter case it forms a variety of the sort of work termed *guipure*.

Stitches in netting are always counted by knots.

The beauty of netting consists in its firmness and regularity. Loops longer than the others of the same kind should be avoided. All joins in the thread must be made in a very strong knot; and, if possible, at an edge, so that it may not be perceived.

JEWELLED DOYLEYS.

THE RUBY.

Materials.—1 oz. ruby-coloured beads, No. 2, and one reel, No. 16 Messrs. W. Evans and Co.'s Boar's-head crochet cotton.

BEGIN by threading all the beads on the cotton; then make a chain of 8

JEWELLED DOYLEYS.   THE RUBY, BY MRS. PULLAN.

stitches, and close into a round. All the doyley is done in Sc, except the edge.

1st Round.—+ 1 Ch, 1 Sc on Sc, + 8 times.

2nd Round.—+1 Ch, 2 Sc on 2 Sc, + 8 times. It will be observed that instead of the usual way of increasing by working two stitches in one, a chain-stitch is made, and one Sc only is worked on each Sc.

3rd Round.—+ 1 Ch, 3 Sc on Sc, + 8 times.

4th Round.— + 1 Ch, 4 Sc on Sc, + 8 times.

5th Round.— + 1 Ch, 5 Sc on Sc, + 8 times.

6th Round.—+ 1 Ch, 6 Sc on Sc, + 8 times.

7th Round.— + 1 Ch, 7 Sc on Sc, + 8 times.

1st Bead Round.— + 2 cotton, 6 beads, + 8 times.

2nd Round.— + 4 beads, coming over 2 cotton, and 1 bead at each side, 5 cotton over 4 beads, + 8 times.

3rd Round.— + 2 beads over the centre 2 of 4, 8 cotton, + 8 times.

4th Round.— + 3 beads, the first 2 over 2, 3 cotton, 1 bead, 4 cotton, + 8 times.

5th Round.— + 7 beads (the first over first of last round), 5 cotton, + 8 times. End with 1 bead on the last stitch.

6th Round.— + 6 beads, (1st on 1st), 6 cotton, 1 bead, + 8 times.

7th Round.— + 3 beads, 10 cotton, 1 bead, + 8 times. End with 2 beads.

8th Round.— + 3 beads, 10 cotton, 2 beads. + 8 times. End with 3 beads.

9th Round.— + 3 beads, 11 cotton, 3 beads, + 7 times, 3 beads. This round is not perfect.

10th Round. + 3 cotton over cotton, 1 bead, 4 cotton, 4 beads, 1 cotton, 3 beads, + 8 times.

11th Round. + 2 cotton, 9 beads, 3 cotton, (over 1 bead, 1 cotton,) 3 beads, + 8 times.

12th Round.—3 cotton over 2, + 7 beads, 5 cotton, 4 beads, 2 cotton, + 8 times.

13th Round.— + 1 cotton, 5 beads, 5 cotton, 3 beads, 1 cotton, 2 beads, 1 cotton, + 8 times.

14th Round.— + 4 cotton, (over 1 cotton, 2 beads,) 3 beads, 5 cotton, 4 beads, (the last on last of 3,) 4 cotton, + 8 times.

15th Round.— + 2 cotton, 5 beads, (the last on last of 3,) 3 cotton, 6 beads, 5 cotton, + 8 times,

16th Round.— + 13 beads, 1 cotton, 2 beads, 6 cotton on 5, + 7 times. Eighth time, 4 cotton only on 3.

17th Round.— + 9 beads, 1 cotton, 4 beads, 2 cotton, (last over 1 cotton,) 3 beads, 4 cotton over 3, + 7 times. Eighth time, 3 cotton on 2.

18th Round.— + 9 beads, 1 cotton, 5 beads, 2 cotton, 5 beads, 2 cotton on 1, + 7 times. Eighth, 1 cotton.

19th Round.— + 5 beads, 5 cotton, 5 beads, 10 cotton, (over 9 stitches,) + 8 times.

20th Round.— + 3 beads, 8 cotton, (over 7 stitches,) 5 beads, 5 cotton, 1 bead, 4 cotton, + 8 times.

21st Round.— + 3 beads over 3, 10 cotton (making 1), 5 beads, (beginning on 2nd of 5,) 3 cotton, 2 beads, 4 cotton, + 8 times.

22nd Round.— + 3 beads on 3, 12 cotton, (making 1,) 9 beads, 4 cotton, + 8 times.

23rd Round.— + 3 beads on 3, 6 cotton, 4 beads, 3 cotton, 7 beads, (on centre 7 of 9,) 5 cotton, + 8 times.

24th Round.— + 3 beads on 3, 6 cotton on 5, 6 beads, 14 cotton, + 8 times.

25th Round.— + 4 beads, (beginning over 1st of 3,) 7 cotton, (on 5 and 1 bead,) 5 beads, 14 cotton, + 8 times.

26th Round.— + 1 cotton over 1 bead, 4 beads, 3 cotton, 1 bead, 3 cotton, 4 beads, (over last 4 of 5,) 13 cotton, + 8 times.

27th Round.— + 2 cotton on 1 cotton, 8 beads, 3 cotton, 4 beads, 13 cotton, + 8 times.

28th Round.— + 3 cotton over 2 C and 1 B, 6 beads, 3 cotton, 4 beads, 14 cotton, + 8 times.

29th Round.— + 4 cotton, 3 beads (the 1st over 2nd of 6), 3 cotton, 5 beads, 16 cotton, + 8 times, 5 cotton.

30th Round.— + 9 beads, beginning on 2nd of 3, 21 cotton, + 8 times.

Do one round of cotton only, and then one of beads.

BORDER.— + 2 Sc cotton, 15 beads, 2 cotton, 13 chain with a bead on each, miss 12, + 8 times.

2nd Round.— 2 slip on 2 cotton, + 2 Sc with cotton, on the first 2 beads, 1 bead, 1 cotton, * alternately 6 times, 1 cotton, 5 Ch, with beads, 1 Sc with bead on 4th of 13, 7 Ch with beads, miss 5 of 13, Sc with bead on next, 5 Ch with beads, + 8 times.

3rd Round.— + 2 Sc with cotton on 2nd Sc and 1 bead, * 1 bead, 1 cotton, * 5 times, 1 cotton, 5 Ch with beads, 1 Sc with bead on 4th of 5, 6 Ch with beads, 1 Sc on 4th of 7 with beads, 6 Ch with beads, Sc with bead on 2nd of 5 Sc, 5 Ch with beads, + 8 times.

4th Round.— + 2 Sc cotton as before, * 1 bead over cotton, 1 cotton over bead, * 4 times. 1 more cotton, 5 Ch with beads, 1 Sc with bead on 4th of 5, 6 Ch with beads, 1 Sc with bead on 4th of 6, 6 Ch with bead, 1 Sc with bead on 3rd of next 6, 6 Ch with beads, 1 Sc with bead on 2nd of 5, 5 Ch with beads.

These Doyleys must be washed with white Windsor soap and soft water only. When quite clean rinse them in fresh water, and hang them before a fire, or in the air to dry. When nearly dry, pull them out into shape. On no account use any starch, nor an iron. Beads, when of good quality, and properly washed, will remain for years uninjured.

———

To KNOW THE TERMINATION OF A ROUND IN D'OYLEYS, &c.—This is often thought a difficulty, even by experienced workers, after the first few rounds are done; and frequently the pattern is destroyed by an error in the calculation. This difficulty may be remedied at once, by attention to the following rule:—Take a thread very opposite in colour to that of your work, and only a few inches long. When only two or three rounds are done and it is still perfectly easy to see the end of the round, draw the needleful of thread through the chain of the last stitch. Do the same with every other round, so that the coloured thread finally runs in a straight line from the centre to the edge. It will save much trouble and many blunders, especially when working the Jewelled D'Oyleys.

THE WORK-TABLE FRIEND.

INSTRUCTIONS FOR TAPESTRY-WORK AND EMBROIDERY.

THE materials for tapestry-work and embroidery. These may be classed under the names of wool, silk, chenille, braid: beads, straw, and a variety of other fancy materials, are also brought into use; and a knowledge of the proper mode of using them, and the varieties of each which are made, is one of the most useful things it is possible for the amateur needlewoman to know. We will, therefore, take them seriatim.

WOOL. German wool (or Berlin wool, as it is commonly called) is the most beautiful material manufactured for canvas - work. The vast variety of shades, the exquisite tints produced, the softness and evenness of the fabric, are beyond all praise. We speak of Berlin wool *as it ought to be ;* for no article is more frequently of inferior quality. From damp, or bad packing, or many other causes, it is frequently crushed and injured, and in that state is not fit to be used for good work. Berlin wool is supposed to be all dyed, as well as made, abroad; at present a large proportion is entirely produced in our own country, which is little, if at all, inferior to the foreign. Berlin wool is made only in two sizes, namely 4-thread, and 8-thread; unless the latter is specified in receipts, the other is always implied. Berlin wools are either dyed in one colour, or in shades of the same colour, or (*very rarely*) in shades of several colours. Technically, a silk or wool, dyed in shades of the same colour, going gradually from light to dark, and from dark to light again, is termed an *ombré* or *shaded* wool or silk, whereas *chiné* is the term employed when there are several *colours* used. There are, also, what are called *short* and *long* shades ; that is, in the former the entire shades, from the lightest to the lightest again, will occur within a short space, a yard or so; whereas, in *long* shades, the gradation is much more gradually made. We notice these apparently trifling differences, in our "instructions," that our readers may comprehend the importance of obtaining precisely the proper materials for each design. If we pre-

scribe a certain article, it is because *it* and no other will give the effect. For instance, in a gentleman's purse, given in p. 170, we advised clear glass beads, threaded on cerise silk,—and the reason was the peculiarly rich effect produced by the coloured silk shining through transparent glass. Yet many of our readers may inquire whether it would not be quite as well with all steel beads:—of course the silk could not be seen through them. Thus, a change of material, which might appear of no consequence whatever, would completely spoil the effect of the design.

A new material has been recently introduced, termed Crystal wool. It looks very brilliant and pretty, but is not well adapted for long wear.

FLEECY WOOL is the sort of wool used for polkas and other large articles. No material has been more improved of late, both in texture and dye. Some of the tints are quite as brilliant as those we so much admire in Berlin wool. It is made in 4, 6, 8, and 12-threads, and is much cheaper than German wool. It does very well for grounding large pieces of tapestry.

SHETLAND WOOL is very fine and soft, but it is not much used.

SILKS. *Netting silk* is so generally known it requires no description. It is, however, made in various sizes, and, of course, the selection of a wrong size often spoils the dimensions of a piece of work. Three sizes are in general use, but there are extra fine and coarse.

FILOSELLE is a silk much used for crochet-work, and for grounding canvas. Its make has been greatly improved of late years, — indeed, some kinds work with almost the richness of floss, at one quarter the expense ; it is not suited for fine work. It is dyed in some very rich tints, but not any great variety.

FLOSS SILK is a very beautiful and expensive material ; if largely used, care should be taken to economise it as much as possible. Generally speaking, if floss is used in cross-stitch, half the stitch is done with wool, and it is then finished with silk. It is chiefly employed in embroidery.

CHENILLE is of two kinds. *Chenille à broder* (the finest sort), and *chenille ordinaire*, which is stiff, and about the thickness of a quill. The extreme richness of the appearance of chenille, makes it suitable for any work requiring great brilliancy; as, the plumage of birds, some flowers, and arabesques. Silk canvas is much embroidered with chenille; but it is extremely expensive, and very soon injured by dust. It should only be employed for articles intended to be glazed, such as pole-screens, the tops of workboxes, and screens.

BRAIDS are of various kinds. Russian silk braids are generally employed for dresses, slippers, &c.; but, for many of these, the new ALBERT braid recently manufactured in England for ourselves, is much richer and more effective. Russian silk braid is generally narrow, and the plait is of that kind which we term Grecian,—all the strands going from the edge to the centre. In French braid, on the contrary, you can distinguish the plait of every two strands over each other. French braid, in silk, is very little used in this country. Slippers, and other small articles, worked in braid, have the effect greatly improved by laying a gold thread on one or both sides of the braid. VICTORIA, ADELAIDE, or CORONATION braid (for the same article has been called by all these various names), is a cotton braid, which, when laid on net or muslin, looks something like satin-stitch. It is composed of thick and thin parts, alternately, and is made in only two sizes.

ALBERT BRAID is a sort of silk cord, made in many beautiful colours. It is intended for either application, in braiding, and being *raised*, looks extremely well, with very small outlay of time or money.

Gold and silver braids are often used in Mosaic-work, and for slippers, blotting-cases, &c. The MOSAIC braid, which is comparatively cheap, is generally used.

A new material has just been manufactured for crochet, called Crystal Twine. It is made in gold, silver, and various colours, and is very brilliant.

We have already described the perforated patterns, used in marking embroidery designs. Canvas-work is always done by the thread; and, in selecting the canvas and pattern, the scale we have already given (in page 149), for the sizes of the former, will be found extremely useful.

Placing the canvas in a frame, technically termed *dressing the frame*, is an operation which requires considerable care. The frame itself, especially for a large piece of work, should be substantially made: otherwise the stress upon it will be apt to warp it, and drag the canvas. If this occurs to any extent, the injury can never be repaired.

After herringboning the raw edges of the canvas, sew them, *by* the thread, to the webbing of the frame,—that is, to the top and bottom. Then stretch the ends till the canvas is extended to its utmost length, put in the pegs, and brace the sides with fine twine. If the canvas is too long for the frame, and any part has to be rolled over the end, let the wood be first covered with a few thicknesses of silver paper.

Sometimes, to save the trouble of grounding, a design is worked on cloth, over which canvas is laid. Whenever this is the case, the cloth must be carefully damped, to remove the gloss, before being put into the frame. Then, as cloth will always stretch much more than canvas, it must be cut a little smaller both ways. The raw edges of the cloth should be turned in, and tacked to the canvas before they are framed. Some people withdraw the threads of canvas after the work is done; but it has a much richer effect, if the threads of canvas are cut close to the outer stitches; and if there are any small spaces in the pattern, where the ground should be seen, they may be worked in wool of the colour of the ground.

Should a piece of work be a little drawn, when taken out of the frame, damp the back well with a clean sponge, and stretch it again in the frame in the opposite direction. Whenever Berlin-work is done on any solid thick material, as cloth, velvet, &c., a needle should be used with an eye sufficiently large to form a passage for this wool. This prevents the latter from being crushed and impoverished as it passes through.

It only remains for us to describe the different stitches used in tapestry-work. There are only five kinds,—CROSS-STITCH, TENT-STITCH, TAPESTRY-STITCH, GERMAN-STITCH, and IRISH-STITCH.

CROSS-STITCH is generally known. The

SIMPLE COLLAR IN SATIN STITCH, BY MRS. PULLAN.

needle is brought up in one pole of the canvas, and down on another, two threads higher and more to the right. The slanting thread is then crossed in the opposite direction. Some workers do a line of half stitches, and then cross them; but this plan is apt to spoil the smooth even surface which the work should present. A cross-stich covers two threads in each direction.

TENT-STITCH occupies one-fourth the space of cross-stitch. It is taken from one hole to the next above, and on the right hand side of it.

TAPESTRY-STITCH crosses two threads of the canvas in the length, and one in the width. It is sometimes called Gobelin-stitch, because the Gobelin tapestry is worked in it. It is not suited for coarse canvas; and, in working from a Berlin pattern, *two* stitches must be counted as one square.

GERMAN-STITCH is worked diagonally, and consists of the first part of a cross-stitch, and a tent-stitch alternately worked.

IRISH-STITCH is worked parallel with the selvages of the canvas. None of the stitches cross the threads in the *width*. In the first row, take the thread alternately over four and two threads; in all future rows take the stitches over four threads,— which, as they rise, first from the long and then from the short stitch, will produce the same appearance in others.

With regard to wools, they should never be wound, as the least handling crushes the pile and spoils them. Chenille needs still more careful handling.

To stiffen large pieces of work, wet the wrong side thoroughly with a sponge and dry it rapidly before a fire (the wet side nearest the fire), before removing it from the frame.

We have said but little of the introduction of beads in canvas-work. They have the double merit of being at once brilliant and durable. The Germans are, however, so tenacious of the monopoly, it is quite a favour to obtain from them the varieties of shades and colours. They are, however, scarcely less numerous than those of wool. We ourselves, as a great favour, have obtained all the colours made in seed-beads, a number considerably exceeding 300.

THE WORK-TABLE FRIEND.

NETTED PURSE.

Materials.—3 skeins of scarlet netting silk of the finest size, 2 skeins of fine and pure gold thread, and a skein of coarse sewing-silk of each of the following colours: dark blue, green, white, purple, and brown. Harlequin tassels, and slides for a garniture. Netting meshes, No. 15 and this width.

THIS purse is done in the ordinary diamond stitch, and every one who has the slightest knowledge of netting may do it. Our instructions in pages 178 and 179 will thoroughly teach those who may be unacquainted with the various requirements for netting.

The netting is done entirely with the scarlet silk, and the pattern is formed by darning afterwards with the gold thread and the other colours.

Make a foundation of 62 stitches. Then with the finest mesh work a round of 60 stitches only. Do 56 rounds in this manner. Take the large mesh, and do one round with it. With the small mesh work the next round, as follows: miss 1 stitch, net the second as usual, *then* the missed stitch. Repeat this all round. Do another round with the large mesh, and one as before with the small. Then instead of working rounds, work backwards and forwards, the following: + 3 rounds plain with the small mesh; one with the large, one with the small, taking the second stitch before the first,—one again with the larger and one with the small as before, + 4 times. End with three plain fine rows, and close into a round. Do alternately a large plain and small twisted row, twice: then 56 rounds with the small mesh.

We must now refer to the engraving. The reader will see two rows of diamonds, and above, between, and below, these, a line of vandykes, the threads being marked leaning to the right, instead of, (as in the body of the purse,) to the left. These vandykes are darned in gold thread; begin four diamonds from the first large round; + darn in a direct line towards the left, across 9 diamonds, raising one bar, and crossing the next; darn up again, raising

NETTED PURSE, BY MRS. PULLAN.

NETTED MAT, BY MRS. PULLAN.

those bars which before were crossed. The diamond should be filled by 6 threads, three each way. Fill the next line, and the succeeding in the same way; then darn across three diamonds only, instead of nine; keeping the slope of the upper line, + repeat all round the purse.

From the lowest point, miss 5 holes, sloping towards the left, reckoning that which the gold thread enters, but does not cross, and repeat the gold darning. Do the same again for the third round of van-dykes. The diamonds between are then darned as represented. The diamonds are darned over 5 holes, the colours coming in the following order. A, purple: B, blue;

C, brown; D, green; the white is white in the engraving also.

Draw up the ends of the purse, sew on the tassels, and slip on the slides.

NETTED MAT.

Materials. — 6 skeins of white Berlin wool, and 6 pink ditto. 1 bone mesh in width, and one No. 11.

With the large mesh work one round of 32 stitches, with the pink wool. Then 5 rounds with the fine mesh. Take the large mesh; + 4 stitches in 1, miss the next; + repeat all round.

FLORAL MAT, BY MRS. PULLAN.

Do 2 more rounds with the fine mesh. A point. Nine stitches, turn; 8 stitches, turn; 7 stitches; turn the work, do 6 only, always omitting the last; turn, do 5; turn, do 4; turn, do 3; turn, do 2; turn, do 1. Break off the wool, leaving an end, which must be neatly fastened off. Repeat all round.

Darn a diamond at each point with white wool, and draw up the centre.

Do another mat with the white wool, in exactly the same manner, and darn three diamonds on it with the pink. Draw it up; lay it over the pink, with every point coming between two points of the latter, as seen in the engraving, and sew them together in the centre.

FLORAL MAT.

Materials.—Five shades of crimson Berlin wool, from brown to light cherry — 4 skeins of each; white, 2 skeins; and lilac, 1 skein; 1 skein of shaded green crystal wool; 1 skein of gold coloured crochet silk, and 1 ball of gold crystal twine. 2 yards of cord to work over will also be wanted.

WITH the darkest wool, work as closely

as possible over the end of the cord, and form it into a round. Work on it another round, increasing sufficiently to keep it flat, and using the same wool.

2nd Round.—(Same colour, and white.) + 3 white, 3 brown, + 7 times in the round.

3rd Round.—(Same colours.) 5 white over 3, 3 brown on brown. + 7 times.

4th Round.—(Next crimson and white.) + 6 white over 5, 5 crimson on 3. + 7 times.

5th Round.—(Crochet silk, and next crimson.) + 7 silk over 6 white, 6 crimson over 5. + 7 times.

6th Round.—(Next shade and silk.) Do 3 silk over the centre of 7 silk, and cover the intermediate space with the wool, increasing sufficiently to keep the mat quite *flat,* and to cover the cord on which you are working.

7th Round.—(Lightest crimson and silk.) + 1 silk on the centre of 3 silk, now cover half the space between it and the next three, with the light wool; then do a single stitch with the crochet silk, only instead of working over the cord, insert the hook in the centre of the 5 *crimson* in the 4th round; then continue with the lightest wool. + 7 times in the round. Fasten off the cord, over which you have been working.

8th Round.—With a bone hook, and the darkest wool, working very slackly, + Dc under both sides of the chain, 1 Ch, Dc under the same stitch, miss 3. + all round.

9th Round.—(Next shade.)—Dc under a chain, + 1 Ch, Dc under the same, Dc under the next. + all round.

10th Round.—(Next shade.) Like the last, but with 2 Ch instead of one.

11th Round.—(Next shade.) Like the 1st, but with 3 chains.

12th Round. — (Lightest shade.) — Sc between any two Dc that have no chain between them, + 4 Ch, 3 Dc under the chain of last round, 1 Ch, 3 Dc under the next chain, 1 Ch, 3 Dc under the next, 1 Ch, 3 Dc under the next, 4 Ch, Sc after the next Dc stitch. + repeat 9 times in the round.

13th Round.—With the silk, + Sc on the first Sc of last row, 3 Ch, Sc under the chain before the first 3 Dc stitches, + 4 Ch, Sc under the 1 Ch, + 3 times,

4 Ch, Sc after the next 3 Dc, 3 Ch. + 9 times.

Now, with the gold cord, work on the same round as you worked the 8th round on; that is, on the edge of the last round over the cord; Sc on the centre one of the 3 stitches missed in the 8th round, + 5 Ch, Sc on the centre of the next 3, + all round.

Observe that this and the following rounds are to be in the front of the mat, the open part already done falling back, and being quite *separate* from this.

2nd Round of gold twine. Sc under the centre of every chain of 5, with 6 chain between.

3rd to 7th inclusive.—The same, with 7 Ch between.

Take a piece of thin cardboard, and make a round 10 inches wide. Cover it on both sides with green silk or twill, running the edges neatly together. Tack the mat on it, running it round at the edge of the cord first, and then by the chains of the 11th round, which should completely cover this foundation, leaving the scalloped edge of the 12th and 13th rounds as a border. The gold net-work is left quite loose. Now make 4 dark leaves, and 4 light with the crystal wool: thus, 20 Ch, take a morsel of wire 1½ finger long, and hold it in while working 1 Sc, 2 Sdc, 1 Dc in the same stitch as the last, 1 Dc, 1 Stc, 1 Tc in the same, 9 Tc, 1 Tc and 1 Stc in one, 1 Stc, 1 Dc, 1 Sdc, 3 Sc in one at the point, 1 Sdc, 1 Dc, 2 Stc, 1 Tc in the same as the last, 10 Tc, 1 Stc in the last, 2 Dc, 1 Sdc in the last, 1 Sc, 1 Slip. Fasten off by plaiting the end of wool with the two ends of wire.

All the 8 leaves are to be done alike.

THE FLOWERS.—With common wool make a chain of 5, close into a round.

1st Round.—1 Dc in every stitch, with 1 chain between.

2nd Round.—Using a different colour Dc on every stitch with one chain between.

Make 16 flowers, some white, some lilac, and some crimson.

Make every two leaves and four flowers into a little bouquet, and tack them down on the mat, at equal distances, as near as they can be to the outer edge of the cord-work, and under the gold net-work. Then tack down the edges of the latter, at the same place as the wool was fastened to the lining (the chain of the 11th round).

TRIMMING IN BRODERIE ANGLAISE, BY MRS. PULLAN.

THE WORK-TABLE FRIEND.

TRIMMING IN BRODERIE ANGLAISE.

Materials. French muslin; W. Evans & Co.'s Boar's Head sewing cotton, No. 40; and Moravian embroidery cotton, No. 70.

This scallop trimming is given in the full dimensions, and the pattern may therefore be traced from it, and drawn on the muslin. When this is done, tack the end of the strip on a piece of *toile ciré*, and work it; then remove the toile to the next piece. In tacking it on, it is not sufficient to fasten the edges only together; the needle should be taken between the flowers, and in every part of the pattern, so as to completely fasten the muslin to the foundation; without, however, carrying the thread across any part which would have to be cut out in the working. The parts where the muslin is to be entirely removed when the pattern is worked, are distinguished in the engraving by being quite black. In the round holes, a morsel is cut out of the centre, with the scissors, and the space enlarged with a stiletto. Where the holes are of other shapes, the piece to be cut out must

be the same shape, but very much smaller. All the parts that are perfectly *white* are to be worked in buttonhole-stitch, graduated according to the depth required. The eyelet holes are sewed round, with Boar's-head sewing-cotton; but every part should be traced with embroidery-cotton, before it is cut out at all. The Moravian embroidery-cotton is proper for the edge and all the buttonhole work.

Have the embroidery nicely washed, after working, before cutting out the edges.

BRUSSELS POINT-LACE.

Materials. The Point-lace cottons of Messrs. Walter Evans & Co., of Derby.

This lace, the design for which may be traced from the pattern, is in the simplest style, though not, on that account, less beautiful. Each scallop contains one sprig in rich heavy stitches, on a fine and closely guipured ground. The Raleigh bars which form that ground, are done in No. 160 Mecklenburgh thread; the edge, in close buttonhole stitch, with Raleigh dots on each small scallop, in No. 100 of the same. The foundation-stitch, in which

BRUSSELS POINT LACE, BY MRS. PULLAN.

the leaves, and every alternate petal of the flowers, is worked, is done in No. 120, Boar's-head sewing cotton; and the spotted lace for the other petals, in No. 140, Mecklenburgh, as also the Mechlin wheels which form the small flowers.

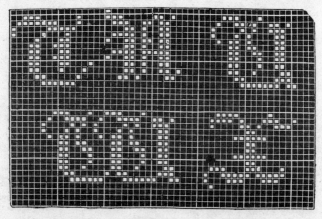

LETTERS IN SQUARE CROCHET, BY MRS. PULLAN.

DEEP POINT-LACE EDGING, BY MRS. PULLAN.

THE WORK-TABLE FRIEND.

DEEP POINT-LACE.

Material.—French white cotton braid, No. 9, and the Point-lace cottons of Messrs. W. Evans and Co., of Derby.

THIS lace, designed for the upper part of the same sleeve given in another portion of this work, is done to correspond with it. The whole outlines are made in the braid ; the leaves are then filled in entirely with Brussels lace, done in Boar's-head, No. 90 the veinings being worked over it, in radiating Venetian bars, with Mecklenburgh, No. 100. The edge is done with No. 80, and the ground with No. 120, Mecklenburgh thread : the Mechlin wheels and the rosettes also are done in the latter.

The rose is represented as done, almost entirely, in Brussels lace ; but if the rows are alternately worked in Fenetian, it will be an improvement. It is done with No. 90, Boar's-head, and the English lace with No. 120, of the same.

Rather more than one perfect pattern of this lace being given, the full size, nothing can be easier than to draw any length from it.

VASE MAT.

Materials.—½ oz. of scarlet crystal wool ; ½ oz. of stone ditto ; ½ oz. of black wool ; 3 skeins of white ditto ; 6 yards of rather fine cotton cord.

WITH the black wool, cover the end of the cord, and form it into the smallest round you can. Do two more rounds

VASE MAT, BY MRS. PULLAN.

with the black, increasing sufficiently to keep the round flat.

3rd Round.—Scarlet and black. + 1 scarlet, 3 black, + 10 times in the round, the last black coming over the *last but one* of the previous round, and one scarlet over the last.

4th Round.—+ 1 black over scarlet, 1 scarlet over the same, 3 black, 1 scarlet all 4 over 3 black, + 10 times.

5th Round.—+ 2 black over 1 black, 1 scarlet over scarlet, 3 black over 3 black, 1 scarlet over scarlet, + 10 times.

6th Round.—+ 3 black over 2, 5 scarlet over 2 scarlet and the 3 black between, + 10 times.

7th Round.—Join on the white. + 3 black over 3 black, 1 scarlet, 1 white, 2 scarlet, over 1 scarlet, 1 white, 1 scarlet, + 10 times.

8th Round.—+ 3 black over 3 black, 7 scarlet over the scarlet and white, + 10 times.

9th Round.—+ 3 black over 3 black, 3 scarlet, 2 white over 1 scarlet, 3 scarlet, + 10 times.

10th Round.—+ 4 black over 3 black, 9 scarlet over scarlet and white, + 10 times.

11th Round.—+ 5 black over 4 black, 3 scarlet, 4 white over 3 scarlet, 3 scarlet, + 10 times,

12th Round.—+ 6 black over 5, 10 scarlet over scarlet and white. + 10 times.

13th Round.—+ 6 black over 6, 2 scarlet over 2, 7 black over 6 scarlet, 2 scarlet, + 10 times.

Cover one round completely with black, increasing sufficiently to cover the cord, and keep the work flat. Then do two rounds of scarlet and stone, by working each alternately over one pattern, *or a 10th part of the round*. In the second round, scarlet comes over scarlet, and stone over stone, the number of stitches being increased enough to cover the cord, which you now cut off.

Now with the white wool and a very fine hook, do a round of open square crochet. A 2nd and 3rd must be done, increasing enough in the round to keep it flat, by making 3 chain instead of 2 about 12 times in the 2nd round, and 24 times in the 3rd.

Four rounds of fringe must now be worked, in scarlet and stone, each coming over the same colour in the last round over the cord. The way of working this fringe being quite new, we must try to describe it. Take a rather large darning needle, and thread it with scarlet. Also take a mesh two-thirds of an inch wide. Hold the mat with the edge on which you are about to work over the finger. Make a knot in the end of the wool, and slip the

WATCH-HOOK IN CROCHET.—BY MRS. PULLAN.

needle *upwards*, through the last stitch of a stone stripe, then *down* through the 1st scarlet.

Pass the wool round the mesh, then slip the needle up the next scarlet-stitch, and pass it under the thread of wool from the stone to the scarlet-stitch. Slip the needle down in the same stitch, let the wool go over the mesh, and up the next scarlet, then under the threads of the last stitch, down through the same, and so on, until you have fringed all the scarlet stripe; when you get opposite the stone-colour, use a needleful of stone-wool; and repeat these colours 5 times in the round.

The 2nd, 3rd, and 4th rounds of fringe are to be worked on the 3 rounds of white wool.

Our friends who work crochet will please to refer to our INSTRUCTIONS (page 5) for all the terms we use.

From not noticing these terms, many of our friends have done their patterns wrong. They will observe, that whenever two or more colours are worked together, over a cord or otherwise, the stitch is Sc.

WATCH-HOOK IN CROCHET.

Materials.—2 shades of green, and 2 shades of pink or crimson wool; also a skein of claret

N

crystal wool; 1 skein of gold-thread, No. 10; a reel of cannetille, and piece of coarser wire; also a mother-of-pearl watch-hooks.

WITH the crystal wool make a chain of four, and form it into a round.

1st Round. — 2 Sc stitches in every stitch.

2nd Round. — 2 stitches in every stitch, inserting the hook under both sides of the chain in every stitch, in this and all the following rounds.

3rd Round. — 2 Sc stitches in every one of the eight in the preceding round.

4th Round. — Increase eight stitches in the round, at equal distances, which will be done by working two in every other stitch.

5th to the 11*th Round.* — Sc all round, increasing eight stitches, at equal distances, in every stitch. Fasten off.

FLOWERS, of which fourteen will be required for the pair of watch-pockets, six being of one shade, and eight of the other. Every flower has five petals, which are worked thus:—Take the pink or crimson wool, make 5 ch. Take a finger-length of cannetille, and work round the chain, miss 1—1 Sc, 1 Sdc in one stitch, 2 Dc in the next, 2 Stc in the next, 2 Sdc in the next, 1 Dc in the same, 1 Sdc and 1 Sc in the same. Bend the wire, and make 1 Sdc in the same stitch, then 1 Dc, and 2 Stc in the same, 2 Stc in the next, 2 Dc in the next, 1 Sdc and 1 Sc in the last, in which work also a slip-stitch and fasten off. This forms one petal, and five will be required for each flower.

The eye of the flower is made with gold thread. 1st. 5 ch, close it into a round by a slip-stitch on the 1st chain.

2nd Round.—3 ch, slip stitch on the slip stitch, ＋ 3 ch, slip stitch on the last stitch and on the one next to it, ＋ 4 times. Fasten off. When you have done 14 of these, proceed to make up your flowers. Take a piece of fine wire, double it, and slip it through the centre of the little golden star; arrange the petals round, and fix them in their places, by covering the wire and all the ends with green wool, worked closely round it. Then take some very fine yellow silk, and sew each point of the star down to one of the five petals.

THE LEAVES.—With the green wool, 18 ch, take a piece of green cannetille,

three times as long as the 18 chain, hold it in, and work on the chain,—1 Sc, 1 Sdc, 1 Dc, 2 Dc in the next, 1 Dc in the next, 1 Sdc in the next, 1 Dc in the next, 1 Stc in the next, 2 Stc in the next, 1 Stc in the next, 1 Dc in the next, 1 Sdc in the next, 2 Dc, 2 Sdc, 1 Sc, 1 ch. Bend the wire, and do 1 Sc stitch in the stitch in which you worked the last Sc; 2 Sdc, Dc, 1 Sdc, 1 Dc, 1 Stc, 2 Stc in one, 1 Stc in the next, 1 Dc, 1 Sdc, 1 Dc, 2 Ddc in one, 2 Dc, 1 Sc, 1 slip stitch in the last stitch. Fasten off.

Do 40 leaves, half the number being of each shade.

Cut two rounds of cardboard, the size of the rounds already made in crystal wool. Cover them with silk on one side, drawing up the other, and covering it with the woollen round. Sew them together at the edges. Take a piece of stout wire, large enough to go more than twice round the circle. Hold the ends together, having bent it into the form seen in the engraving, and cover the ends with green wool rolled round it; place the leaves and flowers on the wire, as seen in the engraving, covering in the ends, and joining them to the thick wire, by winding on the green wool. When the whole of the wire, including the loop by which it is to be suspended, is covered, sew the round to it, and add the mother-of-pearl hooks.

BENEFITS OF RETIREMENT.—He must know little of the world, and still less of his own heart, who is not aware how difficult it is, amid the corrupting examples with which it abounds, to maintain the spirit of devotion unimpaired, or to preserve, in their due force and delicacy those vivid moral impressions, that quick perception of good, and instinctive abhorrence of evil, which form the chief characteristic of a pure and elevated mind. These, like the morning dew, are easily brushed off in the collisions of worldly interest, or exhaled by the meridian sun. Hence the necessity of frequent intervals of retirement, when the mind may recover its scattered powers, and renew its strength by a devout application to the Fountain of all grace.

HYACINTH-GLASS MAT.

HALF an ounce of shaded Green, two skeins of six shades of Scarlet—all 4-thread Berlin Wool; tne lightest shade of Scarlet to be a bright Geranium colour, the darkest a rather light claret, the third shade from the lightest to be a military scarlet. Four yards of White Skirt Cord, the size of ordinary Blind Cord. No. 2 Penelope Hook.

To form the Cup.

WITH Green wool work Dc over the Cord for eight rounds, encreasing in the 2nd round two stitches into every loop, the next round the same, the next round one in every 2nd stitch; and so on in proportion as the encreasing may be necessary, till of sufficient size for a Hyacinth Glass. The bottom of the Mat should be one round larger than the size of the Glass. Then work an additional round without encreasing, but drawing the cord rather tightly about every twelve stitches. Now work eight rows up the side, without encreasing, being careful to draw the cord at intervals: fasten off neatly, and turn the Mat inside out.

For the First Row of Leaves.

Take the four lightest shades, and commence with the darkest: make 12 chain, turn back, work 4 Dc up, 6 L; and into the end loop work 7 L; now work down the chain 6 L, 4 more Dc.

Fasten on the next shade; work 5 Dc up, 5 L, 2 L into every loop of the 7 L excepting in the centre loop, where work 3 L instead of 2, 5 L down the leaf, 5 Dc.

Fasten on the next shade; 6 Dc up, 4 L, 2 L into every loop of the 14 L, with 3 L into the centre loop.

Next shade: take some wire drawn from white ribbon wire, and work a row of Dc all round, enclosing the wire in the stitches; fasten off neatly. Eight of these light leaves will be required.

For the Broad and Dark Leaves.

Commence with the darkest shade; make 9 chain, turn back, work 1 L into every loop except the last, when work 7 L.

Next shade; 7 L, with 2 L into every loop of the 14 L, with 3 L into the centre loop; now 7 L down.

Next shade the same.

Military scarlet; Dc over the wire as in

the first leaves, taking care to bend the end of the wire after the first and last stitches are made, to prevent it slipping. Seven of these leaves will be sufficient.

With lightest wool sew on the first circle of leaves at the points, leaving about an inch and a half above the cup; then with some wool sew each leaf together just where the top of the cup reaches, cutting of the wool every time—not carrying it on. Then, with darkest wool, sew on the outside leaves, taking care that neither ends of wool or wire show; then attach these also, about an inch from the bottom; now mould them into shape with the finger and thumb.

KNITTED TOILET COVER.

STEEL Needles No. 14; 12 reels of No. 6 Evan's Boar's Head Cotton.

CAST on 258 stitches, and knit 12 plain rows. Then begin the pattern, knitting 10 plain rows at the beginning and end of each row. (*The pattern is to be repeated till long enough for the table.*)

By bringing the cotton forward, in the KNITTED *rows, a stitch is made, but in the* PEARLED *rows it will be necessary to put the cotton* ROUND *the needles, to make a stitch; but in every place, the expression "bring forward" signifies making a stitch.*

1st Row.—K 5, K 2 +, Tf, (a) K 1, Tf, K 2 +, K 4.

2nd Row.—P 3, P 2 +, Tf, P 3, (a) Tf, P 2 +, P 4.

3rd Row.—K 5, Tf, K 2 +, (a) K 4, K 2 +, Tf, K 4.

4th Row.—P 4, Tf, K 2 +, P 1, (a) P 2 +, Tf, P 5.

5th Row.—K 3, K 2 +, Tf, K 5, (a) Tf, K 2 +, K 2.

6th Row.—P 4, Tf, P 2 +, P 1, (a) P 2 +, Tf, P 5.

7th Row.—K 1, K 2 +, Tf, K 1, Tf, K 2 +, Tf, K 3, (a) Tf, K 2 +, Tf, K 1, Tf, K 2 +.

8th Row.—P 1, * Tf, P 3, Tf, P 2 +, P 3, (a) P 2 +, Tf, P 3, Tf, P 3 +, *repeat* from *, *and end the row by* P 2 + *instead of* 3 +.

9th Row.—K 1, Tf, K 2 +, K 1, K 2 +, Tf, K 2 +, * K 1, K 2 +, Tf, K 2 +, K 1, K 2 +, Tf, (*end the row knitting* 1 *instead of Tf*).

Hyacinth-Glass Mat.   By Mrs. Warren.

10th Row.—Tf, P 2 +, P 1, P 2 +, Tf, P 3, * Tf, P 2 +, P 1, P 2 +, Tf, P 1.

11th Row.—K 2, Tf, K 2 +, K 2, Tf, K 3 +, * Tf, K 2, K 2 +, Tf, K 1.

12th Row.—P 2, Tf, P 2 +, P 5, * P 2 +, Tf, P 3.

13th Row.—K 4, Tf, K 2 +, K 3, * K 2 +, Tf, K 3.

14th Row.—P 4, Tf, P 2 +, P 1 * P 2 +, Tf, P 5.

15th Row.—K 6, Tf, K 3 +, * Tf, K 5.

16th Row.—Pearled.

17th Row.—As 1st row, but beginning and ending the row at (*a.*)

18th Row.—P 1; then continue the row from (*a*) in 2nd row, ending each pattern with P 2 instead of P 3.

19th Row.—As 3rd row, beginning at (*a.*)

20th Row.—As 4th row, beginning at (*a.*)

21st Row.—K 3; continue as 5th row,

beginning at (*a,*) and ending K 2 instead of K 5.

22nd Row.—As 6th, beginning at (*a.*)

23rd Row.—K 2; continue as 7th, from (*a,*) ending with K 1 instead of 3.

24th Row.—P 1; continue as 8th, from (*a,*) ending P 2 instead of 3.

25th Row.—As 9th, beginning at (*a*).

26th Row—P 1; continue as 10th, from (*a,*) ending P 2 instead of 3.

27th Row.—P 2 +; continue as 11th, beginning at (*a*), end the row by P 2 + (*taking off a border stitch with the last stitch of the pattern*) instead of 3 +.

28th Row.—P 2; continue as 12th, from (*a,*) ending P 3 instead of 5.

29th Row.—K 2; continue as 13th, from (*a,*) ending K 1 instead of 3.

30th Row.—As 14th, beginning from (*a.*)

31st Row.—K 2 +; continue as at 15th.

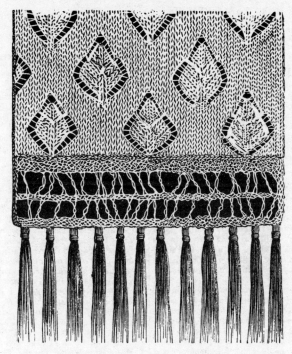

Knitted Toilet Cover. By Mrs. Warren.

ending the row by **K 2 +**, taking an edge stitch with the last of the pattern, instead of 3 +.

32nd Row.—Pearled ; begin again at the 1st row.

(It will be seen that at the 17th row the pattern is begun in the middle, in order to make the leaves fit in well ; therefore that and the following rows are worked from "a" to "a ;" that is, commencing the row at (a), and ending with the first part of the row.)

For the Fringe.

Cast on 9 stitches.

1st Row.—K 4, * cotton twice round, K 2 +, repeat from *, K 1.

2nd Row.—K 3, P 1, K 2, P 1, K ; K 2 +.

3rd Row.—K 5, * cotton twice round, K 2 +, repeat from *, K 1.

Cut some cotton 6 inches long, take eight lengths ; take the 1st stitch, and knit it with these eight lengths taken all together, instead of knitting it with the single cotton, keeping the ends of these lengths even ; then put the stitch from the right-hand needle to the left, and knit it with the cotton ; K 2 more, P 1, K 2, P 1, K 3, K 2 +.

5th Row.—K 4, * cotton twice round, K 3 +, repeat from *, K 1.

6th Row.—Same as 2nd.

7th Row.—K 3, * cotton twice round, K 3 +, repeat from *, K 1.

8th Row.—The same as 4th row.

Now begin as at 1st row.

THE WORK-TABLE FRIEND.

["No. 16 Evans's Boar's-head Cotton," for Lady's Netted Cap, is omitted at p. 132.]

D'OYLEY.

No. 16 Evans's Boar's-head Cotton   No. 4 Penelope Hook.

1st Round.—Make 13 chain, unite, • 9 chain, Dc *under* this circle, *repeat* from • 9 times more—in all, 10 loops of 9 chains; regulate them, and fasten off. (*Every round must be commenced afresh.*)

2nd Round.—5 L *under* the 9 chain, 1 chain, *repeat* 9 times more.

3rd Round.—In the 1 chain work 2 L, 3 chain, 2 more L in same loop, 4 chain, *repeat.*

4th Round.—In the centre loop of the 3 chain work 2 L, 3 chain, 2 more L in the same loop, 4 chain, Dc *under* 4 chain, 4 chain, *repeat.*

5th Round.—In the centre loop of the 3 chain work 2 L, 3 chain, 2 more L in the same loop, 4 chain, Dc *under* 4 chain, 7 chain, Dc *under* 4 chain, 4 chain, *repeat.*

6th Round.—Dc in the centre loop of the 7 chain; now 15 chain, turn back, 1 L into the 9th loop from hook, 3 chain, 1 L into 4th loop, 3 chain, Dc into loop where commenced; 1 chain, turn round on the finger, Dc *under* the the 3 chain, 5 L *under* 3 chain, 5 L *under* next 3 chain, 5 L *under* the chains at the point of the leaf, 3 chain, 5 more L *under* same, 5 L under next 3 chain, 5 L *under* last 3 chain, Dc into same loop where commenced; 5 chain, Dc into the centre loop of the 3 chain; make 15 chain; then work another leaf exactly the same, only uniting at the first 5 L, into the 6th L of former leaf. (*After this leaf is completed, make 5 chain, then repeat.*)

7th Round.—Dc into the 1st L of the 5 L nearest the 3 chain; now Dc into every loop till the centre loop of the 3 chain, then Dc twice into this centre loop, with 1 chain between each Dc stitch, then 2 Dc stitches more; now Dc down to the end of the 5 L; make 1 chain, and *repeat* into next leaf.

8th Round.—Dc into the increased loop of last row which is between the 2 Dc stitches at the point of the leaf, 5 chain, Dc into 4th loop, 5 chain, Dc into the 4th

loop from the increased loop in next leaf. *Repeat.*

9th Round.—Dc into the Dc stitch at the point of the leaf; now make 15 chain, and make another leaf precisely as before (*taking care to make the last Dc stitch come into the loop where the 15 chain commenced*); 4 Dc *under* the 5 chain, 3 Dc into 3 loops of next 5 chain, then 15 chain, and make another leaf as before, only uniting at 5th L stitch into the 6th L of 1st Leaf; now 1 Dc *under* the remaining 2 chain of the 5 chain, 4 Dc *under* next 5, and *repeat.*

10th Round.—The same as the 7th, only omitting the 1 chain between the leaves. (*This round must be worked very tightly.*)

11th Round.—Dc between the two leaves, where the two leaves are joined together. (*There will be no stitch made there in the previous round, but still this can be done.*) Make 9 chain, turn back, Dc into 7th loop from the hook (*this forms a small circle*); turn on reverse side, 5 chain, 1 L *under* the small circle, 5 chain, 1 L *under* same; 7 chain, 1 L *under* same, 5 chain, 1 L *under* same, 5 chain, Dc *under* same; now Dc into the point of the next leaf (*that is, where the Dc was made with the 5 chain*); turn on reverse side, Dc into 5 chain, 5 L *under* same, Dc *under* same; *repeat* this over the Flower (*after the last Dc stitch, Dc into the top of next leaf, then 5 chain, Dc between the two leaves*); 11 chain, turn back, 1 L into 8th loop from hook, 3 chain, Dc into the same loop where the 11 chain commenced; 1 chain, turn round on the finger, Dc *under* the 3 chain, 5 L *under* same, unite into 3rd L of Flower, 5 L *under* the next chains; 3 chain, 5 more L *under* same, 5 L *under* next 3 chain, Dc into loop where commenced; 5 chain, Dc into the top of next leaf, 5 chain, Dc between the leaves; and make another Flower as the first, but uniting at first 3 L of Flower, into the 5th L of the leaf last made.

TULIP-SHAPED MAT FOR A TOILETTE BOTTLE.

THREE shades of Scarlet, the middle tint to be military Scarlet, the darkest a Claret, and the lightest a bright Geranium colour—2 skeins of each; 3 skeins of bright maize colour; ½ an ounce of emerald tint shaded green—all 4-thread Berlin wool: 3 yards of ordinary-sized blind cord. No. 2 Penelope hook.

WITH shaded Green work 14 stitches

D'Oyley. By Mrs. Warren.

over the end of blind cord, then double round in as small a circle as possible, and increase in the first two rounds 1 stitch in every loop of preceding row; then continue at regular intervals to increase in every row until there are 11 rows, taking care that in the last row there are 147 stitches *only*, and that the row terminates exactly opposite to the end of cord where it was commenced. This can easily be seen, and the rows ascertained, by counting; fasten off the cord neatly. Now, without breaking off the wool, work 21 Dc stitches along, then turn on reverse side, and turn back, but without making the extra stitch (*which is always done in a straight piece of work, to prevent the decreasing; but here decreasing is required, therefore avoid making it*). Now work

ridged crochet, by working backwards and forwards till decreased to a point. (*This ridged crochet is made by working into the outside loop instead of the inside one, and turning back every row*). Now work 6 more points the same. In commencing the 2nd point, begin in the last stitch of the 21 Dc stitches in last point: now the Mat will have the appearance of a star. Draw some wire from some white ribbon wire, and with the Maize wool work Dc all round these points, enclosing the wire; but begin on the wrong side of the Mat, as these points will turn up. After the first stitch is made over the wire, bend the wire to prevent its slipping, and at the end the same; but previous to this, stretch the wire well.

With Claret, Dc into a stitch at the bottom of a point, then make 5 chain, Dc into

Tulip-shaped Mat for a Toilette Bottle.   By Mrs. Warren.

·very 3rd stitch up the point, taking care that a 5 chain comes immediately over the top of the point (*this must be particularly attended to*); then work the same down the point. There should be about eight of these chains of 5 on each side of a point, exclusive of the one on the top of the point; but be careful not to bend the wire in this row.

Next row, Scarlet: Dc into the last 5 chain at the end of a point; then Dc into the first 5 of next point, but without making any chains between; then 5 chain, Dc into every 5 till the point, where make 7 chain, Dc *under* same; then 5 chain, Dc *under* 5 till the bottom of the point, where you must unite both together as before.

Lightest Scarlet; the same as last row.

Maize colour: Dc *under* the 7 chain at the point, 7 chain, Dc *under* same, 5 chain, Dc *under* 5 for 5 times. By counting the Dc stitches there will be 6 Dc from the point; now count 5 chains of 5 from the top of next point; Dc into this 5th chain,

without making any chains between; this draws the two points together about midway. Now 5 chain, Dc up the point, then *repeat* at the top as before.

Bend the mat into shape.

--------◆--------

GOOD ACTIONS IN WOMAN.—Let women be deeply and practically persuaded that the favour of God is far above every earthly blessing; that one act of charity or self-denial is better worth than the most flattering display of wit and accomplishments, with all the brilliancy of beauty to lend them lustre. So shall the loveliness of women be twice lovely: so shall the evening as well as the morn of life shine with unclouded brightness; and He, " before whose face the heavens and earth shall flee away," smile on them in that awful hour, when the charms of the fair, and the wisdom of the wise, shall alike be vain, and holiness alone retain its value.— *Bowdler.*

BROAD TRIMMING FOR PETTICOATS

THE IVY, BY MRS. PULLAN.

THE WORK-TABLE FRIEND.

THE IVY.

Materials.—3 shades of green wool (2 skeins of each); 1 skein of black ditto; 1 reel of cannetille, and 1 of thicker wire.

FOR THE LARGEST LEAF.—With the darkest wool make a chain of 16 ; take a long piece of cannetille (about 12 inches), bend the wire underneath the last chain leaving a piece for the stem, and crochet down the chain ; over the wire 1 Sc, 1 Sdc, 9 Dc, 4 Sdc ; bend the wire back, so as to work up the same side, 1 Sc, 1 Sdc ; turn the leaf in your hand, and bend the wire down ; make 8 Ch ; turn, and on the chain do 7 Sc, which will bring you to the wire at the end of the leaf ; work down over the wire 12 Sdc ; again bend the wire, and crochet over it 4 Sc, 4 Sdc, 8 Dc, 1 Sdc, 1 Sc.　Bend the wire down, and crochet 2 Sc, 5 Sdc.　Make 9 chain, on which do 8 Sc.　Then work down the remainder of the leaf 7 Dc, 2 Sdc, 2 Sc ; turn back, and work up the leaf 6 Sc, 5 Sdc, 5 Dc, 1 Sdc ; again bend the wire

down, and work over it 4 Sc, 16 Sdc, which will bring you back to the beginning of the leaf.　Take a slip-stitch, and fasten off.

All the leaves are done in the same way, only with a smaller number of stitches ; the lightest shades of the wool being used for the smallest leaves.　Each leaf is done separately, the ends of the wire being twisted together, and covered closely with the same wool as the leaf itself is made of, for which purpose about half a yard should be left at the end of every leaf.

When the last and smallest leaf is made, a piece of the thicker wire should be held in with the ends, and covered with them. It is to be long enough to mount all the leaves upon.　These are attached in the usual way, by having the ends of wire held to the main stem, and the wool wound round them all together.　In covering the stem with wool, the tint should be gradually changed from the lightest to the darkest.　Indeed, generally speaking, the shades selected for the foliage of the same

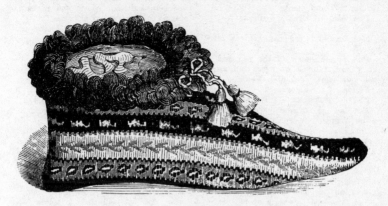

TURKISH SLIPPER IN KNITTING, BY MRS. PULLAN.

spray, must be the closest that can be procured.

For the Fruit.—Take eight bits of cannetille, each 2 inches long. Bend each into the form of a hair-pin, and wind a little ball of black wool round the centre. (It must be much less than a pea). Pinch the sides of the wire close together, and cover with green wool. Mount some of these in a little bunch, and leave the others detached; join them to the stem in the same way as the leaves.

Sometimes these fruit may be made of the lightest green wool. They will then represent the unripe berries.

The Ivy, as well as all the other flowers we have given, has been copied from Nature.

TURKISH SLIPPER, IN KNITTING.

Materials.—Two shades of olive-green wool each 6 skeins; black, 18 skeins; white, 4 skeins; yellow, 8 skeins; scarlet, 16 skeins; purple, 1 skein; pink, 20 skeins. W. Boulton and Son's tapered knitting needles, Nos. 17 and 16; and netting meshes, 1 inch and ¾ inch wide.

With the lightest green wool, cast on 146 stitches, with No. 17 needles.

Knit and purl alternately 6 rows, increasing 10 at one end of the needle, and 7 at the other, while doing them

Observe, the even rows are purled, and the odd knitted throughout—1, 3, 5, 7, 9, 11, &c. are knitted.

2, 4, 6, 8, 10, &c. are purled.

7th Row.—No. 16 needles. Join on the black, without fastening off the green, and alternately knit a stitch of green, and a stitch of black, increasing two stitches at the end of the row. Fasten off green.

8th Row.—Join on the red. Purl one red on every black stitch, and a black on every green, of last row. Do not break off the black. Increase two at the end.

9th Row.—Red. Knit. Increase 2 at the end of every row until further orders.

10th Row.—Red. Purled.

11th Row.— + 4 red, 2 black, + repeat to the end.

12th Row.—Join on the yellow and white, 2 red on the centre two of four red, one black over the first and last red, one yellow over one black, and one white over the other.

Seen on the right side, this pattern looks thus:—2 red, 1 black, 1 yellow, 1 white, 1 black.

13th Row.—The same colours. + 1 red over the last black, 1 black over white, 1 white over yellow, 1 yellow over black, 1 black over red, 1 red, +.

14th Row.—Break off the yellow and white. Purl black over those two colours

of last row, and red over the red and black.
Do not break off black.

15th Row.—All red. Knitted.

16th Row.—All red. Purled.

17th Row. — 1 red and 1 black alternately.

18th Row.—Fasten off the red, and on
the yellow, 1 black on every red, and 1
yellow on every black of last row.

Fasten off the black.

19th and 20th Rows.—All yellow.

21st Row.—Fasten on the dark green, 4
yellow, 2 green, + repeat.

22nd Row.— + 2 yellow over 2 green,
2 green, 2 more yellow, + repeat. Fasten
on purple, without breaking off the green.

23rd Row.— + 3 yellow which come
over the 2 green of the 21st row, and one
yellow beyond, 3 purple, coming over one
yellow, and 2 green of 22nd row, + repeat.

24th Row.— + 3 purple over 3 yellow,
3 yellow over 3 purple, + repeat. Fasten
off the purple.

25th Row.— + yellow on the 3 yellow,
and the next purple, green on the other
2 purple.

26th Row.—This row being purled, do
two green before the two green of last
row, and all the others yellow.

27th and 28th Rows.—All yellow. Break
off green.

29th Row.—Join on the red. 1 yellow
and 1 red alternately. Fasten off the yellow,
and join on the black.

30th Row.—Black over red, red over
yellow.

31st and 32nd Rows.—All black.

33rd Row.—Join on the dark green, +
3 red, 1 black, 2 green, 3 black, + repeat.

34th Row.— + black over the 3 black
and the 2 green, green over the one black,
2 white on 2 red, 1 red on red, + repeat.
Fasten off green.

35th Row. + Black over last red, 1 red
on white, 1 white on white, 1 red on green,
5 black on black, +.

36th Row.— + 1 red on the red over
one green, 1 red on white, 1 black on red,
1 red on black, 5 black, + repeat.

37th Row.—Black.

38th Row.—Black. Purl off 65 stitches,
on one needle. Purl the remainder of the
rows without increasing at the end. Join
on the yellow.

39th Row.— + 1 yellow, 1 black, + 32
times, 1 yellow. Leave the remaining

stitches on the needle and take a third
needle to knit backwards and forwards
these 65 for the front of the shoe.

40th Row.—Join on the red. One red
on yellow, and 1 yellow on black throughout the row.

41st Row.—Knit all red.

42nd Row.—Purl all red.

43rd Row.— + 2 black, 3 red, + repeat.

44th Row.— + 1 red on the centre of 3
red, one black on each of the others, 1
yellow on the nearest black, 1 white on
the other + repeat.

45th Row. — + 1 red on the black
before the one white, 1 black on white, 1
white on yellow, 1 yellow on black, 1
black on red, + repeat.

46th Row.— + Black on the white and
yellow, red on all the others. + repeat.

47th and 48th Rows.—All red.

49th Row. — + 1 red, 1 yellow, +
repeat.

50th Row.— + 1 Black on yellow, 1
yellow on red + repeat.

51st and 52nd Rows.—All black.

Cast off these 65 stitches, with the 65
left on a needle at the 38th row, knitting
a stitch from each needle together. You
will thus join up the front of the foot.
Now take up stitches at the instep edge of
the stripe down the front of the foot, and
with three needles form them into a round,
taking a fourth to knit with.

1st Round of the instep.— 1 Black, 1
yellow alternately.

2nd Round.— 1 Red on every yellow, 1
yellow on every black.

3rd Round.—All red. Continue all red.

4th Round.— + knit 2 together, pass
the wool over the needle twice to make a
stitch, + repeat all round.

5th Round.— Knit all round, treating
the two threads round the needle as one
stitch.

6th Round.—Purled. Cast off.

For the toe. With a fine needle take
up the edge of the two sloping pieces at
the toe, from the last green row to the
ends of the 38th row. Let there be one
stitch taken up on the green stripe, 9 on
the red, and the same on the yellow, with
7 on the black.

With one of the coarse needles, take up
9 stitches at the front of the foot. Join
on the black wool, and knit 8 of these 9
stitches on the right side of the slipper,

slip the last, knit the first of the side stitches off a fine needle, pass the slip-stitch over. Now purl eight stitches, and with the last, purl one off the other fine needle. Knit and purl alternately these nine stitches, taking off one from a fine needle, with the last stitch, at the end of every row, until you have done, with black wool equal to the black stripe. Join on the yellow and continue in the same way, only the nine stitches must gradually be decreased to five by purling 2 together. It is also necessary, every alternate purled and knitted row, to take two instead of one, off the side needle. When as much is done as will equal the yellow stripe, join on the red wool, and continue in the same way, decreasing the five stitches to one, and knitting off all those of the side needles.

For the Sole. Turn the slipper on the wrong side, and take up, with the fine needles, all the original cast stitches, as well as the *one* stitch left at the toe, and the edges of the green stripe. Join on the dark green wool. Knit the stitches at the edge of the green stripe, and 65 cast on ones, + knit two together, + eight times; knit the remainder to the toe.

Repeat this round.

Hold the two needles nearest the toe together, and cast off 17 stitches from each, knitting two stitches together.

Do another round, knitting three together four times at the heel, then cast off, in the same way, twenty more from each side.

Do another round and cast off the remainder in the same way.

Fasten off all the ends.

These slippers are lined with a row of netting, two yards long, done on the small mesh, with pink wool. It is tacked inside the slipper, backwards and forwards, from the toe to the heel, lining the sole and sides, but coming across the front only once, just beneath the instep.

A netted frill of black wool, done with the widest mesh, is made long enough to go round the entire top of the slipper once, and twice across the front. A plaited cord of black and yellow wool, with a red tassel at each end, is run in the open hem round the ankle.

Cork soles may be added if desired, but for invalids, the slippers without soles are incomparably warm and soft.

The receipt is for the right foot; for the left the joins in front should be at the other side, and the increase at the ends of the first green stripe must be reverted.

Those who are not *au fait* at knitting, may work these slippers in crochet. In either case, care must be taken not to draw the wools. It may interest our friends to know that the original pattern for this beautiful slipper was brought to us from Constantinople, by a lady of the highest rank. The effect depends much on the choice of tints.

"WHATSOEVER thy hand findeth to do, do it *with thy might*," said the wisest man that ever lived: but, comprehensive as is the "whatsoever," there is scarcely a maxim or a precept in the pages of Holy Writ so constantly disregarded. Women, especially, suffer themselves to acquire habits of dawdling through life, as if time was some great enemy, whose existence it was wise to regard as little as possible. They seldom do anything with their might; and, as a natural consequence, rarely do anything perfectly well. To *excel* seems to be no point of ambition with them. And yet, when left to their own resources, as too many are, what degree of merit less than surpassing excellence will enable a woman to find more than mere bread in any employment she may endeavour to obtain? As a governess, a *little* music,—a smattering of French, will be of no service, as an ornamental needlewoman, skill, taste and rapidity of execution are all necessary; in all other paths by which a woman would attain independence, the same superior skill is necessary; and whenever that surpassing excellence has been attained, it ensures ultimate comfort to the possessor of the talent—it is better than a fortune.

In the day of prosperity, then, do not disdain to acquire some one art by which you may, if needs be, earn your bread; and spare no pains to acquire that art thoroughly Be contented with nothing short of perfection. Learn all you can, of the most efficient teachers; and whilst taking their lessons, put all your own powers, mental and physical, in the work. In short, whatsoever thy hand findeth to do, do it with thy might.

FLOWERS IN CROCHET—THE TULIP—BY MRS PULLAN.

THE WORK-TABLE FRIEND.

THE TULIP.

Materials. Light yellow wool, 6 skeins; 2 skeins of light *vert* d'Islay; 1 skein of claret; and a reel of two sizes of cannetille.

THE FLOWER. For a petal make 27 Ch; take a quarter of a yard of cannetille, and work over it, on the chain, 2 Sc, 1 Sdc, 2 Dc, 2 Stc, 15 Tc, 2 Tc in each of the next 4 stitches, which will bring you to the end of the chain; 3 Tc in the stitch at the end; bend the wire round, in the shape of a hairpin, and work over it, on the other side of the chain, 2 Tc in each of the next 3 stitches, 15 Tc, 2 Stc, 1 Dc, 1 Sdc, 2 Sc. Slip-stitch at the base, and work round the petal as follows, taking every stitch *under* both sides of the chain, 4 Sc, 1 Sdc, 2 Dc, 2 Stc, 19 Tc, 1 Stc in the same stitch as the last Tc. 2 Dc, 2 Sc in each of the next 3; bend the wire, and work on the other side, to the base of the petal, in Sc; make a slip-stitch and fasten off.

Six of these petals are required for each flower.

THE LEAF. Make a chain of 43 stitches; take a piece of thick wire, slip the end in the last chain-stitch, and work over it 3 Sdc, 3 Dc, 26 Tc, 5 Dc, 6 Sdc; bend the wire, and round the point work 5 Sc; down the side, 6 Sdc, 5 Dc, 26 Tc, 3 Dc, 3 Sdc. Work all round this leaf in Sc, taking every stitch under both sides of the chain, and holding in the wire. Make a slip-stitch at the end, and fasten off.

Several leaves should be made in the same way, but of various sizes.

Before making up the tulip, do 4 pieces of chain-stitch, with the claret wool, rather more than an inch long; join the ends together; take a piece of rather short wire, long enough to make the stem of a tulip when doubled; bend it in the middle, in the shape of a hairpin, and twist round the top a small ball of light green wool, the size of a pea. Arrange round it the 4 claret chains, and 3 of the petals; twist the green wool round them, and then add the other 3 petals. Continue to twist the wool round, until you come to the end of the wire.

Tulips may, of course, be made in any other colour that is to be found in Nature;

MANDARIN SLEEVE, IN EMBROIDERY, BY MRS. PULLAN.

and they as well as the leaves may be a little smaller or larger. The wire that goes round the outer part of the petals, should be drawn a little, to give the edge the *hollow* form proper to the flower.

MANDARIN SLEEVE, IN EMBROIDERY.

Materials. Half a yard of French muslin, and W. Evans & Co.'s Moravian cotton, No. 70, and No. 50. Boar's-head sewing cotton.

WE give in the engraving a diminished representation of half the sleeve, which should be made with a tight under-sleeve to correspond.

This pattern has the merit of being effective, with small outlay of time and trouble.

It is done entirely in raised button-hole and satin-stitch, with the exception of a scallop of graduated eyelet-holes, between the outer edge and the muslin. Those parts which are perfectly white are worked in raised satin-stitch, the black parts of the fruit being merely holes pierced with a stiletto, and the veinings of the leaves being done in open-hem. The stems and tendrils are neatly sewed over, and the Moravian cotton is used exclusively for this work. The sewing cotton, is for the graduated eyelet-holes in the scallops, which by some accident have been omitted by the engraver. The Moravian cotton saves a great deal of time, as one stitch has the appearance of several.

KNITTED BASSINET QUILT, OR COUVRE-PIEDS, BY MRS. PULLAN.

THE WORK-TABLE FRIEND.

KNITTED BASSINET QUILT, OR COUVRE-PIEDS.

Materials.—1 lb. of white 6-thread fleecy wool, ¼ lb of blue or pink ditto, a pair of wooden knitting needles, No. 8, eagle card-board gauge, and a coarse crochet-hook and rug-needle.

THIS pretty quilt is quite a suitable piece of knitting for a beginner in the art; it is so simple, and has so elegant an effect. It may be done in cotton, if preferred; but we advise wool to be used, as so much warmer. We counsel those who teach young people to knit, to attend particularly to the ·INSTRUCTIONS given at page 59; and especially to insist on their pupils' hands being held, and fingers used according to the directions there given. Skill being once acquired in this pretty and useful art, is never lost; and it can be practised when illness, or age, or any other cause prevents one doing work that

requires very good sight. It has, therefore, recommendations which no other work possesses, and should be cultivated by every woman, no matter what her station.

For a bassinet quilt cast on 135 stitches, or any other number which can be divided by 24, and leave 15 over. At the beginning of every row slip off a stitch, without knitting, putting the needle in as if you were going to purl it, and at the end knit a stitch, taking it through the centre instead of the front of the loop, as is usually done. These stitches are not reckoned in the receipt, as they are invariably the same.

1st Row.—Knit 13, + make 1, slip 1, knit 1, pass the slip-stitch over, * 6 times knit 12 + repeat to the end of the row.

2nd Row, and all the other alternate rows are purled.

3rd, 5th, 7th, 9th, 11th Rows.—Like 1st

13th Row.—Knit 1, + * make 1, slip

SCALLOP BORDER IN BRODERIE ANGLAISE, BY MRS. PULLAN.

1, knit 1, pass the slip-stitch over * 6 times, knit 12 + repeat to the end of the row, which will end with the +, make 1, slip 1, knit 1, pass the slip-stitch over + 6 times.

15th, 17th, 19th, 21st, and 23rd Rows. — Like the 13th.

24th Row.—Purled like all the other alternate rows. This completes one pattern, and the twenty-four rows are to be repeated until the piece of knitting is as long as is desired, when cast off. Now thread a large rug-needle with wool of the other colour; fasten it on at the corner of one of the plain squares; take the needle through the centre of the square, to the opposite corner, and then the next, in a diagonal line downwards, returning in the same stitches, twisting the needle in every loop of wool. When all the plain squares are thus worked in one direction, do them in the same way from corner to corner in the opposite direction. Thus every plain square will have a coloured cross on it, the open squares being left without.

A bassinet quilt might be done in stripes of two colours, each being worked with the other colour. For this purpose, cast on 39 stitches only for each stripe, and make them an uneven number, 3, 5, or 7, so that the same colour may be at each edge. They must be neatly sewed together. When the centre of the quilt is done, work one round of open square crochet, with three stitches close together in every corner. In these open squares knit a fringe 3½ inches deep, and composed of the two colours.

SCALLOP BORDER IN BRODERIE ANGLAISE.

Materials.—Thick French muslin, and W. Evans & Co.'s embroidery cotton, No. 30.

THIS edging is very well adapted for trimming articles of dress for ladies and children. It has the further merit,—to amateurs,—of being very easily done. The full-size being given, any length of pattern may be drawn from it. Tack it on a strip of *toile ciré*, and work the edge first, in close button-hole stitch; then the flower, beginning with the *centre* which must be cut out, and the row edges sewed over in overcast, before the other pieces are cut away.

All the black portions of the engraving are to be cut out.

THE USE OF LITTLE TIME.—One of the hours, each day wasted on trifles or indolence, saved, and daily devoted to improvement, is enough to make an ignorant man wise in ten years—to provide the luxury of intelligence to a mind torpid from lack of thought—to brighten up and strengthen faculties perishing with rust—to make life a fruitful field, and death a harvest of glorious deeds.

o

THE WORK-TABLE FRIEND.

CIGAR-CASE IN CROCHET.

Materials.—Black crochet silk, 4 skeins; white ditto, 1 skein; blue, 1 skein; green (Vert-islay), 4 skeins; apricot, 1 skein; scarlet, 1 skein; crimson, 1 skein. All these are to be of a coarse size. Use Boulton & Son's Crochet-hook, No. 19.

WITH the black silk make a chain of 112 stitches, close it into a round, and do 14 rounds.

1st Round of pattern.—Blue and black, + 3 blue, 11 black, + 7 times. End with 3 blue, 10 black, 1 pink.

2nd Round.—(Same colours.) 2 blue, + 11 black, 3 blue, + 7 times; 10 black, 2 blue.

3rd Round.—(Same colours.) 2 blue over 2, + 5 black, 3 blue, 2 black, 4 blue, + 7 times. 5 black, 3 blue, 2 black, 2 blue.

4th Round.—(Same colours.) + 3 blue, 2 black, 6 blue, 1 black, 2 blue, + 8 times. Fasten off the black, and join on the apricot.

5th Round.—+ 1 apricot on the centre of 5 blue, 13 blue, + 8 times.

6th Round.—(Same colours.) + 12 blue, 2 apricot, coming over the last of 13 blue and 1 apricot, + 8 times.

7th Round.—(Same colours.) + 1 apricot, 5 blue, 4 apricot, 2 blue, 2 apricot, + 8 times.

8th Round.—(Same colours.) + 2 apricot, 3 blue, 6 apricot, 1 blue, 2 apricot, + 8 times. Fasten off the blue, and add the crimson.

9th Round.—+ 4 crimson on centre 4 of 6 apricot, 3 apricot, 1 crimson, 6 apricot, + 7 times, 4 crimson, 3 apricot, 1 crimson, 4 apricot, 2 crimson.

10th Round.— + 5 crimson (over 4 C, and 1 A), 3 apricot, 1 crimson, 3 apricot, 2 crimson, + 7 times, 5 crimson, 4 apricot, 1 crimson.

11th Round.—(Add white.) + 4 crimson, 3 white (which come over centre 3 of 7 crimson), 2 crimson, 4 apricot, 1 crimson, + 7 times. 8th time finish with 3 apricot, 2 crimson.

12th Round.—(Add green.) 2 crimson, 2 white, 3 green, 1 white, 2 crimson, 2 apricot, 2 crimson, + 8 times.

13th Round.—(Same colours.) + 1 crimson, 1 white, 2 green, 2 white, 2 green, 1 white, 1 crimson, 2 apricot, 2 crimson, + 8 times.

14th Round.—+ 1 white, 2 green, 1 white, 2 green, 1 white, 1 green, 1 white, 1 crimson, 2 apricot, 2 crimson, + 7 times. The 8th time 1 apricot, 2 crimson.

15th Round.—+ 1 white, 3 green, 1 white, (over 1 white), 4 green, 1 white, 1 crimson, 1 apricot, 2 crimson, + 7 times. 8th time do 3 crimson, instead of 1 crimson, 1 apricot, 2 crimson. Fasten off the apricot.

16th Round.—+ 1 white, 4 green, 2 white, 2 green, 1 white, 4 crimson, + 7 times. The 8th time only 3 crimson.

17th Round.—+ 1 white, 2 green, 2 crimson, 2 green, 3 white, 4 crimson, 1 white, 6 green, 3 white, 4 crimson, + 3 times. 4th time, 1 white, 2 green, 2 crimson, 2 green, 3 white, 4 crimson, 1 white, 6 green, 7 white.

18th Round.—+ 4 green, 2 crimson, 2 green, 6 white, 8 green, 6 white, + 3 times. 4th time, 4 green, 2 crimson, 2 green, 6 white, 17 green. Fasten off white.

19th Round.—+ 3 crimson, 25 green, + 3 times; 3 crimson, 23 green.

20th Round.—+ 5 crimson, 23 green, + 3 times, 5 crimson, 20 green. Join on black.

21st Round.—+ 9 crimson, 2 green, 1 crimson, 16 green, + 3 times, 9 crimson, 2 green, 1 crimson, 5 green, 2 black, 2 green, 3 black, 5 green.

22nd Round.—+ 3 crimson, 1 green, 7 crimson, 5 green, 2 black, 2 green, 3 black, 5 green, + 3 times, 3 crimson, 1 green, 7 crimson, 4 green, 3 black, 1 green, 5 black.

23rd Round.—+ 8 green, 2 crimson, 1 green, 3 crimson, 5 green, 3 black, 1 green, 5 black, + 3 times, 8 green, 2 crimson, 1 green, 3 crimson, 2 green, 14 black.

24th Round.—+ 6 green, 3 crimson, 6 green, 13 black, + 4 times.

25th Round. — + 7 green, 3 crimson, 6 green, 12 black, + 3 times, 7 green, 3 crimson, 6 green, 3 black, 3 white, 8 black.

26th Round.—+ 6 green, 3 crimson, 6 green, 3 black, 3 white, 7 black, + 3 times; 6 green, 3 crimson, 4 green, 3 black, 3 white, 3 black, 3 green, 4 black.

CIGAR-CASE IN CROCHET, BY MRS. PULLAN.

27*th* Round.—3 green, + 1 crimson, 2 green, 2 crimson, 5 green, 3 black, 3 white, 3 black, 3 green, 4 black, 2 green, + 3 times; 1 crimson, 2 green, 2 crimson, 2 green, 4 black, 3 white, 3 black, 5 green, 3 black.

28th Round.—3 green, + 1 crimson, 2 green, 2 crimson, 5 green, 3 black, 3 white, 3 black, 3 green, 4 black, 2 green, + 3 times; 1 crimson, 2 green, 2 crimson, 3 green, 3 black, 3 white, 3 black, 5 green, 3 black.

29th Round.—3 green, + 4 crimson, 5 green, 3 black, 3 white, 3 black, 5 green, 3 black, 2 green, + 3 times; 4 crimson, 4 green, 3 black, 4 white, 2 black, 3 green, 1 black, 1 green, 2 black.

30th Round.—5 green, + 2 crimson, 6 green, 3 black, 4 white, 2 black, 3 green, 1 black, 1 green, 2 black, 4 green, + 3 times; 2 crimson, 4 green, 5 black, 3 white, 3 black, 1 green, 1 black, 2 green, 1 black, 13 green.

31st Round.— + 5 black, 3 white, 3 black, 1 green, 1 black, 2 green, 1 black, 12 green, + twice; with 10 green only the 3rd time.

32nd Round.— + 2 black, 4 white, 1 black, 2 white, 2 black, 2 green, 1 black, 15 green, + repeat between the crosses with 14 green only, *twice*, and with 12 the 4th time.

33rd Round.— + 2 black, 7 white, 2 black, 3 green, 1 black, 8 green, 1 black, 5 green, + 2nd, 3rd, and 4th time with 4 green for 5.

34th Round.—+ 2 black, 1 white, 3 black, 2 white, 5 black, 2 green, 1 black, 6 green, 2 black, 4 green, + 4 times.

35th Round.— +7 black, 1 white, 1 black, 2 white, 3 black, 1 green, 2 black, 4 green, 3 black, 4 green,+4 times.

36th Round.—+ 8 black, 4 white, 2 black, 2 green, 7 black, 5 green, + 3 times. The 4th time, do 6 green for 5.

37th Round.—+ 4 black, 1 scarlet, 2 black 2 white, 4 black, 3 green, 5 black, 7 green,+3 times. The 4th time, 8 green, instead of 7.

38th Round.—+ 2 black, 2 scarlet, 2 black, 1 white, 4 black, 5 green, 5 black, 7 green, + 3 times. The 4th time do, instead of 7 green, 3 green, 1 black, 2 green, the last of which will come over the seventh of 8 green, in 37th row, five on blue.

39th Round.—+ 3 black, 2 scarlet, (over 2 S,) 2 black, 1 white, 2 black, 1 blue, 3 black, 3 green, 2 black, 1 green. 3 black, 2 green, 1 black, 2 green, + 3 times. The 4th time, leave out 1 black, 2 green, at the end.

40th Round.— + 6 black, 3 scarlet, 3 black, 1 blue, 3 black, 4 green, 3 black,— 1 green, 2 black, 2 green, + 4 times.

41st Round.— + 3 black, 2 scarlet, 1

WAISTCOAT, BRODERIE EN LACET, BY MRS. PULLAN.

black, 3 scarlet, 2 black, 2 blue, 2 black, 5 green, 2 black, 2 green, 2 black, 2 green, + 4 times.

42nd Round.— + 2 black, 4 scarlet, 1 black, 1 scarlet, 3 black, 2 blue, 5 black, 6 green, 1 black, 4 green, + 4 times.

43rd Round.— + 3 black, 4 scarlet, 3 black, 3 blue, 5 black, 4 green, 1 black, 5 green, +4 times.

44th Round.— + 3 black, 4 scarlet, 4 black, 2 blue, 1 black, 2 blue, 3 black, 9 green, + 3 times. The 4th time, 6 green.

45th Round.— + 3 black, 4 scarlet, 4 black, 5 blue, 2 black, 3 green, 3 crimson, 4 green, + 3 times. 4th time, 5 green.

46th Round.— + 4 black, 4 scarlet, 3 black, 4 blue, 2 black, 2 green, 2 crimson, 2 green, 1 crimson, 4 green, + 3 times. The 4th time, 3 green only.

47th Round.—+ 3 black, 3 scarlet, 3 black, 1 scarlet, 2 black, 4 blue, 2 black, 1 green, 2 crimson, 3 green, 1 crimson, 3 green, + 3 times. 4th time, 2 green.

48th Round.—+ 3 black, 3 scarlet, 5 black, 1 scarlet, 2 black, 2 blue, 2 black, 2 green, 2 crimson, 2 green, 1 crimson, 3 green, + 4 times.

49th Round.—+ 3 black, 3 scarlet, 5 black, 1 scarlet, 2 black, 1 blue, 2 black 3 green, 2 crimson, 6 green, + 4 times.

50th Round.—+ 3 black, 3 scarlet, 2 black, 1 scarlet, 2 black, 1 scarlet, 2 black, 1 blue, 2 black, 3 green, 3 crimson, 3 green, 1 crimson, 1 green, + 4 times.

51st Round.—+ 3 black, 6 scarlet, 2 black, 1 scarlet, 2 black, 1 blue, 2 black, 4 green, 5 crimson, 2 green, + 3 times, 4th time, 3 green.

52nd Round.—+ 3 black, 4 scarlet, 2 black, 1 scarlet, 2 black, 1 blue, 4 black, 4 green, 3 crimson, 4 green, + 3 times. 4th time, 6 green. Fasten off blue and scarlet.

53rd Round.—+ 13 black, 6 green, 3 crimson, 6 green, + 3 times. 4th time 7 green.

54th Round.—+ 11 black, 3 green, 3 crimson, 2 green, 2 crimson, 7 green, + 4 times.

55th Round.—+ 2 black, 2 green, 7 black, 2 green, 5 crimson, 1 green, 2 crimson, 7 green, + 4 times.

56th Round.—+ 1 black, 4 green, 4 black, 2 green, 1 black, 3 green, 5 crimson, 1 green, 3 crimson, 4 green, + 3 times. 4th time, 6 green.

57th Round.—+ 1 black, 2 green, 2 black, 9 green, 9 crimson, 5 green, + 3 times. 4th time, 6 green.

58th Round.—+ 3 black, 10 green, 5 crimson, 3 green, 1 crimson, 6 green, + 4 times.

59th Round.—+ 3 crimson over the centre of 5 crimson, 25 green, + 4 times.

60th Round the same.

Now repeat backwards, from the 18th to the 1st pattern round. Do 4 rounds in black, then gradually diminish by working 2 stitches together, at regular intervals, 8 times in every round, until 8 stitches only are left.

The Cigar-case must be made up at a shop.

Observe that this Case is to be worked in the German style; that is, instead of *finishing* a stitch with a new colour, finish with the old, so that the upper part of the stitch is of one colour, and the lower of another.

Although 112 are really in every round, the new part of the pattern often begins in a different place; in some rounds there will be more or less than the right number. This is caused by the pattern, and the directions must be explicitly followed.

WAISTCOAT, BRODERIE EN LACET.

Materials.—A waistcoat-piece of satin or cloth. Russia silk braid, 1 knot, and sewing silk.

OUR own taste would decidedly lead us to select black as the colour for the cloth or satin which is to form the waistcoat; with braid in dark blue, green, or violet. The silk must correspond with the braid. Black does not show sufficiently on black to compensate for the time and trouble the work requires, unless the outer edge of the silk braid have a fine gold thread laid on, which gives the pattern relief, but would not be suitable for any but full dress.

For a wedding, a white silk corded waistcoat, with white braid, edged with gold thread, may be worn.

The point stitches which fill the flowers and leaves are to be done with sewing silk. English and Venetian lace are the most suitable. The veinings of leaves and petals are done in Venetian bars, and all the stems are filled with point d'Alençon or herringbone stitch.

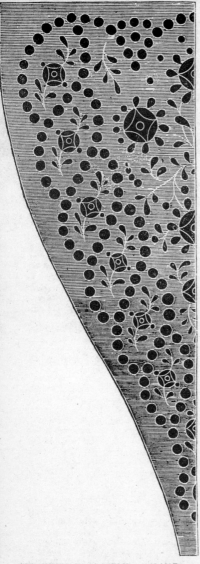

CHEMISETTE IN BRODERIE ANGLAISE.

THE WORK-TABLE FRIEND.

CHEMISETTE IN BRODERIE AN-GLAISE.

Materials. — French muslin, and W. Evans & Co.'s Moravian cotton, No. 70, and embroidery cotton, No. 40.

THIS chemisette is drawn on a scale about one-third the size of the full chemisette, one-half the pattern being given complete. A very slight knowledge of drawing should enable a lady to increase her own patterns. To do so, divide the engraving into a certain number of squares, by lines drawn completely across it, at the half and quarters, both perpendicular and horizontal. Take a piece of writing-paper rather larger than the full-sized pattern, and after lightly tracing out the proper shape, divide it also into the same number of squares, placed at equal distances.

Nothing can be simpler, after this, than to draw the whole design, increasing every part proportionably so that it shall occupy the same space in the large square that it does in the small one.

A very little practice will enable any one to do this correctly.

When two halves of a design correspond, one only need be drawn. If transferred to tracing paper, which is the work of a few minutes, one half can be marked on the muslin from the one side, and one from the other.

A piece of French muslin, the shape of the entire front of the chemisette, is to be used, and the centre only worked. A collar, open at the back, is worn with it.

The design is to be traced with embroidery cotton, and sewed with the Moravian, except the stems, for which the former is to be used. All the eyelet-holes and other parts which are *black* in the engraving, are cut out in working, except the diamond - shaped centres of the flowers, which have only a small eyelet-hole in the middle.

BRAIDED SLIPPER, BY MRS. PULLAN.

THE WORK-TABLE FRIEND.

BRAIDED SLIPPER.

Materials. — Red morocco, Russia black silk braid, 1 knot, 10 skeins of gold thread, No. 3, and 4 reels of gold silk.

WE have succeeded here in giving our readers a section of the design large enough to permit the pattern to be traced from it, if the slippers are intended for a lady. For a gentleman, a little increase is necessary.

The morocco for the slippers is first to be cut out in the proper shape, each front being in one piece, and the back in another. The engraving gives one half the design

BREAD-CLOTH, BY MRS. PULLAN.

for each part. After marking with a perforated pattern, go over the design with a rather thick solution of gum-water and flake white. When dry, run on the braid with one of the strands of the same, a length of the braid being previously cut off for the purpose. Take every stitch *across* the braid, not along the centre.

The gold thread is to be laid on each side of it, and sewed down with China silk of the same tint. If it be thought that the quantity of gold makes the slippers too expensive, it can be laid only on the *outer* edge of the silk braid. Albert braid is not suitable for working on morocco.

The ends of the braid and of the gold thread must be drawn through to the wrong side, with a coarse rug needle.

Morocco can be procured in various colours. Purple, with Vert-islay braid; green, with French blue, and various others, are pretty combinations.

BREAD CLOTH.

Materials.—5 reels of Messrs. W. Evans & Co's Boar's-Head Crochet cotton, No. 24, with Boulton's Crochet-hook, No. 18.

MAKE a chain of 160 stitches, and work on it one row in Dc.

2nd Row.—Begin with 1 chain, and work 2 Dc in each of the two first Dc of last row. One Dc in each of the others, except the two last, in both of which work 2, and end with a chain stitch.

The remainder is to be worked from the design, in ordinary square crochet, but as there is first an increase of a square at each end, and afterwards a decrease, to the same extent in every row, the space in the centre only being without either increase or diminution, we will describe the way in which the decrease is so effected as to leave a regular edge; the increase being always done as we have described in the 2nd row. There are two close squares at each end.

FOR THE DECREASE.—Slip on the first stitch, Sc on the next, Sdc on the next, Dc on the fourth, do three more Dc, 2 Ch, which form the first open square in the line. At the other extremity reverse the process, working on the four last stitches, 1 Dc, 1 Sdc, 1 Sc, 1 slip.

In all the succeeding rows that are decreased, make the slip stitch on the first Dc stitch of the previous row, at each end, thus shortening every row by three stitches.

The edge being of two close squares, allows for all the ends being worked in, which should invariably be done.

Work one row of open square crochet all round, with the Dc stitches sufficiently close at the corners to set flat; and in every square knot a fringe of twelve or sixteen strands, and 2 inches deep.

PATENT WOOL,

USED ONLY FOR KNITTING.

THE articles for which this material is chiefly used are—antimacassars, couvre-pieds, table and bed-covers. It is purchased in balls, of large or small dimensions, according to the article to be made, as each is adapted for a certain purpose, and for *no other*. With each ball is sold a printed paper, directing the number of stitches to be cast on, in order to make the article, and the size of the needles to be employed. The wool is dyed in so peculiar a manner, that when the directions are correctly followed, bouquets or stripes of flowers, of every varied hue, according to those of nature, appear on a white, chocolate, or other ground. In knitting, it will be found that a small knot occurs at intervals in the ball of wool. This knot *should* come exactly at the end of *every* row; and if by any chance it does not, the row must be undone, and knitted more or less tightly, according to the previous deficiency. Fringes to trim all articles knitted with patent wool, and, of course, to match in pattern and ground, can be obtained.

Like all patent articles, these wools and fringes are dear in proportion to many other work-materials, 4s. 6d. being the lowest price for the smallest ball of worsted.

It may be useful to observe that there are two qualities of this patent wool sold—worsted, and Berlin wool; the latter is nearly half as dear again as the former.

The stitch employed is that known as moss stitch, produced by alternately knitting and purling a single stitch. The knitted stitch must always have a purled one above and below it, and *vice versâ*. To produce this, always begin a row with the *same* stitch as you concluded it with: thus, if your last stitch be knitted, knit the first also.

Always cast on with plain Berlin wool, white or coloured.

EMBROIDERED SCENT-BAG.

Materials.—A square of silk canvas, rather more than twice the size represented in the engraving; a skein of ombré green netting silk, one of rose ditto; a little violet, blue, and yellow netting silk; ¾ yard of white silk fringe, some white satin, pot-pourri, &c.

ALL the foliage, various as it is, is worked with the one skein of green silk, a needleful of the darkest part being taken for some of the leaves, the very lightest tints being selected for others, and the medium colours for the remainder. The leaves are done in the usual way; the veinings up the centre in half-polka stitch. Besides all the foliage, another part of the design is also worked in green; that is, all the sprays of heath, the dots of which only are worked in scarlet, in French knots. The China-asters are done in shades of violet, with yellow eyes, also worked in French knots. The petals of those flowers are done by using a double thread in the needle. The forget-me-nots are worked in French knots; five blue ones form a small circle, with a yellow one in the centre for the eye. In working the roses, begin at the heart of the flower, threading your needle so as to use the silk double. Take care

EMBROIDERED SCENT-BAG, BY MRS. PULLAN.

that both the ends are of the same tint, either the darkest or the lightest. Having made a single French knot, with green silk, in the eye of the flower, begin to work round it, in stitches partly laying over each other, and gradually longer, until the heart is entirely worked. The outer petals are to be done in the usual embroidery-stitch, with a single thread, and in such a tint as shall correspond with the outer part of the heart of the flower.

This embroidery requires to be worked in a frame.

To make it up, fill a muslin bag, of the proper size, with any pleasant scent, and cover it again with white silk or satin. Tack on the canvass on one side, sewing it round the edges, and add the fringe.

_____

BRIOCHE CUSHION, BRAIDED ON MERINO.

Materials.—Four pieces of coloured French Merino, and one piece of each of four colours of Albert-braid.

The quantity of merino required for this cushion is three-eighths of a yard, which will cut into four pieces of the form given in the engraving. As the sections of the braid are usually all of different colours, four pieces, each containing the quantity named, will make four cushions; or if two colours only are used, two pieces will suffice for two.

The design given in the engraving is to be enlarged to the necessary size for the cushion; pricked for pointing, and then the same paper will do to mark every section. After using the paper-pattern with prepared pounce, remove it,

BRIOCHE CUSHION, BRAIDED IN MERINO, BY MRS. PULLAN.

and go over the whole design with a solution of flake white and gum water.

The braiding is to be done in the usual way, the stitches being always taken across the thin part of the braid.

In selecting the merinos, violent contrasts should be avoided. The tints should be all either dark or light. Crimsons, greens, dark blue, and claret, go well together; but if light pinks and blues are among the shades, the *joining* colours should be stone, drab, and a warm slate.

In arranging the braids, the same colours should be selected. Green, dark blue, or violet looks well on orange merino, orange on green or blue, pink on stone, or gray, dark blue on claret, crimson on green.

If preferred, eight pieces may be cut to form the round, instead of four; but, in any case, there should be no strong contrasts, and four different colours are quite enough to look well.

———

A FASHIONABLE LADY OF THE FOURTEENTH CENTURY.—Her head was encircled with a turban, or covered with a species of mitre, of enormous height, from the summit of which ribbons floated in the air, like the streamers from the head of a mast. Her tunic was half of one colour and half of another; a zone, deeply embroidered and richly ornamented with gold, confined by her waist; and from it were suspended in front two daggers, in their respective pouches. Thus attired, she rode in the company of her knight to jousts and tournaments.—*Lingard's History of England.*

TOILET COVER IN CROCHET, BY MRS. PULLAN.

THE WORK-TABLE FRIEND.

TOILET COVER IN CROCHET.

Materials. 12 reels Messrs. W. Evans & Co.'s Boar's-head crochet cotton, No. 12.

THE pattern consists of a handsome square, with a rich border on three sides. A foundation chain of 400 stitches must be made, which will allow for a close square at each edge of the toilet. To correspond with this edge, do one row of Dc, before beginning to work the pattern from the engraving.

The entire centre square is given, but not the whole of the front of the border. When the centre of each row is reached, however, it will be very easy to work the remainder backwards. The whole cover is done in square crochet. The border may be added all round, if desired; but this form being a perfect square, is not so suited for a toilet table.

It may be trimmed either with fringe, (done like that of the anti-macassars lately given,) or with a handsome crochet lace, several designs for which we have furnished

CHESTNUT-BASKET, FOR THE DESSERT TABLE.

Materials. Half a yard of pink glazed calico; ditto of flannel; 3½ yards of pink satin ribbon, 1½ inches wide; and seven reels of Messrs. Walter Evans and Co.'s Boar's Head crochet cotton,

CHESTNUT-BASKET FOR THE DESSERT-TABLE, BY MRS. PULLAN.

No. 12. An average worker will use W. Boulton and Son's crochet-hook, No. 16.

THIS elegant novelty for the dessert table consists of a square of crochet, edged with lace, which is afterwards folded into the form seen in the engraving. It is lined with pink glazed calico and flannel, (the former being on the outside); a knot of pink ribbon is placed at each corner, and in order to cover the opening in the centre, a double round of flannel, of the proper dimensions, is quilted with a similar piece of pink calico, and tacked so as to form a lid. It is decorated with bows of pink ribbon, which entirely cover it.

The inner square of the toilet-cover first given would do well for this purpose, working it on a foundation of 262 stitches and with one row of Dc, and one of open square crochet before the pattern is begun.

The nearest centre is to be filled with the initials of the owner, and should be drawn on checked paper, of not more than 31 squares, and worked in.

For the border which is worked all round.

1st Round.—✛ 1 dc, 1 ch, miss 1 ✛ repeat all round, without missing any at the corners.

2nd Round.—✛ 1 dc, 3 ch, miss 3 ✛ all

FUSCHIA SMOKING-CAP.

round, missing only 1, in several stitches at the corners

3rd Round.— + 3 Dc, (the centre on 1 Dc, 6 Ch), miss 6, 1 Dc, on Dc, 6 Ch, + repeat all round.

4th Round.— + 3 Dc, on 3 Dc, 4 Ch, miss 4, 5 Dc, 4 Ch, miss 4, + repeat all round.

5th Round.— + 1 Dc, on the centre of 3 Dc, 3 Ch, miss 3, 3 Dc, 3 Ch, miss 3, 3 Dc, 3 Ch, miss 3, + repeat all round.

6th Round.— + 3 Dc, over 3 Dc, in the 4th row, 4 Ch, miss 4, 5 Dc, 4 Ch, miss 4, + repeat all round.

7th Round.— + 3 Dc, over 3 Dc, 6 Ch, miss 6, 1 Dc over the centre of 5 Dc, 6 Ch, miss 6, + repeat all round.

8th Round.— + 5 Sc, (coming over 3 Dc, and 1 chain on each side), 4 Ch, miss 4, 5 Dc, on 3, 4 Ch, miss 4. +

9th Round.— + 3 Sc, on the 3 centre of 5 Sc, 4 Ch, miss 1 S, and 3 Ch, 10 Dc, over the 5 Dc, and one chain on each side, 4 Ch. +

10th Round.— + Sc on centre of 3 Sc, 5 Ch, miss 4, 1 Sc, 5 Ch, miss 3, 1 Sc, 5 Ch, miss 2, 1 Sc, 5 Ch, miss 3, 1 Sc, 5 Ch. +

Cut out the rounds of flannel and calico nearly of the diameter of the square of crochet, not including the edging. Fold it into the form seen in the engraving; then make it up as directed.

FUSCHIA SMOKING-CAP.

Materials.—A piece of velvet or cloth, thirteen-sixteenths of a yard long, and eight inches deep; Russian braid, soutache, or gold braid, and a tassel to correspond.

THIS smoking-cap may be made to suit almost any person, as cloth with ordinary Russia braid, and a plain silk tassel, may be employed; or if intended to be very handsome, a rich velvet, with pure gold braid, and a gold bullion tassel, may be used; or if a soutache be employed, on either cloth or velvet, a French passemen-

DESIGN FOR FUCHSIA SMOKING-CAP.

terie tassel will be suitable. Perhaps one of the richest caps would be produced by plain crimson velvet and gold braid.

The length we have given will allow of the crown being taken off; the head-piece should be about twenty-two inches, without turnings in. In this space the design should be repeated five times. A very little care will enable a worker to enlarge the design for herself, by drawing a single pattern in the required space, and then transferring it from place to place through the entire length. It is worked in two lines of braid; one forms the upper, and the other the under part of the pattern.

———

MUSLIN EMBROIDERY

FOR

GAUNTLET OR BISHOP SLEEVES.

Materials. — French muslin, and Messrs. W. Evans and Co.'s Royal Embroidery Cotton, Nos. 40 and 50.

THERE is a pretty way of making sleeves now, which, as it imparts warmth, will probably be much in vogue in cold weather. A strip of muslin, deep enough to reach from the wrist to above the elbow, is embroidered in a rich, bold design along one edge; not, however, quite close to it. The design should be from four to six inches

MUSLIN EMBROIDERY FOR GAUNTLET OR BISHOP SLEEVES.

deep; but as the dress-sleeves are not very large, the former depth will probably suffice. The edge is worked in button-hole stitch, as if it were intended to be cut out; but, instead of that, the muslin is gathered into an embroidered band, and formed into a pretty bishop sleeve.

The design we now give is extremely well adapted for this purpose.

The holes forming the diamonds are traced, pierced, and sewed over, as is the design in the centre of each; but the various parts of the flower in the scallop are overcast, and being very open, should be traced with a double thread, to make it stronger. The edge should also be considerably raised.

For gauntlet sleeves, the scallop must be cut out, and the work formed into a frill and set on a band.

The design is given of the full size, in order that our readers may be able to trace it themselves. Take the pattern from the book on tracing paper; lay the muslin evenly on a table, with a strip of blue marking paper over it; place the tracing paper above that, and then go over the design with the point of a pencil.

BRODERIE SCALLOPING FOR FLOUNCES, ETC., BY MRS. PULLAN.

P

CORAL-BORDERED HANDKERCHIEF, BY MRS PULLAN.

BRODERIE SCALLOPING FOR FLOUNCES, &c.

Materials.—Muslin, either Swiss or Jaconet, suitable for the purpose for which the work is intended, with Evans's Royal Embroidery Cotton, No. 24 or 30.

OUR space only permits us to give one-half of a scallop of this beautiful pattern, so simple, yet effective, as to recommend itself to every one who is accustomed to wear rich and handsome embroidery.

It is done in the ordinary way of bro-derie Anglaise, each of the black parts being cut out, and the edges sewed closely round. The round holes are made with a stiletto. The border, which consists of a series of round and oblong holes, is to be worked entirely in the closest button-hole stitch, the work of which is so managed that the edging of one hole closely touches that of the preceding, and thus a border is formed without any extra line.

This design makes extremely handsome mandarin sleeves, three patterns being re-quired for each sleeve.

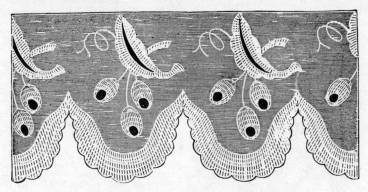

EDGING IN FRENCH EMBROIDERY, BY MRS. PULLAN.

THE WORK-TABLE FRIEND.

EDGING IN FRENCH EMBROIDERY.

Materials.—French muslin, with W. Evans and Co's. Royal Embroidery cotton, No. 24, and Moravian, No. 30.

This section is given the full size, so that the design may be traced from it. The edging consists of an indented scallop, considerably raised and covered with graduated overcast stitch. The three flowers are also done in raised button-hole stitch, the stiletto being used for piercing the small eyelet hole in each. The leaf is worked in satin stitch, with a veining sewed over a thread down the centre. The stem is done in the same manner. The tendril is simply traced and sewed over. The Moravian cotton is used for tracing and raising the work, the embroidery cotton for sewing it over.

FAIRY PURSE.

Materials.—A skein of the finest French netting silk, a little Vert Islay and bright crimson silk, 4 skeins of gold thread, and trimming similar to that seen in the engraving. A fine netting needle, and steel mesh, Nos. 13 and 16.

The black silk which forms the foundation of this purse is exceedingly fine, not exceeding Evans's Boar's-head cotton, No. 100. It is not made in England, where for a long time past, the art of netting has been comparatively much neglected. The appearance of this purse, when worked, is the most delicate and fairy-like imaginable. Begin on a thread foundation, by working with the fine mesh four stitches. Withdraw the mesh from two of them.

1st Round.—Do two stitches in every stitch, beginning with the first, of course ; and for the sake of convenience, withdrawing the mesh from two whenever there are four on it. There will now be eight stitches in the round, every alternate one of which is short.

2nd and following Rounds. — Net 2 stitches in every short stitch, and 1 in every other. Continue increasing thus until there are 60 stitches in the round. Do 40 rounds without any increase.

Take the large mesh, and do a plain round.

With the fine mesh do a round of Egyptian stitches, in the following manner : Miss the first stitch, take up the second with the needle, but in the *reverse* way to that in which it is usually done, namely from above instead of below, drawing it through the first loop. Having netted that, do the first loop in the usual way, taking it through the second. Repeat this all round. Do a plain round with the fine mesh, then repeat these three rounds, beginning where you use the large mesh. Five more rounds must be done with the small mesh, and then the

FAIRY PURSE, BY MRS. PULLAN.

small points, forming the lace at the top of the purse ; of these there should be twelve,—consequently there will be five stitches on the first row ; turn the work, and do four over the five ; turn again, and do three on the four ; turn again, and net two on the three, which forms the point of this vandyke. Fasten off, and commence on the next stitch for the succeeding one.

There are to be twelve in the round. When all are done, work one row of netting all round the points, with the same (that is, the *fine*), mesh. The darning only, now remains to be done.

It will be found on examining the end of the purse, that four lines of close stitches radiate from the centre. This is where the two stitches were netted in one in every round. The line of holes on each side of this is to be darned in gold thread, the needle being taken to one square beyond the last round of increase on one side, and merely up to it on the other. The pure white parts of the engraving represent the gold darning. The triangular spaces between must also be darned, two opposite divisions being filled with gold, one with green, and the fourth with crimson. A single row of holes is left between the triangular and the line of gold, the longest row of the former covering twelve holes, and each succeeding one having one less.

Leaving four vacant holes, or three threads, from the top of a triangle, darn with gold, in a direct line over thirteen holes, (or 14 threads). Do another line parallel with it, not sloping either upwards or downwards, but maintaining the same distance from the darned piece below ; + bring your needle out at the bottom, and slip into the next line of netting, on which darn over six holes only. Leave off at the top of this line, and darn across 2 only, sloping downwards. Do three lines of netting across 2 only, then 1 across 3, the uppermost of which is a hole higher. + Now darn across 13 holes of the next line, and in the two lines following, keeping the space of 4 holes between the lower part of this darning and that at the bottom of the purse. Repeat between the crosses, to form one pattern.

The lower part of the gold being done, begin again at the second line over 13 holes, but at the **top** of that line.

The remainder may be darned from the pattern, the spots being alternately crimson and green.

The points of the border are also darned.

Complete the purse by running in the cord and adding the tassels.

THE WORK-TABLE FRIEND.

HARLEQUIN HAND-SCREEN IN NETTING.

Materials.—A very fine netting-needle, a steel mesh, No. 15, 18 skeins of gold thread, No. 3, 1 skein of white netting silk, 1 scarlet, 1 bright green, 3 black, all very fine ; a pair of hexagon screen-mounts covered with black satin, 1½ yards of black silk fringe, ditto scarlet chenille gimp, ditto black. Of course the scarlet gimp must be of the same shade as the silk.

THE ground of this beautiful screen is done in netting, with black silk ; the pattern is afterwards darned in, with the coloured silks, and the gold thread. The common netting stitch, only, is used in it.

On a foundation thread do six stitches ; then on every one of these, do two, beginning with the first stitch, so as to form a round. It will be seen that the stitches are alternately long and short. In the second, and all the following rounds, do one stitch in every stitch, *except the short one*, which will be found to occur six times in every round, and in which the two stitches must always be worked until there are 25 stitches in each of the six sides. Then do ten rounds without increasing at all, and the foundation is complete.

On examining this piece of netting, it will be seen that a stripe of apparently closer work marks each division. This is darned with gold thread, so as to *fill* a row of holes on each side of the division. The star seen in the engraving represents this, and it will be observed that it does not extend to the extremities of the screen, but only as far as it is increased.

The divisions being thus clearly marked, it becomes extremely easy to darn them. The six triangles in the centre are in gold, which covers *nine* holes, that is to say, crosses *ten threads* in the longest line, leaving one line of holes between it and the darning of the star. To make the triangular-shaped piece, let every line be one hole shorter than the preceding, until one only is filled. There should be a clear line of holes on both sides of the point. From the two upper corners of this gold start two similar triangles, having one hole, *but no bar* between them and the gold. In two sections these are darned in white ; in two they are green ; in the remaining two, scarlet. The

same colour is always seen in two opposite divisions. In the engraving, the white are represented as quite white. A small diamond partially fills up the space : it is four lines wide ; and across four holes. Between two scarlets, the diamond is white ; the scarlet is between two greens ; and the others are green. Twelve triangles darned in gold are placed, base to base, with the coloured ones, the points being, of course, reversed : and between these two, another triangle, which is always of the same colour as the diamond in that division. The two upper diamonds, also, correspond with these. All the darned parts are placed at *one hole* distance from the others.

Great care must be taken, in darning netting, not to contract it at all. When done, it is to be stretched on a hexagon frame, covered on both sides with black

HARLEQUIN HAND-SCREEN IN NETTING,
BY MRS. PULLAN.

LADY'S RETICULE, BY MRS. PULLAN.

description of the arrangement of the colours. We trust our friends will not think us unnecessarily so; since, in truth, on the peculiar way of placing them depends the harmony of the *tout-ensemble*. Even so trifling a matter requires consideration, if we would obtain a satisfactory result.

This screen will harmonize with almost any style of furniture.

LADY'S RETICULE.

Materials.—6 yards of gold cord, 1 skein of gold thread, No. 1, and 3 skeins of silk of any bright colour that may be desired, blue, green, or cerise, being the most suitable. The trimming consists of a handsome tassel, a cord, and 2 small gold balls.

THE gold cord here introduced is a Parisian novelty, which is extremely pretty as well as durable, and much used for purses, bags, work-baskets, &c.

It is about the thickness of very fine window-blind cord, and very brilliant, though not, of course, made of pure gold. The way of using it in crochet is to work over it, in the same way as over ordinary cord for mats, but instead of taking the stitches closely together, and so completely covering the cord, they must be far apart, and with very long chains to them, so that the gold is the principal thing visible and the silk is comparatively little seen.

Begin by working on the end of the cord and closing it into a round, on which work with such an increase as will keep the circle perfectly flat, until it is large enough to form the bottom of the reticule, say four and a half inches in diameter. Now hold the cord so as to form the sides, and work on it, still in the same straggling manner, until a depth of about two and a half inches or more is done. Fasten off the gold cord.

With the silk only do a Dc stitch in every stitch, with one chain between 2nd and following rounds. Dc under chain, 1 Ch. repeat all round.

This part must be about as deep as the corded piece. For the edging + Sc on a chain, 5 Ch, miss 3 Dc and the intervening chain + repeat all round.

2nd Row.— + 1 Sc, 1 Dc, 3 Stc, 1 Dc, 1 Sc every chain of 5 + all round.

3rd Row.—With the gold thread. Sc

satin. The fringe and two cords are added, the black being the outer one. Finally, the handles are adjusted. We may, perhaps, have appeared rather prolix in our

INFANT'S SHOE, EMBROIDERED IN CHAIN STITCH, BY MRS. PULLAN

on every stitch of the last round, and on every Sc of the round preceding.

Run in the cords for strings, in the top line of Dc and chain.

As the reticule is only intended to hold a handkerchief, it need not be very large. Worked in the same manner, and with the same materials, but not exceeding three inches in diameter, it makes a very strong and novel purse for a lady. As it is not flat, however, it is not suitable for the pocket.

INFANT'S SHOE, EMBROIDERED IN CHAIN-STITCH.

Materials.—Pink silk, a few skeins of white sewing silk, white sarsenet ribbon, three quarters of an inch wide. Muslin and flannel

THIS very pretty and comfortable little shoe is to be embroidered entirely in chain-stitch. The pattern is given so clearly in the engraving, that no difficulty can occur in drawing it. It must be marked on the silk in the ordinary manner. The size of the shoe must be suitable for the child, and a paper pattern should first be prepared, of a very ample size, as the quilted lining of the shoe takes up a considerable space. Mark out the silk, allowing a very ample margin in every direction, making the toe in one piece, the ankle-piece for another, and the sole for the third. Cut out pieces of muslin and flannel to correspond, and quilt them together in small diamonds with sewing-cotton.

Work the pattern on the silk; then make up the shoe very neatly, running the sole in parallel lines from heel to toe, taking the needle through the thicknesses of silk, flannel, and muslin.

Bind the upper part of the shoe with a fine piping cord, covered with silk; and pierce holes for the tie, sewing them round with silk of the same colour as the embroidery.

If gros de Naples is thought too delicate or expensive a material, fine French merino of any pretty colour may be used for this shoe.

Although we have already said much concerning the articles suitable for bazaars, we cannot help here remarking, that nothing more certainly commands a sale than pretty shoes and other articles for infants. especially the kind of which we here give a specimen.

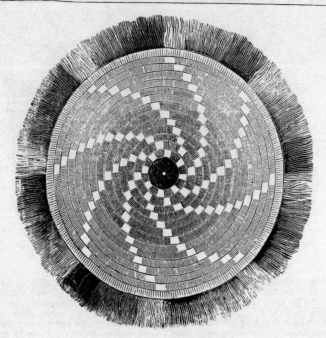

SMALL LAMP-MAT, BY MRS. PULLAN.

SMALL LAMP-MAT.

SUITABLE WORK FOR A BEGINNER.

Materials.—7 shades of crimson wool, varying from very dark to light, and 2 skeins of maize-coloured crochet silk, with 4 yards of cotton-mat cord. Of the 2 lightest and 3 darkest colours, 1 skein only will be required. Of the others, 2 skeins.

WITH the darkest wool, work a few stitches over the end of the cord, and close it into a round, on which, with the same shade, work another round, increasing sufficiently to keep it flat. Another must be done with the same shade. Join on next tint, and work three rounds with it, increasing sufficiently to make it flat, and making enough stitches to cover the cord completely. With the next shade do three more rounds in the same way. Repeat it also with the 4th shade. With the 5th shade, do only two rounds; and with the 6th and 7th, one will be enough. Cut the end of the cord in a slanting direction, so as to terminate it gradually.

Thread a coarse embroidery needle with the maize silk, and work five stitches over the cord of the last round but one, then over the next, and all the others to the centre, not straight down, but in a curved direction (something like one of the spokes of a Catherine's wheel.) Do eight of these curved lines, at equal distances from each other, and all meeting in the centre.

For the border, work over a mesh with the tapestry needle, as in ordinary rug-work, taking a double needleful, both of silk and wool. Four stitches are to be taken in silk, immediately opposite the five stitches on the cord; then four of each shade of wool, from the darkest to the lightest, which should occupy the space to the next silk. Cut the edges of the fringe.

BRAIDED SOFA CUSHION, BY MRS. PULLAN.

THE WORK-TABLE FRIEND.

BRAIDED SOFA CUSHION.

Materials.—A square of fine cloth, with 2 knots of each of 2 colours, in Albert-braid. Sewing silk to correspond.

In selecting the colours for a sofa cushion, the furniture and hangings of the room must be considered. The cloth should be of the principal tint, and the braid such as will go well with it. A French blue ground harmonizes with orange and black braid; a green with crimson and black; gold colour with blue and black, or violet and green. Nothing can exceed the rich appearance of the Albert braid, when two colours are thus laid on, parallel with each other.

In beginning to braid, draw the end through to the wrong side of the cloth, then sew it down, with ordinary sewing silk, taking the stitches always over the *thin* parts of the braid, by which means they are perfectly invisible.

It is much easier to braid with the new material than with the flat silk braid, (usually termed Russia silk), as the latter is apt to work unevenly, except in very expert hands.

In braiding with two colours, do the entire cushion with the brightest tint first; after which sew the other, *close to it,* but on the inside. In the engraving, the white line represents a rich crimson braid, and the black line is the black ground being a very handsome green cloth.

The pattern, which is given completely in miniature, must be enlarged to the proper size (about half a yard square). The back of the cushion may be of plain cloth or silk. Cord and tassels to correspond, should finish the edge and corners.

GENTLEMAN'S LONG PURSE IN NETTING.

Materials.—2 skeins of the finest black netting silk, 6 skeins of gold thread, No. 0, 2 very handsome tassels in black and gold, and slides to correspond. A very fine netting-needle, and mesh, No. 17.

BEGIN on 4 stiches, made on a thread only as a foundation. Draw two off the mesh, and work 2 on each of the four forming them into a round, and never keeping more than two stitches together on the mesh. Continue to work round and round, making two stitches in every small stitch, and by so doing, increasing four stitches in every round, until there are 60 altogether, when you will do 49 rounds, without any increase.

After this, instead of working round, work backwards and forwards 50 rows. Again close for a round, with the same number of stitches (60), and make 49 rounds. To decrease for the end, net two stitches together 4 times in every round, until only four stitches remain. The two stitches must be taken together invariably at the quarters.

The pattern is darned entirely in gold. A star is first done at each side of the lines forming the increase or decrease, and the remainder is worked from the engraving. The pattern, which occupies 15 stitches, is repeated four times at each end. A simple ziz-zag pattern, done on each side of the opening, strengthens as well as ornaments it.

In darning netting, always work in one direction, if the pattern inclines so ; but where (as in the present case) there is a *centre* to each design, the darning must radiate from it in opposite directions, the right side being to the right, and the other being reversed.

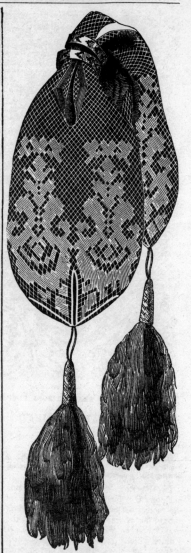

GENTLEMAN'S LONG PURSE IN NETTING, BY MRS. PULLAN.

CHEESE DOYLEY IN CROCHET, BY MRS. PULLAN.

THE WORK-TABLE FRIEND.

CHEESE DOYLEY, IN CROCHET.

Materials.—Messrs. W. Evans and Co.'s Boar's-head crochet cotton, No. 24. Crochet hook, No. 20.

MAKE a chain of eight stitches, close it into a round, and work three rounds of Sc, increasing always sufficiently to keep the work flat.

4th Round.—Dc, increasing as before.

5th Round.— + 3 Dc in one, miss 1, + all round.

6th Round.— + 3 Dc in one, miss 1, 3 Dc in 1, miss 2, + all round.

7th Round.—Like 6th.

8th Round.—Dc in every stitch, with 2 in one, twelve times in the round.

9th Round.— + 2 Dc in 1, 2 Dc in 1, 3 Ch, miss 2, 3 Dc over 2, 3 Ch, miss 2, + 12 times.

10th Round.— + 3 Dc over the centre 2 of 4 Dc, 3 Ch, 5 Dc, (over 3 Dc and one chain on each side), 3 Ch, + 12 times.

11th Round.— + 2 Dc on the centre one of 3 Dc, 3 Ch, 3 Dc, (over 1 Ch and 2 Dc, 2 Ch, miss centre one of 5 Dc, 3 Dc, 3 Ch), + 12 times.

12th Round.— + 1 Dc, (over 1st of 2 Dc, 3 Ch, miss 3, 3 Dc, 4 Ch, miss 4, 3 Dc, 3 Ch, + 12 times.

13th Round.— + 1 Dc over 1 Dc, 3 Ch, miss 2, 5 Dc, 2 Ch, miss 2, 5 Dc, 3 Ch, + 12 times.

14th Round.— + 1 Dc over 1 Dc, 3 Ch, 14 Dc (over 5 Dc, 2 Ch, 5 Dc,) 3 Ch, + 12 times.

15th Round.— + 1 Dc over 1 Dc, 4 Ch, miss 3, 14 Dc over 14, 4 Ch, + 12 times.

16th Round.— + 4 Dc over 1 Dc and one chain on each side, 4 Ch, 12 Dc over centre 12 of 14, 4 Ch, + 12 times.

17th Round.— + 7 Dc over 4 Dc, and

BRODERIE EDGING, BY MRS. PULLAN.

sue chain on each side, 4 Ch, 11 Dc over 10, 4 Ch, + 12 times.

18th Round. — + 4 Dc over 1 Ch, and 3 of 7 Dc, 2 Ch, miss 1 Dc, 4 Dc over 3 Dc and 1 chain, 4 Ch, 9 Dc over centre 9 of 11, 4 Ch, + 12 times.

19th Round. — + 4 Dc, beginning on the last chain stitch before 4 Dc, 5 Ch, miss 2 Ch and 1 Dc on each side, 4 Ch, 7 Dc on centre 7 of 9, 4 Ch, + 12 times.

20th Round. — + 4 Dc as before, 4 Ch, 1 Dc on the centre of 5 Ch, 4 Ch, 4 Dc, (on the last 3 Dc, and a chain stitch beyond), 4 Ch, 5 Dc, 4 Ch, + 12 times.

21st Round. — + 4 Dc as before, 4 Ch, 4 Dc, (doing 2 on the 1 Dc of last round), 4 Ch, 4 Dc, 4 Ch, 3 Dc on centre of 5 Dc, 4 Ch, + 12 times.

22nd Round. — + 4 Dc, as before, 4 Ch, 8 Dc, (over 4 Dc, and one chain at each end,) 4 Dc, 4 Ch, 4 Dc 4 Ch, 1 Dc on centre of 3, 4 Ch, + 12 times.

23rd Round. — + 4 Dc as before, 4 Ch, 4 Dc, 3 Ch, miss the centre 2 of 8 Dc, 4 Dc, 4 Ch, 4 Dc, 3 Ch, 1 Dc, on 1 Dc, 3 Ch, + 12 times.

24th Round. — + 4 Dc as before, 4 Ch, 4 Dc, 6 Ch, (over 3 Ch, and 1 Dc, at each side) 4 Dc, 4 Ch, 4 Dc, 5 Ch, + 12 times.

25th Round. — + 4 Dc, (beginning on the last of 5 Ch,) 5 Ch, miss 4, 4 Dc, 3 Ch, 2 Dc, (on centre 2 of 6 Dc,) 4 Dc, 5 Ch, 4 Dc, 3 Ch, + 12 times.

26th Round. — + 9 Dc, (coming over the last 3 Ch, and 3 Dc, on each side,) 4 Ch, miss 3, 1 Dc on centre of 5 Ch, 4 Ch, miss 3, 4 Dc, 6 Ch, 4 Dc, 4 Ch, miss 3, 1 Dc, 4 Ch, miss 3, + 12 times.

27th Round. — + 7 Dc on centre 7 of 9 Dc, 4 Ch, 4 Dc on 1 Dc, and 1 chain at each side, 4 Ch, 4 Dc, 4 Ch, 4 Dc, 4 Ch, 4 Dc, over 1 Dc, and 1 Ch, at each side, 4 Ch, + 12 times.

28th Round. — + 5 Dc over centre 5 of 7, 4 Ch, 7 Dc, (over 4 Dc and 1 Ch at each side,) 4 Ch, 10 Dc, over 4 Ch, and 3 Dc, at each side, 4 Ch, 7 Dc over 4 Dc, and 1 chain at each side, 4 Ch, + 12 times.

29th Round. — + 3 Dc, (over centre 3 of 5 Dc,) 4 Ch, 4 Dc, 2 Ch, miss centre one of 7 Dc, 4 Ch, 4 Dc, 9 Dc over centre 8 of 10 Dc, 4 Ch, 4 Dc, 2 Ch, miss centre 1 of 7 Ch, 4 Dc, 4 Ch, + 12 times.

30th Round. — + 1 Dc, 4 Ch, 4 Dc,

+ Ch, 4 Dc, 4 Ch, 7 Dc, 4 Ch, 4 Dc, 4 Ch,
4 Dc, 4 Ch, + 12 times.

31st Round. — + 1 Dc, on 1 Dc, 3 Ch,
4 Dc, 3 Ch, 1 Dc, 3 Ch, 4 Dc, 4 Ch, 5 Dc,
4 Ch, 4 Dc, 3 Ch, 1 Dc, 3 Ch, 4 Dc,
3 Ch, + 12 times.

32nd Round. — + 1 Dc, on 1 Dc, 2 Ch,
4 Dc, 3 Ch, 4 Dc, (on 1 Dc, and 1 chain
on each side), 3 Ch, 4 Dc, 4 Ch, 3 Dc,
4 Ch. 4 Dc, 3 Ch, 4 Dc, (on 1 Dc and 1
chain on each side), 3 Ch, 4 Dc, 2 Ch, +
12 times.

33rd Round. — + 4 Dc, (beginning on
the 2nd of the last 4 Dc,) 3 Ch, (coming
over the first 1 Dc, of last row, and 1
chain on each side,) 4 Dc, 3 Ch, 7 Dc (over
4 Dc and 1 chain on each side), 3 Ch,
4 Dc, 4 Ch, 1 Dc, 4 Ch, 4 Dc, 3 Ch, 7
Dc, (as former), 3 Ch, + 12 times.

34th Round. — + 9 Dc, beginning on
2nd of the 1st 4 Dc, 3 Ch, miss 3, 9 Dc,
(over 7 Dc, and 1 chain on each side,)
3 Ch, miss 3, 4 Dc, 7 Ch, (over 1 Dc, and
3 Ch on each side), 4 Dc, 3 Ch, miss
3, 9 Dc, 3 Ch, miss 3, + 12 times.

35th Round. — + 5 Dc, beginning on
the 3rd of the 1st 9 Dc, 4 Ch, miss 4,
11 Dc, 4 Ch, miss 4, 4 Dc, 3 Ch, miss 3,
4 Dc, 4 Ch, miss 4, 11 Dc, 4 Ch, miss 4,
+ 12 times.

36th Round. — + 1 Dc, on the centre
of 5 Dc, 5 Ch, miss 5, 13 Dc, 5 Ch, miss
5 7 Dc, (over 3 Ch, and 2 Dc, at each
side,) 5 Ch, miss 5, 13 Dc, 5 Ch, miss 5,
+ 12 times.

37th Round. — + 17 Dc, (over the last
13 Dc, and 2 Ch, on each side), 7 Ch,
miss 7, 17 Dc, as before, 6 Ch, miss 6,
1 Dc, on the centre of 7 Dc, 6 Ch, miss 6,
+ 12 times.

This is the end of the round. The lace
which follows is not only extremely suitable for doyleys generally, but also any
edgings in which lightness and durability
are essential. When used detached from
the doyley, make a chain of any number
of stitches, divisible by 28, and do on it
a row of Sc.

1st Pattern Row. — + 1 Dc, 1 Ch, miss
1 + repeat all round.

2nd Pattern Row. — + 17 Sc, 13 Ch,
miss 10, + repeat all round.

3rd Pattern Row. — + 15 Sc, (over
centre 15 of 17), 5 Ch, 1 Dc on the 5th
Ch, * 1 Ch, miss none, 1 Dc, * 4 times,
5 Ch, + repeat all round.

4th Pattern Row — + 13 Sc on centre
of 15, 5 Ch, 1 Dc on Dc, * 2 Ch, 1 Dc
on 1 Dc, * 4 times, 5 Ch, + repeat all
round.

5th Pattern Row. — + 11 Sc over 11
centre of 13, 5 Ch, Dc on every Dc, with
3 Ch between, 5 Ch, + repeat all round.

6th Pattern Row. — + 9 Sc over 11, 5
Ch, Dc on every Dc, with 4 Ch between,
5 Ch, + all round.

7th Pattern Row. — + 7 Sc over 9, 5 Ch,
Dc on every Dc with 5 Ch between, 5 Ch,
+ repeat all round.

BRODERIE EDGING.

Materials—French muslin, Messrs. W. Evans
and Co.'s Royal embroidery cotton, No. 30, and
Boar's-head crochet cotton, No. 70. A piece of
toile ciré.

This pattern is engraved so that the
design may be transferred from it to the
muslin, using a solution of indigo with
thin gum water, and a sable brush. All
the parts marked with a cross are to be
entirely cut out, after being traced round
with not less than three thicknesses of
cotton. They are then to be worked
closely in button-hole stitch. The edge is
also to be worked closely in button-hole
stitch, graduated as in the engraving, and
very much raised in order to give a thick
and rich appearance to the edge.

The embroidery cotton is to be used for
all this, and the Boar's-head cotton for the
English lace.

VERY PRETTY CROCHET EDGING,
FOR TRIMMING PETTICOATS, ETC.

WITH rather fine cotton, such as Evans's
Boar's-head Crochet Cotton, No. 30, make
a chain of the required length, or a little
longer, and work on it one row of Sc.

1st Pattern Row. — + 1 Dc, 2 Ch, miss
2, + repeat to the end.

2nd. —1 Sc, on Dc, + 6 Ch, Sc on next
Dc but one, + repeat to the end.

3rd. —Sc under chain of 6, + 3 Ch,
8 Dc under next chain of 6, 3 Ch, 1 Sc
under next Ch, + repeat to the end.

4th. — + 7 Dc over 8, 6 Ch, + repeat.

5th. — + Sc under Ch, 8 Ch, slip on 5th
of 8, 3 Ch, Sc under same chain of 6 in last
round, 4 Ch, 5 Dc over 7, 4 Ch, + repeat.

6th. —Dc in loop formed of 8 Ch, + 3 Ch,
Dc under same, + 5 times, 3 Ch, 3 Dc over
5, 3 Ch.

DOYLEY IN PORTUGUESE GUIPURE, BY MRS. PULLAN.

THE WORK-TABLE FRIEND.

DOYLEY, IN PORTUGUESE GUIPURE.

Materials.—Messrs. W. Evans and Co.'s Boar's-head crochet cotton, No. 30, and Mecklenburgh No. 8. A netting-needle, No. 22, and meshes, No. 8, 10, 12, and 17. Ivory gauge.

THE great popularity of our antique point patterns, and the gratifying proofs we daily receive, that our descriptions are found to be sufficiently clear to be of practical value, induce us to present our readers with the first of a series of specimens of the beautiful Portuguese guipure.

The foundation of this lace is invariably square netting; and the pattern is darned on it, frequently in many highly ornamental stitches.

For the netting, with the Boar's-head cotton, and mesh No. 17, work one stitch on a foundation. Turn the work, and do two in one. Continue to turn the work backwards and forwards, always netting two stitches in the last stitch, until there are 55 in the row. Then, instead of doing two in one, do two together, as one, at the end of every row, until one stitch only is left. Damp the

ANTIMACASSAR IN CROCHET. BY MRS. PULLAN.

square and pin it out, to give it a little stiffness before proceeding with the darning.

This is done with Mecklenburgh thread. We will call it *cloth* darning, as the appearance, when worked, is precisely that of linen cloth. Each square is filled up by four threads, two each way, crossing each other. When two or more squares in a continuous line are to be darned, the threads are taken from the one extremity to the other. Each of the little rounds in the corner is to be formed by darning a cluster of four holes, two each way. This naturally forms a square. The rounded appearance is afterwards given by a tracing in double thread all around.

Any initial may be darned in the centre of this doyley.

For the edging.—With the Boar's-head cotton and mesh, No. 8. Do 12 stitches in the square at the corner, and in every ninth from it.

2nd Row. Mesh No. 10. Net a stitch in every stitch.

3rd Row.—Mesh No. 12. Net a stitch in every stitch, except at the corners, where net two stitches in every stitch.

4th Row.—Mesh No. 17. Net a stitch in every stitch.

All these shells are done separately on the doyley, and are afterwards connected at the points with it by means of a needle and thread.

ANTIMACASSAR IN CROCHET.

Materials.—Evans & Co.'s Boar's-head crochet cotton, Nos. 8 and 12, with 8 oz of turquoise blue beads, No. 3. Boulton & Son's crochet hook, No. 17.

The entire upper part, including the narrow border, is to be worked in open square crochet from the engraving, a foundation chain of 295 stitches. No. 12 Evans' Boar's-head cotton must be used for this purpose. The decreasing at the edges in the upper part is to be done in the mode already directed in our former pages.

The border is to be done in Sc, on the wrong side of the upper part; for it is to be remembered that the beads always appear on the reverse side.

AN EASTER OFFERING—A BASKET OF EGGS, BY MRS. PULLAN.

THE WORK-TABLE FRIEND.

AN EASTER OFFERING—A BASKET OF EGGS.

Materials. 1 skein maize crochet silk; 4 skeins of green Berlin wool, all different shades; 1 skein white ditto; 2 yards each of four shades of green wire chenille; 1 skein fine green ditto; 1 ball silver twine; 1½ yard crochet cord.

WITH the darkest green wool, work a chain of 12 stitches. Holding in the crochet cord, work on both sides of the chain, doing as many stitches as will completely *cover* the cord; at the ends of the chain several stitches must be done in one. Turn quite round the second, cover 4 stitches more, and join on the white.

1st Round.—5 white, 1 green, which comes just at the centre of a side, 5 white, 1 green, 5 white on 3, 1 green (at the centre of the end) 5 white on 3, 1 green, 5 white, 1 green (opposite green), 5 white, 1 green, 5 white on 3, 1 green (at the centre of end), 5 white on 3, 1 green on the last green before white.

2nd Round.— + 5 white on 5, 2 green on 1, 5 white on 5, 2 green on 1, 6 white on 5, 3 green on 1, 6 white on 5, 2 green on 1, + twice.

3rd Round.— + 6 white on 5, 3 green on 2, 6 white on 5, 3 green on 2, 8 white on 6, 4 green on 2, 8 white on 6, 3 green on 2, + twice.

Do two rounds with maize silk on white, and the two succeeding shades of green on green, increasing in every part enough to keep the work flat. Instead of the last stitches of green, with the lightest shade do *one* stitch, then with maize silk do a *long stitch* to the centre of the 2 green in 2nd round, + 5 light green, 2 maize, 5 more green, long stitch with maize on the centre of green in the 2nd round, + all round, doing a greater number of green at the ends of the oval, the long maize stitch always coming at the *centre* of a green stripe.

FOR THE EDGE.—Fasten on the end of the darkest chenille at the centre of one side, sewing it with silk of the same colour; bend about an inch and a quarter into a loop, and sew it at the distance of

CROCHET TOILET CUSHION, BY MRS. PULLAN.

half an inch; continue to make and sew these loops all round.

With the second, third, and fourth shades, join on at the middle of a loop of the previous round; and, forming a similar, but always rather longer loop, sew to the middle of the next. The lightest shade is the last.

FOR THE HANDLE.—Cover two pieces of round satin wire, each half a yard long, with the maize silk, in crochet. Wind round one some of the fine chenille; sew it on at the middle of each side to the bottom of the basket, bending it into the form seen in the engraving. Bend the other so as to cross it at the top and sides. Wind the chenille round it, and round both where they join, and sew it down also.

FOR THE FLOWERS.—Light green wool, 7 Ch, close into a round. 1 Dc in 1 Ch, 1 Ch, miss none.

2nd Round.—(Silver twine.) + 1 Dc under Ch, 2 Ch, miss Dc, + all round. Sew on in groups, as in the engraving.

CROCHET TOILET CUSHION.

Materials. ½ a yard of purple satin; 3 reels of Messrs. W. Evans & Co.'s Boar's-head crochet cotton, No. 34, with Boulton & Son's crochet-hook, No. 2.

MAKE a chain of 156 stitches; close it into a round, and do one round of open square crochet. In all the following rounds the directions are to be repeated thirteen times within the crosses.

1st Round.—+ 10 Dc, 3 Ch, miss 2, +

2nd Round.—+ 11 Dc over 10, 3 Ch, miss 3, +.

3rd Round.—+ 12 Dc over 11, 3 Ch, miss 3, +.

Q

4th Round.—+ 13 Dc over 12, 3 Ch, miss 3, +.

5th Round.—Begin on the second Dc, + 11 Dc over centre 11, 3 Ch, Dc on centre of 3 Ch, 3 Ch +.

6th Round.—+ 11 Dc over 11, 3 Ch, Dc over Dc, 3 Ch, +.

7th Round.— + 9 Dc, (beginning on the second of 11 Dc), 3 Ch, miss 2, 1 Dc, 3 Ch, miss 3, 1 Dc, 3 Ch, miss 2, +.

8th Round.—+ 7 Dc, (beginning on second of 9), 3 Ch, miss 3, 1 Dc, 5 Ch, miss 5, 1 Dc, 3 Ch, miss 3, +.

9th Round.—+ 5 Dc, (beginning on the second of 7), 3 Ch, miss 3, 1 Dc, 8 Ch, miss 7, 1 Dc, 3 Ch, miss 3, +

10th Round.—+ 3 Dc, (beginning on second of 5), 4 Ch, miss 4, 10 Dc, 4 Dc, miss 4, +.

11th Round.— + Begin on the third of the first 4 Ch, + 7 Dc, (over 6 stitches), 3 Ch, miss 3, 5 Dc, 4 Ch, miss 3, 1 Dc on centre of 3 Dc, 4 Ch, miss 3, +.

12th Round.—Begin on the third of the last 4 Ch, + 8 Dc, 4 Ch, miss 4, 6 Dc, 7 Ch, +.

13th Round.—, + 7 Dc, beginning on the first of 8 Dc, 5 Ch, miss 5, 5 Dc, 8 Ch, +.

14th Round.— + 6 Dc, beginning on the first of 7, 5 Ch, miss 5, 5 Dc, 5 Ch, +.

15th Round.— + 5 Dc, beginning on second, 3 Ch, miss 3, 4 Dc, 5 Ch, miss 4, 1 Dc, 9 Ch, +.

16th Round.— + 5 Dc, beginning on the second, 3 Ch, miss 3, 3 Dc, 4 Ch, miss 4, 3 Dc, 10 Ch, +.

17th Round.— + 4 Dc, beginning on third, 3 Ch, miss 3, 7 Dc, 7 Ch, miss 6, 1 Dc, 8 Ch, +.

18th Round.— + 10 Dc, beginning on third, 7 Ch, miss 6, 1 Dc, 7 Ch, miss 6, 1 Dc, 7 Ch, +.

19th Round.— + 6 Dc, beginning on third of 10, 6 Ch, miss 5, 1 Dc, 7 Ch, miss 7, 1 Dc, 7 Ch, miss 7, 1 Dc, 6 Ch, +.

20th Round.—Open square crochet all round.

BAND. *1st Row.*—Sc.

2nd Row.— + 1 Dc, 1 Ch, miss 1, + all round.

3rd Row.— + 1 Dc, 3 Ch, miss 3, + all round.

4th Row.— + 1 Dc on centre of 3 Ch, 3 Ch, miss 3, + all round.

5th Row.— + 17 Dc, beginning on 1 Dc, 3 Ch, miss 3, + all round.

6th Row.— + 3 Dc, on first three of 17, 3 Ch, miss 3, 1 Dc, 3 Ch, miss 3, 1 Dc, 3 Ch, miss 3, 3 Dc, 3 Ch, miss 3, + all round.

7th Row.— + 3 Dc on first 3 Dc, 3 Ch, miss 3, 11 Dc, 3 Ch, miss 3 + all round.

8th Row.— +3 Dc over first 3 of last round, 3 Ch, miss 3, 3 Dc, 3 Ch, miss 3, 1 Dc, 3 Ch, miss 3, 1 Dc, 3 Ch, miss 3, + all round.

9th Row.— + 17 Dc, beginning over the second 3 of last round, 3 Ch, miss 3, +.

10th Row.—Like 3rd.

11th Row.—Like 4th.

12th Row.—Like 2nd.

BROAD EDGING.—To be worked on the last row, + 16 Sc, 5 Ch, miss 5, 4 Dc on 3 stitches, 5 Ch, miss 5, +.

2nd Row.— + 14 Sc, beginning on second, 5 Ch, 7 Dc over 4 Dc and 1 chain at each end, 5 Ch, +.

3rd Row.— + 12 Sc, beginning on second, 5 Ch, 10 Dc, (over 7 and 1 Ch at each end), 5 Ch, +.

4th Row.— + 10 Sc, beginning on second, 5 Ch, 14 Dc, (over 10 Dc, and a chain at each side,) 5 Ch, +.

5th Row.— + 8 Sc, beginning on the second, 5 Ch, 18 Dc, (over 14, and a chain at each side), 5 Ch, +.

6th Row.— + 6 Sc, beginning on the second, 5 Ch, 23 Dc, (over 18, and 1 Ch at each side), 5 Ch, +.

7th Row.—Sc on every stitch of last row, with a loop of 5 Ch at every fifth stitch.

NARROW EDGING.—Worked at the top of the band. Do the first four, and the last rows of the broad edging.

To make up this cushion. Cut two rounds of calico, the size of the crochet round (allowing for turnings in besides). Unite these by a calico band, the width of the worked one, doing the centre or inner round first, and then the outer. Stuff well with bran, cover with satin, and tack on the crochet cover. Place a handsome toilet bottle, or a small glass of flowers in the middle.

Many Bands and Edgings given in this book are very suitable for trimming children's dresses and many other purposes.

PELOTE À L'IMPERATRICE, BY MRS. PULLAN.

THE WORK-TABLE FRIEND.

PELOTE A L'IMPERATRICE.

Materials. 3 skeins of fine black netting silk; 6 skeins of black sewing silk; 3½ yards of satin ribbon, 1½ inches wide, blue, pink, or any other bright colour; ½ a yard of sarsenet, of the same colour.

Having just given an elegant specimen of the most fashionable English style of toilet cushion, we now contrast it with the form most prevalent among the *élégantes* of Paris. The *Pelote à l'Imperatrice* is a high small cushion, covered with silk or satin; the top and frill only are decorated with crochet or netting.

The covering of the one before us is in darned netting; a piece of square netting is to be done with the fine black silk, and then darned, according to pattern, with the ordinary silk. This is tacked over the top of the cushion.

For the lace, begin on one stitch, increasing at each edge, as in square netting, until you have twenty stitches. Then increase at one edge only for six rows; after which, while still increasing at the same edge, decrease, by taking two together at the other edge, fourteen rows. The next time you come to this edge, leave as many stitches at the end as may correspond with the other side of the scallop. Repeat from the part when you cease to increase on one side.

When enough edging is done, darn it, as in the engraving. Line the edge with satin ribbon; set it on full. Cover the joining of the top and frill with black velvet ribbon, trimmed with bugles, and finish with knots of ribbon.

This cushion may also be done in cotton, for which purpose use Messrs. Evans and Co.'s Boar's Head Crochet Cotton, No. 16. It must then be darned with Royal Embroidery Cotton, No. 40.

HIEROGLYPHIC PURSE.

Materials. 2 skeins of bright cerise silk; 1 skein of black ditto; 6 skeins of gold thread, No. 3; with Boulton & Son's crochet hook. No. 23. French garniture.

Make a chain of four stitches, with the black silk, and close it into a round.

Two rounds all black, doing two stitches in every stitch.

1st Pattern Round. — Black and Gold, + 2 black on 1 black, 1 gold on 1 black, + 8 times.

2nd Pattern Round.—The same colours. + 2 black over 2 black, 2 gold on 1 gold, + 8 times.

3rd Pattern Round.—1 black in the last stitch, + 3 more black, 1 gold on the last, 1 black, + 8 times.

4th Pattern Round. — + 4 black on 4, 2 gold on 1, + 8 times.

5th Pattern Round.—+ 1 gold on 1 black, 3 black on 2 black, 3 more gold, + 8 times.

6th Pattern Round.—+2 gold, 1 black on the centre of 3 black, 5 gold, + 8 times.

7th Pattern Round. — + 2 gold, 1 cerise over 1 black, 4 gold over 3, 1 black over 1 gold, 1 gold, + 8 times.

8th Pattern Round. — + 2 gold, 1 cerise over 1, 4 gold, 1 black over black, 2 gold on 1, + 8 times.

9th Pattern Round. — + 1 gold, 3 cerise, 2 gold, 3 black, 1 gold, + 8 times.

10th Pattern Round. — + 2 cerise, 2 gold over 1 cerise, 2 cerise, 2 black, 1 gold over the centre of 3 black, 2 black, + 8 times.

11th Pattern Round. — + 2 cerise, 2 gold, 2 cerise, 2 black, 2 gold on 1, 2 black, + 8 times.

12th Pattern Round. — + 1 gold and 1 cerise on 1 cerise, 5 more cerise, 1 gold and 1 black on 1 black, 5 more black, + 8 times.

13th Pattern Round. — + 1 gold on black, 1 gold on gold, 1 gold on cerise, 4 cerise, 3 gold, 4 black coming on the centre 4 of 6 black, + 8 times.

14th Pattern Round. — + 1 gold on black, 4 more gold, 2 cerise, 5 gold, 2 black, + 8 times.

15th Pattern Round.—All gold, without any increase. Fasten off the black.

16th Pattern Round. — + 2 cerise, 2 gold, + repeated all round.

17th to 18th Pattern Round.—All cerise.

HIEROGLYPHIC PURSE, BY MRS. PULLAN.

19th Pattern Round.—3 C, 4 G, 5 C, 3 G, 1 C, 6 G, 2 C, 3 G, 4 C, 1 G, 3 C, 2 G, 7 C, 2 G, 1 C, 4 G, 5 C, 4 G, 3 C, 3 G, 3 C, 2 G, 2 C, 3 G, 3 C, 4 G, 5 C, 3 G, 3 C, 6 G, 7 C.

20th Pattern Round.—2 C, 1 G, 1 C, 4 G, 4 C, 1 G, 6 C, 1 G, 1 C, 6 G, 1 C, 5 G, 3 C, 2 G, 1 C, 3 G, 5 C, 3 G, 2 C, 2 G, 1 C, 1 G, 1 C, 3 G, 2 C, 1 G, 4 C, 5 G, 3 C, 2 G, 2 C, 2 G, 2 C, 6 G, 4 C, 3 G, 3 C, 6 G, 1 C, 6 G.

21st Pattern Round.—5 C, 4 G, 3 C, 1 G, 1 C, 4 G, 1 C, 1 G, 1 C, 6 G, 1 C, 1 G, 2 C, 2 G, 3 C, 4 G, 1 C, 1 G, 3 C, 5 G, 2 C, 2 G, 1 C, 1 G, 1 C, 3 G, 1 C, 1 G, 8 C, 3 G, 3 C, 2 G, 1 C, 2 G, 1 C, 3 G, 2 C, 3 G, 3 C, 3 G, 3 C, 2 G, 2 C, 2 G, 1 C, 6 G.

22nd Pattern Round.—4 C, 1 G, 2 C, 1 G, 4 C, 1 G, 3 C, 1 G, 2 C, 1 G, 4 C, 3 G, 3 C, 2 G, 9 C, 1 G, 1 C, 3 G, 2 C, 1 G, 3 C, 2 G, 1 C, 1 G, 1 C, 3 G, 1 C, 5 G, 4 C, 3 G, 4 C, 3 G, 2 C, 2 G, 4 C, 2 G, 3 C, 3 G, 3 C, 2 G, 2 C, 2 G, 1 C, 2 G, 2 C, 2 G.

23rd Pattern Round.—2 C, 2 G, 3 C, 1 G, 4 C, 1 G, 2 C, 1 G, 3 C, 1 G, 4 C, 3 G, 2 C, 2 G, 2 C, 1 G, 2 C, 6 G, 1 C, 2 G, 2 C, 3 G, 2 C, 2 G, 1 C, 2 G, 4 C, 4 G, 5 C, 3 G, 4 C, 4 G, 1 C, 2 G, 4 C, 2 G, 3 C, 3 G, 3 C, 2 G, 2 C, 2 G, 1 C, 2 G, 2 C, 2 G.

24th Pattern Round.—1 C, 4 G, 3 C, 3 G, 1 C, 1 G, 1 C, 4 G, 1 C, 1 G, 4 C, 3 G, 2 C, 2 G, 3 C, 1 G, 1 C, 2 G, 5 C, 1 G, 2 C, 5 G, 4 C, 2 G, 4 C, 3 G, 6 C, 3 G, 3 C, 2 G, 2 C, 1 G, 1 C, 3 G, 2 C, 3 G, 1 C, 7 G, 5 C, 2 G, 5 C, 2 G.

25th Pattern Round.—1 C, 4 G, 3 C, 2 G, 2 C, 1 G, 6 C, 1 G, 4 C, 3 G, 3 C, 4 G, 2 C, 3 G, 7 C, 5 G, 4 C, 3 G, 1 C, 1 G, 1 C, 2 G, 4 C, 5 G, 2 C, 4 G, 5 C, 6 G, 2 C, 7 G, 5 C, 9 G.

26th Pattern Round.—2 C, 2 G, 4 C, 1 G, 3 C, 8 G, 4 C, 3 G, 4 C, 2 G, 3 C, 4 G, 7 C, 3 G, 6 C, 4 G, 1 C. 1 G, 6 C, 3 G, 4 C, 2 G, 7 C, 4 G, 3 C, 7 G, 5 C, 9 G.

27th and 28th Pattern Round.—All cerise.

29th Pattern Round.—2 gold, 2 cerise, alternately.

30th Pattern Round.—2 gold over 2 cerise, 2 black over 2 gold, alternately all round.

31st to 32nd Pattern Round.—All black.

33rd Pattern Round.—1 C, 5 G, 1 C, 5 G, 3 C, 3 G, 3 C, 2 G, 5 C, 2 G, 1 C, 8 G, 4 C, 5 G, 4 C, 5 G, 3 C, 3 G, 3 C, 4 G, 3 C, 2 G, 3 C, 2 G, 3 C, 4 G, 2 C, 8 G, 2 C, 3 G, 2 C, 8 G.

34th Pattern Round.—1 C, 5 G, 1 C, 5 G, 2 C, 5 G, 3 C, 2 G, 3 C, 2 G, 2 C, 8 G, 3 C, 7 G, 5 C, 2 G, 3 C, 5 G, 1 C, 6 G, 3 C, 2 G, 2 C, 2 G, 3 C, 4 G, 1 C, 1 G, 3 C, 1 G, 2 C, 6 G, 2 C, 8 G, 1 C.

35th Pattern Round.—1 C, 2 G, 7 C, 2 G, 1 C, 2 G, 3 C, 2 G, 3 C, 2 G, 1 C, 2 G, 3 C, 3 G, 2 C, 3 G, 2 C, 9 G, 3 C, 2 G, 4 C, 2 G, 2 C, 1 G, 1 C. 2 G, 2 C, 2 G, 4 C, 2 G, 1 C, 2 G, 1 C, 1 G, 2 C, 2 G, 2 C, 1 G, 3 C, 1 G, 3 C, 4 G, 3 C, 1 G, 3 C, 2 G, 3 C.

36th Pattern Round.—1 C, 11 G, 1 C, 2 G, 3 C, 2 G, 4 C, 3 G, 4 C, 2 G, 4 C, 2

G, 1 C, 4 G, 3 C, 4 G, 1 C, 2 G, 3 C, 1 G, 1 C, 2 G, 4 C, 2 G, 2 C, 2 G, 5 C, 4 G, 1 C, 1 G, 2 C, 2 G, 3 C, 3 G, 5 C, 2 G, 7 C, 2 G, 4 C.

37th Pattern Round.—1 C, 11 G, 1 C, 2 G, 3 C, 2 G, 4 C, 3 G, 4 C, 2 G, 4 C, 2 G, 1 C, 3 G, 5 C, 3 G, 1 C, 2 G, 2 C, 2 G, 1 C, 5 G, 1 C, 2 G, 2 C, 2 G, 2 C, 1 G, 2 C, 4·G, 1 C, 1 G, 2 C, 2 G, 3 C, 3 G, 5 C, 2 G, 6 C, 2 G, 5 C.

38th Pattern Round.—5 C, 3 G, 5 C, 2 G, 3 C, 2 G, 3 C, 2 G, 1 C, 2 G, 3 C, 3 G, 2 C, 3 G, 1 C, 2 G, 2 C, 3 G, 2 C, 2 G, 1 C, 6 G, 5 C, 1 G, 1 C, 2 G, 2 C, 2 G, 1 C, 1 G, 2 C, 2 G, 2 C, 3 G, 2 C, 2 G, 2 C, 1 G, 3 C, 1 G, 3 C, 4 G, 4 C, 2 G, 5 C, 1 G.

39th Pattern Round.—3 C, 7 G, 4 C, 5 G, 3 C, 2 G, 3 C, 2 G, 2 C, 8 G, 1 C, 1 G, 3 C, 3 G, 3 C, 1 G, 2 C, 4 G, 3 C, 4 G, 1 C, 2 G, 2 C, 2 G, 1 C, 4 G, 7 C, 4 G, 1 C, 1 G, 3 C, 1 G, 2 C, 6 G, 2 C, 9 G.

40th Pattern Round.—3 C, 7 G, 5 C, 3 G, 3 C, 2 G, 5 C, 2 G, 1 C, 8 G, 1 C, 1 G, 3 C, 3 G, 3 C, 1 G, 3 C, 2 G, 3 C, 2 G, 1 C, 2 G, 1 C, 2 G, 2 C, 2·G, 2 C, 2 G, 8 C, 4 G, 2 C, 3 G, 2 C, 8 G, 1 C, 8 G, 1 C.

41st and 42nd Pattern Round.—All black.

43rd Pattern Round.— + 2 black, 2 gold, + alternately.

44th Pattern Round.— + 2 gold, over 2 black, 2 cerise +.

Do three rounds of Sc, with cerise only, and then 10 rounds of open crochet, with one chain, instead of 2, and the Dc, being always taken *under* the chain.

From the 33rd to 40th Round, inclusive, black may be used instead of crimson.

For the Lace. — Black. Work on the last round but two. + 1 Dc, 3 Ch, miss 3, + all round.

2nd Round.—Black and gold. Black, 6 Sc, (beginning on chain before a Dc, 4 Ch. Gold 1 Dc on ditto. Black, 4 Ch.

3rd Round.—Black, 4 Sc, on centre 4 of 6, 4 Ch. Gold, 4 Dc. Black, 4 Ch.

4th Round.—Black, 2 Sc on centre of 4, 4 Ch. Gold, 8 Dc (over 4). Black, 4 Ch.

Run in the cords, above the lace. **Add** the balls and tassels.

THE WORK-TABLE FRIEND.

COIFFURE A L'EUGÉNIE.

Materials.—Two strips of black filet, each 4 inches wide ; one skein of cerise, and one of Vert-islay silk (French); twelve skeins of gold thread, No. 1; and a garniture.

WE present to our readers a genuine Parisian coiffure, with bracelets *en suite*. In Paris, where every day develops some new proof of taste and ingenuity, and where the elegance of all the minor appendages to dress is only equalled by its richness, the coiffure à l'Eugénie has had a *succès* which has astonished even the designer. It is so gay, so brilliant, yet so elegant, and withal so becoming to everybody, that it is universally approved of.

We must first explain the materials. The *filet* is a cheap and excellent loomimitation of hand-netting. It is true this may be done by the hand; but the expense of silk, and the waste of time, will make it at least ten times as expensive. We should therefore advise every one to purchase the imitation in preference.

The French silks used in darning it are also very superior to the English both in make and dye. Perhaps our readers will be surprised at one skein only of each being named, if they are not aware that one skein of French contains at least as much as six English.

The trimmings are composed of silk, beads, and passementerie. Twenty-four tassels are required, and two gold buttons. Of the tassels, eight are longer than the remainder, and have some extra ornamentation. We give a diagram of one (*a.*) The lower part is a wooden mould, covered with floss ; above it a cornet, in gold passementerie, with a large white bead between it and the ball of seed beads above. Another large glass bead, above the latter, finishes the tassel. The eight longer tassels have either another gold ball, or one of the diamond-shaped ornaments seen in the button, and composed of silk and gold, or any other fanciful device. The colours are usually varied in the short and long tassels ; for instance, if the silk of the former be in cerise, in the others it will be green. The cords also are different.

The button (*b*) is in gold passementerie, the lozenge on it in vert-islay and gold, and the small *macaroon* (as it is called), in cerise and gold ; thus blending all the colours.

The diagram (*c*) gives the mode of netting stitch by stitch, the longest length being across nine holes. The Vandykes

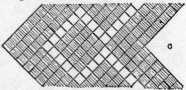

are cut out after darning. One edge is done in one colour, the other in the second, and all the diamonds in gold thread, the ends being carefully fastened off. Each end must be finished in a point, to which the longest tassel is sewed. The others form pendents at each side.

The head-dress is in one length of 1¼ yard with two extra ends, each 1¼ fingers. It goes round the front of the head, and then twines round the plaits at the back, the four ends drooping low on the shoulders. The bracelets are in two pieces each. One goes round the black elastic, which forms the foundation; the other is converted into two ends and a small bow. A gold button is placed on each, and the ends are trimmed like those of the coiffure.

Blue and claret, blue and cerise, and many other combinations are very pretty; and for mourning, gray with silver may be worn. There is a great difference in the value of the trimmings. Some are a guinea or more; but very pretty ones, with all the requisite silks, net and gold thread, may be had for that price.

WORK-TABLE FOR JUVENILES;

OR, LITTLE MARY'S HALF HOLIDAYS.

"OH dear mamma, only see what a miserable afternoon it is; how it is pouring! Do you think there is any chance at all of its clearing up?"

"Indeed, my love, I fear there is not. But how fortunate that it is a half-holiday, and that you are not obliged to go in the rain to school, or else to lose your place in class."

"Yes, mamma, but I should have had such a pleasant game with my cousins. Now, I have nothing to amuse myself with."

"What, no books! no work! What has become of the pretty workbox your kind aunt gave you from the Christmas-tree? And the nice set of books that were your uncle's present? You were greatly delighted with them at the time, but I fear you have ceased to care for them entirely. I never see the workbox open."

"Because work is such a dull amusement, dear mamma! Stitch! stitch! stitch! Like the poem you were reading to me one day."

"Ah! my dear child. If you had to toil for your bread as some poor little girls have to do,—children as young as yourself, dear Mary, perhaps as tenderly loved and delicately nurtured, — then, indeed, you might have cause for that heavy sigh

of weariness. But you, happily, have no care, no need to toil; all that is required of you is to render yourself a source of comfort and happiness to your dear papa, who works so hard to give his little daughter everything that is good for her. He knows what a resource needlework is to a woman, and is very anxious you should be expert at it; and, if I remember rightly, your box is stored with every implement you can possibly require. Indeed I thought it one of the handsomest gifts on the Christmas-tree."

"So it was, mamma. And how splendid the tree looked when it was lighted up; there was not such a pretty one at any of the other parties we went to. Oh, mamma! how I do wish you would let me have a party, and a tree, next Christmas!"

"I would, with pleasure, my love, if I could afford the expense. But you would not like to have no presents on them suitable for your uncles or aunts; and to purchase such is beyond my power."

"Why could I not make some, mamma? Helen made a great many of the handsomest things on their tree. Why could not I do so?"

"Why, indeed? Except that you think stitch! stitch! stitch! is such a very dull amusement."

"Oh, mamma! — pray forget I ever said so! If I were working to please you, or papa, or anybody I loved, it would not be dull."

"No, my love! To toil for those we love can never be a dull or a painful task to a woman, even if the toil be great, and the thanks small. But when it is merely the light and elegant occupation of a few hours a week, it is indeed a pleasure. And so, my little girl, if you will really take pains to work well and diligently, I will furnish the materials, and teach you how to use them; and I think there is no doubt you will find by December that you have abundance of the principal decorations for a very elegant Christmas-tree. But remember, if once you begin, I shall expect you to persevere; and till then you will not have much time to spare for play on any half-holidays."

"Indeed, mamma, I will persevere. But you are quite sure you will like me to spend every half-holiday in fancy-work? I heard you say, the other day, that it was very wrong of Miss Clayton to spend so much time in crochet and embroidery."

"Very true; but have you never heard that what may be right for certain people, and under certain circumstances, may be quite wrong when actors and situations are altered? Miss Clayton's only aim is her personal decoration; whatever she does is for herself only,—to have her collars and handkerchiefs elegantly embroidered, to decorate her *own* apartments, these are the objects of her industry, and the time so selfishly wasted might be employed in relieving her invalid mother of the care of her house, and in teaching her younger sisters. Therefore, I said she was wrong; but your motive is a different one. And in itself, Mary, needlework is an elegant amusement, giving exercise to some of the best qualities of a woman. Diligence, patience, perseverance, and a great many other virtues are brought into exercise, and taste and refinement are cultivated."

"I think my half-holidays will be very pleasant ones, mamma!"

"I hope they will; when you are doing work you quite understand, I shall be able to read to you, also. But we may as well begin at once. Where is your work-box? Let us see what it contains."

"In the top are knitting and netting-needles, meshes, and crochet-hooks."

"Let us examine them. Really, these crochet-hooks are very nice. What beautiful ivory handles!—and see, Mary, there are figures engraved on them, 12, 15, 18, 21, 24. Five sizes, selected from the coarsest to the finest."

"How very convenient, mamma; to know the number of the hook, without using a gauge! Even Helen says, she never can tell how to gauge a crochet-hook."

"It is indeed very difficult; and the idea of engraving the number on the handle, is an excellent one. Then, look at the hook itself; just what a crochet-hook ought to be, perfectly smooth, and tapering very gradually to the point, without any of the sharpness which makes some crochet-hooks so like fish-hooks."

"If I had had one of these hooks, when I was making your anti-macassar,

mamma, I should not have torn my finger so much. Don't you remember I was obliged to wear a sheath, it was so sore?"

"Yes, my dear; Mr. Boulton's hooks are certainly beautiful. It would be almost impossible to work badly with one. I do not wonder, now I compare these hooks with common ones, that he got a prize-medal at the Exhibition. These knitting-needles, too, are beautifully tapered; pointed, without being sharp. It must be quite a pleasure to work with them!"

"And here is an ivory gauge, mamma. This is quite a new thing, is it not? Your gauge is made of card-board?"

"Yes; and as the holes are apt to be injured by thrusting too large a needle through them, the ivory one is a great improvement. These gauges are cut out of the best part of the tusk, slices of which are sawn off, to make these rounds. I have been told that they would not answer the purpose, if cut lengthways from the ivory. I believe these gauges are also an invention of Mr. Boulton.

"Well, it is very useful; and see, mamma, what a stock of sewing-needles of all sorts! then there are pins of different sizes, and some needles with sealing-wax heads. What are they for?"

"To use instead of pins for any fine and delicate work. The smallest pins almost will leave a mark in a piece of French cambric, or in velvet, for instance: and, if such substances require to be pinned, these fine needles are used for the purpose."

"In this division of the work-box, mamma, there are sewing-silks of all colours, wound on cards. Then there are scissars, stiletto, knife, and two bodkins, besides two thimbles. But, mamma, is this ivory thimble of any use, or is it only for ornament?"

"It is intended to be worn when you are doing embroidery, or any other very delicate work; as the silver thimbles sometimes become damp from the heat of the hand, and injure the delicate tints of silks. I think we have now examined every thing except the sewing-cottons. These are, I see, the same as are used in the needlework designs in the *Family Friend*,—Evans's Boar's-head cottons."

"Yes, mamma, I see they have a Boar's-head on the label. Why is that?"

"I have understood it is the family crest of the manufacturers. For many years this cotton has been celebrated for its strength and evenness; indeed, from its being universally considered as the standard cotton we may conclude it has superior qualities. Some day I should like to take you over a cotton manufactory. You would like to see the process by which the raw cotton is made into such a beautiful material as this reel of thread, marked No. 150."

"But surely, mamma, there cannot be any great difference in the quality of cotton. It seems to me that a reel of cotton is a reel of cotton; and that one is as good as another."

"Is there any difference between the quality of this bit of calico at 3d. a yard, and a piece of India muslin? Both are the produce of the same plant. There is nearly as much difference between one kind of sewing or crochet cotton and another. Even the raw cottons vary greatly in quality and value. Egypt, America, and the South Sea Islands furnish it. The Boar's Head Cotton is made of the best."

"What a number of people must have been employed to get together the contents of this box. An elephant has been killed for the thimble and gauge, mines have been dug for the steel and silver, silkworms have given the silk, the cotton, too, has been grown in foreign lands; is there anything else, mamma?"

"You have forgotten the mother-of-pearl handles, my dear; for these pearls have been fished up from the Persian Gulf, or the coast of Ceylon. And the box, itself, Mary, is of one of the most beautiful manufactures of modern times. It is called *papier maché*."

"Papier maché—that means mashed paper, mamma, does it not? But this solid substance cannot be paper?"

"Indeed it is; and by a number of very curious processes soft paper is converted into this beautiful box. Some day you shall see a papier maché manufactory. Meantime, my love, this long, weary, dull afternoon has passed; and here comes Sarah with the tea."

"Mamma! surely it cannot be six o'clock! How quickly the time has gone! But I have done no work!"

"No; but next half-holiday we will begin in good earnest. Meantime, I will give you a most appropriate companion for your work-box, in which you will find all sorts of pretty patterns, and instructions for stitches in crochet, knitting, and other work. You must learn to understand all the terms before we begin."

"So I will, mamma,—and many, many thanks! I am sure I ought to take pains, since you are so kind. How pleasant my half-holidays will be, and how delightful it will be to give presents of my own making!"

"I am glad you think so, dear child. May you ever find your own happiness in seeking to make that of others! There is no surer way of attaining it:

'They who joy would win,
Must *share* it: *Happiness* was born a twin.'"

(*Continued at p.* 265.)

GOLD-FISH GLOBE MAT.

(*Designed by Mrs. Warren.*)

THIS Mat is intended for a Globe whose dimensions are thirty-one inches round the thickest part of the Globe. But for whatever size it may be required, be careful to let the bottom of the Mat extend rather more than an inch beyond the size of the bottom of the Globe; then it can be made of any size, small or large, as required. 3 shades of Emerald Green, 4 thread Berlin wool, half an ounce of each shade; one ounce of shaded Scarlet, 8 thread Wool; 1 reel of No. 10 Evans's Drab Boar's-head Cotton; 20 yards of white skirt Cord, the size of ordinary blind-cord. Nos. 1 and 2 Penelope Hooks.

WITH lightest green make 14 Dc stitches over the end of the cord, and double it in as small a circle as possible, by uniting: this makes 1 row. Work 7 more rows, increasing in the first 3 rows, by working 2 stitches into every stitch of the preceding row; then increase at regular intervals throughout the bottom of the Mat, as may be required. After working 8 rows with the lightest shade, work 8 rows of next shade, then 5 rows of the darkest shade; draw the cord tight, at an interval of every 12 stitches in this last row: this will form an edge to stand up round the bottom of the Mat. On this, with the same colour, work 6 rows without increasing, drawing the cord after every few stitches. This rim, as indeed all the rest, must be perfectly smooth and even.

GOLD-FISH GLOBE MAT, BY MRS. WARREN.

With next shade lighter, work a row, increasing 1 in every 4th stitch, being careful not to draw the cord in this or either of the following rows; then 2 rows without increasing, then 1 row, increasing 1 in every 5th stitch. Then, with lightest shade, 1 row without increasing; then cut off the cord, and fasten it neatly. Then 5 chain, Dc into every 4th loop (*that is, having 2 clear loops between each Dc stitch*); fasten off neatly, and turn the whole inside out, having the right side of the work for the Globe to stand in.

For the Border.

With Drab Cotton ; No. 3 Hook.

1*st Row.*—1 L *under* the 5 chain, 5 chain, 1 more long *under* same, 5 chain, *repeat.*

2*nd and* 3*rd Rows.*—1 L *under* every 5 chain, with 5 chain between each.

4*th Row.*—The same, only making 6 chain.

5*th Row.*—The same, only making 7 chain.

Keep the inside of the Mat in front, turn down the Border all round, at the last 5 chain row, having the outer edge of the Border turned to the outside of the Mat.

8 Thread Scarlet Wool—No. 1 Hook.

Make *under* every 5 chain, 1 stitch thus:—*Place the hook under the 5 chain, draw the wool through, and then through the loop on the hook ; then twist the wool over the hook, and draw it again through the loop on the hook.* All this forms but one stitch, and must be worked very loosely, so much so, that each loop is full an inch long; it looks like a small ruche of wool, when finished. When this row is completed pull the outer edge out well, then the row now done will have the appearance of being worked on the surface of the cotton.

Now, *under* every 7 chain work two stitches precisely the same.

The Border now resembles a frill, which must be arranged and pinned on the edge of the Mat, as shown in the engraving: then sew it neatly through with Green wool.

PARISIAN ESSUIE-PLUME, BY MRS. PULLAN.

PARISIAN ESSUIE-PLUME.

Materials.—1 skein of black netting silk, 1 skein of violet ditto; 1 skein maize, with a small quantity of any other bright colours you may happen to have; such as crimson, claret, blue, green. Also common black cloth, sufficient for six rounds, the size of the crochet work, and a French button.

With the black silk, make a chain of 8; close it into a round, and work one round of Sc, doing two stitches in every stitch.

2nd Round. — Sc all round, with 2 stitches in every alternate stitch, all black.

3rd Round.—Do 2 stitches in every 3rd stitch, all round, in black.

4th Round. — Black and maize, + 1 maize, 3 black, + 8 times.

5th Round.— + 2 maize on 1, 3 black, + 8 times.

6th Round.—Maize, violet and black. + 1 maize, 3 violet, 1 maize on 1 maize, 3 black on black, + 8 times.

7th Round.— + 1 maize, 2 violet on 1, 1 maize, 3 black, + 8 times.

8th Round.—1 maize, 2 violet, 1 maize, 4 black on 3, + 8 times.

9th Round.—+1 maize and 1 violet on 1, 2 violet, 1 violet and 1 maize on 1, 2 black on centre 2 of 4, 1 maize on black, + 8 times.

10th Round.—1 maize and 1 violet on 1, 1 violet,+ 2 maize on 2 centre of 4 violet, 2 violet, 1 maize, 2 black on 2, 1 maize, 2 violet, + 7 times, 2 maize, 2 violet, 2 black, 2 maize.

11th Round.— + 3 violet, 1 maize on the same as the last violet, 3 violet, 2 maize, (over 1 maize 1 black), 1 black on same, 2 maize, + 8 times.

12th Round.— + 4 violet, 1 maize on maize, 4 violet, 3 maize (over 1 black and a maize on each side), + 8 times. Fasten off black.

13th Round.— + 4 violet, 1 maize on violet, 2 maize on 1 maize, 1 maize on violet, 4 violet, 1 maize on centre of 3, + 8 times, 4 violet, 4 maize on 3.

14th Round.—+ 11 violet, 3 maize on 2 centre of 4, + 8 times.

15th Round.— + 4 violet, 1 maize, 2 violet on 1, (the 6th of 11), 1 maize, 4 violet, 4 maize on 3, + 8 times.

16th Round.— + 1 maize, 2 violet, (on centre 2 of 4), 2 maize, 2 violet, 2 maize,

2 violet, 2 maize, 2 black on centre 2 of 4 maize, 1 maize, + 8 times.

17th Round.—4 maize, + 4 violet, (over 2 violet, and 1 maize at each side), 5 maize (on two violet and a maize at each side) 4 black, 5 maize as before, + 7 times, 4 violet, 5 maize, 7 black.

18th Round.— + 1 maize over the last of 5, 4 violet, 1 maize, 5 blue, 2 blue, (on centre 2 of 4 black), 5 black, + 8 times. Observe that when the blue is introduced in this and the following rounds, the other colours are to be substituted in the repetitions. If 4 colours are used, the blue may be in the 1st and 5th; orange on 2nd and 6th, green on 3rd and 7th, and crimson on the remainder. But if every one of the eight patterns is done in a different colour the pattern will be still better.

19th Round.— + 2 maize, 2 violet, (on centre 2 of 4), 2 maize, 4 black, 5 blue, (on 2 blue and 1 black on each side), 4 black, + 8 times.

20th Round.— + 1 black, 2 maize, 1 violet, 2 maize, 3 black, 3 blue, 1 maize, (on 2nd of 5 blue), 1 blue, 1 maize, 3 blue, 2 black, + 8 times.

21st Round.— + 2 black, 3 maize, 3 black, 3 blue, 2 maize, 1 blue on 1 blue, 2 maize, 3 blue, 1 black, + 8 times.

22nd Round.— + 3 black, 1 maize, (on centre of 3), 6 black, 2 maize, 3 blue, 2 maize, 4 black, + 8 times, do 9 more black.

23rd Round.— + 2 maize, (the 1st on 6th black), 5 blue, 2 maize, 13 black, + 8 times. The last time the 13th comes over a maize.

24th Round.— + 2 maize, 3 blue, 2 maize, 15 black, + 8 times.

25th Round.— + 2 maize, 1 blue, 2 maize, 18 black, + 8 times.

26th Round.— + 3 maize, (over 1 blue and 1 maize, on each side), 21 black, + 8 times.

27th Round.—1 maize on the centre of 3, and all the rest black, increasing so as to keep it flat.

28th Round.—All maize.

29th Round.—Violet, + 4 Dc in one chain, 1 Ch, miss 3, + repeat all round.

30th Round.—Maize. Sc on every Dc stitch of last row, and *across* the chain stitch, taking up the centre of 3 missed stitches in the 28th round.

Cut several rounds of black cloth rather smaller than the crochet. Pierce a hole in the centre, and screw on the button.

POINT LACE COLLAR.

Materials.—The Point-lace cottons of Messrs. W. Evans and Co., of Derby, with their No. 1 Mecklenburgh thread.

THIS collar is done in the antique style and is distinguished by that grotesque character so often seen in old point lace.

The outlines are done in Mecklenburgh, No. 1; and the ground is composed entirely of various bars, the pattern on which is heavy, and for the most part in antique stitches. These are respectively to be worked in the following threads:—

No. 1. FOUNDATION STITCH.—No. 100 Mecklenburgh.

No. 2. SEVILLE LACE STITCH.—No. 120 Mecklenburgh.

No. 3. OPEN DIAMOND STITCH.—Boar's Head Cotton, No. 120.

No. 4.—This stitch is a variety of the foundation stitch, and occurs in different parts of the collar. The open lines are produced by leaving the space of two stitches wherever there is an open stitch, whether the lines are to be worked across, or in zig-zags, or other fantastic forms. It is done in Mecklenburgh, No.100.

No. 5 is FAN LACE, done in Mecklenburgh, No. 80.

The English Lace is done in Boar's-head, No. 90; and the Spotted Lace in No. 120 of the same.

All the bars are done in Mecklenburgh, No. 100.

The edge is done in the following way: Every point consists of six loops. Make the three at the base, tack them down with a second needle and thread, and cover the first, second, and half the third with buttonhole stitch, adding the Raleigh dots when required. Take the needle and thread from the centre of the third loop to that of the second, and from that to the first; tack the two made loops down, and over one and *half the other*, with buttonhole stitch; then make the loop at the point; work that, and also the two half loops left.

Afterwards cover the outline thread of the collar with button-hole stitch.

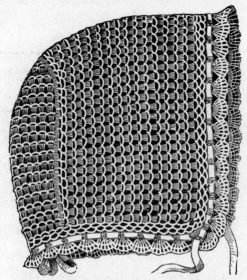

CHILD'S NIGHT-CAP, BY MRS. PULLAN.

THE WORK-TABLE FRIEND.

CHILD'S NIGHT-CAP.

Materials.—1 oz. of W. Evans and Co.'s knitting-cotton No. 24, with hook No. 18.

BEGIN by doing the crown, which is in the form of a horse-shoe. Make a chain of 38 stitches.

1st Row.— + Miss 2, 3 Dc in the next, 1 Ch, + 12 times. End with miss 2, 3 Dc in the last chain.

2nd Row.—Turn the work. 2 Ch, + 1 Sc under 1 Ch, 3 Ch, + repeat to the end. Finish with a Sc stitch on the first of 2 missed, at the beginning of the last row.

3rd Row.—Turn the work. 2 Ch, + 3 Dc, on centre one of 3 Ch, 1 Ch, + repeat to the end. Finish with 3 Dc on the first, and 2 Ch in the previous row.

Repeat the 2nd and 3rd rows 13 times more. Then for 4 times omit the last repetition of the pattern, so as to decrease at each edge 3 stitches in every row. Fasten off.

For the Front.—Sc on the original chain, before the last 3 Dc of first row. + 3 Ch, Sc under the stitch in which 3 Dc are worked, + repeat all round the crown except the original chain which forms the neck, * turn 3 Ch, + Sc on centre of 3 Ch, 3 Ch, + to the end of the row, * repeat between the stars.

Having the work now on the wrong side, repeat the 3rd and 2nd rows of the crown until fourteen of each are done. Then three rows completely round the cap, like the first part of the front.

Open hem.—1 Dc under chain, + 2 Ch, 1 Dc under next chain, + repeat all round.

BORDER.—5 Tc under 1 chain, + 4 Ch, miss 2 Ch and 2 Dc, 5 Tc under the next, + repeat all round.

2nd Row.— + 1 Dc after 1 Tc, * 1 Ch, 1 Dc after next Tc, * 3 times, 2 Ch, + repeat.

3rd Row.— + 1 Sc under the chain of 2 in last round, and the chain of 4 in 1 Ch, 3 Ch, 1 Sc under 1 Ch, 3 Ch, 1 Sc

ROUND DOYLEY IN CROCHET, BY MRS. PULLAN.

under each Ch, 3 Ch, 1 Sc under next, 3 Ch, + repeat all round. Run narrow ribbon in the open hem.

ROUND DOYLEY IN CROCHET.

Materials.—Messrs. W. Evans and Co's Boar's Head crochet-cotton No. 16; crochet-hook No. 18.

Make a chain of 8, close it into a round, and work *under* it 12 Dc stitches.

1st Round.— + 1 Dc 2 Ch, miss none, + 12 times.

2nd Round.— + 2 Dc over 1, 3 Ch, miss 2 Ch, + 12 times.

3rd Round.— + 4 Dc, (over 2, and 1 Ch, at each side,) 3 Ch, miss 1 Ch, + 12 times.

4th Round.— + 6 Dc, over 4 and a chain at each side, 3 Ch, miss 1, + 12 times.

5th Round.— + 8 Dc over 6 and 1 Ch at each side, 3 Ch, miss 1, + 12 times.

6th Round.— + 6 Dc, beginning on 2nd of 8, 2 Ch, miss 2, 1 Dc, 2 Ch, miss 2 + 12 times.

7th Round. — + 5 Dc (on centre 4), 3 Ch, miss 3, 1 Dc, 3 Ch, miss 3, + 12 times.

8th Round.— + 3 Dc (on centre 3 of 5,) 2 Ch, miss 2, 1 Dc, 2 Ch, miss 1, 1 Dc, 2 Ch, miss 1, 1 Dc, 2 Ch, miss 2, + 12 times.

9th Round.— + 2 Dc (on centre 1 of 3), 3 Ch, miss 3, 1 Dc, 2 Ch, miss 2, 1 Dc, 2 Ch, miss 2, 1 Dc, 3 Ch, miss 3 + 12 times.

10th Round.— + 1 Dc, on 2nd of 2, 2 Ch, miss 1, 1 Dc, 2 Ch, miss 1, 1 Dc, 2 Ch, miss 2, 1 Dc, 2 Ch, miss 2, 1 Dc,

2 Ch, miss 1, 1 Dc, 2 Ch, miss 2, + 12 times.

11th Round.— + 9 Dc over 7, 2 Ch, miss 2, 7 Dc, 2 Ch, miss 2, 1 Dc, 2 Ch, miss 2, 1 Dc, 2 Ch, miss 2, 13 Dc (over 10), 2 Ch, miss 2, + 6 times.

12th Round.— + 21 Dc (over 18) 2 Ch, miss 1, 1 Dc, 2 Ch, miss 2, 9 Dc (over 8), 2 Ch, miss 1, 4 Dc, 2 Ch, miss 2, 1 Dc, 2 Ch, miss 2, + 6 times.

13th Round.— + 1 Dc, 2 Ch, miss 1, 19 Dc, 2 Ch, miss 2, 7 Dc, 2 Ch, miss 2, 1 Dc, 2 Ch, miss 1, 1 Dc, * 2 Ch, miss 2, 1 Dc, * 3 times, 2 Ch, miss 2, + 6 times.

14th Round.— + 10 Dc, 2 Ch, miss 2, 1 Dc, 2 Ch, miss 2, 1 Dc, 2 Ch, miss 2, 13 Dc, * 2 Ch, miss 2, 1 Dc, * 4 times, 2 Ch, miss 2, 3 Dc, + 6 times.

15th Round.— + 16 Dc, * 2 Ch, miss 2, 1 Dc, * twice, 2 Ch, miss 2, 4 Dc, 2 Ch, miss 2, 1 Dc, 2 Ch, miss 2, 13 Dc, 2 Ch, miss 2 +.

16th Round.— + * 1 Dc, 2 Ch, miss 2, * twice, 7 Dc, 2 Ch, miss 2, 1 Dc, 2 Ch, miss 2, 4 Dc, 2 Ch, miss 2, 11 Dc (over 10), 2 Ch, miss 2, 12 Dc, + 6 times.

17th Round.— + * 10 Dc, 2 Ch, miss 2, * twice, 13 Dc, 2 Ch, miss 2, 1 Dc, 2 Ch, miss 1, 1 Dc, 2 Ch, miss 1, 1 Dc, 2 Ch, miss 2, 1 Dc, 2 Ch, miss 2, + 6 times.

18th Round.— + 7 Dc, 2 Ch, miss 2, 7 Dc, 2 Ch, miss 2, 13 Dc (over 12), * 2 Ch, miss 1, 1 Dc, * twice, 2 Ch, miss 2, 1 Dc, 2 Ch, miss 2, 4 Dc, 2 Ch, miss 2, 1 Dc, 2 Ch, miss 2, 3 Dc, + 6 times.

19th Round.— + 18 Dc over 16, 2 Ch, miss 2, 16 Dc, * 2 Ch, miss 2, 1 Dc, * 3 times, 2 Ch, miss 2, 7 Dc, 2 Ch, miss 2, + 6 times. The last time close the round and begin the next on the last of 7 Dc.

20th Round.— + 19 Dc (over 18), * 2 Ch, miss 2, 1 Dc, * twice, 2 Ch, miss 2, 4 Dc (over 3), 2 Ch, miss 2, 10 Dc (over 8), 2 Ch, miss 2, 1 Dc, 2 Ch, miss 2, 1 Dc, 2 Ch, miss 2, 4 Dc, 2 Ch, miss 2, 1 Dc, 2 Ch, miss 2, + 6 times.

21st Round.— + 19 Dc, * 2 Ch, miss 2, 1 Dc, * 5 times, 2 Ch, miss 2, 7 Dc, 2 Ch, miss 2, 1 Dc, 2 Ch, miss 2, 4 Dc, 2 Ch, miss 2, 1 Dc, 2 Ch, miss 2, 1 Dc, 2 Ch, miss 2, + 6 times.

22nd Round.— + 10 Dc, 2 Ch, miss 2, 4 Dc, * 2 Ch, miss 2, 1 Dc, * 7 times, 2 Ch, miss 2, 4 Dc, 2 Ch, miss 2, 1 Dc,

2 Ch, miss 2, 4 Dc, † 2 Ch, miss 2, 1 Dc, † twice, 2 Ch, miss 2, + 6 times.

23rd Round.— + 8 Dc, * 2 Ch, miss 2, 1 Dc, * 11 times, 2 Ch, miss 1, 1 Dc, 2 Ch, miss 1, 1 Dc, 2 Ch, miss 2, 4 Dc, + 2 Ch, miss 2, 1 Dc, + 3 times, 2 Ch, miss 2, + 6 times.

Or 1 round of open square crochet, missing 1 only sometimes, instead of two. The border : + 1 Sc, 6 Ch, miss 5, 1 Sc, 11 Ch, miss 8, + all round.

2nd Round.— + 5 Dc. on centre 5 of 11 Ch, 4 Ch, Dc on 2nd of 6 Ch, 4 Ch, miss 2, 1 Dc, 4 Ch, + all round.

3rd Round.— + 7 Dc on 5, 4 Ch, Dc on 2nd of 4 Ch, 4 Ch, Dc on next chain, 4 Ch, + all round.

4th Round.— + 7 Dc on 7, 5 Ch, Dc on 2nd of 4 Ch, 6 Ch, Dc on next stitch, 5 Ch, + all round.

5th Round.— + 7 Dc on 7, 5 Ch, Dc on 2nd of 6 Ch, 6 Ch, miss 2, Dc on next, 5 Ch, + all round.

6th Round.— + 5 Dc, beginning on 2nd of 7, 6 Ch, Dc on 2nd of 6, 8 Ch, miss 2, 1 Dc, 6 Ch, + all round.

7th Round.— + 3 Dc on 3 centre of 5, 6 Ch, Dc on 2nd of 8 Ch, 10 Ch, miss 4, Dc on the next, 6 Ch, + all round.

8th Round.— + Sc on 1st of 3 Dc, 6 Ch, miss 1, Sc on the next, 6 Ch, miss 6, 2 Dc, 3 Ch, miss 3, 2 Dc, 3 Ch, miss 3, 2 Dc, 6 Ch, + all round.

This edging makes a nice trimming for Children's drawers.

———

PLEASURES OF ACTIVE LIFE.—None so little enjoy life, and are such burdens to themselves, as those who have nothing to do. The active only have the true relish of life. He who knows not what it is to labour, knows not what it is to enjoy. Recreation is only valuable as it unbends us; the idle know nothing of it. It is exertion that renders rest delightful, and sleep sweet and undisturbed. That the happiness of life depends on the regular prosecution of some laudable purpose, or lawful calling, which engages, helps, and enlivens all our powers, let those bear witness who, after spending years in active usefulness, retire to enjoy themselves—they are a burden to themselves.

[BRAIDED LOUNGING CAP, BY MRS. PULLAN.

THE WORK-TABLE FRIEND.

BRAIDED LOUNGING CAP.

Materials.—Three-quarters of a yard of rich blue velvet, one piece of *soutache*, gold and silver blended, one yard of cord to match, and a bullion tassel of the same metals.

WE regret that the size of this design enables us to give only the general appearance: nothing can, however, exceed it in richness or beauty, whilst at the same time the materials are not exceedingly expensive; and the labour is such as any one can accomplish in a couple of days.

Soutache is the generic name under which all braids and gimps are known in France. Some are exceedingly simple. Others, like the one with which our lounging cap was worked, are extremely ornamental. This one, with several others, was made indeed expressly for ourselves.

Some have chenille and gold or silver mingled; others are of silk only; many are shaded in one or two colours, and these are very beautiful.

The depth of the head-piece is about six inches and a half, without allowing for turnings in. It is set full round a crown of about five inches in diameter. The design, which is a rich braiding pattern, occupies a depth of four inches, and the crown is entirely covered with it. The velvet must be marked as in ordinary braiding patterns. Of course, any combinations of colours may be used. Cerise or crimson and gold look very well on purple or green. All violets on green; green on claret or black. The tassel should then be of gold only.

When braided, the cap must be neatly made up by lining with silk, and finishing round the head with gold cord.

THE WORK-TABLE FRIEND.

AUSTRALIAN PURSE.

Materials.—One skein of Groseille silk, ½ a skein black do. (both French), 10 skeins gold thread, No 1. Gilt chalice, tassels and cord to correspond. Boulton and Son's crochet-hook, No. 23.

Make a chain of 7, with the groseille silk, close it into a round.

1st. Round.—+ 1 Dc, 1 Ch, miss none, + 7 times.

2nd to 12th Round.— + 1 Dc, 2 Ch, miss 1, + all round. This part, when twelve rounds are done, should just fit the chalice and have 140 stitches.

1st pattern Round.—Sc in every stitch.

2nd Round.— + 6 groseille, 2 gold, 7 groseille, 4 gold, 1 groseille, + 7 times.

3rd Round.— + 3 groseille, 4 gold, 5 groseille, 2 gold, 2 groseille, 2 gold, + 7 times.

4th Round.— + 4 groseille, 2 gold, 2 black, 2 gold, 4 groseille, 1 gold, 4 groseille, 1 gold, + 7 times.

5th Round.— + 4 groseille, 1 gold, 4 black, 1 gold, 4 groseille, 1 gold, 4 groseille, 1 gold, + 7 times.

6th Round.— + 3 groseille, 2 gold, 4 black, 2 gold, 3 groseille, 2 gold, 2 groseille, 2 gold, + 7 times.

7th Round.—+ 1 groseille, 4 gold, 4 black, 4 gold, 2 groseille, 4 gold, 1 groseille, + 6 times.

The 7th end with 5 gold, no groseille.

8th Round.— + 2 gold, 3 black, 1 gold, 2 black (on centre 2 of 4), 1 gold, 3 black, 4 gold, 2 groseille (on centre 2 of 4 gold), 2 gold, + 7 times.

9th Round.— + 1 gold, 12 black, 2 gold, 4 groseille, (over 2 and 1 gold at each side), 1 gold, + 7 times.

10th Round.—The same.

11th Round.—Like 8th.

12th Round.—5 gold, + 4 black on 2 black and 1 gold on each side, 4 gold, 2 groseille, (on centre 2 of 4 gold), 2 groseille, 4 gold, + 7 times.

13th Round.— + 4 black on 4, 2 gold, 4 groseille, 4 gold on 4, 4 groseille, 2 gold, + 6 times. The 7th time end with 5 groseille, 1 gold.

14th Round.— + 4 black on 4, 1 gold, 4 groseille, 2 gold, 2 black, 2 gold, 4 groseille, 1 gold, + 7 times.

AUSTRALIAN PURSE, BY MRS. PULLAN.

15th Round.— + 1 gold, 2 black (on centre 2 of 4), 2 gold, 4 groseille on 4, 1 gold, 4 black, 1 gold, 4 groseille, 1 gold, + 6 times. 7th time, 5 groseille.

16th Round.— + 4 gold (over 2 black and 1 gold at each side), 4 groseille, 2 gold, 4 black on 4, 2 gold, 4 groseille, + 7 times.

17th Round.— + 4 gold over 4, 2 groseille, 4 gold, 4 black on black, 4 gold, 2 groseille, + 7 times.

R

18th Round.— + 1 gold, 2 groseille, on centre 2 of 4 gold, 4 gold, 3 black, 1 gold, 2 black (on centre 2 of 4 black), 1 gold, 3 black, 3 gold, + 7 times.

19th Round.— + 4 groseille, 2 gold, 12 black, 2 gold, + 7 times.

20th Round.—The same. These two rounds forming the centre of the pattern, the remainder can be worked *backwards* from those already done. After completing the design, do four rounds with the groseille alone, in Sc, and then six in the same colour, of open square crochet.

FOR THE LACE.—With the black silk, 1 Dc under Ch, 3 Ch, Dc under the same, miss 1 square.

2nd Round.—Gold, + 6 Dc under every chain of 3, 2 Ch, + repeat all round.

3rd Round.—Black Dc under the 2 Ch, + 3 Ch, Dc under the same, Dc under the next 2 Ch, + repeat all round.

4th Round.—Gold, like 2nd.

Stitch the chalice on the lower part of the purse, and add tassel and cords.

NETTED MUSIC-STOOL COVER.

Materials.—Evans & Co.'s Boar's-head crochet cotton, No. 12. Royal Moravian ditto, No. 12. Ivory mesh, No. 9, (using the ivory gauge).

BEGIN with eight stitches, and work two in every one, commencing with the first. In the following rounds, do two in every short stitch, and one in every other.

THE BORDER.—Begin on one stitch. Net two in one. Turn the work, and net one in the first and two in the second. Continue to net backwards and forwards, always doing two stitches in the last stitch, until there are fourteen in the row +. Now increase only at the end of every alternate row, for sixteen rows; the next row, instead of netting every stitch, leave the last eight, thus forming the first Vandyke, +. Repeat between the crosses,

MUSIC-STOOL, BY MRS. PULLAN.

until you come to the *last* point, which must be done thus:—Do the first two rows as usual; then, instead of *increasing*, you will decrease, by netting two together, at that edge where before you enlarged.

(*A*).—This is a section of the top, from which the pattern is to be darned.

(*B*).—A section of the darned border.

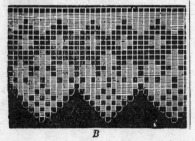

B

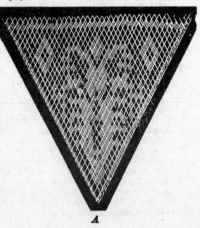

A

THE WORK-TABLE FRIEND.

MOURNING PURSE.

Materials.—1½ skeins black crochet silk, No. 2 (French), 9 skeins of silver thread. Tassels as represented in the engraving, of black and silver, and slides to match. Boulton and Son's crochet hook, No. 21.

Of course this purse can be made in any other combinations of colours, and being extremely simple, is very suitable for a learner.

Make a chain of five, and close it into a round with the silk.

1st Round.—Sc, 2 in 1 all round.

2nd Round. — Silver and black, + 1 silver, and 1 black, + 10 times.

3rd Round.— + 1 silver on silver, 2 black on 1, + 10 times.

4th Round.— + 2 silver on 1, 2 black on 2, + 10 times.

5th Round.— + 3 silver on 2, 2 black on 2, + 10 times.

6th Round.— + 4 silver on 3, 2 black on 2, + 10 times.

7th Round.— + 5 silver on 4, 3 black on 2, + 10 times.

8th Round.— + 1 silver on the same stitch as last black, 1 more silver, + 3 black on centre 3 of 5 silver, 2 silver, 2 black on centre 1 of 3, 2 silver, + 9 times. 3 black, 2 silver, 2 black.

9th Round.— + 1 silver on last stitch, 1 more silver, + 2 black, 1 silver, (on centre of 3 black) 2 black, 2 silver, 1 black, 2 silver, + 9 times.

10th Round.— + 1 black, 3 silver, 1 black, 2 silver, 1 black, + 9 times. The 10th time finish with 2 black.

11th Round.— + 2 silver, 2 black, 1 silver, 2 black, 2 silver, 2 black on 1, + 9 times. The 10th 2 black on 2.

12th Round.— + 1 black, 2 silver, 3 black, 2 silver, 3 black, + 10 times.

13th Round.— + 2 black, 5 silver, 4 black, + 10 times.

14th Round.— + 3 black, 3 silver, 5 black, + 10 times.

15th Round.— + 4 black, 1 silver, 6 black, + 10 times.

16th Round.—All silk, without increase.

17th and *18th Round.*—All silk, + 5 Dc in 1, miss 4 + 22 times. In the 18th and all following rounds, the 5 Dc are worked in the centre of the 5 Dc of the previous one.

MOURNING PURSE, BY MRS. PULLAN.

19th Round.—The same, in silver, with 1 chain between every 5 Dc.

Repeat these three rounds, 2 in silk, and 1 in silver, 5 times.

For the opening, with silk only, + 1 Dc, 1 Ch, miss 1, + work backwards and forwards 20 rows.

Form again into a round, and work the

LADIES' WORK-BAG, BY MRS. PULLAN.

17th, 18th, and 19th rounds, as before, but 7 times instead of 5.

To close it up, work a row of Sc, taking the stitches of both sides.

Work round the opening in Sc, with silver thread.

LADIES' WORK-BAG.

Materials.—French silks of the following colours. White, scarlet, emerald green, yellow (not orange), black, rose, scarlet-cord, and tassels of all the colours combined. Boulton and Son's crochet-hook, No. 24.

We must observe that bags of the most ornamental description are now greatly used by Parisian belles, for holding the handkerchief, purse, &c. They are very small, and are made in crochet, netting, or embroidery. We would not whisper the atrocity to even the winds, nevertheless it is a fact, that these same exquisite pieces of workmanship are the rage among gentlemen, for *tobacco-pouches*. The only difference is, that the lady's reticule is lined with silk or satin, and the gentleman's *blague* with lamb-skin.

With the black silk, make a chain of 336 stitches, and close it into a round.

1st. Round.—Black, + 13 Sc, 3 Sc in 1, 12 more Sc, miss 2, + 12 times.

2nd Round.—Yellow. The same.

3rd, 4th, and 5th Rounds.—Black. The same.

6th Round.—Yellow. The same.

7th Round.—Scarlet, + 7 Sc, 3 Ch, miss 3, 3 Sc, 3 Sc in 1, 3 Sc, 3 Ch, miss 3, 6 Sc, miss 2, + 12 times

8th Round.—Yellow. Like 1st.

9th and 10th Rounds.—Scarlet. The same.

11th Round.—Scarlet and white, + 10 scarlet, 1 white, 2 scarlet, 3 scarlet in 1, 2 scarlet, 1 white, 9 scarlet, miss 2, + 12 times.

12th Round.—+ 8 scarlet, 3 white, 2 scarlet, 3 scarlet in 1, 2 scarlet, 3 white, 7 scarlet, miss 2, + 12 times.

13th Round.—+ 8 scarlet, 1 white, 4 scarlet, 3 scarlet in 1, 4 scarlet, 1 white, 7 scarlet, miss 2, + 12 times.

14th Round.—Scarlet and green, + 6

scarlet, 3 green, 4 scarlet, 3 scarlet in 1, 4 scarlet, 3 green, 5 scarlet, miss 2, + 12 times.

15*th* Round.—Scarlet, green, and black, + 3 scarlet, 3 green, 1 black, 3 green, 3 scarlet, 3 scarlet in 1, 3 scarlet, 3 green, 1 black, 3 green, 2 scarlet, miss 2, + 12 times.

16*th* Round.—Scarlet and green, + 5 scarlet, 1 green, 7 scarlet, 3 scarlet in 1, 7 scarlet, 1 green, 4 scarlet, miss 2, + 12 times.

17*th* Round.—Same colours, + 4 scarlet, 3 green, 6 scarlet, 3 scarlet in 1, 6 scarlet, 3 green, 3 scarlet, miss 2, + 12 times.

19*th* and 20*th* Rounds.—All scarlet, like 1st.

The following rounds are worked in the same way, in the following colours.

21*st* Round.—Yellow.
22*nd* Round.—Red.
23*rd* Round.—Yellow.
24*th*, 25*th*, 26*th* Rounds.—Black.
27*th* Round.—Yellow.
28*th* Round.—Red.
29*th* Round.—Green.

Repeat the stripe of scarlet, from 9th to 20th rounds inclusive, substituting the following colours. White for scarlet, scarlet for white, red for black. Use green as in scarlet stripe.

Reverse the colours from 21st to 29th inclusive, that is, begin with the green, and end with the yellow round.

Now follows another pattern stripe, with green ground, for scarlet, scarlet for green, white for white, and black for black. In working the two plain green rounds which finish the stripe, miss 2 as usual, but work only *one* stitch in every one of the others.

Do a round of yellow, one of green and one of yellow, in the same way, then 4 black, decreasing so that you have 98 stitches in the round.

Black and scarlet, + 13 black, 1 scarlet, + 7 times.

2*nd* Round.—+ 5 black, miss 2, 5 black, 3 scarlet, + 7 times.

3*rd* Round.—+ 4 black, miss 2, 3 black, 5 scarlet, + 7 times.

4*th* Round.—+ 2 black, miss 2, 1 black, 7 scarlet, + 7 times.

5*th* Round.— + 1 black, 7 scarlet on 7, + 7 times.

6*th* Round.—+ 1 yellow on centre of 7 scarlet, 6 scarlet, + 7 times.

7*th* Round.—+ 3 yellow, (on 1, and a scarlet on each side,) 3 scarlet, + 7 times.

8*th* Round.—+ 1 scarlet on the centre of 3, and 4 yellow between + 7 times. Gradually close with yellow.

Now on the original chain do 1 round yellow, 1 green, 1 scarlet, 1 yellow, with 3 in one at each point, and missing 2 at the lower part. Line and trim as in the engraving.

EDUCATION OF GIRLS.—There is some sound advice on this subject in the following passage:—" There are several faults which are common to girls brought up in indolence and timidity: they are incapable of a firm and steady conduct; there is a good deal of affectation in those ill-founded alarms, and those tears that they shed so easily. We must begin by treating them with indifference; we must repress our too tender love, little flatteries, and compliments. We must teach them to speak in a concise manner. Genuine good taste consists in saying much in a few words, in choosing among our thoughts, in having some order and arrangement in what we relate, in speaking with composure; whereas women in general are enthusiastic in their language. Little can be expected from a woman who does not know how to express her thoughts with correctness, and how to be silent. Girls are timid and full of false shame, which is a source of dissimulation. To correct this, we must lead them to discover their thoughts without disguise; when they are tired, to say so; and not oblige them to appear to enjoy books, or society, while fatigued by them. When they have unfortunately acquired the habit of disguising their feelings, we must shew them, by examples, that it is possible to be discreet and prudent without being deceitful, and tell them that prudence consists in saying little, and distrusting ourselves more than others, not in dissembling speeches. Simplicity and truth excite more confidence, and succeed better even in this world, than dissimulation.

SHELL-PATTERN MAT, BY MRS. PULLAN.

THE WORK-TABLE FRIEND.

SHELL-PATTERN MAT.

Materials.—Two ounces of white satin bugles, 1 ball gold-twine, 6 shades of crimson, and 6 of green Berlin wool, (4 skeins of each,) 1 skein of white wool, and eight yards of cotton cord.

WITH the lightest crimson wool, work on the end of the cord 14 stitches, and close it into a round.

1st Round.—(Same crimson and white). + 1 white, 1 crimson, + 12 times.

2nd Round.—(Same colours). + 3 white, 1 crimson, + 12 times.

3rd Round.—(Same colours, and darkest green). + 1 green, 3 white, 1 green, 1 crimson, + 12 times.

4th Round.—(Same green, white, next crimson). + 2 green, 1 white, (on centre of 3,) 2 green, 1 crimson, + 12 times.

5th Round.—(Same crimson, and next green). + 5 green, 2 crimson on 1, + 12 times.

6th Round. — (Next darkest crimson, next lightest green). + 6 green on **5, 2** crimson on 2, + 12 times.

7th Round.—(Next lightest green, same crimson). + 6 green over 6, 3 crimson on 2, + 12 times.

8th Round.—(Next lightest green, same crimson). + 7 green on 6, 3 crimson on 3, + 12 times.

9th Round.—(Next crimson, and lightest green). + 5 green on the centre 5 of **7,** 5 crimson on 3, and a green at each side, + 12 times.

10th Round. — Work round with the next crimson, increasing sufficiently to cover the cord.

11th Round.—(Next crimson, and gold twine). + 2 gold, 2 crimson, + all round, increasing to keep it perfectly flat.

Now one round of the darkest crimson will complete the centre of the mat.

A shell. Darkest green, 11 Ch, 2 Dc, in every chain, with 1 Ch after *every* Dc.

Next green, 2 Dc under every chain, with 1 Ch after every Dc.

MOUSQUETAIRE CUFF, IN MUSLIN EMBROIDERY, BY MRS. PULLAN.

Next lightest green, Dc under every chain, with 1 Ch between the Dc. The same with the next lightest green, loosely. String 40 bugles on a bit of white Berlin wool. Fasten it to one end of the last row, and hold it along the edge. Fasten on the gold thread. + Do 1 Ch, then 1 Dc under the chain of green, leaving a bugle under the gold Ch, +. Repeat this, so that the bugles, with the gold thread above them, form the edge. This shell is then twisted into the form seen in the engraving, and sewed to one-sixth of the round, a single string of 12 bugles also being entwined with it. Two more shells in green, and 3 crimson ones form the border, being sewed alternately round the edge of the mat.

MOUSQUETAIRE CUFF, IN MUSLIN EMBROIDERY.

Materials.—French muslin, and Messrs. W. Evans and Co.'s Royal Embroidery Cotton, No. 60.

This is one of the newest Parisian patterns for a Mousquetaire sleeve, which is worn, more than any other style, in morning dress. The sleeve itself is a full plain bishop, with a narrow band at the wrist, and to this the cuff is attached. It falls back over the arm. It is particularly becoming to a small hand, besides being both more elegant and more suitable for morning wear than the mandarin and pagoda sleeves which leave the entire arm, up to the elbow, unprotected.

The design must be enlarged to the size required, exactly to fit the wrist. It should be fastened by double gold buttons.

It is worked almost entirely in raised button-hole stitch, the centres of the flowers, and the clusters of eyelet-holes only being pierced with a stiletto. The holes in the border are pierced, and worked round in button-hole stitch. The flowers in satin-stitch.

Our readers will, we think, be pleased with the novel and beautiful design which is now submitted to their appreciation.

THE WORK-TABLE FRIEND.

HAND-SCREEN IN RAISED BERLIN WORK.

Materials.—⅔ of a yard of white silk canvas, ¼ yard wide ; a suitable Berlin pattern, a paper of rug needles, some ivory meshes, and all the silks and Berlin wool that may be required for the pattern.

THE demand there is at the present moment for raised Berlin work (or velvet wool work, as it is sometimes called), would go far to prove the truth of the adage, that there is nothing new under the sun : this very work having, a year or two ago, been considered quite out of date, since little or none of it had been done for many previous years. By *Raised Berlin work*, we understand a piece of work done from a Berlin pattern, in which the principal parts, whatever they may be, are worked in relief.

In a flower piece, the flowers themselves are thus raised. In the design we selected for our hand-screen, the bird only is worked in relief. You will begin, therefore, by placing the canvas very evenly in a frame, and doing all those parts of the design

which are to be worked in the usual way. Then remove the canvas, cover up those parts completed, and begin by threading, with the different wools, as many needles as you have shades. A *stitch* in raised work occupies as many threads as an ordinary cross-stitch, that is, two in height, and two in width. Take the needle threaded with the first shade used at the lower part of the pattern, and the left hand side ; hold a mesh evenly along the canvas below the line of two horizontal threads to be worked, and slip the end of the wool under the mesh. Insert the needle under two threads in height, and *one* in width from *left* to *right*, keeping the end of the wool on the right of your stitch. Now take a similar stitch from right to left, inserting the needle two threads in width from the first stitch, and bringing it out *in the same place*. Pass the wool round the mesh, and you are ready to do the second stitch, and all the following ones, in precisely the same way. When a new shade is to be introduced in the row, instead of passing the wool of the old one round the mesh, leave it hanging over it, and introduce the new one under the mesh. At any distance *in the same row*, a shade may be re-introduced merely by bringing it again under the mesh. When one row is done, proceed to the next with a new mesh, and it will be found convenient not to withdraw the mesh from a row until two or three lines beyond it are completed. The meshes should be wide in proportion to the dimensions of the flower or other pattern to be worked, but never less than half an inch. It follows, as a matter of course, that raised work requires a much larger quantity of wool than an ordinary piece of Berlin work.

When all the pattern is completed, the canvas, if not silk, will require grounding ; but all small articles, such as pole and hand-screens, should be done on silk canvas. Cutting the raised work is an art of itself, and requires much more practice than any amateur is likely to possess, to do it well. It is usual to send the work to a shop, accompanied by the original pattern, and to have it done there by people accustomed to it. Those who like to try for themselves, must have a pair of long thin scissors, with which they cut the loops ; and then the mass of ends must be formed into the shape of the natural article. **In** flowers, for instance, each petal must be thinned at the edges, and raised in the middle; in birds, the head must be rounded, the form of the wings, tail, and body perfectly preserved. A large glass bead makes the eye of the bird.

If done correctly, there should be no ends, knots, or other irregularities on the wrong side of this raised work. Each stitch appears, at the back, in the form of a V, and all are as distinct as in a Berlin pattern, the ends being entirely on the right side. For better security, it is advisable to brush over the back of the raised work with thick gum-water. It must be borne in mind that the thicker and more raised the work, the oftener it may be re-cut, and thus renovated.

There are several other ways of doing the stitch of raised work; but after giving a fair trial to all, we have found that described in our present article, the best and firmest that can be done; and for this reason we have no hesitation in recommending it.

The screen, when completed, must be stretched on a hexagon wire frame, covered with satin, and trimmed like the netted ones, with fringe, cord, and handles. Ivory handles are the most suitable for anything that is worked in white silk canvas.

WORK-TABLE FOR JUVENILES;
OR,
LITTLE MARY'S HALF-HOLIDAYS.

(*Continued from p.* 249.)

" Now, my little daughter, if you are quite ready, we will begin our preparations for your Christmas tree. See, I have brought you down a box of materials of all kinds, which will be indispensable for your work. I hope you will take great care of them, for some are very expensive."

" Indeed I will, dear Mamma! How good you are to supply me so well. Here are wools, purse-silks, beads, gold-thread, —in short, it seems to me you have thought of everything."

" At all events, Mary, there are materials enough to occupy you for some time. But we must not waste our half-holiday in talking. Have you resolved what to begin with?"

" No, Mamma; but it should be something very easy, and which can be quickly finished. I should like to do some trifle in crochet."

" Then suppose you make one of the miniature smoking caps that are used to protect the burners of Hadrot Lamps from smoke. They look very pretty, and are useful also. If you work hard you will get one done in an hour or so."

" Oh, then I shall begin something else this evening. What shall I want, Mamma?"

" A little wool of three different colours —say, white, black, and blue—and some steel beads. Also, a little common string to work over, and a crochet hook, No. 18."

" I suppose the hook is to be fine, because the cord is fine, Mamma; for you told my cousin the other day to use a hook No. 15, with wool for her mat."

" Just so. But I do not like the dark blue you have chosen: it is too strong a contrast with the white. Besides, I think if you choose your coloured wools of the kind called crystal, the effect will be better. The cap is done in two parts. Begin with that round the head, by covering the end of the cord with 62 stitches in white wool. Close it into a round. The next round is to be black and white. It is done in rather a curious way, for though the black wool is drawn over the cord in every alternate stitch, every stitch is finished with white. Can you manage it?"

" Oh yes, Mamma. See, the chain above the cord is always white, but the string itself is covered alternately with white and black stitches."

" Quite right. We will call these black half-stitches. The next round is blue and white. + 3 white, 1 blue, 1 half-white (like the half-black), 1 blue, 1 half-white, 1 blue + 8 times in the round, so that you increase 2 stitches. In the next two rounds you do 3 white over the 3 white, and five blue over the white and blue. In the next round you will use all three colours, and hold the cord rather looser, so as slightly to increase the round. Continue to do 5 blue over 5, but have a black half-stitch on the second of the 3 white. In the next round, still holding the cord slacker, do 6 blue over 5, and white and black as in the last. In the following round work 7 blue on 6, and in the next 8 over 7, with the black half-stitch between 2 white. This round finishes the head-piece."

"And the crown, I suppose, is begun in the centre, Mamma?"

CAP FOR HADROT LAMP.

"Yes, my dear. Cover the end of the cord with 8 stitches in white wool. Close it into a round, which should be as small as possible. Work another round all white, with 2 stitches in every one. The next round has every alternate stitch half-black, and there are 26 altogether in the round, which is a sufficient increase to keep the work flat. Blue and white are used for the four following rounds, which I will describe. 1st—+ 3 blue, 1 white + 9 times; 2nd— + 4 blue over 3, 1 white over the white + 9 times; 3rd—+ 5 blue over 4, and 2 white over 1, + 9 times. In the 4th round there is a blue half-stitch over the 1st, 3rd, and 5th of the five blue, and all the rest are white. In the following round——"

"Stay, Mamma, one minute. I am afraid I have not done this very well. The cord shows between the stitches."

"Because you have dragged the wool and made it poor and thin. All kinds of wool, and the best Berlin especially, require most light and delicate handling, or their beauty is destroyed. It was to avoid this that I made you put the skeins over your arms, instead of winding them."

"Must I waste this wool, then, Mamma? It seems a pity, as it is not soiled at all."

"No: but it will be necessary to do an extra stitch here and there. You must manage, however, not to destroy the design. Let the blue half-stitches come as they did before, but increase a little on the white. Now do a round of black half-stitches, and the rest white, which will make the last before joining to the head-piece. Do not cut off the cord, but holding the head-piece and crown together, crochet the edges of both, with black wool over the twine. Fashion it off by cutting the end in a slanting direction, and working till it is quite concealed."

"And the beads, Mamma—you have forgotten them."

"No; they are put on afterwards with a little sewing silk. Trim the edge of the crown with a succession of slanting rows of them, each row containing five beads. A row of eight is also sewed up the centre of each white stripe in the head-piece, and finally a tassel and cord is formed and added, to make the tiny smoking-cap as complete as its larger original."

"Then here is one thing quite done, Mamma. Can you not tell me of something else which I might be able to finish before bed-time? What is this small round bit of cloth for? It is too little for a mat."

"It is for a pen-wiper; and I do not know that you could choose anything better for an afternoon's work. It is certain to be useful, and will look very gay and brilliant on the lighted tree. You will want, besides the cloth, which is ready marked with the pattern, some sewing silk, gold thread, beads, bugles, and a French essuie-plume button."

"What colour shall the silk be?"

"I think black will have the richest effect, with scarlet cloth and gold. That skein is too fine. Take a coarser one, or your work will hardly show. The entire design of the centre must first be worked in chain-stitch (or tambour-stitch); then lay a line of gold thread on each side of it, sewing it down with China-silk of the same colour. Finally, work a scallop of raised button-hole stitch all round, with black silk."

"And the beads and bugles, Mamma?"

"Are for a fringe, which you will easily make. Thread your needle double with black silk, and make a knot in it. Now bring out your needle between two of the scallops. Thread a bugle on—now eight or ten beads—now another bugle. Draw the needle through the *point* of the scallop, and take a stitch to secure it. Run the needle through the last bugle, then through the same number of beads and another bugle. Fasten between this scallop and the

"Suppose then you do a pretty pair of watch-pockets in straw-work? They would be useful and ornamental too. You must trim them to correspond with her bed-furniture; so that you can notice what colour it is when you go there next. It will gratify your aunt to receive such a gift, because it will prove you have be-

PEN-WIPER.

next. Continue this fringe all round. Add rounds of cloth, and fasten on the button, by piercing a hole through all the cloth, and thrusting in the shank, then screwing on the top.

"You have forgotten one thing, Mamma. How do you fasten the ends of gold thread?"

"Gold thread, braids, soutaches, &c., always have the ends concealed by drawing them through the *wrong* side, and sewing them down. A coarse sewing or rug needle may be used for this purpose."

"Well, Mamma, if I do not quite complete this to-night, at least I shall finish it before my next holiday; and then I want to begin something for Aunt Ellen—something handsomer than these little things."

stowed thought and care upon it; for it is not the value of a present, but its being really a proof of affectionate remembrance which renders it valuable to the receiver. And now that I perceive you are interested in the work I have proposed to you, and that these conversations have the effect of encouraging you to a proper employment of your time, I shall have much pleasure in affording you any assistance in my power, for my earnest desire is to see you industrious and happy. Pollock says truly:—

"'By nature's laws immutable and just,
Enjoyment stops when indolence begins;
And purposeless, to-morrow, borrowing sloth,
Itself heaps on its shoulders loads of woe,
Too heavy to be borne.'"

LADY'S RETICULE, BY MRS. PULLAN.

LADY'S RETICULE.

Materials.—8 yards of gold or silver bourdon; 4 skeins of scarlet, green, or royal blue silk (English); skein of gold thread, No. 1; cord, with tassels at the extremities; and two handsome double tassels to match with the silk and bourdon. Use crochet hook No. 16 or 17.

WITH the silk make a chain of 13 stitches. Now hold in the end of the bourdon, and work a Sc stitch in every alternate stitch of the chain, with 2 chain after every Sc stitch. At the end of the 13 chain do a Sc stitch three times in the same stitch, still with 2 chain between. Work in the same way on the other side of the original 13 chain, thus forming the foundation and centre of the bottom of the basket. Continue working round this foundation, still maintaining the oblong form, until a piece 5 inches long by four wide is done. In the few first rounds it will be necessary to make 2 chain between, and work on every alternate stitch of the previous round, but afterwards it will suffice to make 1 chain only, and miss 1 or none as may be requisite to keep the shape. In working over bourdon, however, the chain stitches must always be *long*, to admit of the gold being clearly seen between every 2 Sc stitches.

When the oval piece is finished, make the sides of the basket, by continuing to work over the bourdon, holding it so as to form an upright circle round the oval. The first round is done with 1 Sc, 1 Ch, missing 1, and having no increase in the size. All the following rounds are done entirely in Sc, the stitch of which is, however, long enough to allow the bourdon to be seen between every two stitches. 12 rounds, without any alteration of size, form this part of the reticule. Fasten off the bourdon. With the silk do 1 round thus :— + 1 Dc, 1 Ch, miss none, + all round.

2nd to *14th.*—+ Dc under chain, 1 Ch miss Dc stitch, + all round.

15th.—Gold thread. + 5 Dc under 1 Ch, miss 2 Dc, and the 1 chain between them, +, repeat all round. Fasten off.

Take 3 lengths of bourdon and plait them for the handle, which (as seen in the engraving) comes outside the silk part of the bag, and has the ends drawn through an opening in the silk and fastened down securely. Then run in the cords, beneath the gold-lace edge, and add the tassels.

NETTED CURTAINS, BY MRS. PULLAN.

CHILDREN'S DRESSES, BY MRS. PULLAN.

NETTED CURTAINS.

Materials.—Messrs. W. Evans and Co.'s Boar's Head Cotton, No. 8, and Royal Embroidery Cotton, No. 16. A bone mesh, about a quarter of an inch wide, will make a nice-sized diamond.

THE entire curtain is to be done in ordinary diamond netting, on which the design is afterwards to be darned. The number of stitches must depend entirely on the length required for the curtains. It will require 36 for each pattern; and as, with the mesh we have given, about five patterns will make the depth of a yard, it will be easy to calculate precisely the number of stitches required for curtains of any given length. With regard to the width, this also must necessarily depend on the size of the window. Each stripe occupies 38 rows, or 19 squares, the border being of the same dimensions; and any number of repetitions can be made. Curtains are extremely pretty if worked in alternate stripes of darned netting, and a fancy stitch which is not darned. In page 178 we gave some instructions for netting, which it may be useful to read from time to time.

The design for the border itself would perhaps be preferred, by some people, to the flower stripes. A very handsome netted lace border should be worked on one side, and at the bottom of each curtain.

A GOSSIP ON CHILDREN'S DRESS.

WE should hardly merit our title—*Treasures in Needlework*—could we, in our discussions on dress and toilet, overlook that portion of it which relates especially to the family—to those little people in whose nice appearance papas take so much pride, and at whose frocks and pelisses, and other items, mammas often labour so assiduously. Undoubtedly it is easy to dress a child handsomely, if we have some taste and plenty of money ; for it is very easy to enter one of the Lilliputian warehouses, and select most elegant and tasteful articles of children's dress—if we have but money enough to pay for them. But, alas! most mammas, to whom expense is a consideration, know to their cost that they could buy a handsome dress or bonnet, or cloak, for themselves, for very little, if anything, more than the miniature articles needed for baby would amount to. And, after all, what is it? A mere scrap of muslin, or jean, or merino—a yard or two of work—a little braid—there really seems nothing in it. The exquisitely nice *work* put into these articles is, however, a heavy item in the expense; and inasmuch as it furnishes employment to many who once occupied a good position in the world, and even now are obliged to maintain a respectable appearance, we are far from thinking that this beautiful and often tedious work is in the least degree overpaid, or advising those who can afford to purchase it, to waste their own time over its execution. But for one mother who can afford so to indulge her taste, and employ the skilled labour of others, at least ten feel that it is their imperative duty to labour themselves—not to earn, but to save; and to such, we trust our hints on the prevailing *modes* for the nursery may be acceptable. Undoubtedly there is hardly a pleasure so great in the whole range of woman's joys as that of preparing the wardrobe of the precious little being whose advent she so earnestly expects. It is a sacred happiness; a mingling of all the most human and most elevated sentiments —of love, hope, fear, and devotion—that can enter the human heart. The love of children seems to be so implanted in a woman's heart, that, destitute of it, she is hardly worthy of the name; and most confidently do we believe that a nature (whether man's or woman's) has much of the angel left in it still, that can enjoy the society and join in the frolics of a young child—that can meet, open-eyed, the pure gaze of infancy, and return the soft caress, and echo the merry laugh, of the happy romping child. We should feel that there

was some uncorrupted corner in the heart of such a man or woman, whatever crimes or errors might have defaced their own purity. To love one's *own* child, indeed, is no merit. It is merely rejoicing over our unspeakable wealth. "It would be unwise," says Coleridge, "to call that man wretched who, whatever else he suffers, as to pain inflicted or pleasure denied, has a child for whom he hopes and on whom he doats." And if this be true of the father, it is undoubtedly more so of the mother— at least during the early periods of childhood, when her sorrow and suffering are still fresh in her recollection. Little should we envy the feelings of the woman who, whatever her wealth or position, could coolly *purchase* every article for the wardrobe of the little being who would first give her the name of mother. A robe, a cap, a something, however trifling, should be the work of her own hands. What other fingers could so neatly and tastefully ornament the appropriate clothing of "the loveliest little cherub in the world,"—a being that, although existing without an equal, belongs, as we know, to every mother, poor or rich ?

But to return to the toilet. We scarcely ever remember the time when taste, comfort, and health were so well combined as in the present modes of dress for the rising generation. White is, of course, very much worn by girls of all ages, and boys under four years. The material employed, however, for little boys' dresses is either jean or twilled cambric; the former is most suitable, especially for pelisses. Both pelisses and dresses are very much trimmed with that open work on thick muslin, known by the term *broderie Anglaise*. It is much more suitable than any other kind, as, having seldom any open hem, it both washes and wears better. Worked trimmings that have an open-hem should be avoided by every one who does not desire the trouble of putting on fresh work two or three times before the article itself is worn out. It is very pretty, certainly; but that is all.

The pelisse given in our engraving is of white jean, trimmed with *broderie* and Russian white cotton braid. This latter is a thicker and more substantial fabric than the French cotton braid. It is also of a different make. Probably our friends will recognise the difference at once if we say that Russian braid is plaited like the Grecian plait, in which the hair is often dressed; whereas, the French braid is like an ordinary plait of five, seven, nine, or any other number. For fine thin muslin, the French braid should be used, but the other is best for all stout materials. The pelisse is made with a tight, high body, fastening behind, and braided up the front. The skirt has three widths of jean. The worked insertion is set between two, and is edged at each side by wide worked borders, sloped off towards the waist. A frill of the same is round the neck, and the deep cape is also trimmed with it. The pelisse just takes four yards of this work, and one strip of insertion of the length of the skirt. When it is desired to have the power of subsequently enlarging the dress, it is advisable not only to leave ample turnings-in at the seams of the body, but to cut it longer in the waist than is required, and to turn up an inch or so neatly. The skirt also should have an inch and a half, or more, turned in at the top, not merely of the jean itself, but of the work. The sleeves, too, should have a tuck in them, near the shoulder. White always looking new when it is clean, it is quite worth while to practise these little pieces of economy. The dress may thus be made to look as good the second year as the first.

Pelisses for babies are made and trimmed in just the same way. Little girls and small boys wear sashes with them, either of rich broad ribbon, or of sarsenet. If the latter, half the width of the sarsenet is quite ample for the bows and streamers. Boys of three or four years old wear handsome silk girdles more frequently than sashes. Frocks are trimmed with the same kind of work as pelisses, only the pattern is invariably a handsome Vandyke. Usually the bottom of the skirt is edged with work, above which, alternate tucks and insertion are placed, quite up to the waist. We will shortly give a pretty pattern for a child's dress. Sashes for in-doors are frequently worn in the Scotch scarf style, over the left shoulder, and under the right arm, the bows and streamers being fastened in front at the right side. This style is very pretty for any but very young children. Coloured dresses, in *de laine*, or any similar material, are worn braided as represented in the engraving. The body made in folds, *en*

cœur, and scalloped epaulettes and sleeves trimmed in a running pattern with braid.

Feathers are almost universally worn; for children in arms, they are placed so as to droop on the *left* side, as being most convenient for the nurse. Otherwise, they are placed on either side, and very frequently two handsome ostrich plumes are fastened by a band of ribbon in front of the hat, one falling on each side, so as nearly to surround the crown.

(*Continued at p.* 288.)

DOMESTIC ENDEARMENTS.—It is held to be a sure sign of a mind not poised as it ought to be, if it be insensible to the pleasures of home, to the little joys and endearments of a family, to the affection of relations, to the fidelity of domestics. Next to being well with his own conscience, the friendship and attachment of a man's family and dependents seems to me one of the most comfortable circumstances of his lot. His situation, with regard to either, forms that sort of bosom comfort or disquiet that sticks close to him at all times and seasons, and which, though he may now and then forget it, amidst the bustle of public or the hurry of active life, will resume its place in his thoughts, and its permanent effects on his happiness, at every pause of ambition or of business.

LADIES' SHOES.—If shoes were constructed of the shape of the human foot, neither too large nor too small, and making an equal pressure everywhere, corns and bunions of the feet would never exist. But, unfortunately, shoes are seldom made after this fashion; and in ladies' shoes especially there are generally two signal defects—first, the extremity of the shoe is much too narrow for that part of the foot (namely, the toes) which it is to contain; and secondly, for displaying as much of the foot as possible, the whole of the tarsus and metatarsus is left uncovered, and the pressure of the shoe in front is thrown entirely upon the toes. The toes are thus first squeezed against each other, and then pushed out of their natural position; and thus it is that corns of the feet are generated.

TIGER-LILY MAT PATTERN, BY MRS. PULLAN.

THE WORK-TABLE FRIEND.

TIGER-LILY LAMP MAT.

Materials.—3 yards of crochet-cord; 1 skein maize crochet-silk; a little of each of 3 shades of green crystal wool; 1 skein plain light green ditto; 5 shades of scarlet (4 skeins of each of the two lightest); 3 skeins white; a yard of scarlet and green chenille; and a little dark crystal cord. Also some green twilled calico, card-board, and a little wire.

WITH the darkest scarlet wool cover the end of the cord, and close it into a round. Work one round more.

2nd Round.—(Same scarlet, and green.) + 3 green, 3 scarlet, + 7 times in the round.

3rd Round.—(Same colours.) + 5 green on 3, 3 scarlet, + 7 times

4th Round.—(Next scarlet, and green) + 7 green on 5, 3 scarlet on scarlet, + 7 times.

5th Round.—(Next scarlet, and silk.) + 4 silk, 1 long silk taken on centre of 5 green in third round, 4 more silk (all 9 on 7 green), 5 scarlet on 3, + 7 times.

6th Round.—(Next scarlet, and silk.) + 4 silk on centre 3 of 9, and all the space between closely covered with scarlet. + 7 times.

7th Round.—(Lightest scarlet, and silk.) In this round a single long stitch is taken with the silk, on the centre of the 3 scarlet in the third round, and all the rest of the round is wool. Fasten off the cord.

With the darkest scarlet, and a coarse hook, do a round thus: + 1 Dc, 1 Ch, miss 1, +

8

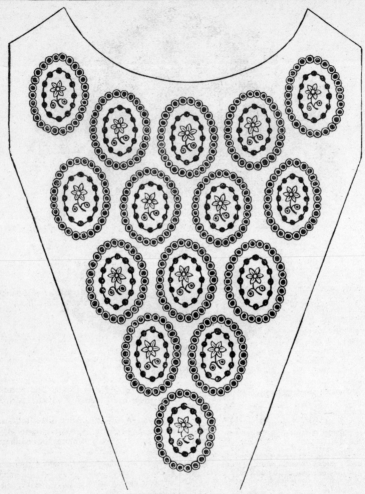

MEDALLION CHEMISETTE, BY MRS. PULLAN.

2nd Round.—+ 1 Dc under chain, 1 chain all round.

Cut a round of card-board 3 inches in diameter larger than the mat. Cover it on both sides with the calico, run together at the edge; tack the wool-work down in the centre, so that there is a margin of 1½ inch

all round. On this margin the flowers are sewed.

THE FLOWERS.—These are six in number, three white and three scarlet. All are made exactly alike. Make a chain of 16 stitches with the white wool. Cut a piece of wire four inches long; hold it in, and

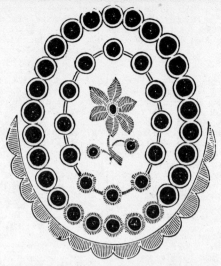

MEDALLION COLLAR PATTERN, BY MRS. PULLAN.

work on one side of the chain thus : miss 1, 1 slip, 1 Sc, 1 Sdc, 9 Dc, 1 Sdc, 1 Sc, 7 Sc ; bend the wire down the other side of the chain—2 more Sc in the same stitch, 1 Sc in the first on the other side of the chain, 1 Sdc, 9 Dc, 1 Sdc, 1 Sc, 1 slip. Twist the ends of the wire, with those of wool, together, and for each flower make 5 petals. For the scarlet, one side of the petal is done with the lightest shade, the other with the next to it. Some ends of the crystal cord, and four pieces of chenille, each an inch long, are fastened in the centre of each flower. The green chenille is put in the scarlet flowers, and scarlet in the white.

THE LEAVES.—18 are to be made, 6 in each shade of the crystal wool. Cut 18 pieces of wire, each five inches long. Make a chain of 18 stitches. Hold in the wire even with the chain, on which work (missing the first stitch) 1 slip, 1 Sc, 1 Sdc, 11 Dc, 1 Sdc, 1 Sc. In the stitch at the point do 4 Sc, bending the wire down the other side of the chain ; do 1 Sc, 1 Sdc, 11 Dc, 1 Sdc, 1 Sc, 1 slip. Fasten off as for the petals.

Sew the flowers, each with three leaves,

at equal distances on the border of the mat, so as completely to conceal the calico.

MEDALLION CHEMISETTE AND COLLAR.

Materials.—French muslin, with Messrs. W. Evans and Co.'s royal embroidery cotton, Nos. 40 and 60.

WE have selected the accompanying design for the readers of our TREASURES, because, being able to give one perfect pattern from which the whole can be drawn, it will be found particularly useful to those of our friends who are too far from large towns to have many facilities for obtaining novelties.

The medallion style (of which this is a specimen) is just now extremely fashionable in Paris, and is worked in two ways, suitable either for the novice or the practised needlewoman. The medallion itself is always of rather a solid, heavy character, the sprig within being in satin-stitch instead of broderie ; but the spaces between the medallions, both in the chemisette and the collar, are either left of the plain muslin, or worked in bars, with the muslin between them cut

away. The former effect will be seen in
our engraving. The latter has the appearance of Irish guipure, the ground looking
like that of some of our specimens of point
lace.

The present design can be worked in
either manner.

In order to draw the pattern, first cut
out the collar and front of the habit-shirt
in muslin (leaving ample margins); then,
in the latter, mark with a pencil the portion you wish worked. Cut out a piece of
tracing-paper the size of the collar and of
the embroidered part of the habit-shirt, and
copy off the full-sized medallion, which we
give, on a separate piece. Lay this under
the tracing-paper, to draw the centre of
the five medallions round the neck. When
this is traced, shift the pattern for the neck,
and so on till all are completed. The collar
is to be drawn in the same way, beginning
with the centre.

From the pattern thus prepared, any
number of collars may be traced on the
muslin with a taper brush or soft quill,
dipped in a solution of indigo and gum-
water.

The outer circle of holes in the medallion is done in button-hole stitch, with
No. 40 cotton; the inner ones are simply
sewed over with the same. The petals and
stem of the flower in satin stitch, with
No. 60; the eyelet holes with the same
cotton, overcast. The scallop is in graduated overcast stitch, with No. 40. Should
the ground between the medallions be
barred, the bars must be done in the irregular way seen in the mousquetaire collar,
given in a subsequent part of this work.
They must be traced, closely covered with
button-hole stitch, and then the spaces between them cut out.

KNITTED EDGING FOR DRAWERS.

Materials.—The Boar's-head Crochet Cotton,
No. 12, 16, or 20 of Messrs. W. Evans and Co.;
needles to correspond.

CAST on 15 stitches, and do one plain row.

1st Pattern Row.—Knit 3, make 1, knit
2 together, knit 3, make 2, knit 2 together,
make 2, knit 2 together, make 2, knit 2
together, knit 1.

2nd Row.—Knit 3, purl 1, knit 2, purl 1,
knit 2, purl 1, knit 5, make 1, knit 2 together knit 1.

3rd Row.—Knit 3, make 1, knit 2 together, knit to the end of the row.

4th Row.—Knit 2, make 2, knit 2 together, make 4, knit 3 together, knit 1, knit
2 together, make 2, knit 2 together, knit 3,
make 1, knit 2 together, knit 1.

5th Row.—Knit 3, make 1, knit 2 together, knit 3, purl 1, knit 4, purl 1, knit 1,
purl 1, knit 2, purl 1, knit 2.

6th Row.—Knit 18, make 1, knit 2 together, knit 1.

7th Row.—Knit 3, make 1, knit 2 together, knit 3, make 2, knit 4 together, +
make 2, knit 2 together, + 4 times, knit 1.

8th Row.—Knit 3, purl 1, + knit 2,
purl 1, + 4 times, knit 5, make 1, knit 2
together, knit 1.

9th Row.—Knit 3, make 1, knit 2 together, knit to the end.

12th Row.—Cast off 8, knit 2 together,
knit 6, knit 2 together, knit 3, make 1,
knit 2 together, knit 1.

THE PRAYERS OF CHILDREN. — The
practice, I believe, is universal, among all
parents who feel it to be their duty to
bring up their children in the " nurture
and admonition of the Lord," to begin as
early as possible to lead them to unite in
the prayers which are made with them,
and also to pray for themselves. This is
regarded as an essential element of their
religious training; while an abundant experience shews what a mighty influence it
has upon their future religious develop-
ment and character. The recollection of
the times and circumstances when the pious
mother prayed with her little one, and
taught him how to offer up his own prayer,
and of the morning and evening devotions
of the family circle where he heard the
voice of a venerated father supplicating the
throne of grace, clings to his memory through
all the changing scenes of life, and often
in the waywardness or recklessness of youth,
and the irreligious worldly-mindedness of
manhood, rouses his conscience to give its
faithful admonitions, and produces the most
salutary and hopeful impressions upon his
heart. How many it has rescued from
ruin! How many it has been the means,
under Divine grace, of turning from the
broad way of destruction into the path of
life!—*Rev. T. H. Gallaudet*

JEWELLED DESSERT MAT, BY MRS. PULLAN.

THE WORK-TABLE FRIEND.

JEWELLED DESSERT MAT.

Materials.—Messrs. W. Evans & Co.'s white of ingrain pink boar's-head crochet cotton, No. 10, 2 reels ; and 1 oz. emerald beads, No. 2.

BEGIN by threading all the beads on the cotton. Make a chain of four stitches, and close it into a round.

1st Round.—+ 1 Ch, 1 Sc on one of 4 Ch, 1 Ch + 4 times.

2nd Round.—+ 1 Ch. 3 Sc, coming on 1 Sc, and a chain at each side, 1 Ch + 4 times.

On referring to the engraving, two diagonal lines, crossing in the centre of the mat, and dividing it into 4 parts, will be seen. All the increasing is done by making *two chains* at each of these corners, *in every round of the mat,* thus increasing 8 stitches in the entire round. For the sake of making the directions clear, we give these chains at the beginning and end of every quarter. The pattern is formed entirely of beads.

3rd Round.—+ 1 Ch, 5 Sc, 1 Ch + 4 times.

4th Round.—+ 1 Ch, 7 Sc, 1 Ch + 4 times.

5th Round.—+ 1 Ch, 9 Sc, 1 Ch + 4 times.

6th Round.—+ 1 Ch, 11 Sc, 1 Ch + 4 time.

7th Round.—+ 1 Ch, 1 cotton, 2 beads, 1 cotton, 1 bead, 3 cottons, 1 bead, 1 cotton, 2 beads, 1 cotton, 1 Ch + 4 times.

8th Round.—+ 1 Ch, 2 cotton, 5 beads, 1 cotton, 5 beads, 2 cotton, 1 Ch + 4 times.

9th Round.—+ 1 Ch, 4 cotton, 1 bead, 1 cotton, 2 beads, 1 cotton, 2 beads, 1 cotton, 1 bead, 4 cotton, 1 Ch + 4 times.

10th Round.—+ 1 Ch, 4 cotton, 3 beads, 1 cotton, 3 beads, 1 cotton, 3 beads, 4 cotton, 1 Ch + 4 times.

11th Round.—+ 1 Ch, 6 cotton, 4 beads, 1 c, 4 beads, 6 c, 1 Ch + 4 times.

12th Round.—+ 1 Ch, 9 c, 1 b, 1 c, 1 b, 1 c, 1 b, 9 c, 1 Ch + 4 times.

13th Round.—+ 1 Ch, 8 c, 4 b, 1 c, 4 b, 8 c, 1 Ch + 4 times.

14th Round.—+ 1 Ch, 8 c, 3 b, 1 c, 3 b, 1 c, 3 b, 8 c, 1 Ch + 4 times.

15th Round.—+ 1 Ch, 10 c, 1 b, 1 c, 2 b, 1 c, 2 b, 1 c, 1 b, 10 c, 1 Ch + 4 times.

16th Round.—+ 1 ch, 10 c, 5 b, 1 c, 5 b, 10 c, 1 Ch + 4 times.

17th Round.—+ 1 ch, 11 c, 2 b, 1 c, 1 b, 3 c, 1 b, 1 c, 2 b, 11 c, 1 Ch + 4 times.

18th Round.—+ 1 Ch, 35 c, 1 Ch + 4 times.

19th Round.—+ 1 Ch, 1 b, 3 c, 1 b, 13 c, 1 b, 4 c, 1 b, 13 c, 1 Ch + 4 times.

20th Round.—+ 1 Ch, 2 b, 1 c, 3 b, 10 c, 1 b, 1 c, 2 b, 1 c, 4 b, 14 c, 1 bead on a chain stitch + 4 times.

21st Round.—+ 1 Ch, 6 b, 2 c, 2 b, 1 c, 1 b, 4 c, 2 b, 1 c, 6 b, 1 c, 2 b, 2 c, 1 b, 4 c, 2 b, 1 Ch + 4 times.

22nd Round.—+ 1 bead on chain, 3 b, 2 c, 1 b, 2 c, 1 b, 2 c, 1 b, 3 c, 1 b, 1 c, 5 b, 2 c, 1 b, 5 c, 1 b, 2 c, 2 b, 5 ＼ 2 b, 1 c, 1 bead on chain + 4 times.

23rd Round.—+ 1 Ch, 1 c, 1 b, 2 c, 4 b, 1 c, 1 b, 5 c, 4 b, 1 c, 1 b, 2 c, 4 b, 4 c, 1 b, 7 c, 4 b, 2 c, 1 Ch + 4 times.

24th Round.—+ 1 Ch, 4 c, 4 b, 3 c, 1 b, 2 c, 1 b, 1 c, 4 b, 3 c, 4 b, 6 c, 1 b, 8 c, 5 b, 1 Ch + 4 times.

25th Round.—+ 1 Ch, 2 c, 5 b, 4 c, 2 b, 2 c, 4 b, 1 c, 1 b, 1 c, 4 b, 8 c, 3 b, 5 c, 4 b, 2 c, 1 b, 1 Ch + 4 times.

26th Round.—+ 1 Ch, 4 c, 4 b, 2 c, 2 b, 4 c, 2 b, 1 c, 1 b, 4 c, 4 b, 4 c, 3 b, 8 c, 2 b, 1 c, 1 b, 4 c, 1 Ch + 4 times.

27th Round.—+ 1 Ch, 2 c, 6 b, 2 c, 1 b, 5 c, 3 b, 3 c, 6 b, 4 c, 1 b, 12 c, 3 b, 5 c, 1 Ch + 4 times.

28th Round.—+ 1 Ch, 1 c, 5 b, 3 c, 6 b, 3 c, 2 b, 1 c, 5 b, 3 c, 6 b, 13 c, 3 b, 4 c, 1 Ch + 4 times.

29th Round.—+ 1 Ch, 4 c, 4 b, 1 c, 1 b, 4 c, 4 b, 1 c, 1 b, 4 c, 4 b, 2 c, 1 b, 4 c, 5 b, 11 c, 1 b, 5 c, 1 Ch + 4 times.

30th Round.—+ 1 Ch, 5 b, 5 c, 2 b, 1 c, 5 b, 3 c, 6 b, 4 c, 2 b, 2 c, 5 b, 13 c, 6 b, 1 Ch + 4 times.

31st Round.—+ 1 Ch, 3 c, 1 b, 6 c, 3 b, 3 c, 6 b, 2 c, 1 b, 6 c, 3 b, 4 c, 7 b, 11 c, 1 b, 4 c, 1 Ch + 4 times.

32nd Round.—+ 1 Ch, 2 c, 2 b, 8 c, 2 b, 1 c, 1 b, 4 c, 4 b, 2 c, 2 b, 5 c, 2 b, 1 c, 1 b, 5 c, 5 b, 8 c, 6 c, 1 Ch + 4 times.

33rd Round.—+ 1 Ch, 1 c, 2 b, 10 c, 4 b, 1 c, 1 b, 1 c, 4 b, 5 c, 2 b, 3 c, 4 b,

1 c, 1 b, 2 c, 5 b, 7 c, 2 b, 9 c, 1 Ch + 4 times.

34th Round.—+ 1 Ch, 3 c, 1 b, 10 c, 1 b, 1 c, 4 b, 3 c, 4 b, 3 c, 1 b, 4 c, 1 b, 1 c, 4 b, 4 c, 5 b, 6 c, 1 b, 10 c, 1 Ch + 4 times.

35th Round.—+ 1 Ch, 5 c, 2 b, 10 c, 4 b, 1 c, 1 b, 2 c, 4 b, 1 c, 1 b, 7 c, 4 b, 1 c, 1 b, 3 c, 5 b, 6 c, 2 b, 9 c, 1 Ch + 4 times.

36th Round.— + 1 Ch, 7 c, 1 b, 2 c, 3 b, 6 c, 1 b, 1 c, 4 b, 3 c, 1 b, 2 c, 1 b, 2 c, 2 b, 4 c, 1 b, 1 c, 5 b, 3 c, 1 b, 9 c, 1 b, 2 c, 3 b, 5 c, 1 Ch + 4 times.

37th Round.—+ 1 Ch, 9 c, 2 b, 3 c, 1 b, 7 c, 2 b, 1 c, 6 b, 2 c, 2 b, 2 c, 1 b, 5 c, 2 b, 1 c, 7 b, 9 c, 2 b, 3 c, 1 b, 5 c, 1 Ch + 4 times.

38th Round.—+ 1 Ch, 15 c, 1 b, 8 c, 1 b, 1 c, 2 b, 1 c, 4 b, 5 c, 1 b, 6 c, 1 b, 1 c, 2 b, 1 c, 5 b, 13 c, 1 b, 6 c, 1 Ch + 4 times.

39th Round.—+ 1 Ch, 14 c, 2 b, 12 c, 1 b, 4 c, 1 b, 4 c, 1 b, 10 c, 1 b, 5 c, 1 b, 11 c, 2 b, 8 c, 1 Ch + 4 times.

40th Round.—All cotton, increasing as usual at the corners.

41st Round.—A bead on every stitch.

BORDER, in which a bead is dropped in *every* stitch, whether Ch, Sc, or Dc.

1st Round.—+ 1 s, 5 Ch, miss 4 + all round, except at corners, when miss 2.

2nd Round.—5 Dc on centre of 5 Ch, + 4 Ch, 1 Sc on centre of next 5 Ch, 4 Ch, 5 Dc on centre of next 5 Ch + all round.

————

LADY'S NIGHT-CAP, IN CROCHET.

Materials. — 6 reels of Messrs. Evans and Co.'s Boar's-head Crochet Cotton, No. 24.

THIS is a very pretty pattern for a lady's night-cap, and one which will be found equally comfortable and becoming.

THE CROWN.—Make a chain of 73 stitches.

1st Row.—Miss 1, 2 Sc, + 4 Ch, miss 3, 1 Dc, 4 Ch, miss 3, 3 Sc, + 6 times. The seventh time end with 1 Sc, 1 Dc, 1 Tc. Turn the work.

2nd Row.—3 Ch, Dc on the Dc, 4 Ch, + 2 Sc, under the first chain of 4, 1 Sc on 1 Dc, 2 Sc, under the next chain of 4, 7 Ch, + 7 times. Dc on the 1st chain of previous

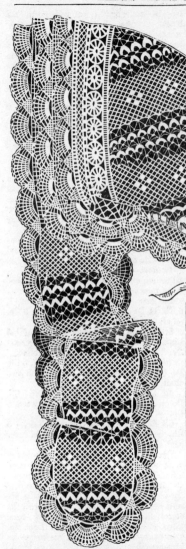

the + is merely to increase gradually the width of the crown.

3rd Row.—Turn the work. 3 Ch, Dc on the Tc ; 4 Ch, 2 Sc under Ch, 1 Sc on Dc, 2 Sc under Ch, + 6 Ch, Dc on centre of 5 Sc, 4 Ch, 3 Sc under chain of 7 + to the end, at which increase a little.

Repeat the 2nd and 3rd rows twice more, increasing a little at the end of every row, and then do the 2nd row only, still increasing. Observe the Tc stitches always come exactly over each other.

Next Row (9th).—7 Ch, 5 Dc under the 4 Ch, 3 Sc over Sc, + 10 Dc under chain, 3 Sc on centre of 5 + to the end. Finish to correspond with the beginning.

10th Row.—Turn the work. 3 Ch, miss none, 4 Sc on nearest 4 Dc, + 6 Ch, 3 Sc on centre 3 of 10 Dc +. Repeat to the end. After the last 3 Sc, 4 Ch, Sc on 4th of 7 Ch at the beginning of the last row.

11*th* like 3*rd*, but begin with 3 Sc under Ch of 4. Continue increasing till further orders.

12*th* like 2*nd*.

13*th* like 9*th*.

14*th* like 10*th*.

15*th* like 3*rd*.   16*th* like 2*nd*.

17*th*.—5 Ch, Sc under Ch, 5 Ch, miss 3, 1 Sc, + 5 Ch, Sc under Ch, 5 Ch, Sc on 1st Sc, 5 Ch, Sc on last Sc, + to the end. Do 2 Sc (with a chain of 5 between) at the end of the row.

18*th*.—+ 5 Ch, Sc under Ch + repeat to the end, doing it twice in the last stitch.

19*th*, 20*th*, like 18*th*.

21*st*.—+ 5 Ch, Sc under chain + 4 times *, 5 Dc on Sc of last row, Sc under the next chain † 5 Ch, Sc under Ch † 7 times * Repeat between the stars to the end. Increase as usual.

22*nd* like 18*th*. When you come to the 5 Dc, do a Sc under the centre one, instead of under the chain as in the other parts.

row, 4 Ch, Tc on the missed stitch at the beginning of first row.   The work after

23rd like 21st, with this difference, 5 Dc are done on the Sc *before* that worked on the centre of 5, then Sc under chain, 5 Ch, Sc under centre of next chain, and 5 more Dc on the next Sc. 2 spots are thus made, with an interval of 5 Ch and 2 Sc between them.

24th like 22nd.

25th.—The spot here occurs exactly over that in the 21st row. As each row is increased at the end, there will therefore be more than 4 repetitions of the chain before the first spot occurs. The spots in rows 21, 23, and 25 now form a diamond.

Do five rows more like 18th.

31st like 3rd, 32nd like 2nd. Cease increasing. 33rd like 3rd, 34th like 2nd.

Repeat from the 9th to the 34th rows again, decreasing at the end of every row after the repetition of the 16th. Do again as far as the 14th, having gradually lessened the size till you end with nearly the same number of stitches you began with. This completes the crown.

THE LAPPETS.—These are begun like the crown, in a chain 2 inches long. In the course of the first 14 rows they are increased in width to 4 inches. About a quarter of a yard is done of this width, after which there is a gradual decrease to the width of 3 inches. When a length of nearly half a yard is done, add an inch extra by making a chain of that length *at one edge of the lappet*, and do 12 rows more, gradually increasing another inch on the same side.

Observe that in the two lappets the increase must take place on opposite sides.

NECK-PIECE. — Make a chain of 85 stitches, miss 4, 1 Dc, + 3 Ch, miss 4, 1 Dc +, repeat to the end.

2nd and 6 following rows, + 5 Ch, Sc under Ch +, repeat to the end.

Sew the two ends of this piece with the foundation chain at the top to the two lappets.

FRONT.—45 Ch, miss 1 Sc on 2nd + 5 Ch, miss 3, Sc on 4th + to the end. 2nd and following rows + 5 Ch, Sc under chain of last row +, repeat to the end. Do a piece long enough to go from ear to ear, the quantity depending on whether, or not, the wearer likes the cap to come low over the ears or not. A piece 12 inches in length will probably suit most people. Now sew this to the lappets from the straight edge about two inches. The

lappets and head-piece row form the front. At the other edge do on the last worked piece thus: Fasten the thread on the nearest loop of the lappet, and do 4 Dc on it. Then the same on every loop of that edge of the head-piece, and on the nearest loop of the other lappet.

THE WHEELS.—8 Ch, form it into a round, under which do 24 Dc.

2nd round.—+ 2 Dc under one stitch, 2 Ch, miss one stitch + 12 times.

3rd.—Sc in every stitch.

Do as many of these as will go from one end to the other of the last row, to which they must be sewed, close enough to touch. They must also be sewed together.

On the opposite edge of the wheels, fasten on to the lappet 5 Ch, 7 Sc on a wheel + 5 Ch, 7 Sc on next wheel + to the end. Finish with 5 chains, and fasten on to the other lappet. Do a Dc stitch on every stitch of this row.

THE BORDER.—To be worked in one continuous line round the front, lappets, and neck. Dc on every stitch, all round.

1st Row.— + 11 Sc, 17 Ch, miss 11, + all round, except at the ends of the lappets, when miss 7 only.

2nd Row.— + 9 Sc over centre 9 of 11, 5 Ch, 11 Dc on centre 11 of 17 Ch, 5 Ch, + all round.

3rd Row.— + 7 Sc over centre 7 of 9, 5 Ch, Dc after 1st Dc, * 1 Ch, Dc after next Dc, * 8 times, 5 Ch, + repeat all round.

4th Row.— + 5 Sc on centre 5 of 7, 5 Ch, Dc on every Dc of last round, with two chain between, 5 Ch.

5th Row.— + 3 Sc on centre 3 of 5, 5 Ch, Dc on every Dc, with 3 chain between, 5 Ch, + all round.

6th Row.— + Sc on centre of 3 Sc, * 5 Ch, Sc under Ch, * 10 times, 5 Ch, * repeat all round.

Two other frills which trim the front are done in precisely the same manner, but on a foundation made of a chain of the requisite length, on which is worked one row of open square crochet. These two frills are sewed on with the needle. As seen in the engraving, they are carried round the ears. Bows of ribbon may be added if desired. The neck is drawn in with narrow white sarsenet ribbon.

———◆———

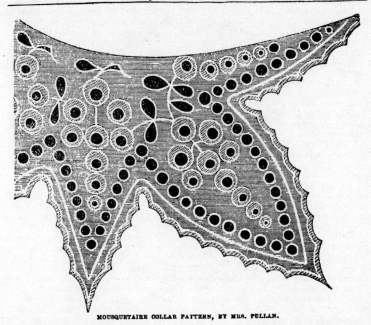

MOUSQUETAIRE COLLAR PATTERN, BY MRS. PULLAN.

THE WORK-TABLE FRIEND.

MOUSQUETAIRE COLLAR.

Materials.—French Muslin, and Messrs. W. Evans & Co's. Royal Embroidery Cotton, No. 50.

THIS collar has the merit of being very rapidly and easily worked, as well as very effective when done. For many of our friends, it will be found quite as large as is desirable, and it is a design which can very easily be enlarged. When marked on the muslin, with a piece of *toile ciré* underneath, every part is to be traced.

The white line between the eyelet-holes and the edge is simply sewed over; the edge itself is done in raised button-hole stitch, the stitches being all of an equal length, not graduated. The grapes are done in graduated overcast; the other parts are simply sewed over.

All those parts which are quite black in the engraving, are either cut out, or pierced with a stiletto. There is no satin stitch in this collar.

JEWELLED DOYLEYS.

THE TURQUOISE.

Materials.—1 reel of Messrs. W. Evans & Co's Boar's Head Crochet Cotton No. 16, and 1 oz. of Turquoise beads, No. 2.

HAVING threaded all the beads on the cotton, make a chain of eight, close it with a round, and work 1 Sc on every stitch, with one chain between.

2nd Round.—+ 2 Sc, 1 Ch, miss none, + 8 times in the round.

3rd Round.—+ 3 Sc, 1 Ch, miss none, + 8 times.

4th Round.—+ 4 Sc, 1 Ch, miss none, + 8 times.

5th Round.—+ 5 Sc, 1 Ch, miss none, + 8 times.

6th Round.—+ 6 Sc, 1 Ch, miss none, + 8 times.

7th Round.—+ 7 Sc, 1 Ch, miss none, + 8 times.

8th Round.—+ 8 Sc, 1 Ch, miss none, + 8 times.

TURQUOISE DOYLEY PATTERN, BY MRS. PULLAN.

9th Round.—+ 9 Sc, with a bead on every one, 1 Ch, + 8 times.

10th Round.—2 cotton, + 5 Sc, beads, 2 cotton, 1 bead, 2 cotton, + 8 times.

11th Round.—+ 3 cotton, 3 beads (on centre 3 of 5), 3 cotton, increasing one, 3 beads, the second coming over 1 bead, + 8 times.

Observe that the *increasing* in every round takes place on the cotton stitches only, and not by working 2 in 1, but by making a chain stitch.

12th Round.—+ 4 cotton, 1 bead (on centre of 3), 3 cotton, 5 beads (over 3 and a cotton on each side), + 8 times.

13th Round.—4 cotton, + 1 bead (over 1) 3 cotton (over 2), 3 beads, 1 cotton on centre of 5 beads, 3 beads, 3 cotton, + 8 times.

14th Round.—+ 1 bead over 1, 3 cotton over 2, 3 beads, 4 cotton (over 1 cotton and a bead on each side), 3 beads, 3 cotton, + 8 times.

15th Round.—+ 1 bead on 1, 3 cotton, 4 beads, 3 cotton (over 2), 4 beads, 3 cotton, + 8 times.

16th Round.—+ 1 bead on 1, 4 cotton on 3, 11 beads, 3 cotton + 7 times. The 8th time, 3 cotton on 2.

17th Round.—+ 3 beads (the second over 1 bead), 4 cotton, 9 beads (on centre 9 of 11), 4 cotton, + 8 times.

18th Round.—+ 5 beads (on 3, and a cotton stitch on each side), 4 cotton, 7 beads (on centre 7 of 9), 4 cotton, + 7 times. The 8th time 5 cotton at the end.

19th Round.— + 5 beads over 5, 5 cotton, 5 beads on centre 5 of 7, 5 cotton, + 7 times. The eighth time, 5 beads, 5 cotton, 5 beads on centre of 7.

20th Round.—+ 3 cotton, 1 bead on centre of 5 cotton, 3 cotton, 3 beads on centre of 5, + all round.

21st Round.—+ 3 cotton, 3 beads (the 2nd on 1 bead, 3 cotton, 1 bead on centre of 3, + 16 times.

22nd Round.—4 cotton over 3, + 5 beads, (over 3, and a cotton at each side), 6 cotton (making 1), + 16 times.

23rd Round.—+ 5 beads over 5, 2 cotton, 2 beads, 2 cotton, 5 beads over 5, 7 cotton over 6, + 8 times.

24th Round.—1 cotton, + 3 beads (on

centre 3 of 5), 2 cotton, 4 beads, 2 cotton, 3 beads (on centre 3 of 5), 4 cotton, 1 bead on centre of 7 cotton, 4 cotton, + 8 times.

25th Round.—1 cotton, + 1 bead on centre of 3, 3 cotton, 4 beads on 4, 4 cotton (making one), 1 bead on centre of 3, 4 cotton, 3 beads (the second over 1), 4 cotton, + 8 times.

26th Round.—4 cotton, over 1 bead and 2 cotton, + 2 beads, 2 cotton on centre 2 of 4 beads, 2 beads, 7 cotton, 5 beads, over 3 and a cotton at each side, 7 cotton + 8 times. The 8th end with 5 cotton only.

27th Round.—+ 4 beads, 2 cotton over 2, 4 beads, 5 cotton, 5 beads over 5, 5 cotton + 7 times. The 8th end with 3 cotton.

28th Round.—+ 3 beads, 2 cotton, 4 beads, 2 cotton, 3 beads, 4 cotton, 3 beads on centre 3 of 5, 4 cotton + 8 times.

29th Round.—3 beads on 3, 2 cotton on 1, + 6 beads, 4 cotton making 1, 3 beads, 3 cotton, 1 bead on centre of 3, 3 cotton, 3 beads, 4 cotton on 3, + 7 times. The 8th time end with 3 cotton on 2.

30th Round.—+ 1 bead, 2 cotton, 2 beads on centre 2 of 6, with a chain between, 2 cotton, 1 bead, 4 cotton, 4 beads, 3 cotton (the centre over 1 bead), 4 beads, 4 cotton, + 8 times.

31st Round.—+ 2 cotton, 5 beads (over 2, 1 Ch, and a cotton on each side), 5 cotton, 3 beads, 2 cotton, 3 beads, 2 cotton, 3 beads, 3 cotton, + 8 times.

32nd Round.—+ 1 cotton, 7 beads, 3 cotton, 3 beads, 2 cotton, 5 beads, 2 cotton, 3 beads, 2 cotton, + 8 times.

33rd Round.—+ 2 cotton, 5 beads (on centre 5 of 7, 8 cotton, 7 beads, 6 cotton) + 8 times.

34th Round.—+ 3 cotton, 3 beads on centre 3 of 5, 10 cotton, 5 beads, 7 cotton, + 8 times.

35th Round.—+ 5 cotton making 1, 1 bead on centre of 3, 12 cotton, 3 beads on centre 3 of 5, 8 cotton, + 8 times.

36th Round.—+ 5 cotton, 1 bead on 1, 14 cotton (making 1), 1 bead on centre of 3, 9 cotton, + 8 times.

Do one round of cotton only, and increase eight stitches in the round. Then a round with a bead on every stitch.

THE BORDER.—*1st Round.*—No beads. 1 Dc, + 3 Ch, Dc under the same stitch, Dc in the 4th from this. + all round.

2nd Round.—With beads on *every* stitch. + Sc on second of 3 Ch, 2 Ch, 5 Dc under the next chain, 2 chain. + all round.

EMBROIDERED SCREENS.

Materials.—Round frames and ivory handles; blue satin, white *chenille à broder*, pearls, and gold bullion and thread; blue fringe.

THIS pair of screens is a very suitable wedding gift, and can be rapidly and easily worked.

EMBROIDERED SCREEN.

The pattern being marked on the satin, the leaves are formed entirely of white chenille, worked in ordinary embroidery stitch; and the pearls, which are of various sizes, form the bunches of grapes. The tendrils are in gold bullion, and the fibres of the leaves in gold thread. When the pearls are put on, a thread of chenille may be carried entirely round them. They are to be mounted in the ordinary way, and either finished with a cord or a quilling of ribbon, with gold cord laid in the centre.

POINT-LACE UNDER-SLEEVE, BY MRS. PULLAN (*Page* 158.)

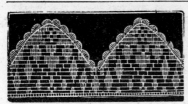

CROCHET LACE BORDER.

THE WORK-TABLE FRIEND.

HANDSOME CROCHET LACE.

Materials.—Cotton suitable for the material to be trimmed. The following will be requisite:— For toilet covers, or anti-macassars, Messrs. W. Evans and Co.'s Boar's Head Crochet Cotton, No. 12. For petticoats, the same make, No. 28; for children's drawers, dresses, &c., No. 24 or 30. With ordinary workers No. 24 cotton will make an edge two inches wide at the point of the Vandyke.

MAKE a foundation chain of any length required, but counting such a number of stitches as may be divided by 65.

(If this border is to be worked round an anti-macassar or other article in crochet, no foundation chain will be required.)

1st Row.—+1 Dc, 1 Ch, miss 1 + to the end.

2nd Row.—+ 2 Dc, 3 Ch, miss 3, 1 Dc, 3 Ch, miss 3, 1 Dc, 5 Ch, miss 5, 4 Dc, 6 Ch, miss 6, 1 Dc, 6 Ch, miss 6, 2 Dc, 6 Ch, miss 6, 1 Dc, 6 Ch, miss 6, 4 Dc, 5 Ch, miss 5, 1 Dc, 3 Ch, miss 3, 1 Dc, 3 Ch, miss 3, 1 Dc, + repeat to the end. In future rows, to prevent repetition, it is to be understood that as many stitches are always missed as there are chains.

3rd Row.—+ 3 Dc, 5 Ch, 3 Dc, 5 Ch, 2 Dc, + 3 times, 2 Ch, † 2 Dc, 5 Ch, † 3 times. 3 Dc, 5 Ch, 2 Dc, + to the end.

4th Row.—+ 4 Dc, 3 Ch, 5 Dc, 10 Ch, 4 Dc, 6 Ch, 2 Dc (over 2 Ch, in last row), 6 Ch, 4 Dc, 10 Ch, 5 Dc, 3 Ch, 3 Dc, + to the end.

5th Row.—+ 3 Dc, 3 Ch, 7 Dc, 4 Ch, 1 Dc, 5 Ch, 2 Dc, 6 Ch, 4 Dc, 6 Ch, 2 Dc, 5 Ch, 1 Dc, 4 Ch, 7 Dc, 3 Ch, 2 Dc, + to the end.

6th Row.—+ 2 Dc, 5 Ch, 5 Dc, 4 Ch, 3 Dc, 7 Dc, 1 Dc, 6 Ch, 2 Dc, 6 Ch, 1 Dc, 7 Ch, 3 Dc, 4 Ch, 5 Dc, 5 Ch, 1 Dc, + to the end.

7th Row.—+ 1 Dc, 2 Ch, 3 Dc, 2 Ch, 3 Dc, 4 Ch, 5 Dc, 8 Ch, 1 Dc, 8 Ch, 1 Dc, 8 Ch, 5 Dc, 4 Ch, 3 Dc, 2 Ch, 3 Dc, 2 Ch, + to the end.

8th Row.—+ 6 Dc, 3 Ch, 3 Dc, 4 Ch, 7 Dc, 4 Ch, 1 Dc, 6 Ch, 2 Dc, 6 Ch, 1 Dc, 4 Ch, 7 Dc, 4 Ch, 3 Dc, 3 Ch, 5 Dc, + to the end.

9th Row.—This row is the first of the point. Each is done separately, the ends being worked in. Begin on the 2nd Dc of last row, with a slip stitch. 1 more slip, 1 Sc, 2 Dc, 1 Ch, 3 Dc, 5 Ch, 5 Dc, 3 Ch, 1 Dc, 6 Ch, 6 Dc (over 2, and 2 Ch, at each side), 6 Ch, 1 Dc, 3 Ch, 5 Dc, 5 Ch, 3 Dc, 1 Ch, 2 Dc, 1 Sc, 2 slip.

10th Row.—Slip on 1st Dc of last row. 1 slip, 1 Sc (on Ch), 3 Dc, 6 Ch, 3 ?t. 3 Ch, 1 Dc, 5 Ch, 10 Dc (on 6 and 2 Ch at each side), 5 Ch, 1 Dc, 3 Ch, 3 Dc, 6 Ch, 3 Dc, 1 Sc, 2 slip.

11th Row.—Slip on Sc, 1 Sc, 2 Dc, 1 Ch, 3 Dc, 3 Ch, 1 Dc, 2 Ch, 4 Dc, 4 Ch, 10 Dc (on 10), 4 Ch, 4 Dc, 2 Ch, 1 Dc, 3 Ch, 3 Dc, 1 Ch, 2 Dc, 1 Sc, 1 slip.

12th Row.—Slip on 2nd Dc, 1 Sc on 1 Ch, 3 Dc, 3 Ch, 10 Dc (on 4 Dc and 3 Ch at each side), 4 Ch, 4 Dc (on 4 centre of 10), 4 Ch, 10 Dc, 3 Ch, 3 Dc, 1 Sc, 1 slip.

13th Row.—Slip on 1st of 3 Dc, 1 Sc, 1 Dc, 3 Ch, 10 Dc on 10, 2 Ch, 8 Dc (on 4 and 2 Ch at each side), 2 Ch, 10 Ch, 3 Ch, 1 Dc, 1 Sc, 1 slip.

14th Row.—1 slip on Sc of last row, 1 Sc, 4 Dc, 2 Ch, 4 Dc (on centre 4 of 10) 3 Ch, 5 Dc, 2 Ch, 5 Dc, 3 Ch, 4 Dc, 2 Ch, 4 Dc, 1 Sc, 1 slip.

15th Row.—Slip on 2nd of 4 Dc, 1 Sc, 14 Dc, 4 Ch (over 2 Ch and 1 Dc at each side), 14 Dc, 1 Sc, 1 slip.

16th Row.—Slip on 1st of 14 Dc, 1 Sc, 9 Dc, 4 Ch, 2 Dc (on centre 2 of 4 Ch, 4 Ch, 9 Dc), 1 Sc, 1 slip.

17th Row.—Slip on 2nd Dc, 1 Sc, 4 Dc, 4 Ch, 2 Dc, 2 Ch (over 2 Dc), 2 Dc, 4 Ch, 4 Dc, 1 Sc, 1 slip.

18th Row.—Slip on the 2nd Dc, 1 Sc, 4 Dc, 3 Ch, 2 Dc, 3 Ch, 4 Dc, 1 Sc, 1 slip.

19th Row.—Slip on 2nd Dc, 1 Sc, 4 Dc, 2 Ch, 4 Dc, 1 Sc, 1 slip.

20th Row.—Slip on 2nd Dc, 2 Sc, 2 Dc, 2 Sc, 1 slip. This forms the extreme point. When all are done, work round the whole of the Vandykes in Sc, then the following shell. + 1 slip, 1 Sc, 2 Dc in next, 2 Dc in next, 2 Dc in next, 1 Sc, + all round.

For round d'Oyleys this edge may be used, by missing *fewer* than the number of chain in the early rows. It is best to do the corners of antimacassars by working enough *chain* for one complete pattern at each corner, and then sewing it in full.

WORK-TABLE FOR JUVENILES;

OR, LITTLE MARY'S HALF-HOLIDAY.

(*Continued from p.* 267.)

"WELL, my dear, I am glad to see you ready for work again. I almost thought the temptation of joining your cousins in their pic-nic would have been too great to be resisted. And, of course, had you chosen so to employ a day which I considered as your own, I could not have been displeased at it."

"You are very kind, dear Mamma. And I should have liked very much to have gone out with my cousins; but I am very happy working by your side. And when I think of the pleasure of giving these things at Christmas, I feel I cannot relinquish it for any present enjoyment. Besides, I am to do something to-day for my aunt; and you remember, dear Mamma, how very kind she was to me when I was ill last year."

"I do indeed, Mary ; and I am glad you, too, have not forgotten it. Let not your gratitude be like that of too many people—what a very clever man once called *a lively sense of favours to come.*"

"I don't quite understand that, Mamma. How can we feel grateful for a kindness we have not yet experienced ?"

"It means, my dear girl, that we too frequently show attention and respect to those who have, as we think, the power of benefiting us in future, than to those from whom we have already received favours. Do you not remember some lines on this subject in your favourite 'Lady of the Lake?'"

"Oh, yes, Mamma. It is in the song when Fitz James leaves the island :—

"' Not faster yonder rowers' might
    Fling from their oars the spray,
Not faster yonder rippling bright
    That tracks the shallop's course in light
    Melts in the lake away, —
Than men from memory erase
    The benefits of former days.' "

"It is too true of the world in general. Let it not be so of ourselves. In denying yourself the little pleasure of going out, and devoting your time to the gratification of another, you are conquering any inclination to selfishness, and giving all the little

you can give, your time and your thoughts, to one who well deserves your affection. But we must to work if we would accomplish anything this afternoon. Here are all the materials for your watch-pockets. You will see what they are."

"Here are six yards of pink satin ribbon, about an inch wide, some pink sarsnet, some card board, black net, and plaited straw. What kind of straw is it, Mamma?"

"It is called straw-beading, and is employed in the same way that split straw was once used; but as it is flexible, and to be had in any length, it is much more easily worked. Besides the things you have mentioned, there is some pink sewing silk, and a little stiff muslin. Now you have all your materials complete, and I have only to show you how to use them. Begin by cutting out the shape for the back of the watch-pocket.

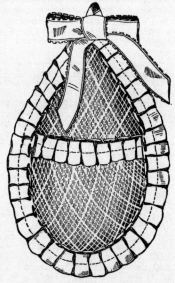

BACK OF A WATCH-POCKET.

Here is a drawing of it. It is 7 inches long, and 4½ in the widest part. Mark the depth of three inches from the bottom, and form this into a half round, then cut it into a point from the widest part to the top. The lower part, which is for the pocket, is thus three inches deep, and the top four inches. You will require two pieces of card-board of this shape and size, which must be covered on both sides with pink silk. Tack them together round the edges."

"These pieces are for the backs. Are the fronts of the pockets made of card-board, too?"

"No; you will use the stiff muslin for them. They must be in the half circle form, 3 inches deep, but 5½ inches wide at the top. They must also be covered with silk on both sides. Now cut out two pieces of black net, rather larger than the backs, and two more (also allowing for turnings in) for the fronts. Do you remark anything peculiar in the net?"

"It is like the imitation netting you brought from Paris, mamma; is it not? The holes are perfect diamonds, and much larger than in any of our English net."

"Yes, it is part of that I brought with me. Being so open, it is easy to slip the straw through it. Take the end of the straw, pass it under two threads and over three, in one line. Cut it off close to the edge of the net. Run in as many lines as you can in the same direction, but with intervals of four holes, five threads between them. Cross them with others in the same way, both straws passing under the *same* hole when they cross. All the four pieces of net must be worked in the same way, and then tacked on, to cover the silk on one side. Now sew the fronts to the backs. The ribbon trimming must now be prepared. It is to be quilled in the centre, in the way called *box* quilling; that is, one plait must be to the right, and the next to the left. Do enough for the top of each pocket separately, and put it on, then a length to go completely round. Finish each pocket with a knot of ribbon at the point, and a small loop to pin it to the bed."

"Do you know, Mamma, I was inclined to think you had not matched the sarsnet and ribbon well; the sarsnet looked so much the darker. Now they correspond perfectly. How is that?"

"You forget that the sarsnet is covered with net, which softens the depth of the tint considerably. Had the covering been muslin, it must have been still deeper, to correspond with the uncovered ribbon. It is for want of the consideration of these small points that there is so frequently a want of harmony in the tints of amateur needlewomen."

"And now, Mamma, what next? for I have a good deal of spare time still."

"You said you would like to work papa a pair of slippers, so I have contrived a design for you, which will use up all your remnants of wool. We will call it the dice pattern. Of each colour you may use, you will require two shades with black and

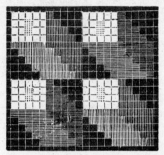

DICE PATTERN FOR SLIPPERS.

white. You can mark on your canvas the outline of the slippers with a soft pen and ink; then work from the drawing I have made, beginning at the toe. You may use any number of colours, only let them be well chosen, and falling in stripes. Do not put green and blue, or any other two colours which do not blend well, close together. You may try the effect with shades in the following order: violet, orange, green, crimson, blue. That part which is quite white in the drawing is done in white wool, and there are two spotted squares which are to be black. Then the upper side of each die is in the darker shade of whatever colour may be used, and the under light. Fill it up with black. If you work on Penelope canvas you will find it much easier."

"Well, Mamma, these slippers will occupy all my spare time until my next holiday. Will you think of something pretty for my cousins before that time?"

"I will do my best, my dear; and we will see whether we cannot find some present suitable for each. You know one is very fond of work, and the other of writing."

"Yes; and she writes verses. Only think of that, Mamma! Real verses! They call her the little poet."

POINT LACE STOMACHER OF AN INFANT'S DRESS.

"Well, my love, it is a glorious name, and, perhaps, may help us in our selection for her. But now it is really time for you to put away your work for this evening."

A GOSSIP ON CHILDREN'S DRESS.

IN resuming our notice of children's dress from page 272, we give a pattern for the point-lace stomacher of an infant's dress, and also a broderie cap-crown for the wear of one of these miniature specimens of humanity; and we trust that our lady friends will be glad of these designs, since so many are now quite *au fait* at both styles of needlework.

The stomacher, which necessarily we give on a reduced scale, should be enlarged to the usual dimensions for a frock of the 2nd size. The pattern is one which can be very readily enlarged ; and as the two halves correspond, one only need be done on tracing paper, before transferring it to the coloured paper on which it is to be worked. The only materials required are Messrs. Walter Evans and Co.'s Point Lace Cottons. All the flowers, leaves, and stems, are filled in foundation stitch, and are represented by being perfectly *white* in the engraving. The grounding, except at the top and round the extreme edges, is in Raleigh bars. At the top there is a small section filled in with English Lace, and Brussels Lace makes the outer border.

All the outlines are done with No. 12 Mecklenburgh, Brussels and English lace with No. 90 Boar's Head, English bars and Kuitian bars with No. 120 Mecklenburgh, foundation stitch in No. 70 Boar's Head, Raleigh bars in No. 140 Mecklenburgh, and Mecklin wheels in No. 90 Boar's Head. All these different threads form a part of the set of point lace cottons of Messrs W. Evans and Co.

The cap-crown is given of the full dimensions, and the design must be traced from the engraving on fine French cambric, in the usual manner for muslin work. All the black parts of the engraving are cut out; or, if round, formed by piercing holes with a stiletto. The whole pattern is simply traced and sewed over, with a thread held in, except the border, which is worked in very fine button-hole stitch. Evans's royal embroidery cotton, No. 70, should be used for this purpose.

Infants' morning caps are, in our opinion, much prettier if made of plain cambric, with the crown only worked, than if the whole cap is embroidered, unless the embroidery be of the very best description, and this is too expensive to be universally attainable. Tac runnings should always be stitched, and the needlework generally of the neatest and finest description. In another page we purpose giving some of the fancy stitches used in making babies' frocks, hoods, &c. At present we shall conclude by describing an extremely pretty

BRODERIE CAP-CROWN FOR INFANTS.

dress for a little girl ten or twelve years of age.

The skirt is of coloured silk, made very full, but without flounces. A white muslin body, low and with short sleeves, is worn with this. It is perfectly plain, except in front, the stomacher only being made in alternate bands of embroidery, and gathered muslin, from the top to the waist, in the form of a V. A worked edging finishes the top. Over this a white muslin jacket, low round the neck, open to the waist (so as to show the stomacher), and with mandarin sleeves, coming a little below the elbow, is worn. It is trimmed all round with deep rich broderies, and fastened round the waist with a sash to correspond with the dress. This style of dress is very useful for wearing out the skirt of a frock, when the body has become too small, or is otherwise unusable. The hair, by the way, is worn in a knot very low at the back of the head. That from the top of the forehead is combed quite back, with a parting at each side. When the hair displays a tendency to grow low on the brow, this mode of wearing it is a certain preventive.

NETTED SHELL EDGING.

Materials.—Messrs. W. Evans and Co.'s Mecklenburg thread. No. 7; one wooden mesh, three-quarters of an inch wide; one round bone, No. 11; and one ditto, No. 9.

WITH No. 9 mesh do two rows or rounds, as the case may be.

3rd Round.—Take the largest mesh, and work four in every alternate stitch.

4th Round.—Smallest mesh. Net one in each of the three loops on one of the second row, and miss the loop which passes over the missed one.

5th Round.—Net a stitch in every stitch, with the same mesh.

6th Round.—Largest mesh. Do six stitches in one. + Pass the needle through the next, in the next: and over the mesh, then through the next, and at the fourth do + again in one. Repeat from the cross as often as required.

7th Round.—With the finest mesh do a stitch in every stitch, including the loop passed through the centre of the third.

8th Round.—Same mesh. A stitch in every stitch.

T

ROUND D'OYLEY.

THE WORK-TABLE FRIEND.

ROUND D'OYLEY.

Materials.—Evans's Boar's-head Crochet Cotton, No. 8.

8 Chain, unite and work.

1st Row.—1 Dc 4 chain 8 times.

2nd Row.—1 Dc into space made by 4 chain of last row, 6 chain, repeat.

3rd Row.—8 long into space made by 6 chain of last row, 3 chain, repeat.

4th Row.—6 long, beginning on second long of last row, 4 chain, repeat.

5th Row.—4 long, beginning on second of 6 long in last row, 6 chain, repeat.

6th Row.—2 long, beginning on second of 4 long in last 4 chain, 1 long in space made by 6 chain of last row, 4 chain, repeat.

7th Row.—1 long between 2 long of last row, 6 chain, 1 long with 6 chain after into each of the two next spaces, repeat.

8th Row.—16 double crochet into first space of last row, 3 chain, 1 Dc into next space, 3 chain, repeat.

9th Row.—16 Dc on Dc of last row, 4 chain, Dc on Dc, 4 chain, repeat.

10th Row.—16 Dc on Dc of last row, 6 chain, Dc on Dc, 6 chain, repeat.

11th Row.—14 Dc, beginning on second of the 16 in last row, 4 chain, 1 Dc in space made by first 6 chain of last row, 4 chain, 1 Dc in next space, 4 chain, repeat.

12th Row.—12 Dc, beginning as before, 4 chain, 1 Dc in first space, 4 chain, (1 long, 3 chain, 1 long) in middle space, 4 chain Dc in next space, 4 chain, repeat.

13th Row.—10 Dc, beginning as before, 4 chain, 1 Dc, with 4 chain after it in each of the two next spaces, 1 long (3 chain, 1 double long, 3 chain, 1 double long, 3

THE PARSONAGE LEAF-MAT.

chain, 1 long) in centre space, 4 chain, 1 Dc, with 4 chain after it in each of the next 2 spaces, repeat.

14th Row.—8 Dc, beginning as before, 4 chain, 1 Dc, with 4 chain after it into all but the centre space, in which work (1 double long, 3 chain, 1 double long) 4 chain, 1 Dc, with 4 chain after into the other spaces, repeat.

15th Row.—6 Dc, beginning as before, the remainder of the row to be the same as the last.

16th Row.—4 Dc, beginning as before, the remainder of the row the same as the last, except that in the centre space work long, instead of double long stitches.

17th Row.—2 Dc, beginning as before, 5 chain, 1 Dc in every space, repeat.

This D'Oyley, if worked according to the above, will form a centre, surrounded by leaves, which must be nicely pulled out, and laid one overlapping the other. The effect is very pretty. The above directions are not suited for wool; but to work one in the latter material, proceed like our next.

THE PARSONAGE LEAF-MAT.

Materials—Of white, black, and six shades of green, each three skeins, and one ball of silver twist.

Begin with white.

Work as far as the 8th row the same as in the D'Oyley before described.

8th Row.—Begin with black wool, and work, 14 Dc in space made by 6 chain of last row, 3 chain, Dc in next space, 3 chain, repeat.

9th Row.—12 Dc, beginning with darkest green on second of 14 Dc in last row, 4 chain, Dc on Dc, repeat.

SECOND SHADE.

10th Row.—10 Dc, beginning on 2nd Dc as before, 6 chain, Dc on Dc, repeat.

THIRD SHADE.

11th Row.—8 Dc beginning as before, 4 chain, 1 Dc in space made by first 6 chain of last row, 4 chain, 1 Dc in next space, 4 chain, repeat.

FOURTH SHADE.

12th Row.—6 Dc, beginning as before, 4 chain, 1 Dc in first space, 4 chain (oblong, 3 chain 1 long) in centre space, 4 chain, 1 Dc in next space, 4 chain, repeat.

FIFTH SHADE.

13th Row.—4 Dc, beginning as before, 4 chain, 1 Dc with 4 chain after it into all but the centre space in it, work (1 long 3 chain, 1 double long, 3 chain, 1 double long, 3 chain, 1 long,) 4 chain, 1 Dc with 4 chain after it into each of the remaining spaces, repeat.

SIXTH SHADE.

14th Row.—2 Dc, beginning as before, the rest of the row the same as the last.

15th Row.—With silver-twist, work 1 Dc, 5 chain in each space missing the 2 Dc of last row.

Now, with a bit of silver-twist, tie down every alternate leaf, passing the twist through the end of the leaf and the 4 chain next the two long in the 6th row. Spread out the remaining leaves nicely.

THE IMPERIAL WORK-BAG.

Materials.—Three skeins of French Vertu-islay silk, twelve skeins of gold thread, No. 2, and imperial trimmings.

THIS truly elegant little bag is made in three pieces—namely, the two sides, and the band connecting them. The pattern is in gold, on a green ground. The clasp is gilt, and the trimmings are of green and gold intermixed, and are studded with small emeralds. The sides being alike, the description of one will suffice.

Make a chain of 16, fasten off. Now begin with another chain of 15, Sc on the first chain of 16, and with 15 Ch. Fasten off at every row.

2nd Row.—3 Ch, Sc on all the other row, 4 Ch. Work in the ends in every row.

3rd Row.—Begin to use the gold. 2 Ch, 20 silk, 2 gold, 3 silk, 2 gold, 3 silk, 2 gold, 21 silk.

4th Row.—3 Ch, 7 silk, 2 gold, 3 silk, 2 gold, 3 silk, 2 gold, 2 silk,+ 4 gold, 1 silk, + twice, 4 gold, 2 silk, 2 gold, 3 silk, 2 gold, 3 silk, 2 gold, 8 silk, 2 chain. Observe that the first and last Sc stitches of a row are always worked on the chain stitches of the previous row.

5th Row.—1 Ch, 5 s, 2 g, 2 s, 4 g, 1 s, 4 g, 1 s, 4 g, 2 s, 2 g, 3 s, 2 g, 3 s, 2 g, 2 s, 4 g, 1 s, 4 g, 1 s, 4 g, 2 s, 2 g, 5 s, 2 chain.

6th Row.—1 Ch, 5 s, 4 g, 2 s, 2 g, 3 s, 2 g, 3 s, 2 g, 18 s, 2 g, 3 s, 2 g, 3 s, 2 g, 2 s, 4 g, 6 s, 1 Ch.

7th Row.—1 Ch, 3 s, 2 g, 2 s, 2 g, 29 s, 1 g, 18 s, 2 g, 3 s, 2 g, 3 s, 1 Ch.

8th Row.—2 Ch, 3 s, 4 g, 10 s, 2 g, 20 s, 2 g, 21 s, 4 g, 3 s, 2 Ch.

9th Row.—1 Ch, 6 s, 2 g, 12 s, 2 g, 15 s, 1 g, 3 s, 2 g, 22 s, 2 g, 6 s, 1 Ch.

10th Row.—1 Ch, 21 s 2 g, 10 s, 1 g, 3 s, 2 g, 2 s, 3 g, 31 s, 1 Ch.

11th Row.—1 Ch, 3 s, 2 g, 17 s, 2 g, 3 s, 1 g, 4 s, 3 g, 1 s, 3 g, 2 s, 3 g, 8 s, 2 g, 17 s, 2 g, 3 s, 1 Ch.

12th Row.—1 Ch, 3 s, 4 g, 16 s, 5 g, 5 s, 3 g, 1 s, 3 g, 1 s, 4 g, 6 s, 4 g, 16 s, 4 g, 3 s, 1 Ch.

13th Row.—2 Ch, 5 s, 2 g, 17 s, 1 g, 1 s, 2 g, 4 s, 4 g, 1 s, 3 g, 1 s, 4 g, 6 s, 5 g, 17 s, 2 g, 5 s, 2 Ch.

14th Row.—1 Ch, 15 s, 1 g, 7 s, 2 g, 3 s, 8 g, 1 s, 3 g, 1 s, 3 g, 9 s, 5 g, 26 s, 1 Ch.

15th Row.—1 Ch, 5 s, 2 g, 9 s, 3 g, 4 s, 4 g, 2 s, 2 g, 1 s, 2 g, 7 s, 8 g, 5 s, 4 g, 22 s, 2 g, 4 s, 1 Ch.

16th Row.—1 Ch, 4 s, 4 g, 8 s, 5 g 2 s, 4 g, 2 s, 1 g, 1 s, 1 g, 1 s, 3 g, 1 s, 13 g, 5 s, 2 g, 22 s, 4 g, 3 s, 1 Ch.

17th Row.—1 Ch, 6 s, 2 g, 9 s, 6 g, 1 s, 4 g, 1 s, 2 g, 2 s, 1 g, 1 s, 3 g, 1 s, 2 g, 3 s, 6 g, 2 s, 4 g, 25 s, 2 g, 5 s, 1 Ch.

18th Row.—18 s, 7 g, 1 s, 3 g, 1 s, 2 g, 4 s, 3 g, 1 s, 4 g, 8 s, 6 g, 4 s, 4 g, 24 s.

19th Row.—5 s, 2 g, 12 s, 3 g, 1 s, 4 g, 1 s, 3 g, 5 s, 9 g, 7 s, 7 g, 2 s, 6 g, 17 s, 2 g, 5 s.

20th Row.—4 s, 4 g, 13 s, 2 g, 2 s, 2 g, 3 s, 4 g, 2 s, 2 g, 1 s, 3 g, 1 s, 2 g, 4 s, 1 g, 1 s, 8 g, 1 s, 8 g, 15 s, 4 g, 4 s.

21st Row.—5 s, 2 g, 11 s, 6 g, 6 s, 5 g, 2 s, 1 g, 1 s, 4 g, 4 s, 6 g, 1 s, 3 g, 1 s, 1 g, 1 s, 2 g, 1 s, 3 g, 16 s, 2 g, 5 s.

22nd Row.—18 s, 9 g, 5 s, 3 g, 4 s, 10 g, 2 s, 4 g, 1 s, 1 g, 3 s, 1 g, 2 s, 3 g, 23 s.

23rd Row.—4 s, 2 g, 12 s, 6 g, 4 s, 1 g, 1 s, 6 g, 3 s, 4 g, 9 s, 3 g, 1 s, 1 g, 2 s, 3 g, 2 s, 4 g, 17 s, 2 g, 4 s.

24th Row.—3 s, 4 g, 16 s, 2 g, 3 s, 1 g, 1 s, 2 g, 1 s, 3 g, 3 s, 3 g, 1 s, 2 g, 3 s, 4 g, 2 s, 1 g, 3 s, 5 g, 1 s, 1 g, 1 s, 2 g, 16 s, 4 g, 3 s.

25th Row.—4 s, 2 g, 12 s, 6 g, 2 s, 1 g, 1 s, 1 g, 2 s, 2 g, 8 s, 3 g, 2 s, 8 g, 2 s, 1 g, 1 s, 5 g, 3 s, 1 g, 18 s, 2 g, 4 s.

IMPERIAL WORK-BAG, BY MRS. PULLAN.

26th Row.—17 s, 7 g, 2 s, 5 g, 1 s, 2 g, 6 s, 1 g, 1 s, 1 g, 2 s, 10 g, 1 s, 2 g, 1 s, 4 g, 1 s, 2 g, 1 s, 5 g, 19 s.

27th Row.—3 s, 2 g, 11 s, 6 g, 4 s, 1 g, 1 s, 4 g, 1 s, 12 g, 5 s, 1 g, 1 s, 1 g, 2 s, 8 g, 2 s, 3 g, 3 s, 6 g, 1 s, 5 g, 13 s, 2 g, 3 s.

28th Row.—2 s, 4 g, 11 s, 6 g, 1 s, 1 g, 1s, 1 g, 1 s, 7 g, 5 s, 1 g, 1 s, 1 g, 1 s, 4 g, 4 s, 2 g, 1 s, 3 g, 5 s, 4 g, 2 s, 5 g, 11 s, 4 g, 2 s.

29th Row.—3 s, 2 g, 15 s, 2 g, 1 s, 4 g, 1 s, 2 g, 1 s, 4 g, 5 s, 1 g, 1 s, 1 g, 1 s, 7 g, 4 s, 2 g, 7 s, 3 g, 1 s, 2 g, 2 s, 2 g, 12 s, 2 g, 3 s.

30th Row.—19 s, 2 g, 1 s, 5 g, 1 s, 2 g, 1 s, 3 g, 4 s, 3 g, 1 s, 1 g, 1 s, 9 g, 2 s, 1 g, 2 s, 3 g, 3 s, 2 g, 5 s, 3 g, 17 s.

31st Row.—4 s, 2 g, 12 s, 5 g, 1 s, 3 g, 2 s, 1 g, 2 s, 2 g, 3 s, 4 g, 2 s, 1 g, 1 s, 6 g, 4 s, 7 g, 3 s, 4 g, 1 s, 4 g, 11 s, 2 g, 4 s.

32nd Row.—3 s, 4 g, 11 s, 5 g, 1s, 3 g, 6 s, 2 g, 2 s, 4 g, 2 s, 1 g, 2 s, 10 g, 1 s, 5 g, 3 s, 4 g, 2 s, 3 g, 10 s, 4 g, 3 s.

33rd Row.—4 s, 2 g, 11 s, 5 g, 2 s, 2 g, 11 s, 4 g, 2 s, 1 g, 4 s, 4 g, 3 s, 7 g, 3 s, 4 g, 1 s, 3 g, 12 s, 2 g, 4 s.

34th Row.—17 s, 5 g, 3 s, 1 g, 11 s, 3 g, 3 s, 1 g, 4 s, 1 g, 2 s, 1 g, 1 s, 8 g, 2 s, 2 g, 2 s, 1 g, 1 s, 3 g, 19 s.

35th Row.—6 s, 2 g, 9 s, 4 g, 5 s, 6 g, 11 s, 1 g, 4 s, 1 g, 2 s, 4 g, 2 s, 2 g, 2 s, 6 g, 17 s, 2 g, 5 s.

36th Row.—5 s, 4 g, 8 s, 2 g, 6 s, 8 g, 6 s, 7 g, 2 s, 1 g, 2 s, 3 g, 1 s, 1 g, 2 s, 9 g, 1 s, 2 g, 13 s, 4 g, 4 s.

37th Row.—Miss first and last stitches of last row, as you now begin to diminish. 5 s, 2 g, 9 s, 1 g, 7 s, 9 g, 3 s, 10 g, 1 s, 1 g, 1 s, 6 g, 5 s, 4 g, 4 s, 2 g, 13 s, 2 g, 4 s.

38th Row.—Miss as in last. 15 s, 1 g, 6 s, 4 g, 1 s, 6 g, 2 s, 10 g, 1 s, 1 g, 1 s, 5 g, 2 s, 1 g, 1 s, 2 g, 5 s, 6 g, 17 s.

39th Row.—Miss 2. 5 s, 2 g, 13 s, 4 g, 1 s, 6 g, 1 s, 12 g, 2 s, 5 g, 1 s, 2 g, 1 s, 2 g, 1 s, 1 g, 1 s, 1 g, 2 s, 5 g, 10 s, 2 g, 5 s.

40th Row.—Miss 1. 3 s, 4 g, 12 s, 4 g, 2 s, 2 g, 1 s, 2 g, 1 s, 7 g, 1 s, 5 g,

NEPAUL SMOKING CAP.

2 s, 4 g, 1 s, 2 g, 1 s, 2 g, 1 s, 1 g, 1 s, 2 g, 2 s, 4 g, 9 s, 4 g, 3 s.

41st Row.—Miss 1. 3 s, 2 g, 13 s, 2 g, 1 s, 2 g, 2 s, 1 g, 2 s, 1 g, 1 s, 3 g, 1 s, 3 g, 1 s, 5 g, 1 s, 11 g, 1 s, 10 g, 10 s, 2 g, 3 s.

42nd Row.—18 s, 3 g, 10 s, 2 g, 1 s, 3 g, 1 s, 6 g, 1 s, 10 g, 1 s, 10 g, 15 s.

43rd Row.—Miss 1. 6 s, 2 g, 10 s, 4 g, 2 s, 6 g, 4 s, 1 g, 2 s, 6 g, 1 s, 9 g, 3 s, 8 g, 8 s, 2 g, 5 s.

44th Row.—Miss 1. 4 s, 4 g, 13 s, 6 g, 2 s, 2 g, 4 s, 2 g, 1 s, 4 g, 2 s, 7 g, 5 s, 7 g, 7 s, 4 g, 3 s.

45th Row.—Miss 1. 4 s, 2 g, 8 s, 5 g, 1 s, 5 g, 1 s, 6 g, 5 s, 4 g, 1 s, 1 g, 1 s, 4 g, 9 s, 3 g, 10 s, 2 g, 3 s.

46th Row.—13 s, 4 g, 2 s, 5 g, 1 s, 8 g, 3 s, 4 g, 1 s, 2 g, 32 s.

47th Row.—Miss 1. 6 s, 2 g, 3 s, 3 g, 3 s, 1 g, 2 s, 1 g, 3 s, 9 g, 1 s, 5 g, 2 s, 2 g, 8 s, 4 g, 11 s, 2 g, 5 s.

48th Row.—Miss 1. 4 s, 4 g, 2 s, 5 g, 1 s, 1 g, 2 s, 1 g, 3 s, 8 g, 1 s, 1 g, 1 s, 2 g, 3 s, 1 g, 1 s, 2 g, 2 s, 1 g, 2 s, 6 g, 10 s, 4 g, 3 s.

49th Row.—5 s, 2 g, 3 s, 4 g, 2 s, 2 g, 1 s, 1 g, 4 s, 7 g, 1 s, 1 g, 6 s, 1 g, 1 s, 5 g, 2 s, 3 g, 3 s, 2 g, 9 s, 2 g, 4 s.

50th Row.—Miss 1. 9 s, 2 g, 3 s, 1 g, 1 s, 3 g, 6 s, 4 g, 1 s, 2 g, 1 s, 6 g, 2 s, 3 g, 1 s, 6 g, 13 s.

51st Row.—Miss 1. 5 s, 2 g, 1 s, 6 g, **3** s, 2 g, 5 s, 4 g, 1 s, 3 g, 1 s, 6 g, **6 s, 2 g, 1 s, 7 g, 5 s, 2 g, 5 s.**

52nd Row.—Miss 1. 3 s, 8 g, 2 s, 1 g, 1 s, 3 g, 9 s, 4 g, 3 s, 5 g, 5 s, 2 g, 1 s, 7 g, 4 s, 4 g, 3 s.

53rd Row.—4 s, 2 g, 2 s, 6 g, 1 s, 5 g, 6 s, 5 g, 1 s, 7 g, 5 s, 1 g, 1 s, 8 g, 5 s, 2 g, 4 s.

54th Row.—10 s, 4 g, 1 s, 6 g, 5 s, 5 g, 2 s, 6 g, 5 s, 1 g, 1 s, 2 g, 1 s, 5 g, 11 s.

55th Row.—Miss 1. 5 s, 2 g, 6 s, 1 g, 1 s, 3 g, 1 s, 5 g, 1 s, 5 g, 1 s, 1 g, 1 s, 5 g, 5 s, 1 g, 1 s, 2 g, 1 s, 4 g, 4 s, 2 g, 5 s.

56th Row.—4 s, 4 g, 4 s, 3 g, 4 s, 5 g, 1 s, 4 g, 2 s, 1 g, 3 s, 3 g, 3 s, 2 g, 2 s, 1 g, 2 s, 4 g, 3 s, 4 g, 4 s.

57th Row.—Miss 1. 4 s, 2 g, 5 s, 2 g, 1 s, 2 g, 2 s, 5 g, 1 s, 4 g, 1 s, 8 g, 3 s, 3 g, 1 s, 1 g, 1 s, 3 g, 6 s, 2 g, 4 s.

58th Row.—Miss 1. 10 s, 4 g, 2 s, 1 g, 1 s, 3 g, 1 s, 3 g, 2 s, 8 g, 4 s, 3 g, 17 s.

59th Row.—Miss 1. 4 s, 2 g, 3 s, 4 g, 1 s, 2 g, 9 s, 1 g, 1 s, 6 g, 6 s, 2 g, 1 s, 4 g, 5 s, 2 g, 4 s.

60th Row.—Miss 1. 2 s, 4 g, 3 s, 8 g, + 1 s, 1 g, + 3 times, 1 s, 2 g, 1 s, 5 g, 7 s, 7 g, 3 s, 4 g, 2 s.

61st Row.—3 s, 2 g, 5 s, 7 g, 1 s, 3 g, 2 s, 3 g, 4 s, 1 g, 1 s, 1 g, 6 s, 1 g, 1 s, 4 g, 5 s, 2 g, 3 s.

62nd Row.—11 s, 5 g, 2 s, 4 g, 1 s, 3 g, 6 s, 1 g, 5 s, 1 g, 16 s.

63rd Row.—8 s, 2 g, 9 s, 7 g, 7 s, 5 g, 7 s, 2 g, 8 s.

64th Row.—7 s, 4 g, 9 s, 6 g, 18 s, 4 g, 7 s.

65th Row.—8 s, 2 g, **12 s, 3 g, 20 s,** 2 g, 8 s.

66th Row.—All silk.

67th Row.—8 s, 2 g, 35 s, 2 g, 8 s.

68th Row.—7 s, 4 g, 33 s, 4 g, 7 s.

69th Row.—Like 67th.

70th Row.—All silk.

71st Row.—10 s, + 2 g, 3 s, + 6 times, 2 g, 10 s.

72nd Row.—9 s, + 4 g, 1 s, + 6 times, 4 g, 9 s.

73rd Row.—Like 71st.

Now do 8 rows of plain silk.

For the band, make a chain of 180 stitches, and do two plain rows.

1st Pattern Row.—+ 3 g, 9 s, + 15 times.

2nd Row.—+ 3 g, 4 s, 1 g, 4 s, + repeat as before in this and following rows.

3rd Row.—+ 4 g, 3 s, 1 g, 3 s, 1 g, +

4th Row.—+ 4 g, 2 s, 3 g, 2 s, 1 g, +

5th Row.—+ 3 g, 2 s, 1 g, 1 s, 1 g, 1 s, 1 g, 2 s, +

6th Row.—+ 3 g, 1 s, 7 g, 1 s, +

7th Row.—+ 3 g, 1 s, 1 g, 1 s, 3 g, 1 s, 1 g, 1 s, +

8th Row.—+ 5 g, 1 s, 3 g, 1 s, 2 g, +

9th Row.—+ 1 s, 1 g, 1 s, 1 g, 2 s, 3 g, 2 s, 1 g, +

10th Row.—+3 g, 2 s, 5 g, 2 s, +

11th Row.—+ 1 s, 1 g, 3 s, 5 g, 2 s, +

12th Row.—+ 1 s, 1 g, 4 s, 3 g, 3 s, +

13th Row.—.+ 6 s, 3 g, 3 s, +

Now two plain rows.

This bag must be made up nearly like a miniature carpet-bag, the band gradually sloped at the ends. Line it with watered silk.

NEPAUL SMOKING CAP.

Materials.—Three skeins of black netting silk, and one of blue ditto (French). 18 skeins of gold thread, No. 1. A passementerie tassel, combining gold, blue and black, and some black silk and calico.

THE rage that there is, at present, for all articles in embroidered netting, its beauty and delicacy, and, above all, its extreme simplicity, will render the novel application of this style of work popular among our friends; while as the habit of smoking is (alas, for us!) becoming daily more general, it is to be hoped that those preventatives of the annoyance of it which our continental neighbours adopt, will become as universal as among them. The great *lightness* of netted work in comparison with crochet or velvet, commends it especially to those who dislike any weight on the head.

The cap is commenced in the centre of the crown, eight stitches being made, and formed into a round. On each of these, two are worked; you then increase in the same way as in the purse we have given in a previous page, by netting *two* in every small stitch, and one in every other until the necessary size is obtained. This should

DARNING PATTERN.

be 2½ inches in each of the eight divisions, *not stretching them out.* Hitherto the netting had formed a perfect octagon: to make it round, it will be necessary to continue the work without any increase, until the piece is 7½ inches across. By stretching it out it will now be also 24 round. The crown being done, continue without any increase for the head, which is 3½ inches deep.

The darning is done in gold thread and blue silk. The white lines represent the gold darning. The spots only are in silk; all this part may be done from the diagram on the preceding page, and which gives it stitch for stitch. A piece of *toile ciré* or stiff paper should be tacked underneath the netting, previous to its being darned.

To make it up, a cap, of the dimensions we have given, should be made of the twilled calico, and covered on both sides with black satin. The netting is stretched over this.

POINT LACE COLLAR.

Materials.—Italian braid, or the best French white cotton braid, No. 7, with the point lace cottons of Messrs. W. Evans and Co., of Derby.

In giving two different kinds of braid as materials for this collar, we have been influenced by the consideration of the expense

POINT LACE COLLAR.

of Italian braid. There can be no question as to the beauty or actual value of a collar worked with Italian braid, rather than with cotton braid; but a very pretty article may be made with the inferior material, which must, however, be the best of its kind, and sewed down at both edges, like Italian braid.

The engraving gives so clear a delineation of the stitches, that we have only to refer to it. The pattern, enlarged to the proper size, and lined with calico or linen must be entirely braided first; then the English lace, worked with No. 70, Evans's Boar's-head, and the open English lace, done with No. 90 of the same thread, are to be used to fill up the spaces, as seen in the engraving. The Mecklin wheels, and English rosettes, are done in No. 120, Mecklenburg; the Raleigh bars, which form the ground, in No. 100, and the Sorrento edge in No. 80.

KNITTED PURSE.

Materials.—One skein of blue silk, one-half of claret, and a small quantity of orange (all French). Silk slides and tassels to correspond. Also two knitting needles, No. 19.

CAST on, with the blue silk, 85 stitches and purl one row.

1st Pattern Row.— + Slip 1, knit 1, pass the slip-stitch over, make 1, knit 1 + repeat to the end. Knit the last stitch.

2nd Row.— + Purl 2 together, make 1, purl 1 + to the end. Purl the last stitch.

Do these two rows, alternately, 4 times with the blue. Join on the claret, and do the 1st and 2nd row with it.

11th Row (Claret).— + Knit 4, knit 2 together + to the end. Knit the last.

12th Row.—Join on the orange. Purl 1 + make 3, purl 2 together, purl 1, purl 2 together + till 4 stitches only are left. Purl them plainly.

13th Row.—Knit all except the centre of the three made stitches, which must be purled.

14*th Row.*—Purled.

15*th Row.*—Knit 2 + slip 1, knit 1, pass the slip-stitch over, knit 4 + repeat to the end, when you knit five. Join on the claret.

16*th Row.*—Purl 3 + purl 2 together, make 3, purl 2 together, purl 1, + repeat to the end.

17*th Row.*— + Knit 3, purl 1, knit 2, + repeat to the end.

18*th Row.*—Purled. Join on the blue.

19*th Row.*— + Knit 2 together, knit 1, make 1, + repeat to the end.

20*th Row.*—Purled.

21*st Row.*—Like 19th. The two that are knitted together being the plain one and the made one of that row.

22*nd Row.*—Purled. Join on the orange.

23*rd Row.*—Like 19th.

24*th Row.*—Purled.

25*th Row.*—Knitted. Join on claret.

26*th Row.*—Purl 1, + purl 2 together, purl 1, make 1. + repeat to the end.

27*th Row.*—Knitted.

28*th Row.*—Purled.

29*th Row.*—Knit 5, + slip 1, knit 1, pass the slip-stitch over, make 1, knit 4, + repeat to the end. Knit those that are left over the last pattern.

30*th Row.*—Purl to the two preceding the last made stitch, + purl together reversed these two, make 1, purl 1, make 1, purl 2 together, purl 1, + purl the last 3.

31*st Row.*—Knit 3, knit 2 together, + make 1, knit 3, make 1, slip 2 together, knit 1, pass the two slip over, + repeat to the end.

32*nd Row.*—Purled.

33*rd Row.*—Like 29th.

34*th Row.*—Like 30th.

35*th Row.*—Like 31st.

36*th Row.*—Purl to the nearest made stitch, + make 1, purl 2 together, reversed, purl 1, purl 2 together, make 1, purl 1. + repeat to the end. Purl the last 4 stitches.

37*th Row.*—Knit 4, + make 1, knit 2 together, knit 1, slip 1, knit 1, pass the slip stitch over, make 1, knit 1, + repeat to the end. Knit the last 3.

38*th Row.*—Like 36th.

39*th Row.*—Like 37th.

40*th Row.*—Like 38th.

41*st Row.*—Knit 5, + make 1, slip 2 together, knit 1, pass the 2 slip stitches

KNITTED PURSE, BY MRS. PULLAN.

over, make 1, knit 3, + repeat to the last 5, which knit.

42*nd Row.*—Purled.

43rd Row.—Knit 1, + knit 2 together, make 1, knit 4, + repeat to the end.

44th Row.—Purl till you come to the two preceding the nearest made stitch. + Purl them together, reversed, make 1, purl 1, make 1, purl 2 together, purl 1, + repeat to the end. Purl the 2 odd stitches at the end, without making one before them.

45th Row.—Knit 4, + make 1, slip 2 together, knit 1, pass the two slip over, make 1, knit 3, + repeat to the end.

46th Row.—Purled.

47th Row.—Knitted.

48th Row.—Purled. Join on the orange.

Repeat the 19th to the 28th inclusive, doing 3 rows in orange, 4 in blue, and the remaining 3 in claret, then join on the orange.

59th Row.—Knit 4, + knit 2 together, make 3, knit 2 together, knit 1, + to the end.

60th Row.—Purl every stitch except the second of the 3 made, which knit.

61st Row.—Knit 2, + knit 2 together, knit 4, + to the end.

62nd Row.—Purled. Join on claret.

63rd Row.—Knit 1, + knit 2 together, make 3, knit 2 together, knit 1, + repeat to the end.

64th Row.—Like 60th.

65th Row.—Knitted. Join on blue.

Do about 3 inches with blue, like the first and second rows, then repeat *backwards* the first part—that is, the 26th, 27th, and 28th, in claret, 59th and 65th as before, 19th to 24th as before. Join on the claret, do two rows, one knitted and the other purled, then repeat the 29th to 46th inclusive, with claret, and the remainder as far as the 65th as before. End like the commencement. Cast off.

Sew up the edges of the two ends, and tack up the blue piece in the centre. Slip it over a bit of stout card-board, to stitch it, tacking the ends also. Damp and let it dry. Take it off, and turn it.

WORK-TABLE FOR JUVENILES.

OR, LITTLE MARY'S HALF-HOLIDAY.

(*Continued from p. 288.*)

" WELL, my little daughter, I suppose you have been half afraid that I should not return from Paris in time for your holiday. However, you see I am here, ready for our lesson, and I have seen so many new and pretty things, that I hardly know which to choose for you to do."

" Pray let it be something very easy, as well as pretty, dear mamma. I should like to make a work-basket, or something of that sort, which would be useful to grandmamma, and look well on our tree besides."

" Then, indeed, my child, you will almost think me a conjuror; for I have brought you all the necessary materials for making the prettiest thing of the sort that, I think, was ever seen. Here they are! First, there is a frame of wire, then a little wadding, black filet,—which is, you know, the imitation netting of which you made your watch-pockets,—netting-silks, gimps, and satin ribbon. Besides these, there is a piece of black satin, and some black sarsnet ribbon. You will require a little *toile ciré*, which I dare say your work-box will furnish."

" But can you not give me any idea of the appearance of this basket, mamma? I never feel as if I could do anything unless I had some notion of what it would be like when completed."

" Here is a sketch for you, my dear;

MODEL WORK-BASKET.

and though no drawing will faithfully represent the extreme elegance of the basket, yet it will, as you say, give you a notion of the general effect."

" It is, indeed, very pretty. I see the sides are transparent; they, I suppose, are made of the filet."

" Yes; and you will begin by cutting a piece of the netting long and deep enough for the four sides, as it is joined only at one of the corners. Take great care to cut it accurately, or your flowers will not run evenly. It must be cut to appear in diamonds, not in squares. Another piece will be required for the bottom of the basket. On these a pattern must be darned in coloured silks. I have drawn you one which will do nicely for the sides."

DARNING PATTERN.

"It is very small, is it not, mamma?"

"It is intended that one of these designs shall be seen in each compartment of the basket. You will see that there are three on each side, and two at each end—ten altogether—so that the pattern is to be repeated that number of times."

"How shall I manage to keep them at equal distances, mamma?"

"I think I should fold the length of netting into ten parts, and run a white thread to mark each separate piece. Now you will require three colours for the darning; what will you choose?"

"What do you think of sky-blue, with maize and scarlet? They would be very pretty, would they not?"

"Very; but then all the trimmings must be in sky-blue, and as you want something rather effective for candle-light, I would suggest that a rich crimson or scarlet would be a better predominant colour. With it you might have green and gold, or green and blue."

"Green and blue form a mixture that I cannot fancy to be pretty, mamma. Do you like the effect of it?"

"Not much; but it is very fashionable. The French introduce it into everything, and call it *préjugé vaincu*, or, prejudice conquered."

"Well, I am afraid, mamma, that my prejudice is unconquerable; so, if you please, we will have maize and green in preference. How am I to use these colours?"

"Do the upper part of the design in scarlet, the lower in green, and the spots up the centre, and between the designs, in maize. In darning, work half the design, from the centre, leaning towards the right hand, and the other half towards the left."

"Am I to use the same pattern for the bottom of the basket?"

"Not in its present form; but if you repeat the design, *reversed*, from the lower part, so as to leave the *points* for the ends, it will be very suitable. You may add a star or diamond, or something very simple, to fill the spaces at the sides. When all the darning is done, detach the cardboard which forms the bottom, tack the wadding down on one side of it, and cover it on this side with the black satin and netting, and on the other with the black satin only. Now all the frame-work of the basket is to be entirely covered with the narrow sarsnet ribbon I have given you for the purpose, the short wires being covered, and the ends secured, before the handle, top, and bottom of the frame are done. Stretch the netting which forms the sides very carefully on. Sew it at the joint, and also at the edges of the net. Now quill the satin ribbon in the centre, into a full and handsome plait; trim the handle with it. Sew the pasteboard bottom in, and add the gimps round the top, while one only may be used for the lower part."

"I might easily add a cover, might I not, mamma?"

"You might, my dear; but in that case the basket should be lined with satin, of some good colour, and the piece of netting you did for the bottom would form the upper part of the top. In the inner part of the cover you might then add a double-stitched ribbon across, to hold scissors, stiletto, &c. But your basket, though more useful, perhaps, would not be so light and elegant as it is at present."

"If you think so, mamma, we will have it so, and for once let well alone."

———

SQUARE NETTED ROSE ANTIMACASSAR, BY MRS. PULLAN.

THE WORK-TABLE FRIEND.

SQUARE-NETTED ANTIMACASSAR.

Materials.—Messrs. W. Evans and Co's. Boar's-head Crochet Cotton, No. 10, and Knitting Cotton, No. 4. Bone meshes.

THE foundation of this antimacassar is in square netting, which is made, as many of our readers will remember, by beginning with one stitch only, and netting two in that one; then-turning the work, and making one in the first stitch and *two* in the second. Again turn the work, and do two in every stitch except the last, in which *two* must be made. This last row must be repeated until the extreme width is attained, which, in this case, is 113 stitches. The triangular piece now made is one-half the antimacassar. For the other half, instead of making two in one at the end of the row, you will net the last two together *as one.* It would answer the same purpose, as far as the decreasing is concerned, to omit the last stitch at the end of the row; but the edges then do not correspond with those of the first part.

When the square is finished, let it be washed, and rinsed in starch water; after which it is to be pinned neatly on a pillow to dry, and it will then be much easier to darn, the holes having taken the proper square form.

THE BORDER, which must now be done, is very simple. With the same mesh as you have used for the square, do two rounds. Then with the ¾-inch mesh do one round thus—+ 5 stitches in one, one stitch in the next. + all round.

2nd.—With the small mesh net a stitch on every stitch of 5. Miss the single one.

3rd.—Same mesh. 4 stitches over 5. Miss the intervening.

4th.—Same mesh. 3 stitches over 4. Miss the loop between.

5th.—Same mesh. 2 over 3. Miss the loop between.

The darning is now to be done from the engraving. The extreme coarseness of the cotton employed for this part fills it up rapidly, and makes it look very well. It is extremely suitable for those whose sight is not very good.

Our ingenious neighbours, the Parisians, have invented a material which exactly imitates hand netting, and the meshes of which are the proper size for this kind of work. This will save the trouble of doing the *ground* to those ladies whose time is valuable.

POLE-SCREEN, IN GERMAN EMBROIDERY.

Materials.—Silk canvas, or perforated cardboard, 16 inches by 12. Beads, gold, steel, blue steel, black, white, opal, and gray blue (3 shades), green (2 shades). Gamboge yellow, shades of green and scarlet wool, and shades of lilac and crimson chenille, and 12 graduated pearls.

As many of our readers will desire to have some idea of the German embroidery, in which beads, as well as wool, chenille, and silks, are used in shades, we shall at once endeavour to gratify them, so far as the capabilities of engraving and description will permit. Where so large a variety of shades and colours is introduced into a single design (as is necessarily the case in even the simplest Berlin pattern), the resources of the engraver do not allow us to represent each one, or enable us to give what may properly be termed a working pattern. But as such patterns partly worked, and with the proper materials for completion, may readily be procured, a general description will probably be as useful as an elaborate one, and also be less trying to the patience of the worker.

POLE-SCREEN, IN GERMAN EMBROIDERY.

The design here represented consists of an elegant basket of flowers, suspended, as it were, by a double-headed arrow, in a rich scroll frame.

These flowers are done entirely in chenille, and the foliage in wool, worked in tent-stitch. The basket is outlined with gold beads, filled in with the shades of blue and the white. The pearls will be observed in the engraving forming the lower part of the basket, and beneath them are seen leaves alternately dark and light. The dark ones are worked in shades of red wool; the light in the green beads, intermixed with gold. Beneath these, again, are scallops formed of white, opal, gray, black, and steel.

The arrows and cord suspending the basket are done in gold beads, and the arrow heads in shades of blue. The entire framework of the scrolls surrounding the basket is in gold beads, the spaces between the outlines being filled with scarlet chenille, green wool, white, opal, black, steel, and gold beads.

Those who remember the beautiful pieces of beadwork that were in the German department of the Great Exhibition, will comprehend not only the richness of such a mixture of materials, but the impossibility of representing it adequately, either by an engraving or a written description. We may add, that we have no claim to the merit of this design, which was one of the most beautiful exhibited in the department we have indicated, in the Crystal Palace.

BABY'S BOOT.

EMULATION. — Those natural inclinations of the human mind ought to be encouraged to the utmost (under proper regulations) which tend to put it upon action and excelling. Whoever would wish his son to be diligent in his studies, and active in business, can use no better means for that purpose than stirring up in him emulation, a desire of praise, and a sense of honour and shame. Curiosity will put a youth upon inquiring into the nature and reason of things, and endeavouring to acquire universal knowledge. This passion ought therefore to be excited to the utmost, and gratified, even when it shews itself by his asking the most childish questions, which should always be answered in as rational and satisfying a manner as possible.—*Dignity of Human Nature.*

BABY'S BOOTS.

Materials.—White silk, and fine lilac embroidering silk.

THESE useful and elegant little boots are made of silk or merino, wadded with fine flannel. The toes are made in one piece, the soles in another, the heels in another.

The soles are simply wadded and quilted; the fronts and heels are embroidered. The former have a double row of herring-bone all round them, and a small flower worked in satin-stitch in the centre. The heels are merely herring-boned all round.

As these shoes come up very high on the ankle, they are extremely suitable for cold weather.

Another very pretty baby's boot may be made of chamois leather, and decorated with beads. It is cut entirely in one piece, sewed up the front, and gathered in rather at the toe   Many-coloured beads should trim it, in imitation of the American-Indian mocassin.

POCKET-BOOK, EMBROIDERED IN APPLICATION.

Materials.—A piece of fine cloth, 13 inches by 9   A yard of narrow black ribbon velvet, a little black velvet, gold thread, No. 2 (3 skeins). An ounce of black glass beads, No. 2. Also a red button. A little silk cord, of the colour of the cloth, will also be required; and satin or sarsenet to line the pocket-book.

THIS pretty kind of pocket-book will commend itself to our readers as being at once very useful and very quickly done. The term "embroidered in application" is used to describe that kind of work in which the pattern is produced by one sort of material being cut out in any given design, and laid on another. The edges are finished with gold thread, gold-coloured Albert braid, or, in short, any material which the worker may fancy.

These pocket-books, which are exceedingly fashionable in France, have the design in three separate compartments,— always, be it understood, on the same piece of cloth. The centre one is, of course, the full size. The front is like it, but slightly sloped from the middle. The flap is cut in the form seen in the engraving.

EMBROIDERED POCKET-BOOK IN APPLICATION.

It may either be simply lined, and closed up the sides, to contain cards or work; or it may be formed into a regular pocket-book, with a place for a pencil, a ribbon down the back to hold some paper. In this case, a thin card-board should be inserted, on both sides, between the silk and the cloth, and a piece nearly the size of the two, and bent in the centre, should also have silk gummed on one side of it, to form a cover for the paper.

The design of this pocket-book is vine-leaves and grapes. The leaves are cut out in velvet, and tacked down on the cloth: the edges, stems, and veinings are entirely in gold thread, sewed closely on. The ends are drawn through to the wrong side. The grapes are formed of clusters of black beads, each one being composed of seven—a centre one, and six close round it. The border is narrow black velvet ribbon, laid on; and at each edge, black beads, placed at regular intervals, with about the space of two between every two, make a pretty finish.

The silk cord is used to conceal the sewing by which the cloth and lining are joined.

Watered silk is preferable to plain for linings.

Thin kid, velvet, or satin may be used for these pocket-books instead of cloth.

Gum is frequently brushed along the back of the work when done; but it needs a very practised hand to do this without spoiling it. Indeed, the process of lining and making up altogether, is better done at a warehouse than by amateurs.

IMPERIAL PURSE.

Materials.—1½ skein of brilliant scarlet silk, ¼ a skein of black ditto, and less than that quantity of emerald green, and Napoleon blue. Six skeins of gold thread. Passementerie trimmings, and an imperial clasp. All the silk is French.

THIS purse is the first of the kind introduced into England. That it is patronized by the Emperor of France is the reason it is termed Imperial. The clasp, which is placed in the centre of the purse, is of a most unique construction. It is a small gold box, with a painting on each side, representing one of the public buildings of Paris. The interior, lined with velvet, is large enough to hold two or three sovereigns. Besides this clasp, the Imperial purse requires (as we may see in the engraving) the usual number of slides and tassels for any long purse.

With the scarlet silk make a chain of 5, close it into a round, and do two Sc in every chain stitch.

2nd Round.—2 Sc in every stitch.

3rd Round.—+ 1 Sc in 1, 2 Sc in next. + 10 times. Continue to increase by doing two in one ten times in every round, until there are 120 stitches in the round.

1st Pattern Round.—Scarlet and gold. ⊤ 2 scarlet, 1 gold, 3 scarlet. + all round.

2nd Round.—Same colours. + 1 scarlet, 3 gold, 2 scarlet. + all round.

3rd Round.—Same colours. + 5 gold, 1 scarlet. + all round.

4th Round.—All gold.

IMPERIAL PURSE.

5th and *6th Rounds.*—All black.

7th Round.—Scarlet and black + 18 black, 1 scarlet, 11 black. + 4 times.

8th Round.—Same colours, with gold. + 17 black, 1 scarlet, 1 gold, 1 scarlet, 10 black. + 4 times.

9th Round.—Same colours. + 16 black, 1 scarlet, 3 gold, 1 scarlet, 9 black. + 4 times.

10th Round.—+ 1 black, 5 scarlet, 9 black, 1 scarlet, 5 gold, 1 scarlet, 8 black. + 4 times.

11th Round.—+ 1 scarlet, 5 gold, 1 scarlet, 7 black, 1 scarlet, 3 gold, 1 scarlet, 3 gold, 1 scarlet, 7 black. + 3 times. The 4th, end with six black, 1 scarlet.

12th Round.—+ 7 gold, 1 scarlet, 5 black, 1 scarlet, 3 gold, 1 scarlet, 1 black, 1 scarlet, 3 gold, 1 scarlet, 5 black, 1 scarlet. + 3 times. The 4th time end with 1 scarlet, 4 black, 1 scarlet, 1 gold.

13th Round.—+ 2 gold, 3 black, 3 gold, 5 scarlet, 3 gold, 1 scarlet, 3 black, 1 scarlet, 3 gold, 5 scarlet, 1 gold. + 3 times. The 4th, end with 4 scarlet, 2 gold.

14th Round.—+ 1 gold, 1 black, 3 green, 1 black, 3 gold, 3 scarlet, 3 gold, 1 scarlet, 5 black, 1 scarlet, 3 gold, 3 scarlet, 2 gold. + 3 times. The 4th, 2 scarlet, 3 gold.

15th Round.—+ 1 black, 5 green, 1 black, 3 gold, 1 scarlet, 5 gold, 1 scarlet, 3 black, 1 scarlet, 5 gold, 1 scarlet, 3 gold. + 3 times. The 4th time end with 2 gold.

16th Round.—+ 1 black, 7 green, 1 black, 5 gold, 1 scarlet, 3 gold, 1 scarlet, 1 black, 1 scarlet, 3 gold, 1 scarlet, 5 gold. + 3 times. The 4th time end with 4 gold.

17th Round.—+ 1 black, 9 green, 1 black, 3 gold, 1 scarlet, 1 blue, 1 scarlet, 3 gold, 1 scarlet (over 1 black), 3 gold, 1 scarlet, 1 blue, 1 scarlet, 3 gold. + 4 times. 1 gold over 1st black.

18th Round.—+ 1 black over 1st of 9 green, 7 green, 1 black, 3 gold, 1 scarlet, 3 blue, 1 scarlet, 5 gold, 1 scarlet, 3 blue, 1 scarlet, 3 gold. + 4 times. End with gold over 1st black.

19th Round.—+ 1 black over 1st green, 5 green, 1 black, 3 gold, 1 scarlet, 5 blue, 1 scarlet, 3 gold, 1 scarlet, 5 blue, 1 scarlet, 3 gold. + 4 times. End as last.

20th Round.—+ 1 black over 1st of 5 green, 3 green, 1 black, 3 gold, 1 scarlet, 7 blue, 1 scarlet, 1 gold, 1 scarlet, 7 blue, 1 scarlet, 3 gold. + 4 times. End as before.

21st Round.—(Centre row)—+ 1 black over 1st of 3 green, 1 green, 1 black, 3 gold, 1 scarlet, 9 blue, 1 scarlet, 9 blue, 1 scarlet, 3 gold. + 4 times.

The following 20 rounds must correspond with those already done, working them backwards, from the 20th to the 1st. Then 19 rows of open square crochet (working backwards and forwards), terminating in a row of Sc, will complete one end. The other is done precisely like it. Slip on the rings before sewing on the clasp.

———◆———

CHEMISETTE IN IRISH GUIPURE.

THE WORK-TABLE FRIEND.

CHEMISETTE AND COLLAR IN IRISH GUIPURE.

Materials.—French muslin, and Messrs. Evans and Co.'s Royal Embroidery Cotton, Nos. 50 and 61.

It has already, we think, been explained to our readers that the term Irish guipure is applied to that style of embroidery on muslin in which the ground is formed of bars, sewed over, and with the spaces between cut out; the pattern itself is thus represented solid on an open ground. It has a prettier effect than is produced by almost any kind of muslin work, and is not less simple than elegant.

Our page does not indeed permit us to give such designs of the full dimensions; but having a conviction that very many of our fair friends are competent to enlarge patterns for themselves, we are encouraged to hope that our instructions for this purpose are useful, and we venture to repeat them, as adapted to this particular pattern.

Take a piece of fine French muslin, amply large for the front of a chemisette, and lightly trace on it the outlines of the embroidered part of one, from any pattern you may have. Mark the form of the neck, the depth of embroidery on the shoulders, and from their extreme points carry two lines down to meet each other at the bottom of the front.

Those who wear their dresses very open will of course require a much larger space embroidered, than they would if only a small part of the chemisette was intended to be visible. Mark the same upon transparent tracing-paper. Draw an oval medallion on common writing-paper, very neatly and accurately; let it be an inch and three quarters long, by nearly an inch and a half wide. Mark the pattern on it, as given in the engraving. When drawn correctly with a pencil, mark it with ink. Now, lay this under the tracing-paper, on one side of the centre of the neck, and transfer it; shift the medallion under the clear paper for each new one to be drawn, until all are done. Between this line and the next, leave the width of one medallion, this space being afterwards filled up with bars and flowers.

If half the chemisette is thus drawn on tracing-paper, it will suffice. Lay on the muslin a sheet of blue tracing-paper (coloured side downwards), and on this the transparent paper. Trace over the half pattern with a sharp-pointed pencil, and from the reversed side draw the other half. The same plan should be pursued with the collar. When marked, tack a piece of toile ciré under the muslin, trace and work it.

All the parts entirely white are to be em-

U

COLLAR IN IRISH GUIPURE.

broidered in satin stitch: those marked in lines show the muslin ground, while the parts cut out are represented by the black. The bars should be traced twice over, and buttonholed with extreme neatness. The edges of the medallions must be considerably raised. Use the coarser cotton for tracing, and No. 60 for working.

DARNED NETTED NECK-TIE.

Materials.—A cross piece of French filet, ⅞ long by 6 inches wide, a little maize, cerise, and vert-islay crochet silk, and a yard of silk fringe,

coloured silk; the scrolls within that border at the ends, in cerise; the upper part of the flower is also in cerise, and the lower in green. The edge is cut out close to the darning, and then trimmed with fringe.

This is one of the prettiest and most useful objects upon which a lady can bestow her attention and skill, and forms a most acceptable present to a friend. The workmanship is simple, and presents no difficulties whatever. Our young friends will be surprised at the effect it produces when finished.

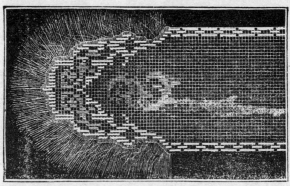

DARNED NETTED NECK-TIE.

two inches deep, which may either be black, or of any colour that will match the silk.

THIS pretty scarf is a Parisian novelty. The entire border is darned in maize-

The design may be worked from the engraving; but those who prefer it can purchase the materials with one end completed.

PARISIAN WHAT-NOT.

THE WORK-TABLE FRIEND.

PARISIAN WHAT-NOT IN APPLICATION.

Materials.—A piece of pale blue moiré silk, claret velvet, pure gold braid, gold thread, and gold and ruby beads.

THE Parisian what-not is an article of furniture very little known in England, where, however, it deserves, from its usefulness and elegance, to be generally adopted. It is a sort of embroidered pocket, standing on a table against the wall, to contain odds and ends of all descriptions. The back, made of silk, and covered with cardboard, is quite flat, the foundation is nearly a half-round, and the front takes that form. It sometimes has cords, by which it is suspended to the wall. These what-nots are worked in braiding, canvas work, crochet, or embroidery.

The beautiful specimen we now give, is of embroidery in application. The entire pattern is cut out in claret velvet, laid on a light blue moiré ground. The edges of the flowers, &c., are worked with gold thread; the stems with coarse gold cord. The fibres of the leaves and the thorns in gold bullion. The eye of the flower is imitated by gold and ruby beads. The scroll, also formed of velvet, is edged with gold braid, and all the pattern on it is worked on the same.

When made up, the bottom of *strong* cardboard is to be covered, as well as the back, with light blue moiré, like the front,

on the inner side, and with claret on the outer. The front is to be lined with thin cardboard only. The work covers it on one side, and blue moiré on the other. A cord, to match, finishes the edges; and also, if desired, serves to suspend it to the wall.

MAMMA'S WORK-BASKET.

Materials.—A piece of white filet, a little blue crochet silk, a frame, some white and blue satin, cardboard, and blue gimps; a yard of blue satin ribbon.

COVER your frame with white satin on the outside, and blue in the interior, the bottom

MAMMA'S WORK BASKET.

being slightly stuffed with wadding. The sides are put in rather full. For the pockets you will take a piece of blue satin double the depth of the basket, fold it in two, with a thickness of fine wadding scented with pot-pourri within it, and sew it in six pockets in the inside, plaiting in the fulness at the bottom, and concealing the stitches with a chenille gimp, which also edges the top.

The outside of the basket is covered with the white netting, darned according to the design, in blue silk. It is edged at the top with three different gimps, and at the bottom with two, of blue and white intermingled. The handles are neatly covered with chenille, and further decorated with a hard gimp, besides being finished with bows and ends.

This is a most elegant and appropriate Christmas gift. It may be made in any other colour, if desired; but should crimson or any deep colour be used, *black* filet would be more appropriate than white.

CIGAR-CASE IN APPLICATION.

Materials.—Brown Russia leather, a little green and scarlet ditto; a small quantity of white, black, and scarlet silk braid, and two yards of gold ditto.

THE ordinary Russia leather forms the

CIGAR-CASE.

leather; the inner part, engraved in horizontal lines, is scarlet leather. Both the green and scarlet are very thin, and are cut out in the forms seen in the engraving. The edges of the different leathers are sewed together closely, through a piece of linen which lines the entire case. The engraving is two-thirds the size of the original.

The gold braid is marked in the engraving by a narrow *double* line. It will be seen that it covers the joins of the different leathers, and also forms a knot in the centre. The outer line of braiding is scarlet; that on the green is white, and on the scarlet leather is black.

This sort of cigar-case is made up *à ressort*, as the French term it; that is, with a gilt frame, in the same way as the *porte-monnaies* usually are done.

HARLEQUIN WATCH-POCKET.

Materials.—Black filet, 14 skeins of gold thread, any crochet silks you may have by you, a little black satin, stout cardboard, and 2¼ yards of coloured cord.

THIS pretty watch-pocket is in two parts. The front, which is embroidered entirely

HARLEQUIN WATCH-POCKET.

ground of this cigar-case. The black part of the engraving represents the green

over, and the back, of which the upper part only is worked.

The vandykes are done in gold thread; the spots in silks of as many different colours as possible. The cardboard, cut out in the shapes seen in the engraving, is covered on both sides with a piece of dimety, under the black satin. The netting is sewed over, and the edges finished with a handsome cord, which also serves to suspend the pocket.

The silks used for darning the spots should be as brilliant and as varied as possible.

ALGERINE BRACELET.

Materials.—Gold Bourdon 8 yards, gold thread and extremely fine ditto (mi-fin), cerise, or blue embroidery chenille, and 8 gold buttons.

THE bracelet is in two parts ; the piece which goes round the wrist, and the butterfly-like ornament in the centre. Draw on white paper a braiding pattern according to the design: tack down the bourdon on it, taking the stitches *across* and never *through* it. To make the paper more substantial, it may be lined with a piece of *toile-ciré*. Thread a long needle with the fine gold thread, and proceed to edge the bourdon with the coarse gold thread on one side, and the fine on the other. The thread is put on *plain,* but the chenille is formed into little loops, nearly close together. They are attached to the bourdon by a sort of *darning* backwards and forwards. Pass your needle over the bourdon, and under the gold thread; let it go *round* the gold thread, *under* the bourdon, and through a little loop of chenille. Then again over the bourdon, and under the gold thread. It need not be done very closely; but when one part of the bourdon

ALGERINE BRACELET.

crosses another, take a few stitches across both to secure them. Sometimes the chenille and gold thread must change places,

as the former is always to form the *outer* edge of the bracelet. The ornament for the centre must be worked in just the same way, and then attached to the bracelet. Two buttons are placed there, and two to fasten the wrist.

MENAGERE, IN EMBROIDERED NETTING.

Materials.—A strip of black filet, 18 inches by 6, 12 skeins of gold thread, or one of maize silk (French), 1 skein Napoleon blue ditto. Cerise satin, black silk, a morsel of kerseymere, &c.

THE pattern may be darned on the filet from the engraving. The vandyke is in

MENAGERE.

gold thread; the spots are in silk. Or all the spots may be done in silks of any colours, taking care that no two of the same are near each other.

The piece of filet is square at one end, and pointed in the other. It is to be lined with satin of a different colour, and also with an inner lining of black silk. At the pointed end is a pocket of coloured silk, neatly stitched. At the other end is also a pocket, with two pieces of kerseymere neatly bound round with ribbon, for needles. Between the two pockets a double piece of the same coloured silk, stitched at intervals of three-fourths of an inch down the entire length, is intended for skeins of coloured silks, cottons, &c. Finish with black and gold cord, and ribbon strings.

THE CHRISTMAS-TREE.

Our lady readers will find in the following pages, dedicated to their use, some pleasing patterns for Christmas presents.

It was a beautiful idea, emanating from the north, that gave to us the Christmas-

CHRIST-ANGEL FOR CHRISTMAS-TREES.

Tree; and it is pleasing to see how readily this trophy of the mirthful, present-giving season, has been adopted by us, and by our neighbours on the Continent. Symbolical of nature and art, the green branch and the ingenious productions of fancy, possess a charm to which young and old are susceptible; and we have looked upon the gay ornament, resplendent with tinselled finery, and surrounded with a joyous group of laughter-loving faces, with peculiar satisfaction. In our young days we had no such accession of strength to a Christmas party; ours were the good old-fashioned time-worn practices of our forefathers, still, we are glad to say, observed in part, though not with the hearty spirit of other days. But these, like all other sublunary things, are subject to the inevitable laws of change.

For instructions how to make a Christmas-Tree, our readers are referred to Vol. VI. (New Series) of the FAMILY FRIEND. A large engraving represents the tree which was imported from Germany, and prepared expressly for the pages of that publication. The artist has introduced the various ob-

jects attached to the branches at the time the sketch was taken, so that an accurate resemblance is preserved. The figure at the top of the tree is the Christ-angel, or Christ-child. The annexed engraving represents one of these curious little figures, which are rudely carved by the Pyrenean peasantry to amuse their children. Our artist has faithfully copied the original, even in its uncouth shape, in order that those of our friends who have not travelled in the countries where they are made may have some idea of the CHRIST-ANGEL.

IMPERATRICE PORTE-MONTRE.

Materials.—Black filet, finest size, 4 skeins gold thread, a little vert-islay crochet silk, 6 yards of satin ribbon to match, 1 inch wide; 2 yards gold cord; 2 of green and gold ditto. Cerise satin, wadding, flannel, cardboard, and two watch-hooks.

This very novel appendage to the bed has almost less work than any other article for

IMPERATRICE PORTE-MONTRE.

the same purpose. Begin by cutting two pieces of cardboard, eight inches long, and

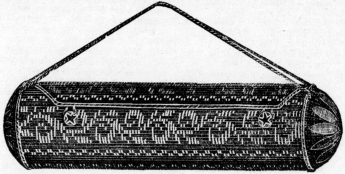

LADY'S NETTING CASE.

in the form and proportion seen in the engraving. Cover this with flannel on one side, and with a thick coating of wadding on the other. It is to be considerably thicker along the centre than at the edges. Over this, on both sides, sew the satin.

Darn the filet in gold, and vert-islay silk, according to the design given. Those parts which are nearest each other are in silk, as are the other parts engraved in the same way; the rest are in gold. These pieces of filet are sewed over the *wadded* sides of the foundation.

The edge is then finished with a silk cord. The ribbon, quilled along the centre, is then sewed on, a little within the edge, and the stitches concealed with the gold cord. Add a loop of cord, and bows at the top, and the hook, as indicated in the engraving.

LADY'S NETTING CASE.

Materials.—1 skein Maize Crochet Silk, 1 skein Napoleon Blue, 1 ditto Cerise, 1 ditto Black (all French), fine and coarse Cord to match, Black and White Sarsenet, and two Passementerie Buttons.

THIS elegant little reticule is made in three pieces; two small rounds for the ends, and that which forms the *body* of the basket. All the pattern is done in small square crochet—that is, with one chain only, instead of two, between every two Dc.

FOR THE ROUNDS.—With cerise silk make a chain of 4, close it into a round, and work 2 Sc stitches in every stitch.

1st Round.—+ 1 Dc, 3 Ch, miss none, +

8 times. Fasten off the cerise, and join on the blue and maize.

2nd Round.— + 3 Dc maize (coming on 1 Dc, and a chain on each side), 2 Ch blue, miss 1, + 8 times.

3rd Round.— + 4 maize Dc on 3, 2 blue chain on 2, + 8 times.

4th Round.— + 6 maize Dc on 4, 2 blue chain on 2, + 8 times.

5th Round.— + 7 maize Dc on 6, 3 blue chain on 2, + 8 times.

6th Round.—Begin with the maize silk on the second of 7 Dc in last round, + 5 maize Dc, 3 Ch blue, 1 blue Dc on 2nd of 3 Ch in last round, 3 Ch blue, + 8 times.

7th Round.— + 3 maize Dc on centre 3 of 5, now with blue, 2 Ch, 1 Dc on 2nd of 3 Ch, 2 Ch, 1 Dc on Dc, 2 Ch, miss 1, 1 Dc, 2 Ch, + 8 times.

8th Round.—All blue, common open square crochet, missing sometimes only one, and sometimes 2 stitches, to increase the round.

Do two rounds more of open square crochet, with the blue silk, and fasten off. Both the ends of the case are done in the same way.

Now make a chain of 190 stitches with the black silk.

1st, 2nd, and *3rd Rows.*— + 1 Dc, 1 Ch, miss 1, + repeat. Join on maize.

4th Row.— + 5 Dc maize, 1 Ch, 1 Dc, 1 Ch black, + repeat to the end. Join on cerise, and fasten off the black.

5th Row.— + 1 maize on the 1st maize. 1 Ch, 1 Dc, 1 Ch cerise, 4 Dc maize, + repeat to the end.

6th Row.—All cerise, 1 Dc, 1 Ch, miss 1, + to the end. 7th the same.

8th Row.— + maize, 2 Dc, cerise 1 Ch, 1 Dc, 1 Ch, 1 Dc, 1 Ch, 1 Dc, 1 Ch; maize 9 Dc, cerise 1 Ch, 1 Dc, 1 Ch, 1 Dc, 1 Ch; maize 9 Dc, cerise, 1 Ch, 1 Dc, 1 Ch, 1 Dc, 1 Ch; maize 3 Dc, + to the end.

9th Row.— + maize, 2 Dc, cerise 1 Ch, 1 Dc, 1 Ch, 1 Ch, 1 Ch, maize 13 Dc, cerise 1 Ch, 1 Dc, 1 Ch, 1 Dc, 1 Ch, maize 9 Dc, cerise 1 Ch, 1 Dc, 1 Ch, maize 3 Dc, + repeat to the end.

10th Row.— + maize, 2 Dc, cerise 1 Dc, 1 Ch, 1 Dc, maize 7 Dc, cerise 1 Ch, 1 Dc, 1 Ch, maize 5 Dc, cerise * 1 Ch, 1 Dc. * 6 times; 1 Ch, maize 3 Ch, cerise 1 Ch, 1 Dc, 1 Ch maize 1 Ch, + repeat to the end

11th Row.— + cerise, 1 Ch, maize 3 Dc, cerise, 1 Ch, maize 5 Dc, cerise * 1 Ch, 1 Dc * 3 times, 1 Ch, maize 3 Dc, cerise † 1 Ch, 1 Dc, † 3 times, 1 Ch, maize 13 Dc, + repeat to the end.

12th Row.— + maize 4 Dc, cerise 1 Ch, maize 5 Dc, cerise 1 Ch, * maize 3 Dc, cerise 1 Ch, 1 Dc, 1 Ch, * twice, maize 5 Dc, cerise 1 Ch, maize 3 Dc, cerise † 1 Ch, 1 Dc † 3 times, 1 Ch. maize 1 Dc, + repeat to the end.

13th Row.— + cerise 1 Ch, maize 5 Dc, cerise 1 Ch, maize 3 Ch, cerise 1 Ch, 1 Dc, 1 Ch, maize 5 Dc, cerise 1 Ch, 1 Dc, 1 Ch, maize 9 Dc, cerise 1 Ch, 1 Dc, 1 Ch, maize 5 Dc, cerise 1 Ch, 1 Dc, + repeat to the end.

14th Row.— + cerise 1 Ch, 1 Dc, 1 Ch, maize 5 Dc, cerise * 1 Ch, 1 Dc * 5 times, 1 Ch, maize 9 Dc, cerise 1 Ch, 1 Dc, 1 Ch, maize 3 Dc, twice + repeat to the end.

15th Row.— + cerise * 1 Ch, 1 Dc * 5 times, 1 Ch, maize 13 Dc, cerise 1 Ch, maize 3 Dc, cerise 1 Ch, maize 5 Dc, cerise * 1 Ch, 1 Dc † 3 times, 1 Ch, maize 3 Dc, + repeat to the end.

16th Row.— + cerise * 1 Ch, 1 Dc * 6 times, 1 Ch, † maize 3 Dc, cerise 1 Ch, 1 Dc, 1 Ch, † twice, maize 7 Dc, cerise 1 Ch, 1 Dc, 1 Ch, maize 5 Dc, + repeat to the end.

17th Row.— + cerise 1 Ch, 1 Dc, 1 Ch, 1 Dc, 1 Ch, maize 9 Dc, cerise 1 Ch, 1 Dc, 1 Ch, maize 5 Dc, cerise 1 Ch, 1 Dc, 1 Ch, 1 Dc, 1 Ch, maize 13, Dc + repeat to the end.

18th Row.— + cerise 1 Ch, 1 Dc, 1 Ch, maize 9 Dc, cerise 1 Ch, 1 Dc, 1 Ch, 1 Dc,

1 Ch, maize 3 Dc, cerise * 1 Ch, 1 Dc * 4 times, maize 9 Dc, cerise 1 Ch, 1 Dc, + repeat to the end.

19th and 20th Row.—All cerise, like 6th and 7th.

21st Row.—Like 5th : 22nd, like 6th.

This completes one stripe. Do four rows of black only, then repeat the stripe, from the 4th row, using blue always instead of cerise ; after an interval of four rows of black, as before, repeat the red stripe, which completes the crochet.

To make up this case, cut two rounds of thin cardboard, nearly the size of the crochet rounds, and a piece the size of the square. Cut off the corners at one end of the square, as seen in the engraving ; cover one side with black sarsenet, and the other with white, with a piece of dimity between the latter and the cardboard. Sew the crochet row on the black side. The rounds must have a thick stuffing of wadding under the black silk, higher in the centre than at the edges, in order to give them the round appearance seen in the engraving. Sew them in their places; edge all with a fine cord, and put two strings of a thick cord to form a handle. The loops for the buttons are made by leaving them in the cord as you sew it on.

Observe, in using two colours in this netting-case, you must work in invisibly the one not in use; no threads must be left at the back.

Black filet, darned in the pattern, is very pretty instead of crochet.

WORK-BASKET A LA MATHILDE.

WE do not give this article as one which

WORK-BASKET A LA MATHILDE.

our friends may themselves imitate, but rather for the sake of showing them what exquisite articles are prepared in Paris for the Etrennes of the season.

As we have the same form, however, and all suitable trimmings, those who would like to make one themselves can readily do so, substituting black filet, embroidered in gold, for the horsehair, embroidered in straw, of which this is composed. The bottom of the basket is a sort of canework, of black horsehair, crossed by diagonal bars of *bourdon or* in one direction, and scarlet chenille in the other.

The sides are a sort of fancy net, made in horsehair, and embroidered with straw. A lace edging of the same materials, shaded with scarlet chenille, forms the border.

The edges, and frame-work generally, are decorated with *bourdon or*, scarlet, and green chenille; and three triple tassels, of silks of various colours, with gold, finish each side of the handle.

We should recommend the coarse filet for the bottom of this basket, not embroidered, but with cross bars of chenille and bourdon, as already described. Whenever two cross each other, let them be fastened down with white and green chenille alternately. The sides may be of fine filet, and embroidered with scarlet and gold, in any simple design. The wire frame being entirely covered with satin ribbon rolled round it, may be finished by holding a piece of bourdon on, and winding the chenille round it and the wire together, but *not closely*. Bourdon is twisted across both handles, to connect them. These baskets are intended to be full of *bonbons* when presented.

PANIER D'OCCASION.

This is a new and very pretty work-basket suitable for a drawing-room table. A wire frame is the foundation of it; the other materials are cerise, white ditto, white wool, cerise cord, white gimp, and a small piece of white satin, or watered silk, and cerise. A round, about 4½ inches in diameter, is formed very substantially of wire: this forms the base. Another round is made 8½ inches in diameter. These are

connected by wires, which are repeated eight times in the round. First, two wires, three-quarters of an inch apart, are placed to connect the two rounds. It will be well

WORK-BASKET FOR DRAWING-ROOM.

to put all these 16 wires on first, at the quarters and half-quarters of the circle. In each of the spaces between, two other wires connect the rounds; but instead of being put straight up, they are bent into a zigzag form, increasing in size so as to fill up the space between the wires. Another wire is taken and bent into eight points, to form the feet. All these wires must be very closely and securely connected, to make the basket as solid as it should be. A piece of stout cardboard forms the bottom.

The zigzags are to be closely covered with cerise chenille. The pairs of upright wires have white wool wound round them, to connect them. It is done thus: thread a coarse tapestry needle with the wool, bring it over, and once round a wire, then over and once round the other of the pairs all the way up. A piece of chenille is worked up the centre on the inside, and a piece put straight up on the outside, to conceal the stitches. The round of cardboard must then be covered on one side with white, and on the other with cerise, and sewed in the bottom of the basket with the white side uppermost. A little chenille cord is put all round, inside, to conceal the stitches. The supports are covered with cerise, and white wound round them, and a cerise chenille cord goes inside. Finish with broad white gimp.

THE WORK-TABLE FRIEND.

MEDALLION PURSE A L'ECOSSAISE.

Materials.—1 skein of white silk, half a skein of black ditto; 10 skeins of gold thread, half a skein of each of light and dark red, and light and dark green; also a little of 2 pinks, 2 blues, and 2 oranges. Medallion chalice, 2 rich Passementerie tassels, cord, and slides.

THIS exquisite little purse is particularly suitable for a bridal present, especially to a

MEDALLION PURSE A L'ECOSSAISE.

Scotch lady: the design itself is in harmony with the chalice, which is similar to one recently described by us, only round, instead of square. The paintings on ivory are the same. The pattern of the purse consists of four little bouquets of flowers, on a white ground, surrounded by gold, forming a medallion; the ground itself being a rich Scotch plaid.

With the white silk make a chain of 8 stitches; close it into a round, and work on it three rounds of Sc, increasing eight stiches in every round. Then do one round thus:—
+ Dc, 1 Ch, miss none. + all round.

Next Round.—+ Dc under chain, 1 Ch, Dc under next Ch, 2 Ch. + repeat all round.

Continue to increase until in the 10th, Dc

round, there are 132 stiches, when do 4 rounds Sc only.

1st Pattern Round.—White and gold, + 4 white, 4 gold, 3 white. + all round.

2nd Round—Same colours. + 3 white, 6 gold, 2 white. + all round.

3rd Round—Same colours. + 1 white, 10 gold. + all round. Fasten off white.

4th and 5th Round.—All gold.

6th Round.—All black.

7th Round.—Gold, black, light and dark red, and green. + 1 gold, 1 black, 3 light red, 1 dark red, 2 light green, 1 gold, 1 black, 2 dark green, 1 dark red, 8 dark green, 1 dark red, 2 dark green, 1 black, 1 gold, 2 light green, 1 dark red, 3 light red, 1 black. + 4 times

8th and 9th Round.—The same.

10th Round.—+ 1 gold, 1 black, 6 dark red, 1 gold, 1 black, 14 dark red, 1 black, 1 gold, 6 dark red, 1 black. + 4 times.

11th Round.—Like 7th Round.

12th Round.—Same colours. + 1 gold, 1 black, 3 light red, 1 dark red, 2 light green, 1 gold, 9 black, 2 dark green, 1 dark red, 8 gold, 1 dark red, 2 dark green, 1 black, 1 gold, 2 light green, 1 dark red, 3 light red, 1 black. + 4 times.

13th Round.—+ 1 gold, 1 black, 3 light red, 1 dark red, 2 light green, 1 gold, 1 black, 1 dark green, 12 gold, 1 dark green, 1 black, 1 gold, 2 light green, 1 dark red, 3 light red, 1 black. + 4 times.

14th Round.—+1 gold, 4 black, 1 dark red, 2 black, 18 gold, 2 black, 1 dark red, 4 black. + 4 times.

15th Round.—+ 1 gold, 1 black, 3 gold, 1 dark red, 7 gold, 8 black, 7 gold, 1 dark red, 3 gold, 1 black. + 4 times.

16th Round.—+ 1 gold, 1 black, 3 light green, 1 dark red, 1 light green, 4 gold, 2 black, 8 gold, 2 black, 4 gold, 1 light green, 1 dark red, 3 light green, 1 black. + 4 times.

17th Round.—+ 1 gold, 1 black, 3 light green, 1 dark red, 4 gold, 2 black, 10 gold, 2 black, 4 gold, 1 dark red, 3 light green, 1 black. + 4 times. Fasten on white, and off dark red.

18th Round.—+ 1 gold, 1 black, 3 dark red, 4 gold, 1 black, 3 gold, 8 white, 3 gold, 1 black, 4 gold, 3 dark red, 1 black. + 4 times.

19th Round.—+ 1 gold, 1 black, 3 light red, 3 gold, 2 black, 2 gold, 10 white, 2 gold, 2 black, 3 gold, 3 light red, 1 black. + 4 times.

20th Round.—+ 1 gold, 1 black, 2 light red, 3 gold, 2 black, 2 gold, 12 white, 2 gold, 2 black, 3 gold, 2 light red, 1 black. + 4 times.

21st Round.—✚ 1 gold, 1 black, 2 light red, 3 gold, 1 black, 2 gold, 4 white, 3 dark green, 1 white, 2 dark green, 5 white, 2 gold, 1 black, 3 gold, 2 light red, 1 black. ⊤ 4 times.

22nd Round.—✚ 1 gold, 1 black, 1 light red, 3 gold, 2 black, 2 gold, 5 white, 4 dark green, 5 white, 2 gold, 2 black, 3 gold, 1 light red, 1 black. ✚ 4 times.

23rd Round.—✚ 1 gold, 1 black, 1 light red, 3 gold, 1 black, 2 gold, 3 white, 6 dark green, 7 white, 2 gold, 1 black, 3 gold, 1 light red, 1 black. ✚ 4 times.

24th Round.—✚ 1 gold, 1 black, 1 light red, 3 gold, 1 black, 2 gold, 4 white, 3 light red, 3 dark green, 1 white, 3 light green, 2 white, 2 gold, 1 black, 3 gold, 1 light red, 1 black. ✚ 4 times.

25th Round.—✚ 1 gold, 1 black, 3 gold, 2 black, 2 gold, 4 white, 1 light green, 3 light red, 5 light green, 3 white, 2 gold, 2 black, 3 gold, 1 black. ✚ 4 times.

26th Round.—✚ 1 gold, 1 black, 3 gold, 1 black, 2 gold, 4 white, 2 light green, 1 light red, 4 light green, 3 light red, 4 white, 2 gold, 1 black, 3 gold, 1 black. ✚ 4 times.

27th Round.—✚ 1 gold, 1 black, 3 gold, 1 black, 2 gold, 1 white, 4 light green, 3 dark red, 2 light green, 6 light red, 2 white, 2 gold, 1 black, 3 gold, 1 black. ✚ 4 times.

28th Round—✚ 1 gold, 1 black, 3 gold, 1 black, 2 gold, 2 white, 2 light green, 5 dark red, 2 light red, 2 light yellow, 3 light red, 2 white, 2 gold, 1 black, 3 gold, 1 black. ✚ 4 times.

29th Round.—✚ 1 gold, 1 black, 3 gold, 1 black, 2 gold, 3 white, 3 gold, 1 black, 2 gold, 3 dark pink, 2 gold, 1 light pink, 3 white, 2 gold, 1 black, 3 gold, 1 black. ✚ 4 times.

30th Round.—✚ 1 gold, 1 black, 3 gold, 1 black, 2 gold, 4 white, 5 light yellow, 1 dark green, 2 dark pink, 2 gold, 2 dark pink, 2 white, 2 gold, 1 black, 3 gold, 1 black. ✚ 4 times.

31st Round.—✚ 1 gold, 1 black, 3 gold, 1 black, 2 gold, 2 white, 2 dark green, 1 dark yellow, 1 dark green, 3 dark yellow, 1 dark green, 6 light pink, 2 white, 2 gold, 1 black, 3 gold, 1 black. ✚ 4 times.

32nd Round.—✚ 1 gold, 1 black, 3 gold, 1 black, 2 gold, 2 white, 6 dark green, 2 dark blue, 2 light pink, 1 light green, 2 light pink, 3 white, 2 gold, 1 black, 3 gold, 1 black. ✚ 4 times.

33rd Round.—✚ 1 gold, 1 black, 3 gold, 2 black, 2 gold, 3 white, 3 light green, 4 dark blue, 2 light green, 4 white, 2 gold, 2 black, 3 gold, 1 black. ✚ 4 times.

34th Round.—✚ 1 gold, 1 black, 1 light red, 3 gold, 1 black, 2 gold, 2 white, 2 light green, 2 white, 2 dark blue, 1 light red, 1 dark blue, 4 light green, 2 white, 2 gold, 1 black, 3 gold, 1 light red, 1 black. ✚ 4 times.

35th Round.—✚ 1 gold, 1 black, 1 light red, 3 gold, 1 black, 2 gold, 3 white, 1 light green, 1 white, 2 dark blue, 2 light red, 2 dark blue, 2 light green, 3 white, 2 gold, 1 black, 3 gold, 1 light red, 1 black. ✚ 4 times.

36th Round.—✚ 1 gold, 1 black, 1 light red, 3 gold, 2 black, 2 gold, 4 white, 6 light blue, 4 white, 2 gold, 2 black, 3 gold, 1 light red, 1 black. ✚ 4 times.

37th Round.—✚ 1 gold, 1 black, 2 light red, 3 gold, 1 black, 2 gold, 5 white, 1 light blue, 1 white, 2 light blue, 5 white, 2 gold, 1 black, 3 gold, 2 light red, 1 black. ✚ 4 times.

Now repeat backwards from the 20*th Round* to the 1*st*, inclusive of both ; after which do 6 rounds of white Sc only, and then two rounds of open square crochet.

Edge.—Gold. 2 Dc under Ch. ✚ 3 Ch, 2 Dc under the same, 2 Ch, 2 Dc under next. ✚ all round.

Sew on the chalice to cover all the open work at the bottom ; run in the strings, cover the ends with the slides, and add tassels.

WORK-TABLE FOR JUVENILES;

OR, LITTLE MARY'S HALF-HOLIDAY.

(*Continued from p.* 299.)

"Mamma, among all the people for whom I have made so many things, *you* have been entirely left out. And yet, I think, if any one has a right to some of my work, it is yourself, to whose affection I owe it that I can work at all. When my Aunts and all the party were so pleased with my work, I could not help thinking that they ought to have thanked you for it, far more than me ; for, if it had not been for you, very little of it would have been finished."

" My dear child, I consider a thorough knowledge of the use of the needle so great a blessing to a woman, that I could not forgive myself if I did not try to give it to you. Next to a love of literature, I think a love of work is the greatest security for a woman not becoming a frivolous, useless mortal, finding pleasure, or, at all events, seeking it, anywhere save in the precincts of her own home. When I see young ladies spending their mornings in yawning over the fire, or paying morning calls, or in some other equally useless way, and their evenings at balls and parties, I cannot help regretting, for their sakes, that they have not some employment in which they feel sufficient interest to induce them to be actively employed at home."

"But, Mamma, if you do not approve of parties, why did you allow us to have one this Christmas, and take such pains to make it pleasant to us all ?"

"My dear girl, I do not object to parties; but I object to any one whom I love being so fond of them as to be unable to spend an evening alone with her own family, or even quite by herself, without feeling weary. To go into society, or to do anything else, merely to get rid of time, shows a state of mind truly deplorable; and I cannot but heartily pity those who find life so wearisome."

"And I suppose, Mamma, when you see one of those young ladies, you feel inclined to say,

'Had she been a daughter of mine,
I'd have taught her to hem and to sew.'

I know I have felt very glad indeed you taught me. But, after all, surely every young lady can work ?"

"I am sorry to say very many young ladies have but a most limited accquaintance with the needle and its uses. For an occupation to be really agreeable to us, we must be well acquainted with it. That is why I have insisted on your being able to do every kind of plain work in the neatest manner; and now you find how easy all fancy work really is, when the other is mastered."

"And very glad I am of it, Mamma; and now I am in hopes that you will let me do a piece of work for you; something that will be really useful, and yet pretty, and that you may be able to keep."

"Well then, my dear girl, I really want an urn mat, and I think we may, by a little ingenuity, contrive a new and easy pattern for one, which you shall work for me   What

colour of wool have you the most shades of ?"

"There is a pretty apple-green, of which I have a quantity; there are ten shades of it.

PATTERN FOR AN URN-MAT.

There are some nice ambers, also, which may serve."

"They will do very well. Have you any Albert braid that will harmonize well with both those colours ?"

"There are two shades of lilac; they would not be amiss, I think, with either colour."

"No. That will do very well. Now get a piece of canvas,—of the ordinary kind, not the Penelope. Cut off a piece about 18 inches square, besides the hems. You will want a little maize filoselle, as well as all the other materials. We will take the green wool, the two shades of violet Albert braid, with the filoselle, for the centre of the mat, and the ambers for the border. Thread a needle with the brightest wool, and work ten long stitches, over ten threads, in the centre of the canvas, for the middle square. Sew down a line of the darkest Albert braid completely round, drawing in the ends through the canvas.   It should cover one thread all round. Completely round this work with the filoselle in tent stitch, but over two threads. Beyond this again, a row of the lightest Albert, on one thread."

"This, I suppose, makes the centre square in the drawing."

"Yes; and with the same wool you will work again round, always over ten threads in depth, except at the corners, where each stitch must be a thread shorter than the previous one, till it comes to a point. All the stitches must radiate from the centre. When the square of wool is worked, the two lines of Albert braid, with the filloselle between them, are to follow. Each shade of green must successively be taken, and a square worked in it, until the outer one is done in the tenth or darkest shade. The two lines of braid, with a line of filoselle between them, divide every two shades of wool."

"This is very easy indeed, Mamma; and I see from the drawing how I am to go on; except the diagonal lines which cross the mat. How are they done?"

"They are stitches of maize filoselle, taken, as you see, at the corners of each square. They cover the joinings of the woollen part only."

"Perhaps, Mamma, as I can finish this at my leisure, you would now show me how to do the fringe."

"With pleasure; and it will not take five minutes to do so. You must have a woollen mesh, about an inch and a half wide; take your light amber wool, and wind it round the mesh 24 times; cut off the end. With a stout needle, threaded with black thread, sew all these loops together, at one edge of the mesh; and then slip them off, and sew on the canvas close to the last round of work, and exactly in the centre of one side. Repeat in the same way, and with the same shade, on each side of this; then with the next, and all the successive ones, until the darkest comes at the corners. They must be sewed near enough to each other to form a handsome fringe, but not quite close. When finished, it may be cut, if you like; but I think I prefer it in loops. You can line your mat with stiff card-board, and cover it with green glazed calico."

"Then, Mamma, I will finish this some other time, and perhaps you will now help me to devise some pretty way of working the little basket for which you got me the frame from Paris. It is so different to the other, I hardly know how to do it."

"I see. The spaces are alternately wide and narrow, and the narrow ones would not show the chenille well, even if it were not crushed to pieces in drawing it through. Suppose you take some of those pretty white satin beads and let them fill up the space, as

they will about do. Then I would thread them on gold twine, as whatever they are threaded on will show, and you can twine it round the wires, so as to keep them at equal distances. Now the wide spaces may be filled in chenille, worked backwards and forwards between the wires; and the bows of wire round the top, and the handles, may be covered with it."

PATTERN OF BASKET.

"It will look rather plain, will it not, round the edge?"

"You may finish it with a row of satin beads, threaded in the gold twine, and worked in crochet all round. Thread three first on the twine; thrée Sc on the wire, 2 Ch; drop a bead, and Sc again, on the wire. Repeat all round."

"Thank you, Mamma; this little basket will be useful for a thousand purposes; and it is as pretty and as easy as any one can desire. And now let me thank you for all your kindness in explaining this work to me. With such assistance, dear Mamma, I can readily produce the pretty articles which have so pleased the friends to whom I have presented them."

"It is always a pleasure, my dear child, to encourage the industrious and grateful."

(*Continued at p* 325.)

BERLIN WHAT-NOT.

THE WORK-TABLE FRIEND.

BERLIN WHAT-NOT.

Materials.—Penelope canvas, No. 24; claret and light blue filoselle, maize crochet silk, blue wool, a shade darker than the filoselle, black crochet silk, blue beads, No. 2 ; round gold of two sizes, the same size, black velvet shamrocks, and stars.

THE design consists of alternate stripes of blue and claret, divided by narrow bands of maize.

Begin by marking the form of the What-not on the canvas. Then, exactly in the centre take the blue stripe, which occupies 44 stitches in width. + with the blue wool; take straight stitches across four threads, 45 times ; then 5 across 32. This is one side of a square in which the velvet stars are placed. Fill up the spaces left by the star, and five threads beyond. Repeat. +. Fill up the opposite side with the blue floss, leaving 8 threads between the floss and the wool. Thus opposite the wide part of the wool will be floss worked over 4 threads only ; and *vice versa*. Velvet stars are placed in both. The 8 stitches between are worked with black silk, in two times of cross stitch, stitches being over four threads. Two rows of gold beads, with a row of blue beads between them, are placed on this cross stitch.

As the long stitches across 32 threads would be apt to get loose, they are neatly stitched down in the centre.

Each point of the star is finished with three *small* gold beads ; the centre has four, forming a diamond, with a blue one in the middle.

On each side of the blue stripes take a line of maize, across 6 threads.

The claret stripe occupies 26 stitches in width. Begin by gumming on the shamrocks back to back, and nearly to touch. Put 3 small gold beads on each point, and a diamond of eight in the centre, with five blue beads within it, and one at the top and bottom. Place these double shamrocks three quarters of an inch apart. Fill up with claret filoselle, which stitch down the centre of the stitches, which are, of course, when *between* the shamrocks, the 26 threads across.

This What-not, made up with stout cardboard, and finished with card to match all the colours, may be lined either with claret or blue silk.

CROCHET WORK-BASKET.

Materials.—4 reels of Messrs. W. Evans and Co.'s red or dark blue Boar's Head Crochet Cotton, No. 10; 4 oz. of chalk white beads, No. 1; a little cardboard; sarsnet and ribbon to match the cotton, and stout wire.

THE lower part of this basket, as seen in the engraving, is done in crochet, as is also the handle. When made up, this part is lined with thin card-board and sarsnet ; a piece of strong card-board, two inches wide in the centre, and pointed at the ends, covered on both sides with sarsenet, is sewed on for the bottom, the lace falling below it; a piece of sarsenet, with a hem at the top in which ribbon strings

CROCHET WORK-BASKET.

are run, forms the upper part. The handle is lined with card-board and wire, to make it more substantial, as well as with the sarsenet.

Thread all the beads on the cotton, and work in Sc, dropping the beads on the wrong side. Fasten off at the end of every row, working in the ends of the previous one. Make a chain of 39 stitches, and do one row of Sc.

1st pattern Row.—8 cotton, 23 beads, 8 cotton.

2nd Row.—7 cotton, + 1 bead, 1 cotton + 12 times, 1 bead, 7 cotton.

3rd Row.—6 cotton, 27 beads, 6 cotton.

4th Row.—5 cotton, 1 bead, 1 cotton, 2 beads, 21 cotton, 2 beads, 1 cotton, 1 bead, 5 cotton.

5th Row.—4 cotton, 4 beads, 23 cotton, 4 beads, 4 cotton.

6th Row.—3 cotton, 1 bead, 1 cotton, 2 beads, 10 cotton, 5 beads, 10 cotton, 2 beads, 1 cotton, 1 bead, 3 cotton.

7th Row.—2 cotton, 4 beads, 10 cotton, 2 beads, 3 cotton, 2 beads, 10 cotton, 4 beads, 2 cotton.

8th Row.—2 cotton, 1 bead, 1 cotton, 1 bead, 10 cotton, 2 beads, 2 cotton, 1 bead, 2 cotton, 2 beads, 10 cotton, 1 bead, 1 cotton, 1 bead, 2 cotton.

9th Row.—2 cotton, 3 beads, 10 cotton, 1 bead, 2 cotton, 1 bead, 1 cotton, 1 bead, 2 cotton, 1 bead, 10 cotton, 3 beads, 2 cotton.

10th Row.—2 cotton, 1 bead, 1 cotton, 1 bead, 6 cotton, 5 beads, + 1 cotton, 1 bead + 3 times; 1 cotton, 5 beads, 6 cotton, 1 bead, 1 cotton, 1 bead, 2 cotton.

11th Row.—2 cotton, 3 beads, 6 cotton, 1 bead, 4 cotton + 1 bead, 1 cotton + 3 times; 1 bead, 4 cotton, 1 bead, 6 cotton, 3 beads, 2 cotton.

12th Row.—2 cotton, 1 bead, 1 cotton, 1 bead, 6 cotton, 1 bead, 3 cotton, + 1 bead, 1 cotton + 4 times, 1 bead, 3 cotton, 1 bead, 6 cotton, 1 bead, 1 cotton, 1 bead, 2 cotton.

13th Row.—2 cotton, 3 beads, 6 cotton, 1 bead, 2 cotton. + 1 bead, 1 cotton, + 5 times, 1 bead, 2 cotton, 1 bead, 6 cotton, 3 beads, 2 cotton.

14th Row.—2 cotton, 1 bead, 1 cotton, 1 bead, 6 cotton, + 1 bead, 1 cotton, + 8 times; 1 bead, 6 cotton, 1 bead, 1 cotton, 1 bead, 2 cotton.

15th Row.—2 cotton, 3 beads, 6 cotton, 1 bead, 2 cotton, + 1 bead, 1 cotton + 5 times; 1 bead, 2 cotton, 1 bead, 6 cotton, 3 beads, 2 cotton.

16th Row.—2 cotton 1 bead, 1 cotton, 1 bead, 4 cotton, 3 beads, + 1 cotton, 1 bead + 7 times; 1 cotton, 3 beads, 4 cotton, 1 bead, 1 cotton, 1 bead, 2 cotton.

17th Row.—2 cotton, 3 beads, 3 cotton, 2 beads, 2 cotton, + 1 bead, 1 cotton + twice; 1 bead, 5 cotton, * 1 bead, 1 cotton * twice; 1 bead, 2 cotton, 2 beads, 3 cotton, 3 beads, 2 cotton.

18th Row.—2 cotton, 1 bead, 1 cotton, 1 bead, 3 cotton, 1 bead, 2 cotton, + 1 bead, 1 cotton + twice; 1 bead, 2 cotton, 3 beads, 2 cotton, * 1 bead, 1 cotton, * twice; 1 bead, 2 cotton, 1 bead, 3 cotton, 1 bead, 1 cotton, 1 bead, 2 cotton.

19th Row.—2 cotton, 3 beads, 2 cotton, 2 beads, + 1 cotton, 1 bead + 3 times; 2 cotton, 5 beads, 2 cotton, * 1 bead, 1 cotton, * 3 times; 2 beads, 2 cotton, 3 beads, 2 cotton.

20th Row.—2 cotton, 1 bead, 1 cotton, 1 bead, 2 cotton, 1 bead, + 1 cotton, 1 bead, + 3 times; 2 cotton, 7 beads, 2 cotton, * 1 bead, 1 cotton, * 3 times; 1 bead, 2 cotton, 1 bead, 1 cotton, 1 bead, 2 cotton.

21st Row.—2 cotton, 3 beads, 2 cotton, 1 bead, 2 cotton, + 1 bead, 1 cotton, + 3 times; 3 beads, 1 cotton, 3 beads, * 1 cotton, 1 bead, * 3 times; 2 cotton, 1 bead, 2 cotton, 3 beads, 2 cotton.

22nd Row.—2 cotton, 1 bead, 1 cotton, 1 bead, 2 cotton, + 1 bead, 1 cotton, + 3 times; 1 bead, 2 cotton, 2 beads, 3 cotton, 2 beads, 2 cotton, 1 bead, * 1 cotton, 1 bead, * 3 times; 2 cotton, 1 bead, 1 cotton, 1 bead, 2 cotton.

23rd Row (centre row).—2 cotton, 3 beads, 2 cotton, 1 bead, 2 cotton, + 1 bead, 1 cot-

+ 3 times, 2 beads, 1 cotton, 1 bead, 1 cotton, 2 beads, * 1 cotton, 1 bead * 3 times, 2 cotton, 1 bead, 2 cotton, 3 beads, 2 cotton.

Now repeat backwards from the 22nd to the 2nd, inclusive of both, and this completes one pattern. Four are required for a bag. On finishing the last pattern, do the first row over again, to perfect the design.

Sew up the work, and do the lace all round it, at both edges.

FOR THE BAND.—Make a chain of three-eighths of a yard long, and do 1 row of Sc. On the two following rows, drop a bead on *every* stitch except the first and last three.

In the next two, after doing 3 stitches without beads, do 2 with, and 2 without, alternately to the end, except the last 3, which should be plain. Then drop a bead on every stitch for two more rows, and end with one of cotton.

FOR THE LACE.—+ 3; slip with no bead, 5 Sc with. + repeat all round.

2nd.—Sc on every stitch, with a bead on each stitch.

3rd.—+ Sc on centre of 3, 8 Ch. + repeat, with a bead on each stitch.

SOVEREIGN PURSE IN CROCHET.

Materials.—1 skein of dark blue purse-silk, 1 skein of apricot or salmon ditto, 1 gilt clasp, and 3 rows of gold beads.

MAKE a chain of 80 stitches with the blue silk, and close it into a round. Do one round of Sc.

1st Pattern Round. — Both colours, +2 blue, 2 apricot, 1 blue, + repeat all round.

2nd Round.—+ 1 blue, 4 apricot, + all round.

3rd Round.—Like 2nd.

4th Round.—Like 1st.

5th Round.—All blue.

6th Round.— + 9 blue, 3 apricot, 8 blue, + 4 times.

7th Round.—+ 10 blue, 3 apricot, (so that the first comes over the second apricot of last round), 7 blue, +4 times.

8th Round.— + 11 blue, 1 apricot, 8 blue, + 4 times.

9th Round. — + 7 blue, 3 apricot, 1 blue, 1 apricot, (which should come over

SOVEREIGN PURSE, IN CROCHET, BY MRS. PULLAN.

the 1 apricot of last round), 1 blue, 3 apricot, 4 blue, + 4 times.

10th Round.— + 6 blue, 1 apricot, 1 blue, 3 apricot, 1 blue, (over 1 apricot of last round), 3 apricot, 1 blue, 1 apricot, 3 blue, + 4 times.

11th Round.— + 6 blue, 5 apricot, 1 blue, 5 apricot, 3 blue, + 4 times.

12th Round.— + 6 blue, 11 apricot, 3 blue, + 4 times.

13th Round.— + 7 blue, 4 apricot, 1 blue, 4 apricot, 4 blue, + 4 times.

14th Round.— + 5 blue, 2 apricot, 2 blue, 1 apricot, 3 blue, 1 apricot, 2 blue, 2 apricot, 2 blue, + 4 times.

15th Round.— + 4 blue, 1 apricot, 2 blue, 4 apricot, 1 blue, (on the centre of

MOUSQUETAIRE COLLAR, BY MRS. PULLAN.

three blue), 4 apricot, 2 blue, 1 apricot, 1 blue, + 4 times.

16th Round.—Like 12th.

17th Round.—Like 11th

18th Round.—Like 10th

19th Round.—Like 9th.

20th Round.—Like 8th.

21st Round.— + 6 blue, 2 apricot, 2 blue, 2 apricot, 8 blue, + 4 times.

22nd Round.— + 5 blue, 9 apricot, 6 blue, + 4 times.

23rd Round.— + 4 blue, 5 apricot, 1 blue, 3 apricot, 7 blue, + 4 times.

24th Round.— + 6 blue, 2 apricot, 1 blue, 1 apricot, 1 blue, 2 apricot, 7 blue, + times.

25th Round.— + 9 blue, 1 apricot, 10 blue + 4 times.

26th Round.— + 8 blue, 3 apricot, 9 blue, + 4 times.

27th Round.— + 8 blue, 4 apricot, 8 blue, + 4 times.

28th Round.— + 8 blue, 4 apricot, 3 blue, 1 apricot, 4 blue, + 4 times.

29th Round.— + 9 blue, 7 apricot, 4 blue, + 4 times.

30th Round.— + 11 blue, 3 apricot, (or the centre three of 7 apricot), 6 blue.

31st Round.—All blue.

Now repeat the 1st to 4th pattern rounds, when fasten off the apricot, and do two rounds of Sc with the blue.

V

1st open Round.—(All blue to the end), + 1 Dc, 1 Ch, miss 1, + all round.

2nd 3rd and 4th Rounds.—Dc under chain, 1 ch, miss Dc stitch of last round.

Work one side of the purse, backward and forwards in the same way, gradually decreasing at each edge, to fit the clasp. Do the same at the other side.

For closing the end, do one round of apricot silk; then holding the two sides together, Sc a stitch of each with blue. Add the fringe and clasp.

MOUSQUETAIRE COLLAR.

Materials.—3 yards of Italian braid, and the Point Lace Cottons of Messrs. W. Evans and Co., Boar's Head Cotton Manufacturers, Derby.

The Mousquetaire is the name given to the very becoming style of collar, recently introduced from France. It is of rather a large size, and in deep points, as seen in the engraving. About seven are the usual number in a collar, but nine may be made if it is intended for a stout person.

The depth, also, must be regulated by the taste of the wearer. We have seen them almost five inches deep; but at present, this size looks peculiar; four inches, reckoning to the point of every Vandyke, may be considered as a medium size, and we would recommend that the pattern should be increased to that scale.

The pines are outlined in Italian braid, which is represented in the engraving by the clear broad white lines. Evans's Mecklenburgh thread, No. 1, forms the outline of the leaves, and other parts. The leaves are made as heavy as possible, being filled with foundation-stitch, with a line of open-work in the veinings only. For this stitch, Evans's Boar's-head cotton, No. 120, must be used. Within the Italian braid is a similar width, worked in open diamond-stitch, with No. 150 Boar's-head; and the centre of each pine is in spotted lace, done with 140 Mecklenburgh. The bars which make the groundwork of the collar, forming a beautiful guipure, are done in 120 Mecklenburgh; as in all the most valuable old point, they are very variously worked—some are quite plain, some merely spotted with Raleigh dots, and others have small semicircular loops on them.

The outline of the collar within the lace edging, which completes it, is a simple line of No. 1 Mecklenburgh thread, closely covered with button-hole stitch. The edging itself must be worked first. This is done by tacking down a thread to correspond with the first row of loops. Cover two of these, and half a third with button-hole stitch; then take back the needle to the middle of the second loop, and after leaving a thread to form a loop there, take a tight button-hole stitch to secure it. Repeat this to the centre of the first loop, and the two being made, cover one, and half the other with button-hole stitch. Take the needle to the centre of the first of these, to form the loop at the *point* of the scallop, work it in the same way, and then cover the half loops left. Thus each scallop is done in succession; the line adjoining the Vandyke, only being outlined.

Care must be taken so to arrange that every Vandyke has a scallop at the point of it.

FEMALE OCCUPATION.—Women in the middle rank are brought up with the idea that if they engage in some occupations, they shall lose "their position in society." Suppose it to be so; surely it is wiser to quit a position we cannot honestly maintain, than to live dependent upon the bounty and caprice of others: better to labour with our hands than eat the bread of idleness: or submit to feel that we must not give utterance to our real opinions, or express our honest indignation at being required to act a base or unworthy part. And in all cases, however situated, every female ought to learn how all household affairs are managed, were it only for the purpose of being able to direct others. There cannot be any disgrace in learning how to make the bread we eat, to cook our dinners, to mend our clothes, or even to clean the house. Better to be found busily engaged in removing the dust from the furniture, than to let it accumulate there until a visitor leaves palpable traces where his hat or his arm have been laid upon a table.

THE WORK-TABLE FRIEND.

THE SANSPAREIL WORK-BAG.

Materials.—2 Oval medallions; a piece of black filet 18 inches by 6; a little Vert-islay, cerise, and white silk; gold thread; green cord, tassels, and satin, and white silk; 10 steel rings.

THIS unique little bag was a part of our collection of fancy work at the fancy-fair held at Drury Lane; and we believe, at the time, it was acknowledged to be a gem. The medallions form the centre, round which the embroidered netting, lined with satin and silk beneath it, is gathered.

The pattern for the netting, of which we give a diagram, is worked in gold and cerise for the flowers, and green for the leaves. Each edge is so darned, and between them the space is filled by small spots of white and gold.

When embroidered line the filet with satin, under which is white silk, and run the edges neatly together before gathering it. Then set it round the medallion. The ends which meet at the top of each, are to be drawn up; cover the rings with crochet, and set five at each side; through these the cords are drawn, and the ends are concealed by bullion slides. The tassels are placed at the centre of each end.

Join on the maize.
1st Pattern Round.—+ 4 S, 1 M, 9 S, 1 M, 5 S, + 6 times. Join on Vert-islay.
2nd Round.—+ 3 S, 3 M, 7 S, 1 M, 1 V, 1 M, 4 S, + 6 times.
3rd Round.—+ 2 S, 1 M, 1 S, 1 M, 1 S, 1 M, 5 S, 1 M, 3 V, 1 M, 3 S, + 6 times.
4th Round.—+ 1 S, 3 M, 1 S, 3 M, 4 S, 1 M, 3 V, 1 M, 3 S, + 6 times.

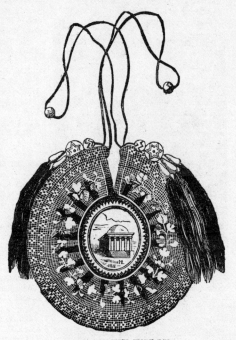

THE SANSPAREIL WORK-BAG.

CIGAR-CASE, IN CROCHET.

Materials.—5 skeins scarlet silk, 4 pale Vert-islay do., 2 black, 3 maize, 1 white, with Boulton's crochet hook, No. 20.

CONTRACTIONS used in this design :—S, scarlet; B, black; M, maize; V, Vert-islay; W, white. The entire work is done in Sc (single crochet).

With the scarlet silk make a chain of 120 stitches; close it into a round, and do three rounds of this silk only.

5th Round.—+ 2 S, 1 M, 1 S, 1 M, 1 S, 1 M, 4 S, * 1 M, 1 V, * 3 times; 1 M, 2 S, + 6 times.
6th Round.—+ 4 S, 1 M, 5 S, 1 M, 3 V, 1 M, 3 V, 1 M, 1 S, + 6 times.
7th Round.—+ 2 S, 2 M, 1 S, 2 M, 3 S, 1 M, 3 V, 1 M, 3 V, 1 M, 1 S, + 6 times.
8th Round.—+ 1 S, 1 M, 5 S, 1 M, 1 S, * 1 M, 1 V, * 5 times; 1 M, + 6 times.
9th Round.—+ 1 M, 2 S, 3 V, 2 S, * 1 M, 3 V, * 3 times, + 6 times. Fasten off scarlet.

10th Round.—+ 2 M, 5 V, 2 M, 1 V, * 1 M, 1 V, * 5 times, + 6 times.   Join on black.

11th Round.—+ 1 V, 1 M, 2 V, 1 B, 2 V, 1 M, 1 V, 3 M, 1 V, 3 M, 1 V, 3 M, + 6 times.

12th Round.—All maize.

13th Round.—All black.

14th and 15th Round.—All Vert-islay.

CIGAR-CASE IN CROCHET.

16th and 17th Round.—All scarlet.

18th Round.—Scarlet and maize, + 19 S, 3 M, 18 S, + 3 times.

19th Round.—+ 1 8 S, 5 M, 17 S, + 3 times.

20th Round.—+ 18 S, 2 M, 1 S, 2 M, 17 S, + 3 times.

21st Round.—+ Like 19th.

22nd Round.—+ 16 S, 2 M, 1 S, 3 M, 1 S, 2 M, 15 S, + 3 times.

23rd Round.—+ 15 S, 11 M, 14 S, + 3 times.

24th Round.—+ 15 S, 5 M, 1 S, 5 M, 14 S, + 3 times.

25th Round.—+ 2 M, 13 S, 11 M, 13 S, 1 M, + 3 times.   Join on Vert-islay.

26th Round.—+ 3 M, 13 S, 2 M, 1 S, 1 V 1 M, 1 S, 2 M, 13 S, 2 M, + 3 times.

27th Round.—+ 1 S, 2 M, 16 S, 1 M, 1 V, 1 M, 16 S, 2 M, + 3 times.   Join on black.

28th Round.—+ 3 M, 13 S, 1 M, 1 S, 1 M, 1 V, 1 B, 1 V, 1 M, 1 S, 1 M, 13 S, 2 M, + 3 times.

29th Round.—+ 2 M, 2 S, 3 M, 7 S, 1 M, 1 S, 2 M, 1 V, 3 B, 1 V, 2 M, 1 S, 1 M, 7 S, 3 M, 2 S, 1 M, + 3 times.

30th Round.—+ 1 M, 2 S, 5 M, 4 S, 1 M, 1 S, 2 M, 2 V, 5 B, 2 V, 2 M, 1 S, 1 M, 4 S, 5 M, 2 S, + 3 times.

31st Round.—+ 1 M, 2 S, 2 M, 1 S, 2 M, 3 S, 3 M, 2 V, 4 B, 1 V, 4 B, 2 V, 3 M, 3 S, 2 M, 1 S, 2 M, 2 S, + 3 times.

32nd Round.—+ 2 M, 1 S, 5 M, 1 S, 2 M, 3 V, 5 B, 3 V, 5 B, 3 V, 2 M, 1 S, 5 M, 1 S, 1 M, + 3 times.   Join on white.

33rd Round.—+ 1 W, 1 M, 2 S, 3 M, 1 S, 1 M, 2 V, 6 B, 7 V, 6 B, 2 V, 1 M, 1 S, 3 M, 2 S, 1 M, + 3 times.

34th Round.—+ 1 W, 3 M, 3 S, 1 M, 1 V, 6 B, 11 V, 6 B, 1 V, 1 M, 3 S, 3 M, + 3 times.

35th Round.—+ 1 B, 2 W, 2 M, 1 S, 1 M, 1 V, 4 B, 17 V, 4 B, 1 V, 1 M, 1 S, 2 M, 2 W, + 3 times.

36th Round.—+ 1 B, 3 W, 1 M, 1 S, 1 M, 1 V, 2 B, 9 V, 1 B, 1 V, 1 B, 9 V, 2 B, 1 V, 1 M, 1 S, 1 M, 3 W, + 3 times.   Fasten off scarlet.

37th Round.—+ 2 B, 2 W, 2 M, 1 V, 3 B, 8 V, 5 B, 8 V, 3 B, 1 V, 2 M, 2 W, 1 B, + 3 times.

38th Round.—+ 1 V, 2 B, 2 W, 1 M, 1 V, 2 B, 9 V, 5 B, 9 V, 2 B, 1 V, 1 M, 2 W, 2 B, + 3 times.

39th Round.—+ 2 V, 1 B, 2 W, 1 M, 1 V, 2 B, 10 V, 3 B, 10 V, 2 B, 1 V, 1 M, 2 W, 1 B, 1 V, + 3 times.

40th Round.—+ 2 V, 1 B, 2 W, 1 M, 1 V, 2 B, 7 V, 2 B, 2 V, 1 B, 2 V, 2 B, 7 V, 2 B, 1 V, 1 M, 2 W, 1 B, 1 V, + 3 times.

41st Round.—+ 1 V, 2 B, 2 W, 1 M, 1 V, 2 B, 3 V, 2 B, 3 V, 2 B, 1 V, 1 B, 1 V, 2 B, 3 V, 2 B, 3 V, 2 B, 1 V, 1 M, 2 W, 2 B, + 3 times.

42nd Round.—+ 2 B, 2 W, 2 M, 1 V, 3 B, 1 V, 4 B, 2 V, 2 B, 1 V, 1 B, 1 V, 2 B, 2 V, 4 B, 1 V, 3 B, 1 V, 2 M, 2 W, 1 B, + 3 times.

43rd Round.—+ 1 B, 3 W, 1 M, 1 V, 1 M, 1 V, 7 B, 3 V, 1 B, 1 V, 1 B, 1 V, 1 B, 3 V, 7 B, 1 V, 1 M, 1 V, 1 M, 3 W, + 3 times.

44th Round.—+ 1 B, 2 W, 2 M, 1 V, 1 M, 1 V, 7 B, 1 V, 1 B, 2 V, 3 B, 2 V, 1 B, 1 V, 7 B, 1 V, 1 M, 1 V, 2 M, 2 W, + 3 times.

As there is now a centre to each pattern, it will be sufficient to write as far as the middle stitch only, observing that you will always work *backwards* from *b* in each round, omitting the first stitch, whatever that may be. Thus, if you begin with 2 black, you will end the pattern with *one*, and so on. As hitherto, the design is repeated thrice in the round.

45th Round.—1 W, 3 M, 3 V, 1 M, 2 V, 4 B, 3 V, 1 B, 1 V, 1 B, *b* 1 W. This 1 white is the centre stitch, after working which, go back from 1 B to the last, which you will not repeat.

46th Round.—1 W, 1 M, 6 V, 2 M, 7 V, 2 B, *b* 3 W.

47th Round.—4 M, 6 V, 4 M, 2 V, 2 B, *b* 5 W.

48th Round.—1 M, 1 V, 2 M, 10 V, 2 M, 4 W, *b* 1 B.

49th Round.—2 M, 2 V, 1 B, 4 V, 4 B, 3 V, 1 M, 2 W, *b* 3 B.

50th Round.—1 M, 2 V, 3 B, 1 V, 8 B, 2 V, 1 M, 2 W, *b* 1 B.

51st Round.—1 M, 3 V, 1 B, 2 V, 9 B, 1 V, 1 M, 1 W, *b* 3 B. Fasten off white.

52nd Round.—1 B, 6 W, 4 B, 3 V, 2 B, 2 V, 1 M, *b* 3 B.

53rd Round.—2 B, 4 V, 4 B, 5 V, 2 B, 1 V, 1 M, *b* 3 B.

54th Round.—1 B, 5 V, 4 B, 2 V, 2 B, 1 V, 2 B, 1 V, 1 M, *b* 3 B.

55th Round.—7 V, 4 B, 2 V, 2 B, 1 V, 1 B, 1 V, 1 M, *b* 3 B.

56th Round.—1 V, 1 B, 11 V, 2 B, 1 V, 1 B, 1 V, 1 M, *b* 3 B.

57th Round.—3 B, 10 V, 4 B, 1 V, *b* 3 B. Fasten on the scarlet.

58th Round.—3 B, 2 V, 2 B, 4 V, 1 B, 1 V, 3 B, 1 V, 1 M, 1 S, *b* 3 B.

59th Round.—1 V, 1 B, 2 V, 2 B, 6 V, 4 B, 1 V, 1 M, 2 S, *b* 1 B.

60th Round.—3 B, 1 V, 4 B, 4 V, 3 W, 1 V, 1 M, 2 S, *b* 3 B.

61st Round.—3 S, 4 B, 4 V, 2 B, 1 V, 2 M, 4 S, *b* 1 B.

62nd Round.—1 B, 4 S, 1 B, 3 V, 5 M, *b* 17 S. Fasten off the Vert-islay.

63rd Round.—2 B, 4 S, 4 M, 10 S, *b* 1 B.

64th Round.—1 B, 3 S, 3 M, 7 S, 1 M, 4 S, *b* 3 B.

65th Round.—2 B, 1 S, 2 M, 2 S, 7 M, 3 S, 1 M, 2 S, *b* 1 B.

66th Round.—2 B, 2 M, 2 S, 2 M, 1 S, 2 M, 2 S, 4 M, 2 S, *b* 3 B.

67th Round.—1 B, 2 M, 1 S, 2 M, 1 S, 1 M, 1 S, 2 M, 1 S, 2 M, 2 S, 3 M, *b* 3 B.

68th Round.—1 B, 1 M, 2 S, 2 M, 6 S, 2 M, 1 S, 2 M, 1 S, 2 M, *b* 1 B.

69th Round.—1 B, 3 M, 11 S, 2 M, 2 S, 1 M, *b* 1 B. Fasten off black.

70th Round.—1 M, 1 S, 3 M, 12 S, *b* 7 M.

71st Round.—1 S, 5 M, 11 S, 2 M, 1 S, *b* 1 M.

72nd Round.—1 M, 1 S, 3 M, 14 S, *b* 3 M.

73rd Round.—2 M, 1 S, 1 M, 16 S, *b* 1 M.

74th Round.—+ 1 M, 39 S, + 3 times.

Repeat from the seventeenth round backwards to the first, which completes the design. Then divide the round into eight, and decrease by omitting a stitch at each division until it is closed. It must be mounted at a warehouse.

+ + * * These marks, used in this and *every other design where they occur*, indicate repetition between two similar marks in the same round or row. Thus, the 9th round, if written without them, would be 1 M, 2 S, 3 V, 2 S, 1 M, 3 V, 1 M, 3 V, 1 M, 3 V, *six times over*. A very little care and attention will enable any worker to understand the terms, which have also been explained at full length repeatedly.

WORK-TABLE FOR JUVENILES;

OR,

LITTLE MARY'S HALF-HOLIDAYS.

(*Continued from p.* 317.)

"THIS is our last half-holiday, dear mamma, before the real Christmas holidays begin; and we are so busy preparing for the examination, that I shall have very little time for more work until then; so I hope that you have some very pretty and very easy articles to suggest, which will serve to decorate the Christmas tree."

"I think, this time, your wishes will be fully realised. What say you to this pretty *allumette-stand*, so useful during the winter months? You could make a pair well in an hour; and how effective they are! The contrast of their brilliant colours against the dark-green tree will be exceedingly striking."

"It looks too pretty to be very easy, mamma. What are the materials employed?"

MATCH-STAND PATTERN.

"First, a wire frame, of the form you see; then about twelve yards of each of two-coloured chenilles; say cerise and Napoleon-blue, or blue and orange, or green and white. You will also require a bodkin, and a needleful of silk of each of the two colours.

"Observe that the stand has the form of a vase. The frame of the upper part is in six flutes, the wires being alternately bent in and out. Take a long needleful of chenille, threaded on a bodkin, fasten the end at the bottom of one of those flutes, and bring it out *over* one of the inner wires; pass it round an outer wire, and under the next inner one, so as to come out over it. Then again round the outer vire. Repeat backwards and forwards on these three wires to the top. Take another colour, and cover the next flute in the same way, passing the chenille over two *new* wires, and one of the inner ones already done. Repeat this, first with one colour, and then with the other, all round. There will be three stripes of each. Secure the ends with a needle and fine silk. The wire which goes round the top of the frame is covered alternately with each of the two colours, merely by twisting it closely round. Each stripe is finished with the opposite colour; thus, if you choose cerise

and green, the green stripe will be headed with cerise, and *vice versâ*."

"And the foot, mamma? How is that done?"

"The six branches are covered with a stripe of the two colours rolled round them; but all the rest is done in the darkest and most durable shade, whatever that may be."

"Then, I suppose, I should make some *allumettes*, to fill them."

"Yes, strips of various-coloured papers, rolled into pretty forms, make very suitable ones; but as that is work that requires but little light, suppose you occupy yourself now with something else. I see your allumette-stand has almost got finished whilst I have been talking of it."

"It is, indeed, quickly done. What a pleasure to have a kind of work which takes so little time, at a season like this, when all are anxious to get as much done as possible in a short space What is the next thing to think of, mamma?"

"A pen-wiper in application; a kind of work which is now most fashionable. You know that application means that one

PEN-WIPER PATTERN.

substance or colour is gummed on another, and the edges sewed over with some sort of ornamental work or braid. This is in green velvet, on claret cloth; the edges of the velvet are covered with gold braid, and a line of black beads laid along the centre of the velvet, is also edged on each side with gold thread. Black glass beads are dotted here and there over the pattern.

"How is that row of beads put on, mamma? If I sew them on one at a time, there will be large spaces between."

"Yes; you will find it better to thread them on a length of black silk, and then, with another needleful of silk, take a stitch across the thread, *between every two beads.* The silk on which you thread them should be very coarse, but you will sew them over with fine. You may, if you like, put a trimming of gold beads, or black bugles, round the pen-wiper."

"The button for the centre is very pretty."

"Yes, it is an eagle, in carved ivory; look at the eyes, how exquisitely they are finished! Everything ornamental is now made in Paris with some sort of imperial emblem or decoration, and the eagle is the favourite."

"Well, it is the king of birds, and makes a kingly appearance here, with its white wings glistening on the dark velvet. And now I think I have a very pretty collection of presents for my tree; and the rest of the decorations may be purchased, I suppose."

MATERNAL TUITION.—No man can sympathise with a child's feelings so truly, so intimately as woman; he is deficient in the kindness which in her overflows: from her heart she pours out nourishment to the infant mind, which man's intellect in vain attempts to supply. No education, from which the mother virtually or actually is excluded, can suffice and satisfy; no education can be normal in which woman has no part; for without her, though the understanding may be brought out, the will which yields not to hard and harsh motives, but to soft and inviting spontaneities,— which does not and cannot respond to mere intellectual teaching, but answers only to sympathetic persuasions, — must remain comparatively dormant. Christian morals taught by female lips cease to be syllogistic disputations, and become at once living principles, receiving illustration not only in the pictures of fancy, and the moving shapes of strong imagination, but in the affectionate reality, true loving-kindness, good-will and well-being, which live in woman.—*Heraud's Essay on Education.*

POLE SCREEN, EMBROIDERED IN APPLICATION.

THE WORK-TABLE FRIEND.

POLE SCREEN, EMBROIDERED IN APPLICATION.

Materials.—Rich dark silk, satin of various colours, green velvet leaves, of different shades, gold thread and braid, and green and gold soutache. Also a pole screen, which must be made at a cabinet maker's, with silk at the back, and glass in front.

THIS piece of work is extremely tasteful.

BRAIDED TRAVELLING BAG.

The large flowers are of bright-coloured satin laid under the silk or satin which forms the ground of the whole, and which is cut away in those parts. The leaves are of velvet, gummed on. The outlines, where they join, are covered with gold braid, but the stems and tendrils are of soutache.

Gold thread is used for the divisions of the petals, and for outlining the leaves.

BRAIDED TRAVELLING BAG.

Materials.—A piece of cloth about 15 inches by 11 for each side of the bag, and a piece of soutache of any suitable colour to correspond with it. The cloth must be marked with any pretty design.

THE only way in which amateurs can mark patterns is, as may be supposed, at once tedious and troublesome ; and it is always better to purchase the cloth ready marked, because those whose business it is to do such things, being required to prepare them in hundreds or thousands, have mechanical facilities which enable them to mark the designs much better than any private persons can, as well as at a very moderate cost.

The pattern we give for this bag is extremely pretty, and well suited for the ornamental soutaches made in Paris for these purposes. There is a vast variety of designs, as well as colours. Perhaps green cloth with violet. or crimson soutache, makes as pretty a bag as any.

The bag may be made up with a steel clasp, or in the ordinary way, which is much less expensive.

THE WORK-TABLE FRIEND.

EMBROIDERED ANTIMACASSAR.

Materials.—A square of netting, or imitation netting, 86 holes up the side; Messrs. W. Evans and Co.'s Boar's Head Crochet cotton, Nos. 10 and 16; and Knitting cotton, No. 4.

WE give a quarter of an Antimacassar in this very ancient style of work, which is particularly suitable for many purposes of decoration, and especially for church work. It is also well adapted for doyleys, bed-quilts, and similar articles.

The pattern is formed by darning with various cottons, on ordinary square netting.

EMBROIDERED ANTIMACASSAR.

Many stitches are used for this purpose. In another part of this work we give our readers very clear and elaborate descriptions of the leading stitches. In the antimacassar before us, however, very few are used, and some are already known to our readers. As much of the effect is produced by using the cottons most adapted for the stitch, the worker will do well to be careful to have precisely that which has been employed by ourselves in the original design.

The outer border occupies two lines of holes, and the pattern is so worked as to fill up alternately a space in the upper and the under line. Fasten on at a knot, in the corner; + pass the needle over one of the side-threads, and under the other of a lower square; then over the lower line and under the upper of the upper square, round the knot to the left, then round the one to the right, down the square, and repeat from the cross. Go in this way entirely round the antimacassar; then by treating the lower squares as upper ones, and always letting the threads cross each other as in ordinary darning, the effect will be produced. We call this Chess-board stitch.

Honey-comb stitch forms the next border. The threads, instead of being taken round the knots, are always on the bars of thread between. Take a series of stitches on the upper bars of the squares to be filled up *one on each*, letting the thread cross over the bar between every two squares. When this is done along the upper line, do the same along the lower; but between every two stitches pass the needle under the side bars and over the loop of thread of the previous row. This pattern occupies a depth of six holes, leaving a row of two between it and the last. The spots seen on it are done by filling a square of four holes with very close darning, done by twisting the threads together, in passing backwards and forwards, and then making a round of cotton on four threads. The Vandyke honeycomb forming the diamonds is done in the same way as the other. For all this use No. 16.

The ornamental spots are also done in darning, or with twisted thread.

The flower in the centre is done in cloth darning, as described in the Portuguese Guipure Doyleys in this work. The very coarse knitting-cotton is used for this purpose, and also for the twisted thread which forms the outline.

As it is very difficult to describe these stitches clearly, we advise our readers to obtain pattern-pieces of netting, with all the stitches marked on them.

To excel in this kind of work, requires something like the same head for calculation that makes a good chess-player; and any one who piques herself on playing that game well, ought to try this work, which will, undoubtedly, delight her.

EMBROIDERED CIGAR-CASE.

THE WORK-TABLE FRIEND.

EMBROIDERED CIGAR-CASE.

Materials.—Rich dark-green or blue velvet; ¼ oz. of dead gold bullion, and the same quantity of bright gold.

IT has always been a sentiment with us that a gift in needlework, to be really valuable to the receiver, should, if possible, bear some evidence that its presentation was a matter of forethought rather than impulse; and for this reason, we would introduce, if possible, the crest or initals of the person to whom a cigar-case or other article is to be given, because it implies that the thoughts as well as the fingers of the worker were employed in the service of her friend,—a circumstance which cannot fail to add much to the gratification which a gift is calculated to afford.

In this present design, therefore, it has been our aim to show the manner in which initials may be arranged to form a suitable centre for a cigar-case. On the reverse side is a small spray of roses and buds, the border being the same on both sides. It will be seen that the letters employed are of a very simple character, the scrolls added to the centre one being merely to give it that extra length which the oblong form of the article demands.

We have already described the mode of embroidering with gold bullion. The fine parts have merely a succession of pieces of bullion sewed down in half-polka stitch; but the wide and heavy parts are raised by having a thickness of yellow floss underneath, over which the bullion is laid. It is to be observed that each part is raised in proportion to its width.

The greater part of the design is worked in the dead gold; the brilliant kind is introduced judiciously into those places where the light falls, as also into the upper parts of the roses, the knots of the border, and the upper part of the leaves on the reversed side. The heart of the rose is formed by little knots of bullion which are very easily made. Bring up the needle, threaded with yellow silk, on the right side, pass it throught a bit of bullion one-fourth of an inch long, and slip the needle down in the same place. The bright bullion is to be used for this purpose.

Velvet, satin, or kid when put in a frame to be embroidered should be lined with fine but stout linen, which makes the work much firmer, and the article more durable.

Shaded silks, instead of gold bullion, look very well for this style of embriodery. Ombré violet on green velvet, scarlet or amber on blue, and almost any colour on black, look well. Ladies' card-cases may be worked in the same way.

SPANISH UNDER-SLEEVE.

Materials.—1 oz. of white Pyrenees wool, and 4 knitting needles, No. 14.

CAST on 60 stitches, namely 20 on each of 3 needles. close it into a round, and knit 1 round.

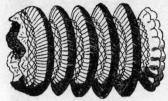

SPANISH UNDER-SLEEVE.

1st Pattern Round.—+ knit 1, make 1, knit 3, knit 3 together, knit 3, make 1 + 6 times.

2nd Round.—Plain knitting,

3rd Round.—Like 1*st*.

4th Round.—Plain knitting.

5th Round.—Like 1*st*.

6th Round.—Plain knitting.

7th Round.—+ purl 8, purl 2 together,+ 6 times.

8th Round.—Purled.

9th Round.—+ make 1, slip 1, knit 2 (not together), pass the slip-stitch over the two. + all round.

10th Round.—Plain knitting.

11th Round.—knit 2. + make 1, slip 1, knit 2 as before, and pass the slip-stitch over the two. + all round. End with make 1, slip 1, and pass it over the two first of the round, the first of which you must put on the third needle.

12th Round.—Plain knitting.

13th Round.—Like 9*th*.

14th Round.—Plain knitting.

15th and 16*th Rounds.*—Purled.

17th Round.—+ make 1, knit 1, + all round.

18th to 39*th Round.*—+ make 1, knit 2 together + all round.

40th Round.—Knit 2 together all round.

41st Round.—Purled.

Repeat from 8*th* to 41*st Round* inclusive, 4 times more, and then as far as the 16*th Round* only.

EDGE.—+knit 3, make 1,+. *2nd Round.*—Plain knitting. *3rd Round.*—+ knit 3, make 1, knit 1, make 1. + all round. *4th Round.*—Plain. *5th Round.*—+ knit 3, make 1. + all round. *6th Round.*—Plain. Cast off.

A second edging is knitted under this, by taking up, with a fine knitting-needle, the back of the stitches of the last purled round, and doing 6 rounds before beginning the pattern of the edging, which must be exactly like the upper one.

If wished extremely warm, these sleeves may be knitted with Berlin wool.

Done in Berlin wool, with one puffing only, and then a couple of inches of ribbed knitting, this pattern makes a most comfortable and elastic glove-top. It will not interfere with the fur cuffs, but will effectually warm the wrists.

THE WORK-TABLE FRIEND.

DEEP CROCHET LACE.

Materials.—Mess's. W. Evans and Co.'s Boar's-head Crochet Cotton, No. 4. 8. or 12. In the last number, the lace will be fully four inches deep.

WE have much pleasure in presenting our readers with the above design for a very deep and handsome crochet lace, suited for counterpanes, toilet covers, and all similar purposes.

Make a chain of the required length, taking care that the number of stitches are divisible by 24.

1st Row.—Dc.

2nd Row.—+ 1 Dc, 2 Ch, miss 2. + repeat to the end. The directions between + + are always to be repeated.

3rd Row.—+3 Dc, 9 Ch, miss 9. +.

4th Row.—Join on. 3 Ch over 3 Dc. + 3 Dc, 3 Ch, miss 3 +.

5th Row.—+ 3 Dc, 9 Ch, miss 9. +.

6th Row.—Join on. 6 Ch, miss 6. + 4 Dc on centre 3 of 9 chain, 9 Ch, miss 9. +.

7th Row.—Join on. 3 Ch. + 4 Dc, coming on the last three of 6 chain and 1 Dc, 2 Ch, miss 2 Dc, 4 Dc, 5 Ch, miss 5, 2 Dc, 2 Ch, miss 2 Dc, 2 Dc, 2 Ch, +.

8th Row.—Join on. 6 Ch, + 4 Dc (over 2 Ch and a Dc on each side), 6 Ch, miss 6, 4 Dc, 2 Ch, over 2 Ch, 4 Dc. +.

9th Row.—Join on. 2 Dc, 12 Ch + 6 Dc, 2 Ch over 2 Ch, 6 Dc, 12 Ch. +.

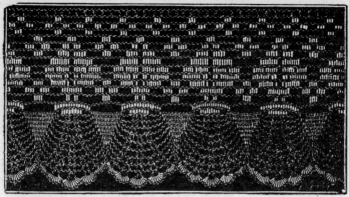

DEEP CROCHET LACE.

10th Row.—Join on. + 1 Ch, miss 1, 4 Dc, 6 Ch, miss 6, 4 Dc, 1 Ch, miss 1, 4 Dc, 2 Ch (over 2 Ch), 4 Dc. +.

11th Row.—5 Dc. + 6 Ch, over 6 Ch, 6 Dc, 1 Ch, miss 1, 2 Dc, 2 Ch (over 2 Ch), 2 Dc, 1 Ch, miss 1, 6 Dc +.

12th Row.—3 Dc. + 3 Ch, miss 3, 4 Dc (on centre 4 of 6 Ch), 3 Ch, miss 3, 5 Dc, 1 Ch, miss 1, 1 Dc, 2 Ch over 2 Ch, 1 Dc, 1 Ch, miss 1, 5 Dc. +.

13th Row.—3 Ch. + 4 Dc, over 3 Ch, and first of 4 Dc, 2 Ch, miss 2, 4 Dc, 4 Ch, miss 4, 8 Dc, 4 Ch, miss 4 +.

14th Row.—6 Ch. + 4 Dc, coming over 2 Ch and a Dc on each side, 9 Ch, miss 8, 2 Dc, 2 Ch over centre 2 of 8 Dc, 2 Dc, 9 Ch, miss 8.

15th Row.—2 Dc. + 12 Ch, miss 12, 16 Dc. +.

16th Row.—+. 12 Sc on 12 Ch, 5 Ch, miss 4, 8 Dc on centre 8 of 16 Dc, 5 Ch, miss 4. +.

17th Row.—+ 11 Sc over 12, 5 Ch, Dc on 3rd Dc, 3 Ch, Dc on same, 1 Ch, miss 2, Dc on next Dc, 3 Ch, Dc on same, 5 Ch. +.

18th Row.—+ 9 Sc, beginning on 2nd Sc, 5 Ch, Dc under the Ch of 3, 3 Ch, Dc under the same, 2 Ch, Dc under the next Ch of 3, 3 Ch, Dc under the same, 5 Ch. +.

19th Row.—+ 9 Sc on 9 Sc. 5 Ch, Dc under chain of 3, 3 Ch, Dc under same, 3 Ch, over 2 Ch, Dc under next chain of 3, 3 Ch, Dc under same, 5 Ch. +.

20th Row.—+ 7 Sc beginning on the 2nd Sc of last row, 5 Ch, Dc under the 1st chain of 3, 3 Ch, Dc under same, 2 Ch, Dc under 2nd chain of 3, 3 Ch, Dc under same, 2 Ch, Dc under 3rd chain of 3, 3 Ch, Dc under same, 5 Ch. +.

21st Row.—Like 20*th*.

22nd Row.—+ 5 Sc, beginning on the 2nd of 7 Sc, 5 Ch, Dc under 1st chain of 3. 3 Ch, Dc under same, 3 Ch, Dc under next chain of 3, 3 Ch, Dc under same, 3 Ch, Dc under next chain of 3, 3 Ch, Dc under same, 5 Ch. +.

23rd Row.—+ 5 Sc on 5, 5 Ch, * 2 Dc under next chain of 3, 3 Ch, Dc under same, 1 Ch * 5 times. 4 more chain +.

24th Row.—+ 3 Sc, beginning on the 2nd of 5 Sc, 5 Ch, * Dc under 1st chain of 3, 3 Ch, Dc under same, 2 Ch, * 5 times; 3 more chain +.

25th Row.—+ 1 Sc on 2nd of 3 Sc, 5 Ch * Dc under 1st chain of 3, 3 Ch, Dc under the same, 2 Ch, * 5 times. 3 more Ch +.

26th Row.—+ Sc under chain of 5, close to the 1st Dc, * 1 Ch, 6 Dc under 3 Ch, 1 Ch. Sc under 2 Ch, * 4 times; 1 Ch, 6 Dc under 3 Ch, 1 Ch, Sc under chain of 5. +.

Sc is working a stitch without putting the thread round the hook.

Dc is working with the thread once round the hook.

When two *similar* marks as + + or * * occur in a row, the repetitions are to take place between those two similar marks, for any specified number of times, or throughout the length if no number is mentioned.

VENETIAN POINT COLLAR.

THE WORK-TABLE FRIEND.

VENETIAN POINT COLLAR.

Materials.—1 piece of best Paris cotton braid, No. 7, and the Point Lace cottons of Messrs. W. Evans and Co. of Derby.

BEGIN by laying on the braid as you do the Italian, sewing it down at *both* edges. A great variety of stitches is introduced into this collar. We will describe first those worked in the flowers round the neck, as one or two are entirely new. The one nearest the end of the collar is in an open foundation stitch worked by doing four stitches close together, and then leaving enough space for four. In the following row the four stitches are worked on the thread between every two sets of stitches. The second flower is done in Seville lace; the third in open diamond; the fourth in Cadiz lace; the fifth in a new stitch which we must call Star stitch. It is worked thus :—1*st Row.*—+ 6 foundation stitches, miss the space of 3, 1 stitch and again miss the space of 3. + Repeat. 2*nd Row.*—The same, the close stitches coming just over those of the previous row. 3*rd Row.*—+ miss the first 3 stitches, 1 stitch, miss the other 3, and do 3 on each side of the single stitch of last row. +. The 4*th Row* is stitch for stitch like the 3rd. Repeat these four rows to

fill up the space. Use Evans's Mecklenburg thread, No. 100. For the Seville and Cadiz lace use No. 120. For the open diamonds, Boar's Head, 150. For the spotted lace, Mecklenburg, No. 80. The large flower at the corner of the collar is done in Cadiz and Spotted lace, with the same thread as those stitches were before worked in. The next flower is in English lace, with Evans's Boar's Head, No. 70. The third is Venetian, with No. 90. The fourth contains a new stitch which we will call Close Spotted lace. Join on the thread on the right hand; take it across the widest part of the space to the left, and fasten on the braid with a button-hole stitch. + Work on the braid and over the thread 5 foundation stitches, miss the space of 3. + repeat to the end of the row. Take the thread again across from right to left, and work backwards, doing a stitch over every stitch and three on the space. The third row and every alternate is like the first, but working, of course, on the second, instead of on the braid; and the fourth, and all other intermediate, like the second. Use Evans's Mecklenburg, 140.

A reference to the engraving will show that the ground is entirely in Raleigh bars, and the small spaces in rosettes, both worked in Mecklenburg, 100.

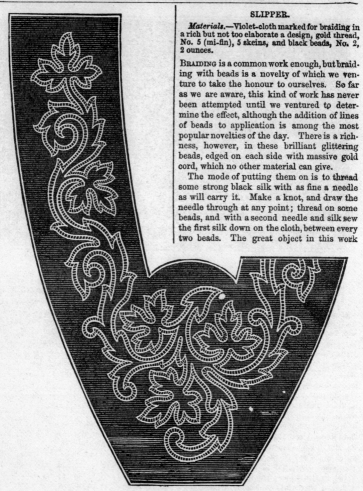

PATTERN OF SLIPPER.

SLIPPER.

Materials.—Violet-cloth marked for braiding in a rich but not too elaborate a design, gold thread, No. 5 (mi-fin), 5 skeins, and black beads, No. 2, 2 ounces.

BRAIDING is a common work enough, but braiding with beads is a novelty of which we venture to take the honour to ourselves. So far as we are aware, this kind of work has never been attempted until we ventured to determine the effect, although the addition of lines of beads to application is among the most popular novelties of the day. There is a richness, however, in these brilliant glittering beads, edged on each side with massive gold cord, which no other material can give.

The mode of putting them on is to thread some strong black silk with as fine a needle as will carry it. Make a knot, and draw the needle through at any point; thread on some beads, and with a second needle and silk sew the first silk down on the cloth, between every two beads. The great object in this work

An edging of Sorrento is to finish the collar, using Mecklenburg, No. 80.

———

is to take care that the beads do not lie too close together.

The gold thread is sewn down on each side, with silk of the same colour, the ends being drawn to the wrong side.

For inkstand mats, and many other things, bead braiding will be found very effective

THE WHEEL AND SHAMROCK ANTIMACASSAR.

THE WORK-TABLE FRIEND.

THE WHEEL AND SHAMROCK ANTI-MACASSAR.

Materials.—Messrs. W. Evans and Co.'s Boar's Head crochet cotton, No. 10, and turquoise beads, No. 1.

As this antimacassar is made in separate pieces, it will suffice to thread a few rows of beads on the cotton at a time. For the same reason, it may be made of any required dimensions, and it may or may not have a border: but if one is desired, it should be of close crochet, with the pattern in beads, and a deep fringe beyond it.

A WHEEL.—Make a chain of eight, close it into a round, and work under it 16 Sc stitches. + 9 Ch, dropping a bead on every stitch, miss one of the 16, and Sc under the next + 8 times. Slip-stitch on 4 of the first 9 Ch. Sc on the next two of the 9 * 3 Ch, Sc on the 4th, 5th, and 6th of the next 9 chain * all round. End with slip-stitch on the 1st and 2nd of the first 3 chain. + 8 Ch, Sc under the next chain of 3. + 7 times. 8 Ch, Sc on 2nd slip-stitch. To complete the wheel do under each chain of 8, 1 Sc, 10 Dc, 1 Sc, dropping a bead on every stitch.

A SQUARE.—6 Ch, close it into a round. + 3 Sc under chain, 5 Ch, + 4 times, * 1 Sc on 2nd Sc, 4 Dc under chain, with a bead on each, 5 Ch, 4 Dc with a bead on each, under the same Ch * 4 times. Slip-stitch up the first 4 Dc. + 5 Ch, Sc under 5 Ch of last round, 6 Ch, Sc under same, 5 Ch, Sc under same; 8 Ch, Sc under the next chain of 5.

Last Round.—1 Sc, 4 Dc under the chain of 5, *2 Ch*, 4 Dc, 1 Sc under same, 1 Sc, 4 Dc under chain of 6, *2 Ch*, 4 Dc, 1 Sc under same, 1 Sc, 4 Dc under chain of 5, *2 Ch*, 4 Dc, 1 Sc under same. 1 Sc under chain of 8. Do this all round, dropping a bead on every stitch. The two chains which are printed in italics are those places where the squares are to be connected with the other pieces. It will be seen that the last round forms four shamrocks. The centre leaf of each shamrock (coming at the point of the square) is to be united to the point of another square; while those at the sides are to be joined to the rounds.

A bead is dropped on every Dc stitch.

SWISS LACE HABIT-SHIRT.

Materials—Very fine soft net, and jaconet muslin, Messrs. W. Evans and Co.'s Boar's Head sewing cotton, No. 50, and Royal Embroidery cotton, No. 40, with a sewing needle, No. 4, as well as that suitable for fine muslin.

THE design being marked on the muslin, the net (of which the entire habit-shirt is made) is laid underneath it. The whole pattern is then traced with Royal Embroidery cotton, the stitches being taken very closely together, so that a *thread* of net may be taken up at every

SWISS LACE HABIT-SHIRT.

one to the other, drawing the threads of the muslin together, to leave the holes clear. Pierce another little hole, and take a stitch or two from the second to the third, and so continue, something like veining. When the entire design is worked in *Point d'échelle*, the outline threads are to be sewed over; that forming the border to be done in button-hole stitch. After this the muslin may be cut away, and the design appears in heavy flowers on a light net ground.

The effect is extremely rich and beautiful, and there is not a great deal of work in it, compared with what is found in many less effective designs.

FRENCH PELOTE DE LIT.

Materials.—A wire frame, two skeins of crimson chenille, of different shades, and a little wire chenille of a light shade; also a little yellow satin, wadding and cardboard.

THIS forms a pendant to a Dahlia Porte-montre. Instead of a pair of watch-pockets,

FRENCH PELOTE DE LIT.

stitch. Just within this thread, throughout the entire design, a row of very small holes is worked, forming what is called *Point d'échelle*, or *Ladder-stitch*. To do this, thread the coarse needle with Boar's Head cotton, fasten it on, and pierce two small holes with it, immediately inside the tracing thread. Take two or three stitches between the two holes; that is, from

the present fashion is to have *one* watch-hook, and a pin-cushion to match.

The pelote is made precisely like the watch-hook, except in the centre, which, instead of a hook, has a soft cushion, formed of a round of cardboard, wadded thickly, and covered with yellow satin.

THE WORK-TABLE FRIEND.

WARM MITTENS, IN KNITTED EMBROIDERY.

Materials.—White or Black Pyrenees wool, 1 skein; a little of the other colour, of 2 greens, dark pink, and orange, and half a skein of lighter pink.

WE have, in various parts of this work, presented to our readers specimens of the beautiful bead-work of Germany (such as the pole screen in page 301 of this volume), the work-baskets and other elegant trifles of Paris, and the lace for which Italy

MITTEN, IN KNITTED EMBROIDERY.

was so long famous. The muslin work of Switzerland and the knitting of Turkey have also appeared in our columns—to say nothing of the many designs, in every style, which we have ourselves originated. The cordial reception that our various patterns, selected with great care, have received, has stimulated us to yet further researches, with the hope of opening new sources of enjoyment from this important and pleasing branch of domestic art.

We now present a specimen of the beautiful knitted embroidery for which the peasantry of the Pyrenees have been long and justly celebrated. They have indeed advantages which we have not hitherto possessed in the exquisite texture of the wools, which are not only incomparably softer than Shetland, but also take dyes of a far more brilliant character. There is supposed to be some peculiar quality in the water of those mountain streams, which imparts this exquisite tint to some of the colours.

And now for the term KNITTED EMBROIDERY. EMBROIDERY is, strictly speaking, ornament of any sort worked on a plain ground; thus, we know embroidery is done with cotton on cambric for a handkerchief; with gold on velvet for a shoe; with silks on silk, satin, or leather, and so on. This, we see, is different to those kinds of ornamentation in which colours are *woven in* to form the pattern, as is the case with crochet. Now, some few patterns have from time to time appeared in which the pattern, in one colour, is knitted into another; and this, having something of the effect of embroidery, we have called by that name. We now mean, however, to introduce our readers to a kind of knitting which really deserves the name we apply to it, as the design is *darned in* after the article is made. The only thing to be observed, however, is, that the darning is strictly imitative of the knitting-stitch; this is, however, so easily done, that any one taking a rug-needle with a bit of wool in it can do it without a moment's study.

In this mitten we will suppose all the groundwork to be white, with some few stripes of dark pink.

With the dark pink wool cast on 96 stitches, that is 24 on one needle, and 36 on each of two others. Form it into a round, and do two purled rounds. Fasten on the white wool and begin pattern.

1st, 3rd, 5th, 7th, 9th, 11th Rounds.—+ Knit 1, make 1, knit 4, knit 3 together, knit 4, make 1, + all round.

2nd, 4th, 6th, 8th, 10th, 12th Rounds are plain knitting.

Fasten on the pink, and do four rounds, then nine rounds with the white, four more with the pink, and at least one inch with the white.

To form the thumb. Knit all the round

w

but the last two stiches, make 1, knit 2, make
1. Do two rounds without increase.

4th Round.—Knit all but the last four.
Make 1, knit 4, make 1.

Two more rounds plain.

7th Round.—Knit all but the last six.
Make 1, knit 6, make 1.

Two more plain rounds.

Continue to increase in this manner, always
having two more at the end of the round, and
making one before and after these, until the
thumb has about 30 stiches, when take three
more needles, divide the 30 stitches on them,
and cast on six more before forming them
into a round. Knit a plain round; then 6
more rounds, knitting two together over the
new stitches once in every round, then 8
or 10 more rounds, fasten on the pink, purl 2
rounds with it, and cast off. Continue the
round, taking up six stitches where you cast
them on for the thumb, and gradually taking
them all in, by knitting two together *at this
part* once in every round until all are used.
Do about a dozen more rounds, then four
with pink, nine with white, four more with
pink, three white, two purled rounds pink,
and cast off not too loosely.

The mitten being done, wash it, dry, and
stretch it on a card, making it long rather
than wide, and darn on it the design we here

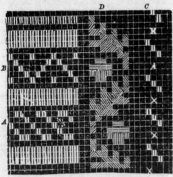

DARNING PATTERN.

give, each square being to represent one
stitch, done exactly to imitate knitting-stitch.
A for the lower band of 9 white rounds,
alternately light and dark pink. *B* for the
upper band; the Vandyke dark green, the
spots light. *C* the three stripes up the back
of the hand, one in the centre, the other at

each side of the wide stripe. The orange
spot is indicated by a cross, the rest black. *D*
the broad stripe. One is in two shades of
green, with pink spots; the other has the
same colours reversed. The engraving shows
the places where the two shades are used, the
lighter being uppermost, both in scroll and
spot.

There is the space of three stitches between
every two stripes. The narrow pattern of
orange and black also runs up the thumb.

Mittens are extremely pretty with the
entire pattern darned in one colour; such as
lavender on white, for mourning; or green or
brown on white.

WORK-TABLE FOR JUVENILES;

OR, LITTLE MARY'S HALF-HOLIDAY.

(*Continued from p.* 327.)

"MAMMA, have you seen any of those pretty
doyleys, made entirely of beads, that look
almost like painted glass? I should so very
much like to do some, if they are not very
difficult or expensive."

"They are not either; on the contrary,
they are singularly simple, and the materials
cost but a trifle. The beads are very large
ones—about a quarter of an inch in length—
and made in many brilliant colours. About
two bunches of each will suffice for a small
doyley, or half as much again for a large one.
You will want a small wooden frame, with
pegs in it on two opposite sides, not quite
half an inch apart, and rather thick, to keep
the two threads separate. Take a reel of
Messrs. W. Evans and Co.'s Boar's Head
cotton, No. 4, and thread on it alternately
twelve beads of one colour and twelve of
another, doing as many of each as there are
pegs on one side of the frame. Fasten the
thread on the peg at the end of one side.
Carry it in a straight line to the peg at the
opposite side, and round it, leaving six beads
there; now bring it round the second peg on
the first side; continue working thus backwards and forwards, leaving six beads at every
peg, until the whole frame is filled with lines
of thread, at equal distances, in one direction."

"What are these six beads for at each peg
mamma?"

"They are to form the fringe at two sides

of the doyley. You will find in these bunches some beads which are considerably smaller than the others. These you must put aside, as the beads employed must be as nearly as possible the same size. Now fasten on a long thread at one of the other sides of the frame, and on your needle as many white beads as you have bars of thread, *except one.* Carry

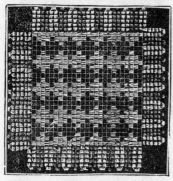

BEAD DOYLEY.

your needleful of thread, with all the beads, under the entire line of threads, close to the fringe, pushing up the beads, so that one comes between every two threads. Now run your needle in each bead, *over* the threads in the opposite direction, and the row is thus secured. The second, and all following rows, are done in the same way; but after completing each alternate row, thread on six beads before proceeding to the next."

"But how shall I make the pattern, mamma?"

"The simplest you can have is a series of stars in beads of one colour, on a ground of another. As we have begun with white, we may as well make that the ground. Thread the beads regularly.   + 3 white, 1 blue, 2 white.   + repeat as often as you may require it, ending, however, with three white instead of two. This is the first row after that of plain white. For the next, begin with two white; then three blue, three white alternately, ending with two white. For the third one white, five blue, alternately, ending with one white. The fourth row is like the second; and these four make one pattern. You must, however, finish your doyley with

the first row, and a line of plain white beads beyond it."

"But in order to form a pattern, it seems to me there must be a certain number of pegs, mamma?"

"Very true; sixteen pegs on each side will do a very good-sized doyley in this pattern. But I am sure you could easily vary your design by arranging any pattern on a bit of checked paper, and working from it. When all the doyley is completed, except the fringe of one side, remove it from the frame, and add this fringe, carrying your needle down two or three beads, and up the next row to fasten it. Loops of beads are also to be placed at the corners, and your doyley is finished.'

"Well, it certainly is very easy, and pretty too; and I suppose it will wash very well. I shall certainly make a set. And now, mamma, what do you think of my doing a work-basket for myself, with one of these wire frames and a little fancy cord. See! I have some satin cord of cerise, and Marie Louise blue, and some cerise silk and ribbon. I think I can manage to make a very pretty basket."

"I suppose you mean to use your cord instead of chenille, and wind it from one bar of the frame to another. It will certainly make a very strong basket, and a much cheaper one than of chenille. You will have first to cover

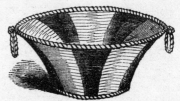

PATTERN WORK-BASKET.

all your wire with the narrow cerise ribbon, and also to make a cardboard bottom, covered with silk; you may put a little wadding on the inner side. Now I would wind some of the blue cord evenly round the upper and lower round of the frame, and also the handles. Then wind the cord across every two wires, backwards and forwards; let each space be of one colour. As the cord is thick, and the second colour is wound round each wire, it must not be done too closely. When each division is filled, and the cardboard sewed in, the basket is complete.

CIGAR-CASE IN CROCHET.

THE WORK-TABLE FRIEND.

CIGAR-CASE IN CROCHET.

Materials.—2 skeins of scarlet or cerise silk, 1 black do., ⅓ one maize, all fine French silk. Boulton's crochet hook, No. 23. Worked entirely in Sc.

WITH the scarlet silk make a chain of 4, close it into a round, and work two stitches in each stitch. Next round same.

3rd Round.—+ 1 Sc in 1, 2 Sc in next +, 8 times.

The increase is now regular and progressive. Eight times in each round you will do two stitches in one ; in all the other stitches you will do one only, until you have 144 stitches in the round, when you will do five rounds in the same colour without increase except of two stitches, making 146. The two stitches are to be worked in one at equal distances from each other; thus in the 4th round it will take place on every third stitch ; in the 5th on every fourth, and so on.

Now begin to work the pattern.

1st Round.—30 Scarlet, 4 Black, 5 Scarlet, 4 Black, 60 Scarlet, 4 Black, 5 Scarlet, 4 Black, 30 Scarlet.

As the third of the five Scarlet forms the centre of each side, it will be useful to put a bit of white thread in it, that you may always know when you come to the middle of the pattern.

2nd Round.—18 Scarlet, 4 Black, 7 Scarlet,

6 Black, 3 Scarlet, 6 Black, 1 Scarlet, 4 Black, 18 Scarlet, + twice.

3rd Round.—+ 17 Scarlet, 6 Black, 2 Scarlet, 2 Black, 1 Scarlet, 3 Black, 11 Scarlet, 3 Black.

1 Scarlet, 2 Black, 2 Scarlet, 6 Black, 17 Scarlet, + twice.

4th Round.—*a* 17 S, 2 B, 2 S, 3 B, 1 S, 1 B, 2 S, 2 B, *b* 13 S. Go backwards from *b* to *a* to complete one side, and repeat the whole for the other side, making the entire round. The same directions will be applied to all future rounds.

5th Round.—*a* 15 S, 3 B, 3 S, 3 B, 2 S, 3 B, 4 S, 2 B, *b* 3 S.

6th Round.—*a* 17 S, 2 B, 3 S, 2 B, 3 S, 1 B, 6 S, 2 B, *b* 1 S.

7th Round.—*a* 10 S, 2 B, 5 S, 3 B, 1 S, 2 B, 3 S, 3 B, 5 S, *b* 5 B.

8th Round.—*a* 9 S, 4 B, 3 S, 5 B, 4 S, 3 B, 1 S, 1 B, 3 S, 3 B, *b* 1 S.

9th Round.—*a* 8 S, 3 B, 2 S, 1 B, 4 S, 4 B, 3 S, 1 B, 3 S, 6 B, *b* 3 S.

10th Round.—*a* 8 S, 2 B, 4 S, 1 B, 2 S, 1 B, 2 S, 5 B, 5 S, 4 B, *b* 5 S.

11th Round.—*a* 8 S, 1 B, 7 S, 1 B, 5 S, 2 B, *b* 25 S.

12th Round.—*a* 8 S, 1 B, 5 S, 2 B, 6 S, 4 B, *b* 21 S.

13th Round.—Begin maize silk. *a* 9 S, 1 B, 2 S, 2 B, 5 S, 1 B, 2 S, 4 B, 10 S *b* 1 M.

14th Round.—*a* 11 S, 1 B, 2 S, 2 B, 4 S, 4 B, 11 S, *b* 3 M.

15th Round.—a 10 S, 1 B, 4 S, 2 B, 9 S, 3 M, 4 S, b 7 M.

16th Round.—a 9 S, 1 B, 4 S, 3 B, 8 S, 5 M, 1 S, 5 M, b 1 B.

17th Round.—a 9 S, 1 B, 1 S, 5 B, 8 S, 8 M, b 9 B.

18th Round.—a 8 S, 1 B, 3 S, 3 B, 9 S, 3 M, b 19 B.

19th Round.—a 8 S, 2 B, 9 S, 3 M, 2 S, 4 M, b 17 B.

20th Round.—a 4 S, 7 B. 7 S, 10 M, b 17 B.

21st Round.—a 4 S, 3 B, 3 S, 2 B, 5 S, 6 M, 2 B, 2 M, 8 B, b 3 M.

22nd Round.—a 3 S, 3 B, 4 S, 3 B, 4 S, 2 M, 1 B, 2 M, 12 B, 1 M, b 3 S.

23rd Round.—a 3 S, 3 B, 5 S, 2 B, 4 S, 2 M, 15 B, 1 M, b 3 S.

24th Round.—a 4 S, 3 B, 2 S, 1 B, 1 S, 2 B, 4 S, 2 M, 15 B, 1 M, b 3 S.

25th Round.—a 4 S, 6 B, 2 S, 1 B, 4 S, 3 M, 15 B, b 3 M.

26th Round.—a 5 S, 4 B, 3 S, 1 B, 4 S, 9 M, b 21 B.

27th Round.—a 11 S, 1 B, 6 S, 7 M, b 23 B.

28th Round.—a 10 S, 2 B, 6 S, 4 M, 4 B, 1 M, b 19 B.

29th Round.—a 10 S, 1 B, 8 S, 9 M, b 17 B.

30th Round.—a 6 S, 6 B, 7 S, 9 M, b 17 B.

31st Round.—a 5 S, 3 B, 2 S, 3 B, 6 S, 2 M, 1 S, 5 M, b 19 B.

32nd Round.—a 4 S, 3 B, 4 S, 2 B, 11 S, 1 M, b 23 B.

33rd Round.—a 4 S, 1 B, 3 S, 1 B, 1 S, 3 B, 10 S, 4 M, b 19 B.

34th Round.—a 4 S, 1 B, 4 S, 3 B, 10 S, 6 M, b 17 B.

35th Round.—a 5 S, 1 B, 15 S, 3 M, 2 S, 2 M, b 17 B.

36th Round.—a 5 S, 2 B, 18 S, 3 M, b 17 B.

37th Round.—a 4 S, 6 B, 14 S, 4 M, b 17 B.

38th Round.—a 3 S, 3 B, 2 S, 3 B, 13 S, 3 M, b 19 B.

39th Round.—a 3 S, 2 B, 5 S, 2 B, 6 S, 3 M, 1 S, 4 M, b 21 B.

40th Round.—a 3 S, 3 B, 5 S, 2 B, 6 S, 6 M, b 23 B.

41st Round.—a 3 S, 3 B, 2 S, 1 B, 2 S, 2 B, 8 S, 3 M, b 25 B.

42nd Round.—This is the first round of the middle of the pattern ; in the centre is a space 27 stitches wide by 15 deep intended for the initials. Two old English letters can be arranged extremely well in this space. They should be marked on a piece of checked paper, and the stitches forming the letters worked in maize silk. As this must vary for each different name, we give only the 27 Black which would otherwise occupy the space. Those who do not wish to put initials may work a diamond of Scarlet outlined with maize in the same space. a 3 S, 5 B, 3 S, 2 B, 6 S, 4 M, b 27 B.

43rd Round.—a 4 S, 3 B, 4 S, 2 B, 5 S, 5 M, b 27 B.

44th Round.—a 11 S, 2 B, 6 S, 4 M, b 27 B.

45th Round.—a 11 S, 1 B, 8 S, 3 M, b 27 B.

46th Round.—a 10 S, 1 B, 10 S, 2 M, b 27 B.

47th Round.—a 3 S, 7 B, 2 S, 1 B, 7 S, 3 M, b 27 B.

48th Round.—a 4 S, 3 B, 4 S, 2 B, 6 S, 4 M, b 27 B.

49th and centre Round.—a 5 S, 9 B, 4 S, 5 M, b 27 B.

Then repeat backwards from the 48th to 1st inclusive ; after which do 5 rounds of Scarlet, and then 5 rows of each side separately, which completes the work.

FRENCH PURSE.

Materials.—1 skein of bright scarlet silk, ½ do. maize and white, a little black, emerald-green, and Napoleon blue. Slides and tassels to correspond.

WITH the scarlet silk make a chain of 104 stitches ; close it into a round, and do two rounds of Sc.

1st Pattern Round.—Scarlet and maize, + 13 S, 1 M, 12 S, +. The repetitions occur four times in every round.

2nd Round.—+ 12 S, 3 M, 11 S, +.

3rd Round.—+ 11 S, 5 M, 10 S, +.

4th Round.—Like 2nd.

5th Round.—+ 8 S, 2 M, 3 S, 1 M, 3 S, 2 M, 7 S, +.

6th Round.—+ 10 S, 1 M, 1 S, 3 M, 1 S, 1 M, 9 S, +.

7th Round.—Like 3rd. *8th.*—Like 2nd.

9th Round.—+ 7 S, 1 M, 1 S, 1 M, 3 S, 1 M, 3 S, 1 M, 1 S, 1 M, 6 S, +.

10th Round.—+ 8 S, 3 M, 1 S, 3 M, 1 S, 3 M, 7 S, +.

11th Round.—+ 7 S, 13 M, 6 S, +.

12th Round.—+ 8 S, 11 M, 7 S, +.

13th Round.—+ 11 S, 5 M, 10 S, +.

14th Round.—+ 6 S, 1 M, 1 S, 1 M, 3 S, 3 M, 3 S, 1 M, 1 S, 1 M, 5 S, +.

15th Round.—+ 5 S, 5 M, 3 S, 1 M, 3 S, 5 M, 4 S, +.

16th Round.—+ 6 S, 5 M, 1 S, 3 M, 1 S, 5 M, 5 S, +.

17th Round.—+ 7 S, 13 M, 6 S, +.

18th Round.—Scarlet, maize, and blue.
+ 10 S, 3 M, 1 B, 3 M, 9 S, +.

19th Round.—+ 5 S, 1 M, 1 S, 1 M, 3 S,
1 M, 3 B, 1 M, 3 S, 1 M, 1 S, 1 M, 4 S, +.

20th Round.—+ 4 S, 7 M, 2 B, 1 M, 2 B,
7 M, 3 S, +.

21st Round.—+ 3 S, 7 M, 2 B, 3 M, 2 B,
7 M, 2 S, +.

22nd Round.—+ 4 S, 5 M, 4 B, 1 M, 4 B,
5 M, 3 S, +.

FRENCH PURSE.

23rd Round.—+ 9 S, 1 M, 2 B, 3 M, 2 B,
1 M, 8 S, +.

24th Round.—3 S, 4 M, 4 B, 5 M, 4 B, 4 M,
2 S.

25th Round.—+ 2 S, 7 M, 3 B, 3 M, 3 B,
7 M, 1 S, +.

26th Round.—+ 1 S, 9 M, 3 B, 1 M, 3 B,
9 M, +. Fasten off scarlet, and begin
black.

27th Round.—1 Black, 5 M, 1 Black, 3 M,
2 Blue, 3 M, 2 Blue, 3 M, 1 Black, 5 M, +.

28th Round.—1 Black, 6 M, 1 Black, 3 M,
2 Blue, 1 M, 2 Blue, 3 M, 1 Black, 6 M, +.

29th Round.—+ 2 Black, 5 M, 1 Black, 3
M, 2 Blue, 1 M, 2 Blue, 3 M, 1 Black, 5 M,
1 Black, +.

30th Round.—+ 3 Black, 3 M, 2 Black, 3
M, 2 Blue, 1 M, 2 Blue, 3 M, 2 Black, 3 M, 2
Black, +.

31st Round.—+ 8 Black, 3 M, 5 Blue, 3 M,
7 Black, +.

32nd Round.—+ 7 Black, 3 M, 7 Blue, 3
M, 6 Black, +. Fasten off Blue.

33rd Round.—+ 6 Black, 15 M, 5 Black,
+. Fasten on the Green.

34th Round.—+ 3 Black, 6 M, 1 G, 1 M,
2 G, 1 M, 2 G, 1 M, 1 G, 6 M, 2 Black, +.
Fasten off Black.

35th Round.—+ 8 M, 1 G, 1 M, 2 G, 3 M,
2 G, 1 M, 1 G, 7 M, +. Fasten on White.

36th Round.—+ 6 M, 1 W, 1 M, 5 G, 1 M,
5 G, 1 M, 1 W, 5 M, +.

37th Round.—+ 4 M, 4 W, 1 M, 9 G, 1 M,
4 W, 3 M, +.

38th Round.—+ 4 W, 3 M, 2 W, 2 M, 5 G,
2 M, 2 W, 3 M, 3 W, +. Fasten off Green.

39th Round.—+ * 3 W, 5 M, * 3 times. 2
W, +.

40th Round.—+ 3 W, 8 M, 5 W, 8 M, 2
W, +.

41st Round.—+ 4 W, 2 M, 1 W, 13 M, 1
W, 2 M, 3 W, +.

42nd Round.—+ 7 W, 2 M, 3 W, 3 M, 3
W, 2 M, 6 W, +.

43rd Round.—+ 6 W, 4 M, 2 W, 3 M, 2 W,
4 M, 5 W, +.

44th Round.—+ 6 W, 4 M, 1 W, 5 M, 1 W,
4 M, 5 W, +.

45th Round.—+ 7 W, 2 M, 1 W, 7 M, 1 W,
2 M, 6 W, +.

46th Round.—+ 11 W, 5 M, 10 W, +.

47th Round.—+ 10 W, 7 M, 9 W, +.

48th Round.—Like 46th.

49th Round.—+ 12 W, 3 M, 11 W, +.

50th Round.—+ 13 W, 1 M, 12 W, +.

Do one round of White only, but without
fastening off the Maize.

52nd Round.—(First decreasing round.)
+ 7 W, 1 M, 6 W, + 7 times. Omit one
stitch in six of the seven repetitions.

53rd Round.—+ 5 W over 6, 3 M (the 2nd)
over 1 M, 5 more W, + 7 times.

54th Round.—+ 4 W, 5 M (over 3 and a
White) on each side, 3 W, + 7 times.

55th Round.—+ 2 W, 7 M (over 3 and a
White) on each side, 2 W, + 7 times. Fasten
off White.

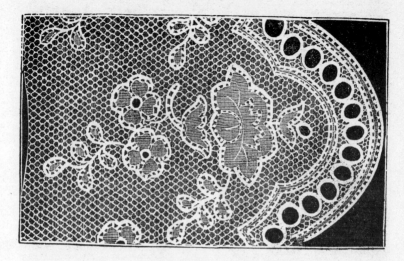

SECTION OF COLLAR, IN SWISS LACE.

56th Round.—+ 5 M, 1 Black on centre 7 M, 4 M, + 7 times.

57th Round.—+ 3 M on 4, 3 Black (the 2nd on 1 Black), 3 M, + 7 times.

58th Round.—+ 2 M on 3, 5 Black, 1 M, + 7 times.

59th Round.—+ 1 M, 5 Black on 5, 1 M, + 7 times. Fasten off Maize.

60th Round.— + 1 Scarlet on M, 5 Black on 5, + 7 times.

61st Round.— + 1 S on S, 3 Black on 4, 1 S on Black, + 7 times.

62nd Round.— + 1 S, 2 Black, + 7 times.

Decrease quite to a point with Scarlet only. Do the other end in the same way, and crochet with the Scarlet a piece 3 inches long for the centre. It is done in open square crochet, and joined in Sc at both ends. Fasten on the trimmings.

FULL-SIZED SECTION OF COLLAR, IN SWISS LACE.

Materials.—Fine soft net, jaconet muslin, Evans' Royal Embroidery cotton, No. 40, and Boar's Head sewing cotton, No. 50. A coarse sewing needle, and fine ones.

HAVING elsewhere described the mode of working Swiss Lace, we content ourselves now with giving a section of a collar of the full size. From it the entire design may readily be traced; and it is to be worked according to the instructions we refer to, the large holes only being pierced with a stiletto, and sewed round.

HUMAN BROTHERHOOD.—The race of mankind would perish did they cease to aid each other. From the time that the mother binds the child's head, till the moment that some kind assistant wipes the death-damp from the brow of the dying, we cannot exist without mutual help. All, therefore, that need aid, have a right to ask it from their fellow-mortals; no one who holds the power of granting can refuse it without guilt.—*Sir W. Scott.*

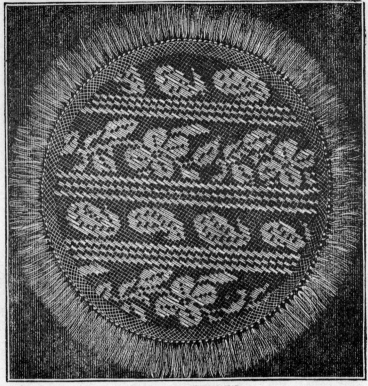

ROUND NETTED ANTIMACASSAR.

THE WORK-TABLE FRIEND.

ROUND NETTED ANTIMACASSAR.

Materials.—Messrs. Walter Evans and Co.'s Boar's Head crochet cotton, No. 4, for the netting, and their knitting cotton, of the same size, for darning. A round wooden mesh, No. 6, will be used.

To produce a piece of round netting, begin with 25 stitches, and increase by doing two in one at the end of every row for fifty rows. Do the same number of rows without either increasing or diminishing, and then the like number decreasing, by netting two together at the termination of every row. You will finish with the same number that you commenced with. This makes the nearest approach to a round that can be obtained in netting. To complete it do four or five rounds of netting, and knot a heavy fringe, four inches deep, in every stitch of the last round.

Nothing can be easier than this fringe-knotting. Take a card of the width the fringe is required, and wind the cotton round it any given number of times (twelve will make a thick fringe). Slip it off the card, and with a coarse crochet hook draw the mass sufficiently far through a stitch to allow the other end to pass through it. Draw this tightly, and when all are done, cut the strands of cotton.

Wash, slightly stiffen, and dry the antimacassar, before darning it. This must be done from the engraving. The thick cotton gives it a rich effect, with very little trouble.

THE WORK-TABLE FRIEND.

CHEESE DOYLEY, IN CROCHET.

Materials.—3 reels of Messrs. W. Evans and Co.'s Boar's Head crochet cotton, with a suitable hook.

MAKE a chain of 8, close it into a round, and work under it 9 Sc stitches.

1st Round.—+ 1 Dc, 1 Ch, miss none, + 9 times.

CHEESE DOYLEY, IN CROCHET.

2nd Round—+ 1 Dc, 1 Ch, miss none, + 18 times.

3rd Round.—+ 1 Dc on Dc, 2 Ch, miss 1, + 18 times.

4th Round.—+ 3 Dc under, 2 Ch, 2 Ch, + all round.

5th Round.—+ 1 Dc under Ch, 5 Ch, + all round.

6th Round—+ 7 Dc under Ch, 2 Ch, + all round.

7th Round.—+ 7 Dc on 7, 3 Ch, + all round.

8th Round.—+ 5 Dc beginning at 2nd on 7, 6 Ch, + all round.

9th Round.—+ 5 Dc on 5, 8 Ch, + all round.

10th Round.—+ 3 Dc, beginning on 2nd, 10 Ch, + all round.

11th Round.—+ 3 Dc on 3, 11 Ch, + all round.

12th Round.—+ 1 Dc on centre of 3, 15 Ch, + all round.

13th Round.—+ 1 Dc on Dc, 19 Ch, + all round.

14th Round.—+ 3 Dc all in the 10th of the 19 Chain, 15 Ch, + all round.

15th Round.—+ 3 Dc all in the centre of 15 Chain, 19 Ch, + all round.

16th Round.—+ 11 Dc, beginning on the 5th of 19 Chain, 12 Ch, + all round.

17th Round.—+11 Dc on 11, 14 Ch, +all round.

18th Round.—+ 9 Dc, beginning on the second of 11, 9 Ch, 3 Dc on centre 2 of 14 Ch, 9 Ch, + all round.

19th Round.—+ 9 Dc on 9, 14 Ch, 3 Dc on 4th of 9 Ch, 7 Ch, 3 Dc on 6 of next 9 Ch, 4 Ch, + all round.

20th Round.—+ 7 Dc, beginning on the second of 9, 3 Ch, 3 Dc on 2nd of 4 Ch, 7 Ch, 3 Dc on 4th of 7 Ch, 7 Ch, 3 Dc on 3rd of 4 Ch, 3 Ch, + all round.

21st Round.—+ 1 Sdc on 1st of 7 Dc, 5 more Dc, 1 Sdc, 3 Sc on 3 Ch, 3 Ch, miss 3 Dc, 7 Sc on 7 Ch, 3 Ch, miss 3 Dc, 7 Sc on 7 Ch, 3 Ch, miss 3 Dc, 3 Sc on Ch, + all round.

22nd Round.—+ 5 Dc on 5 Dc of last round, 4 Ch, 1 Dc on 3rd Sc, 3 Ch, 7 Dc on 7 Sc, 4 Ch, 7 Dc on next 7 Sc, 3 Ch, 1 Dc on 1st Sc, 4 Ch, + all round.

23rd Round.—+ 5 Dc on 5 Dc, 5 Ch, miss 4, 1 Sc, * 4 Ch, miss 4, 1 Sc, * 5 times, 5 Ch, + all round.

24th Round.—+ 3 Dc on centre 3 of 5, 5 Ch, Sc under Ch, * 4 Ch, Sc under Ch, * 6 times, 5 Ch, + all round.

25th Round.—+ 3 Dc on 3 Dc, * 4 Ch, Dc under chain, * 8 times, 4 Ch, + all round.

26th Round.—+ 1 Dc on centre of 3, 6 Ch, close into a loop, 3 Ch, * 3 Dc under Ch, 6 Ch, miss 1 chain of 4, * 4 times, 3 Dc under Ch, 3 Ch, + all round.

27th Round.—+ 21 Dc under loop of 6, 3 Ch, 5 Dc under chain of 6, 6 Ch, 1 Dc under chain of 6, 5 Ch, 2 Dc on 2nd of next 3 Dc, 5 Ch, 1 Dc under next Ch, 6 Ch, 5 Dc under Ch of 6, 3 Ch, + all round.

28th Round.—+ Dc on 1st of 21 Dc, * 2 Ch, miss 1, 1 Dc, * 10 times, 5 Ch, 5 Dc under chain of 6, 5 Ch, 4 Dc (on 2 Dc and a chain on each side), 5 Ch, 5 Dc under next Ch, 5 Ch, + all round.

29th Round.— + 1 Dc, 2 Ch, miss 1, + all round.

VINE-LEAF TRAVELLING CAP, IN APPLICATION.

Materials.—Rich brown cloth, black velvet leaves, small steel rings, black silk, gold braid, and thread.

THIS cap is done in application Our readers may remember the small rings which

TRAVELLING OR SMOKING CAP.

covered with crochet, were used some time ago for purses. The bunches of grapes in this design are formed in the same way; covered with crochet, and sewed on the cloth. The leaves are of velvet, stamped out, and *appliqué* on the cloth, bordered with gold braid on the outside, and with thread on the inside.

For a travelling cap there should be no ears, and as warmth is an object, it should be wadded; but for a smoking cap, ordinary bed-tick is the best lining, with sarsnet inside it. The tick makes it nice and firm; and should be brought down within an inch of the edge.

The ears of the travelling cap are made separately, and are not ornamented, as they are frequently tucked in the cap.

The tassel, of passementerie, is made to unite all the colours of the cap itself.

ANTIMACASSAR, IN FLANDERS LACE.

Materials.—Messrs. W. Evans and Co.'s Boar's Head crochet cotton, Nos. 16 and 20. Bone mesh, No. 12.

Do the foundation in square netting, with No. 16 cotton. Wash, slightly stiffen, and put it in a frame, as it is much easier then to darn it nicely. Flanders lace is worked entirely in the stitch termed cloth-darning, which fills up every square of the design with four threads, two in each direction, crossing each other.

ANTIMACASSAR, IN FLANDERS LACE.

This stitch, which for beauty of effect surpasses all others, may be very easily done by paying attention to two or three rules.

1st, Always begin at the left hand, and work towards the right, outwards.

2nd, Never cross over more than one thread at a time, *except when a single square is to be filled up*, when it will be necessary to go over two.

3rd, Join at the end of a needleful, by knotting on the next with a weaver's knot, cutting the ends closely.

4th, Always take, if possible, the entire length of any line of squares that may have to be filled up.

Begin by any line you please, leaving a few inches of your thread, and take one line to the left and another to the right in the same row of holes, putting the needle under one and over another thread of the foundation; then do the next row above it, if it extends as far to the left; but should it be one square short, cross that square before proceeding to the next line.

Proceed throughout the pattern in the same way.

THE WORK-TABLE FRIEND.

MELON PATTERN SLIPPERS,
IN APPLICATION.

Materials.—Black cloth, claret, or green velvet
(or *velours épinglé*), gold braid and thread, and
beads to match the velvet. The slippers are to
be made in the French form; that is, the fronts
and heels separate.

THIS pattern may be worked in two ways.
Either the pieces composing the sides of the
fruit, and also the leaves, may be cut out of
velvet, and gummed on the cloth, or the pattern being entirely marked on the cloth, those
parts may be cut out, and a piece of coloured
satin being gummed underneath, they will
appear sunk in satin on the cloth. In either
case the edges, after being sewed down, are
to be covered with gold thread. The stems
are made of gold braid, and where wide, have
an Albert braid, of the same colour as the
velvet or satin, between them.

The heart of the fruit is admirably repre-

MELON PATTERN SLIPPER, IN APPLICATION.

sented by beads sewed on at equal distances,
and the veinings of the leaves are in gold
braid.

This design, somewhat modified, of course,
for the different form, is admirably adapted
for a smoking or travelling cap.

SHIELD CIGAR-CASE IN APPLICATION.

Materials.—A piece of rich violet or maroon cloth, black velvet, fine gold braid, gold thread, and black silk.

AT the present moment every sort of work in application is becoming more liked than ever, especially among the Parisians. No matter what the article may be, from a screen or a sofa-cushion to a cigar-case, every piece of ornamental work is sure to have some parts of the design in velvet laid on the cloth,

SHIELD CIGAR-CASE, IN APPLICATION.

or silk on cloth, or leather on leather, or, in short, no matter what combination of materials, but always something of the same sort. If the style of material is uniform, however, the designs are infinitely various. We have already given patterns of groups of foliage and arabesques. The one we now present to our readers is of a totally different character. It is designed to present the appearance of a shield, and in the centre, where a pendent tassel now is seen, the initial of the owner may be embroidered. The pattern, with the corner pieces of the border, is in black velvet, cut out in the proper form, and gummed on the cloth. All the edges are covered with gold braid, which also forms the various scrolls, except those on the velvet itself, which are in gold thread. To work the fringe you will take a succession of stitches with coarse black silk, the length required for the pattern, each one being straight down. At equal distances, say every fifth stitch, appears one in gold thread. The lower part of the tassel is worked in the same way; the upper part slightly raised, and with cross bows of silk.

THE WORK-TABLE FRIEND.

BOURSE A FLACON.

Materials.—3 skeins of rich scarlet crochet silk, 3 of light green, 4 of black, 3 of blue, 2 crimson, 2 white, 16 of gold thread. The tassel should mingle all these colours; besides which, the smelling bottle forming the top, and a handsome ring, will be required.

CONTRACTIONS USED—Lg, green; G + gold; S, scarlet; Bl + blue; C, crimson; W, white; B, black.

All the purse, except that part on which the ring comes, is done in single crochet.

With the scarlet silk, make a chain of 150 stitches, close it into a round, and do 4 rounds of Sc. Join on the gold.

1st Pattern Round.—+ 4 S, 8 G, 7 S, 2 G, 9 S, + 5 times.

2nd Round.—+ 1 G, 4 S, 9 G, 6 S, 2 G, 8 S, + 5 times.

3rd Round.—+ 5 S, 2 G, 4 B, 4 G, 5 S, 2 G, 7 S, 1 G, + 5 times.

4th Round.—+ 5 S, 2 G, 6 B, 3 G, 3 S, 9 G, 1 S, 1 G, + 5 times.

5th Round.—+ 5 S, 2 G, 2 B, 2 G, 3 B, 2 G, 1 S, 4 G, 1 B, 8 G, + 5 times.

6th Round.—+ 1 G, 3 S, 3 G, 2 B, 1 G, 1 Lg, 1 G, 3 B, 5 G, 2 B, 3 G, 3 B, 2 G, + 5 times. Fasten off the scarlet.

7th Round.—+ 6 G, 3 B, 1 G, 2 Lg, 1 G, 2 B, 2 G, 5 B, 2 G, 3 B, 3 G, + 5 times.

8th Round.—+ 1 B, 4 G, 4 B, 1 G, 2 Lg, 1 G, 2 B, 1 G, 6 B, 1 G 3 B, 1 G, 3 B, + 5 times.

9th Round.—+8 B, 1 G, 3 Lg, 1 G, 4 B, 1 G, 1 B, 3 G, 8 B, + 5 times.

10th Round.—+ 2 G, 3 B, 3 G, 3 Lg, 5 G, 1 B, 3 G, 1 B, 2 G, 4 B, 2 G, + 5 times.

BOURSE A FLACON.

11th Round.—+ 2 Lg, 1 G, 1 B, 1 G, 11 Lg, 2 G, 4 B, 3 G, 4 B, 1 G, + 5 times.

12th Round.—+ 1 G, 2 Lg, 1 G, 6 Lg, 5 G, 3 Lg, 6 G, 6 B, + 5 times.

13th Round.—+ 1 G, 2 Lg, 1 G, 3 Lg, 4 G, 8 Lg, 6 G, 5 B, + 5 times. Join on crimson.

14th Round.—+ 1 G, 2 Lg, 1 G, 1 Lg, 2 G, 1 C, 1 G, 2 G, 5 G, 3 Lg, 7 G, 4 B, + 5 times.

15th Round.—+ 4 Lg, 1 G, 2 C, 1 G, 1 Lg, 2 G, 4 B, 2 G, 3 Lg, 1 G, 1 B, 4 G, 3 B, 1 G, + 5 times.

16th Round.—+ 3 Lg, 1 G, 2 C, 5 G, 4 B, 1 G, 1 B, 1 G, 2 Lg, 1 G, 2 B, 3 G, 2 B, 1 G, 1 Lg, + 5 times.

17th Round.—+ 2 Lg, 1 G, 2 C, 3 G, 2 B, 2 G, 2 B, 2 G, 2 B, 1 G, 1 Lg, 1 G, 3 B, 2 G, 1 B, 1 G, 2 Lg, + 5 times. Join on the blue.

18th Round.—+ 1 Lg, 1 G, 3 C, 2 G, 4 Bl, 1 G, 2 B, 1 G, 3 B, 1 G, 1 Lg, 1 G, 6 B, 1 G, 2 Lg, + 5 times.

19th Round.—+ 1 G, 3 C, 1 G, 1 Bl, 1 G, 2 Bl, 1 G, 1 Bl, 1 G, 2 B, 1 G, 3 B, 1 G, 1 Lg, 1 G, 6 B, 1 G, 2 Lg, + 5 times.

20th Round.—+ 3 C, 1 G, 3 Bl, 2 G, 2 Bl, 1 G, 2 B, 1 G, 3 B, 1 G, 1 Lg, 1 G, 1 B, 6 G, 1 Lg, 1 G, + 5 times.

21st Round.—+ 3 C, 1 G, 7 Bl, 1 G, 3 B, 1 G, 1 B, 1 G, 1 Lg, 1 G, 3 B, 1 G, 3 Lg, 1 G, 1 Lg, 1 G, + 5 times.

22nd Round.—+ 3 C, 1 G, 4 Bl, 2 G, 2 B, 1 G, 3 B, 3 G, 5 B, 1 G, 3 Lg, 1 G, 1 C, + 5 times.

23rd Round.—+ 3 C, 1 G, 2 Bl, 2 G, 5 B, 4 G, 4 B, 1 G, 2 B, 1 G, 3 Lg, 1 G, 1 C, + 5 times.

24th Round.—+ 2 C, 1 G, 2 Bl, 1 G, 12 B, 4 G, 2 B, 2 Lg, 1 G, 2 C, + 5 times.

25th Round.—+ 2 C, 1 G, 1 Bl, 3 G, 11 B, 4 G, 2 B, 1 G, 3 Lg, 1 G, 2 C, + 5 times.

26th Round.—+ 2 C, 3 G, 2 Bl, 1 G, 2 B, 4 G, 2 B, 2 G, 5 B, 1 G, 3 Lg, 1 G, 2 C, + 5 times. Fasten on white.

27th Round.—+ 1 C, 1 G, 1 Bl, 1 G, 4 Bl, 1 G, 2 B, 1 G, 2 W, 1 G, 1 B, 1 G, 6 B, 1 G, 2 Lg, 1 G, 3 C, + 5 times.

28th Round.—+ 1 C, 1 G, 1 Bl, 1 G, 2 Bl, 1 G, 1 Bl, 1 G, 3 B, 1 G, 2 W, 2 G, 2 B, 5 G, 2 Lg, 1 G, 3 C, + 5 times.

29th Round.—+ 1 C, 1 G, 2 Bl, 2 G, 2 Bl, 1 G, 3 B, 1 G, 2 W, 1 G, 2 B, 2 G, 4 Lg, 1 G, 1 Lg, 1 G, 3 C, + 5 times.

30th Round.—+ 1 C, 1 G, 6 Bl, 1 G, 3 B, 1 G, 2 W, 1 G, 4 B, 1 G, 3 Lg, 1 G, 1 Lg, 1 G, 3 C, + 5 times.

31st Round.—+ 1 C, 1 G, 5 Bl, 1 G, 4 B, 1 G, 2 W, 4 G, 2 B, 1 G, 3 Lg, 1 G, 4 C, + 5 times.

32nd Round.—+ 1 C, 1 G, 2 Bl, 3 G, 4 B, 1 G, 2 W, 2 G, 2 W, 2 G, 1 B, 1 G, 3 Lg, 1 G, 4 C, + 5 times.

33rd Round.—+ 1 C, **1 G, 1 Bl, 1 G, 7 B,**

1 G, 2 W, 1 G, 2 W, 1 G, 3 B, 1 G, 3 Lg, 1 G, 4 C, + 5 times.

34th Round.—+ 1 C, 4 G, 3 B, 4 G, 4 W, 1 G, 4 B, 1 G, 3 Lg, 1 G, 4 C, + 5 times.

35th Round.—+ 3 G, 2 Bl, 1 G, 3 B, 1 G, 3 W, 1 G, 3 W, 1 G, 2 B, 3 G, 3 Lg, 1 G, 4 C, + 5 times.

36th Round.—+ 2 G, 4 Bl, 1 G, 3 B, 1 G, 5 W, 1 G, 1 B, 1 G, 3 Lg, 1 G, 2 Lg, 1 G, 4 C, + 5 times.

37th Round.—+ 2 G, 2 Bl, 1 G, 2 Bl, 1 G, 2 B, 1 G, 4 W, 1 G, 1 B, 1 G, 5 Lg, 1 G, 1 Lg, 1 G, 4 C, + 5 times.

38th Round.—+ 1 G, 1 Bl, 2 G, 2 Bl, 1 G, 3 B, 1 G, 2 W, 2 G, 2 B, 3 G, 4 Lg, 2 G, 4 C, + 5 times.

39th Round.—+ 1 G, 5 Bl, 1 G, 2 B, 1 G, 2 W, 2 G, 6 B, 1 G, 4 Lg, 1 G, 4 C, + 5 times.

40th Round.—+ 5 Bl, 1 G, 2 B, 1 G, 5 W, 1 G, 6 B, 1 G, 2 Lg, 1 G, 4 C, 1 G, + 5 times.

41st Round.—+ 2 Bl, 3 G, 2 B, 1 G, 6 W, 1 G, 6 B, 1 G, 2 Lg, 1 G, 4 C, 1 G, +.

42nd Round.—+ 3 G, 4 B, 1 G, 3 W, 3 G, 7 B, 1 G, 1 Lg, 1 G, 5 C, 1 G, + 5 times.

43rd Round.—+ 6 B, 1 G, 3 W, 1 G, 4 B, 4 G, 2 B, 1 G, 1 Lg, 1 G, 4 C, 2 G, + 5 times.

44th Round.—+ 2 G, 4 B, 1 G, 2 W, 1 G, 4 B, 1 G, 4 Lg, 1 G, 1 B, 1 G, 1 Lg, 1 G, 4 C, 2 G, + 6 times.

45th Round.—+ 2 Bl, 1 G, 3 B, 1 G, 1 W, 1 G, 3 B, 1 G, 2 B, 1 G, 4 Lg, 2 G, 1 Lg, 1 G, 3 C, 3 G, + 5 times.

46th Round.—+ 2 Bl, 1 G, 3 B, 1 G, 1 W, 1 G, 2 Bl, 1 G, 4 B, 1 G, 3 Lg, 1 G, 1 Lg, 1 G, 3 C, 2 G, 2 Bl, + 5 times.

47th Round.—+ 1 G, 1 Bl, 1 G, 3 B, 3 B, 1 G, 1 W, 1 G, 2 B, 1 G, 4 B, 1 G. 3 Lg, 1 G, 1 Lg, 1 G, 2 C, 1 G, 1 Bl, 1 G, 2 Bl, + 5 times.

48th Round.—+ 2 Bl, 1 G, 4 B, 2 G, 2 B, 1 G, 5 B, 1 G, 2 Lg, 1 G, 2 Lg, 2 G, 3 Bl, 2 G, + 5 times. Fasten off green and crimson.

49th Round.—+ 2 G, 2 B, 6 G, 2 B, 9 G, 3 Bl, 2 G, 4 Bl, + 5 times.

50th Round.—+ 3 B, 2 G, 3 B, 3 G, 2 B, 2 G, 9 Bl, 1 G, 1 B, 4 G, + 5 times.

51st Round.+ 3 B, 1 G, 6 B, 3 G, 1 B, 3 G, 6 Bl, 1 G, 6 B, + 5 times. Fasten off blue.

52nd Round.—+ 3 B, 1 G, 12 B, 7 G, 7 B, + 5 times.

53rd Round.—+ 2 G, 3 B, 5 G, 3 B, 1 G, 13 B, 3 G, + 5 times.

54th Round.—+ 3 G, 1 B, 6 G, 3 B, 2 G, 10 B, 5 G, + 5 times. Join on scarlet.

55th Round.—+ 2 S, 3 G, 3 S, 2 G, 2 B, 5 G, 6 B, 5 G, 2 S, + 5 times.

56th Round.—+ 3 S, 1 G, 4 G 2 G, 1 B, 2 G, 2 S, 10 G, 3 S, 1 G, 1 S, + 5 times.

57th Round.—+ 3 S, 1 G, 4 S, 5 G, 4 S, 7 G, 6 S, + 5 times.

58th Round.—+ 7 S, 5 G, 10 S, 1 G, 7 S, + 5 times.

Now do three rounds of scarlet only. For the round, begin with scarlet and gold. + 9 G, 7 S, 2 G, 12 S, + 5 times.

2nd Round.—+ 1 S, 10 G, 6 S, 2 G, 10 S, over 11, + 5 times. Join on black.

3rd Round.—+ 1 S, 2 G, 5 B, 4 G, 3 S, 7 G, 6 S, over 7, + 5 times.

4th Round.—+ 1 S, 2 G, 7 B, 8 G, 2 B, 3 G, 4 S, over 5, + 5 times.

5th Round.—+ 3, G, 7 B, 3 G, 7 B (over 8 stitches), 5 G (over 6 stitches), 5 times.

6th Round.—+ 1 G, 7 B, 1 G, 8 B, over 10, 5 G, over 6, + 5 times.

7th Round.—+ 3 B, 4 G, 8 B (missing 1), 3 G, 1 B, + 5 times.

8th Round.—+ 3 G, 9 B (over 10), 3 G, 1 B, 2 G, + 5 times. Join on blue.

9th Round.—+ 2 Bl, 2 G, 6 B, over 7, 3 G, 4 Bl, + 5 times. Fasten off black.

10th Round.—+ 4 Bl, 5 G, 6 Bl, + 5 times.

11th Round.—+ 6 Bl, 1 G, 7 Bl, + 5 times.

12th Round.—+ 4 Bl (on 5), 3 G, 5 Bl (on 6), 5 times.

13th Round.—+ 3 Bl, 5 G, 3 B, + 5 times. Join on green.

14th Round.—+ 1 Bl, 3 G, 1 Lg, 3 G, 2 Bl + 5 times.

15th Round.—+ 2 G, 3 Lg, 2 G, 1 Bl, + 5 times.

16th Round.—+ 1 G, 4 Lg, 2 G, + 5 times.

17th Round.—+ 1 G, 3 Lg (on 4), 1 G, + 5 times.

18th Round.—+ 1 G, 2 Lg (on 3), + 5 times.

19th Round.—+ 1 G, 1 Lg, + 5 times. Fasten off.

Now, with scarlet silk, on the original chain, do about four inches of open square crochet, working backwards and forward. Finish by slipping on the ring, sewing on the flacon, and adding the tassel.

_____

THE WORK-TABLE FRIEND.

INFANT'S CAP, IN BEAD EMBROIDERY.

Materials.—6 reels of Messrs. W. Evans & Co's Boar's Head Crochet Cotton, No. 40, Seed Beads, with Lace and Ribbon for Borders.

THE exquisite bead-work of Germany has long been a subject of almost as much wonderment as admiration in England; and since the examination of the beautiful display of that work in the Crystal Palace, it has been an object of ambition with us to attempt to produce something equally rich and elegant. The difficulties in the way of such an achievement were such as would hardly be believed by those who have not tried similar experiments. The grand difficulty was the obtaining of a sufficient variety of beads. To produce the effect of a well-executed painting (which

all good bead-work should do), the shades of the beads should be sufficiently numerous to blend together in the most perfect manner; and in vain we ransacked the city warehouses for the needful varieties. True, we saw hundreds of casks of these tiny beads, and laughed to ourselves at the idea of there being any difficulty in the matter; but when we came to examine them, we found that our utmost research would not enable us to obtain a quarter of the necessary colours. We did, at last, what perhaps it would have been wise to have done at first—applied to the fountain-head, and sent an order to the manufacturer at Berlin for a quantity of every seed bead that was made. The result astonished us. Between three and four hundred colours made their appearance; and it soon became perfectly clear, that if we did not succeed in bead-painting, it would not be for want of materials.

The next consideration was, on what article to employ our skill; and considering crochet as one of the most universally popular kinds of work, and feeling, moreover, that though screens and cushions, and nick-nacks of all sorts, might go out of fashion, that babies never would, and that consequently any article for the wear of those small specimens of humanity could not fail to be generally popular, we have selected a BABY'S CAP as a good example of bead embroidery.

Besides the materials we have enumerated at the head of the article, two ordinary Berlin patterns will be required. One should be a wreath, not more than 28 to 36 squares wide, the other a small bouquet, 30 squares wide, and 24 deep. A few squares more or less do not signify. Choose such a design as will afford a variety of shades and colours. For this reason, roses are always suitable; because, even if not painted in the pattern, you can make one in crimsons, another in scarlets, a third in yellows, while all possible varieties of greens can be introduced in the leaves. White flowers only are inadmissible on a ground of cotton; but in bead-embroidering, in general, we must not forget that there are *shades* of white, as well as of any other colour.

The most troublesome part of the work is the first threading of the beads, which must be done before any part is commenced. Supposing the bouquets round the crown are 25 to 30 stitches wide, about eight of them will be placed round the crown. Take the Berlin pattern, therefore, and thread on every row eight times, beginning with the *last* row, and ending with that containing the stems of the group. For the wreath in front, about 300 stitches will make a large-sized cap, so that if one perfect pattern of the design has 120 stitches, you must, in threading the beads, do two perfect patterns and a-half in every row. Use one reel of cotton for the wreath, another for the bouquets, and begin the cap with a third, commencing with the centre of the crown, thus :—

Make a chain of 6. Close it into a round, and work three rounds on it in Sc, increasing enough to keep it flat.

1st pattern Round.—+ 1 Dc, 2 Ch, miss 1, + 16 times.

2nd Round.—+ 3 Dc on 1 Dc, 2 Ch, miss 2 Ch + 16 times.

3rd Round.—+ 4 Dc on 3, 2 Ch, miss 2 Ch + 16 times.

4th Round.—+ 5 Dc on 4, 2 Ch, miss 2 Ch + 16 times.

5th Round.—+ 6 Dc on 5, 2 Ch, miss 2 Ch + 16 times.

6th Round.—+ 7 Dc on 6, 3 Ch, miss 2 Ch + 16 times.

7th Round.—+ 8 Dc on 7, 3 Ch, miss 3 Ch + 16 times.

8th Round.—+ 9 Dc on 8, 3 Ch, miss 3 Ch + 16 times. Slip on the 1st of 9 Dc.

9th Round.—+ 7 Dc, beginning on the 2nd of 9, 3 Ch, 1 Dc on 2nd of 3 Ch, 3 Ch + 16 times. Slip on 1st of 7.

10th Round.—+ 5 Dc, beginning on 2nd of 7, 3 Ch, Dc on 2nd of 3 Ch, 3 Ch, Dc on second of next three chains, 3 Ch + 16 times. Slip stitch on 1st of 5 Dc.

11th Round.—+ 3 Dc, beginning on 2nd of 5, * 3 Ch, Dc on second of 3 Ch * 3 times, 3 Ch + 16 times.

12th Round.—Dc on centre of every chain and of the three Dc, all round, with 3 Ch, between every 2 Dc.

13th Round.—Dc all round.

Observe that if a *small* cap be required this pattern repeated 12, 10, or even 8 times only, will do, only the foundation round must be smaller, and the first pattern row (which, all the others follow) must have no more repetitions than are desired for the others. For a very small cap eight repetitions of a bouquet would also be too many. The scale on which the cap is designed must not be forgotten in threading the beads.

When this is done, count the number of stitches in the round, and divide it by eight. The number in each eighth *more than in the width of the bouquet* are to be in plain Sc. Work on the wrong side, from the Berlin pattern, dropping the beads in their proper places, and leaving an equal number of plain stitches between every two groups of flowers. There is no increase in this part. Finish with a round of Sc. Fasten off, and resume the open work on the *right* side. Do one round of Sc.

1st pattern Round.—+ 1 Dc, 3 Ch, miss 3 + repeat all round.

2nd Round.—+ 3 Dc (the second coming over 1 Dc) 6 Ch, miss 6, 2 Dc on 1 Dc, 6 Ch, miss 6, all round.

3rd Round.—+ 3 Dc (the last on 1st of 3 Dc), 2 Ch, miss 1, 3 Dc, 3 Ch, miss 3, 2 Dc in one stitch, 1 Ch, miss 2, 2 Dc in 1, 3 Ch, miss 3 + all round.

4th Round.—Begin on the 3rd of the first 3 Ch, + 4 Dc (the centre 2 on 2 Ch), 4 Ch, miss 4, 2 Dc on 1, 1 Ch, miss 2, 2 Dc on 1, 1 Ch, miss 2, 2 Dc on 1, 4 Ch, miss 4, + all round.

5th Round.—+ 2 Dc on centre 2 of 4, 4 Ch, miss 4, * 2 Dc on 1, 1 Ch, miss 2 * 3 times, 2 Dc on 1, 4 Ch, miss 4, + all round.

6th Round.—+ 1 Dc, 1 Ch, miss 1, + all round.

NOTE.—That for a small cap the last 5 of these *six* rounds may be entirely omitted, the worker proceeding immediately after the first to the

FRONT.—1*st Row.*— 3 Dc, + 5 Ch, miss 5, 1 Dc, 5 Ch, miss 5, 3 Dc + repeat until nearly three-quarters of the entire round are done, when finish with 3 Dc, and fasten off. The space left is for the back of the neck.

2nd Row.—3 Dc, 4 Ch, miss 4, + 3 Dc, 5 Ch, miss 5, 1 Dc on centre of 3, 5 Ch, miss 5 + to the end of the row, which must correspond with the beginning.

3rd Row.—3 Dc on 3, 1 Ch, miss 1, + 3 Dc, 3 Ch, miss 3 Dc of last row, 3 Dc, 5

Ch, miss 5 + repeat to the end, which must be like the beginning.

4th Row.—Like 2nd.

5th Row.—Like 1st.

6th Row.—6 Dc, + 5 Ch, miss 5, **3 Dc 3** Ch (over 3 Dc in last row), 3 Dc, + repeat to the end, which must have 6 Dc.

Repeat these six rows again, and the first 3 once more, then a row of Sc, contracting by missing a stitch, if there should be above 12 stitches more than are required for the wreath

OPEN HEM.—2 Dc 3 Ch, miss 3. Repeat to the end.

For the wreath begin on the wrong side, do two rows of Sc before beginning with the beads, and whatever number of stitches may be over, divide equally between the two ends. After the wreath is finished, do 2 rows of Sc, then open hem, 3 rows Sc, then open hem, which is to be worked *all round the cap*, and finally 3 rows of Sc on the front only. Trim with lace border, and run ribbon in the open hem.

PORTUGUESE GUIPURE DOYLEY.

Materials.—Messrs. W. EVANS & Co.'s Boar's Head Crochet Cotton, No 30, and Mecklenburgh thread, No. 8. Netting needle, No. 22, and steel meshes, Nos. 8, 10, 12 and 17.

THIS Doyley is to be worked precisely like the preceding one of the series ; or it will serve for an antimacassar pattern in crochet, using Nos. 4, 8, or 12 Boar's Head cotton.

MODESTY.—One of the most indispensable female virtues, and that which gives them most credit in the world, and individual loveliness, is Modesty. This amiable quality of the soul has such an influence upon the features, air, mind, and character, that everything loses its charm in woman, where this bright diamond is wanting. It inspires us with angelic presence.

PORTUGUESE GUIPURE DOYLEY.

THE WORK-TABLE FRIEND.

SOFA OR CARRIAGE PILLOW, IN CROCHET.

7 shades of Scarlet, 4 thread Berlin Wool ; the 3rd shade from the lightest, to be a bright military Scarlet, the darkest to be nearly black. 7 shades of bright Emerald Green (*Grass Green must never be used*), $\frac{3}{4}$ of an oz. of each shade, except the lightest of both colours—6 skeins of each of these. No. 2 Penelope Crochet Hooks.

1st Row.—With lightest Scarlet make a chain of 9 stitches, unite the ends; 5 chain, Dc *under* the 9 chain; repeat this 5 times more, (*in all, 6 chains of* 5). Cut off the wool, tie it securely at the back. (*This must be done at every row.*)

2nd Row.—Same colour. 2 long *under* the 5 chain; 3 chain; 2 more long *under* the same; 3 chain; repeat this 5 times more.

3rd Row.—Next shaded Scarlet. 2 long *under* the 3 chain, between the 4 long stitch; 3 chain; 2 more long *under* the same; 3 chain; Dc *under* 3 chain, 3 chain; repeat this 5 times more.

4th Row.—Military Scarlet. 2 long *under* the 3 chain, between the 4 long; 4 chain; 2 more long *under* the same; 4 chain; Dc on Dc; 4 chain; repeat this 5 times more.

5th Row.—Palest Green, 3 long *under* the 4 chain, between the 4 long; 5 chain;

X

Sofa, or Carriage Pillow, in Crochet.   By Mrs. Warren.

3 more long *under* the same ; 3 chain ; Dc *under* 4 chain; 5 chain ; Dc *under* 4 chain ; 3 chain, *repeat*.

This forms the centre Star.

Now work 6 more stars, in precisely the same manner, only varying the shades as follows :—Commence with the lightest shade Scarlet, and work the 2nd row with next shade instead of the same ; taking the next shade Green for the outside row ; sew with Green Wool these 6 stars to the points of the centre Star, sewing them also at the side.

Now make 12 stars, beginning with the 2nd shade Scarlet, making the 1st and 2nd rows of the same colour.

3rd Row.—Military Scarlet, same as 3rd row of 1st star.

4th Row.—Next darker shade, same as 4th row.

5th Row.—Next darkest Green.

Sew these 12 stars round the last 6, attaching them as before.

Now make 18 stars, commencing with military Scarlet, making the 2 first rows in the same shade.

3rd Row.—Next darker.

4th Row.—Next darker.

5th Row.—Next darker Green.

Sew these round the other stars.

Make 24 stars, commencing with military Scarlet, but making the 2nd row of the next darker shade, instead of the same.

Use the next two darker shades in gradation, and the next darkest Green.

Sew these stars round the others.

Make 30 stars, commencing with the next shade darker than the military Scarlet; use the 3 darker shades in gradation, and edge with the darkest Green but one. It will be observed, that 7 shades of Scarlet are used on this side, and 6 of Green :

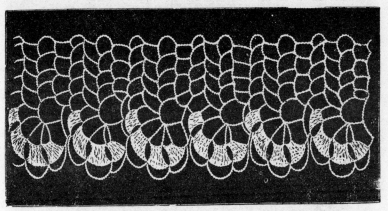

Crochet Edge, worked the short way. By Mrs. Warren.

for the reverse of the cushion, 6 of Scarlet and 7 of Green. Damp well, and press by placing it between folded linen, with a heavy weight upon it, till dry.

Line this side with white cotton velvet, white satin, or watered silk.

For the Reverse.

Make exactly the same number of stars, and worked precisely the same way with respect to the tints, but commencing with the palest Green, instead of Scarlet, and edging the outside row with Scarlet.

This side may be lined either with white or green velvet: make a lining of strong calico, the exact size, fill with 4lbs of feathers.

Trim with green silk cushion cord, and 6 shaded bullion tassels.

Great care must be taken to arrange the colours precisely as the instructions given, as the effect will be to give a most intense and brilliant colour, and in selecting the wools, they should be of the brightest tints.

CROCHET EDGE, WORKED THE SHORT WAY.

No. 20 Boar's Head Cotton. No. 4 Penelope Hooks.

Make a chain of 20 stitches; 1 long, 3 chain; 1 long into 4th loop for 4 times; 5 chain; 1 long into last loop.

(*This row is to be omitted after this time.*)

1st Row.—Turn back 8 chain, 1 long *under* 5 chain; * 5 chain, 1 long *under* the same 5 chain; repeat from * twice more, 3 chain, 1 long *under* every 3 chain.

2nd Row.—Turn back 7 chain, 1 long *under* 1st 3 chain; 3 chain, 1 long *under* every 3 chain; * 3 chain, Dc *under* 5 chain, 4 long *under* same chain; repeat from * 3 times more. (*Always in working this row again, in making the next scallop, after the last *, Dc into Dc of previous scallop.*)

3rd Row.—Turn back 7 chain; Dc *under* 3 chain for 4 times; 3 chain; 1 long *under* 3 chain for 4 times.

4th Row.—7 chain, 1 long *under* 1st 3 chain; 3 chain, 1 long *under* every 3 chain; 5 chain, 1 long *under* 7 chain; now repeat again as at 1st row. The pattern consists of 4 rows only.

ANGER.—As a preventative of anger, banish all tale-bearers and slanderers from your conversation, for it is these blow the devil's bellows to rouse up the flames of rage and fury, by first abusing your ears, and then your credulity, and after that steal away your patience, and all this perhaps for a lie. To prevent anger, be not too inquisitive into the affairs of others, or what people say of yourself, or into the mistakes of your friends, for this is going out to gather sticks to kindle a fire to burn your own house.—*Old Divine.*

COL MOUSQUETAIRE, BRODÉ À JOURS.

THE WORK-TABLE FRIEND.

COL MOUSQUETAIRE, BRODÉ À JOURS.

Materials.—Fine soft Jaconet muslin, narrow Valenciennes insertion, the Royal Embroidery cotton, Nos. 40 and 60, and Boar's Head cotton, 140, of Messrs. W. Evans & Co., of Derby.

THIS collar is in a style but just introduced into Paris. The novelty consists in the intermixture of Valenciennes lace with the muslin, and the working of fancy stitches (technically termed *jours*) in the edge and various other parts. A reference to the engraving will show that one line of lace is placed at a little distance from the neck, and another, in points, is placed at a little distance from it. Between these two is a wreath of leaves, and at each point is a flower pendent from it. The deep scallop within which this flower is

placed has a double line of overcast stitch, the space between the two being filled with an open muslin stitch. The entire ground of the collar is in button-holed bars, or, as this work is technically termed, " *guipure de Venise.*"

This collar is of a very large size, and is certainly one of the richest designs that has ever been seen.

When drawn on the muslin, the first thing is to lay the Valenciennes insertion on it, folding it over where points are to be formed. Take the embroidery cotton, No. 40, and begin to run the edge of the lace at the neck and the muslin together, taking a stitch or two only before you come to the first bar of the ground; run your needle into the muslin where the bar is to connect it, and button-hole over the thread back again to the lace. Run a stitch or two more of the lace and muslin together, and repeat, thus making all the bars as you go along. At the other edge of this line of lace you will make the bars to connect it with the wreath of leaves; and where little circles occur, something like Mechlin wheels, trace them on the muslin, pierce a hole in the centre, and work the overcast on the muslin itself. The edges of the lace are then to be very neatly sewed over with No. 60 cotton, in the finest button-hole stitch.

The other line of lace is to be treated in the same way, after which the small scallops (or *dents*) round the neck may be worked, and the wreath of leaves. These are traced out with double cotton, No. 40, and the edges overcast with No. 60, as narrow as possible. Within this they are worked in raised satin stitch, with the same cotton; and the vein-ings are in the open stitch we shall presently describe, only observing now that the muslin must *not* be cut away. The flower at each point may be worked exactly in the same manner, but the muslin part may afterwards be cut out. The graduated button-hole stitch of the edges must also be worked, and, *lastly*, the open work. The first stitch is that seen in the leaves. We will call it lace-work. Remove the muslin from the *toile-ciré*, take a very fine needle (say Boulton & Son's No.12), and on the wrong side draw out three threads, and leave three in one direction, and three in the contrary one. Fasten on your thread at the raised work, and take a stitch over every three threads, so that the thread is on the wrong side, where two lines cross each other. When every line, in both directions, is thus worked, this lace is completed. At the edge the same stitch is used, but spotted in small stars. This is done after the foun-dation is finished, on four squares, leaving a vacant one in the centre, being darned back-wards and forwards, twisting the thread every stitch, and working two squares in one direc-tion, and two in another. In the flowers at the points, a row of Brussels edging is worked, and then a thread run in every stitch, after which two bars of *point d'Angleterre* are worked across each square, and three in the centre ones.

As may be imagined, these collars are ex-tremely costly. Three guineas and a half was asked for one worked by the designer; and we saw another, done in this style, but still larger, and with sleeves to correspond, for which 1500 francs, or £60, was given !

But the rage for rich and beautiful embroi-dery never was so great as at present.

ARABESQUE PURSE.

Materials.—6 skeins of fawn-coloured silk ; 4 scarlet, 3 black, and 2 bleu ciel ditto, all French small skeins. Algerienne garnitures to match. Fine hook.

WITH the fawn silk make a chain of 112 stitches ; do two rounds of Sc with this silk.

ARABESQUE PURSE.

FIRST PATTERN ROUND.—Join on Scarlet. ✛ 5 Fawn, 1 Scarlet, 2 F, 5 S, 3 F, 5 S, 2 F, 1 S, 4 F, ✛ 4 times. All the repetitions of the pattern between ✛ ✛, will occur four times.

2nd Round.—✛ 6 F, 8 S, 1 F, 8 S, 5 F, ✛ 3rd Round.—Join on Black. ✛ 6 F, 2 S, 5 B, 3 S, 5 B, 2 S, 5 F, ✛ 4th Round.—✛2 S, 3 F, 2 S, 7 B, 1 S, 7 B, 2 S, 3 F, 1 S, ✛ Join on Blue.

5th Round.—╬ 3 S, 2 F, 1 S, 4 B, 3 Bl, 3 B, 3 Bl, 4 B, 1 S, 2 F, 2 S, ╬ No Fawn next round.

6th Round.—╬ 2 B, 4 S, 2 B, 6 Bl, 1 B, 6 Bl, 2 B, 4 S, 1 B, ╬

7th Round.—╬ 3 B, 3 S, 2 B, 2 Bl, 3 F, 3 Bl, 3 F, 2 Bl, 2 B, 3 S, 2 B, ╬

8th Round.—╬ 4 B, 2 S, 1 B, 2 Bl, 5 F, 1 Bl, 5 F, 2 Bl, 1 B, 2 S, 3 B, ╬

9th Round.—╬ 3 B, 2 S, 2 B, 2 Bl, 5 F, 1 Bl, 5 F, 2 Bl, 2 B, 2 S, 2 B, ╬

10th Round.—╬ 2 B, 2 S, 3 B, 2 Bl, 11 F, 2 Bl, 3 B, 2 S, 1 B, ╬ No more Scarlet.

11th Round.—╬ 7 B, 3 Bl, 2 F, 1 Bl, 3 F, 1 Bl, 2 F, 3 Bl, 6 B, ╬

12th Round.—╬ 8 B, 5 Bl, 3 F, 5 Bl, 7 B, ╬

13th Round.—╬ 2 B, 1 Bl, 6 B, 4 Bl, 3 F, 4 Bl, 6 B, 1 Bl, 1 B, ╬

14th Round.—╬ 3 B, 2 Bl, 5 B, 3 Bl, 3 F, 3 Bl, 5 B, 2 Bl, 2 B, ╬

15th Round.—╬ 4 B, 8 Bl, 5 F, 8 Bl, 3 B, ╬

16th Round.—3 B, 2 Bl, 1 F, 4 Bl, 9 F, 4 B, 1 F, 2 Bl, 2 B, ╬

17th Round.—╬ 3 B, 2 Bl, 19 F, 2 Bl, 2 B, ╬

18th Round.—Join on Scarlet. ╬ 2 B, 2 Bl, 2 F, 1 B, 6 F, 3 S, 6 F, 1 B, 2 F, 2 Bl, 1 B, ╬

19th Round.—╬ 4 Bl, 2 F, 1 B, 4 F, 7 S, 4 F, 1 B, 2 F, 3 Bl, ╬

20th Round.—╬ 2 Bl, 3 F, 2 B, 4 F, 2 S, 3 B, 2 S, 4 F, 2 B, 3 F, 1 B, ╬ No more Blue.

21st Round.—╬ 4 F, 2 B, 4 F, 2 S, 5 B, 2 S, 4 F, 2 B, 3 F, ╬

22nd Round.—╬ 2 F, 3 B, 5 F, 2 S, 5 B, 2 S, 5 F, 3 B, 1 F, ╬

23rd Round.—╬ 4 B, 6 F, 2 S, 5 B, 2 S, 6 F, 5 B, ╬

24th Round.—╬ 3 B, 7 F, 2 S, 5 B, 2 S, 7 F, 2 B, ╬

25th Round.—╬ 2 B, 9 F, 2 S, 3 B, 2 S, 9 F, 1 B, ╬

26th Round.—╬ 9 F, 4 S, 3 B, 4 S, 8 F, ╬

27th Round.—╬ 4 F, 1 S, 3 F, 6 S, 1 B, 6 S, 3 F, 1 S, 3 F, ╬

28th Round.—╬ 4 F, 5 S, 3 B, 2 S; 1 B, 2 S, 3 B, 5 S, 3 F, ╬

29th Round.—╬ 4 F, 4 S, 5 B, 1 S, 1 B, 1 S, 5 B, 4 S, 3 F, ╬

30th Round.—╬ 4 F, 2 S, 7 B, 1 S, 1 B, 1 S, 7 B, 2 S, 3 F, ╬

31st Round.—╬ 5 F, 2 S, 15 B, 2 S, 4 F, ╬ Join on Blue. ¦

32nd Round.—╬ 6 F, 1 S, 4 B, 1 S, 2 B, 1 Bl, 2 B, 1 S, 4 B, 1 S, 5 F, ╬

33rd Round.—╬ 5 F, 6 S, 2 B, 3 Bl, 2 B, 6 S, 4 F, ╬

34th Round.—╬ 4 F, 2 S, 6 B, 5 Bl, 6 B, 2 S, 3 F, ╬

35th Round.—╬ 3 F, 2 S, 7 B, 5 Bl, 7 B, 2 S, 2 F, ╬

36th Round.—╬ 3 F, 2 S, 8 B, 3 Bl, 8 B, 2 S, 2 F, ╬

37th Round.—╬ 4 F, 2 S, 4 B, 7 Bl, 4 B, 2 S, 3 F, ╬

38th Round.—╬ 5 F, 2 S, 3 B, 9 Bl, 3 B, 2 S, 4 F, ╬

39th Round.—╬ 6 F, 2 S, 1 B, 11 Bl, 1 B, 2 S, 5 F, ╬

This being the centre round of the design, you will now repeat backwards from the 38th to the 1st, inclusive of both, then do two rounds of plain fawn.

For the centre do about four inches, working backwards and forwards instead of in a round, thus:—1st row, 1 Dc, 1 Ch, miss 1, ╬ repeat to the end. Turn ╬ 3 Ch, 1 Dc under chain, 1 Ch, miss 1, ╬ This last row must be repeated backwards and forwards. When 4 inches are done, close into a round, and do 1½ inch in the same way, still using only the fawn silk. Then 2 rounds of scarlet, * 5 rounds fawn, and 2 rounds scarlet * twice, and 1½ inch more fawn.

Draw up the end. Sew the large tassel on. Crochet up the other end flat, with the opening in the centre of one side, and sew a small tassel at each corner.

Contractions used in this design.—Sc, single crochet; Dc, double crochet; Ch, chain; B, black; Bl, blue; F, fawn; S, scarlet.

For the ground of this pattern, many other colours would look extremely well—a rich Vert-islay, or a claret, or dark blue. We have a vast variety of Algerienne trimmings, suitable for any combination of colours.

———

INDUSTRY.—There is no art or science that is too difficult for industry to attain to; it is the gift of tongues, and makes a man understood and valued in all countries, and by all nations; it is the philosopher's stone that turns all metals and even stones into gold, and suffers not want to break into its dwelling; it is the northwest passage that brings the merchant's ship as soon to him as he can desire—in a word, it conquers all enemies, and makes fortune herself pay contribution.

THE WORK-TABLE FRIEND.

TAMBOURED PURSE.

WITH INSTRUCTIONS IN TAMBOUR WORK.

Materials.—Black soie D'Avignon, a fine steel mesh, green, pink, crimson, violet, and orange silks (a small quantity of each), fine gold thread, a single slide, gold fringe, and a garniture à flacon. A small frame for embroidery is also indispensable.

WE feel great pleasure in introducing this novelty to our readers; and we doubt not of giving satisfaction by our exertions for

TAMBOURED PURSE.

their amusement. We now present to them a style of work very recently introduced into France, although the stitch itself (the tambour stitch) was fashionable in the time of our grandmothers. The peculiarity consists in the using it for embroidery on an open substance like netting, which can only be

done through he medium of a more solid one, which is afterwards pulled out, thread by thread. The material which answers best for this purpose is very fine crape, and the colour most pleasant to work on is pale green.

The implement used for tambour work something resembles a crochet hook, but with this difference, that the tambour needle is separate from the handle; it is about the length of an ordinary needle, and slides into the ivory handle, being kept in its place by a steel screw at the side. This screw is useful as a *rest* for the finger, and greatly aids the execution of the work. We would not, therefore, advise the substitution of the ordinary crochet for the more legitimate instrument, as, though the form of the hook itself is the same, the mode of working is essentially different. Muslin, or muslin and net, ribbon and lace, and many other materials were once frequently embroidered in tambour work; and the mode being the same in all, it remains only to describe the process. First have the design marked, then stretch the materials to be embroidered in a frame, or between two small loops; hold the tambour needle on the upper side, and the silk or cotton *under* the work. Insert the hook in the work, at the base of a stem, or in any other convenient part, and catch over it a loop of the silk, which should be held between the finger and thumb of the left hand, close to the place. A loop being now on the hook, insert it again in the outline about the tenth of an inch off, draw up another loop though the first, and continue the process. It will be found to facilitate the work, if the screw of which we have spoken is turned towards the worker in inserting the hook, and turned from her, towards the left, in withdrawing it. It will be observed from this description that the left hand is always *under* the work, and the right above it. In tambour work the outlines are the *first* worked, and the filling up is done afterwards. In the purse pattern we now give, all the outlines of the design are done in gold thread, and the flowers and leaves are afterwards filled up in their natural colours. The purse itself is in ordinary diamond netting, done in two pieces, seven and a half by four inches. One of these must have the opening left three inches long. The two pieces, after being embroidered, are sewed up the sides, rounded at the corners of one end, and trimmed with gold fringe, as seen in the engraving.

The trimming is a passementerie imitation of the little smelling-bottle now so fashionable for short purses, with tassels and cord to correspond.

ALABASTER DESSERT MAT.

Materials.—2 oz. of alabaster beads, No. 2, and a reel of the ingrain pink Boar's Head crochet cotton of Messrs. W. Evans and Co., of Derby.

THREAD the beads on the cotton, do 3 Ch, Sc on the first, and work 2 Sc on each, dropping a bead on every stitch.

2nd Round.—Increase to 12, still with a bead on every stitch.

3rd Round.—Increase to 20, working in the same way.

4th Round.—Increase to 28, still in the same way.

In the next round you will increase to 35, to be worked thus :—*5th Round.*—+ 3 beads, 2 cotton on 1, + 7 times.

ALABASTER DESSERT MAT.

6th Round.—+ 3 beads on 3, 3 cotton on 2, + 7 times.

7th Round.—+ 1 cotton on first bead, 1 bead on 2nd of 3, 4 more cotton, + 7 times. After the 7th work 1 cotton on 1, and 1 on the 1 bead.

8th Round.—+ 1 more cotton over 1 bead, 2 C, 1 B, 3 more C, + 7 times.

9th Round.—+ 3 C over 2, 3 B (the centre on 1), 2 C, + 7 times.

10th Round.—+ 3 C on 2, 5 B, 1 C, + 7 times.

11th Round.—Crochet with a bead on every stitch, increasing 7, so as to have 70 altogether in the round.

12th Round.—+ 2 C on 1, 4 B, + 14 times.

13th Round.—+ 3 C, 2 B (on centre 2 of 4), 1 C, + 14 times.

14th Round.—+ 3 C on 2, 4 B, + 14 times.

15th Round.—+ 3 C on 3, 6 B on 4, + 14 times.

16th Round.—+ 5 C, 2 B (on centre 2 of 6), 2 C, + 14 times.

17th Round.—Cotton on cotton, and beads on beads, of last round.

18th Round.—+ 4 cotton, 4 beads (over 2 beads and a cotton stitch at each side), 1 cotton, + 14 times.

19th Round.—+ 3 cotton, 6 beads (over 4 and a cotton stitch at each side), + 14 times.

20th Round.—+ 4 cotton, 4 beads, 1 cotton, + 14 times.

21st Round.—+ 4 cotton over 3, 2 B, 2 C, (over centre 2 of 4 beads), 2 B, + 14 times.

22nd Round.—+ 1 B, 2 C, 2 B, 5 C (over 2 and a bead at each side), 1 B, + 14 times.

23rd Round.—+ 4 B (over 2 C and a bead at each side), 7 C, + 14 times.

24th Round.—+ 6 B, 4 C (over 3 centre of 7), 2 B, + 14 times.

25th Round.—+ 5 B, 6 C, 1 B, + 14 times.

26th Round.—+ 1 B, 2 C, 2 B, 2 C, 1 B, 1 chain, 1 B, 2 C, 1 B, + 14 times.

27th Round.—+ 4 C, 3 B, 4 C (over 1 Ch and a bead at each side), 3 B, + 14 times.

28th Round.—+ 4 C, 1 B, 1 C, 1 B, 4 C (over 4), 1 B, 1 C, 1 B, + 14 times.

29th Round.—+ 6 C, 2 B, 3 C (on centre 2 of 4), 2 B, 2 C, + 14 times.

30th Round.—+ 5 C, 4 B, 1 C (on centre of 3), 4 B, 1 C, + 14 times.

31st Round.—+ 5 C, 9 B, 1 C, + 14 times.

32nd Round.—+ 6 C, 7 B, 2 C, + 14 times.

33rd Round.—+ 9 C (over 6, and 2 B), 3 B, 4 C, + 14 times.

34th Round.—+ 10 C, 1 B, 5 C, + 14 times.

Now work the edge thus :—* 7 Ch, miss 7, Sc on 8th, 5 Ch, Sc on next 6 Ch, Sc on the next, 5 Ch, Sc on the next, + repeat this all round. Then on the right side of the doyley, 5 Sc under the chain of 7, 6 Sc under the chain of 5, 7 Sc under the chain of 6, 6 Sc under the chain of 5.

THE WORK-TABLE FRIEND.

JEWEL BOX.

Materials.—Thick common cardboard; white gros de Naples, and white satin, ¾ yard of each; white satin cord; ribbon, 1 inch wide; 1 yard of deep white fringe; 1 reel of white soie d'Avignon; 6 skeins of gold thread; and a skein of pale blue silk.

The foundation of this pretty box is made of cardboard, which may easily be cut out from the engraving. Ten pieces are required, namely, four for the sides, all of the same dimensions, 7 inches at the top, 4½ at the bottom, and 5 deep, gradually sloping equally at both sides, from the widest to the narrowest part. The

JEWEL BOX.

piece for the lid will then, as a matter of course, be 7 inches square, and that for the bottom 4½. The shape of the four pieces forming the stand can be well seen in the engraving; at the upper and narrowest part they are 4½ inches, and about half an inch deep.

The cardboard for this box should be of a kind too thick to sew; the edges should, therefore, be gummed together and bound over with strips of cotton. The inside is then to be lined with silk, and the outer part with satin, a lining of flannel being placed between both these substances and the cardboard. The edges will be sewn together, and covered with the ornamental cord, *inside* as well as out. The lid of the box must be nicely wadded, to raise it, and over the satin covering one of darned netting is laid. It must be done in the square stitch, with the white silk, and a pattern darned on it in gold and blue. A quilling of white satin ribbon trims the lid

of the box; it is laid rather within the edge, which is finished with the same ornamental cords as the other parts.

Square netting is begun on one stitch, in which two are worked; then turn the work, and do one in the first stitch and two in the last. Work backwards and forwards, always doing two in the last stitch of the row, until you have the required length up one side: then net the last two together, at the end of every row, until one stitch only remains.

WORK-TABLE FOR JUVENILES; OR, LITTLE MARY'S HALF-HOLIDAY.

(*Continued from p.* 339.)

" Mamma, I find I have by me some of that pretty gold bourdon of which you taught me to make bracelets in the winter, and I was thinking I might use it to make a knitting basket for you. If you remember, there was a plain one given in the Family Friend some time ago; but I should think, with a little contrivance, I might work a pattern on it, which would be much prettier."

" It certainly would; and at the same time I do not think it would be difficult if you did not choose too great a variety of colours. In working over bourdon, you must not forget that it forms one colour, as well as a ground of itself; and that it is intended to be quite visible. Another advantage of this basket would be, that it would be more solid than those usually made, and would not only hold the cotton well, but would allow of the end of it being drawn through the middle of the cover, so that the reel of cotton would not be liable to be dragged out. It will be a very useful thing, and I shall thank you much for it.

" I shall be delighted, then, to do it, Mamma, if you will give me a little instruction. Perhaps a pine would be as pretty as anything. Can you help me with a design?

" Here is one which will be just the thing. See, your outline shall be white, with red and black in the centre. You require so little silk that you are sure to have enough among your remnants of skeins; the ground would be pretty in blue. Begin by the round for the bottom; do a few stitches on the end of the bourdon, make it into a round, and work round and round over the cord, until you have a piece about three inches in diameter.

" But look, Mamma, you can hardly see the gold at all."

" Because your stitches are too close together.

You must make the upper part of them quite long. Now, hold the bourdon so as to begin to form the sides; and I think you may do two rounds of blue more. Take care not to make the circle any larger. Divide your circle into five, and knot in a bit of thread to

KNITTING BASKET.

mark the divisions. Now do 4 blue, 8 white, 5 more blue, in each of these ; that is, 5 times in the round.

2nd Round.—+ 2 blue, 2 white, 8 red, 2 white, 3 blue + 5 times.

3rd Round.— + 2 white, 11 black, 2 white, 2 blue, + 5 times.

4th Round.—Like *2nd.*

5th Round.—Like *3rd.*

6th Round.—+ 2 blue, 2 white, 6 red, 2 white, 5 blue, + 5 times.

7th Round.— + 4 blue, 6 white, 4 blue, 2 white, 1 blue, + 5 times.

8th Round.— + 6 blue, 5 white, 2 blue, 2 white, 2 blue, + 5 times.

9th Round.— + 8 blue, 6 white, 3 blue, + 5 times.

Now do two rounds of blue only, and then one more, holding in the cord a little, to contract the basket. That will do nicely."

"How shall I make the top, Mamma? It should have some pattern on it?"

"Yes. Begin in the centre, as you did for the basket, and I think you may do three rounds of blue only. Then 5 white, and 5

blue stitches, alternately. Now 2 white, 2 blue over 2 of 5 white, 5 white, and 3 more blue. The next round work in blue until over the 2 blue you do 2 white, 3 black on white, 2 white, then the rest blue. In the next round do 2 white a little in advance of last, 5 red over black, 2 white, and the rest blue. In the next round finish the pine by doing white over red, and all the rest blue. I think you will now require about two rounds of blue only to make your cover fit. You may finish it with a little lace of white, thus:—1 Sc on edge, 2 Ch, miss 1 stitch, 4 Dc in next, 2 Ch, miss 1 stitch, + all round."

"And the handle is also to be made of bourdon, I suppose."

"Yes, and three strips will make a nice strong one. I should cover the two outer ones with black silk and the centre with red, as they will not so readily soil as lighter colours. Use the same colours also for a lace round the top of the basket, which will conceal the ends of the handle. With red silk do 7 Ch, then a single crochet along the top round of the bourdon. Do this all round. For the next, Sc on Sc, 3 Ch, 5 Dc on centre of 7 Ch, 3 Ch. The third round, with black, may be done in Sc on every Dc, chain over chain."

"But supposing I cannot get bourdon, Mamma, or do not wish to go to the expense of it, how can I make such a basket with common cord?"

"Very easily. The colour used for the ground might be made in wool, taking care to put in stitches enough completely to cover it. For the pattern, if you do two stitches instead of one you will find the design quite correct. You may use either wool or coarse crochet silk."

"That will be very easily done, Mamma. Now I want you to give me an idea for some handsome book-markers. Those worked on perforated card are pretty, but they are so very common."

"Besides that, they are hardly handsome enough for our friend's bazaar, which I suppose is the purpose for which you want them. I think I can tell you of a prettier, yet equally simple kind. Have you any gold paper?"

"Plain?—yes, Mamma, here is a morsel."

"That will be enough. Now find some purple silk, and ribbon the same colour, about an inch and a quarter wide. You must now decide what motto you will have. Mark it from the crochet alphabet, on checked paper, and see how many lines you want."

' What will be a suitable motto?"

" *Amitié*, or *Souvenir*, or, if for a Bible, you may take an appropriate one—' *Search the Scriptures.*'"

" I think I will choose *Amitié*, as it is simple and short,"

" Very well. Cut your gold paper into a length of four inches by one. Cut up three inches of it into seven strips, leaving the last inch not cut. Now take a bit of cardboard, an inch and a half wide and five long. Lay the gold paper on one side, along the centre, and fold the uncut part over one end. Cut a morsel of ribbon to cover this end, and as close as you can to the edge run in the end of silk with a needle. Now wind the silk round the card very evenly, and when you come to the cut part of the gold, raise up the strips as they are wanted to form the letters, winding the silk twice round, under the strip, for a stitch. Thus the letters will appear in gold on a silk ground. When the motto is marked, lay a bit of ribbon over the end of the card to cover it, and wind round the silk to the edge. Then fasten off, and add a bow at each end, and a length of ribbon as you may think suitable."

" But though these mottoes do for a bazaar because they would suit every one, could I not find something more *recherché* for any friend of our own."

" Yes, the family motto, whatever that might be, would be far better; because it would prove that your gift had the greatest value it could have; namely that it was the result of *thought of your friend.* Hence it is that initials, mottoes, and devices which suit only *one* are more valued than what might be equally appropriate to your most ordinary acquaintance. Moliere's sentiment is probably that of every human heart,—

" Je veux qu'on me distingue; et, pour le
   trancher net,
L'ami du genre humain n'est point du tout
   mon fait.

THE weakest living creature, by concentrating his powers on a single object, can accomplish something: the strongest, by dispersing his over many, may fail to accomplish anything. The drop, by continued falling, bores its passage through the hardest rock—the hasty torrent rushes over it with hideous uproar, and leaves no trace behind.

THE WORK-TABLE FRIEND.

SPECULUM HAND-SCREEN.

Materials. — A pair of hexagon frames, two small round mirrors, covered ivory or gilt handles, 12 yards scarlet satin ribbon, 1 inch wide, 4 ditto ¾ inch; 2 reels scarlet soie d'Avignon, a little black, green, and white crochet silk; a little gold cord, and deep scarlet fringe.

NOTHING, perhaps, strikes the English visitor in Paris more than the immense number of mirrors which everywhere meets the eye, even in very ordinary hotels and private houses. In England, on the contrary, there is a decided absence of them, which always forms a subject of lamentation to foreigners; one of whom we remember well remarking patheti

SPECULUM HAND-SCREEN.

cally, that it was impossible to live in a house without a mirror,—it was his chief enjoyment.

Assuredly the fashion of the present season will supply any want of this sort. Everything is decorated with bits of looking-glass, and we shall be fain to learn reflection even from our fans and screens.

The present design has a beautiful circular mirror in the centre; the frame being prepared with it attached. The netting, done with the soie d'Avignon, begins with 90 stitches,

BRIDAL GLOVE-BOX.

which are closed into a round. Put a thread at every fifteenth stitch, to mark it. In the first round do two in every fifteenth, and one in every other ; after which do two in every short stitch, and one in all the others, until you have done seventeen rounds, when seven without any increase will complete it. All the pattern is darned in gold but the centre of each arabesque, which in two opposite divisions is white, in two black, and two green.

The frame is covered with scarlet satin, and the border is formed of quilled ribbon, with a gold cord along the centre. The narrow ribbon trims the glass.

————

EARLIEST MANUFACTURE OF COTTON. —Though cotton is a native plant of India, the interior of Africa, and Mexico, and perhaps some other warm countries, and it has been spun into cloth, and furnished the principal clothing of the Hindoos from time immemorial, and of the natives of Mexico at the time of the discovery of America! yet its manufacture seems to have been unknown to the ancient Egyptians, Greeks, and Romans, and to have been first brought into Europe by the Moors, who introduced it into Spain in the ninth or tenth century. It was first introduced into Italy in the thirteenth or fourteenth century, and into Flanders and France at a still later period ; and was not introduced into England until the sixteenth century.

BRIDAL GLOVE-BOX.

Materials.—A card-board frame, 4 ivory feet, white satin, silk wadding-cord, ribbon, and fringe ; and for the embroidery *ombré* lilac, pink and green silks, white ditto, a small quantity of three shades of orange, small bugle pearls, a little white embroidery chenille, gold thread and bullion.

THIS glove-box is beautifully embroidered at the top, with a bouquet of narcissus, lilacs, and ears of barley. The narcissus is embroidered in white Dacca silk, veined with the faintest possible green ; the centre of the flower in orange, with a little scarlet for the edge of the cup. The pearl-bugles are used for the barley ears, each one being surrounded with white chenille, and with the beard represented by morsels of gold bullion, about half an inch long, at the point of each pearl. The bunch of lilacs is, as a matter of course, worked in lilac silk, with a small pearl, surrounded by bullion, in the centre of each. The veinings of the leaves are in gold thread and bullion.

The frame of this box is in strong card-board, with a lining of flannel, both inside and out, between it and the satin. The seams inside are covered with white cord ; the same material covers the outer seams and runs along the edge. The outside of the lid is stuffed to a considerable thickness with fine wadding, over which the embroidered satin is placed. The border is of quilled ribbon, with white fringe round the sides, headed with a handsome cord.

————

THE WORK-TABLE FRIEND.

SCROLL PATTERN PURSE.

Materials.—4 skeins of light blue silk, 12 skeins of gold thread, 2 skeins of claret silk. French trimmings to correspond.

MAKE a chain of 7 with the blue silk; close it into a round, and do 2 Sc stitches in every stitch. Repeat in the next round.

SCROLL PATTERN PURSE.

3rd Round.—+ 1 Sc on 1, 2 Sc on next, + all round.

4th Round.—Join on claret, + 3 blue, 2 claret on one stitch, 2 blue, + 7 times. Join on gold.

5th Round.—+ 2 B, 2 C, 1 gold and 1 claret on one, 1 more C, 1 B, + 7 times.

6th Round.—+ 1 B, 4 C on 3 stitches, 1 G on G, 4 C on 3 stitches, + 7 times.

7th Round.—+ 6 C (on 1 B, 4 C), 1 G on G, 4 C, + 7 times.

8th Round.—+ 1 G, 4 C, 3 G, 4 C, + 7 times.

9th Round.—+ 2 G on 1, 3 C, 2 G, 1 B (on 2nd of 3 G), 2 G, 3 C, 1 G, + 7 times.

10th Round.—+ 2 G, 2 C, 2 G, 3 B, 2 G, 2 C, 2 G, + 7 times.

11th Round.—+ 1 B on 1st G, 2 G on 1 G, 1 C, 2 G, 5 B, 2 G, 1 C, 2 G, + 7 times. Fasten off claret.

12th Round.—+ 2 B, 5 G, 3 B, 5 G, 1 B, + 7 times.

13th Round.—+ 1 B, 5 G, 5 B, 5 G, + 7 times.

14th Round.—+ 5 G, 7 B, 4 G, + 7 times.

You have now 112 stitches in the round. Do three rounds with blue only, decreasing 4 stitches in the course of them.

BORDER.—*18th Round.*—+ 4 G, 5 B, + 12 times.

19th Round.—+ 2 B, 4 G, 2 B, 1 G, + 12 times.

20th Round.—+ 2 B, 3 G, 3 B, 1 G, + 12 times.

21st Round.—+ 2 B, 1 G, 1 B, 4 G, 1 B, + 12 times.

Two more rounds of blue only must be done, increasing two stitches in each round.

BAND.—*24th Round.*—+ 6 B, 5 G, 5 B, + 7 times.

25th Round.—+ 5 B, 7 G, 4 B, + 7 times.

26th Round.—+ 4 B, 9 G, 3 B, + 7 times.

27th Round.—+ 3 B, 5 G, 1 B, 5 G, 2 B, + 7 times.

28th Round.—+ 3 B, 4 G, 3 B, 4 G, 2 B, + 7 times.

29th Round.—Like 27th.

30th Round.—+ 1 G, 3 B, 9 G, 3 B, + 7 times.

Begin claret.

31st Round.—+ 1 C, 1 G, 3 B, 7 G, 3 B, 1 G, + 7 times.

32nd Round.—+ 2 C, 1 G, 3 B, 5 G, 3 B, 1 G, 2 C, + 7 times.

33rd Round.—+ 3 C, 1 G, 1 B, 7 G, 1 B, 1 G, 2 C, + 7 times.

34th Round.—+ 1 G, 3 C, 9 G, 3 C, + 7 times.

35th Round.—+ 1 B, 1 G, 3 C, 3 G, 1 B, 5 G, 1 C, 1 G, + 7 times.

36th Round.—+ 2 B, 1 G, 3 C, 1 G, 3 B, 5 G, 1 B, + 7 times.

37th Round.—╪ 1 B, 3 G, 3 C, 1 G, 1 B, 1 G, 1 C, 5 G, ╪ 7 times.

38th Round.—╪ 5 G, 3 C, 1 G, 3 C, 4 G, ╪ 7 times.

39th Round.—╪ 4 G, 1 B, 1 G, 5 C, 1 G, 1 B, 3 G, ╪ 7 times.

40th Round.—╪ 3 G, 3 B, 1 G, 3 C, 1 G, 3 B, 2 G, ╪ 7 times.

41st Round.—Like 39th.

42nd Round.—Like 38th.

43rd Round.—╪ 1 B, 5 G, 1 C, 1 G, 1 B, 1 G, 3 C, 3 G, ╪ 7 times.

44th Round.—╪ 2 B, 5 G, 3 B, 1 G, 3 C, 1 G, 1 B, ╪ 7 times.

45th Round.—╪ 1 B, 1 G, 1 C, 5 G, 1 B, 3 G, 3 C, 1 G, ╪ 7 times.

46th Round.—╪ 1 G, 3 C, 9 G, 3 C, ╪ 7 times.

47th Round.—╪ 3 C, 1 G, 1 B, 7 G, 1 B, 1 G, 2 C, ╪ 7 times.

48th Round.—╪ 2 C, 1 G, 3 B, 5 G, 3 B, 1 G 1 C, ╪ 7 times.

49th Round.—╪ 1 C, 1 G, 3 B, 7 G, 3 B, 1 G, ╪ 7 times.

Repeat backwards from the 30th to the 10th round, inclusive; then three rounds of blue only, and fasten off. Begin the other end in the same way. Having completed it, add four inches of open crochet for the centre, working it backwards and forwards. Crochet on the other end. Add tassels and slides.

If an imperial clasp be added, the open crochet must be done at *each* end, and the rings put on before sewing on the clasp.

EMBROIDERED SHOE, FOR AN INFANT.

Materials.—White kerseymere, a skein of green *ombré* silk, a skein of scarlet or lilac *ombré* ditto, and one of coarse white sewing silk, also flannel and soft jaconet muslin, for lining.

THIS pretty little shoe, like another of which we have already given the design, is formed of three pieces; namely the sole, the toe, and the heel piece. The two latter are embroidered. On the toe is a small bouquet of flowers and leaves, worked in common embroidery stitch, the shading of the silk producing the requisite variations. Over the instep another small group of flowers is worked. Round the ankle is a line of herring bone, done with the green silk.

When all the embroidery is finished, cut out a lining for each part in flannel and muslin; stitch the front neatly over the instep, on the right side, with white silk; put on the sole on the *wrong* side, and scalop the edge round the ankle, in overcast stitch, add-

EMBROIDERED SHOE.

ing buttons and button-holes. Cork soles may be used if preferred.

IF you would really improve your time, be very careful to be always *doing something*. It is not enough to be *intending* to do. "The fool," it is said, "talks of what he is going to do." The wise man will hardly mention what he has done. It is astonishing what a number of hours may be daily wasted in dreaming of setting about something. The only plan that will insure no waste of time is to assign a certain hour for every employment, and to go directly from one to another at that hour, without one moment's hesitation, taking, however, into that new occupation, all our thoughts, and energies, and heart. But when we speak of putting all our heart and energies into our employment, let us also be sure that the occupation itself is one which is worthy of our destinies as responsible, immortal beings. Whatever can contribute to the happiness of others, or to our own improvement or pleasure, is an occupation in which we may safely engage; but there are some restless and ill-regulated minds that seek diversion in occupation, without the slightest thought as to its ultimate utility.—*Maternal Counsels.*

SLEEVE TRIMMING IN EMBROIDERY.

THE WORK-TABLE FRIEND.

SLEEVE TRIMMING IN EMBROIDERY.

Materials—Muslin, common tape one-third of an inch wide, the Royal embroidery cotton No. 30, and Point lace cottons of Messrs. W. Evans and Co., of Derby.

THIS is a new style of work, very pretty, very durable, and very easily done. Trace the design on muslin in the usual way, increasing it to double the size; then run on the tape in all the broad white lines, and connect it by bars to the medallions, as described in the collar we have given. The medallions themselves are in muslin, the pattern being worked on them in Broderie Anglaise, and a close row of button-hole stitch, over a double tracing thread, forming the outline. At the outer edge, a gradual line of button-hole stitch, and a close narrow one at the upper edge, to connect the tape and muslin, are worked. The entire ground is in Raleigh bars, worked in Evans' Mecklenburgh, No. 120; the English lace, filling some of the spaces, in Boar's Head, No. 70, and the rosette in Mecklenburgh, No. 100. When worked, cut away the muslin underneath.

PATCH-WORK.

THE materials for this design may either be pieces of silk, or beads worked on canvas; but in both cases, to give the proper effect, two shades of each of two colours one other colour and black will be required.

A reference to the engraving will show that in the stars one-half of each section is lighter and the other darker. This part should be worked in two shades of some rich colour. The black part may be done by laying black velvet or narrow satin ribbon on, after the work is otherwise completed; and in this case, as a matter of course, the pieces which they edge must be proportionally larger. Each quarter of the square is also done in two shades, those with the horizontal lines being

PATCH-WORK

the darkest. A third colour is to be used for the small diamonds. As every shade of colour can be obtained in silks, the following combinations will be found pretty :—two violets for the star, 2 ambers for the square, and a a rich emerald green for the diamonds ; or these latter colours may be reversed. Rich blue and brown, or blue and cerise, with amber diamonds, would also look well. The various sections may be enlarged to any required dimensions ; doubled or even trebled ; and the squares may be worked in different colours, if a very gay effect is desired.

If beads be employed, they must be worked by the thread, on canvas which must be selected for the squareness of the meshes. Begin in the centre of a square ; put on 8 stitches in a straight perpendicular line ; let the left row have 8 also, but begun a stitch higher and therefore slanting a little at the top ; suppose five rows are done so ; then make every row one shorter at the beginning but even at the top, until one bead completes the point. This is one section of the square, and if all are worked like it, according to the figure, the space for diamonds will be clearly seen. The black lines will occupy the depth of two beads. As bead work is so fashionable, this design, suitable for a mat, table-cover, or many other purposes, will be found very useful. Care must be taken that the canvas is of such a size that the beads quite cover two threads each way.

———◆———

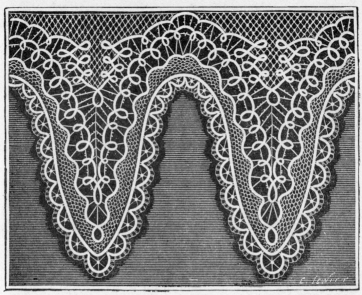

POINT LACE TRIMMING.

THE WORK-TABLE FRIEND.

POINT LACE TRIMMING.

Materials.—French white cotton braid, No. 3, and Messrs. W. Evans and Co.'s point lace cottons.

WE are glad to be enabled to give this design of the full size requisite for working. It is well adapted for sleeves, whether open or otherwise; and for trimming the frock and drawers of a little girl it is equally suitable, the deep points giving it a very rich and antique appearance. The pattern may be taken from the drawing without any difficulty, and the stitches which fill up the spaces are of the simplest character. A single English spot is worked in each loop, and a row of Sorrento edging entirely round it. English lace is worked in the upper part, using No. 50, Boar's Head cotton, and the Brussels lace is worked in No. 90 of the same. The Raleigh and Venetian bars and the edging are done in Mecklenburg, 120.

CORNUCOPIA SMOKING CAP.

Materials—2 Oz black crochet silk, 4 skeins maize, 2 claret, 2 white; 4 ombré green, 3 ditto pink, 3 ditto orange, 1 ditto violet; 2 Napoleon blue. A handsome tassel in passementerie, to correspond.

ALL this cap is done in single crochet, that is, the ordinary close stitch; and every pattern is repeated eight times in the round.

Make a chain of 336 stitches; close it into a round. This will be large enough for general wear; but should the silk be very fine, or the work more than usually tight 42 stitches (or one pattern,) more must be added. Always measure the chain before closing it into a round.

1st Round.—Black.
2nd Round.—Maize.
3rd Round.—Claret.
4th Round.—Black.
5th Round.— + 20 black, 8 maize, 3 black, 1 maize, 10 black, +.
6th Round.—Black, maize, claret, + 18 B, 11 M, 1 C, 1 B, 1 C, 1 M, 9 B, + repeat in every round, eight times between + and +.

Y

7th Round.— + 16 B, 4 C, 10 M, 1 C, 2 M, 9 B, +.

8th Round.— + 15 B, 4 M, 2 C, 6 M, 5 C, 2 M, 8 B, +.

9th Round.— + 14 B, 6 M, 2 C, 6 M, 5 C, 2 M. 7 B, +.

10th Round.— + 13 B, 8 M, 2 C, 7 M, 4 C, 2 M, 6 B, +.

11th Round.— + 12 B, 10 M, 1 C, 6 M, 1 C, 3 M, 2 C, 2 M, 5 B, +.

12th Round.— + 11 B, 11 M, 2 C, 2 M, 2 B, 1 C, 5 M, 2 C, 2 M, 4 B, +.

13th Round.— + 11 B, 12 M, 1 C, 1 M, 3 B, 1 M, 3 B, 3 M, 2 C, 1 M, 4 B, +.

14th Round.— + 10 B, 13 M, 1 C, 10 B, 2 M, 1 C, 1 M, 4 B, +.

15th Round.— + 10 B, 12 M, 1 C, 12 B, 1 M, 2 C, 4 B, +.

16th Round.— + 9 B, 13 M, 13 B, 2 M, 1 C, 4 B, +.

17th Round.— + 9 B, 1 M, 8 C, 3 M, 9 B, 3 M, 3 B, 1 M, 1 C, 4 B, +.

18th Round.— + 9 B, 10 C, 2 M, 8 B, 2 M, 2 C, 1 M, 2 B, 1 M, 1 C, 4 B, +.

19th Round.— + 8 B, 2 C, 7 M, 3 C, 1 M, 8 B, 1 M, 3 C, 1 M, 2 B, 1 M, 1 C, 4 M, +.

20th Round.— :- 8 B, 1 C, 10 M, 2 C, 8 B, 1 M, 2 C, 2 M, 1 B, 1 M, 1 C, 1 M, 4 B, +. Join on blue.

21st Round.— + 8 B, 12 M, 1 C, 4 Blue, 4 B, 1 M, 1 C, 2 M, 1 B, 1 M, 1 C, 1 M, 5 B, +. Join on white.

22nd Round.— + 8 B, 12 M, 1 Blue, 4 White, 1 Blue, 4 B, 1 M, 4 C, 1 M, 6 B, +. Fasten off claret.

23rd Round.— + 8 B, 5 M, 4 Blue, 2 M, 1 Bl, 2 W, 2 Bl, 2 W, 1 Bl, 4 B, 4 M, 7 B, +.

24th Round.— + 8 B, 4 M, 1 Bl, 4 W, 1 Bl, 1 M, 1 Bl, 2 W, 1 Bl, 1 B, 1 Bl, 1 W, 1 Bl, 15 B, +.

25th Round.— + 8 B, 3 M, 1 Bl, 2 W, 2 Bl, 2 W, 1 Bl, 4 W, 2 Bl, 1 W, 1 Bl, 15 B, +. Fasten on green.

26th Round.— + 8 B, 3 M, 1 Bl, 1 W, 1 Bl, 1 B, 1 Bl, 2 W, 1 Bl, 7 W, 1 Bl, 6 B, 1 G, 1 B, 1 G, 6 B, +.

27th Round.— + 8 B, 3 M, 1 Bl, 1 W, 2 Bl, 10 W. 1 Bl, 7 B, 1 G, 1 B, 2 G, 5 B, +.

28th Round.— + 8 B, 3 M, 1 Bl, 8 W, 1 Bl, 3 W, 4 Bl, 3 B, 1 G, 1 B, 2 G, 1 B, 1 G, 5 B, +.

29th Round.— + 8 B, 2 M, 1 Bl, 3 W, 2 Bl, 3 W, 3 Bl, 6 W, 1 Bl, 3 B, 1 G, 1 B, 1 G, 1 B, 1 G, 5 B, +. Fasten on pink and orange.

30th Round.— + 8 B, 1 M, 3 Bl, 2 W, 3 Bl, 2 W, 3 Bl, 3 W, 2 Bl, 2 W, 1 Bl, 3 B, 2 G, 1 P, 1 G, 5 B, +.

31st Round.— + 8 B, 1 Bl, 3 W, 1 Bl, 2 W, 3 Bl, 5 Orange, 2 W, 1 Bl, 1 B, 1 Bl, 1 W, 1 Bl, 3 B, 2 G, 1 P, 1 G, 5 B, +. Fasten off pink.

32nd Round.— + 8 B, 1 Bl, 8 W, 2 O, 3 M, 2 O, 2 W, 2 Bl, 1 W, 1 Bl, 2 B, 4 G, 6 B.

33rd Round.— + 8 B, 1 Bl, 1 W, 1 Bl, 1 B, 1 Bl, 2 W, 2 O, 2 M, 4 G 1 M, 1 O, 3 W, 1 Bl, 1 B, 2 G, 10 B, +.

CORNUCOPIA SMOKING CAP.

34th Round.— + 8 B, 1 Bl, 1 W, 2 Bl, 2 W, 1 Bl, 2 O, 1 M, 6 G, 1 M, 1 W, 2 Bl, 4 G, 2 B, 1 G, 7 B, +.

35th Round.— + 8 B, 1 Bl, 4 W, 2 Bl, 2 O, 1 M, 6 G, 1 M, 2 W, 5 G, 1 B, 2 G, 7 B, +.

36th Round.— + 9 B, 1 Bl, 4 W, 1 Bl, 2 O, 1 M, 5 G, 1 M, 1 O, 1 W, 6 G, 10 B, +. Fasten on pink.

37th Round.— + 10 B, 3 Bl, 2 W, 2 O, 1 M, 5 G, 2 P, 1 W, 5 G, 1 B, 1 G, 9 B, +.

38th Round.— + 10 B, 1 Bl, 4 W, 2 O, 1 M, 3 G, 4 P, 1 B, 4 P, 1 G, 2 B, 3 G, 6 B, +.

39th Round.— + 10 B, 1 Bl, 1 W, 2 Bl, 1 W, 4 G, 1 M, 1 G, 10 P, 1 B, 4 G, 6 B, +. Fasten off maize and orange.

40th Round.— + 10 B, 1 Bl, 1 W, 2 Bl, 7 G, 10 P, 5 G, 6 B, +.

41st Round.— + 10 B, 1 Bl, 3 W, 5 G, 11 P, 6 G, 6 B, +.

42nd Round.— + 11 B, 1 Bl, 3 W, 3 G, 12 P, 6 G, 6 B, +. Fasten off white.

43rd Round.— + 12 B, 4 Bl, 2 G, 13 P, 4 G, 7 B, +. Fasten off blue.

44th Round.— + 10 B, 3 G, 4 B, 1 G, 14 P, 2 G, 8 B, +.

45th Round.— + 9 B, 5 G, 1 B, 4 G, 13 P, 10 B, +.

46th Round.— + 8 B, 7 G, 1 B, 2 G, 14 P, 2 G, 8 B, +

47th Round.— + 7 B, 7 G, 1 B, 3 G, 13 P, 4 G, 7 B, +.

48th Round.— + 7 B, 7 G, 1 B, 3 G, 12 P, 6 G, 6 B, +.

49th Round.— + 7 B, 6 G, 1 B, 5 G, 9 P, 9 G, 5 B, +.

50th Round.— + 8 B, 3 G, 2 B, 5 G, 1 B, 7 P, 2 G, 1 B, 7 G, 4 B, +.

51st Round.— + 8 B, 4 G, 8 B, 2 G, 4 P, 2 G, 1 B, 2 G, 1 B, 6 G, 4 B, +. Join on orange.

52nd Round.— + 15 B, 2 G, 1 B, 10 G, 3 O, 1 G, 10 B, +.

53rd Round.— + 14 B, 5 G, 1 B, 7 G, 1 B, 4 O, 1 G, 2 O, 7 B, +.

54th Round.— + 11 B, 3 G, 2 P, 2 G, 1 B, 8 G, 1 B, 1 G, 6 O, 7 B, +. Fasten off Pink.

55th Round.— + 13 B, 4 G, 1 B, 6 G, 1 B, 2 G, 4 O, 1 G, 3 O, 7 B.

56th Round.— + 11 B, 2 G, 1 B, 1 G, 3 B, 5 G, 1 B, 3 G, 3 O, 2 G, 2 O, 3 G, 5 B, +.

57th Round.— + 13 B, 1 G, 2 B, 2 G, 6 B, 3 G, 7 O, 4 G, 4 B, +.

58th Round.— + 16 B, 4 G, 3 B, 5 G, 6 O, 1 B, 3 G, 4 B, +.

59th Round.— + 17 B, 9 G, 1 B, 4 G, 3 O, 2 B, 2 G, 4 B, +.

60th Round.— + 18 B, 7 G, 3 B, 2 O, 1 G, 3 O, 3 B, 1 G, 4 B, +.

61st Round.— + 19 B, 5 G, 1 B, 2 O, 1 B, 3 O, 1 B, 1 G, 1 B, 3 O, 4 B. Miss a stitch, thus decreasing 8 in the round +.

62nd Round.— + 18 B, 1 G, 6 B, 1 G, 6 O, 1 B, 1 G, 4 O, 3 B, +.

63rd Round.— + 18 B, 3 G, 3 B, 2 G, 3 O, 1 G, 3 O, 1 B, 4 O, 2 B, miss 1, +.

64th Round.— + 18 B, 4 G, 2 B, 4 G, 1 O, 1 G, 4 O, 1 G, 2 O, 3 B, +.

65th Round.— + 18 B, (over 19 stitches,) 8 G, 7 O, 2 G, 3 O, 1 B, +.

66th Round.— + 19 B, 7 G, 5 O, 2 G, 5 O, 1 B, +. Fasten on violet.

67th Round.— + 18 B over 19, 4 G, 3 B, 1 G, 3 Violet, 3 O, 6 B, +.

68th Round.— + 23 B (over 23 stitches,) 2 V, 1 B, 1 O, 2 V, 1 B, 3 V, 5 B, +.

69th Round.— + 20 B (over 21,) 1 O, 3 V, 3 O, 1 G, 1 B, 3 V, 4 B, +.

70th Round.— + 18 B, (over 19,) 3 O, 1 V, 1 B, 3 O, 1 G, 1 B, 3 O, 4 B, +.

71st Round.— + 20 B (over 21 stitches,) 1 G, 1 B, 2 O, 2 G, 1 B, 4 O, 3 B, +.

72nd Round.— + 17 B, 3 V, 2 B, 2 V, 1 B, 2 G, 4 O, 3 B, +.

73rd Round.— + 15 B (over 16,) 1 O, 3 V, 1 B, 3 G, 2 O, 4 B, +.

74th Round.— + 15 B, 2 O, 2 B, 1 O, 3 V 1 O, 3 V, 1 B, 2 G, 7 B, +.

75th Round.— + 18 B, (over 19,) 2 O, 1 V, 1 B, 2 G, 8 B, +.

Now decrease in every round, at each of the eight divisions, working with the black silk only, until only 16 stitches are in the round. Fasten off.

Line the cap with black silk, which may, if preferred, be quilted with a thin lining of dimett. A strip of black patent leather may be added round the head. Sew the tassels on the crown.

In working the colours together, do not hold those in which you are not using, but let them pass loosely at the back, as otherwise the crochet would be too thick in some places.

SUITABLE DRESS is a condition of health. Clothing should be warm, light, and comfortable. Woollen stockings should be worn throughout the winter, and such boots as will effectually preserve the feet from damp. Cloth boots, however thick the soles, are unfit for wet weather, as the ankles are sure to get wet, and they remain a long time damp. By far the most comfortable boots for wet weather are Wellingtons, such as are worn by gentlemen ; the thick leather protects the legs both from wet and cold, and they are much more readily taken off than those that button or lace. We have known several ladies wear them throughout the winter with great satisfaction, and remember well the remark of a distinguished medical man, when some jesting at the Wellingtons was going on: "Ah, Mrs. —— is an enemy to doctors; she knows prevention is easier than cure." Corns which are such a source of annoyance, are generally the result of pressure on some part of the foot, which will always be the case whilst boots and shoes are purchased hap-hazard, like bonnets or gloves. All boots should be made on a last expressly for the wearer ; but of course this cannot be the case when we do not deal regularly with one tradesman. They should be amply long and wide, so as to give the natural tread, which generally is about double the width of the French sole.

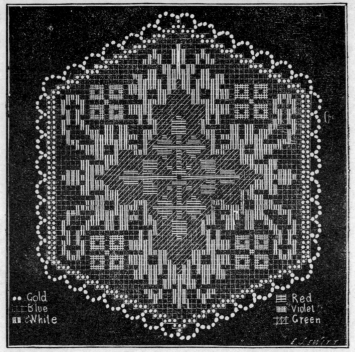

Gold
Blue
White

Red
Violet
Green

E. S. SWITT

GERMAN BEAD-MAT.

THE WORK-TABLE FRIEND.

GERMAN BEAD-MAT.

Materials.—A piece of coarse canvas, and a bunch of each of the following O. P. beads :— Filled red, amber, opal white, clear violet, green, and light blue.

O. P. beads are the large glass beads which are just now having such a rage for mats, table-covers, and similar purposes. They have a most brilliant effect, very nearly resembling painted glass; and being so large, do not try the eyes in the least. There are two ways of using them; either by working on canvas, or by merely threading them. This design is intended for the former kind of work, and must be worked from the engraving, as all the colours are clearly indicated in the cut.

Very strong linen thread (say Evans' Mecklenburgh, No. 7) must be used for putting on the beads, which should cover four threads each way of the canvas. When finished, the canvas is to be hemmed, and the loose border of beads added. Lined with strong cardboard and black cotton velvet, it will make an excellent urn-rug.

GREEK PURSE.

Materials.—5 skeins of Napoleon blue silk, 3 skeins black ditto, and 10 skeins of gold thread, No. 1, marquise garniture, and a fine hook. Work entirely in single crochet.

WITH the blue silk make a chain of 5, close it into a round, and do 2 stitches in every stitch for 2 rounds.   Join on gold.

1st Round.— ╋ 2 blue on 1, 1 gold, ╋ 10 times.

2nd Round.— + 2 blue on 2, 2 gold on 1, + 10 times.

3rd Round.— + 2 blue on 2, 3 gold on 2, + 10 times.

4th Round.— + 3 blue on 2, 3 gold on 3, + 10 times.

5th Round.— + 3 blue on 3, 4 gold on 3 + 10 times.

6th Round.— + 4 blue on 3, 4 gold on 4, + 10 times.

7th Round.— + 4 blue on 4, 5 gold on 4, + 10 times.

GREEK PURSE.

8th Round.— + 5 blue on 4, 5 gold on 5, + 10 times.

9th Round.— + 5 blue on 5, 6 gold on 5, + 10 times.

10th Round.— + 6 blue on 5, 6 gold on 6, + 10 times.

11th Round.— + 6 blue on 6, 7 gold on 6, + 10 times.

12th Round.— + 7 blue on 6, 7 gold on 7, + 10 times.

13th Round.— + 8 blue (on 7 blue, and the first of 7 gold), 5 gold, 1 more blue, + 10 times.

14th Round.— + 9 blue (over 8 and 1 gold), 3 gold, 2 blue, + 10 times.

15th and 16th Round.—All blue.

17th Round.— + 4 blue, 2 gold, 4 blue, + 14 times.

18th Round.— + 3 blue, 4 gold, 3 blue, + 14 times.

19th Round.— + 2 blue, 6 gold, 2 blue, + 14 times.

20th Round.— + 1 blue, 8 gold, 1 blue, + 14 times.

21st Round.— + 1 blue, 2 gold, 1 blue, 2 gold, 1 blue, 2 gold, 1 blue, + 14 times.

22nd Round.— + 4 blue, 2 gold, 4 blue, + 14 times.

23rd Round.—All gold. Join on black.

24th Round.— + 5 blue, 4 black, 7 blue 10 gold, 2 blue, + 5 times.

25th and 26th Round.—The same.

27th, 28th, and 29th Round.— + 2 blue, 10 black, 7 blue, 4 gold, 5 blue, + 5 times.

30th, 31st, and 32nd Round.—Like 24th.

33rd, 34th, and 35th Round.—Like 27th.

Repeat these 12 rounds, substituting gold for black, and black for gold; and then do them again in the original colours, which will bring you to the 60th round, all gold.

Repeat backwards from 22nd to 17th inclusive; then 4 rounds of Sc, and 2 of + 1 Dc, 1 Ch, miss 1 + in blue only.

EDGING.—Gold + Sc under a chain, 1 Ch, miss 1 chain, and 2 Dc, 8 Dc under next chain, 1 Ch, miss 2 Dc, and the chain between them, + repeat all round.

2nd Row.—Black, Sc on every stitch of last round.

Run the cords in the two rounds of open crochet, covering the ends with the small slides. Add the tassel.

Many other colours would look well worked in this design. A rich green or claret might be substituted for blue; and with the latter ground, use blue for black; or groseille would make a rich ground.

DARNED NETTED VANDYKE EDGING.

Materials.—Messrs. Walter Evans and Co.'s Boar's Head Crochet cotton, No. 8, and Royal Embroidery cotton, No. 16. Netting Mesh No. 13.

THIS design is very suitable for the trimming of counterpanes, toilet-covers, antimacassars, and other similar articles. The materials must, of course, vary so as to agree with those employed for the centre of the work; but we have indicated those which are adapted for anything that is not extremely coarse and heavy. The mode of producing vandykes in netting is as follows : — Begin on one stitch as for square netting, and net two in one at the end of every row, until on one side you have as many squares as are needed for the narrowest part of the vandyke, which, in the present instance, will be twenty-four, +. Then increase only in every *alternate*

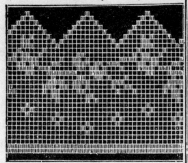

DARNED NETTED VANDYKE EDGING.

row, until you have the number of squares down the point (7 squares) ; in the next row, working to the point, you will leave the last seven squares, which thus form one point, + repeat between the squares until the entire length is done. Darn the design on it in white cotton. This pattern is also suited for trimming for children's drawers ; and if worked on black filet, in coloured silks and gold thread, will be very pretty for the medallion bag described in this work.

CROCHET COUNTERPANE.

Materials.—No. 4 knitting cotton of Messrs. W. Evans and Co., of Derby, with a suitable hook.

THESE patterns may be worked from the engravings in square crochet, and will make an extremely pretty counterpane. Each is to be done separately, and four being sewed together, a small tuft of cotton is to be placed where the squares join. Another extremely pretty way of working a counterpane is to do the squares alternately in netting, darned in a pattern, and in *broderie Anglaise*, on a thick material, such as stout jaconet, or a very fine long-cloth. Of course the thick and open squares are then placed alternately, and the effect is very good. The

designs we give below are well adapted for the netted squares, which should be done in Evans's Mecklenburgh, No. 7, and darned with No. 12. The square must be produced by beginning on one stitch, and increasing at the end of every row, until

CROCHET COUNTERPANE.

you have as many squares up one side as are required. Do one row then without either increasing or decreasing ; after which, net two together at the end of every row, until the last two are taken together. It is well to wash and slightly stiffen the squares before darning them, and also to place them in a frame like that for canvas-work.

CROCHET COUNTERPANE

FLOWER MAT.

THE WORK-TABLE FRIEND.

FLOWER MAT.

Materials.—10 yards coarse crochet cord, 1 skein maize crochet silk, 1 skein white wool, 1 skein black ditto, 12 skeins dark green, and three of each of three lighter shades; 2 bunches of transparent O.P. beads, and 13 round fancy ditto.

OVER the end of the cord work with the black wool, close it into a round, and do one round, increasing sufficiently to keep it flat.

1st pattern Round.—White and dark green, + 6 white, 2 green, + 5 times in the round.

2nd Round.— + 9 white over 6, 2 green on 2, + 5 times.

2rd Round.— + 11 white over 9, 3 green over 2, + 5 times.

4th Round.— + 13 white over 11, 4 green over 3, + 5 times.

Fasten off the white and darkest green, put on the silk, and next shade.

5th Round.— + 13 silk over white, 5 green over 4, + 5 times. Slip-stitch with silk on 2 first silk, so as to begin the next round on the 3rd.

6th Round.— + 10 silk on 9, 10 green (on 5 and 2 green) each side, + 5 times. Slip-stitch on 4 of the first 10 silk.

7th Round.— + 3 silk on centre 2 of 10, then cover the space to the next centre 2, with green wool, + repeat all round. Join on the next lighter shade of green, and work all round with it; only a single stitch in silk must be worked over the middle of the three in last round. Do another round with this wool, and then two with the brightest; after which seven must be worked with the darkest wool only, without any pattern. Thread a coarse rug-needle with the maize silk, and make some stitches in the following places:—Across the first two rounds of green, on the centre of the two stitches; in the centre of the last two rounds of white; in the centre of the 5 green in 5th round across four rounds (that is, to the ninth); and a stitch from the sixth to the 11th round, on each side this one.

Now make the bead border, by placing the 13 fancy beads at equal distances on the first of the 7 dark green rounds. In the next round behind this put 1 clear bead. Then 3, 4, 5, 6, 7, 8, and 9, threading them on very coarse cotton (No. 4, Evans's Boar's Head), and allowing them to form loops. As there are only 7 rounds of crochet, they must be placed rather closer than one on every round after the two first. It forms a sort of shell. Between every two of these place a smaller one, of 1, 2, 3, 4, and 5 beads.

These mats, being very substantial, will be greatly improved by being lined with cardboard and green calico. They are extremely pretty in shades of crimson; or in violet, with green filoselle instead of maize.

SOVEREIGN PURSE.

Materials.—1 skein of fine scarlet silk, 1 ditto white, 1 ditto black, 5 skeins of gold thread, No. 1, clasp with chain, and a few small round gold beads.

EACH side of this purse is done separately, and both precisely alike. With the gold thread make a chain of 4, close it into a round, and do two stitches in each.

2nd pattern Round.—2 Sc in every stitch.

3rd Round.—Gold and black. + 1 gold, 1 black, + 12 times in the round, increasing 8.

4th Round.— + 2 gold on one, 1 black on black, + 12 times.

5th Round.— + 3 gold over 2, 1 black on black, + 12 times.

6th Round.—Add white. + 1 gold, 1 white on 2nd gold, 1 gold, 1 black on black, + 12 times.

7th Round.— + 1 gold and 1 white on gold, 1 white on white, 1 white and 1 gold on gold, 1 black on black, + 12 times.

8th Round.— + 1 gold, 3 white, 1 gold, 1 black, + 12 times.

9th Round.—Add scarlet, and work one on the same stitch as the last black. + 1 black on gold, 1 gold, 1 white, 1 gold, 1 black, 1 scarlet, + 12 times. Fasten off white.

10th Round.— + 2 scarlet, 1 black on gold, 1 gold on white, 1 black on gold, 1 more scarlet, + 12 times, working this round somewhat loosely. Fasten off the gold.

SOVEREIGN PURSE.

11th Round.—Do a black stitch on the gold of last round, and six scarlet between it and the next. Repeat this all round, and then fasten off the black, and do a round of scarlet only, increasing 12 stitches.

12th Round.—Scarlet, white and gold, + 3 scarlet, 2 gold, 2 white, 5 scarlet, 5 gold, 2 scarlet, + 6 times, thus increasing 3 in every pattern.

13th Round.—Join on black, + 5 scarlet (over 3 and 1 gold), 2 gold, 2 white, 4 scarlet (over 3 centre of 5), 2 gold 4 black on centre 3 gold, 2 gold, 1 scarlet, + 6 times.

14th Round.— + 7 scarlet (over 5 and 1 gold), 2 gold, 2 white, 2 scarlet, 1 gold, 2 black, 5 scarlet over 4 black, 1 black, 2 gold, 1 black + 6 times.

15th Round.— + 2 scarlet, 2 gold on one scarlet, 5 scarlet, 1 gold, 3 white, 1 gold on 2nd of 2 scarlet, 2 black, 6 scarlet, 1 black on black, 3 gold on 2, 1 black, + 6 times.

16th Round.— ✛ 1 scarlet. 1 gold, 2 white, 1 gold, 4 scarlet, 1 gold, 2 white, 1 gold on gold, 1 black, 8 scarlet, 1 black on black, 3 gold on gold, 1 black, ✛ 6 times.

17th Round.— ✛ 2 scarlet, 1 gold, 1 white, 1 gold, 4 scarlet, 1 gold, 2 white, 2 gold, 4 white, 5 scarlet, 3 black on 3 gold, 1 scarlet, ✛ 6 times.

18th Round.— ✛ 2 scarlet, 1 gold, 1 white, 1 gold, 4 scarlet, 1 gold, 2 white, 6 gold, 2 white on 1 white, 1 scarlet, 8 scarlet, ✛ 6 times.

19th Round.— ✛ 3 scarlet, 1 gold, 1 white, 4 gold, 2 white, 4 gold, 3 black, 1 gold, 3 white, 5 scarlet, ✛ 6 times.

20th Round.— ✛ 4 scarlet, 1 gold, 4 white, 3 gold, 3 black, 5 scarlet, 2 white, 5 scarlet, ✛ 6 times.

21st Round.— ✛ 5 scarlet, 3 gold, 5 black, 8 scarlet, 1 white, 6 scarlet, ✛ 6 times.

Finish each side with one round of scarlet only, and then crochet the two sides together, as far as the clasp leaves room.

For the edging, fasten on the gold thread, at the beginning of the joining, ✛ 1 Dc, 1 Dc on same stitch, 3 Ch, Dc on same, Dc again on same. 1 Ch, miss 5, ✛ repeat as far as the sides are joined.

Now do 9 Dc under each chain of 3, and 1 Sc under the 1 Ch, which completes the edging.

The neatest way to put on the clasp is to hold it over the edge of the silk, run the needle through a hole, thread a bead, and then return the needle though the same hole ; after which proceed to the next. This looks much prettier than the usual way of putting on a clasp, as no stitches are visible.

DRESS. — Invariably, the apparel of a woman who has the power of selecting her own may be taken as a criterion of her character. In some instances this may seem a harsh judgment ; for there are women who affect to think dress a matter of no consequence, and who make this indifference an excuse for any defect in their attire. But even here, it seems to me, the maxim may be held true ; the want of attention to the details of dress indicates, and very generally accompanies, a large amount of indifference to the feelings of others. A woman should dress to please others, and not herself ; and the sentiment once admitted, that it is of no consequence how she looks, and whether her appearance is pleasing or the contrary, she will hardly stop at this halting-place on the road to complete indifference. On the contrary, she will next discover that it is of no consequence what she says, or how she acts—" she does not care for the opinion of the world ;" or, " there is nobody that cares for her."

It is true that these are not the arguments generally to be heard from the young, who seldom err on the side of indifference, either to the duties of the toilet or to the opinion of the world. But whether the looking-glass engross too much or too little time, it is equally an error for a woman to be ill-dressed, since the attire is an index of the mind so unfailing, so accurate, that we need little more than a single glance at a woman to be able to learn all the most salient points in her character. Do we see a young woman dressed in the extreme of fashion, in a style which neither her purse nor her position warrants ; can we be wrong in imagining her vain and selfish, with the head unfurnished just in proportion as the body is over-dressed ? If, in addition, we observe a soiled stocking or a petticoat, a buttonless sleeve or an ill-fitting shoe ; shall we not feel that indolence and impurity of person will end in tainting the mind ? Can we help fearing that the love of finery, which this style of dress betrays, will prove some day, like Esau's mess of pottage, a temptation too great for her womanly truth and feeling to withstand ? May not the woman who so loves dress be tempted to barter for it that noble birthright, her warm and honest affection for some one who is not in a position to gratify her love of finery ; to exchange her independence for a slavery which will be none the less galling because it is a voluntary sacrifice. From how many temptations is that woman free ; from how many trials .does *she* escape, who has not imbibed in girlhood a love of dress !

And yet we would deprecate almost as much any unwomanly indifference to the choice of attire.

THE WORK-TABLE FRIEND.

POMPADOUR RETICULE.

Materials.—1 skein of bright pink crochet silk; half a skein of blue ditto; half a skein of black ditto; 10 skeins of gold thread, No. 2; and passementerie trimmings.

As our readers will conjecture, this purse derives its name from the union of blue and pink which it contains, and which is popularly termed the Pompadour mixture. The pink should be of the tint called *rose de chine* and the blue, *bleu ciel.*

With the pink silk make a chain of 8, close it into a round, and do a Sc stitch on every

POMPADOUR RETICULE.

stitch, and a chain *after* every one.

1st Round.—Pink and gold. + 2 P on 1, 1 G, + 8 times.

2nd Round.— + 3 P on 2, 1 G on 1, + 8 times.

3rd Round.— + 3 P on 3, 2 G on 1, + 8 times.

4th Round.— + 4 P on 3, 2 G on 2, + 8 times.

5th Round.— + 4 P on 4, 3 G on 2, + 8 times.

6th Round.—Black and pink. + 5 P on 4, 3 B on 3 G, + 8 times.

7th Round.—Same colours. + 5 P on 5, 4 B on 3, + 8 times. Fasten off black.

8th Round.— + 6 P on 5, 4 G on 4 B, + 8 times.

9th Round.— + 6 P on 6, 5 G on 4, + 8 times.

10th Round.— + 7 P on 6, 5 G on 5, + 8 times. Now fasten off the gold and join on the blue.

11th Round.— + 7 P on 7, 6 Bl on 5 G, + 8 times.

12th Round.— + 8 P on 7, 6 Bl on Bl, + 8 times.

13th Round.— + 8 P on 8, 7 Bl on 6, + 8 times.

14th Round.— 8 P on 8, 8 Bl on 7, + 8 times. Fasten off blue and join on gold.

15th Round.— + 9 P on 8, 8 G on 8 Bl, + 8 times. Fasten on black. Do not fasten off the gold.

16th Round.— + 9 P on 9, 8 B on G, + 8 times.

17th Round.— + 9 P, 9 G on 8 B, + 8 times.

18th Round.— + 4 P, 1 G on 5th P of last round, 4 more P, 9 B on 9 G, + 8 times.

19th Round.— + 4 P, 1 G, 4 P, 7 G, + 8 times.

20th Round.— + 3 P, 3 G, 3 P, 4 B, 1 P, 4 B, + 8 times.

21st Round.— + 3 P, 3 B, 3 P, 3 G, 3 P, 3 G, + 8 times.

22nd Round.— + 3 P, 3 B, 3 P, 2 B, 5 P, 2 B, + 8 times.

23rd Round.— + 2 P, 5 G, 2 P, 1 G, 7 P, 1 G, + 8 times.

24th Round.— + 2 P, 5 G, 2 P, 1 B, 7 P, 1 B, + 8 times.

25th Round.—Like 23rd. Fasten off the black and gold, and join on the blue.

26th, 27th, and *28th Rounds.*— + 1 P, 7 Bl, 10 P, + 8 times.

29th and *30th Rounds.*— + 9 Bl, 9 P, + 8 times. Fasten off blue, and join on gold.

31st Round.— + 9 G, 9 P, + 8 times. Join on black.

32nd Round.— + 9 B, 9 P, + 8 times.
33rd Round.—Like 31st.
34th Round.— + 9 B, 4 P, 1 G, 4 P, + 8 times.
35th Round.— + 9 G, 4 P, 1 G, 4 P, + 8 times.
36th Round.— + 4 B, 1 P, 4 B, 3 P, 3 G, 3 P, + 8 times.
37th Round.— + 3 G, 3 P, 3 G, 3 P, 3 B, 3 P, + 8 times.
38th Round.— + 2 B, 5 P, 2 B, 3 P, 3 B, 3 P, + 8 times.
39th Round.— + 1 G, 7 P, 1 G, 2 P, 5 G, 2 P, + 8 times.
40th Round.— + 1 B, 7 P, 1 B, 2 P, 5 G, 2 P, + 8 times,
41st Round.— + 1 G, 7 P, 1 G, 2 P, 5 G, 2 P, + 8 times. Fasten off black and gold, and join on the blue.
42nd, 43rd, and 44th Rounds.— + 10 P, 7 Bl, 1 P, + 8 times.
45th and 46th Rounds.— + 9 P, 9 Bl, + 8 times. Join on black and gold, and fasten off blue.
47th Round.— + 9 P, 9 G, + 8 times.
48th Round.— + 9 P, 9 B, + 8 times.
49th Round.—Like 47th.

Repeat from the 18th round to the 32nd, inclusive of both; then do two rounds of gold, and two open square crochet in pink.

EDGING.—Gold. + 5 Dc under chain, 2 ch, miss 2 squares, + repeat all round.

Run the cords in the two rounds of open square crochet. Cover the ends with the small gold slides, and add the tassel at the bottom of the purse.

TOILETTE FOR CHILDREN.

NEVER was there a time when children's dress was prettier than at present, or more easily made. It has less *façon* about it than we ever remember, at the same time that it is comfortable and suitable for the requirements of these specimens of perpetual motion, to whom anything like confinement is intolerable.

Boys dresses are made, for the most part, to fasten in front; and for children above three years old, moiré, or rich poplins and chalés are most in favour. The skirt is made very full, the body generally tight, except at the back of the waist, where it is slightly fulled in. There is no band at the waist at all, the skirt being set on beneath a thick

piping, and a girdle, with handsome tassels being used instead of a sash.

The trimming for almost all the materials we have named is stamped velvet, to correspond in colour, about one and a-half inches wide. One straight piece is taken up the front, from the neck to the bottom of the skirt, thus covering the hem which forms the opening. A piece on each side is carried up to the shoulder, meets the centre one at the waist, and gradually form robings on the skirt. The short sleeve is trimmed in the way; and an edging of *broderie Anglaise* forms

PATTERN FOR BOY'S DRESS.

a tucker round the neck, and also finishes the sleeves.

High dresses are also very generally made in the same way. The sleeves are small pagodas, and have under-sleeves in the bishop form, either of the same material, or of muslin with embroidered bands. The dresses of younger children are made with full bodies, and are braided in rich patterns, with fancy braids. Amongst these, the Albert braid, which we have already introduced to our readers, is a favourite, as it is very little trouble, and is extremely effective. We have seen a pink French merino, for a little girl, braided in white Albert braid, which had a very beautiful effect; and blue would doubtless look equally well.

PATTERN FOR GIRL'S DRESS.

Out-door dresses (of which we give an engraving) are invariably richly braided round the cape, sleeves, and collar, and down the front. The cape is usually scalloped, and edged with a rich silk fringe. Jackets are very little worn; but we have seen some muslin ones, richly trimmed with *broderie Anglaise*, with waistcoats to correspond, worn over a rich poplin dress.

As to colours, a rich Napoleon blue, and the reddish-brown, termed Adelaide, seem the most popular. The tartan poplins are also great favourites, as they will probably always be, for boys. For little girls, white is decidedly the favourite kind of dress, and the skirt of the robe is frequently one mass of work, terminating in a rich Vandyke trimming. Silk dresses, however, are frequently worn by young ladies of six or seven years old; but they are made in the form seen in our illustration, open from the waist, the front laced across with ribbons, and a full muslin chemisette worn underneath. This is made high up to the throat, where it is trimmed with a lace frill; and attached to it are full sleeves, finished in the same manner. In the dress itself there are *no* sleeves, but merely a small epaulette.

When the dress is made with an ordinary body, the sash is worn across the left shoulder, with large bows and floating ends down the right side, *in front*. Berthas, of embroidered muslin, about four inches deep, set into a narrow band of insertion, and with an edging on the other side, are very generally worn with a plain silk or barege dress. Light materials are always made very full, and with flounces cut bias.

For young children, mull muslin and lace insertions are much used; but jaconet, with the rich heavy *broderie Anglaise* is decidedly the best for little girls, and for boys above a year old.

HARMONY OF DRESS.—A due regard to the harmony of our dress with our position will prevent us from indulging in a taste for finery, or even for elaborate elegance not in accordance with our circumstances; for we should never forget that it is not sufficient for a bonnet or shawl to be extremely pretty, or very cheap, for it to be suitable for us to wear. A lady whose airings are taken in a carriage may very properly wear a bonnet which is elaborately trimmed; but it would be inappropriate for a pedestrian, however becoming to her face. All purchases, then, should be made with a direct reference to our social standing, as well as to the next point of harmony—our personal appearance. To know ourselves, even as far as our faces and figures go, is a knowledge which we can only acquire after some study; nevertheless it is very necessary for every one who would wish to possess that circular letter of recommendation, a pleasing personal appearance. Of course we cannot alter the form of the features, or add to our height, or in any other way remodel ourselves; but we *can* dress with taste and propriety, so as to soften down any defects of nature, and increase the effect of any beauties.

GERMAN PLAID COMFORTER.

Materials.—2 oz. of black and white pearl wool; 1 oz. of black 6-thread fleecy; 1 oz. of red ditto. A pair of large wooden knitting needles, and a coarse bone crochet hook.

THE pearl wool, which is the chief material for this most comfortable *autour-cou*, is a recent invention, and for some purposes extremely pretty. The wool is dyed alternately in two colours—half an inch, or rather more, of each appearing alternately. That in blue and white is extremely pretty;

GERMAN PLAID COMFORTER.

so is the black and white; and for imitating the Scotch plaids, the black and grey form an admirable mixture. Nothing can be simpler than this scarf. With the black wool, cast on 21 stitches, and + do two rows of common knitting. Join on the pearl wool, with a weaver's knot, and do four more rows. Join on the red, and do four,

then with the pearl wool do four more, after which two black, then twelve with the pearl wool, and then repeat from the +. Do any length required in this way. About one and a quarter yard will be ample. By knotting the new wools on, with a weaver's knot, you will be enabled to cut off the ends quite closely.

The stripes *across* the scarf being thus formed, do those in the opposite direction with the coarse crochet hook, alternately in red and black. It is done in tambour stitch. Hold the knitting stretched, and with the right side uppermost; and in the centre of the second stitch from the edge, do two tambour stitches, each over a thread of wool. Then a reverse stitch, like a chain in crochet, on the wool only. Then two more across the threads, and so on. One stripe must be done close to each edge, and two others at equal distances from them.

Observe that the ends of the scarf must correspond, so that you will cast off, not at the end of the pattern, but after the second black stripe, and before the twelve rows of pearl wool. Add a deep fringe, of all the colours combined, and cut off the ends.

EMBROIDERED BRACELET.

Materials.—Ribbon velvet, half oz. of gold bullion, white embroidery chenille, pearls and fancy buttons.

THE velvet most suitable is either maroon or purple, with pearls. If white chenille be thought too delicate, green *ombré* silk may be used for the leaves. After the design is marked on the velvet, a piece of thin fine linen should be gummed with a solution of isinglass lightly at the back. It must then be put in a frame, and worked. All the stems are done in gold bullion; the same material also surrounds the flowers, which are formed of seven seed pearls. Short white bugles are introduced between the pearls.

This kind of embroidery is now much used for napkin rings. The velvet is mounted on a ring of cardboard or light wood; and the initial embroidered on one side.

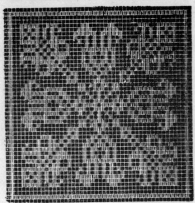

SQUARE FOR A COUNTERPANE IN CROCHET
OR DARNED NETTING.

THE WORK-TABLE FRIEND.

SQUARES FOR A COUNTERPANE IN CROCHET OR DARNED NETTING.

MATERIALS for crochet, Messrs. W. Evans and Co.'s knitting cotton, No. 12 or 16; for netting, making the ground of Boar's Head, No. 4, and darn in the pattern in Royal Embroidery cotton, No. 12. They may also be used for d'oyleys, if worked with finer thread, in Flanders lace. The *cloth-darning*, which distinguishes this beautiful kind of lace, is somewhat difficult to describe in writing; but as many of our readers may desire to have a description given them, we will endeavour to furnish as clear a one as we can.

The appearance cloth-darning presents is that of linen weaving, for in every square four threads (two in each direction) cross each other, as well as those of the square itself, regularly and evenly. By regularly we imply that one thread ought never on any occasion to cross over *two* at a time. To manage this, great care is requisite, as well as some study of the pattern. As a rule, begin at the nearest corner opposite your right hand. In the design before us this has five filled stitches running horizontally on one line. Thread your needle with rather a long thread, and run across these five squares, raising one, and passing over the next; then back again. This brings you back to the starting point.

The next is a single stitch, to be treated in the same way; then two, then one, then six. All these being darned backwards and forwards in *one* direction, you will cross the five horizontal ones forming one side, by darning in the same way, lifting every other thread; then cross the second of the six; then the third, and with this last the single one below it, although it has not yet been darned in the other direction; then the fourth, from which pass to the single one above the fifth; cross that horizontally, and then you will be able to run down to the fifth of the first five. Before running these back again, finish the other three of these five, when you will also *half* do the single one in the centre; to get back to finish this, take a stitch on the netting, at the edge of the square just completed; and observe to take it from *above* if the stitch near it is so, and from *beneath* if otherwise. Cross this horizontally, and you will then be able to complete the single square, half done in the first place; complete the third of the six, also only half done, and pass the thread, as before described, on the edge of the *fourth* of sixth, so as to run horizontally those which have only a single thread down them in the opposite direction. This will bring you down to the corner; complete the crossing of these, and your thread will then be ready to work upwards. Observe that the only occasion where *two* threads are to be crossed together is when a single square, not connected at any side with another, occurs. As it is necessary to fill all these up separately, you go from one side to another, all round, crossing over two threads always, except at the completion. Join on your thread always with a weaver's knot, and cut the ends *quite close*. Pass from one place to another, when quite necessary, by the process already described, technically called cording. Work upwards, and towards the left, and never trouble yourself about incompleted stitches, which you will certainly find an opportunity to finish afterwards. At the same time *study* the design, so that you may, as far as possible, complete as you go on.

TRUE.—A reading people will become a thinking people, and then they are capable of becoming a rational and a great people.

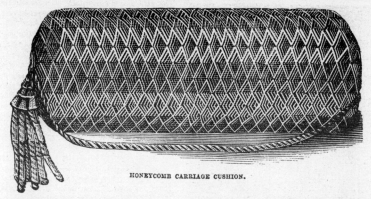

HONEYCOMB CARRIAGE CUSHION.

THE WORK-TABLE FRIEND.

HONEYCOMB CARRIAGE CUSHION.

Materials.—Coarse Penelope canvas, Berlin wool of any colours that may be at hand, but four shades of each; cord, and a pair of tassels.

THE length of canvas required for one of these cushions is a square of about twenty-two inches. It is worked in stripes of four or five different colours, and is particularly useful, as it works up remnants of wool which may be lying-by. It is also one of those simple patterns which require only that the threads should be counted; and it is, therefore, particularly suitable for those whose eyes are not good, or for beginners.

Observe that, in speaking of a stitch in Penelope canvas, we mean a *square*, or two threads each way.

With the darkest wool of any colour, do the first row thus :—Make a knot in the wool, and bring out the needle as near the left hand corner lower side as you can; miss three stitches in length, and five in depth, and slip the needle under the two threads of the third, *towards the left;* then up again to the line in which your needle was first inserted, and slip it under two threads of the *fifth* from it; then to the lower line, + and take up the two threads of the *fourth* from the last of that line; then to the upper line again, the two threads of the fourth from the last; + repeat in this way between the two crosses, for the entire length of the line. Then, with the same shade, bring out the

needle in the same hole as at first, and work another line precisely the same, only upwards instead of downwards, so that the lowest stitch of this row is taken under the same two threads as the upper of the last. The next shade is worked in the same way. Draw out the needle two threads *below* the first, and slip it under two threads (that is, the stitch), in front of it through the length. In the second row, bring out the thread a stitch above it, and work in the same way. The third shade is worked in the same way as regards the second, as that is to the first;

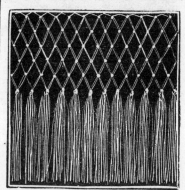

BORDER AND FRINGE.

and the fourth shade, worked precisely the same way, will fill up the space. Every stripe is done in the same way.

OCTAGON ANTIMACASSAR.

To make up the cushion, form a small bolster of ticking, stuffed with flock; and having sewed the edges of the canvas together, draw it over the pillow, and gather up the ends, sewing on a tassel in the centre of each, and a fancy cord to connect the two. This cord is used to slip over the back of a chair, and thus keep the cushion in its place.

OCTAGON ANTIMACASSAR.

Materials.—4 reels of No. 10 Boar's Head crochet cotton of Messrs. W. Evans and Co., of Derby, 2 oz. of knitting cotton No. 8, and an ivory mesh, No. 9.

On a foundation begin with 25 stitches, and increase (by netting two in one at the end of every row) until there are 51 squares at each side. Continue without increasing for 48 rows, and then decrease by netting two together at the end of every row, until 25 loops only are left. The antimacassar should then be washed, and pinned out, that it may form into shape. Place it in a frame to darn, and this may be done extremely well from the engraving; then add the border and fringe. The former is plain netting, with a stitch in every one, except at the corners, when four must be worked in each. This is for the first round; in the succeeding ones, one stitch only is to be worked in each. Finish by knitting on a rich fringe, three inches deep.

PATTERN OF TABLE-COVER.

THE WORK-TABLE FRIEND.

NEW DESCRIPTION OF WORK FOR TABLE COVERS, OTTOMANS, OR PILLOWS.

Materials required for working a table-cover one yard square, four lengths of the pattern for each side. A skein of each of the following coloured Berlin wools—shaded pink (yellow and blue greens), brown, scarlet, purple, orange, gray, and blue. Also one pennyworth of mixed seed-beads, and a yard of puce-coloured cloth, or fine dark tweed.

Directions for Work.—Copy the design on white tissue-paper, and tack it along the edge of your cloth; strain the cloth on a frame, and thread a fine darning-needle with any old wool of one colour. Fill up one side of each leaf, taking long stitches from the end to the top of the leaf. Fill the other side the same way, but with a contrast colour, and then with a crochet-hook draw away the tissue-paper, and sew over one side of the leaf (working from the centre) with the shaded blue-green wool, taking the stitches shorter near the top. Break your shaded

wools into lengths, so that when the last stitches are dark, the next may join in a dark part also. Work the other side of the leaf in the same manner, always being careful not to draw your wool too tightly, as that gives the work a puckered appearance. For the lily use light shaded gray, and fill up the leaves as you do the green; then sew over from the centre. For the pistil, work with yellow-green. The stamens are formed of a row of beads, beginning with four gray glass, the next four white glass, and then five white chalk beads. For the anther, or top of the stamen, work eight gray glass beads across, and then one row over it of pale yellow chalk beads. To work the yellow rose, you fill in the leaves from the bottom, and sew over with the lightest part of the shaded orange, commencing the lower end of the petal with the darker shade, and work across instead of from the centre. For the stamens stitch on yellow chalk beads, light and dark. The green leaves are filled as before directed; but in working over, you take four long

z

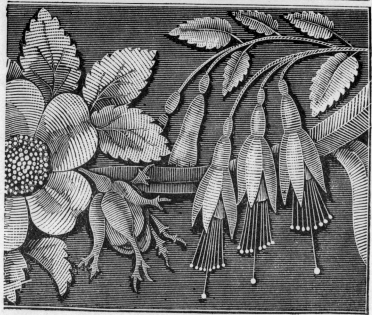

PATTERN OF TABLE-COVER.

stitches from the centre out, then shorter, then long again, to form the mitre of the rose-leaf; work in the dark part of the green, getting lighter towards the top of the leaf. For the fuschia, use the medium shade of shaded crimson, and purple for the inner petals. For the stamens, work with pink silk, placing a white chalk bead at the end of each, and the leaves with yellow-green wool.

Our fair readers can readily work this pattern from the engraving when it is joined. The separation has been made for the convenience of printing.

BEAD URN MAT.

Materials.—Very coarse canvas; opal, amber, dark blue, claret, and two shades of green O. P. beads. Put on the beads with Messrs. W. Evans and Co.'s Boar's Head Crochet Cotton, No. 4.

For all purposes where beads are likely to be subjected to considerable pressure, it will be found better to put them on canvas than to form them into a solid mass simply by thread-ing them together. The design we now give is well adapted to this purpose. The entire

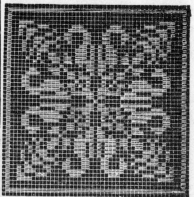

BEAD URN MAT.

ground may be in white beads, and these have better effect when the border is in a

NOTE OR CIGAR CASE IN APPLICATION.

rich dark colour, such as claret, than when paler tints are used. The two shades of green will form the design in the centre, beginning with the darkest for the middle, and allowing the other shade to surround it. The points may be worked in dark blue, and their supports in amber, which will thus intervene between the blue and green, and harmonize with both. The vase-like pattern in the centre of each side will look well in amber.

These beads must be put very evenly on the canvas, and all that vary considerably from the average size must be set aside. Every row must be worked completely before proceeding to the next.

A fringe should be added, made of beads of all the various colours employed in the mat, each loop being of one colour.

This design may also be employed for crochet or Flanders lace.

———

THE powers of memory are twofold. They consist in the actual reminiscence or recollection of past events, and in the power of retaining what we have learned, in such a manner that it can be called into remembrance as occasions present themselves, or circumstances may require.

NOTE OR CIGAR CASE IN APPLICATION.

Materials.—Rich green cloth; ditto velvet; a few emerald beads; gold braid and thread, No. 5.

IN this, as in all other works in application where velvet is employed, it should be of the best quality, and with a short pile, as the other kind is apt to fray out very much at the edges. The leaves are so easy to cut, that the merest tyro cannot fail to prepare this work for herself, if she will draw one corner leaf, and one of the centre ones, and by taking them first on one side and then on the other, arrange them in the required positions. This should be done on a piece of paper the size of the intended case. Then the scrolls and braided border may be added, one half of the border being readily traced from the other. The design should then be pricked, or *pounced*, as it is technically called, and transferred to the cloth. The velvet leaves, nicely cut out, are to be gummed in their places; then the braid sewed down at the edge. The veinings of the leaves are of gold thread, and spots of beads are introduced here and there, as seen in the engraving.

The braid must be laid on evenly, the corners always neatly and sharply turned, and the ends of cord and braid drawn through to the wrong side, and sewed down.

LADY'S WORK-BASKET.

THE WORK-TABLE FRIEND.

LADY'S WORK-BASKET IN BEAD WORK.

Materials. — Perforated card-board; a wire frame, 10 inches by 4, and about 2 deep; a little narrow satin ribbon, broader ditto, fringe, gold thread, and beads of various colours, all No. 2.

We have designed this basket expressly to use up the various beads that are left from other pieces of work, as any and every colour will come into a design like this. The frame may be either purchased or made by the worker, as the wire of which it is composed is not of a very thick kind.

The dimensions we have given are for the bottom of the basket. The upper part must, of course, be proportionately larger, as it is very open. A wire at each corner must connect the two parts of the frame. The handle is also formed of two wires, placed about one inch apart at the bottom, but close together along the upper part. The best way to form these baskets is to cut the various pieces the proper length, and a little over, and join the ends by binding them round with fine wire.

The perforated cardboard, of which the basket is chiefly composed, is in five pieces, namely, for the bottom and four sides. All

are embroidered in beads. For this purpose a Berlin pattern of proper size may be used, and adapted to any beads that the worker may have by her. As there is not the same variety to be found in beads of the required size that we can obtain in wool, and this frequently prevents the adaptation of designs intended for the latter material, a few hints on this subject may not be unacceptable.

The leading colours in beads are
Blue, about four shades.
Orange, about five.
Green, about seven.
Pink, not more than two.
Gray, three.
Lavender, three or four.
White, four.
Bronze, three.
Ruby, one.
Coral, one.
Black.

A little reflection will make it obvious that there exist a great deficiency of shades; but as these beads are manufactured in Venice, and we have not, at present, any way of improving the character of the consignments, all that remains for us to do is to bring as much skill into our work as possible. The blues, oranges, and lavenders, generally run pretty well into shades. The greens are opaque or not, and some have the yellow tinge, and others the blue. By using black for the darkest shade in very dark leaves, a tolerable variety of foliage may be produced; and the addition of some of the leaves in a design in the bronze, or dead-leaf colour, will be an improvement. Gold beads and black ditto are frequently used as extreme shades of bronze, the former for the lightest, and the other for the darkest. With these we may consider we have six tints; and the way in which these should be managed to produce a variety of foliage will, if described, serve as a guide in other colours.

Suppose that, on an average, four shades enter into a single leaf, and you intend to work a group of three leaves in bronze. The lightest you will compose of the four lightest shades,—that is, gold and the three darkest bronzes. For the leaf nearest to it—which, therefore, you would like to make as great a contrast as possible—take black and the three darkest bronzes, and the third leaf may be worked in the bronze only. Other colours, whether for flowers or leaves, must be arranged with similar care.

In the list we have given four whites; these are chalk, alabaster, opal, and clear white. Steel beads are frequently mixed with these in white flowers, and grays and stone-colours are employed to deepen the shades.

With a little ingenuity, therefore, a great variety may be made, and almost any Berlin pattern, or section of one, used. For roses, the two pinks, the coral, an ruby, and even black may be employed. All the dark shades for a dark rose; and pinks, fading into white, for light.

The perforated cardboard being worked, the frame must be entirely covered by winding round it satin ribbon of any predominant colour. Light blue, pink, or crimson, will answer for this purpose. The handle must be covered in the same way. Then the pieces are sewed in at the back of the frame; the fringe is placed at the top, and a quilling of narrow ribbon, with a gold thread run along the centre, forms the heading of the fringe, and the cover of the handle. Bows and ends are placed on each side of the widest part of the latter.

The basket may be worked on silk canvas if preferred.

STAR DOYLEY.

Materials.—2 reels of Messrs. W. Evans and Co.'s Boar's Head crochet cotton, No. 10; 1½ oz. ruby, and 1½ oz. aqua-marine beads, No. 2.

THREAD the beads of one colour on one reel, and of the other on another reel. Begin with the rubies. Make a chain of 4, close it into a round, and work 8 in it, with a bead on every stitch. Do three more rounds with a bead on every stitch, increasing 8 in every one, so that there are at last 32 altogether. Join on the other cotton, and work with both.

1st *pattern Round.* — + 2 cotton on 1, 1 ruby, 2 cotton on one, 1 aqua, + 8 times.

STAR DOYLEY.

2nd *Round.* — + 1 cotton, 3 rubies, the centre over 1, 1 cotton on same as last bead, 3 aquas, the centre on 1, + 8 times.

In future rounds it is understood that each kind of bead goes over the same kind of previous round.

3rd *Round.* — + 1 cotton on 1, 4 beads on 3, + 16 times.

4th *Round.* — + 1 cotton on cotton, 4 beads on 4, + 16 times.

5th *Round.* — + 2 cotton on 1, 4 beads on 4, + 16 times.

6th *Round.* — + 1 cotton, 1 bead on same as last cotton, 5 more beads, + 16 times.

7th *Round.* — + 2 cotton on 1, 6 beads on 6, + 16 times.

8th *Round.* — + 1 cotton, 7 beads, + 16 times.

9th *Round.* — + 1 cotton, 9 beads over 7, + 16 times.

EMBROIDERED HANDKERCHIEF FOR A BRIDAL PRESENT.

10th Round.— + 1 cotton, 9 beads, + 16 times.

Now reverse the colours, putting rubies over aqua-marines, and *vice versa.*

11th Round.— + 1 cotton, 10 beads over 9, + 16 times.

12th Round.— + 2 cotton on 1, 10 beads on 10, + 16 times.

13th Round.— + 1 cotton, 12 beads over 10, + 16 times.

14th Round.— + 1 cotton, 12 beads, + 16 times.

15th Round.— + 2 cotton on 1, 12 beads, + 16 times.

16th Round.— + 2 cotton, 12 beads, + 16 times.

17th Round.— + 1 cotton, 13 beads, + 16 times.

18th Round.— + 1 cotton, 13 beads, + 16 times.

19th Round.— + 2 cotton on 1, 13 beads, + 16 times.

BORDER.—*1st Round.*—Rubies. + 7 chain, with a bead on every stitch, miss 5, 1 Sc, + all round.

2nd Round.—No beads. 1 Sc on 4th bead, + 7 Ch, Sc on the 4th bead of next loop, + all round.

3rd Round.—Aqua-marines. 10 Dc under every chain, dropping two beads on each stitch.

EMBROIDERED HANDKERCHIEF.

To be embroidered in satin stitch, with the Royal Embroidery cotton, No. 50, of Messrs. W. Evans & Co. of Derby.

CHAIR COVER.

THE WORK-TABLE FRIEND.

CHAIR COVER—IN CHINESE DESIGN.

Materials.—For crochet, the Boar's Head crochet cotton No. 12, of Messrs. W. Evans and Co., of Derby. For netting use No. 4 of the same cotton, and darn it with No. 8 knitting cotton. As we consider this mode of working much newer and prettier than crochet, our directions apply to it.

WITH a bone mesh, No. 9, on a foundation do nine stitches; turn and do a stitch in every stitch except the last, in which work two; repeat this, thus increasing a stitch in every row, until there are sixty-four squares up the side. Net sixteen rows without any increase, and then take two together at the end of every row, until you have only the number of loops left with which you started.

The netting thus made must be washed, starched, and carefully pinned out into shape before being darned; and it should always be placed in an embroidery frame for darning. This may be done in the ordinary way, except the faces and heads of the figures, which should be done in cloth-darning, to bring them into contrast with the rest of the design. As it is not possible to get the eyes and mouth at all right by filling up a square, there should be only a little darning on the thread forming the side of the hole; and if the pattern is done in *crochet*, two successive

De stitches must be used, and a longer space of chain left between them.

The introduction of cloth-darning with the ordinary kind, in all these designs, will be found very effective for the lighter parts, such as the branches of trees, &c.

A netted lace may trim the cover, or a fringe may be added. If worked *very fine*, in either crochet or netting, the design will not be too large for a dessert doyley.

BAND FOR THE EDGE OF A CHAIR.

The band we give is intended to go round the edge of the chair, so as to keep the cover in its place. The front and sides are to be worked on the respective parts, in one line, and the back separately; then, if a piece has been allowed at each end of the side parts, sufficiently long to button to that at the back, going round the poles of the latter, the cover will be always in its place, and at the same time can readily be removed to be washed.

CARD-BASKET.

Materials. — O. P. beads of the following colours :—opal, clear white, garnet, light purple, and emerald, filled pink and filled yellow. Also wire, not too stout, to be readily cut.

O. P. beads is the technical name of the large glass beads which have lately been imported in such quantities from Germany, and have been used for mats, and other similar purposes. They, in common with all other bead-work, possess the great advantage over silks and wools of being unspoiled by dust, sun, or wear; they also form a kind of work very suitable for invalids or children, as they are so easily threaded, and do not try the eyes. Perhaps baskets are among the prettiest and most useful articles that can be made in these beads, and the present one will be found extremely simple.

It consists of a centre, four solid sides connected by bars of beads, and a handle.

Each side is made as mats are, that is,

beginning in the centre line. Thread a long needleful of stout thread at each end.

On each needle slip 1 garnet, 1 yellow; now put both needles through 1 yellow; left hand needle, 1 purple; right hand, 1 yellow; both, 1 purple; 1 purple on each; both through 1 yellow; 1 garnet on each; both, 1 yellow; 1 purple on each; both, 1 purple; left hand purple; right, yellow; both, yellow; yellow on each; both, 1 garnet.

This forms the centre row. Knot the two threads, so that they will not slip, and use *one* only to complete the left side, thus :—Slip on another garnet, then pass the needle through last yellow; 1 purple; then through last purple; 1 opal; then through next purple; 1 yellow, and through garnet; 1 yellow, and through purple; 1 opal, and through another purple; 1 purple, then through yellow and garnet at the top.

3rd Row.—Thread on garnet and purple, then through purple, 1 opal, through opal, 1 purple, through 1 yellow, 1 yellow, through another yellow, 1 purple, through 1 opal, 1 opal, through 1 purple, 1 purple, through garnet at the bottom.

4th Row.—1 garnet through last purple, 1 purple, through opal. 1 opal, through purple, 1 purple, through yellow, 1 purple, through purple, 1 opal, through opal, 1 opal, through 1 purple, 1 garnet.

5th Row.—Slip on garnet and opal, through opal, 1 pink, through opal, 1 opal, through purple, 1 purple, through purple, 1 opal, through opal, 1 purple, through purple, 1 opal, through garnet at the end.

6th Row.—1 garnet, through opal, 1 opal, through purple, 1 purple, through opal, 1 purple, through purple, 1 purple, through opal, 1 pink, through pink, 1 pink, through opal and garnet.

7th Row.—1 garnet, 1 opal, through pink, 1 green, through pink, 1 opal, through purple, 1 opal, through purple, 1 purple, through purple, 1 opal, through opal, 1 garnet, through garnet at the end, then catch the needle through the loop of thread at the end, and run it back through the two garnets at the side, as this is a decreasing row. Your needle is now on a line with the edge of the second row of beads, reckoning from the end.

8th Row.—1 garnet, through opal, 1 opal,

through purple, 1 purple, through opal, 1 purple, through opal, 1 pink, through green, 1 pink, through opal and garnet.

9th Row.—1 garnet, 1 opal, through pink,

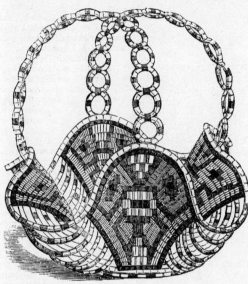

CARD-BASKET.

1 pink, through pink, 1 opal, through purple, 1 opal, through purple, 1 opal, through opal, 1 garnet, slip the needle round the thread from the lower garnet to opal, then up again through this garnet and another.

10th Row.—Through opal, 1 opal, through opal, 1 purple, through opal, 1 opal, through pink, 1 opal, through opal and garnet.

11th Row.—Garnet and opal, through opal, 1 opal, through opal, 1 purple, through purple, 1 opal, through opal; join on a garnet as before, below this; pass the needle through it, and another.

12th Row.—Through opal, 1 opal, through purple, 1 purple, through opal, 1 opal, through opal, 1 opal, 1 garnet.

13th Row.—1 garnet, 1 opal, through opal, 1 purple, through 1 purple, 1 opal, through opal, join on 2 garnet as before.

14th Row.—Through opal, 1 opal, through purple, 1 purple, through opal and garnet.

15th Row.—1 garnet, and one purple,

through purple, 1 opal, through opal. Join on 2 garnet at the edge as before.

16th Row.—Through opal, 1 opal, through purple and garnet.

17th Row.—1 garnet, 1 opal, through opal. Join on 2 garnet at edge as before. Through the opal and garnet at the top, and then add 2 garnet at the side.

Half this piece being done, the other (or right side) is to be made like it, observing that the beads already threaded on the extreme right form the centre row. Four of these must be done.

Now, at the widest part of every piece, add a line of clear white beads, thus:— Fasten the thread to the loop at the edge of the garnet, thread on a bead; slip the needle under the thread between this garnet and the next; thread on 2 beads. Continue to do this for the whole length. By choosing rather small beads you will closely cover the edges of the garnets.

Take a wire three-quarters of a yard long, run it through all these clear white beads of one side, then three clear white, 1 garnet, 2 white, 1 green, 2 white, 1 pink, 2 white, 1 green, 2 white, 1 garnet, 3 white, continue the wire through the white beads of another side, then thread more beads like the first string; join all the four sides together in this way, with a string of beads between them, and twist the ends of wire down together to form the round.

Join the pieces down the sides by strings of beads, strung on thread, shortening the white at each end, so as to leave green over green, pink over pink, &c. Add clear white beads at the small end of each piece, and connect all with a wire, with 11 beads between.

Carry wires down the sides, through the garnet beads, and crossing in the centre, with beads strung on them, to form the ground, and a double handle of wires threaded with beads, crossing and both passing through one bead at regular intervals, must be attached to the middle of each side.

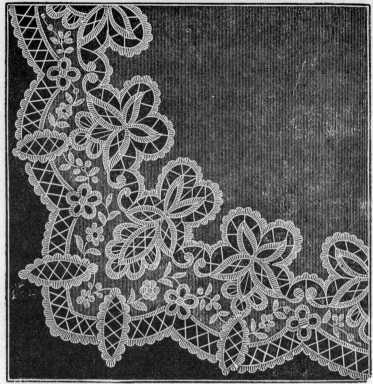

HANDKERCHIEF BORDER.

THE WORK-TABLE FRIEND.

HANDKERCHIEF BORDER—GUIPURE DE VENISE.

Materials.—A square of French cambric, and the Royal Embroidery cotton, Nos. 50 and 70, of Messrs. W. Evans and Co., of Derby.

THE design of this handkerchief is a combination of the open work known as Venetian guipure, with embroidery. This produces a rich and beautiful effect, and is especially adapted for full-dress handkerchiefs.

A quarter of the design, on a reduced scale, is given. The handkerchief, when of the full size, should be five-eighths of a yard square.

As in all the specimens of Venetian guipure, the bars are to be worked first. Run a thread along the tracing, and carry it across to the opposite edge of the open work, in the direction seen in the engraving. Cover this thread with button-hole stitch, and then run the needle a little way along, to form the next bar in the same direction. Observe that when working the lines in the *opposite* direction (which is not to be done until all in one way are completed), you will pass the needle through the bar already made, as the two cross, thus connecting them together.

The bars, and all the tracing, are to be worked in No. 50 cotton, but all the embroidery in No. 70. All the medallions, the large flowers, and every part connected by bars, is to be overcast. The running pattern of Forget-me-nots and leaves *only* to be in satin stitch. The centre of the Forget-me-nots to be pierced, and neatly sewed over.

O. P. BEAD MAT.

O. P. BEAD MAT.

Materials.—2 bunches deep purple beads, 1 opal, 1 pale filled green, 1 clear dark ditto, 1 filled pink, 1 filled red, 1 amber, 1 light blue. Messrs. W. Evans and Co.'s Boar's Head cotton, No. 4.

THIS design is formed by simply threading the beads; consequently, this kind of mat is the same on both sides, and has more the effect of painted glass than of needlework. This appearance is enhanced in no slight degree by the peculiar depth and brilliancy of the purple ground; and we notice it as a hint to our fair friends to exercise great care in the choice of their colours.

This mat is worked from the centre, first to the left, and then to the right; the fringe is afterwards formed, the loops being twisted in each other as the worker proceeds.

The colours to be used are indicated in the engraving thus:—No. 1, opal; No. 2, purple; No, 3, pale green; No. 4, darker green; No. 5, pink; No. 6, red; No. 7, amber; No. 8, light blue. The fringe is formed of 17 beads in each loop, 2 purple, 1 red, alternately; ending with two purple.

At least two bunches of purple, and one of opal, will be required for this mat. Of the other colours, less than one bunch, and of light blue and amber, a *very* few will suffice

TURKISH BAG.

THE WORK-TABLE FRIEND.

TURKISH BAG.

Materials.—Coarse Penelope canvas, and 2 oz. each of Turkey red, blue, and black 8-thread Berlin wool.

WITH the black wool work in ordinary cross stitch a stripe three stitches wide up the edge of the bag, and another fifteen stitches distant from it. Do as many of these black stripes as the width of the bag will allow, each one being fifteen stitches from the last, and three stitches wide. Now work the cross-bars on the second of these lines, by working 9 stitches in length on each side of the bar, parallel with the 9th, 10th, and 11th stitches from the bottom, and at the end of each add a piece which will give it the form of the letter T, carrying the 9 stitches to 12 in length, and five more above and below it in height.

Thus each T comes within three stiches of the bar of black nearest to it. A similar one is placed above this, with 19 stitches missed between the two bars, and 9 stitches between the ends of the T's.

In the next line the cross bar comes pre-cisely between every two of the former, so that a space of *three* stitches is between the new bar and the part which appears to form the top of the T. Of course, at the edges, the bar can be carried on one side only.

The stripes are then filled in alternately with red and blue, the entire design being worked in black.

When these bags are not very large, it is quite as well to make them up at home as to give them to a warehouse. They should be lined with *tick*, within which silk or sarsenet may be placed; but for a bag used in pic-nics, and such matters, nothing is nicer than green oilcloth, merely *tacked* in so as to be readily removed and cleaned.

The edges should be finished with a cord, to correspond with the bag, and the same will serve for handles. To make the top stiff, a whalebone may be run in each.

PHILOSOPHY is the account which the human mind gives to itself of the constitution of the world.

SHAVING BOOK.

THE WORK-TABLE FRIEND.

SHAVING BOOK.

A PRETTY PRESENT FOR A GENTLEMAN.

Materials.—A piece of fine cloth, 8 inches by 16; silk braid, coarse crochet silk of the same colour; black sarsnet, a bit of whalebone, cord, and some old linen.

THIS design cannot fail to be generally useful and ornamental. The cloth is twice as long as it is wide, and forms the cover of the book. It is ornamental on one side only. The outer part of the design is braided; but the initial, or monogram, is done in chain stitch, as this enables the worker to form the points and delicate parts of the letters more perfectly. When completed, it is lined with sarsnet, the edges being sewed together, and the join being covered by an ornamental cord. A piece of whalebone down the back gives it a little stiffness.

Seven pieces of linen, each a little smaller than the cloth, are then hemmed, and a button-hole made in the middle of each. They are thus attached by a button to the centre of the book, and one is readily removed every morning.

No gentleman's dressing-table should be without one of these convenient appendages.

Any of the squares we have given for darned netting would do well for this purpose also. Two would have to be joined together, and an edging worked all round one of them. If lined with ingrain pink gingham, they could be constantly washed without injury.

THE WORK-TABLE FRIEND.

WATCHPOCKET IN CROCHET.

Materials.—Rich ingrain pink Boar's Head Crochet cotton of Messrs. W. Evans and Co., of Derby, No. 10 ; and four ounces of Alabaster beads, No. 2. Crochet hook, No. 17.

THREAD the beads on the cotton, and make a chain of 5, with a bead on every stitch. Close it into a round, and work thus :—

WATCHPOCKET IN CROCHET.

1st Round.— + 1 Sc, 1 Ch, miss none, + 5 times, with a bead on every stitch.

2nd Round.— + 2 Sc, 1 Ch, miss none, + 5 times, with a bead on every stitch.

3rd Round.— + Sc without any beads, increasing after every third stitch.

4th Round.— + 2 cotton, 1 bead, 2 cotton in one, + 6 times.

5th Round.— + 2 cotton in 1, 3 beads (the second over 1 bead), 1 cotton, + 6 times.

6th Round.— + 2 cotton in 1, 5 beads, + 6 times.

7th Round.— + 3 cotton, 3 beads, 2 cotton over last of 5 beads, + 6 times.

8th Round.— + 5 cotton over 3 and 1 bead, 1 bead, 3 cotton, + 6 times.

9th Round.— + 1 bead, 9 cotton (increasing 1), + 6 times.

10th Round.— + 2 beads, 4 cotton on 3, 1 bead, 3 cotton, 1 bead, + 6 times.

11th Round.— + 3 beads, 2 cotton on 1, 3 beads, 2 cotton, 2 beads, + 6 times.

12th Round.— + Sc with a bead on every stitch, and without any increase.

13th Round.—Sc, without any beads, and increasing 12 stitches on the round.

14th Round.—Sc with a bead on every *other* stitch.

15th Round.—Sc, without any beads.

EDGE.— + 3 Sc with a bead on every stitch. 5 chain, also with a bead on every stitch, miss 3 + repeat all round.

2nd Round.— + Sc on 2nd of 3 Sc, 3 Ch, with a bead on every stitch, Sc on centre of 5 Ch, 3 Ch with a bead on every stitch, + all round.

Fasten off, and work on the other edge of the 15th round with a row of Dc, without any beads, extending more than half way of the entire round.

Now commence a chain of 5, close it into a round, and work on it round and round in Sc, increasing enough to keep it flat, till a piece is done as large as the front, *without the edge.* Then hold the two together, and crochet them at the *edge of the Dc,* as far as it goes. Do two more rounds in Sc. Then the shell edging, thus :—

+ 8 Sc, with a bead on every stitch, miss 7, 7 chain, also with a bead on every stitch, + all round.

2nd Round.— + 6 Sc, working over all the 8 except the first and last, and dropping a bead on every stitch, * 1 Ch with a bead, 1 Dc with 2 beads on the stitch, on the first of 7 Ch, * repeat between the stars 7 times, 1 chain with a bead on it, + repeat from + to +.

3rd Round.— + 4 Sc with a bead on each, on centre 4 of 6, * 2 Ch, with a bead on each, 1 Dc with 2 beads on Dc, * 7 times, 2 Ch with bead on each.

This completes the crochet work. Now cut out two cardboard rounds, each the size of front without edge ; cover *one* side of each with pink silk, slightly wadded, and tack them inside the pocket, with the silk sides face to face.

Add bows, and a ribbon to suspend it, and the pocket is completed.

As the cottons of Messrs. W. Evans and

GERMAN BEAD MAT.

Co. are ingrain, these watchpockets may be washed, simply removing the two cardboards and the ribbon. Those whose furniture would not suit with pink, will find a rich new blue, with alabaster beads, or salmon, with turquoise, or a brilliant emerald, with chalk white, very pretty.

———

GERMAN BEAD MAT.

Materials.—O. P. beads of the following colours: red, three shades; purple. four shades; amber; dark green; and clear white. To be made with the Boar's Head crochet cotton, No. 4, of Messrs. Walter Evans and Co., of Derby.

UNLIKE the majority of these bead designs, the present one will be found to have the colours shaded in a thoroughly artistic manner. It will be observed, also, that it is not one of those patterns in which the one half is simply a repetition of the other.

The leaf in the centre is shaded in reds; the depth of tint in the engraving indicating the shade. Throughout the pattern, perpendicular lines indicate this colour; diagonal lines, from left to right, show a dark clear shade of green, which will be found to occur only in the veining of the leaf, and the fringe; plain white squares show the white beads; cross-barred indicate amber; and horizontal lines, deepening into black, show the purple beads. Thus it will be seen, on referring to the engraving, that the leaf is surrounded by white, beyond which a single line of amber, all round, divides it from the purple border. A line of red, and one beyond it of amber, completes the mat.

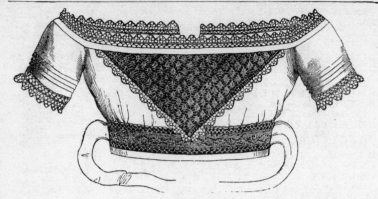

INFANT'S FROCK IN KNITTING.

THE WORK-TABLE FRIEND.

INFANT'S FROCK IN KNITTING.

Materials.—The Boar's Head Crochet cotton, No. 50, of Messrs. W. Evans and Co., of Derby, and a pair of Boulton and Son's knitting needles, No. 21.

THE EDGING.—Cast on seven stitches, and knit one plain row.

1st Row.—Knit 3, make 1, knit 2 together, make 2, knit 2.

2nd Row.—Knit 3, purl 1, knit 2, make 1, knit 2 together, knit 1.

3rd Row.—K 3, M 1, K 2 together, K to the end.

4th Row.—K all but 3, M 1, K 2 together, K 1.

5th Row.—K 3, M 1, K 2 together, M 2, K 2 together, M 2, K 2.

6th Row.—K. 3, P 1, K 2, P 1, K 2, M 1, K 2 together, K 1.

7th Row.—Like 3rd.

8th Row.—Like 4th.

9th Row.—K 3, M 1, K 2 together, M 2, K 2 together, M 2, K 2 together, M 2, K 2 together, K 1.

10th Row.—K 3, P 1, K 2, P 1, K 2, P 1, K 2, M 1, K 2 together, K 1.

11th Row.—Like 3rd.

12th Row.—Cast off 8 stitches, K all the rest but 3, M 1, K 2 together, K 1.

This little edging trims the top and sleeves, also the capes, if any are put to the body. For a first-sized frock, as the edging should be very narrow, the open hem may be so laid on as to cover the muslin hem or runner. Each piece of the edging must be done separately, and when measured, as well as sewn on, must be pulled out in the width, as it is apt to shrink

THE BODICE.—This commences in a point, and gradually increased; while the edging is knitted on it as it proceeds, by a method invented by ourselves.

Cast on 15 stitches, and knit a few rows quite plain; then knit all but 4. Make 1, knit 2 together, make 2, knit 2.

1st Pattern Row.—Knit 3, purl 1, knit 2, make 1, knit 2 together, knit 1, make 1, knit 1, make 1, knit 3, make 1, knit 2 together, make 2, knit 2.

2nd Row.—K 3, P 1, K 2, M 1, K 2 t, K 1, P 3, K 3, M 1, K 2 t, K 4.

3rd Row.—K 6, M 1, K 2 t, K 1, M 1, K 3, M 1, K 3, M 1, K 2 t, K 4.

4th Row.—K 6, M 1, K 2 t, K 1, P 5, K 3, M 1, K 2 t, M 2, K 2 t, M 2, K 2.

5th Row.—K 3, P 1, K 2, P 1, K 2, M 1, K 2 t, K 1, M 1, K 5, M 1, K 3, M 1, K 2 t, M 2, K 2 t, M 2, K 2.

6th Row.—K 3, P 1, K 2, P 1, K 2, M 1, K 2 t, K 1, P 3, M 1, P 2 t, P 2, K 3, M 1, K 2 t, K 7.

7th Row.—K 9, M 1, K 2 t, K 1, M 1, *raise a stitch* by knitting as one a bar of thread, M 1, K 2 t, K 3, K 2 t, M 1, raise 1, M 1, K 3, M 1, K 2 t, K 7.

8th Row.—K 9, M 1, K 2 t, K 1, P 11, K 3, M 1, K 2 t, M 2, K 2 t, M 2, K 2 t, K 1.

9th Row.—K 3, P 1, K 2, P 1, K 2, P 1, K 2, M 1, K 2 t, K 1, M 1, K 3, M 1, K 2 t, K 1, K 2 t, M 1, K 3, M 1, K 3, M 1, K 2 t, M 2, K 2 t, M 2, K 2 t, M 2, K 2 t, K 1.

10th Row.—K 3, P 1, K 2, P 1, K 2, P 1, K 2, M 1, K 2 t, K 1, purl all but the last 15, K 3, M 1, K 2 t, knit all the rest.

11th Row.—Cast off 8, K 3, M 1, K 2 t, K 1, M 1, K 5, M 1, K 3 t, M 1, K 5, M 1, K 3, M 1, K 2 t, knit to the end.

12th Row.—Cast off 8, K 3, M 1, K 2 t, K 1, P 3, M 1, P 2 t, P 6, M 1, P 2 t, P 2, K 3, M 1, K 2 t, M 2, K 2.

13th Row.—K 3, P 1, K 2, M 1, K 2 t, K 1, M 1, raise 1 + M 1, K 2 t, K 3, K 2 t, M 1, K 1 + M 1, K 2 t, K 3, K 2 t, M 1, raise 1, M 1, K 3, M 1, K 2 t, M 2, K 2.

14th Row.—K 3, P 1, K 2, M 1, K 2 t, K 1, purl all but the last 9, K 3, M 1, K 2 t, K 4.

15th Row.—K 6, M 1, K 2 t, K 1, + M 1, K 3, M 1, K 2 t, K 1, K 2 t + twice, M 1, K 3, M 1, K 3, M 1, K 2 t, K 4.

16th Row.—K 6, M 1, K 2 t, K 1, purl all but the last 9, K 3, M 1, K 2 t, M 2, K 2 t, M 2, K 2.

17th Row.—K 3, P 1, K 2, P 1, K 2, M 1, K 2 t, K 1 + M 1, K 5, M 1, K 3 t + twice, M 1, K 5, M 1, K 3, M 1, K 2 t, M 2, K 2 t, M 2, K 2.

18th Row.—K 3, P 1, K 2, P 1, K 2, M 1, K 2 t, K 1 + P 3, M 1, P 2 t, P 3 + twice, P 3, M 1, P 2 t, P 2, K 3, M 1, K 2 t, knit to the end.

19th Row.—K 9, M 1, K 2 t, K 1, M 1, raise 1 + M 1, K 2 t, K 3, K 2 t, M 1, K 1 + twice, M 1, K 2 t, K 3, K 2 t, M 1, raise 1, M 1, K 3, M 1, K 2 t, K to the end.

20th Row.—K 9, M 1, K 2 t, K 1, P all but 12, K 3, M 1, K 2 t + M 2, K 2 t + 3 times, K 1.

21st Row.—K 3, P 1, K 2, P 1, K 2, P 1, K 2, M 1, K 2 t, K 1, + M 1, K 3, M 1, K 2 t, K 1, P 2 t + 3 times, M 1, K 3, M 1, K 3, M 1, K 2 t * M 2, K 2 t * 3 times, K 1.

22nd Row.—K 3, P 1, K 2, P 1, K 2, P 1, K 2, M 1, K 2 t, K 1, P all but the last 15, K 3, M 1, K 2 t, K to the end.

23rd Row.—Cast off 8, K 3, M 1, K 2 t, K 1 + M 1, K 5, 'M 1, K 3 t, + 3 times, M 1, K 5, M 1, K 3, M 1, K 2 t, K to the end.

24th Row.—Cast off 8, K 3, M 1, K 2 t, K 1, P 3 + M 1, P 2 t, P 6 + 3 times, M 1, P 2 t, P 2, K 3, M 1, K 2 t, M 2, K 2.

Repeat these last twelve rows, from 13th to 24th inclusive, as often as required for the depth, always repeating between the crosses once more in every six rows. Thus the repetition will be always *four* times, from 25th to 30th, five times in the next six, and so on, instead of three.

Make it up with muslin, as seen in the engraving.

EMBROIDERED COLLAR.

Materials.—Nansook muslin, and the Royal Embroidery cotton of Messrs. W. Evans and Co., of Derby, No. 30, white and ingrain red.

THIS collar is in quite a new style of work, (see p. 403), the border being very open, connected by bars only, in Point de Venise, the centre of the muslin sprigged over with little flowers; the two parts are connected by a row of open-hem.

Of course the muslin is marked all in one piece, and the design is so simple there can be no difficulty in enlarging it to the required size. The first part to be worked is the bars; then the remainder of the border; after this the little sprigs, which are entirely in satin-stitch, and finally the open-hem. This is done by piercing holes with a very coarse needle, first at one side of the space left for the open-hem, and then at the other, and sewing over with a fine thread (Evans' Boar's-head, No. 60), the threads of muslin between.

The border is sometimes done in scarlet.

POPULAR notions of a beautiful foot are extremely erroneous. It is thought desirable the foot should be very narrow, and tapering at the toe. Now, this is not the form in which feet are made, consequently the modern boot is calculated to produce deformity, and an ungraceful carriage is the result. The only rational bootmaker I ever saw, always sketched the sole on a bit of paper, making his customer stand firmly without a shoe while doing so. Thus the peculiar form of the foot was obtained, and the boot was made to it, instead of the reverse, which is usually the case.—*Maternal Counsels.*

TURKISH CUSHION.

TURKISH CUSHION, IN BERLIN WORK.

Materials.—A square of very coarse Penelope canvas, Berlin wool (eight-thread) of the following colours, yellow, salmon, red, violet, scarlet, green of two shades vert-islay, black, and white. Also rich cord and a single tassel, in which salmon is the prevailing colour.

In one of our engravings we represent the cushion as completely made; the other gives the diagram of one quarter, stitch by stitch. In brioche cushions, generally, the top is formed of six, eight, or more pieces, joined down the sides, and meeting in the centre of the cushion. But the present pattern has all the top in one piece, the design, however, being still in the usual style.

Not the slightest difficulty can be expe-
rienced in working from the engraving, in which the colours are thus represented.

WHITE.—White. This occurs only in the geometrical figure in the centre.

BLACK.—Black squares.

SCARLET.—Horizontal lines.

CRIMSON.—Ditto, but darker.

VERT-ISLAY.—Shaded diagonally. The two shades represented by the degree of darkness.

YELLOW.—White squares, dotted.

VIOLET.—Horizontal lines, like the scarlet, but much darker. This colour occurs only in the little shamrocks between the medallions.

The grounding is to be done in salmon colour, and may be extended to make as large a cushion as can be desired, but generally it

TURKISH CUSHION.

is not more than eighteen inches in diameter.

To make up one of these cushions, take a round piece of millboard for the bottom, and cover it with black twilled calico on both sides, first piercing a hole in the centre. A strip of stout tick, two and a-half or three inches wide, forms the sides, and a round of tick the top. The millboard being covered on *both* sides, you are enabled to sew the tick

EMBROIDERED COLLAR.

to the edges of the calico. Stuff this frame with feathers or flock; sew a band of leather or velvet over the side, and the work in its place. Add the tassel in the centre, and ornamental cord at each edge of the band.

All brioches are made in this way, but when the top is in divisions, a finer cord must be run down to conceal the join in each.

THE WORK-TABLE FRIEND

EMBROIDERED COLLAR.

Materials.—A piece of very fine book-muslin, or French muslin, and Evans's embroidery cotton, No. 50.

THE collar is of one of the newest Parisian shapes, and the design has been arranged especially for the readers of our volume of TREASURES, being of a style that allows us to give a section the full size for working in our pages. The pattern consists of a series of vandykes, which are worked alternately in two different ways. An unequal number is, of course, required to make the ends correspond, and for a moderate sized collar fifteen will be required, whilst a large one will take seventeen. It will be observed that the vandyke at the end of the collar is rather different to the others. To prepare the pattern, first work the circle for the neck on a piece of tracing paper, taking the pattern from any collar you may have that fits well. Then trace the section given in the engraving, on a separate bit of paper.

Transfer that to the larger piece, and draw the remainder by shifting the pattern until one-half the collar is marked, then folding the tracing paper, and drawing the other half from it.

A perfect pattern being thus procured, the muslin is laid over it, and the design marked with indigo, using a very fine sable brush.

The French oil silk, which is green on one side, and black on the other, is the nicest material to work on. The muslin must be tacked on it.

Trace the border first, and run the little button-hole scallops, which form the edge, about three times, taking the thread up the division of each vandyke, and back again to the edge, when doing it for the first time. Then work all the edge very evenly in scalloped button-hole stitch. When one point is done, run the thread up the division between that and the next one : work it down to the scallop again in common close button-hole.

The flowers are done in stitch ; the small holes are pierced with a stiletto, but

FLOWERS IN CROCHET—THE NARCISSUS.—BY MRS. PULLAN.

those which are more open, and occur in every alternate point only, must have a small piece of the muslin cut out.

The stems are run and sewed over *once* only. A little management is required for this. Run the thread up the stem to the flower at the point, which work; then sew back as much of the stem as brings your needle to the next flower.

Repeat the process.

By way of variety, the small flowers may be worked, like the edge, in long button-hole stitch.

FLOWERS IN CROCHET.

THE NARCISSUS.

FLOWERS made of wool, in crochet, have the advantage of being more durable than those in rice paper, wax, or many other substances; whilst the effect of the work is extremely good, provided proper care is taken in the selection of the materials.

A bouquet of flowers made in crochet will form, therefore, an extremely pretty decoration for a drawing-room table; whilst they may also enter into the composition of various other ornaments. Small flowers, such as heart's-ease, may be arranged as a border for a mat; and the ingenuity of our readers will readily supply other modes of using the larger ones.

We will now describe the mode of making the narcissus; observing that it is of the utmost consequence to select the proper shades of wool, in order that the work may present a close imitation of nature.

MATERIALS.—Berlin wool of the following tints: white, yellow, scarlet, and three shades of green (*Vert d'Islay*), a little white florists' wire, and very fine common wire.

Begin by making the petals of the narcissus, in white wool.

15 Ch. — Take a bit of florist's wire, about one finger long, slip the end of it through the last stitch, and hold it even with the chain on which you are about to work. 2 Sc, 3 semi-stitches, 7 Dc, 1 semi-stitch, 3 Sc in one at the end. Work on the other side of the chain, holding in the end of work as well as the wire, 1 semi-stitch, 7 Dc, 3 semi-stitches, 2 Sc, 1 slip-stitch in the last stitch of the chain. Cut off the wool, leaving about two inches, and plait this in with the ends of wire.

Each flower will require six of these petals, which must all be made separately.

The eye of the narcissus is made thus: With the white wool, make a chain of 7 stitches. Cut off the white wool, and join on the yellow, as close as possible to the last chain stitch. Join the chain into a round, and work on it + 1 Sc, 1 Ch, miss none, + 7 times. Cut off the yellow wool, and join on the red, and work a slip-stitch in every stitch of the last round. Fasten off, leaving a small piece of the wool, to sew the eye of the flower to the petals.

Place your six petals in the proper form for a flower, twist the end of the wires together, and sew the eye in its place.

For the stem, take a piece of the coarser wire, about 3 fingers long, bend it into the form of a hair-pin, but pinching it so that the two prongs are *close* to each other. Slip them through the eye of the flower, and bring one prong out on each side between two petals. Pinch them quite close, and twist some green wool round the stem thus formed, so as to cover it entirely.

The lover of Nature will have observed, that there is a slight bulbous swelling in the stem of the narcissus, just below the flower. This is imitated by winding the wool up and down the wire, at that spot, on a space of about the third of an inch, and rather more than an inch from the flower. Do this on your way down the wire.

THE FOLIAGE.—Take any shade of the green wool, and make 50 chain stitches. Cut off a piece of the coarser wire, rather more than double the length of the chain;

slip the end into the last chain stitch, and work on the chain and over the wool, 7 Sc, 37 SDc stiches, 4 Sc, 3 Sc in one, at the point; on the other side, 4 Sc, 37 SDc stitches, 7 Sc, 1 slip stitch at the end. Cut off the wool, and fasten it as you did the petals of the flowers.

Each flower should have three or four leaves, done in the different shades of the green wool. All are to be worked in the same manner, but to differ slightly in size, the darkest being also the *largest* leaves.

Wind some green wool round the flower, holding in first one leaf and then another, covering the ends, and so joining them to the stem of the flower.

To make the leaves larger or smaller than the above, make so many more or less chain stitches, and in the same way alter the number of semi-stitches, to more or fewer.

This contraction, *SDc stitch*, being new to our readers, we will explain the mode of making it, and the purpose for which it was invented.

Between the Sc and the Dc stitch there is a very great difference, as to height. In forming a flower, or leaf, where every change is so very gradually made, a half stitch, larger than the one, and not so large as the other, was very desirable. For this purpose the short double crochet stitch was invented. Proceed exactly as for a Dc stitch, but, when you have three loops on the needle, instead of drawing the wool through two only, and then through the other two, the old one and the one just formed, draw the wool through all three at the same time.

To give the slight variation of size always found in Nature, it will be desirable to make some of the flowers rather smaller than those described.

VISIONS OF THE PAST!—If some of our close, quiet chambers, pleasant rooms we have loved, were suddenly peopled with the phantoms of our old selves as we have appeared in many an awful hour when none saw us but God; if the dumb walls could re-utter our words, the void air revive the impress of our likeness there,—what a revealing it would be! Surely we ought not to judge harshly, but each of us to have mercy upon one another.—*The Head of the Family.*

NETTED VANDYKE TRIMMING.

THE WORK-TABLE FRIEND.

NETTED VANDYKE TRIMMING FOR CHILDREN'S DRAWERS, &c.

Materials.—Messrs. W. Evans & Co's Boar's Head crochet cotton, No. 16, with a bone mesh, No. 9, for the foundation, and the same, with No. 12, for the darning.

BEGIN with one stitch, on which net *two*. Turn the work, and do one in the first stitch, and two in the second. Continue to work in this way,—turning at the end of every row, and always doing two in the last stitch, and one in every other until you have eight stitches in the row—the next row, and every alternate one after that, until the 21st row, when you cut off the thread *near* the knot. The alternate intermediate rows are to be increased, as usual, by working two stitches in one. So far one point, and a section of the upper part of the next, is made. Fasten on the thread on the seventh loop from the point, and repeat from the directions when you have eight stitches in the row, which you will find you have in this, not reckoning, of course, the one to which you attach the thread.

Every point must be done in the same way, except the last, when, in order to make the edge straight, and to correspond with that of the commencement, you will net two together, instead of doing two in one at the end of the 9th, 11th, 13th, and 15th rows from the fastening on.

Wash the length of netting in soft water with white soap, starch it slightly with gum-water, and pin it out evenly to dry. Then tack it on a piece of *toile ciré*, and darn it.

A circle of wheels will be seen in the point. The centre one has an English rosette worked in the middle, the wheel around it being formed by running a thread twice round, and covering it with buttonhole stitch. This occupies four squares of the netting; but in order to give the round form, the threads, which are afterwards covered with button-hole stitch, are taken into the square immediately beyond. The eight squares surrounding this are filled with square herring-bone stitch; that is, with herring-bone stitch worked alternately over each of the four bars of the square. The eight wheels round the centre one are worked like it, but with a wheel instead of a rosette in the middle. The mode of doing the Vandyke pattern must be seen from the engraving itself. The edge is covered with button-hole stitch, dotted with Raleigh bars. The little square in the upper part is done by closely filling certain squares with ordinary herring-bone; in the pattern eight are thus occupied, inclosing a square of four, in which a rosette is worked. The entire upper line of holes is closely darned.

No. 12 cotton is used for all the stitches except the rosettes, wheels, and square herring-bone.

CARD-PURSE.

CARD-PURSE.

Materials.—1 skein of Vert-islay silk, ¼ a skein of Napoleon blue ditto, less than that quantity of cerise and black, 6 skeins of gold thread, a medallion chalice, with chains and ring, 3 rich tassels to correspond with the silk, silk cord, and 2 gold slides.

WE will begin by describing the chalice, which is one of the most *recherché* Parisian patterns. It is nearly flat at the bottom, and square, with a gilt figure at each corner, and a medallion painted on ivory at the centre of each side. These four medallions represent different views in Paris. The Madelaine, the Tuilleries, the Barrière de l'Etoile, and Nôtre Dame are there on the chalice before us. Our readers may suppose that, trifling as this trinket is, it really merits to be considered as a work of art.

The ground of the purse is Vert-islay silk. Begin on a chain of four, which close into a round, and do three Sc stitches in every stitch. In the next round, do three stitches in the *centre* one of every three, and one in each of the others. The piece of crochet thus takes the form of a square,

and you will continue to increase in the same way, by doing 3 stitches in each corner stitch, and one in each of the others, until a piece 1 inch and a-third wide is made. Then begin to work in Dc, with 1 chain after every Dc stitch, still increasing at the four corners only, by working 3 Dc in the corner stitches, with a chain stitch after each, until six rounds are done. There must be 150 stitches in the last round. Then do four rounds of Sc, with the same silk, which will bring you to the

1st Pattern Round—(Green, black, and gold).—+ 3 green, 5 gold, 13 green, 4 black, 4 green, 4 gold, 17 green, + 3 times.

2nd Round.—Same colours, with blue. + 3 green, 1 gold, 4 blue, 1 gold, 9 green, 1 black, 1 green, 2 black, 2 green, 2 black, 4 green, 1 gold, 2 blue, 1 gold, 3 green, 1 gold, 12 green + 3 times.

3rd Round.—+ 2 green, 1 gold, 5 blue, 1 gold, 1 green, 4 gold, 5 green, 2 black, 4 green, 1 black, 5 green, 1 gold, 2 blue, 1 gold, 3 green, 2 gold, 10 green + 3 times.

4th Round.— + 1 green, 4 gold, 4 blue, 1 gold, 4 blue, 1 gold, 4 green, 2 black, 1 green, 1 black, 2 green, 1 black, 5 green, 1 gold, 2 blue, 1 gold, 3 green, 1 gold, 1 blue, 1 gold, 9 green, + 3 times.

5th Round.—1 green, 1 gold, 3 green, 1 gold, 2 blue, 1 gold, 5 blue, 1 gold, 4 green, 2 black, 2 green, 2 black, 6 green, 1 gold, 2 blue, 1 gold, 2 green, 1 gold, 2 blue, 1 gold, 9 green + 3 times.

6th Round.—+ 6 green, 1 gold, 1 blue, 1 gold, 3 blue, 3 gold, 5 green, 2 black, 8 green, 1 gold, 3 blue, 3 gold, 3 blue, 1 gold, 3 green, 1 gold, 5 green, + 3 times. Do 4 more green.

7th Round.—+ 2 green (over last 2 of 6 green), 1 gold, 4 blue, 1 gold, 9 green, 3 black, 4 green, 2 gold, 3 blue, 1 gold, 6 blue, 4 gold, 1 blue, 1 gold, 8 green. + 3 times.

8th Round.— + 3 green, 1 gold, 2 blue, 1 gold, 5 green, 4 gold, 3 green, 3 gold, 13 blue, 1 gold, 5 blue, 1 gold, 2 green, 1 gold, 2 green. + 3 times.

9th Round.— + 3 green, 1 gold, 2 blue, 1 gold, 4 green, 6 gold, 1 green, 6 gold, 4 blue, 7 gold, 5 blue, 1 gold, 2 green, 6 gold, 1 green + 3 times. Begin cerise.

10th Round.— + 3 green, 1 gold, 2 blue, 1 gold, 3 green, 3 gold, 3 cerise, 3 gold, 3 cerise, 7 gold, 2 blue, 1 gold, 2 green, 3 gold, 2 blue, 1 gold, 2 green, 2 gold, 3 cerise, 3 gold. + 3 times.

11th Round.— + 3 green, 1 gold, 2 blue, 1 gold, 3 green, 2 gold, 5 cerise, 1 gold, 5 cerise, 2 gold, 3 green, 1 gold, 2 blue, 1 gold, 5 green, 2 gold, 3 green, 1 gold, 5 cerise, 2 gold. + 3 times.

12th Round.— + 3 green, 1 gold, 3 blue, 1 gold, 2 green, 2 gold, 4 cerise, 3 gold, 4 cerise, 2 gold, 3 green, 1 gold, 3 blue, 1 gold, 6 green, 1 gold, 2 green, 1 gold, 5 cerise, 2 gold. + 3 times.

13th Round.— + 4 green, 1 gold, 2 blue, 1 gold, 2 green, 2 gold, 3 cerise, 1 gold, 3 black, 1 gold, 3 cerise, 2 gold, 3 green, 1 gold, 3 blue, 3 gold, 5 green, 1 gold, 1 green, 3 gold, 3 cerise, 2 gold. + 3 times.

14th Round.— + 1 green, 4 gold, 2 blue, 1 gold, 3 green, 2 gold, 2 cerise, 1 gold, 4 black, 1 gold, 1 cerise, 2 gold, 3 green, 1 gold, 4 blue, 1 gold, 8 green, 1 gold, 3 black, 1 gold, 1 cerise, 2 gold, 1 green. + 3 times.

15th Round.— + 2 gold, 3 blue, 1 gold, 1 blue, 1 gold, 4 green, 4 gold, 4 black, 3 gold, 2 green, 2 gold, 3 blue, 1 gold, 1 blue, 1 gold, 4 green, 4 gold, 4 black, 3 gold, 2 green + 3 times.

16th Round.— + 2 green, 1 gold, 4 blue, 1 gold, 8 green, 1 gold, 3 black, 1 gold, 1 cerise, 2 gold, 2 green, 4 gold, 2 blue, 1 gold, 3 green, 2 gold, 2 cerise, 1 gold, 4 black, 1 gold, 1 cerise, 2 gold, 1 green + 3 times.

17th Round.— + 3 green, 1 gold, 3 blue, 3 gold, 5 green, 1 gold, 1 green, 3 gold, 3 cerise, 2 gold, 4 green, 1 gold, 2 blue, 1 gold, 2 green, 2 gold, 3 cerise, 1 gold, 3 black, 1 gold, 3 cerise, 2 gold. + 3 times.

18th Round.— + 3 green, 1 gold, 3 blue, 1 gold, 6 green, 1 gold, 2 green, 1 gold, 5 cerise, 2 gold, 3 green, 1 gold, 3 blue, 1 gold, 2 green, 2 gold, 4 cerise, 3 gold, 4 cerise, 2 gold. + 3 times.

19th Round.— + 3 green, 1 gold, 2 blue, 1 gold, 5 green, 2 gold, 3 green, 1 gold, 5 cerise, 2 gold, 3 green, 1 gold, 2 blue, 1 gold, 3 green, 2 gold, 5 cerise, 1 gold, 5 cerise, 2 gold. + 3 times.

20th Round.— + 4 gold, 2 blue, 1 gold, 2 green, 3 gold, 2 blue, 1 gold, 2 green, 2 gold, 3 cerise, 3 gold, 3 green, 1 gold, 2 blue, 1 gold, 3 green, 3 gold, 3 cerise, 3 gold, 3 cerise, 3 gold. + 3 times.

21st Round.— + 3 blue, 7 gold, 5 blue, 1 gold, 2 green, 6 gold, 4 green, 1 gold, 2 blue, 1 gold, 4 green, 6 gold, 1 green, 6 gold, 1 blue, + 3 times.

22nd Round.— + 10 blue, 1 gold, 5 blue, 1 gold, 2 green, 4 gold, 5 green, 1 gold, 2 blue, 1 gold, 5 green, 4 gold, 3 green, 3 gold, 3 blue, + 3 times.

23rd Round.— + 1 gold, 3 blue, 1 gold, 6 blue, 4 gold, 1 blue, 1 gold, 10 green, 1 gold, 6 blue, 1 gold, 9 green, 3 black, 4 green, 1 gold, + 3 times.

24th Round.— + 1 green, 1 gold, 3 blue, 3 gold, 3 blue, 1 gold, 3 green, 1 gold, 11 green, 1 gold, 1 blue, 1 gold, 3 blue, 3 gold, 5 green, 2 black, 7 green, + 3 times.

25th Round.— + 2 green, 1 gold, 2 blue, 1 gold, * twice, 10 green, 1 gold, 3 green, 1 gold, 2 blue, 1 gold, 5 blue, 1 gold, 4 green, 2 black, 2 green, 2 black, 4 green, + 3 times.

26th Round— + 2 green, 1 gold, 2 blue, 1 gold, 3 green, 1 gold, 1 blue, 1 gold, 10 green, 4 gold, 4 blue, 1 gold, 4 blue, 1 gold, 4 green, black, 1 green, 1 black, 2 green, 1 black, 3 green, + 3 times.

27th Round.— + 2 green, 1 gold, 2 blue, 1 gold, 3 green, 2 gold, 12 green, 1 gold, 5 blue, 1 gold, 1 green, 4 gold, 5 green, 2 black, 4 green, 1 black, 3 green, + 3 times.

28th Round.— + 1 green, 1 gold, 2 blue, 1 gold, 3 green, 1 gold, 15 green, 1 gold, 4 blue, 1 gold, 9 green, 1 black, 1 green, 2 black, 2 green, 2 black, 3 green, + 3 times.

29th Round.— + 4 gold, 21 green, 4 gold, 13 green, 4 black, 4 green, + 3 times.

Now do four rounds of Sc, with the Vertislay, and then two of open square crochet.

For the Border.—Gold thread, 1 Dc under chain, + 3 Ch, 1 Dc under same, miss one square, and Dc under the next, + all round.

2nd Round.—Cerise 4 Dc under every chain of 3.

3rd Round.—Gold. Dc between the 2 Dc of 1st round, Sc on each Dc of last round.

The chalice is stitched on just above the last open round of the foundation.

LOOKS AND GESTURES.—How frequently is the honesty and integrity of a man disposed of by a smile or a shrug ! How many good and generous actions have been sunk into oblivion by a distrustful look, or stamped with the imputation of proceeding from bad motives, by a mysterious and unseasonable whisper!—*Sterne.*

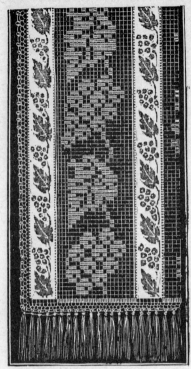

VINE-LEAF ANTIMACASSAR.

THE WORK-TABLE FRIEND.

VINE-LEAF ANTIMACASSAR.

Materials.—Messrs. W. Evans and Co.'s Drab Boar's Head Crochet Cotton, No. 10, and 1½ oz. Emerald or Turquoise beads, No. 2. 5 reels of cotton will suffice for a small Antimacassar.

THREAD all the beads on two reels of the cotton, leaving the other three for those parts in which beads are not used. Begin with a reel on which beads are threaded, by making a chain of 240 stitches, which, as the design occupies 39 stitches, will allow for six repetitions of the pattern, and three plain stitches extra at each end. In giving our directions, we shall omit the mention of the three extra stitches, which must always be worked.

1st Row.—Sc, dropping a bead on every alternate stitch.

2nd Row.—Sc without any beads.

3rd Row.—(1st row of the Pattern.)— + 4 cotton, 2 beads, 33 cotton, + repeat.

4th Row.—+ 3 cotton, 2 beads, 1 cotton, 1 bead, 32 cotton, + repeat.

5th Row.—+ 3 cotton, 4 beads, 1 cotton, 2 beads, 15 cotton, 2 beads, 1 cotton, 3 beads, 8 cotton, + repeat.

6th Row.—+ 1 cotton, 2 beads, 1 cotton, 2 beads, 1 cotton, 2 beads, 1 cotton, 1 bead, 7 cotton, 3 beads, 3 cotton, 8 beads, 5 cotton, 2 beads, + repeat.

7th Row.—+ 2 beads, 1 cotton, 1 bead, 3 cotton, 4 beads, 5 cotton, 2 beads, 3 cotton, 1 bead, 1 cotton, 2 beads, 1 cotton, 2 beads, 1 cotton, 3 beads, 3 cotton, 2 beads, 2 cotton + repeat.

8th Row.—4 beads, 1 cotton, 2 beads, 1 cotton, 2 beads, 1 cotton, 2 beads, 1 cotton, 2 beads, 6 cotton, 3 beads, 1 cotton, 1 bead, 1 cotton, 3 beads, 2 cotton, 2 beads, 4 cotton + repeat.

9th Row.—+ 1 cotton, 2 beads, 1 cotton, 2 beads, 1 cotton, 1 bead, 2 cotton, 2 beads, 1 cotton, 1 bead, 8 cotton, 2 beads, 1 cotton, 1 bead, 1 cotton, 6 beads, 6 cotton + repeat.

10th Row.—+ 4 cotton, 4 beads, 2 cotton, 4 beads, 7 cotton, 2 beads, 3 cotton, 8 beads, 5 cotton + repeat.

11th Row.—+ 2 cotton, 2 beads, * 1 cotton, 2 beads, * 3 times, 7 cotton, 2 beads, 1 cotton, 2 beads, 3 cotton, 2 beads, 3 cotton, 2 beads, 4 cotton + repeat.

12th Row.—+ 1 cotton, 2 beads, * 1 cotton, 1 bead, 2 cotton, 2 beads, * twice, 7 cotton, 1 bead, 1 cotton, 1 bead, 1 cotton, 2 beads, 1 cotton, 1 bead, 2 cotton, 4 beads, 5 cotton, + repeat.

13th Row.—+ 1 cotton, 4 beads, 2 cotton, 4 beads, 1 cotton, 2 beads, 1 cotton, 1 bead, 4 cotton, 3 beads, 1 cotton, 2 beads, 1 cotton, 3 beads, 3 cotton, 2 beads, 4 cotton + repeat.

14th Row.—+ 2 cotton, 2 beads, 1 cotton, 2 beads, 1 cotton, 2 beads, 2 cotton, 4 beads, 6 cotton, 5 beads, 1 cotton, 2 beads, 1 cotton, 1 bead, 2 cotton, 2 beads, 3 cotton, + repeat.

15th Row.—+ 4 cotton, 2 beads, 1 cotton, 1 bead, 2 cotton, 2 beads, 1 cotton, 2 beads, 7 cotton, 5 beads, 1 cotton, 2 beads, 1 cotton, 3 beads, 1 cotton, 2 beads, 2 cotton, + repeat.

16th Row.—+ 4 cotton, 4 beads, 1 cotton, 2 beads, 1 cotton, 1 bead, 2 cotton, 2 beads, 4 cotton, 2 beads, 3 cotton, 12 beads, 1 cotton, + repeat.

17th Row.—+ 5 cotton, 2 beads, 2 cotton, 4 beads, 1 cotton, 2 beads, 1 cotton, 1 bead, 4 cotton, 1 bead, 3 cotton, 3 beads, 1 cotton, 3 beads, 1 cotton, 5 beads, + repeat.

18th Row.—+ 10 cotton, 2 beads, 2 cotton, 4 beads, 9 cotton, 2 beads, 2 cotton, 2 beads, 6 cotton + repeat.

19th Row.—+ 15 cotton, 2 beads, 22 cotton, + repeat.

20th Row.—All cotton.

21st Row.—+ 1 bead, 1 cotton, + repeat to the end.

This forms one bead stripe. Now take a reel of the cotton on which there are no beads, and begin to work on the *right* side.

22nd Row.—Open square crochet.

23rd Row.—1 Dc, + 22 open, 2 close, 13 open, + repeat to the end. (The length is about two patterns.)

24th Row.—1 Dc + 21 open, 2 close, 1 open, 1 close, 12 open, + repeat.

25th Row.—1 Dc + 6 open, 2 close, 1 open, 3 close, 9 open, 4 close, 1 open, 2 close, 9 open, + repeat.

26th Row.—1 Dc, + 1 open, 1 close, 3 open, 8 close, 3 open, 2 close, * 1 open, 2 close, * 3 times, 1 open, 1 close, 7 open, 1 close, + repeat.

27th Row.—1 Ch, + 2 open, 1 close, 1 open, 2 close, 1 open, 2 close, 1 open, 3 close, 3 open, 1 close, 1 open, 2 close, 1 open, 1 close, 3 open, 4 close, 5 open, 2 close, 1 open + repeat.

28th Row.—1 Dc + 3 open, 3 close, 1 open, 1 close, 1 open, 3 close, 2 open, 2 close, 2 open, 4 close, * 1 open, 2 close, * 4 times, 3 open, + repeat.

29th Row.—1 Dc, + 3 open, 2 close, 1 open, 1 close, 1 open, 6 close, 5 open, 2 close, 1 open, 2 close, 1 open, 1 close, 2 open, 2 close, 1 open, 1 close, 5 open, + repeat.

30th Row.—1 Dc, + 2 open, 2 close, 3 open, 8 close, 7 open, 4 close, 2 open, 4 close, 5 open, + repeat.

31st Row.—1 Dc, + 1 open, 2 close, 1 open, 2 close, 3 open, 2 close, 3 open, 2 close, 4 open, 2 close, * 1 open, 2 close, * 3 times, 6 open, + repeat.

32nd Row.—1 Dc, + 1 open, 1 close, 1 open, 1 close, 1 open, 2 close, 1 open, 1 close, 2 open, 4 close, 4 open, 2 close, * 1 open, 1 close, 2 open, 2 close, * twice, 4 open.

33rd Row.—1 Dc, + 1 open, 3 close, 1 open, 2 close, 1 open, 3 close, 3 open, 2 close, 3 open, 4 close, 2 open, 4 close, 1 open, 2 close, 1 open, 1 close, 3 open, + repeat.

34th Row.—1 Dc, + 3 open, 5 close, 1 open, 2 close, 1 open, 3 close, 1 open, 2 close, 4 open, 2 close, 1 open, 1 close, 2 open, 2 close, 1 open, 2 close, 4 open, + repeat.

35th Row.—1 Dc + 2 open, 2 close, 3 open, 12 close, 3 open, 4 close 1 open, 2 close, 1 open, 1 close, 2 open, 2 close, 2 open + repeat.

36th Row.—1 Dc, + 3 open, 1 close, 2 open, 4 close, 1 open, 3 close, 1 open, 5 close, 3 open, 2 close, 2 open, 4 close, 1 open, 2 close, 1 open, 1 close, 1 open, + repeat.

37th Row.—1 Dc, + 8 open, 2 close, 2 open, 2 close, 11 open, 2 close, 1 open, 2 close, 2 open, 4 close, 1 open, + repeat.

38th Row.—1 Dc, + 33 open, 2 close, 2 open, + repeat.

Turn the work on the wrong side, and repeat from the first row to the 38th inclusive (working the open stripe, as before, on the right side). Then repeat the bead stripe again, which forms the width of the antimacassar.

Do one row of open square crochet entirely round the antimacassar, except the extremities of the two open stripes, in each square of which work 3 Dc stitches.

Take the cotton with beads on it, and do the following:—2 Dc, dropping two beads on each, under a chain, + 4 chain 2 Dc as before under the same chain, 4 Ch, 2 Dc as before, under the next chain but one, + repeat all round, and at equal distances on the close part.

The next round is precisely the same, only the 4 Dc, with the 4 chain between, are to be worked under the chain between the Dc of the previous row.

Complete the antimacassar by knotting a fringe on every chain of 4, between the 2nd and 3rd Dc stitches.

A fringe may be knotted all round, if desired; but, in this case, five reels of cotton will not be sufficient.

THE WORK-TABLE FRIEND.

ANTI-MACASSAR, FOR AN ARM-CHAIR.

Materials.—W. Evans and Co.'s Boar's Head Crochet Cotton, No. 4, and 2oz. of stone-blue beads, the size next to seed-beads. Boulton's Crochet-book, No. 14.

This Anti-Macassar is intended to slip over the top of an easy chair, and is therefore a great improvement on the old style of covering which was liable to be displaced with every movement of the head. The Anti-Macassar represented in our engraving consists of two pieces, one of which is made in crochet, and the other either in crochet, marcella, or muslin. The sides and rounded part are sewed together, and thus a bag is formed, open at the bottom, which is slipped over the head of the chair. The border of beads, which is added to the right side only, is not only a pretty finish, but by adding weight to the Anti-Macassar, assists in keeping it in its place. It is necessary to be attentive to two things in the choice of the beads; they must slip easily on the thread, and they must be of a kind that will wash well.

Make a chain of 274 stitches, on which work one row of Dc.

2nd Row.—1 close square at each end, the rest open square crochet.

3rd Row.—1 close, 1 open, 87 close, 1 open, 1 close.

4th Row.—1 close, 1 open, 1 close, 85 open, 1 close, 1 open, 1 close.

5th Row.—1 close, 1 open, 1 close, 42 open, 1 close, 42 open, 1 close, 1 open, 1 close.

6th Row.—The same.

7th Row,—1 close, 1 open, 1 close, 41 open, 2 close, 8 open, 1 close, 33 open, 1 close, 1 open, 1 close.

8th Row.—1 close, 1 open, 1 close, 38 open, 1 close, 2 open, 2 close, 9 open, 1 close, 32 open, 1 close, 1 open, 1 close.

9th Row.—1 close, 1 open, 1 close, 28 open, 2 close, 8 open, 2 close, 1 open, 2 close, 2 open, 1 close, 6 open, 1 close, 1 open, 1 close, 5 open, 1 close, 24 open, 1 close, 1 open, 1 close.

10th Row.—1 close, 1 open, 1 close, 13 open, 1 close, 15 open, 2 close, 8 open, 3

close, 2 open, 2 close, 7 open, 1 close, 5 open, 1 close, 25 open, 1 close, 1 open, 1 close.

11th Row.—1 close, 1 open, 1 close, 13 open, 3 close, 13 open, 2 close, 10 open, 1 close, 1 open, 3 close, 5 open, 1 close, 1 open, 1 close, 1 open, 2 close, 2 open, 1 close, 11 open, 1 close, 13 open, 1 close, 1 open, 1 close.

12th Row.—1 close, 1 open, 1 close, 15 open, 2 close, 5 open, 1 close, 7 open, 1 close, 1 open, 1 close, 5 open, 2 close, 1 open, 1 close, 1 open, 2 close, 7 open, 2 close, 1 open, 4 close, 11 open, 1 close, 14 open, 1 close, 1 open, 1 close.

13th Row.—1 close, 1 open, 1 close, 15 open, 2 close, 1 open, 1 close, 4 open, 1 close, 1 open, 1 close, 5 open, 1 close, 7 open, 4 close, 3 open, 1 close, 7 open, 2 close, 1 open, 2 close, 3 open, 1 close, 7 open, 2 close, 13 open, 1 close, 1 open, 1 close.

14th Row.—1 close, 1 open, 1 close, 16 open, 1 close, 1 open, 1 close, 5 open, 2 close, 5 open, 1 close, 10 open, 1 close, 2 open, 2 close, 3 open, 2 close, 2 open, 4 close, 3 open, 1 close, 6 open, 1 close, 1 open, 1 close, 14 open, 1 close, 1 open, 1 close.

15th Row.—1 close, 1 open, 1 close, 9 open, 1 close, 6 open, 4 close, 6 open, 1 close, 2 open, 1 close, 1 open, 1 close, 1 open, 1 close, 5 open, 2 close, 1 open, 1 close, 1 open, 2 close, 4 open, 4 close, 2 open, 2 close, 1 open, 1 close, 1 open, 1 close, 4 open, 1 close, 1 open, 2 close, 15 open, 1 close, 1 open, 1 close.

16th Row.—1 close, 1 open, 1 close, 10 open, 1 close, 7 open, 2 close, 6 open, 2 close, 1 open, 1 close, 2 open, 2 close, 1 open, 3 close, 2 open, 4 close, 5 open, 2 close, 1 open, 2 close, 5 open, 2 close, 3 open, 1 close, + 1 open, 1 close, + 3 times; 14 open, 1 close, 1 open, 1 close.

17th Row.—1 close, 1 open, 1 close, 10 open, 1 close, 1 open, 1 close, 5 open, 3 close, 4 open, 6 close, 1 open, 5 close, 6 open, 1 close, 1 open, 1 close, 3 open, 4 close, 1 open, 2 close, 2 open, 1 close, 3 open, 1 close, 1 open, 1 close, 1 open, 2 close, 17 open, 1 close, 1 open, 1 close.

18th Row.—1 close, 1 open, 1 close, 11 open, 2 close, 1 open, 1 close, 4 open, 2 close, 6 open, 4 close, 1 open, 4 close, 6 open, 3 close, 6 open, 2 close, 1 open, 4 close, 2 open, 1 close, 1 open, 1 close.

ANTI-MACASSAR, FOR AN ARM-CHAIR, BY MRS. PULLAN.

1 open, 2 close, 2 open, 1 close, 6 open, 1 close, 9 open, 1 close, 1 open, 1 close.

19th Row.—1 close, 1 open, 1 close, 13 open, 2 close, 4 open, 2 close, 4 open, 6 close, 1 open, 5 close, 4 open, 2 close, 2 open, 2 close, 6 open, 2 close, 1 open, 2 close, 2 open, 1 close, 1 open, 2 close, 2 open, 1 close, 6 open, 2 close, 10 open, 1 close, 1 open, 1 close.

20th Row.—1 close, 1 open, 1 close, 12 open, 3 close, 1 open, 2 close, 2 open, 1 close, 1 open, 1 close, 4 open, 9 close, 9 open, 3 close, 2 open, 2 close, 1 open, 4 close, 1 open, 4 close, 2 open, 1 close, 7 open, 1 close, 12 open, 1 close, 1 open, 1 close.

21st Row.—1 close, 1 open, 1 close, 7 open, 1 close, 6 open, 1 close, 1 open, 4 close, 1 open, 1 close, 8 open, 2 close, 6 open, 2 close, 3 open, 5 close, 1 open, 4 close, 2 open, 2 close, 4 open, 2 close, 5 open, 2 close, 2 open, 2 close, 11 open, 1 close, 1 open, 1 close.

22nd Row.—1 close, 1 open, 1 close, 8 open, 2 close, 2 open, + 2 close, 1 open + 3 times, 1 close, 4 open, 5 close, 1 open, 2 close, 3 open, 1 close, 1 open, 2 close, 2 open, 5 close, 1 open, 4 close, 13 open, 1 close, 1 open, 4 close, 13 open, 1 close, 1 open, 1 close.

23rd Row.—1 close, 1 open, 1 close, 10 open, 4 close, 1 open, 4 close, 1 open, 3 close, 2 open, 6 close, 1 open, 3 close, 2 open, 4 close, 3 open, 9 close, 6 open, 2 close, 4 open, 1 close, 1 open, 2 close, 1 open, 2 close, 13 open, 1 close, 1 open, 1 close.

24th Row.—1 close, 1 open, 1 close, 10 open, 2 close, 1 open, 2 close, 2 open, 2 close, 3 open, 3 close, 2 open, 4 close, 3 open, 1 close, 1 open, 1 close, 1 open, 2 close, 1 open, 3 close, 1 open, 2 close, 2 open, 3 close, 1 open, 3 close, 4 open, 2 close, 3 open, 1 close, 1 open, 4 close, 14 open, 1 close, 1 open, 1 close.

25th Row.—1 close, 1 open, 1 close, 11 open, 4 close, 5 open, 2 close, 4 open, 5 close, 4 open, 2 close, 4 open, 5 close, 1 open, 1 close, 3 open, 6 close, 3 open, 2 close, 3 open, 2 close, 2 open, 2 close, 3 open, 1 close, 10 open, 1 close, 1 open, 1 close.

26th Row.—1 close, 1 open, 1 close, 11 open, 2 close, 2 open, 2 close, 1 open, 2 close, 6 open, 2 close, 1 open, 1 close, 4 open, 2 close, 1 open, 4 close, 1 open, 4 close, 1 open, 1 close, 4 open, 5 close, 3 open, 2 close, 3 open, 4 close, 2 open, 3 close, 11 open, 1 close, 1 open, 1 close.

27th Row.—1 close, 1 open, 1 close, 10 open, 1 close, 4 open, 5 close, 3 open, 1 close, 2 open, 1 close, 3 open, 2 close, 4 open, 4 close, 1 open, 6 close, 1 open, 1 close, 3 open, 4 close, 3 open, 2 close, 2 open, 3 close, 5 open, 1 close, 2 open, 4 close, 7 open, 1 close, 1 open, 1 close.

28th Row.—1 close, 1 open, 1 close, 11 open, 4 close, 1 open, 1 close, 1 open, 1 close, 4 open, 2 close, 6 open, 2 close, 3 open, 4 close, 1 open, 3 close, 2 open, 1 close, 1 open, 2 close, 3 open, 1 close, 3 open, 7 close, 8 open, 1 close, 2 open, 1 close, 2 open, 1 close, 6 open, 1 close, 1 open, 1 close.

29th Row.—1 close, 1 open, 1 close, 8 open, 3 close, 1 open, 1 close, 2 open, 5 close, 4 open, 1 close, 3 open, 1 close, 4 open, 3 close, 1 open, 4 close, 3 open, 4 close, 2 open, 2 close, 1 open, 4 close, 1 open, 2 close, 3 open, 3 close, 1 open, 4 close, 5 open, 1 close, 8 open, 1 close, 1 open, 1 close.

30th Row.—1 close, 1 open, 1 close, 7 open, 1 close, 1 open, 1 close, 5 open, 2 close, 1 open, 2 close + 1 open, 3 close + twice, 1 open, 2 close, 2 open, 3 close, 1 open, 5 close, 1 open, 7 close, 2 open, 6 close, 1 open, 2 close, 4 open, 3 close, 1 open, 3 close, 13 open, 1 close, 1 open, 1 close.

31st Row.—This being the first diminishing row begin thus,—miss 1 stitch, slip 1, 1 Sc, 1 Dc,—reverse this in ending the row. All the diminished rows are begun and ended in the same manner. After the Dc stitch, 2 Ch, 1 close, 20 open, 4 close, 1 open, 4 close, 2 open, 11 close, 1 open, 5 close, 1 open, 9 close, 1 open, 2 close, 2 open, 3 close, 1 open, 6 close, 12 open, 1 close, 1 open; end as directed.

32nd Row.—Begin on the Dc, 1 slip, 1 Sc, 2 Dc, 2 Ch, 1 close, 12 open, 1 close, 6 open, 9 close, 2 open, 7 close, 3 open, 2 close, 2 open, 3 close + 1 open, 3 close + twice; 3 open, 2 close, 1 open, 2 close, 1 open, 2 close, 1 open, 4 close, 3 open, 1 close, 8 open, 1 close, 1 open; end as last.

33rd Row.—Begin with slip stitch, over slip, 1 Sc, 2 Dc, 2 Ch, 1 close, 7 open, 1 close, 5 open, 2 close, 4 open, 4 close, 1 open, 4 close, 3 open, 5 close, 2 open, 1 close, 2 open, 2 close, 1 open, 2 close, 1 open, 5 close, 1 open, 2 close, 3 open, 2 close, 1 open, 4 close, 1 open, 1 close, 4 open, 3 close, 9 open, 1 close, 1 open; end.

34th Row.—Slip on the 2nd Dc, 2 Sc, 1 open, 1 close, 7 open, 2 close, 5 open, 4 close, 2 open, 1 close, 1 open, 1 close, 1 open, 1 close, 2 open, 3 close, 4 open, 2 close, 3 open, 2 close, 5 open, 5 close, 5 open, 2 close, 2 open, 4 close, 1 open, 3 close, 2 open, 1 close, 2 open, 2 close, 6 open, 1 close, 1 open; end as begun.

35th Row.—Slip over 1st Dc, 2 Sc, 1 open, 1 close, 4 open, 1 close, 3 open, 5 close, 2 open, 1 close, 1 open, 4 close, 1 open, 4 close, 1 open, 1 close, 3 open, 11 close, 3 open, 2 close, 1 open, 2 close, 9 open, 3 close, 2 open, 1 close, 1 open, 2 close, 2 open, 1 close, 3 open, 1 close, 4 open, 1 close, 1 open; end as begun.

36th Row.—Begin with slip on Dc; 2 Sc, 1 open, 1 close, 4 open, 3 close, 3 open, 1 close, 5 open, 9 close, 4 open, 6 close, 1 open, 6 close, 7 open, 4 close, 5 open, 1 close, 4 open, 4 close, 10 open, 1 close, 1 open; end.

37th Row.—Begin with slip on Dc, 2 Sc, 1 open, 1 close, 5 open, 1 close, 2 open, 1 close, 3 open, 2 close, 1 open, 4 close, 1 close, 4 close, 4 open, 6 close, 1 open, 6 close, 7 open, 1 close, 1 open, 4 close, 8 open, 5 close, 8 open, 1 close, 1 open; end.

38th Row.—Begin with slip on Dc, 2 Sc, 1 open, 1 close, 3 open, 1 close, 6 open, 4 close, 1 open, 3 close, 1 open, 3 close, 2 open, 1 close, 4 open, 4 close, 1 open, 4 close, 2 open, 1 close, 3 open, 2 close, 1 open, 1 close, 14 open, 4 close, 7 open, 1 close, 1 open ; end.

39th Row.—Begin as before ; 1 open, 1 close, 11 open, 3 close, 3 open, 1 close, 5 open, 3 close, 2 open, 3 close, 3 open, 3 close, 3 open, 1 close, 1 open, 6 close, 2 open, 3 close, 11 open, 1 close, 6 open, 1 close, 1 open ; end as begun.

40th Row.—Begin as before ; 1 open, 1 close, 7 open, 3 close, 2 open, 1 close, 3 open, 1 close, 6 open, 4 close, 3 open, 3 close, 8 open, 1 close, 1 open, 2 close, 1 open, 7 close, 3 open, 1 close, 12 open, 1 close, 1 open ; end as begun.

41st Row.—Begin as before ; 1 open, 2 close, 4 open, 2 close, 1 open, 2 close, 1 open, 1 close, 2 open, 1 close, 2 open, 4 close, 3 open, 2 close, 4 open, 1 close, 1 open, 2 close, 1 open, 2 close, 4 open, 2 close, 2 open, 1 close, 1 open, 5 close, 2 open, 2 close, 10 open, 2 close, 1 open ; end.

42nd Row.—Begin as before ; 2 open, 1 close, 5 open, 1 close, 1 open, 1 close, 6 open, 6 close, 1 open, 1 close, 1 open, 3 close, 2 open, 1 close, 1 open, 5 close, 6 open, 3 close, 1 open, 3 close, 1 open, 1 close, 1 open, 2 close, 10 open, 1 close, 2 open ; end as before.

43rd Row.—Begin as before ; 1 close, 1 open, 1 close, 3 open, 2 close, 1 open, 1 close, 7 open, 3 close, 1 open, 3 close, 2 open, 3 close, 2 open, 1 close + 1 open + 3 times ; 2 close, 3 open, 5 close, 1 open, 3 close, 1 open, 1 close, 4 open, 1 close, 6 open, 1 close, 1 open, 1 close ; end as before.

44th Row.—Begin on the 4th Dc stitch, with 1 slip, 2 Sc on the chain of 2, 1 open, 2 close, 13 open, 8 close, 6 open, 5 close, 1 open, 2 close, 2 open, 5 close, 6 open, 4 close, 2 open, 1 close, 2 open, 2 close, 1 open ; end as before.

45th Row.—Begin with slip on Dc, 2 Sc on chain, 2 open, 1 close, 11 open, 1 close, 3 open, 3 close, 1 open, 2 close, 5 open, 2 close, 1 open, 2 close, 2 open, 1 close, 2 open, 1 close, 1 open, 3 close, 1 open, 2 close, 3 open, 1 close, 3 open, 2 close, 2 open, 1 close, 2 open ; end as before.

46th Row.—Slip ; 2 Sc, over 2 Ch, 4 Dc, 1 open (over close), 2 close, 7 open, 2 close, 2 open, 3 close, 1 open, 4 close, 4 open, 1 close, 2 open, 1 close, 8 open, 3 close, 1 open, 4 close, 3 open, 1 close, 2 open, 1 close, 1 open, 2 close, 1 open, 1 close ; end.

47th Row.—Begin as before ; 2 open over 2 close, 1 close, 7 open, 1 close, 1 open, 2 close, 1 open, 1 close, 1 open, 4 close, 3 open, 2 close, 2 open, 4 close, 9 open, 2 close, 1 open, 1 close, 7 open, 1 close, 2 open ; end as before.

48th Row.—Slip on Dc, 2 Sc on chain, 4 Dc, 1 open, 2 close, 4 open, 1 close, 2 open, 4 close, 2 open, 3 close, 3 open, 1 close, 2 open, 2 close, 1 open, 3 close, 7 open, 1 close, 1 open, 2 close, 6 open, 2 close, 1 open, 1 close ; end.

49th Row.—Slip on last of 4 Dc, 2 Sc on Ch, 2 open, 1 close, 3 open, 1 close, 2 open, 4 close, 4 open, 1 close, 6 open, 1 close, 1 open, 1 close, 2 open, 1 close, 7 open, 1 close, 3 open, 2 close, 3 open, 1 close, 2 open ; end.

50th Row.—Slip on Dc, 2 Sc on Ch, 1 close, 1 open, 2 close, 4 open, 3 close, 14 open, 2 close, 8 open, 1 close, 4 open, 1 close, 2 open, 2 close, 1 open, 1 close ; end.

51st Row.—Begin as before, over open ; 2 open, 2 close, 2 open, 1 close, 16 open, 2 close, 14 open, 2 close, 2 open ; end.

52nd Row.—Slip, 2 Sc on Ch, 1 close, 2 open, 2 close, 18 open, 1 close, 12 open, 2 close, 2 open, 1 close ; end.

53rd Row.—Slip, 2 Sc on Ch, 1 close, 2 open, 3 close, 15 open, 1 close, 9 open, 3 close, 2 open, 1 close ; end.

54th Row.—Slip 2 Sc on 2 Ch, 1 close, 3 open, 4 close, 17 open, 4 close, 3 open, 1 close ; end.

55th Row.—Slip ; 2 Sc on 2 Ch, 2 close, 4 open, 3 close, 11 open, 3 close, 4 open, 2 close ; end.

56th Row.—3 close, after beginning as usual, 3 open, 11 close, 3 open, 3 close ; end.

57th Row.—Begin over the open squares, Dc over them ; open over the close end as you begin.

58th Row.—Over the open only ; 1 slip, 2 Sc, 28 Dc, 2 Sc., 1 slip.

The border must be worked on the *wrong* side. Do a row of Sc at the bottom of the Anti-Macassar ; in the next row begin the pattern.

1st Row.—+ 1 bead, 4 cotton, 1 bead,

12 cotton, + repeat to the end in this and following ones.

2nd Row.— + 1 cotton, 1 bead, 3 C, 2 B, 1 C, 1 B, 9 C, +.

3rd Row.— + 1 C, 1 B, 3 C, 5 B, 6 C, 1 B, 1 C, +.

4th Row.— + 2 C, 1 B, 2 C, 5 B, 3 C, 1 B, 1 C, 2 B, 1 C, +.

5th Row.— + 3 C, 2 B, 1 C, 5 B, 1 C, 5 B, 1 C, +.

6th Row.— + 2 C, 1 B, 2 C, 3 B, 1 C, 2 B, 1 C, 4 B, 2 C, +.

7th Row.— + 6 C, 3 B, 1 C, 3 B, 1 C, 4 B, +.

8th Row.— + 6 B, 2 C, 2 B, 2 C, 1 B, 1 C, 3 B, 1 C, +.

9th Row.— + 5 B, 1 C, 5 B, 3 C, 1 B, 2 C, 1 B +.

10th Row.— + 5 C, 4 B, 3 C, 4 B, 2 C +.

11th Row.— + 7 C, 6 B, 1 C, 2 B, 2 C +.

12th Row.— + 1 C, 1 B, 4 B, 7 B, 2 C, 3 B, +

13th Row.— + 5 B, 1 C, 3 B, 1 C, 2 B, 5 C, 1 B, +.

Do one row of Sc, and one of Dc. The one of open square crochet, in every alternate square of which a fringe of 4 inches deep, is to be knotted. It is made by winding the thread on a card of that width, about twenty times. Cut the ends after it is knotted.

When the back, whether of crochet or calico is sewed on, add the following edge round the top and sides.

Open square crochet, at regular distances, all round.

2nd Row.—6 Dc under the chain of every alternate one.

This Anti-Macassar is suitable for a leather chair of ordinary size; it is easy to enlarge the design, by adding any number of stitches that can be divided by 6; and then allowing so many extra open squares, close to the side borders. 6 stitches, allow one at each side.

When the foundation chain is made, hold it across the back of the chair to see if it is large enough. There is a great difference in the size of the same design, if worked tightly or slackly. Good crochet is always *rather* tight.

LADIES' NECK-TIES,
IN APPLICATION.

Materials.—Three-quarters of a yard of cerise sarsenet ribbon 4 inches wide: a small piece of stiff black net; black beads and a few bugles. Of course, ribbon of any other colour would do as well as cerise; for half-mourning, a soft grey is extremely pretty; and for bridal toilette we saw, in Paris, a neck-tie (*cravate*) of white ribbon and blonde, ornamented with pearls and pearl bugles.

Application is the term given to that kind of embroidery in which the design appears in one substance on a ground of a different material. The fabric in which the pattern is to appear, is to be laid over the other, the design being previously marked on it; the two substances are then to be connected throughout all the outlines, either by *chain-stitch*, as in the pattern before us, or by laying on braid, cord, &c. The upper substance is then to be cut away carefully, in all those parts which constitute the ground, and the work is then said to be *appliqué*.

This work is extremely fashionable just now in Paris, for every ornamented article for the toilette. Gilets are about to be introduced in double application; collars, chemisettes, and many other things, are of muslin over net; and cravats and bracelets, *en-suite* of ribbon and blond, are worn by the most distinguished *élégantes*, and have a very rich and novel appearance.

The ribbons chosen for the two articles must correspond, that for the bracelet being about two inches and a half wide. The first thing to do is to prepare a pattern, which may be drawn from the engraving, and enlarged to four inches by five inches; or it may be bought, ready pounced, which saves trouble. The design for the bracelet should correspond. One end of ribbon for each should present the full pattern diminished to two inches and a half by three and a quarter, but the other end must have only the end of the design worked.

The pattern is transferred to the ribbon by the pounced pattern, and marked in the usual manner. The two ends of the broad piece are to be worked, leaving the bit between knot and neck-ribbon. Under each end lay a piece of stiff black tulle, rather larger than the design. This tulle afterwards forms the ground of the pattern, the ribbon being cut away from it. The design is worked in very close chain-stitch, with fine black silk, every part being completed before any is cut away. Two rows of chain-stitch are to be done round the edge, which is finished with a line of sor-

LADIES' NECK-TIE, IN APPLICATION, BY MRS. PULLAN.

rento edging (see the Point-lace Stitches, fully explained in this volume, pp. 36-40), a black bead being threaded on the silk at every long stitch. The same edging should finish that part of the ribbon which forms the knot. Short and long black bugles, and beads, are introduced as seen in the engraving.

The bracelets are worked in the same way, about three-quarters of a yard of ribbon being required for each one. The part which goes over the hand is lined, and has two elastic runners inserted in the usual manner; a band of bows, with one long end falling over the hand, and a short one in the opposite direction is then added, the long end not being more than four inches. The bows must be edged like the knot of the neck-tie.

Very light colours, as pink and blue, as well as white, should be *appliqué* on white net; if chain-stitched with white silk, the effect is still more delicate than if the tints of the ribbon itself be used. Pearls and pearl bugles are only admissible, of course, in evening toilette.

The pattern we have given would be very suitable for muslin on net, as a lappet or neck-tie. The design should be drawn with great accuracy, or the effect will be injured.

HUMAN LIFE.—The whole career of human life is a series of changes; its different periods are histories of transformation, and the whole species is a perpetual metamorphosis. A man of eighty is supposed to have renovated his whole body at least four - and - twenty times. The history of man is ultimately the theatre of vicissitudes, which He alone can review who animates all these figures. He builds and destroys, improves and modifies forms, while He changes the world around him. The wanderer upon earth, the transient ephemeron, can only admire the wonders of this great Agent, in a narrow circle: he enjoys the form that belongs to him in the general choir, adores, and disappears. "*I too was in Arcadia,*" should therefore be the epitaph of all living beings, in the ever-changing, ever-renovating creation.

B B

TRIMMING FOR A CHILD'S DRESS, IN BRODERIE ANGLAISE, BY MRS. PULLAN.

THE WORK-TABLE FRIEND.

TRIMMING FOR A CHILD'S DRESS,
IN BRODERIE ANGLAISE.

Materials.—French muslin, and W. Evans & Co.'s white embroidery cotton, Nos. 40 and 50.

WE give here a pattern for the flounce of a little girl's dress, and the edging for the sleeves and body, such a design hav-ing been considered by us useful to our readers. It is very quickly done, which may be considered as a great recommen-dation. The pattern is given the full size, so that the muslin may be marked from it. All the parts which are black in the en-graving, are cut out of the muslin altogether. These holes are traced round several times and worked over in graduated

CROCHET FLOWERS—HEART'S-EASE—BY MRS. PULLAN.

buttonhole stitches. In working those at the edge of the scallop, the stitches of one must touch those of the preceding one, so as to form, of themselves, an edge, beyond which a scallop of plain raised buttonhole stitch is made. The small leaves should also be cut out, and sewed over.

The tracing should be done with No. 40 cotton, and No. 50 should be used for all the sewing.

The muslin should be tacked on toile cirée, before being worked.

The design given is very suitable for trimming the small mandarin sleeves now worn, and it is particularly adapted for amateur workers, as a good effect is produced with very little trouble.

CROCHET FLOWERS.—HEART'S-EASE.

Materials—Violet-coloured wool, 1 skein; yellow ditto, and green, two shades of each, and 1 skein; a skein of coarse black sewing silk, and some very fine green wire.

THOSE who prefer it, may use fine chenille instead of Berlin wool for these flowers; that material giving the rich velvet-like surface peculiar to the heart's-ease. It is, however, indispensable that flowers made of chenille should be kept under a glass shade, as the least particle of dust destroys them.

For each flower cut five pieces of wire, four inches long. The wire is about the thickness of Evans's Boar's Head Cotton, No. 40.

THE PURPLE PETALS. 8 Ch; take the wire, and hold it in the left hand parallel with the chain, working it in at every stitch; miss 1, 1 Sc in the next, 1 semi-double crochet in next, 2 Dc in the next two, 2 Dc in one in the next, 2 Tc in one in the next, 5 Tc in the last; fold the wire, and work down the other side of the chain; 2 Tc in the first, 2 Dc in the next, 1 Dc in each of the two next, 1 semi-double in the next, 1 Sc in the last. Slip stitch at the end, on the first Sc, and make one chain. Cut off the wool, leaving about 1½ inches. Twist this a little, with the two ends of the wire.

Make two purple petals.

A semi-double stitch is begun like a

double crochet, but after drawing the loop of wool through the chain, when three threads are on the needle, bring a loop of wool through all three at once. It forms a medium stitch between a Sc and a Dc. We need scarcely remind our readers that the *first* stitch of a chain is never counted.

SMALL YELLOW PETALS, of which two are required for every flower. 7 Sc with the darker yellow; hold in a piece of wire, and work on one side of the chain, 1 Sc, 2 semi-double, 1 Dc, 2 Dc in one, 5 Dc in the last; on the other side,—2 Dc in one, 1 Dc, 2 semi-Dc, 1 Sc, 1 slip on the first Sc, 1 Ch; cut off the wool, leaving a small end, and twisting it with the wire.

LARGE YELLOW PETAL, with the lighter shade. 6 Ch; hold in a piece of wire, and work on the chain, 1 Sc, 1 semi-double, 1 Dc in the next, 1 Tc in the same, 1 Tc in the next, and on this Tc a Dc must be worked; 1 Tc in the last, 1 Dc on it, 5 more Tc in the same, 1 Dc on the last, 1 Tc on the first chain stitch on the other side, 1 Dc on it, 1 Tc and 1 Dc on the next, 1 semi-double on the next, 1 Sc on the next; 1 slip stitch and a chain to finish. Cut off the wool, and twist all the ends together ; take a piece of wire 8 inches long, bend it in half, and slip both the points through the heart of the flower ; cover the stem with dark green wool. Take a needleful of black silk, and work five long stitches on the large petal, and three on the small ones, making them of unequal lengths, and radiated from the base.

To make a group of Heart's-ease well, a variety of specimens should be introduced. Some may be entirely purple or golden ; and larger or smaller than the directions given.

The leaves should be made of several shades of green ; and two may be allowed for each flower. 20 Ch ; take a piece of green cannetille, the length of a finger, slip the end in the last chain stitch, and work over it, on the chain, 2 Sc, 2 Sdc, 2 Dc, 1 Sdc, 1 Sc, 1 Sdc, 5 Dc, 1 Sdc, 1 Sc, 1 Sdc, 1 Dc. Bend the wire, and work on the other side of the chain, 3 Sc in one, 1 Dc, 1 Sdc, 1 Sc, 1 Sdc, 5 Dc, 1 Sdc, 1 Sc, 1 Sdc, 2 Dc, 2 Sdc, 2 Sc. Slip a stitch at the end, in the first Sc ; make one chain, and cut off the wool, twisting the end in, with the ends of wire.

CARD-BASKET.

Materials.—2 yards of cotton cord, a skein of Vert-islay filoselle, fine and coarse wire, bright crimson wool, 6 skeins, ditto Vert-islay, 6 skeins ; filled red bugles, fluted white ditto, satin beads. A skein of each of five shades of crimson wool.

WORK over the end of the cord with the darkest wool, and close it into as small a round as possible. Do two rounds more, increasing so as to keep it perfectly flat.

Join on the filoselle and next lightest shade. + 5 wool, 2 silk. + 7 times in the round.

2nd Round.—Same colours. + 4 wool, 4 silk (the centre 2 over 2 silk). + 7 times.

3rd Round.—Next shade of wool, and silk. + 4 wool over 4, 6 silk. + 7 times.

4th Round.—Same colours. + 3 wool on 4, 3 silk, 3 wool (on 2 centre silk of last round), 3 wool. + 7 times.

5th Round.—Next shade, and silk. + 1 silk, 3 wool on centre one of 3, 3 silk, 7 wool, 2 silk. + 7 times.

6th Round.—Lightest shade. + 7 silk, 7 wool, 1 silk. + 7 times.

This completes the foundation of the basket.

The sides are formed of eight leaves, four of each colour, which are placed alternately round the middle, and connected by beads. A rather stout wire is bent, to form the outline of one leaf ; it must be about five inches long, and very pointed at the top.

A finer wire must be doubled over this point, and carried down the centre. Thread a rug-needle with either cerise or green wool, and darn closely backwards and forwards across the edge wires, beginning at the point, and completely covering one leaf. Twist the end of the wool with the wires at the bottom. When all are done, sew them to the foundation of the basket, and put a bit of cardboard, covered with calico, to cover the ends, and form the bottom.

Connect them together by threading one of the fluted bugles (which are upwards of an inch long), and passing it from one leaf to another, as near the *base* as possible. A little higher up, connect them in the same way with a filled red bugle, which, being shorter, brings the two leaves closer together. Two of these red bugles, at intervals, are followed by a white one ; and higher up still, rather less than an inch from the point, two

CARD-BASKET.

of these long white bugles, with a white satin bead between them. These are connected with the last by two more white bugles, forming a triangle from the satin bead and the ends of the fluted white.

The handle is made by covering a wire with wool, and then twisting it over a pencil into the form seen in the engraving. A satin bead is placed in each round, being threaded on wool, and dropped in its place. The wool is then carried twice round the two intermediate wires, so as to keep them in place. One handle is thus made in green, and one in cerise; and they are sewed to the points of leaves, to give the effect seen in the engraving.

Loops of satin beads then form a sort of pendent fringe to the basket, being attached to the point of each leaf, and the satin bead between the two bugles; then from the bugle to the point of the leaf again.

A row of satin beads is also carried down the centre of each leaf.

TAPESTRY.—The term "tapestry" is derived from the Latin word *tapes*, which originally signified "a carpet," or "covering," for a bed or couch, but is now generally applied to the textile fabrics usually made of wool or silk, embroidered with figures, landscapes, and fanciful compositions, sometimes enriched with gold and silver, and even jewels introduced among the various colours. In the olden time the walls were covered with the work. In the middle ages this art was elevated to such a degree, that Raphael was employed to make the designs for the hangings at the Vatican, which were worked at Arras, a town in Artois; and, consequently, we find that tapestry hangings are frequently called *arras*. The arras was hung on wooden frames, and therefore vacant spaces were left between the arras and the walls, which frequently served for concealment; and we find many allusions to it made in Shakspere.

SWISS LACE COLLAR, BY MRS. PULLAN.

THE WORK-TABLE FRIEND.

SWISS LACE COLLAR.

Materials.—The finest Brussels net, and book-muslin, with the point-lace cottons and embroidery thread, No, 70. of Messrs. W. Evans & Co.; also two yards of fine pearl edging.

THIS pattern is in the same style as that generally known to our readers under the name of Swiss Appliqué Lace. The pattern which must be drawn on the muslin, is entirely in that material, the ground being net, and the open parts of the flowers in Point Lace stitches. Among these is one that is quite new to our readers. It is called Brussels spots. Bars and cross bars are made, as for English lace, but instead of the round spot worked where these cross each other, a loop of thread is made, over another needle, between every two threads, by tacking a tight button-hole stitch on the cross. Four of these loops will be made at every cross, and will produce the appearance seen in the engraving. This stitch must invariably be done with the *finest* of the point Lace Cottons, namely No. 150 Boar's-head.

The English Lace is to be done with No. 100, and the English bars (seen in the bud), in Mecklenburgh 121.

After the muslin and net are tacked together, the outlines are to be traced entirely in embroidery cotton. They are then to be sewed over, in No. 70 Boar's-head, with a thread of No. 80 Mecklenburgh held in. A double line of tracing is to be made for the scallops, forming the edge of the collar. It is to be run *within* that in the engraving, and covered with button-hole stitch done in the embroidery cotton. The pearl edging is to be added.

We give the section the full size.

DEEP CROCHET EDGING, BY MRS. PULLAN.

DEEP CROCHET EDGING.

THIS edging is suitable for trimming skirts, &c., for which purpose No. 16 or 20 of W. Evans & Co.'s Boar's-head crochet cotton will be suitable. For children's drawers and frocks, No. 30 of the same manufacture may be used.

Make a chain of the required length, the number of stitches being divisible by 32, with a few over, if the work is to be done in a length. For drawers, and anything else, when the exact quantity for each piece can be ascertained, it is desirable to close the chain in a round, and work round on it.

1st Row.—Dc.

2nd Row.—+ 4 Dc, 3 Ch, miss 3, 4 Dc, 6 Ch, miss 5, 1 Sc, 11 Ch, miss 9, Sc on the 10th, 6 Ch, miss 5, + repeat,

3rd Row.—+ 2 Dc on the first two of 4 Dc, 2 Ch, miss 2, 3 Dc on 3 chains, miss 2, 2 Dc, 6 Ch, miss 4, 1 Sc, * 5 Ch, miss 3, 1 Sc, * 4 times, 6 Ch, miss 4 + repeat.

4th Row.— Begin on the first Dc of last row. + 4 Dc, 3 Ch, miss 3, 4 Dc, 6 Ch, miss 4, 1 Sc, 7 Ch, miss 1 loop, Sc on the centre of the next, 7 Ch, Sc on the centre of the next, 7 Ch, miss 1 loop, Sc

on the 2nd of the 6 Ch of the next, 6 Ch + repeat.

5th Row.—+ 2 Dc on the first two of 4 Dc, 3 Ch, miss 3, 1 Dc, 3 Ch, miss 3, 2 Dc, 6 Ch, miss 4, 1 Sc, 9 Ch, miss the next loop, and Sc on the 3rd of the 7 Ch of the following loop, 3 Ch, miss 1, 1 Sc, 9 Ch, miss 1 loop, Sc on the 2nd stitch of the next, 6 Ch, + repeat.

6th Row.—+ Sc on the first Dc of the last row, 9 Dc on the next 9 stitches, Sc on the next. 3 Ch, miss 3, 1 Sc, 5 Ch, Sc on the 5th of 9 Ch, 18 Ch, miss the small loop and Sc on the 5th of the next 9 chain, 5 Ch, Sc on the 3rd of 6th Ch, 3 Ch, + repeat.

7th Row.—+ Sc on the first Sc of last row, 5 Ch, miss 3, Dc in the 4th, 3 Ch, miss 1, Dc in the 2nd, 5 Ch, miss 3, Dc in the 4th, 7 Ch, miss 3 of the 18 Ch, 5 Dc, 2 Dc in each of the next 2, 5 more Dc, 7 Ch, + repeat.

8th Row.—+ 11 Dc, beginning on the 3rd chain, after the first single crochet of last row, 3 Ch, miss 6, Sc in the 7th, 3 Ch, miss 4, Sc on the 5th, * 5 Ch, miss 4, Sc on the 2nd, * twice, 5 Ch, miss 2, Sc on the 3rd 5 Ch, miss 1, Dc on the 2nd 5 Ch, miss 1, Dc on 2nd, 3 Ch, miss 4, Sc on the 5th 3 Ch, + repeat.

9th Row.—+ Begin on the third of the 11 Dc. + 7 Dc, 6 Ch, miss the 1st chain of 3, Sc under the 2nd, 3 Ch, Sc under the next loop, 5 Ch, Sc under the next, 7 Ch, Sc under the next, 7 Ch, Sc under the next, 5 Ch, Sc under the next, 3 Ch, Sc under the next, 6 Ch, + repeat.

10th Row.—Begin on the 4th of the 6 chain before the Dc stitches. + 1 Sc, 1 Sdc, 9 Dc, 1 Sdc, 1 Sc, 4 Ch, Sc under the next loop, 5 Ch, Sc under the next, 7 Ch, Sc under the next, 9 Ch, Sc under the next, 7 Ch, Sc under the next, 5 Ch, Sc under the next, 4 Ch, + repeat.

11th Row.—Begin on the first Sc stitch. + Sc on Sc, 5 Ch, close into a loop, 1 Sc, 1 Sdc, 1 Dc, 5 Ch, close, * 3 Dc, 5 Ch, close, *twice, 1 Dc, 1 Sdc, 1 Sc, 5 Ch, close. These 5 chains, closed into a loop, form *a picot.* Slip-stitch all the rest of each pattern, making a picot on the centre of every loop, and on every Sc stitch.

APRON. BRODERIE EN LACET APRON.

Materials.—¾ of a yard of broad black silk, either brocaded or *glacé*; 2 skeins of brilliant cerise Russia braid, of the narrowest size, and ¼ of an ounce of sewing silk of exactly the same shade; black girdle.

The pattern given in the engraving is to be enlarged to the full size for an apron; then draw it on good writing-paper, and prick all the outlines, at equal distances, with a coarse needle. The holes should be about eight to the inch, and one half the apron only need be drawn and marked. The pattern so prepared is termed a *pounced pattern.* Lay the paper on the silk, so as to cover one half of it, and rub it all over with fine pounce, using a broad flat stump. Remove the paper, and the design will be clearly seen on the silk. Shake all the particles of pounce off the pattern, then lay it on the other side, and mark the remaining half in the same manner. Grind a little flake-white up with gum-water, and mark over all the outlines with this mixture, using a fine sable brush. When dry, the whole pattern must be braided. Each flower, with its attendant leaves and stem, is done separately. Begin it, therefore, at the end of the stem of each spray, drawing all the ends of braid through the silk with a chenille needle. Before you begin to braid, cut

off two lengths of three-quarters of a yard each and draw out the strands of the braid from these pieces, for running on the remainder.

The flowers are filled in with the sewing silk, in point-lace stitches. The petals of the open rose are alternately filled with Venetian and English lace; a Mechlin wheel being worked in the centre, and a Venetian bar at the base of each petal. The small leaves and stems are done in Point d'Alençon; the small flower has a Mechlin wheel in the centre, and the inner edges are finished with Venetian edging. The petals of the other flower are marked by edged Venetian bars, the spaces between being filled with English bars, taken on every alternate stitch of the Brussels with which the bars are edged.

This sort of work, of which this is the first specimen ever given to the public, is well adapted for children's dresses, bags, and other articles. Pounced patterns may be procured at shops.

VINE-LEAF CARD PURSE.

Materials.—3 skeins of fine crimson purse silk; 2 skeins of black ditto, and 4 skeins of gold thread, the same thickness. A handsome tassel of crimson and black, with gold balls, crimson cord, and 2 gold slides.

Make a chain of 9 stitches with the crimson silk. Close it into a round, in which do 18 stitches.

2nd Row.—(Begin black) + 2 black on one crimson, 1 crimson on crimson + 9 times.

3rd Row.— + 2 black on the 2 black, 2 crimson on 1 crimson + 9 times.

4th Row.— + 2 black on the 2 black, 2 crimson on 1 crimson, 1 crimson on the next crimson, + 9 times.

5th Row.— + 2 black on 2, 4 crimson on 3 + 9 times.

6th Row.— + 2 black on 2, 5 crimson on 4, + 9 times.

7th Row.— + 3 black on 2, 5 crimson on 5 + 9 times.

8th Row.— + 4 black on 3, 5 crimson on 5 + 9 times.

BRODERIE EN LACET APRON, BY MRS. PULLAN.

9th Row.— + 5 black on 4, 5 crimson on 5, + 9 times.

10th Row.— + 6 black, 3 crimson over the centre 3 of 5, 1 black.

11th Row.—Join on the gold instead of the crimson, + 1 black, 3 gold (on the 2nd, 3rd, and 4th of 6 black), 7 black, doing 2 in 1 over 1 crimson, + 9 times.

12th Row.— + 5 gold, 6 black, + 9 times.

13th Row.— + 1 gold, 3 black, 2 gold, 5 black over 4, 1 gold, + 9 times.

14th Row.— + 5 black, 1 gold, 6 black over 5, 1 gold, + 9 times.

15th Row.— + 5 black, 1 gold, 7 black over 6, 1 gold, + 9 times.

16th Row.—All black. Fasten off black.

17th Row.—All gold.

18th Row.—All crimson.

19th Row.— + 5 gold, 1 crimson, + 21 times.

20th Row.—The same.

21st Row.— + 1 crimson, 3 gold, 2 crimson, + 21 times.

22nd Row.—Like 21st.

23rd and 24th Rows.— + 2 crimson, 1 gold (on the centre one of three gold,) 3 crimson, + 21 times.

25th and 26th Rows.—All crimson.

27th Row.— + 2 crimson, 2 black, 8 crimson, 2 gold, 8 crimson, 1 gold, 18 crimson, 1 gold, + 3 times.

28th Row.— + 1 crimson, 1 black, 2 crimson, 1 black, 6 crimson, 4 gold, 7 crimson, 2 gold, 14 crimson, 4 gold, + 3 times.

29th Row.— + 1 crimson, 1 black, 8 crimson, 6 gold, 6 crimson, 3 gold, 10 crimson, 1 gold, 1 crimson, 5 gold, + 3 times.

30th Row.— + 2 crimson, 1 black, 6 crimson, 7 gold, 4 crimson, 1 gold, 1 crimson, 4 gold, 1 crimson, 2 gold, 2 crimson, 1 gold, 2 crimson, 8 gold, + 3 times.

31st Row.— + 3 crimson, 1 black, 4 crimson, 4 gold, 1 black, 3 gold, 4 crimson, 9 gold, 1 crimson, 3 gold, 1 crimson, 2 gold, 1 black, 2 gold, 1 black, 2 gold, + 3 times.

32nd Row—. + 4 crimson, 1 black, 3 crimson, 1 gold, 1 black, 1 gold, 1 black, 4 gold, 4 crimson, 3 gold, 1 black, 5 gold, 1 crimson, 6 gold, 1 black, 1 gold, 1 black, 3 gold, + 3 times.

33rd Row.— + 4 crimson, 1 black, 1

VINE-LEAF CARD-PURSE, BY MRS. PULLAN.

crimson, 4 gold, 2 black, 6 gold, 3 crimson, 3 gold, 1 black, 3 gold, 2 crimson, 6 gold, 2 black, 3 gold, 1 crimson,+3 times.

34th Row.— + 3 crimson, 1 black, 2 crimson, 5 gold, 1 black, 2 gold, 1 black, 3 gold, 4 crimson, 2 gold, 1 black, 4 gold, 1 crimson, 2 gold, 1 black, 3 gold, 1 black, 5 gold.+3 times.

35th Row.—+ 2 crimson, 1 black, 3 crimson, 2 gold, 1 black, 1 gold, 1 black, 2 gold, 1 black, 4 gold, 2 crimson, 5 gold, 1 black, 6 gold, 1 black, 2 gold, 1 black, 6 gold,+3 times.

36th Row.—+ 5 black, 2 crimson, 1 gold, 1 black, 1 gold, 3 black, 5 gold, 2 crimson, 5 gold, 3 black, 3 gold, 1 black, 2 gold, 4 black, 3 gold, 1 crimson, + 3 times.

37th Row.— + 1 crimson, 1 black, 2 crimson, 2 black, 1 crimson, 2 gold, 2 black, 4 gold, 1 black, 3 gold, 1 crimson, 2 gold, 5 black, 4 gold, 3 black, 6 gold, 2 crimson, + 3 times.

38th Row.— + 2 crimson, 1 black, 3 crimson, 1 black, 1 crimson, 3 gold, 4 black, 4 gold, 2 crimson, 3 gold, 3 black, 3 gold, 2 black, 7 gold, 3 crimson, + 3 times.

39th Row.—+ 2 crimson, 1 black, 4 crimson, 1 black, 1 crimson, 2 gold, 1 black, 6 gold, 4 crimson, 5 gold, 3 black, 2 gold, 3 black, 7 gold, + 3 times.

40th Row.— + 2 crimson, 1 black, 5 crimson, 2 black, 1 gold, 1 black, 3 gold, 1 black, 1 gold, 1 crimson, 3 gold, 3 crimson, 2 gold, 2 black, 2 gold, 1 black, 10 gold, 1 crimson, + 3 times.

41st Row.— + 2 black, 2 crimson, 6 gold, 2 black, 2 gold, 1 black, 7 gold, 1 crimson, 3 black, 2 gold, 1 black, 11 gold, 2 crimson, + 3 times.

42nd Row.—+ 3 crimson, 4 gold, 3 black, 2 gold, 1 black, 1 gold, 1 black, 3 gold, 2 black, 3 gold, 1 crimson, 3 gold, 4 black 3 gold, 2 crimson, 3 gold, 2 crimson, 1 black, + 3 times.

43rd Row.—+ 5 crimson, 3 gold, 1 black, 4 gold, 1 black, 2 gold, 2 black, 4 gold, 2 crimson, 2 gold, 1 black, 1 gold, 1 black, 2 gold, 2 black, 2 gold, 6 crimson, 1 black + 3 times

44th Row.— + 3 crimson, 4 gold, 1 black, 6 gold, 2 black, 4 gold, 4 crimson, 2 gold, 1 black, 2 gold, 1 black, 6 gold, 5 crimson, 1 black, + 3 times.

45th Row.— + 2 crimson, 4 gold, 1 black, 1 gold, 1 black, 4 gold, 1 black, 2 gold, 1 black, 6 gold, 2 crimson, 4 gold, 1 black, 6 gold, 4 crimson, 1 black, 1 crimson, + 3 times.

46th Row.— + 1 crimson, 5 gold, 1 black, 1 gold, 1 black, 3 gold, 1 black, 4 gold, 1 black, 6 gold, 1 crimson, 5 gold, 1 black, 5 gold, 3 crimson, 1 black, 2 crimson, + 3 times.

47th Row.— + 1 crimson, 4 gold, 1 black, 6 gold, 1 black, 4 gold, 2 black, 5 gold, 1 crimson, 6 gold, 1 black, 2 gold, 4 crimson, 1 black, 3 crimson, + 3 times.

48th Row.— + 3 crimson, 2 gold, 1 black, 3 gold, 1 crimson, 2 gold, 1 black, 4 gold, 1 black, 1 gold, 1 black, 2 gold, 3 crimson, 1 gold, 1 crimson, 4 gold, 1 black, 3 gold, 2 crimson, 1 black, 3 crimson, + 3 times.

49th Row.— + 2 crimson, 2 gold, 1 black, 4 gold, 1 crimson, 7 gold, 1 black, 2 gold, 1 black, 2 gold, 4 crimson, 5 gold, 1 black, 2 gold, 2 crimson, 1 black, 4 crimson, + 3 times.

50th Row.— + 2 crimson, 2 gold, 1 black, 4 gold, 2 crimson, 3 gold, 1 crimson, 6 gold, 1 black, 2 gold, 4 crimson, 7 gold, 2 crimson, 1 black, 2 crimson, 1 black, 1 crimson, + 3 times.

51st Row.— + 3 crimson, 7 gold, 2 crimson, 3 gold, 1 crimson, 10 gold, 4 crimson, 1 gold, 1 crimson, 4 gold, 2 crimson, 3 black, 2 crimson, + 3 times.

52nd Row.— + 2 crimson, 3 gold, 1 crimson, 2 gold, 4 crimson, 1 gold, 3 crimson, 10 gold, 7 crimson, 2 gold, 7 crimson, + 3 times.

53rd Row.— + 2 crimson, 2 gold, 13 crimson, 1 gold, 2 crimson, 5 gold, 9 crimson, 1 gold, 7 crimson, + 3 times.

Do 2 rounds of crimson only, fastening off the black; then 2 like the 23rd, 2 more like the 21st, and 2 more like the 19th. After this, 1 round of scarlet, and 1 of gold will complete the close part of the purse.

Join on the black, fastening off the others, do 1 round of Sc.

2nd Round.— + 1 Dc, 1 Ch, miss 1, + repeat all round.

3rd Round.— + Dc under the chain, 1 Ch, + repeat.

Do 5 more rounds like the last.

For the frill. Count 3 open rounds, and miss them; on the top of the 4th work with the crimson, + 5 Dc over 1 Dc, 1 Ch, miss 2 Dc, + repeat.

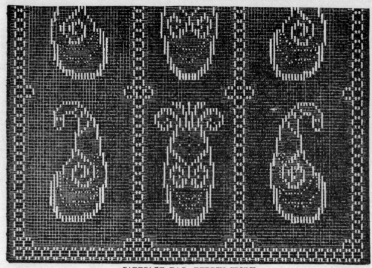

CARRIAGE BAG, BERLIN WORK.

With the gold, do a Sc stitch on every stitch of the last round.

3rd Round.—Crimson, + 5 Dc over the centre of 5 Dc, 1 Ch, + repeat.

4th Round.—Like 2nd.

Run cords in the two rounds above the frill, leaving one, at the top, vacant. Conceal the joins with the small slides; fasten on the tassel.

———

CARRIAGE BAG, BERLIN WORK.

Materials.—Penelope canvas, No. 18. Black, chalk-white, turquoise, blue, and garnet beads, No. 1. Steel beads, No. 12, and fine black crochet silk.

WE have here succeeded in giving our friends a Berlin pattern from which they can work.

The entire pattern of this bag is done in beads, and the ground in common cross-stitch with the black silk. Nothing can be prettier than the effect of this ground, when the design is in beadwork. It throws the beads so completely into relief, that it is a great improvement on wool, and is very much lighter in the hand, which is also desirable, as the beads are necessarily heavy.

Beads are thus distinguished in the engraving:—

Black—Black squares.

White—White lines, as in the outlines of the pine.

Blue—Horizontal lines, as in the inner part of the pine.

Steel—Round dots.

Garnets—Small crosses in the squares.

Ground—Perpendicular lines.

The bag may be either worked with a different pattern in the centre line, as in the engraving, or with the same pine repeated in each division. In the latter case four patterns may be worked in the width and two in depth. The bags require to be made up at a warehouse, and fitted with a padlock.

———

JEWELLED DOYLEY PATTERN.

THE WORK-TABLE FRIEND.

JEWELLED DOYLEY.—EMERALDS AND GARNETS.

Materials.—4 reels of Messrs. W. Evans & Co.'s Boar's Head Crochet Cotton, No. 16, 1 oz. of Garnet beads, No. 2, and 1 oz. of Emerald ditto.

THREAD the garnet beads on one of the reels of cotton, and the emerald on another.

Begin with the reel on which the garnet beads are threaded. Make a chain of 6, close it into a round.

1st Round.—+ 1 Sc, 1 Ch, miss none + 6 times.

2nd Round.—+ 2 Sc, 1 Ch, miss none + 6 times.

3rd Round.—+ 3 Sc, 1 Ch, miss none + 6 times.

Continue to increase in this way, until, in the ninth round, there are 9 Sc in each of the 6 divisions, with a chain after every ring.

10th Round.—+ 10 garnets, 1 Ch, miss none + 6 times. Fasten off the garnet thread, and add on the emerald.

11th Round.—Increase 6 stitches in this round + 3 cotton, 1 bead, 2 cotton + 12 times.

12th Round.—+ 2 cotton, 3 beads (the second over 1 bead), 2 cotton over 1 + 12 times.

13th Round.—+ 1 cotton, 5 beads, 1 cotton + 12 times.

14th Round.—+ 2 cotton, 3 beads (on centre 3 of 5), 2 cotton + 12 times.

15th Round.—+ 3 cotton, 1 bead (on centre 1 of 3), 3 cotton. 1 Ch, miss none + 12 times. Fasten off the emerald, and add the garnet cotton. Do 3 cotton more.

16th Round.—+ 4 cotton, 1 bead (on the 1 Ch of last round), 3 cotton + 12 times.

17th Round.—+ 3 cotton, 3 beads (the centre on 1), 2 cotton, 1 Ch, miss none + 12 times.

18th Round.—2 cotton, 5 beads (over 3 and a cotton at each side), 2 cotton + 12 times.

19th Round.—+ 1 cotton, 7 beads, 1 cotton, 1 Ch, miss none + 12 times. Add on the emerald bead cotton, and work with both, just as you work with variously-coloured silks in purses.

20th Round.—This round has a bead on every stitch. + 3 garnets, 3 emeralds (on centre 3 of 7 garnets in last round), 4 garnets, the 4th on 1 Ch of last round + 12 times.

21st Round.—+ 2 garnets, 1 Ch, 1 cotton over 3rd garnet of last round, 3 emeralds over 3, 1 cotton, 1 Ch, miss none, 3 garnets + 12 times.

22nd Round.—+ 1 garnet, 2 cotton, 5 emeralds (over 3 and a cotton on each side), 2 cotton, 2 garnets + 12 times.

23rd Round.—+ 2 cotton, 7 emeralds, 2 cotton, 1 garnet (on 2nd of 2 garnets) + 12 times.

24th Round.—+ 3 emeralds (coming over 2 cotton and the first of 7 emeralds), 1 Ch, miss none, 1 cotton over 2nd emerald, 3 garnets (on centre 3 of 7 beads) 1 cotton, 1 Ch, miss none, 4 emeralds, +, 12 times.

25th Round.—+ 3 emeralds on 3, 2 cotton, 3 garnets on 3, 2 cotton, 1 Ch, miss none, 4 emeralds on 4, + 12 times.

26th Round.—+ 2 emeralds (on first 2 of 3), 3 cotton (on 1 bead, 1 cotton), 5 garnets (on 3 and a cotton on each side), 3 cotton, 3 emeralds, + 12 times.

27th Round.—+ 2 emeralds on 2, 3 cotton on 3, 2 garnets, 2 cotton on 3rd garnet, 2 garnets, 3 cotton, 3 emeralds, + 12 times.

28th Round.—+ 1 emerald, 3 cotton, 3 garnets, 2 cotton on 2, 3 garnets, 3 cotton, 2 emeralds, + 12 times.

29th Round.—+ 1 emerald on 1, 3 cotton, 2 garnets (on first two of 3), 2 cotton, 1 Ch, miss none, 2 more cotton, 2 garnets, on 2 last of 3), 3 cotton, 2 eme-ralds on 2, + 12 times.

30th Round.—+ 1 emerald on 1, 3 cotton, 2 garnets on 2, 2 cotton, 1 emerald over 1 Ch, 2 cotton, 2 garnets, 3 cotton, 2 emeralds, + 12 times.

31st Round.—+ 1 emerald, 3 cotton, 2 garnets, 1 cotton, 1 Ch, miss none, 1 cotton, 1 emerald on one, 1 cotton, 1 Ch, miss none, 1 cotton, 2 garnets, 3 cotton, 2 emeralds, + 12 times.

32nd Round.—+ 4 cotton, 2 garnets (on 2), 2 cotton, 3 emeralds (the second on one), 2 cotton, 2 garnets, 4 cotton, 1 emerald on 2nd of 2, + 12 times.

33rd Round.—+ 4 cotton, 2 garnets, 2 cotton, 1 Ch, 3 emeralds on 3, 1 Ch, miss none, 2 cotton, 2 garnets, 4 cotton, 1 emerald on 1, + 12 times.

34th Round.—+ 4 cotton, 2 garnets on 2, 3 cotton, 3 emeralds on 3, 3 cotton, 2 garnets on 2, 4 cotton, 1 emerald on 1, + 12 times.

35th Round.—Like 34th.

36th Round.—+ 4 cotton, 3 garnets, 3 cotton, 1 emerald on centre one of 3, 3 cotton, 3 garnets, 5 cotton, + 12 times.

37th Round.—+ 5 cotton, 2 garnets, 3 cotton on 3, 1 emerald on 1, 3 cotton, 2 garnets, 6 cotton, + 12 times. Fasten off emeralds.

38th Round.—+ 5 cotton, 3 garnets, 5 cotton, 3 garnet, 6 cotton, + 12 times.

39th Round.—+ 6 cotton, 1 Ch, miss none, 9 garnets, 1 Ch, miss none, 7 cotton, + 12 times.

40th Round.—+ 8 cotton, 7 garnets (over centre 7 of 9), 9 cotton, + 12 times.

41st Round.—All cotton. Fasten on the emeralds, and do one round, dropping an emerald bead on every stitch. Then do a round in cotton, and afterwards one with a garnet bead on every stitch. Do another round of cotton, and fasten off.

THE BORDER.—Work the cotton on which emeralds are threaded, + Dc, 3 Ch, Dc in same, miss 3, + repeat all round.

2nd Round.—3 Dc under the chain, dropping 2 emeralds on each stitch, + 2 Ch with an emerald on each, 3 Dc under the next chain, with two beads on each, + repeat all round, and fasten off.

SOFA-CUSHION PATTERN.

SOFA CUSHION.

Materials—A large square of blue or black cloth, two pieces of gold-coloured Albert braid, a piece of Groseille ditto, and a piece of suitable French soutache. Cord and four tassels.

THIS consists of a rich centre pattern, and a Greek border, in which handsome scrolls are worked. The Greek pattren should be worked in gold-coloured Albert braid; or on a blue ground, a black braid may be used. Those who do not regard expense may make a very handsome cushion by the application of black velvet on the cloth, for the Greek pattern. Velvet ribbon may be laid on for this purpose; or the design may be cut out of a square of any gold German velvet. In that case, the edges must be finished with black Albert or Russian braid; and a line of black glass beads, No. 1, may be laid along the centre of the velvet. The scrolls within the border are to be braided with a handsome soutache, or with Albert braid. The soutache should be selected with reference to the other colours of the cushion—a remark which applies equally to the braid. Black velvet and braid, with blue in the centre, on a claret ground, would be very rich. On a green ground, two shades of violet braid, with black velvet, might be used.

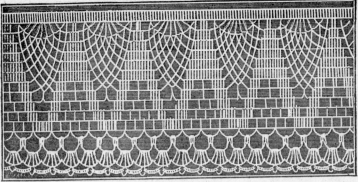

CROCHET EDGING.

THE WORK-TABLE FRIEND.

HANDSOME CROCHET LACE,
SUITABLE FOR TOILET COVERS, ANTIMACASSARS, ETC.

Materials.—Messrs. W. Evans & Co.'s Boar's Head Crochet Cotton, No. 16, with a suitable hook.

MAKE a chain of the required length, and work one row in Dc.

1st Pattern Row.—+ 2 Dc in one, 2 Ch, miss 2, 1 Dc, 2 Ch, miss 3, 1 Dc, 2 Ch, 1 Dc in same, * 2 Ch, Dc in next, 2 Ch, Dc in same, * 3 times; 2 Ch, miss 3, 1 Dc, 2 Ch, miss 2, + repeat to the end.

2nd Row.—+ 4 Dc (over 2 Dc and a chain on each side), 3 Ch, Sc under the chain between the first 2 Dc in one stitch, * 3 Ch, Dc under the next chain, * 6 times; 3 Ch, + repeat to the end.

3rd Row.—+ 6 Dc (over 4 Dc and a chain at each side), 3 Ch, Sc under the chain after the first Sc, * 3 Ch, Sc under the next chain, * 5 times; 3 Ch, + repeat to the end.

4th Row.—+ 8 Dc (over 6 Dc and a chain at each side), 2 Ch, Sc under the chain after the first Sc, * 3 Ch, Sc under the next chain, * 4 times, 2 Ch, + repeat to the end.

5th Row.—+ 10 Dc (over 8 Dc and a chain at each side), 2 Ch, Sc under the chain after the first Sc, * 3 Ch, Sc under the next chain, * 3 times; 2 Ch, + repeat to the end.

6th Row.—+ 12 Dc (over 10 Dc and a chain on each side), 2 Ch, Sc under chain after the first Sc, * 3 Ch, Sc under next chain, * twice, 2 Ch, + repeat to the end.

7th Row.—Begin on the chain stitch before the 12 Dc, + 4 Dc, 3 Ch, miss 2, 2 Dc, 3 Ch, miss 2, 4 Dc, 2 Ch, Sc under chain after first Sc, 3 Ch, Sc under next chain, 2 ch, + repeat to the end.

8th Row.—Begin on the chain before the first 4 Dc, + 4 Dc, 4 Ch, 2 Dc over 2 Dc, 4 Ch, miss 4, 4 Dc, 2 Ch, Dc under the chain of 3, 2 Ch, + repeat to the end.

9th Row.—Begin on the chain stitch before the first 4 Dc, + 4 Dc, 3 Ch, Dc under the chain of 4, 3 Ch, Dc under the next chain, 3 Ch, 4 Dc, beginning on the second of 4, 3 Ch, + repeat to the end.

10th Row.—Begin on the second of the last 4 Dc, + 4 Dc, 1 Ch, miss the second of 3 Ch, 4 Dc, 3 Ch, 1 Dc under Ch, 3 Ch, Dc under next Ch, 3 Ch, Dc under next Ch, 3 Ch, + repeat to the end.

11th Row.—+ 5 Dc, the middle one on the 1 Ch, * 3 Ch, Dc under next chain, * 4 times, 3 Ch, + repeat to the end.

12th Row.—+ Sc over the third of 5 Dc, 6 Ch, Sc on Dc after 3 Ch, 6 Ch, miss 3 Ch and Sc under the next 3, 6 Ch, Sc on second Dc from that, chain 6 Ch, + repeat to the end.

13th Row.—+ 3 Dc under Ch, 5 Ch, + repeat to the end.

14th Row.—+ 1 Dc, 1 Ch, + 5 times under every chain.

15th Row.—+ Sc on the third of 5 Dc, 6 Ch, + repeat to the end.

16th Row.—+ Slip on a Sc stitch, 5 Ch, slip on the same, Sc on each of the 6 Ch of last row. + repeat to the end.

JEWELLED DOYLEY—RUBIES AND MALACHITES.

Materials.—2 reels of Messrs. W. Evans and Co.'s Boar's Head Crochet Cotton, No. 24, half an ounce of Malachites, and the same quantity of Ruby Beads, No. 3.

THREAD the ruby beads on one reel of cotton, and the malachite on another.

JEWELLED DOYLEYS.—RUBIES AND MALACHITES.

Begin with that reel on which the rubies are threaded. Make a chain of 10, close it into a round, and do a Sc stitch in every chain.

2nd Round.—+ 1 Sc, 1 Ch, miss none + 10 times.

3rd Round.—+ 2 Sc, 1 Ch, miss none + 10 times.

4th Round.—+ 3 Sc, 1 Ch, miss none + 10 times.

Continue to increase 10 stitches in every round, at equal distances, until there are 90 stitches in the round, when do two rounds without increase, dropping a bead on every stitch. Join on the other cotton, and do 4 stitches.

1st Pattern Round.—+ 5 cotton on 4, 1 malachite, 4 cotton + The repetition between the crosses occurs 10 times in every round.

2nd Round.—+ 4 cotton, 3 malachite (the 2nd on 1), 4 cotton on 3, +

3rd Round.—+ 3 cotton, 5 m (the 3 centre on 3 m), 3 cotton +

4th Round.—+ 3 cotton on 2, 7 m (the centre 5 on 5), 2 cotton +

5th Round.—+ 2 cotton, 9 m (the centre 7 on 7), 2 cotton on 1 +

6th Round.—+ 2 cotton on 1, 11 m (the centre 9 on 9), 1 cotton +

7th Round.—Rubies and malachites + 1 ruby on the 1st of 2 cotton, 2 cotton, 9 malachites (on centre 9 of 11) 2 cotton + The 10th time these 2 cotton are worked on 1 stitch.

8th Round.—+ 3 r (the 2nd on 1 r), 2 cotton, 7 m (on centre 7 of 9), 3 cotton on 2 +

9th Round.—+ 5 r (the 3 centre on 3), 3 cotton on 2 stitches, 5 m (on the centre 5 of 7), 3 cotton + the last time, 3 on 2.

10th Round.—+ 7 r (the centre 5 on 5), 3 cotton, 3 m (on 3 centre of 5), 3 cotton, + the 10th time 3 cotton on 2.

11th Round.—+ 9 r (the centre 7 on 7), 4 cotton on 3, 1 m (on middle one of 3), 3 cotton +

12th Round. — Cotton; increasing 10 stitches in the round.

13th Round.—+ 5 cotton, 1 r over the centre of 9 r, 3 cotton + 20 times.

14th Round.—+ 3 cotton, 3 r, 3 cotton + 20 times.

15th Round.—+ 2 cotton, 5 r, 2 cotton, + 20 times.

16th Round.—+ 3 cotton, 3 r (on centre 3 of 5), 3 cotton + 20 times.

17th Round.—+ 5 cotton, on 4 stitches, 1 ruby on centre of 3, 4 cotton, + 20 times. The 20th do only 2 cotton.

18th Round.—+ 5 rubies, coming evenly between two diamonds, 5 cotton + 20 times.

19th Round.—+ 5 rubies on 5, 6 cotton on 5 + 20 times.

20th, 21st, and 22nd Rounds.—Rubies on rubies, and cotton on cotton, increasing to 7 cotton on 6 in the last round.

23rd Round.—Both kinds of beads + 2 cotton, 3 malachites on the centre 3 of 7 cotton, 19 cotton + 10 times.

24th Round.—+ 1 cotton, 5 m (over 3 and a cotton on each side), 9 cotton, 1 ruby on the centre of 7 cotton, 8 cotton + 10 times.

25th Round.—+ 2 cotton on 1, 5 malachites on 5, 8 cotton, 3 rubies on 1, and a cotton stitch on each side, 7 cotton + 10 times.

26th Round.—+ 2 cotton, 5 m on 5, 8 cotton on 7, 5 rubies (on 3, and 1 cotton on each side), 6 cotton + 10 times.

27th Round.—+ 4 cotton on 2 and a bead, 3 m on centre 3 of 5, 8 cotton, 7 rubies, 4 cotton + 10 times. Slip stitch on the first four cotton, and first of 3 beads.

28th Round.—+ 2 cotton on 2nd of 3 beads, 5 m, 4 cotton, 7 rubies on 7, 4 cotton, 5 m + 10 times. Slip stitch on the first cotton.

29th Round.—+ 7 malachites, on 5 and a cotton at each edge, 4 cotton, 5 rubies on centre 5 of 7, 4 cotton, 7 malachites as before, 1 cotton on the same as the last malachite + 10 times, then slip stitch on 4 of the first 7 malachites.

30th Round.—+ 4 m, 4 cotton, 3 rubies on centre 3 of 5, 4 cotton, 4 malachites, 2 cotton, 5 malachites (the centre one on 1 cotton), 2 cotton + 10 times.

31st Round.—+ 1 cotton, 4 m, 4 cotton, 1 ruby on centre of 3, 4 cotton, 4 m, 2 cotton, 7 m, 1 cotton + 10 times.

32nd Round.—+ 2 cotton, 4 m, 7 cotton, 4 m, 3 cotton, 1 m on first of 7, 2 cotton on one stitch, 3 m (on centre 3 of 7), 2 cotton on 1, 1 m on last of 7, 1 cotton + 10 times. No more rubies.

33rd Round.—+ 3 cotton, 4 m, 5 cotton, 4 m, 6 cotton, 5 m (on 3 and a cotton on each side), 3 cotton + 10 times.

34th Round.—+ 4 cotton, 4 beads, 3 cotton, 4 beads, 6 cotton, 7 m (on 3 and a cotton on each side), 2 cotton + 10 times.

35th Round.—+ 5 cotton, 4 m, 1 cotton, 4 m, 8 cotton, 5 m (on centre 5 of 7), 3 cotton + 10 times.

36th Round.—+ 4 cotton, 2 m, 1 cotton, 7 m, 1 cotton, 2 m, 7 cotton, 3 m (on centre 3 of 5), 3 cotton + 10 times.

37th Round.—+ 7 cotton, 1 m (on first of 7 m), 1 cotton, 3 m, 1 cotton, 1 m (on last of 7), 11 cotton, 1 m (on centre of 3), 4 cotton + 10 times.

38th Round.—In this round all the stitches are without beads, except over the 1 cotton, 3 malachite, 1 cotton; on which 5 beads are to be worked.

In the following round, 3 malachite are worked on the centre 3 of 5, and all the rest of the stitches are cotton, with an **increase of 10 stitches in the round** In

the next round, one bead is dropped on the centre of 3, all the rest being cotton. The last round is plain.

For the border, with the ruby thread 1 Dc under a stitch + 2 Ch, Dc under the same, Dc under the next + repeat to the end of the round, dropping 2 beads on every Dc stitch.

2nd Round.—5 Dc under a chain, 5 Ch, with beads on every stitch.

CORONET SMOKING-CAP IN APPLICATION

Materials.—Rich dark-blue cloth, 6 inches deep by seven-eighths of a yard long, black silk velvet, gold braid, gold thread, No. 3, and black beads, No. 2. A gold tassel.

THE design is in black velvet, cut out in one entire piece, and gummed on to the cloth. The edges, after being sewed down, are covered with the purest gold braid,

CORONET SMOKING-CAP IN APPLICATION.

which also forms small ornamental loops on the cloth itself. Along the entire centre of the knot, a row of black beads is laid over, and edged with coarse gold thread. The way to put on the beads is to thread them on strong black silk, and then sew the silk down in an even line between every two beads. The gold thread and braid must be sewed on with Chinese silk of the same colour. The design for the crown corresponds with that of the head piece. To make it up it must be lined with silk of the same colour. The head piece is set full into the crown, as will be observed in the engraving. A very long and rich gold tassel completes the cap.

C C

THE WORK-TABLE FRIEND.

SCREEN IN NETTED EMBROIDERY.

Materials.— Two pieces of filet, each large enough for a screen; half a skein of cerise or blue silk (French); 5 skeins of gold thread, No 1. Frame, cord, handles, and black satin.

THE imitation netting is used for these screens, which renders them much easier of

NETTED EMBROIDERY SCREEN.

execution than any pattern we have yet given.

Begin in the centre of the filet, and darn from the engraving. All those parts which are *quite* white are done in gold thread; the shaded, in silk. By an oversight the diamond near the handle is a square out of place. A reference to the others will enable you to rectify this.

The screens are to be mounted in the usual way. Fringe may be added, if desired. We now have fringes, cords, and handles all made to correspond with each other, which is a great improvement when it is desired to give a handsome present.

CONVOLVULUS WATCH-POCKET.

Materials.—Two shades of green chenille, 3 skeins of each, 1 skein brown ditto, 2 blue, 2 white, with a morsel of yellow. A pair of wire frames, a little green satin, wadding, and cardboard; also cord and tassels.

THE wire frame represents the skeleton of a convolvulus flower and leaves, with a loop at the extremity, which serves afterwards

to suspend the article by. The pocket itself is behind the flower. At the back of

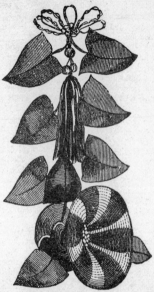

the pocket a round of cardboard, wadded on one side and covered with green satin on both, is sewed, the wadded side being inwards, of course. The front of the pocket is filled in the same way, forming the base of the flower. The leaves are filled in with chenille, which is carried first to the point of the leaf, and then backwards and forwards from one edge to the other, entirely filling up, as far as the base. The two shades of green are used for this purpose; the lightest leaves being those nearest the flower, and the three small ones immediately surrounding it. The brown chenille is used for covering the stems.

The sections of the flower are alternately white and blue (or white and violet, or white and pink may be used for this purpose). The sections of the flower are filled in the same way, and the edge covered, on each division, with the section that fills it. Two or three small loops of yellow chenille are placed in the heart of each flower, and a fancy cord and tassels finish it off. The chenille used is that termed *chenille a broder*

MARYGOLD MAT.

THE WORK-TABLE FRIEND.

MARYGOLD MAT.

Materials.—Scarlet and white Berlin wools, 3 skeins each; green ditto, 2 shades, 8 skeins each; a small quantity of each of 4 shades of green, 8 thread Berlin, and a skein of shaded ditto; cardboard; green sarsenet, very stout wire, and a reel of black and of white cannetille; also a quantity of florists' pistils, and a little green paper and fine common wire.

This mat, the very elegant appearance of which is faithfully represented in the engraving, has a centre of cardboard, covered on both sides with green silk (or black glazed calico may be sewed on one side). The border, which consists of raised flowers and leaves, is of so new a kind, we must beg our readers' especial attentions to the description.

The flower has five petals, surrounding a circle of pistils, within which the stamens are represented by a tuft of green wool. The formation of the flowers is the first care. The eight skeins of green wool of two shades are used for the tuft; and, as there are eight flowers in the mat, one skein of each shade will be used for every flower.

First take a piece of stout wire 2½ inches long for the stem. Take the lightest green, and wind it round a mesh of 1¾ inches wide, holding in a bit of fine wire at one edge. Draw the wool together, and tie the ends of wire as closely as possible. Then cut the loops; bind this at one end of the thick wire, for the centre of the tuft. Treat the dark skein in the same way, and tie it completely *round* the light wool on the thick wire; cut the surface, allowing the centre to be somewhat higher than the sides, and combing it till it forms a smooth ball, without any fibrous appearance of threads. Entirely round this tie the pistils. As every part must be very secure, it is better to use fine wire for fastening each piece than even the strongest thread. The forming of the petals is done in a curious but very effective way. It has this advantage over crochet that it leaves the surface of the wool smooth, and consequently more like nature than any flowers can be for which stitches are employed. Take a bit of card three-quarters of an inch wide, and three pieces of fine white wire, each four inches long. Wind the white wool round two of these pieces together for an inch and a half. Now hold them *above* one edge of the card, and the other piece at the other. Wind the wool round the card, bringing up the end between the two bits of wire at the top. Cross these, drawing them tightly, and again wind the wool round the card, and bring it up between them. Cross them again, always bringing the back one to the front, before taking the front one to the back. Repeat this, drawing them together, and of course compressing the wool between them until nearly the length of an inch is done. Then wind the wool round the two wires, as at the beginning. The piece of wire at the other edge of the card must now be tightly tied, all the wool being drawn together at this edge. Then slip it off the card, and wind the two ends of double wire with the other. This forms a petal, and five are required for each flower. Place these at equal distances round the pistils; tie safely with wire, gum a bit of green paper on for a calyx, making it also cover the thick wire stem, and a flower is complete. Four of the flowers are white; the other four are scarlet; for these the black cannetille must be used.

The leaves are formed by bending a piece of thick wire into the shape seen in the engraving, and proportionately large, and winding the green 8-thread wool between them. As, however, the wires would not be sufficiently covered were the wool merely carried from one side to the other, it should be wound round each wire on coming to it. Always begin at the point of the leaf; you will finish by covering the two ends of wire together. All four shades of green are to be used for these leaves, the large ones being dark. The darkest and lightest will be placed together.

Take the shaded wool and a wooden mesh, half an inch wide, with two long pieces of fine black wire, and work it exactly as you did the petals, but without the third wire, as you do not require that the loops should be drawn up. As fast as the length of the mesh is covered, slip off all but an inch or two, and go on, until at least three yards are worked.

Take a piece of the thick wire, bend it into a round exactly the size of the cardboard one, and work on the flowers and leaves, at equal distances (as seen in the engraving), by bending an inch of the ends, and passing wire round it and the circle at the same time. Any one who will take the trouble to examine a spray of artificial flowers will perceive the way in which all the pieces are united.

Now wind the length of shaded wool round this wire closely enough to completely cover it and then sew it round the cardboard.

WOMAN.—"There is nothing," says Sir Samuel Romilly, "by which I have through life more profited than by the just observations, the good opinion, and sincere and gentle encouragement of amiable and sensible women."

SPANISH POLKA.

FOR A CHILD OF TWO OR THREE YEARS OLD

Materials.—6 oz. claret 4 thread Berlin wool; 1 oz. of white Pyrenees ditto; a pair of knitting needles with heads, No. 8, and another, No. 10.

WITH the claret wool and finest needles cast on 242 stitches, and knit two plain rows. Now tie a bit of white thread at the 36th from each end, and at the 56th from them. These four pieces of cotton serve to mark the places where you are to decrease by knitting three together in every alternate row, after the 24th.

SPANISH POLKA.

Begin the pattern, which is ordinary brioche stitch, adding three stitches at the end of every row, until there are 36 more at each end; in the next row cast on 21 more at the end, and when you come to the end of the next row do the same. Meantime after 24 rows done without decreasing, you will take in three stitches at each of the white threads, in every other row, until you have decreased, in each place, 27 stitches. To produce the proper effect take in first at one side, and then at the other of the white thread, so that a ridge from each side disappears alternately. You may then do 60 rows, without increasing or diminishing. It will be necessary to make button-holes at one edge, at the distance of every 30 rows, thus: Knit 6 stitches, cast 9 off the left-hand needle, by passing one over another without knitting them; then cast on 6 on the right-hand needle, in this way diminishing by 3 at every button-hole; at the other edge do not decrease at all. You now form a gusset

SPANISH POLKA.

437

for underneath the arms by making a stitch on each side the ridge which runs up from the side of the outer decreasings, nearest to the front: at each you will increase 18 stitches in as many rows, as the alternate ones only have the made stitches. **Continue to knit in the brioche stitch.**

In the next row, knit as far as the first 18 stitches. Turn back; cast off the 18, and knit the others backwards and forwards as usual, forming one side of the front, up to the shoulder, for 36 rows; always continuing to make the button-holes at equal distances, if this is the side for them. Now cast off a stitch loosely at the end of every row, until one stitch only is left. Draw the wool through. Now continue the piece for the back, from the gusset; knit across the back, to the end of the other 18 stitches, turn; cast them off, and do 36 rows; then cast off a stitch at the end of every row, until 8 ribs are cast off at each edge. Cast off the remainder. Do the other side of the front to correspond with the first.

FOR THE SLEEVES.—Cast on 99 stitches, knit 2 plain rows, then the brioche stitch. Gradually decrease two ribs at each edge, and knit about 6 inches. Now cast off 24 stitches at each edge, and knit eight rows before casting off the remainder.

THE COLLAR.—Cast on 102 stitches, and do the depth of an inch with the claret wool, and cast off. Then with the white wool, and the same needles, take up stitches along the two ends and one side, and knit one row. *2nd* —+ knit 2, make one by bringing the thread before the needle. + all round. *3rd.*—Purled. *4th.*—+ knit 2, make 1, knit 1, make 1, + repeat to the end. *5th*—Purled. *6th*—cast off. This finishes the collar.

The deep lace frill, which gives so elegant a finish to this polka, is done with the coarse needles in Pyrenees wool. It is double, and is to be done as follows. Cast on 30 stitches, and knit one plain row.

1st Pattern Row.—knit 7. + make 1, knit 2 together, knit 6. + Repeat till 7 only are left. Make 1, knit 7.

2nd Row.—Purl 5. Purl 2 together, + make 1, purl 1, make 1, purl 2 together, purl 3, purl 2 together. + to the end; purl the last 5.

3rd Row.—Knit 4, knit 2 together, + make 1, knit 3, make 1, knit 2 together, knit 1, knit 2 together, + to the end, when make 1, knit 3, make 1, knit 2 together, knit 4.

4th Row.—Purl 3, purl 2 together; + make 1, purl 5, make 1, purl 3 together, + to the end.

These four rows form one pattern, and must be repeated five times, after which do two plain rows, and slip all the stitches on a finer needle.

Do another piece with a depth of only two patterns, and two plain rows. Then holding the two pieces of lace together, knit one row with a stitch off each needle, thus uniting the two frills. Do another plain row, and a series of holes, thus:—Knit 3, + make 1, slip 1, knit 2 (not together), pass the slip stitch over. + repeat to the end, when the last 3 are to be knitted plain. 1 purled row; 1 plain ditto. Cast off. To be sewed round the bottom of the jacket.

To trim the sleeves, cast on 96 stitches, and work in the same way. When three patterns are done, begin the upper frill, to which do two before joining them. Complete like that for the body, and sew on to the sleeve, closing it up the edge.

Now sew up the shoulders, add the collar and sleeves, and plait some white 8-thread fleecy to make the trimming down the fronts and round the neck. The buttons are covered also with pieces of white knitting, so that every part washes.

Those who are not acquainted with brioche stitch may be glad to learn that it is simply— + bring the thread in front, slip 1 as if purling, knit 2 together, +. The wool of which these polkas are made is the finest Spanish.

FEELING.—To feel is amiable; but to feel too keenly is injurious both to mind and body; and a habit of giving way to sensibility, which we should endeavour to regulate, though not eradicate. may end in a morbid weakness of mind, which may appear to romantic persons very gentle and very interesting, but will undoubtedly render its victims very useless in society. Our feelings were given us to excite to action; and when they end in themselves, they are impressed to no one good purpose. This is the chief reason why novels are so dangerous to young persons. My dear daughter will be persuaded that I say this from motives of the tenderest affection to her, and because I would have her not stifle the good and amiable emotions of her heart, but direct them rightly.—*Bishop Sandford*

THE EMERALD DOYLEY.

THE WORK-TABLE FRIEND.

JEWELLED DOYLEY—THE EMERALD.

Materials.—2 oz. Emerald beads, No. 2, and 2 reels of Messrs. W. Evans and Co.'s Boar's Head Crochet Cotton, No. 16.

Begin, as in all bead-work in crochet, by threading the beads on the cotton; and we may here remark (*par parenthèse*) that jeweller bead-needles are the proper instruments to employ. There is not the slightest difficulty in threading any beads whatever with them.

Make a chain of 4, close it into a round, and do 2 Sc stitches in every stitch. Do the same for the second and third rounds.

4th Round.—Drop a bead on every stitch, and after every eighth stitch, work another with a bead on it, in the same, so that you have 36 beads in the round.

5th Round.—Sc, without beads, increasing to 48 stitches.

6th Round.—Sc, with a bead on every stitch, and no increase.

7th Round.—+ 4 cotton on 3, 1 bead, + 12 times.

8th Round.—+ 3 beads (coming over 1 bead and a cotton at each side) 3 cotton, + 12 times.

9th Round.—+ 3 beads on 3, 4 cotton + 12 times.

10th Round.—5 beads (over 3, and a cotton at each side), 3 cotton on 2 + 12 times.

11th Round.—+ 5 beads on 5, 4 cotton on 3 + 12 times.

12th Round.—+ 7 beads (over 5 beads and a cotton on each side), 2 cotton on 2 + 12 times.

13th Round.—+ 7 beads on 7, 3 cotton on 2 + 12 times. Work on in cotton to the centre of 3.

14th Round.—+ 1 bead on centre of 3 cotton, 9 cotton + 12 times.

15th Round.—+ 1 bead on 1 bead, 10 cotton on 9 + 12 times.

16th Round.—+ 3 beads (on 1 bead and a cotton on each side), 8 cotton + 12 times.

17th Round.—+ 5 beads (on 3, and a cotton on each side), 7 cotton on 6 + 12 times.

18th Round.—+ 7 beads (on 5 and a cotton on each side), 5 cotton on 5 + 12 times.

19th Round.—+ 9 beads (on 7, and a cotton on each side), 3 cotton + 12 times.

20th Round.—+ 7 bead on centre 7 of 9), 2 cotton, 1 bead on centre of 3 cotton, 3 cotton (making one), + 12 times.

21st Round.—+ 5 beads (on centre 5 of 7), 4 cotton, 1 bead on 1 bead, 4 cotton + 12 times.

22nd Round.—+ 3 beads (on centre 3 of 5), 4 cotton, 3 beads (on 1 bead and a cotton on each side), 4 cotton + 12 times.

23rd Round.—+ 1 bead (on centre of 3), 4 cotton, 5 beads (on 3, and a cotton on each side), 4 cotton + 12 times.

24th Round.—+ 1 bead on 1, 3 cotton, 3 beads, 1 cotton (on centre of 5 beads), 3 beads, 4 cotton (making 1) + 12 times.

25th Round.—+ 1 bead on 1, 3 cotton on 2, 3 beads, 3 cotton (the 2nd on 1 cotton), 3 beads, 3 cotton + 12 times.

26th Round.—+ 5 cotton (the centre over 1 bead), 3 beads, 5 cotton (on 3 cotton and a bead on each side), 3 beads, + 12 times.

27th Round.—+ 3 cotton (on centre 3 of first 5), 3 beads, 7 cotton (on 5 and a bead at each side), 3 beads, + 12 times.

28th Round.—+ 1 cotton on 2nd of 3, 3 beads, 10 cotton (over 7, and a bead at each side), 3 beads, + 12 times.

29th Round.—In this round 5 beads are worked to come over the *one* cotton of last round, and 2 beads on each side, and 12 cotton stitches between these and the next five. The 12th time do only 6 cotton.

30th Round.—+ 4 cotton, 9 beads, 5 cotton over 4 + 12 times.

31st Round.—+ 2 cotton, 2 beads, 3 cotton, 3 beads (on centre 3 of 9) 3 cotton, 2 beads, 3 cotton + 12 times.

32nd Round.—+ 1 cotton, 4 beads, 2 cotton on 1, 5 beads (on 3 and a cotton on each side), 2 cotton on 1, 4 beads, 2 cotton + 12 times.

33rd Round.—Beads on beads of last round, and cotton on cotton.

34th Round.—+ 2 cotton, 2 beads on centre 2 of 4, 3 cotton, 5 beads on 5, 3 cotton, 2 beads, 3 cotton (making 1 + 12 times.

35th Round.—+ 9 cotton, 3 beads (on 3 centre of 5), 10 cotton + 12 times.

36th Round.—All cotton, increasing twelve stitches in the round.

37th Round.—Without increase, dropping a bead on every stitch.

38th Round.—Like 36th.

39th Round.—Like 37th.

40th Round.—+ 2 Dc in 1, dropping a bead on each, 1 Ch, 2 Dc in same, miss 3 + all round, taking care there is an even number.

41st Round.— + 5 Tc under the 1 Ch, dropping 2 beads on each stitch, 2 Ch, with a bead on each, Sc under the next 1 Ch, 2 Ch, with a bead on each + repeat all round.

WORK-TABLE FOR JUVENILES;
OR,
LITTLE MARY'S HALF-HOLIDAY.

(*Continued from p. 363.*)

"WELL, my little girl. we must now waste no time, for December is approaching, and unless you hasten I fear your Christmas tree will look rather bare"

"Cannot you, dear Mamma, suggest something that could be very rapidly made, and yet look well? I still want a present for a bride; and something pretty for one of my cousins—something she can wear. Besides——"

"For to-day, my dear girl, you have suggested quite enough. For the bride's

present, some article for the decoration of the house would be the most appropriate gift. Let me think! When I was in Paris last, I saw a most beautiful pin-cushion for the toilet-table. If I could remember it sufficiently to describe it to you, I think it would be just the thing you would like."

"And that my new aunt would like too! Do, dear Mamma, try if you cannot think of it. I am sure you will, if you rack your brains sufficiently."

"I think I can, at all events, manage to give you an idea of it. It was something in the style of the *Impératrice* cushion, but flatter and larger round. The cover was of satin. The top was of darned netting trimmed with gold, and having rich passementerie tassels. See, I will make you a drawing of it. You see that it is ornamented

PIN-CUSHION FOR THE TOILET-TABLE.

with tassels. These are in silk and gold. You will find it very little work, and I think it is sure to be admired."

"Suppose we begin then, Mamma What materials are needed?"

"Some cherry-coloured satin, calico, and bran; black netting silk, Napoleon blue crochet silk, gold thread (12 skeins), and five *passementerie* tassels. You will begin by making a cushion 9 inches in diameter, and 3 high at the edges, but raised a little in the centre. It must be tightly stuffed with bran, and covered very neatly with the satin."

"As I can do this, dear Mamma, at another time, perhaps you will tell me now how to go on with the cover."

"Fill a fine netting-needle with the black silk, and begin with five stitches, which form into a round, and do two stitches in every one. Then continue to increase by working always two stitches in a short stitch, and one in every other until there are 29 stitches in every division. Do two rounds without increase. This forms the top of the cushion. For each point work backwards and forwards in a division, always omitting the last stitch until there are two only, when fasten off. The mesh to be used is No. 13. The blue silk is used for darning the flower in each point, the spots and the triangular piece in each division being in gold. Before darning, however, the netting should be damped, and pinned out, which will give it a little stiffness. A narrow edging, in crochet, with the gold thread, may then be advantageously worked all round. To complete the cushion the netting is simply to be laid on the satin, and tacked down at the places where the *passementérie* trimming is added."

"You often use the word *passementérie*, dear Mamma: what does it mean?"

"It is a French term, my dear, for that kind of ornamental work in which gold thread and coloured silks are worked up into certain forms. You have observed that all the French purse trimmings are of this kind, no steel or gilt ornaments being used for them."

"And now for something lasting! Something that will look pretty at very little cost."

"What say you to a pair of gold bracelets? This *bourdon* would make some pretty ones, and you could finish them this

N FOR BRACELET.

ll. Take some gold-
y strong) and a couple

of gold buttons with shanks to them. You will require 3½ yards of bourdon. Cut it into 16 lengths, four of 7 inches, and the remainder divide equally. Half of these are used for each bracelet. Fasten the ends securely, then plait them in a plait of four, as you see in the drawing. There are to be two strands of bourdon used together. When finished fasten these ends also, and work over them in button-hole stitch to secure them. Add a gold button, and a button-hole to each."

"That is soon done, indeed, Mamma; and as they look so beautiful, and cost so little, I think I will do another pair in silver. They would be quite as pretty, and I have enough of the material."

THE WORK-TABLE FRIEND.

DOYLEY IN PORTUGUESE GUIPURE.

Materials.—Messrs. W. Evans and Co.'s Boar's Head Crochet Cotton, No. 30, and Mecklenburgh thread, No. 8. Netting needle 22, and steel meshes Nos. 8, 10, 12, and 17.

DOYLEY.

The foundation is square netting, done with the Boar's Head Cotton, and mesh No. 17. The pattern, which is done with the Mecklenburgh thread, is worked in what is called *cloth darning*, every square of netting which is darned being filled by four threads (two each way), which cross each other as in woven cloth. Of course each square is not darned separately, but the line is continued, whenever the pattern will admit, in the same direction. The outline thread is the same number as that used for the darning, but doubled

It is advisable to wash the piece of netting, and pin it out to dry, in order to give it a little stiffness before it is darned.

EDGE.

In doing the border of these Doyleys, the Boar's Head Cotton and all the meshes are used. Begin with mesh No. 8, and do 12 stitches in one of the holes (take one at the corner first).

Turn the work, and with the No. 10 mesh do a stitch in every stitch. With No. 12 do the same, except at the corners, where *two* stitches are to be worked in every stitch. With No. 17 also net a stitch in every stitch; and if another row be done in the same way, it adds to the beauty of the edge.

The shells are done at the distance of eight holes from each other; they are joined at the points, and the edges sewed to the Doyley with a fine needle and thread.

is admirably calculated to enable them to use up all the fragments of crochet silk which may remain from their purses, and similar articles. It must, however, be the French crochet silk, as the common kind is too coarse to be available for this purpose. They cannot have a single needleful of silk by them of a bright rich colour, which cannot be made available for this pattern, as every fresh scroll or bend may have a new colour. In this design the following tints are used—black, claret, scarlet, crimson, orange, violet, blue, and *three* different shades of green. All that need be attended to, in the working, is that such colours should come near each other as harmonize. In the large pine, for instance, orange, green, and violet are worked in the inner part and the outline is entirely in claret. The two sides of the front must, of course, correspond. It will be seen what scope this gives to the fancy. The only requisite is that no silk shall be used of the same colour as the ground. The gold thread is laid on one side of the chain stitch.

After the work is done, it is brushed over on the wrong side with gum-water. This design is most suitable for ladies' slippers.

HINTS FOR BEAD-WORKERS.

Use jewellers' bead needles.

Beads for pink roses are opaque. For crimson, transparent, and deepening into black.

HARLEQUIN SLIPPER.

HARLEQUIN SLIPPERS EMBROIDERED IN CHAIN STITCH.

Materials.—Fine cloth, of any very dark colour, or of any shade of drab or fawn : fine crochet silk, of all the colours that can be had, and gold thread, No. 2, four skeins. When made up, these slippers are to be trimmed with large bows of bright satin ribbon.

THE pattern we here present to our readers

All shades of greens may be used, black being made the deepest shade for leaves; but olives and browns (for faded leaves) may be introduced with effect.

The beads should be kept in pill-boxes, and when used a few may be turned out into the lids, which being shallow are more convenient than the boxes.

BRACELET IN CROCHET, BY MRS. PULLAN.

THE WORK-TABLE FRIEND.

BRACELET IN CROCHET.

Materials.—One skein of coarse pink crochet silk ; 2 ozs. of the shortest white bugles; a little parchment : ½ a yard of pink sarsenet ribbon, 2 inches wide, and a bracelet snap.

Although, for the sake of clearness, I have given a particular colour for the silk and bugles, other tints will do as well. Light blue silk looks very well with white bugles, and grey or scarlet with black. The ribbon must always match the colour of the silk.

Thread the bugles on the silk—then with a crochet-book, No. 17, begin the largest medallion, thus,—3 Ch, close into a round, and work on it two stitches, on every stitch, dropping a bugle on one, and doing the other plain. Thus there are six stitches in the round. Work every following round in the same manner, so that there are twice as many stitches in it as in the one preceding it. Increase until there are 48 bugles in round. Do one round of slip stitch, without any bugles, and fasten off. There is *one* medallion only of this size.

Medium size, of which there are two. Begin with ⸺ chain, on which drop two bugle⸺ ⸺ n the next round, then 9, ⸺ ⸺ally 36. Finish with a ⸺ , and fasten off.

⸺ ⸺ork like the largest, ⸺ und⸺ of twenty - four ⸺ ⸺ off after a slip ⸺ hese medallions.

Cut two rounds of parchment, for each medallion, but a very little smaller. Put one into the crochet round ; cut out a bit of ribbon, in the form of a round, large enough to cover one side of the other piece of parchment, and to draw up the edges securely on the wrong side. Sew this to the crochet. This raises the centre of each medallion a little.

Fasten the medallions together, as indicated in the engraving, by connecting a small bit at the side, and join the clasp to the two smaller ones.

OCTAGON WATCH-POCKET, in CROCHET.

Materials.—Two reels of W. Evan's & Co.'s Boar's-head crochet cotton ; 2 ozs. of turquoise blue seed-beads, a small piece of blue sarsenet, 1½ yards of blue satin ribbon, an inch wide, and a small piece of cardboard.

The whole of this watch-pocket, with the exception of the edge, is done in Sc. ; the pattern being formed by dropping on beads in certain places, as in the German Purse (see page 6).

Begin by threading the beads on the cotton, which it will be advisable to wind as you proceed, on a reel considerably larger than that from which it was taken.

The watch-pocket is made in two pieces —the octagon, which forms the back, and the small piece bearing the motto, which, when sewed to the large one, holds the watch.

For the Motto Piece.—Make a chain of 32 stitches, and drop a bead on every stitch, in working a row on it.

OCTAGON WATCH-POCKET IN CROCHET, BY MRS. PULLAN.

2nd Row. (Begin this, and every follow-ing row, at the same end.) Drop a bead on every stitch, increasing one stitch at each end.

3rd Row. (Increase one at each end.) 2 bead stitches, 32 cotton, 2 beads.

4th Row. (Increase as before.) 2 beads, 2 cotton, 2 beads, 2 cotton, 3 beads, 3 cotton, 3 beads, 4 cotton, 3 beads, 1 cotton, 2 beads, 3 cotton, 2 beads, 4 cotton, 2 beads.

5th Row. (Increase as before.) 2 beads, 4 cotton, + 1 bead, 2 cotton, + 4 times, 1 bead, 3 cotton, 1 bead, 2 cotton, 2 beads, 1 cotton, 1 bead, 3 cotton, 1 bead, 5 cotton, 2 beads.

6th Row. (Increase as before.) 2 beads, 6 cotton, 1 bead, 1 cotton, 1 bead, 5 cotton, 1 bead, 3 cotton, 1 bead, 3 cotton, 1 bead, 2 cotton, 1 bead, 6 cotton, 1 bead, 5 cotton, 2 bead.

7th Row. (Increase as before.) 2 beads, 7 cotton, 1 bead, 2 cotton, 1 bead, 5 cotton, 1 bead, 2 cotton, 1 bead, 4 cotton, 1 bead, 2 cotton, 1 bead, 6 cotton, 2 bead, 1 cotton 1 bead, 2 cotton, 2 beads.

8th Row. (Increase **as before.**) 2 beads, 9 cotton, 3 beads, 6 cotton, 3 beads, 3 cotton, 2 beads, 2 cotton, 2 beads, 4 cotton, 2 beads, 1 cotton, 2 beads, 3 cotton, 2 beads.

9th Row. (Increase as before.) 2 beads, 10 cotton, 1 bead, 33 cotton, 2 beads.

10th Row. (Increase as before.) 2 beads, 12 cotton, 1 bead, 33 cotton, 2 beads.

11th Row. (Increase one at each end for the last time.) 2 beads, 4 cotton, 2 beads, 7 cotton, 1 bead, 34 cotton, 2 beads.

12th Row. 2 beads, 3 cotton, 1 bead, 2 cotton, 1 bead, 41 cotton, 2 beads,

13th Row. 2 beads, 7 cotton, 1 bead, 40 cotton, 2 beads.

14th Row. 2 beads, 4 cotton, 4 beads, 3 cotton, 3 beads, 4 cotton, 4 beads, 3 cotton 3 beads, 1 cotton, 1 bead, 3 cotton, 3 beads, 3 cotton, 2 beads, 2 cotton, 3 beads, 2 cotton, 2 beads.

15th Row. 2 beads, 4 cotton, 1 bead, 2 cotton, 1 bead, 3 cotton, 1 bead, 2 cotton, 1 bead, 3 cotton, 1 bead, 3 cotton, 1 bead, 2 cotton, 1 bead, 2 cotton, 1 bead, 1 cotton, 1 bead, 2 cotton, 1 bead, 6 cotton, 1 bead, 2 cotton, 1 bead, 4 cotton, 2 beads.

16th Row. 2 beads, 4 cotton, 1 bead, 2 cotton, 2 beads, 2 cotton, 1 bead, 3 cotton, 1 bead, 3 cotton, 1 bead, 5 cotton, 1 bead, 2 cotton, 1 bead, 4 cotton, 4 bead, 4 cotton, 1 bead, 2 cotton, 1 bead, 3 cotton, 2 beads.

17th Row. 2 beads, 5 cotton, + 1 bead, 2 cotton, 1 bead, 3 cotton, + twice; 1 bead, 6 cotton, 1 bead, 2 cotton, 1 bead, 4 cotton, 1 bead, 2 cotton, 1 bead, 3 cotton, 2 bead, 1 cotton, 1 bead, 3 cotton, 2 beads.

18th Row. 2 beads, 6 cotton, 3 beads, 3 cotton, 3 beads, 4 cotton, 1 bead, 6 cotton, 2 bead, 1 cotton, 1 bead, 4 cotton, 3 bead, 2 cotton, 2 bead, 1 cotton, 2 bead, 3 cotton, 2 bead.

19th Row. 2 beads, 20 cotton, 1 bead, 9 cotton, 1 bead, 17 cotton, 2 beads.

20th Row. 2 beads, 21 cotton, 1 bead, 9 cotton, 1 bead, 16 cotton, 2 beads.

21st Row. Like 20th.

22r ⸻ 2 beads at each end; the rest ⸻

⸻ beads, 3 cotton, 2 beads, 2 ⸻ 4 cotton, 3 beads, 3 cotton, ⸻ 3 beads, 3 cotton, 1 bead, ⸻ 's, 5 cotton, 1 bead, 2 ⸻

⸻ 's, 2 cotton, 1 bead, 2

cotton, 2 beads, 3 cotton, 1 bead, 2 cotton, 1 bead, 2 cotton, 1 bead, 1 cotton, 1 bead, 4 cotton, 1 bead, 2 cotton, 1 bead, 5 cotton, 1 bead, 3 cotton, 1 bead, 3 cotton, 1 bead, 1 cotton, 1 bead, 1 cotton, 2 beads.

25th Row. 2 beads, 3 cotton, 2 beads, 2 cotton, 2 beads, 5 cotton, 1 bead, 3 cotton, 1 bead, 4 cotton, 1 bead, 4 cotton, 1 bead, 5 cotton, 1 bead, 2 cotton, 2 beads, 2 cotton, 4 beads, 3 cotton, 2 beads.

26th Row. 2 beads, 8 cotton, 1 bead, 6 cotton, 1 bead, 2 cotton, 1 bead, 4 cotton, 1 bead, 1 cotton, 1 bead, 2 cotton, 1 bead, 5 cotton, 2 beads, 6 cotton, 1 bead, 2 cotton, 1 bead, 2 cotton, 2 beads.

27th Row. 2 beads, 8 cotton, 2 beads, 2 cotton, 1 bead, 3 cotton, 3 beads, 5 cotton, 2 beads, 1 cotton, 4 beads, 4 cotton, 1 bead, 7 cotton, 1 bead, 1 cotton, 1 bead, 2 cotton, 2 beads.

28th Row. 2 beads, 9 cotton, 1 bead, 3 cotton, 1 bead, 15 cotton, 1 bead, 14 cotton, 1 bead, 1 cotton, 1 bead, 1 cotton, 2 beads.

29th Row. 2 beads, 10 cotton, 3 beads, 32 cotton, 2 beads, 1 cotton, 2 beads.

30th Row. 2 beads at each end; the remainder in cotton.

31st Row. A bead on every stitch.

⸻

THE EDGE. Sc under a stitch, + 2 ch, miss 2, Sc under the next, + repeat to the end.

2nd Row, Sc on Sc, + miss one loop, 3 Dc under the next, dropping 2 beads on every stitch, 2 Ch, 3 more Dc in the same way under the same loop. + repeat. End the row with a Sc stitch, and fasten off.

All the ends of thread must be worked in, according to the instructions already given.

For the Octagon. Make a chain of 35 stitches; do one row of Sc. Increase the next, and all succeeding rows, to the 28th.

2nd Row. 2 cotton, 33 beads, 2 cotton.

3rd Row. 2 cotton, 35 beads. 2 cotton.

4th Row. 2 cotton, 2 beads, 33 cotton, 2 beads, 2 cotton.

5th Row. 2 cotton, 2 beads, 35 cotton, 2 beads, 2 cotton.

6th Row. 2 cotton, 2 beads, 37 cotton, 2 beads, 2 cotton.

7th Row. 2 cotton, 2 beads, 19 cotton, 1 bead, 3 cotton, 1 bead, 15 cotton, 2 beads, 2 cotton.

8th Row. 2 cotton 2 beads 14 cotton,

1 bead, 4 cotton, 3 beads, 1 cotton, 3 beads, 15 cotton, 2 beads, 2 cotton.

9th Row. 2 cotton, 2 beads, 16 cotton, 1 bead, 1 cotton, 1 bead, 2 cotton, 2 beads, 1 cotton, 2 beads, 17 cotton 2 beads, 2 cotton.

10th Row. 2 cotton, 2 beads, 18 cotton, 1 bead, 1 cotton, 2 beads, 2 cotton, 1 bead, 20 cotton, 2 beads, 2 cotton.

11th Row. 2 cotton, 2 beads, 20 cotton, 1 bead, 2 cotton, 2 beads, 1 cotton, 2 beads, 19 cotton, 2 beads, 2 cotton.

12th Row. 2 cotton, 2 beads, 9 cotton, 1 bead, 11 cotton, 1 bead, 1 cotton, 3 beads, 1 cotton, 3 beads, 9 cotton, 1 bead, 9 cotton, 2 beads, 2 cotton.

13th Row. 2 cotton, 2 beads, 7 cotton, 3 beads, 11 cotton, 2 beads, 2 cotton, 1 bead, 3 cotton, 1 bead, 11 cotton, 3 beads, 7 cotton 2 beads, 2 cotton.

14th Row, 2 cotton, 2 beads, 5 cotton, 1 bead, 2 cotton, 1 bead, 1 cotton, 1 bead, 31 cotton, 1 bead, 1 cotton, 1 bead, 2 cotton, 1 bead, 5 cotton, 2 beads, 2 cotton.

15th Row. 2 cotton, 2 beads, 5 cotton, 2 cotton, 3 beads, 31 cotton, 3 beads, 2 cotten, 2 beads, 5 cotton, 2 beads, 2 cotton.

16th Row, 2 cotton, 2 beads, 8 cotton, 2 beads, 37 cotton, 2 beads, 8 cotton, 2 beads, 2 cotton.

17th Row. 2 cotton, 2 beads, 9 cotton, 2 beads, 37 cotton, 2 beads, 9 cotton, 2 beads, 2 cotton.

18th Row. 2 cotton, 2 beads, 5 cotton, 5 beads, 2 cotton, 2 beads, 33 cotton, 2 beads, 2 cotton, 5 beads, 5 cotton, 2 beads, 2 cotton.

19th Row. 2 cotton, 2 beads, 6 cotton, 1 bead, 3 cotton, 1 bead, 2 cotton, 1 bead, 35 cotton, 1 bead, 2 cotton, 1 bead, 3 cotton, 1 bead, 6 cotton, 2 beads, 2 cotton.

20th Row. 2 cotton, 2 beads, 7 cotton, 1 bead, 1 cotton, 1 bead, 1 cotton, 1 bead, 41 cotton, 1 bead, 1 cotton, 1 bead, 1 cotton, 1 bead, 7 cotton, 2 beads, 2 cotton.

21st Row.—2 cotton, 2 beads, 5 cotton, 1 bead, 2 cotton, 1 bead, 3 cotton, 1 bead, 41 cotton, 1 bead, 3 cotton, 1 bead, 2 cotton, 1 bead, 5 cotton, 2 beads, 2 cotton.

22nd Row.—2 cotton, 2 beads, 5 cotton, 2 beads, 2 cotton, 5 beads, 41 cotton, 5 beads, 2 cotton, 2 beads, 5 cotton, 2 beads, 2 cotton.

23rd Row,—2 cotton, 2 beads, 8 cotton, 2 beads, 51 cotton, 2 beads, 8 cotton, 2 beads, 2 cotton.

24th Row.—2 cotton, 2 beads, 9 cotton, 2 beads, 51 cotton, 2 beads, 9 cotton, 2 beads, 2 cotton.

25th Row.—2 cotton, 2 beads, 7 cotton, 3 beads, 2 cotton, 2 beads, 47 cotton, 2 beads, 2 cotton, 3 beads, 7 cotton, 2 beads, 2 cotton.

26th Row.—2 cotton, 2 beads, 8 cotton, 1 bead, 1 cotton, 1 bead, 2 cotton, 1 bead, 49 cotton, 1 bead, 2 cotton, 1 bead, 1 cotton, 1 bead, 8 cotton, 2 beads, 2 cotton.

27th Row.—2 cotton, 2 beads, 9 cotton, 3 beads, 55 cotton, 3 beads, 9 cotton, 2 beads, 2 cotton.

28th Row.—2 cotton, 2 beads, 9 cotton, 1 bead, 61 cotton, 1 bead, 9 cotton, 2 beads, 2 cotton.

29th Row.—(Not increased from here.) 2 cotton, 2 beads, 81 cotton, 2 beads, 2 cotton.

30th to 36th Row inclusive, like *29th.*

37th Row.—2 cotton, 2 beads, 5 cotton, 1 bead, 69 cotton, 1 bead, 5 cotton, 2 beads, 2 cotton.

38th Row.—2 cotton, 2 beads, 6 cotton, 1 bead, 67 cotton, 1 bead, 6 cotton, 2 beads, 2 cotton.

39th Row.—2 cotton, 2 beads, 7 cotton, 1 bead, 2 cotton, 1 bead, 59 cotton, 1 bead, 2 cotton, 1 bead, 7 cotton, 2 beads, 2 cotton.

40th Row.—2 cotton, 2 beads, 6 cotton, 1 bead, 1 cotton, 3 beads, 59 cotton, 3 beads, 1 cotton, 1 bead, 6 cotton, 2 beads, 2 cotton.

41st Row.—2 cotton, 2 beads, 7 cotton, 1 bead, 65 cotton, 1 bead, 7 cotton, 2 beads, 2 cotton.

42nd Row.—2 cotton, 2 beads, 5 cotton, 1 bead, 1 cotton, 1 bead, 1 cotton, 1 bead, 61 cotton, 1 bead, 1 cotton, 1 bead, 1 cotton, 1 bead, 5 cotton, 2 beads, 2 cotton.

43rd Row.—2 cotton, 2 beads, 4 cotton, 3 beads, 1 cotton, 3 beads, 59 cotton, 3 beads, 1 cotton, 3 beads, 4 cotton, 2 beads, 2 cotton.

44th Row.—2 cotton, 2 beads, 5 cotton, 2 beads, 1 cotton, 2 beads, 61 cotton, 2 beads, 1 cotton, 2 beads, 5 cotton, 2 beads, 2 cotton.

45th Row.—Like *41st.*

46th Row.—Like *44th.*

47th Row.—Like *43rd.*

48th Row.—2 cotton, 2 beads, 5 cotton, 1 bead, 3 cotton, 1 bead, 61 cotton, 1 bead, 3 cotton, 1 bead, 5 cotton, 2 beads, 2 cotton.

49th to 52nd Row inclusive, like *30th.*

53rd Row.—2 cotton, 2 beads, 15 cotton, 2 beads, 47 cotton, 2 beads, 15 cotton, 2 beads, 2 cotton.

54th Row.—2 cotton, 2 beads, 16 cotton, 2 beads, 45 cotton, 2 beads, 16 cotton, 2 beads, 2 cotton.

55th Row.—2 cotton, 2 beads, 17 cotton, 2 beads, 21 cotton, 1 bead, 21 cotton, 2 beads, 17 cotton, 2 beads, 2 cotton.

56th Row.—2 cotton, 2 beads, 18 cotton, 2 beads, 15 cotton, + 1 bead, 1 cotton, + 5 times; 1 bead, 15 cotton, 2 beads, 18 cotton, 2 beads, 2 cotton.

57th Row.—2 cotton, 2 beads, 8 cotton, 1 bead, 10 cotton, 2 beads, 12 cotton, 2 beads, 1 cotton, 3 beads, 1 cotton, 1 bead, 1 cotton, 3 beads, 1 cotton, 2 beads, 12 cotton, 2 beads, 10 cotton, 1 bead, 8 cotton, 2 beads, 2 cotton.

58th Row.—In this, and every following row, leave out one stitch at each end. 2 cotton, 2 beads, 8 cotton, 3 beads, 8 cotton, 2 beads, 13 cotton, + 1 bead, 1 cotton, + 5 times, 1 bead, 13 cotton, 2 beads, 8 cotton, 3 beads, 8 cotton, 2 beads, 2 cotton.

59th Row.—2 cotton, 2 beads, 7 cotton, 1 bead, 1 cotton, 1 bead, 2 cotton, 1 bead, 6 cotton, 2 beads, 17 cotton, 1 bead, 17 cotton, 2 beads, 6 cotton, 1 bead, 2 cotton, 1 bead, 1 cotton, 1 bead, 7 cotton, 2 beads, 2 cotton.

60th Row.—2 cotton, 2 beads, 6 cotton, 3 beads, 2 cotton, 2 beads, 6 cotton, 2 beads, 33 cotton, 2 beads, 6 cotton, 2 beads, 2 cotton, 3 beads, 6 cotton, 2 beads, 2 cotton.

61st Row.—2 cotton, 2 beads, 8 cotton, 2 beads, 9 cotton, 2 beads, 31 cotton, 2 beads, 9 cotton, 2 beads, 8 cotton, 2 beads, 2 cotton.

62nd Row.—2 cotton, 2 beads, 7 cotton, 2 beads, 10 cotton, 33 beads, 10 cotton, 2 beads, 7 cotton, 2 beads, 2 cotton.

63rd Row.—2 cotton, 2 beads, 4 cotton, 2 beads, 2 cotton, 5 beads, 5 cotton, 31 beads, 5 cotton, 5 beads, 2 cotton, 2 beads, 4 cotton, 2 beads, 2 cotton.

64th Row.—2 cotton, 2 beads, 4 cotton, 1 bead, 2 cotton, 1 bead, 3 cotton, 1 bead, 41 cot⸺ 1 bead, 3 cotton, 1 bead, 2 cot⸺ 4 cotton, 2 beads, 1 cotton.

⸺he Octagon repeat from the ⸺wards to the first, and after ⸺he ends, do an edge all ⸺ like that at the top of the

⸺ watch-pocket, cut out

a piece of card board, the size of the Octagon, and cover it, on both sides, with silk. Sew the shorter pieces on the other, so that the border joins to the slanting lines of beads beginning at the *53rd row.* The Octagon is then to be attached to the cardboard, and ribbons, with a rosette and ends sewed on, to suspend the pocket.

This work, in beads on cotton, has the merit of both wearing and washing well. It does not answer, however, for every kind of bead. Those which are transparent should never be used for this purpose. Care must be taken, also, to adapt the cotton and beads to each other. If the latter are too large the effect will be completely lost.

DOYLEY IN PORTUGUESE GUIPURE.

This Doyley is to be worked in the same style as the others of its class, and with similar materials.

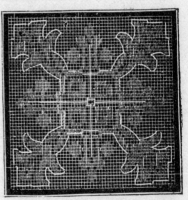

DOYLEY IN PORTUGUESE GUIPURE.

Any of these designs, worked with coarse Boar's Head cotton, instead of Mecklenburg, and darned with No. 4 knitting cotton, would be extremely pretty for square antimacassars.

JEWELLED DOYLEY—THE GARNET.

THE WORK-TABLE FRIEND.

JEWELLED DOYLEY—THE GARNET.

Materials.—1 ounce of Garnet beads, and 2 reels of Messrs. W. Evans and Co.'s Boar's Head Crochet Cotton, No. 10.

MAKE a chain of 4, close it into a round, and do 2 Sc stitches in every stitch.

2nd Round.—The same.

3rd Round.—+ 1 Sc on 1, 2 Sc on 1 + 8 times.

4th Round.—+ 2 Sc, 2 Sc on 1 + 8 times.

5th Round.—+ 3 Sc, 2 Sc on 1 + 8 times.

6th Round.—+ 3 cotton, 2 beads, + 8 times.

7th Round.—+ 2 cotton on 1, 1 more cotton, 2 beads, 1 cotton, + 8 times.

8th Round.—+ 2 cotton, 3 beads, 3 cotton + 8 times.

9th Round.—A bead on every stitch.

10th Round.—+ 3 beads, 2 cotton in 1 + 16 times.

11th Round.— + 5 beads on 3 and a cotton on each side, 2 cotton, 1 bead on the centre of 3, 2 cotton, + 8 times.

12th Round.—+ 1 cotton, 3 beads on centre 3 of 5, 3 cotton, 2 beads on 1, 2 cotton, + 8 times.

13th Round.—+ 2 cotton, 1 bead on centre of 3, 3 cotton, 4 beads, 1 cotton + 8 times.

14th Round.— + 6 beads (over 4), and a cotton on each side, 7 beads, + 8 times.

15th Round.—+ 2 beads (on 3rd and 4th of 6), 12 cotton between them and the next 2. All round.

16th Round.—+ 1 cotton, 3 beads, 1 cotton, 2 beads, 1 cotton, 2 beads, 1 cotton, 3 beads, 1 cotton + 8 times.

17th Round.—+ 6 beads, 3 cotton, 6 beads, 1 cotton + 8 times.

18th Round.—+ 8 beads (on 7 stitches), 1 cotton, 8 beads on 7, 1 cotton, + 8 times.

19th Round.—+ 1 cotton, 3 beads, 2 cotton, 2 beads, 1 cotton, 2 beads, 2 cotton, 3 beads, 2 cotton + 8 times.

20th Round.—+ 6 cotton over 5, 3 beads, 2 cotton over 1, 3 beads, 6 cotton + 8 times.

21st Round.—+ 2 cotton, 6 beads, 4 cotton, 6 beads, 2 cotton + 8 times.

22nd Round.—+ 1 cotton, 7 beads over 6, 2 cotton, 2 beads, 2 cotton, 7 beads over 6, 1 cotton + 8 times.

23rd Round.—+ 1 cotton, 5 beads, 3 cotton, 4 beads, 3 cotton, 5 beads, 1 cotton + 8 times.

24th Round.—+ 2 cotton, 9 beads, 1 cotton on the last, 9 beads, 3 cotton on 2, + 8 times.

25th Round.—+ 1 cotton, 6 beads, 2 cotton, 1 bead, 3 cotton, 1 bead, 2 cotton, 6 beads, 2 cotton, + 8 times.

26th Round.—+ 1 cotton, 2 beads, 1 cotton, 3 beads on 2, 2 cotton, 2 beads, 3 cotton, 2 beads, 2 cotton, 3 beads on 2, 1 cotton, 2 beads, 2 cotton, + 8 times.

27th Round.—+ 4 cotton, 2 beads, 2 cotton, 4 beads, 1 cotton, 4 beads, 2 cotton, 2 beads, 5 cotton + 8 times.

28th Round.—+ 8 cotton, 10 beads (over 9 stitches), 10 cotton on 9 + 8 times.

29th Round.—+ 7 cotton, 4 beads, 1 cotton, 2 beads, 1 cotton, 4 beads, 9 cotton + 8 times.

30th Round.—Work round to the first bead stitch, + 3 beads on the first 3 of 4, 2 cotton, 2 beads, 2 cotton, 3 beads, 18 cotton + 8 times.

31st Round.—+ 2 beads, 2 cotton, 4 beads, 2 cotton, 2 beads, 18 cotton + 8 times.

32nd Round.—Do 6 beads over 4, and a cotton on each side, and all the rest cotton.

The next two rounds the same, increasing sufficiently in the cotton part to keep the work flat.

In the next round, do 4 beads on centre 4 of 6, and the rest cotton, increasing as before.

2 beads on centre 2 of 4, and cotton on all the rest.

Two rounds of Sc with cotton only.

Edge.— + 1 Sc, 2 Ch, miss 1, 1 Dc, 2 Ch, miss 1 +.

2nd Row.— + Sc on Dc, 5 Ch, with a bead on each +.

KNITTED PURSE.

Materials.—Two bunches of steel beads, No. 6; three skeins of fine purse-silk; needles, No. 20.

CAST on 16 stitches on each of three needles, and knit 2 plain rounds.

1st and *2nd Rounds.*—Bring forward, knit 2 together all round.

3rd Round.—Draw up 6 beads ; then bring forward, knit 2 together, bring forward, knit 2 together, *repeat.*

Knit 7 *more* rounds, the same as last.

11th Round.—The same, only drawing up 5 beads instead of 6.

12th, 13th, 14th, and *15th Rounds.*— The same, only drawing but 4, 3, 2, and 1 bead.

16th Round.—Bring forward, knit 2 together, draw up 1 bead, bring forward, knit 2 together.

17th, 18th, 19th, 20th, and *21st Rounds.* —The same as the 16th, only drawing up 2, 3, 4, 5, and 6 beads.

Repeat the 21st round for 19 times more.

41st Round.—The same, only drawing up 5 beads instead of 6.

42nd, 43rd, 44th, and *45th Rounds.*— The same, only drawing up 4, 3, 2, and 1 bead.

46th Round.—Bring forward, knit 2 together, draw up 1 bead, bring forward, knit 2 together, knit 1 at the end of the round; *repeat* to the end of the round, then turn back instead of going on to the next needle.

47th Round.—The same as the 46th.

48th and *49th Rounds.*—Draw up 1 bead, bring forward, knit 2 together, bring forward, knit 2 together, knit 1 at the end.

Repeat the 46th, 47th, 48th, and 49th rounds 5 times more, when there will be 24 rounds knitted flat; then commence to knit round again.

70th Round.—Begin again at the 1st round, and knit till the 45th ; then continue knitting 2 together until the purse is decreased to a point.

The wrong side of the knitting is the right side of the purse.

Finis.

HARRILD, Printer, LONDON.